GEORGE BLAXLAND

Codex Legum Anglicanarum

OR

A DIGEST

OF

PRINCIPLES OF ENGLISH LAW

ARRANGED IN THE ORDER

OF

THE CODE NAPOLEON

Elibron Classics
www.elibron.com

Elibron Classics series.

ISBN 1-4212-4893-X (paperback)
ISBN 1-4212-4892-1 (hardcover)

This Elibron Classics Replica Edition is an unabridged facsimile of the edition published in 1839 by Henry Butterworth, London.

Codex Legum Anglicanarum;

OR,

A DIGEST

OF

PRINCIPLES OF ENGLISH LAW;

ARRANGED IN THE ORDER

OF

THE CODE NAPOLEON.

BY

GEORGE BLAXLAND.

Le Ley est le pluis haut enheritance que le Roy ad, car per le ley il mesme et touts ses subjects sonts rules, et si le ley ne fuit, nul Roy ne nul enheritance serra.—*Anglo-Norman Law Maxim.*

LONDON:

HENRY BUTTERWORTH,

LAW BOOKSELLER AND PUBLISHER,

7, FLEET STREET.

1839.

PREFACE.

THE utility of anything which tends to facilitate the study of the laws of foreign countries, cannot require much urging upon the minds of the members of the legal profession, in a country which must unhesitatingly be considered as the first nation of the mercantile universe—and whose ports, crowded with myriads from all climes and all nations, proclaim it the centre spot of commerce.

In the peace which has now subsisted on the earth for nearly a quarter of a century, traffic has become so absolutely universal with this country, the natives of other realms have so free an intercourse with it for commerce, so easy an access to it for shelter from persecution, religious or political, that contracts of all kinds, marriages, nuptial settlements, wills, and succession to property, may be said daily to take place here between persons, whose native, if not their adopted, homes or domicil, as well as their property, are in different countries; and in the conflict of laws, governing their new and old conditions, which must inevitably ensue, any attempt to render the jurisprudence of two countries so closely neighbouring each other, and between which there is so great an intercourse, as France and England, more known to the students and professors of each, cannot but be desirable. The placing of part of the two systems in juxtaposition, as is here done, must undoubtedly tend to this object. No apology, therefore, can be required for the design of a work of this tendency; but from a person like the author, some sort of excuse or apology may, perhaps, seem to the graver members of the profession requisite to authorize his publication of a work of so wide a range—some reason why it should have been undertaken, by one almost unknown in his profession, and who, by his deficiencies, may be thought to display the English system, so highly and so justly prized as the joint production of successive centuries, to disadvantage by the side of the new-born Code, which is in form so captivating to the imagination; and as the author cannot but participate in something like a similar feeling, he begs to lay before them the following statement of the origin of his undertaking.

Some years back he was in the habit of calling frequently at the counting-house of a gentleman engaged in extensive commercial transactions with France and the Netherlands. On those occasions, a small duodecimo volume, containing the French Code, was often produced to him; and the common but misapplied raillery against the English law, for what is called its uncertainty, the multifariousness of enactments and details, and the consequent immense size of an English law library, received a double force when backed by the assertion, that the volume produced, so diminutive in size, so specious in appearance, contained the whole body of the French law, and that it was thought a few moments' reference to that volume would suffice for finding the law applicable to any given transaction.

Totally ignorant at that time wherein consisted the excellency of a system of law, as a science, both in matter and form, the author, jealous for the system he was studying, conceived that as many rules of English law as there are articles of the French Code could be collected together and arranged in the same order as those of the French Code, and that the execution of this idea would be the best method of determining the value of the two systems, and of meeting the unmeasured ridicule heaped on the English system. With this view he commenced, for his own satisfaction, a collection of the rules and decisions of the English law relating to portions of it, parallel in their application to those of the French Code, article for article. But the phraseology and notions of the English law are so peculiar to it, that his knowledge of that system afforded no assistance, but rather an impediment to the understanding of the French rules of law: and from the difficulty and distastefulness of learning a new phraseology;* from not being perfectly familiar with the notions and the habits

* "We live in the midst of the Common Law; we inhale it at every breath, we imbibe it at every pore; it is interwoven with the very idiom we speak, and we cannot learn another system of laws without learning at the same time another language."—Dr. Du Ponceau on the Jurisdiction of the Courts of the United States, p. 91. The author takes the opportunity of acknowledging here, that in the translation of the Code Napoleon, printed in the Appendix, he has availed himself, to a very great extent, of the labours of a previous translator, an anonymous Barrister of the Inner Temple.

of life which the French law is intended to regulate; from having but little leisure for such occupations, and from other causes, it was long before he made so much progress as to have collected materials enough for a very scanty outline of English law parallel to that of France. In that state it was seen by some gentlemen engaged in commerce with France, who expressed their opinion that such a work would be useful if published; and this encouragement, slight as, coming from a non-professional quarter, it might be considered, added to all the other inducements which influence authors to offer the produce of their labours to the public, determined the author on endeavouring to make his work fit for publication. He was proceeding in his task, and hoped, with a year or more of hard work, to bring it to something near the idea of what he conceived it ought to be, when, from a change in his plans of life, he found himself compelled, either to abandon for an indefinite period the attempt, or publish it in the state in which it is. Having said thus much in justification of his having undertaken this work, and to account for some of the deficiencies which may be detected in it, the author submits himself to the judgment of the profession, venturing at the same time to remind the reader, that, besides the defects arising from this cause, there are others the necessary result of the nature of the work. It has been said a book of travels must always be more or less a book of inaccuracies, and this is still more true of a book on a wide field of law; and the author is entitled to his share of allowance on that score.

It may however, perhaps, be urged by those fearful for the fame of the English system, that some method might have been adopted for facilitating the study of the French law by the English lawyer, less calculated to set forth in glaring contrast the defects of the English system, than that of placing the venerable science of the English Common Law side by side with the code of France, and thus exposing the somewhat distorted figure of the ancient law of this realm by the side of her more trim French neighbour, and thereby giving countenance to those who have so lustily cried out for codifying the laws of England. A higher opinion, however, should be entertained of the English system; there need be no fear that it would, were it but properly set forth, be any loser by the contrast with unprejudiced minds: and the author feels that, if in the subsequent pages it should be thought that the English system appears to disadvantage, the deficiency is not in the system but in the expositor. The truth of this will be evident, if we consider each of the points wherein consist the excellences of systems of law. These are of two kinds: one relating to the nature of those laws; the other to the mode in which they are expressed, and by which that nature is made manifest. Again, the nature of law is of two kinds, formal and material; and the expression of law has also two bearings, namely, the order in which it is arranged, and the language with which it is clothed.

From the arrangement of this work, the differences between the nature of some of the leading principles of the two systems will be obvious to all: with regard to their respective merits in the above points of excellency, a few remarks must here be allowed. As to the nature of the law, there cannot be a doubt, that the first and chief point is, its adaptation to the wants, feelings, and habits of the society which it is to govern. However, to consider the second first (because being by far the minor point it may be speedily dismissed), in the form and the orderly arrangement in which its positive enactments are displayed, it must be admitted, the French codes have decidedly the advantage. But the eight codes, with the ninety or one hundred volumes of bulletins des lois, can only be strictly compared to one portion of our system; for being the enactment of positive laws, it is rather to be compared to our statute-book, than to our common law system. The English statute-book is a disorderly mass of enactments in detail, having no other arrangement than that in which it has been produced by time and unsystematic necessity: the French codes are, like our statute-book, a series of enactments, but arranged (together with legal definitions) in so scientific an order, that, having learned the principle of arrangement, a person would know where to look for a particular rule of law, almost without having seen the book containing them; and certainly this is no small advantage. And as to the language in which it is expressed, there can be no comparison between the terse and almost classic phraseology of the French Code, and even the very best specimens of the cumbrous verbosity of the English statutes. Perhaps, from the nature of English legislation, this defect, not necessarily inherent in the system of law itself, is not to be entirely avoided; but before we think of codifying our laws, let us first learn, at least, the primary and most easily attained requisite, namely, how to express them.

When we turn to the other kind of excellency, namely, the nature of the law, as a different state of society requires a different state of laws to suit it, it must be evident that, as far as the material nature of the rules of each system goes, a person, not well versed in the habits and feelings of each, cannot fairly make any relative estimate of the adaptation of each to its office. The Englishman may know that a particular rule of French law would either not have any bearing at all on English manners and habits, or that it would or would not suit them; but without a thorough knowledge of French manners and habits (except in so far as he presumes they resemble those with which he is acquainted), he cannot form an opinion what bearing that rule has on French society; and so, on the other side, a Frenchman cannot judge of the fitness of any rule of English law to its object: and therefore no opinion will here be ventured on the relative excellence of the rules of the two systems in their respective natures, or in what may be called their material reasons. There is no wish on either side the Channel for a wholesale exchange of rules of law, in order to try them on like new patterns, and see how they fit.

But with regard to what, if it be not thought too logical a term, may be called the formal reason of the law, which consists in the dependency of its rules, the close coherency of notions, and the consequent 'logical deduceableness' and the copiousness of matter which results therefrom; and which, where a positive enactment or decided rule is wanting, enables it to draw from within itself a new rule as a consequence of the old principles, the English law has decidedly and unmeasurably the advantage over the French. And indeed in this consists one of the chief, if not the very chief, excellences of a system of law; for a moment's attention will show, that it is absolutely impossible for any book to contain enactments which shall meet every case. The arrangement of a code may be admirable; the rules which it does contain may be the best that could be applied to the society for which they are intended; and yet after all it may be totally inapplicable, or at least totally inadequate in itself, to meet the exigencies of life, and therefore next to useless. The rules contained in any code, if they consist only of first principles, must of necessity be so general, as to leave the mode and degree of their application almost entirely discretionary with the administrators of the law. If the articles, instead of consisting merely of general first principles, descend to particular rules intended to apply to the facts of individual cases, the chances are, that very few of the cases, under all the circumstances imagined by the legislator, ever happen. As well might an architect attempt to describe all the peculiarities of every house in London in one book, as the legislator endeavour to provide a rule for—what are a hundred times more diverse—all the varieties of rights and relations which exist between persons and persons, and persons and property, modified as they are by human wants, and the whims which a refined state of society produces.

It is by this standard alone, namely, by their being able of themselves to meet all the exigencies that arise in the society which they are intended to regulate, that the relative excellency of the two systems of law is to be judged. Their arrangement without this is evidently nothing. What signifies it that a man knows exactly in what part a given rule of law ought and is to be found, or that it be expressed in the aptest words, if, after all, that rule affects nobody, or is so indefinite as to leave to the judge's discretion its mode of application. Again, as to the material nature of the rule, it can hardly, when the rule itself is, like the society to which it applies, the growth of time, be inapplicable to the society on which it has been formed; and its slight variations are easily rectified.

At first few people, perhaps, will be willing to credit, that the French codes are by no means sufficient in themselves to meet the necessities of the society for which they are formed. The English lawyer, however, need scarcely have his attention directed to the numerous points in any one title of law, not even alluded to in the French codes, on which, in the English system, decisions as extensive in their application as any of the rules of the French Code, not only provide a rule of law, but also show the process and the principles from which that rule was obtained, and thus furnish examples for deciding future cases.

The non-professional reader will, however, be more readily convinced of the inefficacy of the French codes to meet the wants of society, when he is told by so eminent a French lawyer as M. Dupin, in his advice to a student whom he would not willingly overburthen, that, in order first to thoroughly understand what the codes themselves do contain, he must apply not only to the codes, but also to the projects originally prepared of them; the observations made by the various French courts of law on those projects; the discussions which took place in the council and chambers; and the reports and exposés of motions on enacting those projects; all of which are collected in no less than fifteen closely printed octavo volumes. And when he is informed that, to what was originally contained in these codes, numerous additions have been made, to be separately found in upwards of one hundred volumes of bulletins des lois, he may be inclined to think, that there must at least, in this mass of legislation, be sufficient for a nation's utmost wants. But such is not the case; and French law writers are found referring, not to the codes, but to the old systems of the Roman, and the Customary law previously existing in France, to supply the deficiencies of positive legislation, and to explain the meaning of the codes. Hence though we find the one volume of the Code Civil, one of eight codes, expounded, in nineteen octavo volumes, by persons of such undoubted learning as M. Duranton, and numerous commentaries on that and the other codes, by M. Delvincourt and other able men, yet even these have not sufficed to prevent the demand for a publication of a general collection in thirty volumes of the French laws, as they existed before the revolution. Collections of decisions, which multiply by dozens of volumes annually, and numerous other works, besides the whole body of the civil law, might be added to fill up the library required now in France to supply materials for law, under the deficiencies of the codes to meet the exigencies of society. At the sight of this system, so teeming with new laws which seem likely to outstrip in bulk any law hitherto known, the English reader may well enquire why so much outcry has been made for codification in this country, a task for which, to judge from our statute-book, we are peculiarly unfitted; and supposing ourselves as well fitted as any nation, what are we likely to gain, either in point of matter or expression, unless a system of law nominally contained in one volume, but which leaves real practical questions to be decided from other sources be a gain?

Without making further comparisons as to the relative values of the English and French systems of law, it only remains to state the plan on which the author has formed his work.

There was, during the middle ages, so much resemblance between the institutions of England and those of France, and so much was derived from the same source, that a brief historical sketch has been prefixed, attempting to show the origin of some of those points on which the two systems differ, as well as the source of those institutions which are common to both. The progress of English jurisprudence, and the present state of her legal institution, reflect much light on the early history of the French law, and Littleton and other English authors were considered as valid authorities on French customary law before the first revolution. And the French ancient laws often illustrate and explain those of England. Sir F. Palgrave says,* "Evidence is wanting at home concerning institutions, whose principles, clearly displayed in the muniments of France and Gaul, afford the best commentary on our own traditional usages and laws. Marculfus can be employed to interpret a manorial court-roll, and the Vassi, who assemble round the throne of Charlemagne at Aix-la-Chapelle or Ingleheim, will sometimes aid us in developing the station held by the members composing the Witenagemote of the Confessor, or the Parliament of an English king."†

In comparing in the body of the following work, the portions of English law given as parallel with each article of the French law, it will be seen that scarcely one of them is so brief as the French parallel; but this is not because any one rule of English

---

* Rise and Progress of the English Commonwealth, part 1, p. 483

† To the same effect it has been said, "A previous enquiry concerning the original sources of national law is surely necessary for unfolding the design and the principles of our earlier legal institutions, and must afford great facilities towards the comprehending those parts of the present fabric of our jurisprudence, of which the construction is of an ancient date, or which have been fashioned after the ancient model." —Preface of Amos, to Translation of Fortescue.

"Whoever considers how great a coherence there is between the several parts of the law and how much the reason of one case opens and depends upon that of the other, will, I presume, be far from thinking any of the old learning useless which will conduce so much to the perfect understanding of the modern."—Mr. Hawkins' Pref. to Ab. of 1st Inst.

law could not have been expressed in as few words as a parallel rule of French law; it evidently might: for example, the sixth article says, "private agreements must not derogate from the laws which concern public order and good morals;" this is merely a translation of a maxim adopted by the French Code from the civil law,* Conventio privatorum non potest publico juri derogare,† which is also adopted by the English law, and which might be expressed in the English parallel, in the very same words as in the French. But in the first place, it was evident, that the mere enunciation of rules of law, without connection or without reference to the reasons on which they are founded, would render the work uninteresting and unreadable, if not unintelligible. And in the second place, the legislator may propound an enigma, declare it a law, and enact that the judge who shall refuse to determine its meaning, under pretext of not understanding it, shall be punished; but the work of a private author on law, can be of no use to anybody, unless it states, sufficiently to be intelligible, the rule, its principle, and its interpretation and application. In the article, therefore, to which we have above alluded (the 6th), not only the bare rule has been given at greater length than the French parallel, but in the note some of the cases to which it is applicable have been referred to, from whence those wishing further information, may find an almost unlimited supply; and the same observations apply to almost every article in the book. As to some, however, which are adapted solely to the peculiar state of French manners, no parallel English rule is requisite; as, for example, the whole title on adoption.

It has cost no small labour to find decisions of English law parallel to some other portions of the French law, which, from a difference of manners and habits, relate to customs almost unknown to us, and which therefore have, in England, rarely been the subject of legal discussion; and, on the other hand, some rules laid down in the French law are of such a nature, and such an application, that they form part of the ordinary life of every Englishman; and, requiring no legal authority to enforce them, have never, or at least not for centuries, been a subject of dispute,

* Dig. l. 50, tit. 17, l. 46.

† Law Maxim, cited Coke upon Littleton, p. 166; Wingate, Maxims.

or called for the authority of the law to decide them; therefore it has been difficult, and sometimes impossible, to meet with any authority whatever in the English law; and such must inevitably be the case, where the habits of life differ: for example, where shall we discover a direct authority in the English law, that the son cannot compel the father to appropriate his property, to establish that son in life.

In executing this work, the first object has been to find and quote authorities, and state them; whether in the application of principles, in legal decisions, or in the statutory enactments. A great many of the cases referred to in the notes, have not a direct bearing on the point in the text; but, having been collected by the author as materials to be examined and used in the task he had in hand, have often a more immediate reference to other points; though they generally, in an indirect manner, tend to establish the point on which they are cited, and may be usefully referred to. The reader need scarcely be reminded, that all reasonning on abstract law must necessarily proceed in what in logic is called the mathematical method, commencing with definitions of words, definitions of notions, axioms of reason, principles, and rules, with their corollaries and sequences, as applicable to given propositions. The English law might to great advantage have been set forth in this form, and probably some day some master-hand will be found to perform the task; the author dares not to attempt it. But great pains have been taken to find definitions in this work, not only to explain the meaning of words, but because every just definition of a legal notion should express within itself all the rules which form and produce that notion. The rules of law, as it were, define and bound a legal notion, as the imaginary lines of geometry do a mathematical one; thus, for example, take the definition of dower, as it stood before the passing of the late act. Dower * is an estate for life, which the law gives the widow, in the third part of the lands and tenements, of which the husband was solely seized, at any time during the coverture, of an estate in fee or in tail, in possession, and to which estate in the lands and tenements, the issue of such widow might, by possibility, have inherited. The first and most general rule of the law on this subject is, that the law gives the widow a

* Watkins, Principles of Conveyancing, b. 1, c. 1.

certain right in the property of her deceased husband;—the next rule is, that the right given by the law to a widow in her husband's property, is only for her life;—then, that only a third belongs to the wife;—then, that only certain kinds of property, possessed by the husband, are dowable;—then, that only such of those kinds as he was solely seized of;—that dower does not attach to those of which he had been seized, but which he parted with before marriage;—that he must have possessed an estate of inheritance;—then, that property in which he has only a future interest or estate during coverture, is not dowable;—then, that whatever the nature of the property, if the issue of the widow could not, by possibility, have inherited, she is not entitled to dower out of them. Each of these, besides others which it will be seen are contained in it, is a distinct rule or maxim of the law, and goes to the accurately defining, that is, laying the boundaries of the notion of dower. Deprived of any one of these rules, which are almost as numerous as the words, the dower would not attach—the boundary which separates it from other interests would be wanting, and some right let in by the want of that line of fence, would come in to transfer the estate to some other person. By preventing any one of these rules from applying to the estate of the husband, the widow was barred of her dower. The most usual method of barring dower, was by preventing what constitutes a legal inheritance from vesting in him; giving him at the same time a power over the inheritance. A logical definition always consists of the genus and differentia;* and it may be as well here to observe, that what is a characteristic (called in logic, differentia) attaches to each portion of definition, distinguishing it from others. Thus, the being given by the law is the characteristic (differentia) which, added to the idea of the widow's interest (the genus), distinguishes it from another species of widow's interest, namely, jointure; of which the being given by convention or agreement, is the characteristic (or differentia). Thus, in logic, the terms, dower and jointure, are two species of the widow's interest in her husband's lands, which constitutes their genus or common nature, distinguished by being respectively given by law or by convention, as their characteristic or logical differentia. In like manner, the common law rule of

* Whateley, Elements of Logic, p. 132.

the third distinguishes dower from the half of certain customary tenures; and so of the other rules: each has a distinctive quality or differentia, which goes to separate it from some other notion.

Aware, therefore, of the difficulty of forming correct legal definitions, the author has sought carefully for those given by the masters of the law; and has not ventured to alter them to his own fancy, although they are often apparently defective, or redundant.

Next to the definitions stand the rules: and here the author has taken some pains to show the legal maxims bearing on the respective portions of law; believing that, in those maxims (so often borrowed from the civil law), besides the classical phraseology of most of them, are contained the fundamental principles of English law.

Not daring to undertake to translate such of them as are in Norman French or Latin (which to do correctly so as to express their full meaning and no more, would be no easy task), the author abandoned his design of placing before each title such as belonged to it, or putting them into the text; and he has thrown most of the principal ones into the notes, where, in connexion with their application to, and limitation by, decided cases, they may, perhaps, serve a purpose which they otherwise would not; for, as Lord Bacon says, "the naked rule or maxim doth not effect: it must be made useful by good differences, ampliations, and limitations, warranted by good authorities."

A right, without a remedy to enforce it (whatever moral obligation it may have), is a mere legal nullity, and, consequently, rights are only co-extensive with remedies, and are limited by them; it has, therefore, not been possible to exclude from this work, references to forms of law, of which it has been impracticable to give any explanation.

The author, in concluding these observations on his work, cannot but repeat, that if the English law appears on the whole, or in any respect, except in style of expression and arrangement, to disadvantage by the side of the French Code, the blame is to be attributed to the author's having disguised it, and the disadvantage must be placed to the account of his deficiencies; for he need scarcely repeat, that the law relating to persons, which traces its origin from early times, has been formed entirely out of the customs and habits of the people, and therefore must of necessity be the best adapted to their object, of any that can be imagined; and it scarcely requires the assertion, to a professor of English law to render evident, "that the English law of the relations of private life were, for the most part, either settled upon, or have been gradually brought within the true principle; namely, that of deriving from the connexion the greatest advantage to both parties, which, on a comprehensive view of their interests, the particular relation seems qualified to produce." With regard to the second book of this work, it only contains a very small fragment of the parallel subject of English law; and the reader will be totally incapable of seeing from it the truth of the assertion of a person well capable of judging, because well acquainted with it, that though "the judicial system of property received in England is complicated, it is perfect both in theory and for practical objects." And with regard to the third book into which this work is divided, the author need only remind the reader, that the portion of the law of which it treats is the production of men—of learning, at once so extensive, profound, and accurate—of talents and judgment so practised, so acute, as Lord Mansfield, Lord Hardwicke, Lord Eldon, Lord Holt, Lord Tenterden, Baron Bayley, Justice Buller, were; and he must perceive that it can fall but little short of that degree of perfection which human works are capable of attaining; and on the whole, when he considers these things, and sees the origin of the present laws, gathered from our British, Saxon, and Norman ancestors, as well as from the Roman system, he will agree with the great Lord Bacon, that "our laws are as mixed as our language; and as our language is so much the richer, the laws are the more complete."

7, Crosby Square.
29th January, 1839.

☞ It will be observed that this Volume concludes with the Third Title of the Third Book of the Code.

CONTENTS.

Page

BOOK II.—OF PROPERTY.

TITLE I.

TITLE II.

TITLE III.

TITLE IV.

BOOK III.—OF THE MODES OF ACQUIRING PROPERTY.

TITLE I.

TITLE II.

Page

TITLE III.

A BRIEF EXAMINATION

INTO

THE ORIGINAL SOURCES

OF THE

LAWS OF FRANCE AND ENGLAND,

AND AN

HISTORICAL SKETCH OF THEIR DEVELOPMENT.

ACCORDING to one of the most perfect analyses which can be made, the laws relating to the affairs of private individuals have been classed under four heads, or distinct species: first, those relating to persons, their capacities and incapacities; second, the laws of property, its kinds and legal qualities; third, the modes of acquiring property, contracts, and obligations; and, fourth, actions, and means of remedy for breaches of the other kinds of laws.

Analytical division of civil law.

Nearly correspondent to this division are certain distinctions as to the origin and nature of the various species of law, which, as they throw much light on the history of all systems of law whatsoever, will form the basis of the following brief historical sketch of the sources and progress of the laws of France and England to their existing state.

The laws of persons, being all based either on the union of the sexes in marriage, or on natural capacity and incapacity, take their origin in domestic manners and habits, and are framed in accordance with the feel-

Analytical division of civil law.

ings and opinions of the people at large, and above all, their religion, which must be considered as modifying, more or less, or producing the others. The same system of personal laws would not apply to the Asiatic and European, the Christian and the Mahomedan or Pagan, or to the ancient Roman, whose family were his personal goods, and the modern, or even to the ancient Dorian and Ionian Greeks. These laws of persons, with a few of those ranged under the other heads, in which the legislator can but follow and legislate for the habits of the people, may be called the Popular part of municipal law. They are as lasting as a people's manners, and can only be effectually changed by the gradual alteration which takes place under the influence of civilization, accelerated or retarded by the judicious or injudicious interference of the legislature. A legal enactment attempting extensive and abrupt fundamental alterations in this part of law, without a change of popular manners and opinions, must generally be a dead letter, notwithstanding heavy penalties are annexed to its non-performance.

The laws of property, with the rules of succession to it, though in general growing out of the customs of society, are not so mixed up with popular manners and opinions as the personal. Indeed the laws of property are necessarily from their nature complicated; and possessing few features of general interest, the majority of mankind care little about the nature of the incorporeal qualities with which the law may have invested the object of property, provided the results they desire, in the enjoyment and distribution of the corporeal object, be effected by their means.[1] Thus the ancient Roman and modern Frenchman may live under nearly the same system of property-law. The ancient Scythian, the Asiatic Rajh-

[1] Professor Savigny remarks that, respecting some portions of law, non-professional persons take a lively interest; and others they give up, as indifferent matters of legal technicality. Vom Beruf unserer zeit für Gesetzgebung und Rechtswissenschaft.

poot,[1] and the European, may hold his property under a system of tenural or feudal law. This part of the law must be called the artificial or Technical portion. The legislator and the principles of social policy here lead the people; and these laws may be altered fundamentally or entirely, without producing any very great popular feeling, although extensive alteration in a highly civilized country may, and indeed must inevitably, produce great confusion and many unlooked-for disastrous consequences.

Analytical division of civil law.

The law relating to contracts is founded, in all civilized nations, almost entirely on reason, more or less modified by peculiar rules, produced by the positive laws, and the manners and opinions of each country. "It is pleasing," says Sir William Jones, "to remark the similarity or rather identity of those conclusions which pure unbiassed reason, in all ages and nations, seldom fails to draw in such judicial inquiries as are not fettered and manacled by positive institutions; and although the rules of the Pundits concerning succession to property, the punishment of offences, and the ceremonies of religion are widely different from ours, yet in the great system of contracts the pootee of the Indians and the digests of the Romans are by no means dissimilar."[2] This portion of the law, being educed by reason and only accidentally affected by positive laws, may be called the Rational.

The formal, ceremonial, and symbolical part of the law, consisting of the process substituted in the place of the natural right of revenge and self-redress, and of the forms, signs, and ceremonies, by which a legal act or obligation is created so as to bind the party, chiefly takes its origin in the other three kinds of law, and partakes more or less

[1] Pinkerton's Dissertation on the Origin and Progress of the Scythians or Goths. Col. Tod's Annals of Rajast'han.

[2] Sir William Jones's Treatise on Bailments, p. 114.

Analytical division of civil law.

of the character of each, according as it relates to a transaction respecting persons, property, or contracts. But it is also in a great measure governed and alterable by the will of the legislator.

This statement of these general principles, which affect the origin of all laws in the abstract, opens the way for the consideration of the course of events, the progress of legislation, and the spirit and causes which influenced the enactments of the actual laws of France and England. And as we proceed, we shall find that the sources of the systems of law existing in both countries may be traced to three tolerably well-marked periods:[1] namely, first, that in which the races which now inhabit either country were first planted there, or intermingled with the previous occupiers, so as to lay the foundation of manners and of personal laws and relations; and in which property was a consideration of less importance than the rank of the possessor, which determined the state of the property: second, that in which property acquired an almost exclusive importance, and gave to the possessor his peculiar station in life, and in which the technical laws of property were developed out of national manners, personal relations, political expediency, and technical constructions; and, lastly, a period in which the rational part of the law, relating chiefly to contracts and commercial transactions, has been cultivated: the progress of the remedial and symbolical part of the law partaking of the state of society in each of these three periods.

Course of historical events in France.

At the opening of the history of Western Europe, when the first light was thrown on that part of the world by the Roman authors, Gaul and Britain were inhabited by tribes of the great Celtic nation. The Roman republic

[1] We do not mean to assert that the progress of all systems of law necessarily divides itself into three periods, similar to the ones we have pointed out; but only in England and France circumstances caused the different kinds of laws to be developed in three periods.

Course of historica events in France.

was then fast extending its boundaries, and about 56 A.C. Julius Cæsar added Gaul, part of which till then had remained unsubdued, to its dominion; and the country remained nearly five centuries a part of the Roman empire, and subject to the Roman laws.[1]

In England.

In the year 55 A.C., Julius Cæsar first landed his Roman legions on the coast of Britain; but the conquest of the country was not completed until Agricola,[2] about A.D. 79, carried the arms of the succeeding Cæsars into Scotland, and pushed the Roman dominion to its utmost permanent extent in this country. Of the countries conquered by Rome, some were permitted to use their own laws and choose their magistrates, others were not. Agricola finally[3] established the Roman laws as well as Roman government and institutions.[4]

During the two centuries succeeding the subjection of Agricola, some of the most eminent Roman lawyers filled the judicial offices of the most distant provinces; and during the reign of Severus this island was honoured by the presence of jurisconsults of no less renown than

---

[1] Savigny, Geschichte des römischen Rechts in Mittelalter, b. 1, passim; but see the views of the authors quoted in his preface, among the sources used by him. 24 A.

A distinction must be made between the whole body of the laws of Rome, from its foundation to the downfall of the eastern empire, and the code of Justinian, which was not compiled until after the separation of Gaul from the empire. The former has been called the Roman law, the latter the Civil law.

The Roman law therefore used in ancient Gaul consisted of the laws made anterior to that period. The senatus-consulti and plebiscita, the edicts of the prætors, and the opinions of jurisconsults, the works of five of whom Papinian, Ulpian, Paulus, Gaius, and Modestinus, had the force of law expressly given to them. The Theodosian Code, published 438, was, however, the most important. Savigny, v. 1, c. 1.

[2] Tacit. Agric. 14—17.

[3] Selden, Dissertatio ad Fletam, c. 4, s. 1. The Roman law was first established there by Claudius, when Roman colonies were first planted.

[4] As to the laws of the ancient Britons, the Druids being prohibited th exercise of their rights, such nations as were governed by them grew regardless of their authority and ready to receive the Roman law.—Selden's Notes to Fortescue, pp. 11, 12.

Emilianus Papinianus, as Prefect of the prætor,[1] and Ulpian and Paulus, as his assessors.[2] It appears that Papinian taught as well as administered the Roman law at York.

Germanic invasions in France.

In the middle of the third century, 250, the Roman empire was first seriously threatened by the Gothic tribes; but, bribed by the Emperor Gallus with the promise of an annual tribute, the first band of the invaders retreated with their captives and booty, to make known the wealth and weakness of the empire. And from that time swarms of barbarians, Huns, Goths, and Vandals, Alemanni, Burgundians, Franks, and other German tribes, ravaged Europe until the downfall of the western Roman empire, A.D. 476, when Odoacer, the chief of the Heruli, was declared king of Italy. The countries beyond the Alps he resigned to Euric, the king of the Visigoths,[3] who (between A.D. 412 and 450) had spread themselves between the Rhone south of the Durance, the Pyrennees, and the Loire.

The Burgundians, under Gundicher, had previously (A.D. 406 to 413) obtained a settlement in the eastern part of Gaul, between the Jura, the Saone, and the Durance. They acknowledged the supremacy of Euric, and he imposed terms of peace on the fierce Frankish nations, then inhabiting the north of Gaul and Belgium. The Franks were divided into two nations, Salians and Ripuarians; but after Euric's death, Clovis having united Salic Franks with the Ripuarians, subdued successively the Visigoths (between 507 and 542) and Burgundians (about the year 534); and from his reign the French kingdom is generally considered to have commenced. The

---

[1] Selden, Dissertatio ad Fletam, c. 4, s. 3. Leunclav. in vit. Dion. As to the fact of his being in Britain, Dio. Cass. Hist. 76.

[2] Lampridius, in Alex. Sev. Dig. l. 12, tit. de Reb. Creditis, l. 40.

[3] Gibbon's Decline and Fall of the Roman Empire, chap. 38. Savigny's History (Geschichte), vol. ii. c. 1, part 1, of the French edition. A copy of the French translations has been used here, and is the one generally quoted.

Franks, having obtained the supremacy, left the Visigoths and Burgundians to enjoy their possession, and occupied the north of France, between the Rhine, the Scheldt, and the Loire, not however including Brittany and the western part of Normandy, which successfully opposed them.

Germanic invasions in England.

Some time before the final overthrow of the Roman empire the Roman government was obliged to abandon Britain; and, in the year 449, the first band of the Germanic tribes, viz. the Jutes, under their ealdormen, Hengist and Horsa, landed in Kent: and though at first invited to defend the country against the Picts and Scots, having been joined by two other tribes,[1] the Angles and Saxons, eventually, after a fierce protracted struggle, subjugated the whole of that part of the united kingdom called England.

Consequences of the German invasion on the law of France.

In general the Teutonic races, which settled in the western Roman empire, though they carried with them their own customs, by which they themselves were to be governed in their new settlements, did not interfere with the laws they found established there, but allowed the inhabitants to regulate their transactions among themselves, according to the Roman[2] or other law, previously used by them; but for his own government, the barbarian claimed to be judged and protected by his own national laws, as his birthright and charter. So that two systems of law, Teutonic and Roman, were established concurrently through the greater part of Western Europe.[3]

Consequences to the law of England

In England, the desperate resistance made by the Romanized inhabitants was followed by an almost utter

---

[1] See Bede's account of the tribes who invaded Britain. Hist. Eccl. l. 1, c. 15.

[2] Geschichte des römischen Rechts in Mittelalter. As to the cause of retaining so many different laws within the same state, and the probable mode of their acting, see Savigny, cap. 3.

[3] There existed in France the Salic, Ripuarian, Burgundian, Visigothic, and Roman laws. Agobard, in writing to Louis le Debonnaire, says, "It often happens that of five men met together not one has the same law as another."—Agobardi, Ep. ad Lud. P. in Bouquet, tom. vi. p. 356.

extirpation, or at least reduction to slavery, so as no longer to be a people; and with them the Roman law was entirely lost to this country, and the German customary law established in its stead: and if we except a few local customs, which corresponding with the Roman law are said to owe their origin to it, this system of jurisprudence has left no vestiges of its having at one time governed this kingdom.[1]

That it has made a silent though often unrecognized inroad (as it is said, not by reason of empire, but by the empire of reason)[2] into the laws, even the most exclusively customary of modern Europe, is unquestionable, and among others into our own. Some writers have gone so far as to say it is the real but unacknowledged basis of the system, an assertion, however, evidently unfounded. It would, however, be a very interesting subject for the investigation of the legal antiquary, to trace out historically in detail the various parts of our law over which it has exerted a palpable influence.

Course of legislation in France.

The customs of the Germans existed, not in a written code, but in the mind and habits of the people; and when they had settled in Europe, and came in contact with their more polished subjects, the want of written laws became felt; and accordingly we find almost every tribe of the barbarians reducing their laws to writing between the fifth and the eighth centuries. The extant codes of these laws are among the most interesting as well as singular records we have of the early state of any nation; and to these nations, which traced the origin of their laws to them, they possess a double interest, and well merit notice.

It would seem that the law of the Visigoths is the first that was committed to writing. It was formerly held that the Salic laws were compiled by Phara-

[1] Selden, Dissertatio ad Fletam, c. 1, s. 4; c. 5, s. 7.

[2] Non ratione imperii sed rationis imperio.

mond or Clovis; and the question has been much agitated, whether they were reduced to writing before the Salian Franks crossed the Rhine, which would make *that code the more ancient: but it* seems most probable that, though enacted long before, they were not written until after that event; and though perhaps committed to writing shortly after, none of the extant texts of the Salic Digest of Law can be traced back beyond the seventh century. That it was first written in Latin, and not in German, seems undoubted.[1]

The laws of the Visigoths, called Forum Judicum, Evaric, or Euric, who reigned in 466 to 486, caused to be compiled. This is undoubtedly the most perfect and most ample of all the barbarian codes; and to the Roman civilization and the example of the Roman law this superiority is attributable. Another Visigothic king, Alaric son of Euric, caused a collection of Roman laws, or an abridgment of the Theodosian code, to be made and published for the use of his Roman subjects, now known under the title of Breviarium Aniani, but originally called Lex Romana.

The laws of the Burgundians were reformed and published by Gondebaud about the end of the fifth or beginning of the sixth century, and the precise date of 501 has been affixed to them. Sigismund, the Burgundian, did for his Romish subjects what Alaric had done in the south, and published, under the title of Papiani Responsum, a code of Roman law. Another system of laws, namely, that of the Ripuarian Franks, was published by Theodoric, between 511 and 534, and it greatly resembles the Salic law.[2]

---

1 The German student may see a discussion of this question in the history and explanation of the Salic law, by Wiarda Geschichte des Salischen Gezetzes.

2 For authorities on the history and general contents of the early codes of the Frankish invaders, the reader may refer to Savigny's celebrated History (Geschichte, &c.) and to Guizot's Essais sur l'Histoire de France, and Histoire de la Civilization en France, lect. 7, two admirable works.

Course of legislation in France.

From these different sources, in France under the Merovingian and Carlovingian races, the Franks in the north were governed by the Salic and Ripuarian law; the Burgundians in the east by the Gombette code; and in the south of France the Visigothic law continued in force. These laws were however confined to the persons of the conquerors: the vanquished continued to be governed by the Roman laws: the Breviarium Aniani, and the Responsum Papiani for the south and eastern parts: in the north, the previously existing general Roman law, unreduced to a code, continued in force. In matters relating to contracts, marriages, slaves, &c., from a deficiency of the codes of the barbarians, they were themselves obliged frequently to have recourse to the civil law.

Under the first race, from the confusion and strife of the early reigns, and the feebleness of the later ones, no political institution or general system of legislation or administration obtained consistency or permanence. In 752 the last of the Merovingian race was consigned to a cloister, and the mayor of the Palais, Pepin, proclaimed king. Under the Carlovingian race the Frankish kings, with the assent of their subjects,[1] convened in the Champs de Mars, or Mai, enacted many new general laws, under the title of Capitularies.[2] Most of these capitularies were made in the reigns of Charlemagne and Louis le Debonnaire. The capitularies, like the barbarian codes, were all personal or distinct for each race. The penal legislation of Charlemagne is little more than a repetition of those ancient codes. The new

[1] Lex consensu populi fit et constitutione regis. Capitularies of Charles the Bald, art. 6.

[2] The term Capitulary (derived from Capitula, a little chapter) is applied to all the laws of the Frankish kings.

Besides the authorities already quoted, the Capitularies, Précis Historique du Droit Français par Fleury, and Bernardi, de l'Origine et des Progrès de la Legislation Française, have been consulted in the foregoing sketch.

dispositions introduced by him generally softened the ancient legislation, especially as to the chastisement of slaves, though he introduces and freely employs the pain of death in a capitulary destined to restrain the Saxons.

Course of legislation in England.

St. Augustine and the Christian Missionaries brought with them, not only a new religion, but the wants and feelings of civilization; and as soon as the Anglo-Saxon King Ethelbert, who reigned in Kent from 591 to 616, was converted to the new faith, he published, with the consent of his witan, his "doom," or code of law.[1] Bede says[2] it was after the example of the Romans. But the successor of Hengist was not, like Alaric and Theodoric, instructed in the imperial law; and the expression of the historian can refer only to the promulgation of a code or regulation in writing, contrasted with a traditional and customary law. Ethelbert's statute offers no imitation whatever of the Roman policy, and it is Teutonic in language as well as in spirit.[3] All the other Teutonic nations employed the Latin language in their codes, but the laws of Ethelbert are written in Anglo-Saxon. The doom of Ethelbert was followed by the publication of the laws of several of the kingdoms of the Saxon Heptarchy; of which those of Hlothaire and Eadric in 685, and Wihtraed in 699, kings of Kent, and of Ina, about 700, king of Wessex, have come down to us.[4]

After the union of the Heptarchy under one king, the first of the code of laws is that of Alfred, who has been styled Conditor Legum Anglicanarum, and to whom popular tradition has assigned most of the institutions

---

[1] Leg. Æthelb. Prol. in Wilkins' Leges Anglo-Saxonicæ.

[2] Bede, Hist. Eccles. Ang. 2. 5.

[3] Sir Francis Palgrave, Rise and Progress of the English Commonwealth, which see for the nature and course of Anglo-Saxon legislation, part 1, c. 2, p. 44. Savigny also says, the collection of Ethelbert has nothing in common with the Roman law, Hist. v. 2, p. 136; Versuch einer Darstellung der Geschichte des Angelsächsischen Rechts., von George Phillips, n. 213.

[4] Phillips, s. 16. 67; Reeve's History of the English Law, vol. 1.

peculiar to this country, of which the origin is not positively known.[1]

The laws of the Anglo-Saxon kings, Edward the Elder, Athelstan, Edmund, Edgar, and Ethelred, are also extant. Canute, the Dane, repeated in a comprehensive code, published between 1017 and 1033, the laws of his Saxon predecessors; and Edward the Confessor, usually styled Restitutor Legum Anglicanarum, was required by the clergy and nobility, as the price of restoration to the throne of his ancestors, to confirm the laws of Canute.[2] The laws which have gone under the name of Edward the Confessor have been rejected as spurious, and they are supposed to have been collected thirty or forty years after his death.[3] After the battle of Hastings, when by his victory William the Norman had made good his claim to the crown of England, the English with one accord demanded the restoration of the laws and customs known and used by them. To this William assented; and a charter, statute, or capitulary has been preserved of the "laws which King William granted to the people of England after the Conquest (adquisitio), being the same which King Edward his cousin held before him," the substance of which is in a great measure a repetition of the laws of Canute; and those clauses not in the laws of the Danish king seem of Anglo-Saxon origin.[4]

General nature of the Germanic laws in France.

It is evident that the codes of both nations, in their most barbarous state, consisted of little more than a collection of the usages to which the people had been accustomed, reduced to writing by the authority of the

---

1 Stolberg, Leben Alfreds.

2 Palgrave, Rise and Progress, part 1, p. 48.

3 A collection of Anglo-Saxon laws, under the title of Archaionomia sive de priscis Anglorum legibus, was published by Mr. Lambarde in 1568; and an enlarged and corrected edition was published in 1644, by Abraham Wheloc; and, after many additions made by Dr. Wilkins, he published it in his Leges Anglo-Saxonicæ.

4 Palgrave, Rise and Progress, part 1, p. 55.

sovereign with the advice of his witan, or mahl. The chief subject of them is the laws relating to crimes, civil or ecclesiastical, committed with violence.

Almost all of the barbarian codes recognized the principle of allowing a pecuniary penalty to compensate[1] for the breach of the law by freemen; and the principal difference between the one and the other of them is in the mode of punishment, or the amount of pecuniary compensation directed.

Of the Salic law,[2] 343 articles relate to penalties, and 65 to subjects of other natures; and almost the only penalty is the 'wehrgeld,' or 'widrigeld,' composition to the party injured or his family, and the 'fred,' payable to the sovereign for the violation of the law.

The law of the Ripuarians was rather less exclusively a penal code, and the civil law gained a larger share of attention from its framers than the Salic law; but it is still largely occupied with pecuniary penalties, and differs from the Salic law chiefly in the provision for compensation for injuries to the sovereign or the church.

In the law of Burgundy the civil laws occupy nearly as many articles as the penal part; but the character which distinguishes this law from the preceding one is, that corporeal punishment is provided by it as well as pecuniary compensation.

The law of the Visigoths was the work of the clergy at the councils of Toledo, it also admitted of corporeal punishment. Both the Burgundian and Visigothic codes refused to recognize, in the punishment of crimes, the distinction between the Roman population and that of

---

[1] The composition was the first step of criminal legislation beyond the system of personal vengeance. The right which subsisted, concealed under this penalty, is that of each to redress and avenge himself by force: for the offended to make war on the offender. Composition was an inducement to substitute legal redress for war. The offended party long preserved the right to choose between the composition and self-redress—to refuse the wehrgeld, and have recourse to vengeance.—Guizot, Histoire de la Civilization en France, lect. 9.

[2] Guizot, Histoire de la Civilization en France, lect. 9.

their conquerors, and awarded the same compensation and punishment for killing a Roman as a barbarian; while the Salic and Ripuarian laws established a mortifying distinction, and valued the Roman at half the "were" due for a Frank.[1]

The laws of the Salic Franks partake more of the Teutonic character than those of the Ripuarians; and as we advance southward to Burgundy, we find the laws become still less of that character, and the code of the Visigoths in the south, who had been longer in contact with the Romans, and lived within their dominions, is the least German, and most Roman, of any of them.[2]

General nature of the Anglo-Saxon codes.

The Anglo-Saxon laws are of an unmixed Germanic character; and although, previous to, and for some time after the Norman Conquest, laws of three different denominations, namely, West Saxnalage, Myrcenalage, and Danelage[3] existed, yet, as Spelman observes, they seem to have differed rather in their mulcts than in their canon, i. e. in the quantity of fines and amerciaments than in the course and frame of justice. Ethelbert's laws relate only to the amount of the pecuniary fines payable for various transgressions. Those of Hlothaire and Eadric to the system of pledges and warranty intended to prevent theft and larceny, and Wihtraed's affix temporal punishments to spiritual offences.

The laws of Alfred seem to have probably consisted of two statutes, or sets of laws; one for the West Saxons,

---

1 Montesquieu's opinion is, that "The Roman law came to be disused among the Franks, because of the great advantages accruing from being a Frank, a barbarian, or a person living under the Salic law: on the other hand, in the patrimony of the Visigoths, as the Visigoth law gave no civil advantages to the Visigoths over the Romans, the latter had no reason to discontinue living under their own law."—Spirit of Law, l. 28, c. 4.

2 Guizot, Histoire de la Civilization en France.

3 These three denominations seem to have been preserved at the Conquest, though the view generally taken of the laws of Edward the Confessor is thus expressed: "Out of these three laws, Roger Hoveden and Ranulphus Cestrensis inform us, King Edward the Confessor enacted one uniform law, or digest of laws, to be observed throughout the whole kingdom."—1 B.C. 66.

containing Ina laws, and the other for Mercia, to which the laws of Offa, the Mercian king, were appended, which last have not come down to us. The now extant laws of Alfred do not differ in spirit from those of his predecessors, and do not justify the encomiums they have received;[1] though probably, as popular tradition is seldom entirely without foundation, the lost portion of his laws were of a character superior to those we now have.

General spirit of the institutions of the Gauls, Romans, and Germans.

In contrasting England and France, we must remember that the population of the former, whether Saxon or Norman, is almost exclusively of German origin; while among the latter, that race is largely mixed with Celtic and Roman descendants. A remarkable difference is perceptible between the characters of the ancient Gauls and the Germans, as described by Julius Cæsar and Tacitus;[2] and not only the present character and political institutions of the English and French nations, but also much of their respective civil laws, take their peculiarities from this source, particularly in that which (based on the habits of the people, and as durable and unchangeable as their character) we have described as the popular part of the law.

There can be no doubt the spirit and feelings of the ancient Gauls descended to their successors on the soil.[3] Neither the civilized Romans, nor the barbarian invaders, attempted the extirpation of the inhabitants; and the Latin or German, planted in Gaul, imbibed the spirit of

---

[1] Palgrave, Rise and Progress, part 1, p. 45 to 55.

[2] For a comparative view of the ancient institutions of Gaul and Germany, see Melchiori Goldasti, Hamensfeldii Collectio Consuetudinum et Legum Imperialium. At page 1 are, Consuetudines veterum Gallorum Germanorumque conscriptæ à C. Jul. Cæs. lib. 6, de Bel. Gall.; and at page 5, Consuetudines veterum Germanorum conscriptæ à C. Cornelio Tacito in lib. de Moribus Germanorum.

[3] An eminent French lawyer, Pierre Jean Grosley, in his work, Recherches pour servir a l'Histoire du Droit Français, asserts that a large portion of the French customary law existed before Cæsar.

the surrounding people: so that the character of the ancient Celtic Gauls, as described by the Roman authors, continued in the mass of the French population, unchanged either by the Roman or the Germanic invasions.[1] In the south of Gaul the Roman institutions, laws, and manners tended somewhat to modify the Gallic, but the effect of the Germanic customs was scarcely felt. More northward these customs had far more influence, and the legal institutions were more essentially Teutonic. In England, from the Saxon invasion, no traces are found either of the spirit and feelings, or of the positive institutions of either Roman or Celt.[2]

Character of the Gauls.

Throughout ancient Gaul the common people were little better than the slaves of the equestrian and sacerdotal orders. Daring nothing of themselves, and having no share in the public deliberations,—oppressed with debt, heavy tribute, or the violence of the more powerful classes,—they gave themselves up to servitude to the nobles, who exercised the same jurisdiction over them as masters over slaves.[3]

The Roman law, which succeeded that of the Gauls, notwithstanding its inestimable value as a body of rational jurisprudence, tended rather to increase than diminish these principles. Its rights of persons and its rules of the personal relations are the most defective part of the civil law; and it must be admitted by its warmest

---

[1] Nous voyons dans les anciens Gaulois un caractère de valeur, de vivacité, d'hospitalité, qu'on peut aisément reconnaître dans leurs descendans. Elémens de l'Histoire de France par M. l'Abbe Millot, tom. i.—Introduction.

Le Français est tel aujourd'hui qu'il fut dans tous les temps: inconstant, léger; mais brave, généreux, loyal, passionné pour la gloire; Des Magistrats d'Autrefois, &c., par M. Dupin.

For the singular permanence of the Gallo Francia since the time of Cæsar, see Heylin's France Painted to the Life, 46; Palgrave, Rise and Progress, pt. 1, p. 500.

[2] We must however bear in mind the continuance of Borough English in England and Brittany.

[3] Cæsar, de Bello Gallico, lib. 6, c. 12. See the conclusions drawn by Montlosier, De la Monarchie Française, tom. i. pp. 12, 13, 130; Bernardi, de l'Origine et des Progrès de la Legislation Française, p. 5; Fleury, Précis Historique, s. 2.

advocates to breathe a spirit of severity little likely to ameliorate the legal condition of the slave, or to respect the rights of any but the citizen.

Character of the Gauls.

Before the Roman Conquest, security could be obtained by the lower orders of Gaul only by placing themselves in servitude to one of the nobles. The Roman republic and early emperors left the administration of the law much in the hands of the ancient authorities, and that practice never entirely disappeared; though, after the native magistrates were displaced during the later times of the Imperial administration, it very much diminished; and not only the bravery, hospitality, and vivacity of the ancient Gauls, but also the slavish spirit of the commonalty, were inherited by their descendants.

Character of the Germans.

The origin of the popular part of the Anglo-Saxon law is almost wholly Germanic; and an examination of it will serve to exemplify that of the Frankish settlers in Gaul, whose institutions were also essentially of the same character, and prevent the necessity of separate notice.

The system of personal liberty and individual importance, is the foundation of the social state of the Germans. Each free barbarian held himself independent of every one; and everything was left to the whim or caprice of the individual. The only power in the ancient German society, was the will of the freeman. Their nations were formed of a federation of tribes, and their tribes of a federation of individuals. In each state, not only was the union of the several tribes which composed it loose and precarious, but each individual held himself but little connected with the others. The families lived separately, not in cities or towns, but in isolated habitations, at a distance from one another; and each barbarian fixed his independent dwelling on the spot to which a plain, a wood, or a stream of fresh water, had induced him to give the preference.[1]

[1] Gibbon.—Guizot.—Tacitus de Mor. Germ.

Rights of individuals.

There is scarcely anything more visible, and yet more indispensable to be duly observed, than the very different degrees of respect paid by the laws of Rome, Gaul, and Germany to an individual of the human race, and of importance attached to him—as a man; and this is clearly exemplified by a consideration of the law relating to new-born infants. Among the Romans the child was laid at the feet of its father, and unless he lifted it from the ground, it had not a legal right to life; and if he lifted it, it became his property.[1] The Gaul as little esteemed the helpless stranger, and long afterwards the father retained the right of selling his offspring. With the German[2] the child was recognized as entitled to the rights of a human being from the moment it had opened its eyes or uttered a cry. The palpable distinction, thus commenced at the very birth of the individual, went with him through life.

Rights of individuals in England.

Many of the Saxon personal laws and institutions still remain in England; but still more of the spirit of them. If we consider, first, the absolute rights of individuals, we find,—notwithstanding the ignorance and apathy, the habits of drunkenness and brutality with which the Anglo-Saxons, in common with all the German race, were justly chargeable, and though permitting slavery, their freemen[3] were jealous of their persons, and animated with a high sense of honour and independence,—their freedom dif-

[1] Hence, tollere filium, to educate, and non tollere, to expose, Cic. Leg. 3, 8; Suet. Oct. 65; Calig. 5. In his father's house, the adult son of a Roman citizen was a mere thing.—Gibbon, c. 44.

[2] Tacitus (De Mor. Germ.) informs us, that the Germans never exposed their children. It is not, however, intended here to deny that the Visigoths, and other barbarian tribes, especially those in the south of France, permitted exposing them; but as to the Anglo-Saxons, see Wilkins, A. S. L. 19, and n.; Michelet, Origines du Droit Français, b. 1, c. 1.

[3] M. de Savigny says, "I regard the class of freemen as the basis of the Germanic organization; and by this we must not understand a mere negative state of liberty as opposed to slavery; but, on the contrary, the full capacity for and complete exercise of all rights. The expression of dignity, which Mœser uses, renders this idea perfect. The words, dignity and freemen, correspond with those of caput and civis optimo jure among the Romans." Geschichte, v. i. c. 4.

fered materially from the civic liberty of the Romans and other ancient republicans, among whom the individual was sacrificed in the citizen. This spirit and feeling of individual personal independence, which gave to each the liberty of acting solely for his own object, though checked by the Norman Conquest, has ever since been developing itself in England.[1]

Rights of individuals in France.

The laws of the Salic and Ripuarian Franks appear to have a singular respect for the person and liberties of the freeman. The Burgundian laws also retained the guarantees of personal independence, originating in their ancient manners; but the spirit of individual independence was equally unknown to the Celtic Gaul, or to the Roman of the later times, and the imperial laws. Among the Romans liberty existed; but even in the best times of the Republic it was liberty as a citizen, arising

[1] It was this spirit that produced, within a century and a half of the Conquest, the memorable declaration of the Magna Charta. "No freeman shall be taken or imprisoned but by lawful judgment of his peers, or by the law of the land." 9 Hen. III. c. 29. The blot of the qualification of freedom in this article of the charter was gradually wiped out as the progress of time civilized the feelings of men, and having emancipated all classes, permitted this spirit of personal independence to be shared by the freed bondman and emancipated thrall, as well as the ancient Saxon freeman. Statute after statute (in 1289, 5 Ed. II. c. 9; in 1337, 25 Ed. III. c. 4; 28 Ed. III. c. 3) followed this great charter, expressly enforcing freedom from personal restraint, and to prohibit that any man should be taken or imprisoned, by suggestion or petition of the king or his council, unless it be by process of law.

A mere enactment is a dead letter without institutions and remedial process to enforce it, and these the writs of mainprise, de homine replegiando, and habeas corpus provided, by which a prisoner obtained his release from custody, or was bailed into the hands of his mainpernors and fellow-freemen. Pledges and mainpernors are of the same signification: but pledge applies to other things as well as persons, mainpernors of men only.—Mirror, c. 4, s. 9. See also as to appeal for imprisonment in bailable cases, contrary to sufficient bail.—Mirror, c. 2, s. 18. From a very early period, the party injured might have an action of false imprisonment against his gaoler or detainers to recover compensation in damages assessed by a jury. See a bill for false imprisonment, Year Book, 2 Ed. II., 22 Ass. 85, temp.; 22 Ed. III. 1348; Year Book, 14 Hen. VI. 26; 22 Ed. IV. 45.

The habeas corpus act, by reducing to certainty and facilitating the means of obtaining the ancient common law writ of habeas corpus, established the entire sanctity of the person from all but legal restraints, and finally carried to its full extent this inherited spirit of the Saxons.

from the privileges of an association. Under the empire, however, this liberty was but a name for oppression; and though the Visigoths, like the other Germanic nations that settled in Gaul, carried with them the personal independence enjoyed by them in their native land, their habits became conformed to those of the vanquished Celts, and their whole system of law became more or less tinctured with the Roman Administration. In the forum judicum, the Visigothic law, where the Roman superseded the German, the want of guarantees for personal independence is manifested. The fierce barbarian would, no doubt, have resisted personal restraint had it been applied to himself in the first instance; but the principles and maxims of the Roman law and the Celtic spirit gradually infused itself into the whole system, and to these two causes is due the subsequent tyranny under which France so long laboured: for although, in the north, institutions, similar to those of the ancient Germans, existed in the earlier times to keep alive the feelings of individual independence, yet the example of the southern provinces, and the gradual and unobserved substitution of forms of administration, different from those of their ancestors, and more conformable to the spirit of the Roman administration, left the Frank no handle which he could legally employ to resist arbitrary power.

Until shortly before the revolution of 1780, the Celtic spirit of tyranny on the one part, and slavery on the other, continued unchecked in France.

Local organization.

The legal capacity and rights of the private individual, among the Anglo-Saxons, was founded on a system of mutual suretyship.[1]

Tacitus[2] mentions the division of the people into hundreds (centena); and this division, together with the sub-

[1] Leg. Cnut. II. 19. Volumus ut quisque liber homo sit in decima constitutus quum sit major 12 annis: vel posthac nullo libertatis jure sit dignus, &c.

[2] Germ. c. 6.

division into tens (decenna), existed among all the German tribes[1] who overran Europe, as well for some time after as before they left their native forests, and formed a military organization of the people. A tithing-man (decanus) commanded his tithing, or ten; and a hundredary, or ealderman of the hundred (centenarius), the hundreds.[2] The gerefa, graphio,[3] heretoch, or eorl (dux, comes) led united hundreds. The invaders carried the same organization into their new territories, France as well as England;[4] and when permanently settled there they still retained it, at least in England, though in France, from the existence of the Roman population, it seems not to have been so fully established, or so long and generally retained. From thence, in England, arose the existing division of the country into tithings (decenna), also called borghs[5] and hundreds (centena), still headed by the centenarius, or alderman of the hundred, and the decanus, or head tithing-man. Among them there existed no distinction between the citizen and the soldier; all were armed, and ready to protect themselves against the foreign enemy or domestic marauder, and both in England and in France[6] the State endeavoured to make

---

1 Eichhorn, Deutsche Staats und Rechtsgeschichte, s. 18.

2 These offices and titles are found not only in the Anglo-Saxon laws but in the capitularies and the codes of other continental nations.—Car. Magn. Cap. de villis, A.D. 800, s. 10 & 58; Ll. Wisigothorum, l. 9, tit. 2; Ll. Bajavorum, tit. 5.

3 The graphio, graf, grave, or greve, of the continental nations was of a more determinate rank than the Anglo-Saxon gerefa, and corresponded with the Anglo-Saxon eorl; the terms gravio and comes were used as synonymous among the Franks immediately after the Conquest of Gaul.—Savigny, c. 4. The gerefa among the Anglo-Saxons signified any person possessing authority, and was usually associated with some other word indicating the limit of that authority, as scire gerefa (sheriff), hundredgreve, portreeve.—Savigny, History, c. 4, p. 3; Greve, Latinorum lingua nihil expressius sonat quam præfectura, Leg. Ed. Conf. 35.

4 Bernardi, de la Origine et des Progrès de la Legislation Française, p. 23.

5 Borghs or burghs seem synonymous with township, tun, tunginium, which is also used for the Frankish mallum.

6 Montesquieu says, "The division into hundreds is posterior to the establishment of the Franks in Gaul; it was made by Clotharius and Childebert, with a view of obliging each district to answer for the robberies committed in their division: this we find in the decrees of those princes."—Spirit of Laws, b. 30, c. 17.

use of the existing military organization as a system of police. Each head tithing-man, with his fellow tithing-men, was charged to watch and ward, to preserve the peace within the territory in which they had settled,[1] so that ward and tithing became synonymous terms. The district or tithing was made answerable for the robberies committed within its circuit, and was bound to deliver up the robber or pay a fine. Each tithing was made answerable for the appearance of its members[2] when accused of crimes which it was bound to repress.[3]

Frank-pledge.

The members thus became borgh, or pledge for each other; and the community was called a friburg, or frank-pledge.[4] To prevent the institution from falling to decay, every person was obliged, at the age of twelve years, to enrol themselves in some decenary or tithing. The tithing-man was in a more especial manner bound to answer for the good conduct of the others; and a thief who broke the pledge thus given for him by the tithing was said to be untrue to the people, folkentreu.[5] When any of the members accused of crime were not, or could not be, produced to answer the accusation, the tithing was fined.[6] The member who fled, besides thereby tacitly acknowledging that he could not purge himself, rendered his pledge liable on his behalf, and was therefore considered to have forfeited his claim to

Outlawry.

their countenance or protection. He became an outlaw (utlaghe) and friendless man, who might be slain like a wolf, or animal noxious to society, and was thence called wolf's-head, caput lupinum;[7] mercy was never extended to him. The institution was afterwards extended

---

[1] Palgrave, Rise and Progress, part 1, pp. 82, 193.

[2] Leg. Æthebr. I. 1; Leg. Cnut. II. 19; Leg. Ed. Conf. 20.

[3] In this point of view it must be regarded as a system of coercion.—See Palgrave, Rise and Progress, part 1, p. 193.

[4] Leg. Edw. Conf. 20, 32; Jud. Civ. Lund. 3.

[5] Canute II. s. 23, 27; Laws of William the Conqueror, s. 39, term applied to a thief.

[6] Leg. Loth. et Eadr. 2.

[7] He was also called a flyman or flemene.

to civil cases. As the strictness of the responsibility of the tithing relaxed, the penalties attached to absconding became to be considered as too heavy; and the outlaw's life was put under the protection of the law, though his property was forfeited. To this institution the modern laws of outlawry are to be traced. William the Conqueror enforced the law of frank-pledge, as a system of police for the government of his acquired kingdom;[1] and he added to the oath taken by each member when he enrolled himself in his borough, what was afterwards called the oath of allegiance. An examination of the tithings, and a renewal of this oath, called view of frank-pledge, visus franci plegii, took place once every year. Outlawry.

The military organization, thus deducing its existence from ancient Germany, and passed into a system of police, has been brought down in this country to our own times; and the armed leader of the military band of ten or a hundred has been converted into the rustic constable or peace officer, still chosen by his fellow-burghers. In early Anglo-Saxon times, the whole system of personal law thus hung upon this organization of mutual pledgeship, or borgh, by which the government was secured against the escape of offenders, while at the same time the liberty of the accused individual, bailed or intrusted to the hands of his fellow-pledgers, was preserved; and he had a sort of right[2] to call for the countenances of the men of his borgh to become responsible for him, and to swear to their belief of his innocence, if other modes of proof failed.

The Germans certainly had for a long time nothing

[1] Leg. Guil. Conq. 64.

[2] See post. It is obvious, that being in the pledge of borgh was synonymous with in the law, or laghe; for on it depended all the rights of the freeman. See page 20, n. 1. We will not, however, run the changes on in-law and out-law (Gloss. Wilkins, Leg. A. S. utl) laghe or lah, borgh, pledge, burg, district; but there certainly does seem more than a probability that, as some have asserted, laghe is not merely equivalent to borgh-pledge, but also to a district, which is called borgh.—See Bishop Nicholson's Preface to Wilkins' Leges Anglo-Saxonicæ, p. xvi.; and Dreyer, De uso genuino jure Anglo-Saxonici, p. 267.

Municipal institutions.

in common with municipal institutions: towns and cities were unknown to the primitive Germans, who abhorred the very name of a walled town. The protection of the lofty ramparts seemed to them synonymous with degradation and servitude.[1] In England the Anglo-Saxon walled cities were organized like the open country, assuming the form of a hundred or shire; and with the exception of the trading guild, descended from the colleges of operatives, only very scanty vestiges of the Roman municipal institutions can be found.[2] In France it was very different: the cities which constituted the primitive element of the Roman world survived the invasion;[3] and even in the north, where the Franks were most numerous, the forms of the Roman municipal government were retained. Many cities could deduce their institutions from the Roman period until the first French Revolution. Bourges, Perigueux, Boulogne, Tournay, Marseilles, Toulouse, Nismes, afford remarkable exemplifications of this fact.[4]

The civil jurisdiction of the Roman cities was easily adapted to the German constitution.[5] The laws re-

---

1 Palgrave, Rise and Progress, part 1, p. 268.

2 The bourgeoisie of London, as that of the greater part of the larger Saxon cities, formed under the name of the hanse a municipal corporation, to which belonged the police and government of the city. The presence of the king did not change this order of things, and the burgesses could even without his permission assemble and deliberate on their internal affairs. At the head of the elective chiefs of this powerful association was a person, of whom no historian has preserved the name, and whom the only recital in which he figures designates by the title of Hansward.—Thierry, Histoire de la Conquête de l'Angleterre par les Normands.

The recital alluded to is a manuscript Latin poem, on the Surrender of London, discovered in the Royal Library of Brussels. It seems however very doubtful, whether the word Ansgardus, rendered above Hansward, is not a proper name.

3 Professor Savigny's History of the Roman Law during the Middle Ages.

4 M. Raynouard, Histoire du Droit Municipal en France; John of Salisbury, epist. 214; Dubos, Histoire Critique de l'Etablissement de la Monarchie Française dans les Gaules; Palgrave, Rise and Progress, part 1, p. 493, 4; Savigny, History, c. 5. This however is denied by Mably, Observation sur l'Histoire de France, b. 1, c. 2.

5 See part 2 of the 2nd chapter of Savigny's History, v. i., for an account of the judicial organization of the cities of Gaul at the barbaric invasion; and also Guizot' Essais sur l'Histoire de France, Ess. 1.

lating to the municipal system occupy a large space in the Breviarum. These institutions seem, at least in the north, not at first to have been shared by the Germans. When at a later period they became numerous in the cities, they founded among themselves communities similar to those of the Romans: they united to them, and the conquerors and the conquered formed one great community, composed of two distinct elements, under the direction of a college of German Echevins and the Ordo of the Romans,[1] the ancient Decuriones.

During the troubles which ensued in France, the inhabitants of cities established among themselves societies, under the protection of some lord, to guarantee themselves from the tyranny of others, and to be judged by their peers.

Domestic rights, husband and wife.

In their domestic personal relations, from the earliest records we have of the Germans, we discover the high estimation in which they held their females; and they attributed a sanctity or inspiration to them.[2] The rights arising from relation of marriage were the same in kind, though since refined by increased civilization, as they still are in England.[3] The wife was supposed to be under the domestic control of her husband,[4] and she was therefore not included in the frank-pledge, or free-borgh.[5] From this, added to the Christian doctrine of the union of husband and wife as one flesh, arose the legal maxim that they are one person,[6] which still governs this relation in England.

---

1 Savigny, History, v. i. c. 5.

2 Tac. c. 8.

3 Eichhorn, Deutsche Staats und Rechtsgeschichte, s. 52, 56.

4 In mariti sui potestatem pervenerit. Pœnit. Egb. 1; 33 Wilk. Conc. p. 122; Leg. Inæ, 57; Leg. Cnut. II. 74. See Mirror of Justice. The total disability of a woman to contract is almost peculiar to this country.

5 Palgrave, Rise and Progress, part 1, p. 198.

6 The striking contrast between the English and the civil and French laws on this subject would leave little doubt of the Saxon origin of this legal maxim, even if there were no other evidence. It was not known to the Pays coutumier in the north of France. Beaumanoir says, "partnership is formed by marriage," c. 21; and even in Normandy there were no traces of it. M. Houard, in com-

The difference between the German and Gallic manners is scarcely in anything more strongly marked than in the domestic relations. Among the Gauls[1] the men had the power of life and death over their wives and children; and when any father of a family of illustrious rank died his relations assembled, and upon the least ground of suspicion put even his wives to the torture like slaves; and if any discovery was made, they were tortured to death with fire and all sorts of torments.[2]

The Celtic relations of marriage partly gave way before Christianity and the Roman habits;[3] and to this day the French law of marriage is for the most part regulated by the civil law.

The domestic tribunal of the Romans[4] seems to have preceded the family council of the modern French law.[5] The Roman husband summoned the wife's relations, and tried her in their presence. This tribunal decided not only in respect to the violation of the laws, but also of manners, and inflicted arbitrary penalties.

In France, at the time of Charlemagne, the relations

---

menting on the 168th and the 291st section of Littleton, notwithstanding his anxiety to show a perfect similarity between the English and Norman customs, could find nothing to adduce at all similar on this most important and fundamental principle of personal law. The cause of this difference between the continental German customs and the English, is perhaps to be traced to the different states of their respective clergy, who it must be remembered absorbed all the learning of the period. In France the line of ecclesiastics continued unaltered by the barbarian invasion, and the Gallic priest was a Roman, and retained the usage of the Roman law, which regarded the wife as a different person from her husband. The Saxon priest was ignorant of the Roman law, and in administering the law of the secular tribunals, to which he himself was subject, (Alfred, s. 21; Hist. Eliensis, p. 482,) he had no motive for not adding the doctrines of the church to the Anglo-Saxon customary law.

[1] Cæs. de Bel. Gall. b. 6, c. 18; Grosley, Recherches pour servir à l'Histoire du Droit Français, p. 8, &c.

[2] Meiners, in his history of the female sex, maintains that women were never so happy or so virtuous as in Germany, and that before the entrance of the Franks the Gauls knew not how to love or respect them.—Geschichte des weiblichen geschlechts, t. i. p. 198, &c.

[3] Savigny, v. ii. p. 5.

[4] Montesquieu, Spirit of Laws, b. 7, c. 10.

[5] It existed under the ancient coutume of Paris, and other districts.

of man and wife were exceedingly irregular; and a man took and quitted a wife without scruple, and almost without formality. Great disorder resulted from it. There are a great number of dispositions in the Capitularies on the conditions of marriage, the degrees of consanguinity, the duties of husbands to their wives, and the duties of widows, &c. The greater part of these dispositions coincide with the doctrines of the canon law; and it was only under the second, or Carlovingian race, that the distinction between a lawful wife and a concubine began to be made. From that time there could be no legitimate marriage without the benediction of the priest.[1]

Tacitus says the wife did not (as among the Romans) bring the dowry to the husband, but the husband gave one to his wife.[2] According to the laws of our Anglo-Saxon kings, in a contract of marriage, the consent of the female and her friends was first obtained; the bridegroom then gave his pledge, that he desired her that he might keep her according to the laws of God, as a man ought to keep his wife.[3] The next step was to provide respecting the foster lean[4] (the money required to keep the children); and then he signified what he would give her for choosing to be his wife (the morgan gift);[5] which, like modern jointure, was not to vest in her till after the nuptials; and they then fixed what he would give her in case she survived him. After the husband had given the requisite pledges, the marriage was celebrated in the presence of the priest. The ancient Anglo-Saxon laws mention the purchasing a wife; and

---

[1] Capit. vi. 130, 13 B; vii. 59, 105, 179. As to the ritual and forms of marriage, Michelet, Origines du Droit Français cherches dans les Symboles et Formules du Droit Universel, v. i. p. 34.

[2] Tac. c. 18.

[3] Leg. Edm. d. Spons. 1.

[4] Leg. Edm. d. Spons. 2.

[5] Leg. Cnut. ap. Brompton, c. 99. This gift was also made in France by the Teutonic husband. Du Cange v. Morganegiba.

Among the Visigoths the morgengabe might not exceed the tenth of the goods of the husband; among the Franks it might be a third. The donation was called also bankgabe.—Michelet, Origines, p. 47.

if it did not merely mean, as has been supposed, the treaty for her morgan gift, as she might refuse to marry any man,[1] it certainly did not signify the purchase of her as a slave, but a sort of compensation, for the loss of her services and society, paid to her relatives,[2] probably like the modern English damages for seduction.[3]

In Gaul we are told,[4] that whatever fortune the wife brought the husband he was obliged to equal it out of his own estate; and the sum thus produced was left untouched, and went to the survivor. This custom was the forerunner of the community of goods,[5] a species of partnership between man and wife, existing in the modern French laws. Its Celtic origin is beyond all doubt: it existed in Brittany, which so strenuously withstood the Frankish arms and laws, and in other provinces.

The Anglo-Saxon wife (like the modern Englishwoman) was permitted to inherit and possess landed property, to transmit it, and with her husband's consent to sell or alienate it. If she brought forth children, and survived her husband, she was entitled to half his property for dower.

As an index of the comparative estimation of the two sexes, it may be observed, the Visigothic law permitted daughters to inherit land with the brothers.[6] The Salic and the Burgundian laws[7] excluded the daughters from the right of succeeding to land in conjunction with their brothers.

Among the Germans the laws of matrimony were strictly observed. Adultery was very uncommon, and its punishment most severe.[8]

The contact with the conquered Gauls seems to have entirely obliterated the feelings which the Franks, we

---

1 Pœnit. Egb. I. 20; Wilk. Conc. p. 119; Leg. Cnut. II. 72.

2 Leg. Æthelst. 76, 82; Leg. Inæ, 31.

3 Palgrave, Rise and Progress, part 1.

4 Cæs. de Bel. Gall., b. 6, c. 18; Bernardi, de l'Origine et des Progrès de la Legislation Française, p. 6.

5 Bernardi, de l'Origine, &c., pp. 6, 7.

6 Visigothic Law, lib. 4, tit. 2, s. 1.

7 Tit. I, s. 3; tit. 14, s. 1; tit. 51.

8 Tacitus.

may presume, had in their native country, in common with the other German tribes; and incest, adultery, and unlegitimated sexual commerce abounded. But after the reformation effected by Charlemagne, the Frankish subjects could no longer take and quit a wife at pleasure, without form or ceremony, though divorce was tolerated among them in certain cases.[1] And in England a man might lawfully leave his wife for adultery,[2] and marry another; but divorce seems to have been denied for any other cause.[3] A law of the Visigoths enjoins, that the slaves of the house shall be obliged to bind the man and woman they surprise in adultery, and to present them to the husband and to the judge.[4] By the Anglo-Saxon law a fine was imposed for that as for other crimes.[5]

Parent and child.

In another of the domestic relations, there yet remains a distinction, which, while it speaks volumes for the character of the Germanic women, clearly shows the Anglo-Saxon origin of the existing personal laws. According to the Anglo-Saxon law, the condition of the child, as a freeman or slave,[6] followed that of the father,[7] and not that of the mother; as it does in the civil law, and the French and other systems founded on that code.[8]

The authority of the Teutonic father seems to have been very large; but great care was bestowed on youth in consideration of the knighthood or servitude rendered from childhood to manhood. To be surrounded by a band of select youths was the pride and strength of the ancient German chiefs, their ornament in peace, their defence in war; and this, added to their emancipation as

[1] Bernardi, de l'Origine, &c. p. 160.

[2] Egb. Pœnit. I. 19.

[3] Epist. John. VIII. Pont. ad Æthelr. Cant. Archiep. ann. 877; Wilk. Conc. tom. i. p. 195.—See a curious privilege for the wife, Egb. Pœnit. 1, 20.

[4] Law of the Visigoths, lib. 3, tit. 4, s. 6.

[5] Leg. Æthelst. 32.

[6] The same rule still governs the law as to natives and aliens.

[7] Pœnit. Egb. I. 25; Ll. Hen. I. c. 77.

[8] Partus sequitur ventrem: but Lex Angliæ nunquam matris sed semper patris conditionem imitari partum judicat.—Co. Lit. 123, a.

soon as they could carry their arms, and admission to the national councils, corroborates the previous statement, that the same personal importance partly attached to the free-born minor, which afterwards fully invested his manhood.

By the Ripuarian laws, we find that the age of fifteen, the ability to bear arms and majority went together;[1] and among the Burgundians they were of age at fifteen.[2]

The ancient Gauls never suffered their children to come openly into their presence until they were of age to bear arms: the appearance of a son in public with his father before he reached manhood, was accounted dishonourable;[3] and partly to the Celtic view of the relation of parent and child, and partly to the paternal authority allowed by the Roman law, which was far too unlimited, is perhaps to be attributed the great authority of the French father, which however was still greater before the Revolution.

Ranks of the people.

The terms "caldormen," signifying chief, and "to set in ealdre," to make ruler, like the Latin term senator or senior, and the Arabian sheik, seem to indicate that the eldest or aged governed; but that use of these words perhaps arose out of the primeval form of patriarchal government, or else it might have originated in the practice of election, in which the people naturally put themselves under the most experienced man: and therefore, as age generally brings experience,[4] the terms ruler and elderman become synonymous. But, although the practice of choosing chiefs existed, it must not be supposed that an equality subsisted throughout the nation; for, on the contrary, the Germanic tribes,[5] especially the Anglo-Saxons, seem to have been divided, if not into castes, at least into well-defined classes, consisting of, 1st, the Royal Family, or class of ealdormen, to which the

---

1 Tit. 81.
2 Tit. 87.
3 Cæs. de Bel. Gall. c. 6.
4 Leg. Edw. Conf. 35.
5 Savigny, Geschichte, v. i. c. 2.

supreme authority was confined; and though lost by one individual, the sovereignty could not depart from the race:[1] 2nd. The nobility (eorlcunden, or class of eorls or thane-born),[2] the hands or compurgatory oath of one of whose members was, when a great or king's thane, of six times as much weight as one of the lower order of freemen; and when a minor thane, or radecnight, of three times: 3rd. The lowest class of Saxons, recognized as free and part of the people, were the ceorls, or villeins. Theowes, serfs or slaves, were not included in the commonweath.[3] A ceorl might voluntarily resign his freedom; and the criminal and insolvent debtor were liable to be sold to slavery.

Among the Germans, slaves (who were chiefly rural, and rarely domestic) were treated with great lenity. To strike a slave, or fetter him, was a rare occurrence. Sometimes, indeed, they were killed in moments of anger, but not by a course of severity.[4]

---

[1] Phillips, Angelsachsischen rechts. s. 68; Turner, History of the Anglo-Saxons, v. 4, b. 4, c. 1.

[2] Thane (from Thegnean, Thenians [A. S.], Dienen [Germ.], to serve) originally signified "minister," or servant of the Anglo-Saxon monarch. The title was afterwards extended to all landed proprietors who were neither aldermen nor churls.

[3] The master answered in the burg for his slaves.—Cnut. II. 19, 28; Wilkins, 136, 139.

Palgrave, Rise and Progress, part 1, pp. 9, 10, 11, 12, 13, 14. Though the person of a ceorl was free, the services due from him might be transferred by bequest or sale: Palgrave, p. 17. Proofs are wanting of any abridgment of the personal liberty of the ceorl anterior to the accession of Henry Plantagenet: p. 18. And the Anglo-Saxon principles of personal freedom emancipated the villeins in England at an earlier period than in France. Sir T. Smith says that the lower orders of clergy were very zealous in procuring the manumission of villeins. A preamble to the manumission, by Henry VIII., recites that the act is pious and meritorious with God, who created all men free. A commission of Queen Elizabeth is preserved in Rymer for giving freedom to such of her villeins as chose to pay a composition. Sir T. Smith states that in his time he never knew any instance of a villein in gross. On Charters of Manumission, see Hickes, Diss. Epist.; Madox, Formulare Anglicanum; Robertson, Charles V. v. i. n. 20; on the use of the term slave, s. 1, 1 Ed. 6, c. 3; on the latest testimonies to the existence of villeinage in England, Hallam, v. ii. p. 393.

[4] Tacitus, c. 25.

The state of villeinage was established in Gaul before it was invaded by either Roman or barbarian; and during the time of the Romans, there were in that country a vast number[1] of slaves, both domestic, who served within the house, and rural, whose occupation lay without the rustici, agricolæ, aratores, adscriptii, coloni, of the Roman law. The Gallic master had the power of life and death over his slaves.[2] Notwithstanding the respect shown for the freemen in the Salic law, for the slaves, and even the cultivators of the soil, the enactments of that law are of a brutal cruelty, abounding in tortures and other corporal punishments. A capitulary, however, deprived the master of the power of punishing his slaves with death.[3]

An Anglo-Saxon ceorl was called a twihændman; a minor thane, a sixhændman; and a major thane, a twelfhændman; designations which signify the relative value of their hands, or compurgatory oaths. A vestige of this superior confidence in the word and honour of the noble is left in the existing English law, which takes, in certain cases, the evidence of a peer on his honour instead of his oath.

Among the Franks, as among the Anglo-Saxons, there were, besides the Royal Family, three classes of men: 1st, the nobles; 2nd, freemen (lidi liti lassi, &c.); 3rd, slaves.[4] The great distinction which existed between the noble classes and the freeman, has been thought to indicate that the pre-eminence of the former was established by the conquest by them of another tribe, to whom they left their freedom, while they established a superiority over them.

In England, the ranks and titles of the Imperial

---

[1] Bernardi, de l'Origine, &c., p. 83.

[2] Gregor. Turon. V. 3.

[3] Capit. Add. iv. 49.

[4] The rank of each class is clearly defined by the Frankish and Anglo Saxon laws in the amount of the fine, or wehrgeld, imposed on the murder of so individual of either rank.

Roman government were entirely swept away, and Teutonic names and institutions substituted, which continue to the present time, as earl, shire-reeve, &c. In France, the early Merovingian kings[1] affected to continue the imperial administration; the Roman titles were retained, and the sovereign distributed the conquered provinces among his Teutonic heretochs and graphios, and assigned to them the same offices as the emperors had given to their consuls, rectors, and presidents. But though his officers took the titles of their Roman predecessors, duke and count (dux, comes), they were animated with a totally different spirit, and were rather military chiefs than ministerial officers.

Besides hereditary ranks, another distinction has been pointed out as existing at the time of the invasion, in the state of the Germans, viz. between their relations to each other in their tribes, and as bands of warriors; and some writers have endeavoured to show that totally distinct classes of individuals composed these two associations.

In the military band of the ancient Germans, no man entered but of his own accord; the warrior chose his own chief and companions, and undertook nothing but by an act of his own will. In the constitution of an army, although there may exist a great degree of liberty, yet equality cannot subsist with command and the patronage of a chief over his companions, but a military or aristocratic subordination becomes indispensable, and at an early period a leader or king was chosen by the invaders out of the royal or superior race.[2] When a band took possession of a district, the chief appropriated vast do-

[1] Clovis was invested with the dignity of Consul and Patrician by Anastasius, the Emperor of the East.—Garnier, Origine du Gouvern. Franç., p. 18; Millot, Elemens de l'Histoire de France, p. 11; Histoire Critique de l'Etablissement de la Monarchie Française dans les Gaules, par M. Dubos.

Mr. Alleyn, in his learned work, Inquiry into the Rise and Progress of the Royal Prerogative, shows that much of our monarchical theory of government is derived from the Roman empire. Not only the Norman but the Anglo-Saxon copied the continental theories and institutions.

[2] Gregor. Turon. Hist. 2, 9.

mains: the greater part of the warriors who had followed him continued to live around him and with him at his table, without any property specially their own. The chief disposed of his great means; the others were merely warriors; and a great number of freemen fell into a very inferior condition. The Anglo-Saxon laws speak of folghers;[1] and the Frankish laws talk constantly of freemen living in the lands of another, and reduced almost to the same state as coloni.

When a tribe seated themselves in a new district, nearly the same personal relations would continue as in the old country.

Nobility among the Germans was originally independent of the king, who was only the head among equals: but in subsequent times the sovereign became the source of honour; and contact with him, while it called for a return of service and dependence, gave the freeman a new importance. The voluntary companions (comites) of the prince, mentioned by Tacitus, were converted into the men who had vowed fealty to the king (qui sunt in trusti regis),[2] and are called in the formularies of Marculfus by the title of the king's antrustios;[3] by the earliest French historians leudes and fideles, and by those of a later date vassals.[4]

Besides these nobles of the sovereign court, were the followers of the inferior chiefs, who established themselves at a great distance from each other, and occupied vast domains: their houses, at a later period, became castles. The villages formed around them were peopled by men no longer their equals, and the commonwealth was divided into "hlafords"[5] and "men," in feudal

---

1 The lord was answerable as the pledge of his follower.

2 Sal. L. tit. 44, art. 4.

3 l. 1, form 18.

4 Montesquieu, b. 3, c. 16; Guizot, Essais sur l'Hist. de Fran. Ess. 4, c. 2, s. 3.

5 'Hlaford,' by contraction 'lord,' originally signified distributor of bread. In the ancient times of England, the chief of a great house, whose table nourished many men, was so called.—Thierry, ii. 162; Etymol. Dict.; Phillips, Angelsachsischen Rechts, n. 370.

language, lords and vassals. An Anglo-Saxon freeman (not a hlaford) might be attached to a superior, to whom he was bound by fealty,[1] and from whom he could claim a legal protection or warranty, when accused of any transgression.[2] That military service, or the obligation of defending the country, and, therefore, of following to the war the leaders from the highest to the lowest in subordination, was due of common right, is indisputable; and the organization in tens and hundreds facilitated the arrangement.

Laws of property.

When we come to the consideration of the laws of property[3] among the Anglo-Saxons, we find a very large portion of the law occupied with enactments for the preservation of cattle[4], and such like property. As to landed property, a difficulty meets us at the outset, for there are found so few laws relating to the subject, that it has long been a perplexed question of history, whether the feudal system existed among them or not.[5] This question seems to depend greatly upon the determination of the problem, whether that system is the peculiar law of any particular nation, or one of the laws of universal prevalence which arise as necessary consequences of certain circumstances, and must always be found in any country in which, while lands are possessed by the soldiery of a conquering army in reward for their service, the country continues to be held by them under a feeling of insecure dominion, which preserves the relation of soldier and general, leader and follower, lord and vassal. The latter opinion seems to bear the greatest

[1] Form of oath.—Leg. Æthelst. II. App. s. 1.

[2] Item diximus quod quis pro domino suo pugnet impune, si Dominum quis oppugnet; ita Dominus pro hominibus suis pugnare debet.—Leg. Ælfr. 38; Palgrave, Rise and Progress, p. 14.

[3] Phillips, Versuch einer Darstellüng der Geschichte des Angelsachsischen Rechts, Sachenrecht, s. 133, 145.

[4] Theft of cattle was most severely punished.—Leg. Wihtr. 26; Leg. Ælfr. 9.

[5] See the discussion of this subject by Bishop Nicholson, in the Preface to Wilkins, Anglo-Saxon Laws, p. 4.

appearance of truth, when we consider that a system of military tenure, partially resembling that of feuds, existed among the ancient Scythians and Scandinavians, in Rajast'han in Asia, and in Bornou in Africa, as well as in Europe. One thing, however, is evident from the numerous laws relating to cattle, and the few to be found on the subject of lands, that landed property had not during the Anglo-Saxon period that exclusive importance which it obtained when feudalism was fully established.

Among the ancient Germans, the land was vested, not in individuals, but in the nation in common.[1] Every year they made a new division of the arable lands; and, to avoid disputes, suffered a great part of their territory to lie waste.[2] Among the Germans there were vassals, but no fiefs, because the princes had no lands to give; though the magistrate elected to superintend the annual division of the lands, being the representative of the whole, may be conceived to have held the same situation as the warrior-chief, who afterwards regulated the division of the spoil, and, becoming more powerful, called upon his followers to vow fealty in return for their shares.

After the conquest of Gaul, the Franks, Salic and Ripuarian, took what land they pleased, making no regulations but among themselves. The Visigoths and Burgundians at first entered into an arrangement, that the Roman population should provide for their subsistence; and the barbarian took possession of the Roman villa as the "guest" of the proprietor. Afterwards, in Burgundy and among the Visigoths, the barbarians took possession of two-thirds of the land and one-third of the bondmen.[3]

During the period we are now considering, there is no

---

[1] Hence the doctrine, that all land is held of the crown, which personifies the nation.—Palgrave, Rise and Progress, p. 67.

[2] Tacitus, de Mor. Germ. c. 26; Cæsar, 6, 21.

[3] Savigny, History, v. i. c. 5, part 1, Kingdom of Burgundy; ib. part 2, Kingdom of the Visigoths.

doubt there were three sorts of landed possessions in France, namely, allodial lands, benefices, and tributary lands; but as the state of the proprietor determined the state of his land rather than, as in the next period, the state of the land the condition of the proprietor, and as the condition of the land was not decidedly marked during the early part of this period, the consideration of these three kinds of territorial right more properly belongs to the next.

In England, the Anglo-Saxons, like the Franks, took unrestricted possession of the lands. Each clan or tribe settled throughout the country, formed a township[1] (tun, from tynan, to enclose) either under the authority and protection of a military or a hereditary chief of the superior classes, who held the lands in demesne;[2] or without such chief, when the lands of the township belonged to the community,[3] and a head was chosen by the members. Where the lands were held by a chief, or hlaford, in demesne, he granted out portions (when, by charter, called bocland, terra codicillaris) to the men of the township. When held by the community (and called folkland, terra popularis),[4] the elected head seems to have done so; the right of possession by the individual was called a læn, and was usually for life, sometimes in perpetuity.[5] Lands retained in the hands of the hlaford, and cultivated by his serfs for the support of his household, were called inlands (terra dominicalis); the rest, let out to ceorls, for a certain rent or service, were called outlands (terra tenementalis).[6]

Among them, the possession of the country under the military organization before mentioned, and the existence of the relation of hlaford and man, suggests the extreme probability of the existence of a feudal law without that

---

1 See note 5, page 21.

2 Palgrave, Rise and Progress, v. i. pp. 65, 66.

3 Leg. Edou. II. 5.

4 Ib. Domesday, v. i. p. 23, b. 27, b. 47, 52, 54.

5 Palgrave, Rise and Progress, p. 66.

6 Spelman, Feuds, c. 25.

subtilty of system, and without much of the oppressiveness introduced after the conquest. It is certain that, as to some lands, the kings and thanes granted portions as the price of military service: the property of the land remaining in the lord, the tenant held it as a loan. The claim of the heir to the benefice of his ancestor was not absolute; and, as he might be unable or unwilling to perform the required duties, the lord might refuse to renew the grant; and to prevent that, and also as a consideration for a renewal of the grant, a relief, or heriot, was rendered on the death of the tenant. In some districts, the female tenant was in the wardship of the lord, who disposed of her person and land. Egbert, educated as he had been under Charlemagne, probably encouraged the tendency existing in England to the feudal system, which he had found, from his experience on the continent, where the feudal system existed already, increased the power of the superior lord.[1]

We postpone the further consideration of the feudal law until the period after the conquest, when, from the confiscation which followed the revolts of the Saxons against William the Norman, and from the consequences deduced from his mode of regranting them to his followers, the subjection of the land to the feudal law seems to have been completed in England as well as France.

Law of contracts.

Of the rational part of the law little exists which can be traced to the Saxons. Rude and unlettered, their contracts and bargains were formed on visible and corporeal acts more than on verbal agreements, and seldom on written ones. In the latter case, the seal of the party supplied the place of his signature, or verified his mark or cross.

The Anglo-Saxon laws are not very abundant on this subject. We find the general rule, that a man's agreement must be cautiously observed,[2] and the form in

[1] As to the existence of the feudal law among the Anglo-Saxons, see Palgrave, Rise and Progress, c. 19.

[2] Leg. Ælf. I.

which a man discharged or purged himself of a debt on *his oath.*[1] It seems that no purchase, and even no contract or bargain could be made except in the presence of a certain number of witnesses, or the gerefa; and if anything was sold without observing this law, the thing was to be forfeited.[2] Live animals, as well as other things, could not be bought without pledges; but there was a special law in favour of butchers, then called fleshmongers, buying, killing, and selling cattle,[3] on certain days, without pledges. Where the purchaser of an article discovered any defect in it, he might return it to the seller, unless the latter swore he knew nothing of the defect when he sold it.[4] Such being the barren state of the law as to contracts in general, we are surprised to find the rude legislator providing respecting pledges;[5] and even as to bailments to keep,[6] or to use.[7] The compensations (bote and wite) payable to a person for injuries to himself or his family, would seem to belong to the class of imperfect contracts, obligations ex delicto; but they have been already mentioned, and they are too well known to require further comment.

Among our neighbours, the law of contracts was in a more advanced state, owing to the continuance of the knowledge of the Roman laws. The Burgundian laws contain many dispositions respecting contracts, marriages, gifts, wills, &c., for which it is evidently indebted to the Roman law. The Visigothic law is still more full from this source; and even the Franks themselves were obliged frequently to have recourse to the Roman law, because their codes contained few regulations on the subject.

---

1 Leg. Æthelst. II. App. s. 11.

2 Leg. Loth. & Eader. 16; Leg. Edou. I.; Leg. Æthelst. I. 12; Leg. Æthelr. I. 4; Leg. Cnut. II. 22; Leg. Edou. Conf. 38.

3 Leg. Edou. Conf. 39.

4 Leg. Inæ, 56, according to a prescribed form of oath; Leg. Æthelst. II. App. s. 9.

5 Leg. Inæ, 49; Leg. Cnut. II. 18; Leg. Guil. Conq. 42.

6 Leg. Ælfr. 17. 7 Ib. 19.

Symbolical and ceremonial actions.

In the early history of all nations the untutored mind of man was incapable of the abstraction which conveys legal rights from one to another by mere word of mouth, or by writing, but required some palpable act or some symbolical form to create, transfer, or extinguish a right. The chief business of the early Roman jurists consisted in the preservation and accurate application of formal acts, which among the ancient Italic races appear to have been even more fixed and regular than those of the Teutonic tribes.[1] In a more enlightened age, the legal forms were derided and observed by the Roman lawyers.[2] The Anglo-Saxons brought their legal forms with them. It is not to be expected that the formal acts of the Germans in France should long exist in presence of the more advanced and more rational ones of the Roman law.

When we examine the formal and symbolical part of law as it existed among the Anglo-Saxons,[3] though we find the actual forms and ceremonies nearly obsolete, yet their spirit and principles remain. Thus land was conveyed by delivery of earth and stone, of a rod, branch, &c.[4] After writing became known and practical, a deed or charter was drawn up as a memorandum, collateral to the form or ceremony; a record that the investiture was duly made in the presence of witnesses.[5]

In these symbolical acts, the right of property and the right of usufruct were and still are distinguished. Seisin (or the freehold) was not given by the rod, but on the soil, by turf, stone, &c. The owner of the soil granted the usufructuary possession by the symbol of rod or

---

1 Savigny, Beruf.

2 Gibbon, c. 46.

3 Hickes, Dissert. Epist. p. 50.

4 Ingul. Hist. p. 901; "Absque scripto vel charta, tantum cum domini gladio vel corni vel tenementa, cum calcari, cum striguli, cum archi, nonnulla cum sagitta, cratera et plurima."—Palgrave, Rise and Progress, part 1, p. 141; Concilia, v. i. p. 63.

5 Palgrave, Rise and Progress, p. 141; Michelet, Origines, t. i. b. 2, c. 3.

branch; and in manors where the freehold or right of property is in the lord of the manor, the customary tenure is still given by the rod, and not by delivery of part of the land. In all deeds operating at common law, the livery of seisin is still made, or supposed to be made, by actual delivery of part in the name of the whole property.[1]

Courts were summoned by sound of bell (called mot, or mote-bel);[2] by the delivery of a token, such as weapon, hammer, or other symbol, which passed from hand to hand; and in judicial proceedings the parties were summoned before the court by delivery of similar tokens.[3] In actions relating to land, called real actions, the warning or summons to appear before the court was given by erecting a white stick or wand (baculus nunciatorius) on the party's land; and it is only at a very recent period that a written mandate entirely superseded the symbol as a summons. The mace, or hammer, seems to have been the ensign of authority, and to have been used to measure lands and domains. In cases of contest as to the extent of jurisdiction, over a river for example, the public officer or beneficiary seems to have assumed or contended for a jurisdiction as far as he could throw a hammer or mace;[4] and when his companions

---

[1] Palgrave, Rise and Progress, part 1, p. 141; and see Palgrave, Anglo-Saxon Period, Family Library, p. 151; who also remarks (in Rise and Progress, p. 141), "These ceremonies correspond in spirit with the Roman mancipation, which transferred the dominium directum, or right of ownership of the soil, and the Roman tradition, which conferred a right of enjoyment only dominium utile. Tradition was effected by the delivery of a symbol; the mancipation by a fictitious sale before witnesses. The right to the soil was vindicated by bringing a turf from the land, which was delivered to whom the prætor adjudged the possession. The livery of seisin by the Roman tribunal bears the nearest affinity to the forms of the Gothic law."—Heineccius Vocabularius; Cod. Theod. b. 8, tit. 12; Ll. IV. 8, 9; Spence's Inquiry, 32, 34.

[2] Leg. Edou. Conf. 35.

[3] Palgrave, Rise and Progress, part 1, p. 142; Michelet, Origines, t. ii. p. 131.

[4] Notre seigneur de Mayence s'avancera lui même à cheval dans le Rhin; aussi loin qu'il pourra lancer dans le Rhin le Marteau de marechal, aussi loin

ceded to a man a portion of earth, the man took a hammer, and whirling it round, threw it as far as he could, and so far he became entitled to the land. The numerous forms of the early Germanic laws have become for the most part so obsolete, that, however interesting, more space cannot here be allotted to them.[1]

Remedial institutions of courts of justice.

The courts of justice among the Anglo-Saxons were as numerous as the divisions of the country; and each district had within itself a power of redressing grievances. The gau, tithing and township had its folkmote, in which the tithing-man presided;[2] each hlafordswic its halmote, or court-baron. Superior to these was the hundred gemote, in which the alderman of the hundred presided;[3] and scyregemote, or county court, held before the bishop and the alderman, and afterwards before the sheriff[4] alone, was inferior only to the witangemote of the nation.[5]

The king, or supreme ruler, is, in the early stages of the civilization of a people, not only the leader in war and peace, but the supreme judge; and so we find him, among the Anglo-Saxons, possessed, from the earliest period, of a transcendant jurisdiction over all their tribunals; and our sovereigns have inherited this authority.[6]

The freemen[7] decided all things in the assembly of

---

s'etendra sa juridiction;" and the Count of Nassau had as far in the Rhine as a man on horseback could throw a hammer.—Michelet, Origines, v. i. l. 2, c. 1.

1 For further information on this subject, see Michelet, Origines.

2 The Gauding was equivalent to the Concilium described by Tacitus.—Eichhorn, Deutsche Staats und Rechts, Geschichte, s. 18.

3 Leg. Edou. Conf. 32.

4 The English sheriff is called vicecomes, a term which is also used together with vicarius and advocatus in the writs of the Frankish monarchs.—Savigny, c. 4, p. 3.

5 As to the origin and formation of the witangemote, see Phillips, Angelsachsischen Rechts, s. 70.

6 Palgrave, Rise and Progress, part 1, p. 279; Allen, Inquiry into the Rise and Progress of the Royal Prerogative.

7 The freemen of the Anglo-Saxon law, the frilingi of the Saxons, the rachimburgii of the Franks, the original prud'hommes of the French, and the arimani of

each burgh. Justice was then rendered by the freemen themselves, under the direction of their aldermen. Questions of law, or rather custom, as well as questions of fact, were submitted to their decision.[1]

The jurisdiction of the Anglo-Saxon township consisted of deciding the disputes of its members. Whether the township was under the protection and authority of a hlaford or not, an officer, elected by the tenantry, and called gerefa (or tungerefa, or reeve, or tunginus), presided at the folkmote of the township,[2] who, in after times of the Normans, took the name of bailiff of the district. The courts of the township and the halmote, like the modern courts baron of manors, could only be exercised by the head, with the participation of the inhabitants; without suitors it could not act.[3]

In the hundred courts, each town was represented by four of its members and the gerefa, and the priest seems also to have attended,[4] over whom presided the alderman of the hundred (centgrave, hundredarius); and these, with the thanes and landlords, with the bishop, formed the hundred court.[5] Each hundred or township, in ancient demesne, was represented at the shiremote by twelve jurors; and the four men and reeve of the township completed the assembly. The judges of this high remedial tribunal appear to have been specially charged to protect the people against the abuses of power.[6]

The Anglo-Saxon kings, with their witangemote, appear to have made journeys through the kingdom twice a year, to administer justice in person, as the last resort

---

the Lombards; in Latin, called boni homines, liberi homines, and in our own English law probii et legales homines.—Savigny, History, c. 4, on Freemen. German seems to be the same as ariman, ehreman, herman, sounds easily confounded by a foreigner.

[1] Eichhorn, Deutche Staats und Rechts, Geschichte, s. 18.

[2] Palgrave, Rise and Progress, pp. 81, 2.

[3] Ib. p. 79.

[4] Ib. p. 82.

[5] Ib. p. 98; every landlord in person or by his gerefa, pp. 117, 119.

[6] Ib. p. 119.

to their subjects, and to punish oppression; a practice continued with more or less regularity by the Norman monarchs,[1] until the alteration of manners, and the increasing technicality of the laws, excluded the person of the sovereign from his courts: in some of which he is still, however, supposed to be present.

In the Saxon period, the art of writing was almost wholly confined to the clergy, who necessarily became the king's scribes. The king's chaplains, notaries, or secretaries[2] were therefore the constant attendants of the supreme tribunal, in order to compose and transcribe his mandates or writs, and to take care of, and to read as well as write, his royal charters when required. They thence became a permanent branch of the royal court, and keepers of the records deposited in the royal chapel. At the head of the king's chaplains was the chancellor[3] (a name of office which can be distinctly traced back to the time of Edgar), who also kept the king's signet, or royal seal; and, as early as the introduction of the clergy into England, in the time of Ethelbert, we find a referendarius, or keeper of the king's signet,[4] whose name and office were evidently borrowed from the Continent,[5] and who was probably also the chancellor, as the two titles are used indiscriminately.

---

[1] King John, Henry III., Edward I., and Edward II. administered criminal justice in person.

[2] Cancellarius was used in the 6th century as synonymous with amanuensis, tabellio, or notarius.—Savigny, t. i. c. 2, n. 104.

[3] As to the Frankish referendary, chancellor, and apocrisiary, or arch chaplain, see Bernardi, de l'Origine et des Progrès de la Legislation, pp. 46, 7.

[4] Augumundus was referendarius of Ethelbert. — Somner's Canterbury, 46. Arfastus, Bishop of Thetford, was chancellor in the time of the Conqueror.—Mont. 132 to 64.

[5] The king's chaplains of England corresponded with the "clerks of the palace" of the Frankish monarch.—Hincmar, ep. de ordine Palatii, s. 10. The king's chaplains were shrewd and learned clerks. When they followed the king into the witenagemote, increasing deference would be paid to their discretion and wisdom; and the bench of the "clerks of the chapel," or "chancery," may be considered as engrafted upon the great council of the empire.—Palgrave, Rise and Progress, part 1, p. 552.

In France, in consequence of the concurrent existence of the Roman as well as the Germanic population, two systems of administration were required to carry the two into execution. Accordingly, each had their different courts, officers, and judges, as well as different modes of procedure. For the Roman subjects, the same courts existed after the invasion as under the Imperial government; and the Frankish kings exercised the right of appointing or confirming the judges and other officers, as the emperors had done.[1] The Frank, like the Saxon, was to be judged by his peers, and the system employed for the Franks was at first similar to that of the Anglo-Saxons; and in opening the most ancient laws of the Franks, as well as the other Teutonic nations, it is found that the assemblies of the freemen (rachimburgi) in each district or canton, were held very frequently, every week or month. All the affairs of the district were carried on there: the judgments were given, not only in criminal but also in civil matters; and almost all the transactions of life were performed there, sales, donations, &c.

When once the people were established in Gaul, the assemblies became less frequent, and so difficult, that it was necessary to employ coercive means to make the freemen attend. Passing to the middle of the 8th century, each county has only three assemblies in the year, and often none. When they no longer continued to assemble, it was necessary to find some means of supplying their place; and at the end of the 8th century, under Charlemagne, the system was changed. The absence of the

---

[1] Palgrave, Rise and Progress, part 1, p. 179. Over their Roman subjects the Frankish monarchs governed according to the forms aud maxims of the imperial law. The Roman emperor had been absolute in legislative and executive authority; and this species of domination was gradually imposed by the Franks, to a considerable extent, on their own people. Though the guild was assessed in the folkmote according to the declaration of the arbogast and salogast, yet transgressions against the sovereign were punished according to the spirit of the imperial consistory.—Ib. p. 36. See, as to the preservation of the ancient Roman forms in the cities, Savigny, c. 5.

body of freemen, or rachimburgii, was remedied by the scabini, or special echevins.[1] In each county, five, seven, nine, or twelve freemen were named as scabini, on whom was imposed the duty of attending the county assembly, and judging the processes, in the meantime without excluding the other freemen. The grafio, originally elected by the people, had become the delegate of the Frankish sovereign; and in him was vested the chief executive authority in the centenæ or council, though he took no part in the judging. The centenarius, centgrave, or tunginus, acted in subordination to the grafio, though elected, like the scabini,[2] by the people. The scabini decided both the law and the facts of the case. In many districts an immunity, or the right of administering justice (forming what was called des justices seigneuriales), was granted to the count, or other lord of the benefice,[3] to the exclusion of all external authorities.[4]

The early Frankish monarchs, like the Anglo-Saxon, administered justice in person;[5] and as early as the time of Clovis,[6] the king's residence was called the Aula Regia (Royal Court). The extensive dominions of Charlemagne, and his numerous occupations, prevented the possibility of his administering justice in person. He instituted certain officers,[7] called missi dominici, or regii, to make

---

1 Car. Mag. c. 3, A.D. 803; c. 1, A.D. 809, s. 22; Lud. Pii, c. 5, A.D. 819, s. 4; Lotharii, c. 30, A.D. 824, s. 3.

2 Bern. de l'Origine, &c. b. 1, c. 8. 3 Ib. p. 44. 4 Ib. p. 48.

5 Louis XIII. was desirous to sit in judgment upon the trial of the Duke de la Valette, and sent to some members of the parliament and of the privy council for their opinion, which was against his so doing.—Montesquieu, l. 6, c. 6.

6 Vita S. Vedasti apud script. rer. Francic, t. ii. p. 371.

7 The officers who presided at the mallum of the Frankish freemen, or rachimburgi, were like our modern judges presiding over a jury, required to know the law.—See Baluz, Capitularia Reg. Fr., App. c. 111, a. 803, add. c. 5, a. 803, art. 19; v. i. pp. 396, 400.

As the judges could not know all the customs, which were not written in any authentic form, it was necessary that either the parties agreed respecting them, or proved them by witnesses: whence it happened that all the questions of law reduced themselves to facts, on which it was necessary to make inquests par turbes (by multitudes), as is still the case in England, to a certain extent, on questions as to the custom of merchants, and other customs.

judicial circuits,[1] and to act in his name[2] and stead; and under the presidency of one of the missi dominici of the court, or of his substitute, justice was administered by the echevins. Except in the presence of the missi dominici, the temporary representatives of the sovereign, and sometimes to their exclusion, the local and resident magistrates (whether those named by the emperor, dukes, counts, graphios, centenaries, or those deriving their authority from holding domains of him, vassals or beneficiaries) continued to exercise their jurisdiction.

Modes of trial.

The most simple mode of trial was by the country (judicium parium). It has been a question, whether trial by the country was the same in those days as in these; whether there were institutions similar to the modern petty jury for criminals, or the jury in civil cases; but there seems not to exist a ground for doubt that the negative is the correct opinion. The practice of making presentments or arraignments by twelve men was universal among the Germans. Thus the Anglo-Saxon law directs that twelve thanes, with the sheriff of the county, shall make inquiry into offences. They possessed the power of accusation, but not of trial; and their office closely corresponded with that of the modern English grand jury. The duty of the twelve scabini or echevins in France was also of a similar nature; but the ancient trial by the country was before the jurors of the courts, consisting of the freemen or peers in general.[3] If the fact was notorious, or within

---

[1] Cap. Wormatiense, A.D. 829, II. 2. In 853, and only in this year, is preserved an exact account of the distribution of the Imperial commissioners, the missi dominici, as they were sent through the kingdom. From this it appears, that France was divided into eighty-six districts, or territorial circuits, which were distributed between twelve companies of missi, which, consisting of forty-three missi, at the head, or at least the first named of each mission, was a bishop.—Cap. Car. Calv. tit. 14.

[2] Bernardi, de l'Origine, b. 2, c. 8.

[3] Trial by a tribunal of sworn witnesses elected out of the popular courts, for the decision of rights of property, may be traced in the Anglo-Saxon period, but not in criminal cases.—Palgrave, Rise and Progress, part 1, p. 256.

the knowledge of the judges, they decided from the notoriety of the fact; and, in the trial by witnesses, the Anglo-Saxon jurymen were the witnesses of the fact, and not the triers of the truth of the evidence given before them by other witnesses: so that the old Anglo-Saxon trial by jury thus was essentially different from the modern tribunal for trying an issue bearing the ancient name.[1]

If direct proof could not be obtained, the mode of trial was suited to a barbarous period, when the mind of the judges, unable to estimate circumstantial evidence, rejected it entirely.

One of the methods resorted to for defect of direct evidence was compurgation.[2] The party accused was permitted to bring a number of persons, called his conjurators or compurgators, who laid their hands[3] on the gospel halidame, or altar, and he laid his hands over all the rest. He was permitted to swear by God, and all the hands that were under his, that he was not guilty of the charge[4] laid to him; and the persons whose hands were so given for him, declared on their oaths that they

---

[1] An institution resembling the modern jury existed under the Roman republic, Savigny, Geschichte, s. 2; and in the early ages of the empire, conformably to the ancient customs, we find the judge, or person to whom the jurisdiction belonged (prætor, governor of the province, or municipal magistrate), when a process came before him, merely determined the rule of law, the legal principle by which it was to be governed. He established what we call the point of law; and then designated a citizen, called judex, who examined and decided the point of fact. Little by little, as the imperial despotism established itself, and the ancient liberties disappeared, the intervention of the judex became less regular. The magistrate decided, without recourse to him, certain questions, called Extraordinariæ cognitiones. Dioclesian formally abolished the institution in the provinces, and the entire jurisdiction belonged to the governors.—Guizot, Histoire de la Civilization en France, lect. 2. See Montesquieu, b. 11, c. 18.

[2] Leg. Loth. et Ead. V.; Leg. Æthelst. I. 9; Leg. Edou. I.

[3] The compurgatory oath of an earl was equal to that of six ceorls; the oath of a minor thane (one without sufficient land to constitute a lordship) to three ceorls. A ceorl was called twihændman: hence a minor thane was a sixhændman, and an earl a twelfhændman.—Palgrave, Rise and Progress, part 1, p. 19.

[4] As to the form of oath used by the plaintiff and by the defendant, see Leg. Æthelst. II. App. ss. 2, 3, 4, 5, 6.

believed he had sworn the truth.[1] Originally, the compurgators seem to have been taken from the relations of the accused.[2] A man accused was considered as a man attacked, and his friends followed him to the tribunal as to a combat; afterwards they were selected from the decenna, the privilege being denied to those not in the frank-pledge.[3]

When the evidence was defective, and compurgation could not be obtained or allowed, resort was had to certain modes of deciding the question, called the judgment of God (judicium Dei). These were, the ordeals of fire and water, hot iron, or boiling water,[4] and trial by battle. It seems doubtful, however, whether the latter was adopted in England before the Norman conquest.

The Salic law is nearly silent as to legal procedures;[5] it assumes them as already existing; and it is only here and there that we find traces of appearance before tribunals, witnesses, judges' proofs, boiling water, conjurators, &c.

In the Ripuarian and Burgundian codes they are more frequently mentioned; and in the latter the legal combats or duels are more especially regulated.[6]

Evidence or records of legal proceedings.

Originally the proceedings, evidence, and judgment were all carried on publicly, in France as well as in

---

[1] It was not until about the time of Henry VI., 1422 to 1461, that assumpsit became the remedy applicable to all cases of debt on simple contract, till trover was generally adopted instead of detenue, and Chancery proceedings in preference to the action of account, that trial by jury superseded that by wager of law; and it is only very recently that wager of law was formally abolished. Reeve, History of the Law, H. 4, 5, 6; 3 & 4 William IV. c. 42, s. 13; 2 Barn. and Cres. 538; see 3 B.C. c. 22.

[2] As to compurgation among the Franks, Ducange, verbo Compurgatores Sacramentum.—Leg. Burgund. tit. 8, capit. b. 3, c. 23.

[3] Palgrave, Rise and Progress, part 1, p. 218.

[4] Leg. Inæ, 77.

[5] Montesquieu says (Spirit of Laws, b. 28, c. 13 & 14), that "the Salic law differed from that of the Ripuarian and other barbarous nations, in not allowing the negative proofs of compurgations and judicial combat;" but it is evident that the Salic laws treats them as methods in existence, on which it was not necessary to legislate.

[6] Leg. Burgund. c. 45.

England. Legal proceedings were wholly oral; and the memorials of the court were entrusted to the memory of the witan, the judges by whom decrees were pronounced; and they remembered, or "recorded in their breasts," the proceedings. Proof of legal proceedings was made by testimony of living witnesses;[1] and a person was appointed recorder for that purpose. The rolls to which this testimony was afterwards committed were figuratively called records, and are now substituted for the oral testimony.[2]

The ancient laws and customs were recorded in the county court by the testimony of the representatives of the community, who were the judges as well as the witnesses. Instead of opening a book to decide a contested custom, the king's officers were obliged to appeal to the virtual delegates of the people, and to be confronted by their authority. This popular branch of the remedial tribunal could not be lopped off; and the scabini and jurors, from being the witnesses of the law, became the legislators.[3]

Roman law retained by the clergy in France.

In France, besides these Germanic laws and institutions, the Roman law continued in force; and not only were the institutions of the Roman municipalities retained to a very great extent in the cities of that kingdom, but also, besides a large mass of the inhabitants, the clergy, as a body, continued to be judged by the rules and principles of the Roman law, afterwards modified by the canon law. The forms of the proceedings of the ecclesiastical tribunals were those of the Roman law. We are told that in France the notaries succeeded the tabelliones of the empire, and, following the models bequeathed to them by their predecessors, preserved the forms and expressions of the imperial administrations of justice.[4]

---

[1] Palgrave, Rise and Progress, p. 143.
[2] Ib. p. 146.
[3] Palgrave, p. 150.
[4] Savigny, v. ii. p. 371.

Among the Anglo-Saxons, the clergy, though they occasionally studied the Roman law, were not subject to it: they were tried by the secular laws and tribunals, like other subjects. Not in England.

Such were the general spirit and principal features of the laws and institutions, established or retained by the Teutonic tribes, on their settlement in France and England, during the first period of our legal history. It is not, however, to be supposed that they continued unaltered during the whole of that period: indeed, they were scarcely established before material changes took place, especially in France, which, owing to the mixture of the conquered, Gauls and Romans, with the conquerors, Franks, Burgundians, and Visigoths, contained within itself more principles of change, and a greater variety of legal institutions, to amalgamate into new ones, than England did. Connection of the first and second periods of legal history.

It is interesting to observe the manner in which the institutions of this first period were superseded by others in France, which led the way to the principles of the second period of our history. England, from being at that time in a lower degree of civilization, naturally imitated its neighbour, even during the Saxon period; and, after the Conquest, adopted very many of her institutions.

After the fall of the Merovingians, Charlemagne endeavoured to re-establish the central sovereign power, which had perished with the Roman empire. The attempt was successful while his powerful mind directed affairs, and for a moment a central power appears in the west; but after his death it was lost. He had reformed many of the national usages; he attempted to lessen the ancient jurisdictions of the centennæ, and to substitute the Royal courts. During his reign the graphio and the missus were invested with their judicial functions by the authority of the crown; and the administration of justice tended to concentration in his courts. Charlemagne died Course of events after the final settlement of the Germans in France.

in 814; and with him fell the central government.[1] It is clear that at the general national assemblies, held under him, he was the cause of their assembling, the centre of every movement, and the soul which animated the whole. His son, Louis le Debonnaire, succeeded to his empire, but not to the energy and ability of his character. The quarrels between Louis le Debonnaire and his sons, and the quarrels of his sons among themselves, commenced the anarchy of which France was so long the prey. Rebellion followed rebellion, accompanied by a feeble administration, and a neglect of any definite system of policy. A number of weak princes successively seized the throne; and each was fully occupied in preserving his own authority against a rival, or in humbling a brother prince.

A continuation of the policy of Charlemagne might have completed the centralization of the judicial power in the hands of the sovereign; but an uniform system of policy was necessary, to give consistency to the institutions of Charlemagne, among a nation composed of several different races, of which not only each race had a separate legislation of its own, but each district or township.[2] The successors of Charlemagne, occupied with their own personal station, had not time either to conceive, or to carry into execution, such a scheme of policy. After being prolonged awhile, under Louis le Debonnaire and Charles le Chauve, but evidently with

---

[1] Millot, Elemens de l'Histoire de France, v. i. p. 128 to 196; Dubos, Histoire Critique de l'Establissement de la Monarchie Française dans les Gaules; Guizot, Histoire de la Civilization en France, lect. 25; Essais sur l'Histoire de France, ess. 3; Fleury, Precis Historique, s. 14; Bernardi, de l'Origine, b. 2.

[2] Among all the German tribes the legislative authority was originally belonging to each township, or gau; and the earliest laws of the Goths were termed Byelagines, or Bye-laws, that is, laws of the By, or habitation.—Jornandes de Rebus Gesticis, c. 2; Palgrave, 79.

In England to this day the inhabitants of a town (in certain cases even without any particular customary right), the freeholders of a court leet, a borough, or an upland town, by custom and various others, may make bye-laws, 2 Danv. 457; Mo. 579, 584; 1 Ins. 110.

less and less force and effect, the general assemblies,[1] the missi dominici,[2] and all central and sovereign administration disappeared, though the local government of the great officers and vassals continued. Each successive prince, anxious to gain and preserve the adherence and assistance of the hereditary counts and powerful barons, though in one sense his own official representatives, was unable to attend to the repression of their usurpations.

The disorder of the kingdom was increased by the ravages of the Normans, and the wars between the dukes and counts, and all who had strongholds of retreat.[3] The consequence of all this was, that, towards the end of the 9th century, twenty-nine petty states had been erected, in which the graphio, or comes, of Charlemagne, had become, under the name of duke, count, or viscount, the actual sovereign; and at the end of the 10th century, instead of twenty-nine, there were at least fifty-five little states of this kind, seignories, duchies, counties, or viscounties, in which the lord was sovereign, invested with a power more or less absolute, according to the previous state of the population, and the share they had in legislation, the anarchy of the district or the power of the lord. Some have attributed this to the incapacity of the successors of Charlemagne; others have imputed it to the avidity of the dukes, counts, and other royal officers; others, to the Normans:[4] but they all seem to have concurred, that when Hugh Capet obtained the throne, A.D. 987, he was only master of his own demesnes, the duchy of France and the county of Paris, and feudal superior of the great vassals of the crown.[5]

During this anarchy, the differences of races had dis-

[1] At the end of the tenth century there remained scarcely a trace of the ancient Mahls, Champs de Mars, de Mai, or German pleas.

[2] Guizot, Histoire de la Civilization en France, lect. 24; Bernardi, de l'Origine, p. 99, 100, and b. 3, c. 2.

[3] Bernardi, de l'Origine, p. 165.

[4] Ibid. b. 2, c. 9; b. 3, c. 1 & 2.

[5] And even in his own domains the lords of Chamont, Clermont, Montlhery, Montmorency, Coucy, and others, were sufficiently powerful to dispute his authority.

appeared; and the descendant of the Roman or Frank, instead of being governed by distinct codes of law, was governed by the local customs which had grown out of the amalgamation of the races and their laws.[1] In each seignory, formed by the feudal subdivision of the territory, particular laws arose; no two lordships were governed by precisely the same laws.[2] The customs and privileges of each district had succeeded to the various national laws of Franks, Burgundians, Visigoths, and Romans.

The consequences of the toleration of the law, existing in France at the time of the establishment of the Germanic tribes, now became manifest. In those parts where the Franks predominated in number over the conquered, a customary law, founded on a mixture of their barbarian codes, and the previous institutions of the conquered Gauls, arose. In the south, where the original inhabitants greatly outnumbered their conquerors, the Germans settled there united and formed one people with the Gallic population, and adopting the same laws and institutions, the Roman law continued in operation. France was thus divided into two districts, one governed by customs (loi coutumiere), the other by the Roman law (droit ecrit). The Loire formed the south limit of the Frankish Gaul, and served for a boundary to the two districts of France, of which the southern one was called Pays du Droit Ecrit, and the other Pays du Droit Coutumier.

In comparing the customs of the east and western parts of the French kingdom, many of the differences are easily accounted for, when we consider that the

---

[1] L'Abbé Fleury says, "The disorders of the 10th century confounded the Roman and barbarian laws, so that at the commencement of the third race of kings there was no other law in France than an uncertain usage, to which the learned joined the study of the Roman law; and their decisions, mixed with this ancient usage, formed the customs afterwards written by public authority."—Precis. Historique du Droit Française, s. 1.

[2] Guizot, Histoire de la Civilization en France; Essais sur l'Histoire de France, Ess. 3.

Franks of Austrasia, separated from those of Neustria by the vast forest of Ardennes, and placed on the borders of the Rhine, of the Moselle, and of the Meuse, necessarily soon differed greatly from the Franks of Neustria, settled in the west, and the middle of France. The Rhine alone separated the former from ancient Germany. They lived in continual relation, hostile or pacific, with the German people, who inherited the right banks, and were therefore less separated from the institutions and manners of ancient German society than the Neustrian Franks. The organization of the Austrasian Society was the *most perfect and most faithful* image of the ancient manners, and less of Roman or Gallic elements is therefore met with.

The customs thus found (partially reformed and altered, though but little, by the lapse of time) continued to form the civil law of France down to the period of the Revolution.

Course of events in England.

In England, from the time of Egbert (828), notwithstanding the occasional disputes of the succession to the crown, and the anarchy caused by the Danish invasion, the crown retained its power, and continued to make, with more or less regularity, its judicial circuits; and the later Anglo-Saxon and Anglo-Danish kings, with their witangemote, though they appear to have respected the different laws of the various races which inhabited this country, yet possessed and retained the power of legislating for the whole kingdom. William the Conqueror, we have seen, preserved the main fabric of the Anglo-Saxon jurisprudence.[1] Under William II. the

[1] It has been imagined that the Conqueror, in reality, though not in form, entirely abrogated the Anglo-Saxon, and introduced the whole Norman system of jurisprudence, and that the existence at this day of laws and institutions similar to those of the Anglo-Saxons is to be accounted for by their gradual re-introduction. M. Howard has endeavoured to show that the laws of Edward the Confessor had no consanguinity to the laws of William I. (Anc. Loix); but his arguments are strongly answered by Mr. Kelham, in the preliminary discourse to the laws of King William, subjoined to his Dictionary of the Norman, or old French language; and M. Thierry, an author fully inclined to magnify the changes

absolute will of the arbitrary monarch prevailed over law and custom; but his reign was too short to effect any great change, and his successor, Henry I., restored the law of the Confessor. Under Stephen neither government nor law existed in England; and had this state of public affairs continued long, there can be no doubt each feudal baron would have established his domains as an independent state, acknowledging perhaps a mere superiority to the king. On the accession of Henry II. to the throne he confirmed the charter of his grandfather; and thus, until his time, the Anglo-Saxon laws were nominally retained;[1] although many consequences naturally resulted from the Conquest, and the changes made in the executive details; and from the strictness of the feudal doctrines, the technicality of the property system had greatly increased.

First legal consequences of the Norman Conquest.

A conquest,[2] like that of the Normans, could not but be followed by important, though not immediate alterations, especially relating to the forms of legal proceedings.

---

effected by the Conquest, admits that neither William nor his successors attempted any very extensive alterations, or ever showed any great hatred for the Saxon laws, civil or military.—Conquête de l'Angleterre par les Normans.

Sir F. Palgrave, whose learning and research give a weight to his assertions respecting English history, says, "Notwithstanding the ascendency of the Normans, the usages and customs of Anglo-Saxon England were retained with much greater pertinacity than those in countries where no foreign ruler attained the throne. When William won England, Gaul and Germany had already forgotten the Salic and Ripuarian laws. Scarcely had the Capets established themselves on the throne, when all the barbarian codes of the Carlovingian empire seem to have passed away. The venerable Capitularies sank into repose. The changes in English policy were effected principally by the slow operation of internal causes; by usages which modified the state, by the common assent which altered or revoked the law, and by the silent establishment of new forms and proceedings, creating new channels for the administration of the government."—Rise and Progress of the English Commonwealth, part I, p. 654.

[1] The rebellions of the Normans against William I., the usurpations of William II., Henry I., and of Stephen, and the necessity of the kings seeking the aid of the Anglo-Saxons, gave the vanquished people an importance they would not perhaps otherwise have acquired.

[2] The term conquest, in the Norman law, signifies the same thing as purchase (acquisitio) in the English law.—See Norman Coust. compared with Littleton, by M. Howard, Anciennes Loix.

The confiscations which followed the successive efforts made by the Anglo-Saxons had an immediate effect on the technicality of the law of property; for in granting the forfeited lands the Conqueror attached feudal service to them, and before the end of his reign the whole kingdom was subjected to the feudal system. He seems, however, to have left the rights affecting these newly-granted lands much as he found them, both as between the occupiers and tenants, and the new grantees, and also as between the several new grantees who stood in the situations of the previous holders.[1] Besides which, these confiscations enriched the sovereign, and were one reason why the king and his successors, as legislators, were enabled to give a degree of uniformity to the laws, and why the Royal courts were enabled to preserve their authority over the most powerful subjects, and produced regularity in the administration of justice. The offices in gift of the Conqueror were bestowed on the Normans, and other foreigners, who had assisted him in his enterprise. This employment of functionaries educated under a different system was followed by the introduction of proceedings which had afterwards the effect of displacing the old jurisprudence,[2] particularly in the king's council, or witangemote, which now assumed the name of Curia Regia, or Aula Regis; and with the Conquest a new era

---

[1] Shortly after the Conquest (1072) we find the Norman nobles, to whom the confiscated estates were granted, appealing to the Anglo-Saxon modes of trial, and to Anglo-Saxon jurors, to testify the rights enjoyed by their respective predecessors, or holders of the land.—See De Placit. apud Pinenden in Lanfrancum Archiep. et Odonem Baj.; Spicilegium ad Eadmerum, p. 197; De Contentione in Gundulfum et Pichot. Textus Roffensis, p. 149; Monasticon, v. i. p. 478.

[2] Palgrave, Rise and Progress, part 1, p. 240. It has generally been supposed and asserted, by our first writers, that the Conqueror attempted to substitute the Norman for the Saxon tongue, and enacted that the former should alone be legally used: but this is quite a mistake, though in after ages fashion seems nearly to have effected what the Conqueror never contemplated. D. Barrington, in his observations on the Statute de Scaccario, is the first to point out the erroneousness of the opinion that an immediate change of language took place at the conquest.—Observations on the Ancient Statutes; Luder's Tract on the Use of the French Language in our Laws, &c.

of legal documents commenced. The Normans were litigious to a proverb, and showed themselves, immediately after the Conquest, extremely prodigal of documents, deeds, and legal process.[1]

An important institution, closely resembling the modern system, becomes visible about this time, and probably was introduced from Normandy, and that is, the employment of inquests,[2] for the presentment of the customs of the land, and the rights of the people and of the crown. Previously, in England, the whole township, hundred, or county were summoned to attest their laws and customs, as well as to judge and decide on facts; to declare the law, and to decide the fact, were equally their office. But the custom of having inquisition made by an inquest or jury, who represented the whole community, had previously been in use in Normandy,[3] and was adopted by the Conqueror, not only in legal cases, but also in fiscal matters.[4] Inquests were employed to make the survey for Domesday-book; and they have since been employed to obtain information as to forfeitures, escheats, &c., so that the king can only be informed of his rights through the medium of the people in inquest. The same system was applied to the general assembly of the nation. In 1080, William the Bastard caused an inquisition to be made by the most noble and wisest of each county, and on their witness caused to be put in writing the ancient customs of the Anglo-Saxons and Danes.[5] The Archbishop of York and the Bishop

1 Thierry, Histoire de la Conquête de l'Angleterre par les Normands.

2 In the Norman law the term Inquest, "Enquete," was substituted for jury, "Jurée."

3 When the Norman villeins rose in 996 against the nobility, they elected two representatives from every clan, or sept, who appeared on behalf of their constituents, at a general assembly.—Palgrave, Rise and Progress, part 1, p. 126, 245, 6; Grand Coustumier, c. 68, 69. 103, 245.

4 Cum rex ipse regisque proceres loca nova perlustrarent, facta est inquisitio diligens.—Dialogus de Scaccario, in notes ad Matth. Paris.

5 Electi sunt de singulis comitatibus 12 viri sapientiores, quibus jurejurandis injunctum erat coram rege Willelmo ut quod possent, legum suarum et consuetu-

of London, it is said, wrote them with their own hands. William I., to gratify his foreign clergy, separated the ecclesiastical from the foreign tribunals.[1] At the Conquest the practice of trial by legal combat was established, if not introduced, for his Norman followers.[2]

Revival of the study of the Roman law.

About this period of history the first light of the revival of ancient learning appeared in an extraordinary renovation of the Roman law, as a science; an event which, though it here demands our notice from the important effects which about this time it produced in the laws of both countries, yet relates chiefly to the part of the law which belongs to the third period of our history, and on which its influence was far more direct than on the popular or technical laws of either nation. After the Frankish invasions the church in France, and other parts of the continent, continued to follow the Roman law, which under the second race of French monarchs received from them considerable attention and study: at that time among the ecclesiastics there were persons who made it a profession to instruct pupils in it;[3] and the Roman law continued to subsist and be practised in Western Europe from the fall of Rome. The Justinian code, from the time of its promulgation, had been all but unknown to Western Europe: Britain, Gaul, Spain, and the chief part of Italy had been separated from the empire before the promulgation of that code. The sudden and brilliant renovation of the

dinum sancita patefacerent, nil pretermittentes, nil addentes.—Th. Rudborn in Angliâ Sacrâ, p. 259.

[1] The ultimate tendency of this measure was to set free the civil judge from the more learned ecclesiastic, and thus to leave the rude system of Anglo-Saxon jurisprudence to the administration of simple laymen, unversed in the despotic practice, as well as the science of the Roman law.

[2] Anglicus se purgat per judicium ferri, Francigena se defendat per bellum, et si Anglicus non audeat probare per bellum, defendat se Francigena pleno juramento.—Leg. Willelm. nothi apud Johan Brompton.

[3] Precis Historique du Droit Française, par L'Abbe Fleurys; and see the whole of the 6th chapter of Savigny's Geschichte, &c., for proofs of the study of the Roman law throughout Europe, and even in England, by ecclesiastics during the Saxon period.

science of Roman law and the study of the Justinian code, which commenced about the 12th century, has generally been attributed[1] to the discovery of the Pandects at Amalfi, about the year 1128, which it was supposed gave the first stimulus to the study. This has now been clearly proved to be an erroneous opinion:[2] for while the rest of Europe was separated from the empire before these codes were formed, the victories of Belisarius and Narses, the generals of Justinian, had reconquered Rome from the barbarians, and the code of their imperial master was established in his re-acquired dominions; and though Rome was again lost, the exarchate of Ravenna long continued to acknowledge the authority of the Eastern empire, and to administer its new codes.[3]

Not far from Ravenna, where there had thus been preserved more than elsewhere a number of copies of the books of Justinian, is Bologna. From Ravenna some copies were carried to Bologna; and there Irnerius, a man of a prompt and active spirit, devoted to study, met with these books, and read and re-read them with curiosity and avidity. Alone, without master, he gave himself to their study. He perceived their value, and commenced teaching them, and the study became more appreciated. Such was the cause of the renovation of the Roman law, and the origin of the famous school of Irnerius at Bologna.[4]

Though interdicted by the Pope—jealous for the canon law—the study was notwithstanding pursued with ardour

---

[1] Blackstone's Commentaries; Hume's History of England.

[2] The six ages preceding Irnerius offer the most complete proofs of the continued existence of the Roman law, but they present few traces of scientific cultivation.—Preface to Savigny's History of the Romans in the Middle Ages; and for a confirmation of this assertion, see the two first volumes of that work.

[3] As to the preservation of the Roman system of administration in Ravenna, see Savigny's History, v. i. c. 5, s. 7; Ravenna and Rome under the Pope and the Emperor.

[4] "We have certain proofs, that in the 11th century Ravenna had a school of law; and it is easy to conceive that a neighbouring city, Bologna, adopted this institution."—Savigny, History of the Roman Law during the Middle Ages.

throughout Europe. One of our Anglo-Norman prelates, Theobald, visiting Italy, brought over with him a professor of the new study, the celebrated Vacarius,[1] who commenced teaching it in the University of Oxford; and though it was forbidden by Stephen,[2] it continued to be studied at Oxford.[3]

Further alterations in the remedial part of the English law.

We now come to the reign of Henry II., a prince whose acts, as well as the assertions of his historians, show him to have been wise and intelligent. In his hereditary office of grand seneschal of France, he must have become well acquainted with the details of judicial policy. His confirmation of the charter of Henry I. professed to restore the Anglo-Saxon laws, the memory of which had been handed down from generation to generation, a charter precious to the people: but the several causes mentioned as introduced at the Conquest, and perhaps the operation of the study of the civil law, had already produced many extensive alterations.

The most striking change which had taken place by this time was in the constitution of juries. In trial by witnesses the Anglo-Saxon, we have seen, was judged by the whole body of his peers assembled in the mote, and who, being the witnesses also, constituted the jurors of the court. At the time of the Conquest,[4] a practice of selecting, in certain cases, an inquest of a certain number, instead of the whole court, had been introduced,

---

1 History of Vacarius, by Wenck. Lipsia, 1820. 8vo.

2 Selden, Dissertatio ad Fletam, c. 8, s. 1. De usu apud majores nostros juris Justiniani à tempore Stephani (quo primum huc allatum est) per Henrici secundi, Richardi primi et Joannes Regum tempora.

3 John of Salisbury says, the more the study of Roman law was persecuted, the more it flourished.

4 By the law of Normandy (Grand Coustumier, c. 68, 69, 103) criminals were tried by an inquest of twenty-four men of the country, summoned by the serjeant from the neighbourhood where the crime was committed, who were to be those best informed of the truth of the matter, and how it happened. Jurors, or recognitors as they were called in Normandy, were in like manner the witnesses of the fact in civil cases.—Palgrave, Rise and Progress, part 1, p. 245.

and its use was greatly extended. Henry II.[1] introduced by a statute, emphatically called the Grand Assize, a species of trial by jury on a writ of right, giving the tenant or defendant the choice of deciding his right either by a jury or by battle. This, and the assize of novel disseisin, and other assizes [2] or statutes of Henry, paved the way to the adoption of juries, greatly to the exclusion of the more barbarous modes of trial by battle, ordeal, and compurgation. From this time a jury of the hundred court for the trial of causes may be considered to have consisted of a definite number instead of the whole body, or an indefinite number of collected freemen. They still, however, continued to be selected as witnesses as well as judges of the facts of the case:[3] they were directed to be taken from the neighbourhood (de vicineto); and if any of the persons chosen on a jury in a case were ignorant of the circumstances, others were to be taken in their stead until twelve were unanimous.[4] They afterwards gradually became, and still continue to be, in the modern form, rather the judges and deciders of question of fact, from evidence brought before them by other persons as witnesses, than from their own personal knowledge of the circumstances.[5]

---

[1] For the alterations effected at the time of Henry II., or by him, see Palgrave, Rise and Progress, part 1, pp. 241, 244.

[2] It is curious to observe the coincidence between the feudal laws of England, France, and Jerusalem, which is perhaps not more conspicuous in anything than the doctrine of novel disseisin, as it is laid down in the French writers, the assize of novel disseisin of Henry and the assizes of Jerusalem. In the latter code it is enacted, that when one disseised would recover seisin, he must come before the seignor, and say, "Li Sir, tel et le nome m'a de nouveu dessaisi de tel chose et die de quoi, &c., et si vous mescrées que enci ne sort come je vous ay dit faites le enquete et me faites si com vous devés par l'assize et usage de cet royaume com de nouvele dissaisine." Then the seignor shall command two or three of his men to inquire, &c., c. 63.

[3] Brac. l. 3, de Corona, c. 22; Mirror, s. 38.

[4] Palgrave, Rise and Progress, part 1, pp. 246—260.

[5] Among the Franks, before such institutions were superseded in their country, as in England at this day, the jurors, until they gave their verdict, were to be kept without meat or drink.—Car. Magni, cap. 2, A.D. 805, s. 11; cap. 3, A.D. 805, s. 15; cap. 1, A.D. 809, s. 16.

The Conqueror continued the judicial eyres, which the Anglo-Saxon kings had been used to make, in substance, though not in form; and in person held three judicial eyres or sessions of his aula regia every year, in the different parts of England.[1] When he visited his continental dominions, he appointed[2] justiciars, who administered justice in his stead. These two practices were followed by his successors; but the business of the king's court increased, and the law became, under the hand of the Norman lawyers, more subtle and refined, and rendered the duty of the supreme administrator of justice both important and onerous. Henry's time was much divided between his French and English dominions; and in 1170 we find him appointing "barones errantes," whose office much resembled that of the missus of Charlemagne, and from whom the circuits of the modern justices in eyre are deduced. The jurisdiction of the justices in eyre was exercised by means of the jurors of the hundred, who had superseded the twelve thanes, scabini, and four men and reeve of the township.[3] The assizes of Clarendon, enacted at Clarendon, and recorded at Northampton by Henry II., about A.D. 1176, increased the rigour of the preceding laws. These assizes are said to have been given as the rule for the guidance of the justices in eyres, and they were known by the name of Capitula Itineris.[4]

When the king held his placita he was accompanied by his court (aula regia), which had supplied the place of the witangemote of the Saxons. The members of the ordinary court[5] were most probably selected at the pleasure of the sovereign and the convenience of the clerks and barons. The clerks of the king, with the chancellor at their head,

---

[1] Saxon Chron. 1067, 8, 1086, 7; Palgrave, Rise and Progress, p. 288.

[2] Odo and William Fitz Osborn were the first appointed, A. D. 1067.—Ordericus Vitalis, l. 7, p. 213; Guil. Malms. l. 3, f. 6; Palgrave, Rise and Progress, p. 290.

[3] Ib. part 1, pp. 92, 3, 5, 6.

[4] Assis. Clarend. apud Wilkins, p. 832.

[5] See post, as to the extraordinary Curia Regia.

were the king's scribes, and made out his writs. They were usually ecclesiastics. Particular branches of business were referred to separate committees, selected by the king, when occasion required, out of a larger body; and the committees, assuming by degrees a permanent independent existence, formed the origin of our courts of Common Pleas, Exchequer, and Chancery; while from the main body, in which the king presided, is derived the King's Bench, in which the sovereign is still presumed to be always present.[1]

From the end of the reign of Henry II. the records of the royal court (curia regia) are preserved, and have been recently published;[2] and they seem to have been enrolled, at least from the early part (before the seventh year) of the reign of this prince;[3] but the exact period at which the pleadings of the suitors were first thus reduced to writing, and preserved among the rolls of the court, instead of being merely recorded by or committed to the memory of the freemen of the court, seems doubtful.

Feudal laws.

This cursory notice of the alterations effected in the forms of judicial proceedings, leaves us at liberty to consider the law of property, particularly as to land, which characterises this period of the legal history of both countries, and which almost exclusively occupied the attention of the lawyers; and, reacting on the laws of persons, out of which it had arisen, affected, and materially modified their relations, as well as the law of contracts.

The important consequences of the stricter doctrines of the feudal law had had time, in the hands of the subtle Norman lawyers, to work upon the law of property, though at first the change was rather in name than reality; and at the time when Henry II. ascended the throne (A.D. 1154), and during his reign, the Anglo-Saxon law had arrived at the greatest height of feodality,

---

[1] Palgrave, Rise and Progress, part 1, pp. 290, 1.

[2] Rotuli Curiæ Regis, published by the Record Commission, and edited by Sir F. Palgrave.

[3] Introduction to Rotuli Curiæ Regis.

with its burthens and appendages, as the French laws had done, about two hundred years earlier, some time before Hugh Capet was chosen king, in 987.

Different accounts of the feudal law.

So many accounts, all widely differing from each other, have been given of the origin of the feudal system, that it is useless to attempt to reconcile them. According to the notions still most commonly received in this country, it has been imagined that the leaders of the barbarian invaders took possession of the country, and parcelled it out among their chief followers, who subdivided their allotments among their officers, who again divided it among the soldiers, upon various conditions, as that of defending them in military service, or supplying a certain article of subsistence as a rent.[1] This and other theories,[2] with which the writers of the last century pleased themselves, seem to have been abandoned by the universal consent of those who have more recently investigated this subject.

Origin of the feudal relations.

The dependence out of which the feudal system originated was by no means universal in the first instance. After the invasion of France, there were, as before remarked, three ways in which land was held, namely, as allodial, as beneficiary, and as tributary.[3]

On settling in Gaul, a large number of the invaders separated themselves entirely from their leaders, and obtained possession of lands in allodium[4] (franc-aleux), quite independent of all relation and all duty. Their lands have been dignified by the high name of fiefs of the sun (fiefs du soleil). Others of the barbarians continued round the leader or general, as his followers and companions, and shared his board, either to plan new

[1] Blackstone, Com. 45; Robertson, Charles V., v. i.

[2] Sir F. Palgrave says, "The popular theory of the feudal system, propagated by Robertson, Montesquieu, &c., is erroneous, and this theory of systematic divisions has been generally abandoned on the Continent. If true, it is only true of Normandy and of the Norman conquests in Britain and the south;" part 1, p. 496.

[3] Guizot, Essais sur l'Histoire de France, Ess. 4, c. 1; Bernardi, de l'Origine, &c., pp. 22, 23.

[4] Guizot, Ess. 4, c. 1, s. 61.

invasions, or to live idly at his table, and took possession of no lands. Others, still continuing in connection with their chief, took possession, or had grants, of land for their lives, as a benefice. From this possession of land, in continuance of the relation of follower and leader, seems to have gradually grown the feudal system.[1] Other lands were held by persons tributary to some chief or invader. These tributary lands, and those in allodium, were eventually absorbed in the feudal system.

The relation between the leader and his followers was of two sorts; either like the voluntary and personal enlistment of the soldier under the general, or that of a patriarchal tribe following its head or chief member.[2] But it was rather in the form of a band of warriors, voluntarily formed under a leader, for conquest and pillage, than a migratory tribe, that the Germans invaded Europe; and although the relation of a tribe continued partly to exist even there, it necessarily partook more of the character of a military than a patriarchal government.

When the Germans were established in Gaul, and lands were appropriated, this relation was at first personal: the superior granted out, to those who retained connection with him, lands for life, or other period. It has been supposed that at first these grants were originally only for one year, like the annual distributions which took place in Germany before the invasion; but no sooner was the new country acquired, than many of the institutions of the vanquished inhabitants were adopted. From the first, feuds are found to have been held for all the four periods of the will of the grantor,

---

[1] Sir F. Palgrave, however, says, "The feudal system was created by the union of Roman laws and barbarian usages. The personal relation of lord and vassal was founded on the Teutonic antrustionship, or homage, not perhaps without Celtic mixture: but the tenure of beneficiary land was borrowed from the Roman jurisprudence."—Rise and Progress, part 1, p. 495.

[2] Guizot, Histoire de la Civilization en France, lect. 3, cours de 1830; Essais sur l'Hist. de France, Ess. 4, c. 1, s. 2.

for years, for life, or in perpetuity; and these were not successive stages of the feudal system, but states all existing in every epoch. From the first, the grants for life were most frequent.

Definition of a feud.

A feud, or benefice,[1] has been defined "a right which the vassal hath in land, or some immoveable thing of his lord's, to use the same, and take the profits thereof, hereditarily, rendering unto his lord such feudal duties and services as belong to military tenure, the mere propriety of the soil always remaining to the lord."[2]

General character of the feudal law

Although the feudal system had peculiarities in each of the different countries where it obtained, the general characters common to the feud throughout Western Europe are such as seem essentially to belong to a military connection, or naturally arise out of it. This relation of general and soldier is merely personal, and between those of the invaders who continued, as before observed, the relationship of the leader and follower, or the head and the rest of his tribe, was, after they were settled in Gaul,

---

[1] The word feud has been derived by some from the Latin word "fides," implying fidelity to a sovereign; by others from the word "emphyteusis;" and by others from the Teutonic words "fee," "fe," recompense, and "od," possession. The latter seems the most likely derivation, and places the feod in contradistinction to the alod. The term "feudum" does not appear to have been used until the 9th century, the word "beneficium" being applied from the 5th century up to that period. This was probably owing to the two languages having been hitherto kept distinct, and the Latin taste of the ecclesiastical scribes was unwilling to use a word so evidently of barbarian origin; but by that time the mixed language of modern France had been formed by the admission of some German roots into the corrupt Latin.—See Origin of the Romance Languages.

[2] The following are some of the various definitions given of a fee, feud, or fief:

Quid est feudum jus prædio alieno in perpetuum utendi fruendi; quod pro beneficio dominus dat ea lege, ut accipit sibi fidem et militiæ munus aliudve servitium exhibeat.—Cujas.

Est feudum beneficium, seu benevola et libera rei immobilis, aut æquipollentis concessio, cum utilis dominii translatione; retenta proprietate, seu dominio directo, sub fidelitate, et exhibitione, servitiorum honestorum.—Craig.

Definitio feudi varie traditur. Verior et receptior est illa, quam tradit Raynal feudum est benevola, libera et perpetua concessio rei immobilis vel æquipollentis, cum translatione utilis dominii, proprietate retenta, sub fidelitate et exhibitione servitiorum.—Dumoulin, 114. As to the signification of the term "fief," see Guizot, Histoire de la Civilization en France, lect. 2, cours 1830.

of the same nature as before.[1] The tie in Germany had been personal, it continued so in Gaul; neither party could substitute another in his stead without the consent of the other. Where fiefs were for a limited period, or for life, the relation was obvious; in hereditary tenure, the primitive idea of a voluntary engagement between the giver and the beneficiary was also continued. Each time either a grantor or a beneficiary died, another person, the heir, being substituted in his stead, it became necessary to renew the personal relation; and formal acts were necessary to place them in the same situation as had existed before. It was necessary the heir of the deceased beneficiary should do some formal act, to signify his becoming the vassal of the suzereign; and that the suzereign should formally accept him, and place him in the same relation as had existed with his ancestor. Hence the origin of Homage,[2] Fealty,[3] and Investiture. By the first, the tenant offered himself, and the lord accepted him as his homo, antrustion,[4] man or vassal. By the second, the tenant swore fidelity to his lord; and by investiture, the lord put the tenant in possession of the land, as a stipend for the duties to be performed, and warranted it to him.[5]

The relation became afterwards to be regarded in precisely the reverse point of view—viz., as territorial instead of personal. The grant of the land was considered

---

[1] The right of commendation (selecting a military leader) continued long after the settlement of the German tribes in the Roman provinces. The inferior Saxon noble might leave his land held of a superior hlaford, and commend himself to any other; and the same right existed among the Franks.—See Commendation in the Capitularies, Domesday book, v. ii. 182 b, 188 b, 309, 321.

The ceorl was unable to depart from the land: he had however an interest in it.—Palgrave, Rise and Progress, pp. 16, 17.

[2] Glanville, Tractatus de Legibus et Consuetudinibus Regni Anglice, l. 9, c. 1; Bernardi, de l'Origine et des Progrès de la Legislation Français, p. 190, as to the repugnance to the Dukes of Normandy to do homage in person.

[3] Leg. Hen. I. c. 5.

[4] Antrustionship was equivalent to homage.—De Antrustione Regis Marculfus, Form. 1, 18.

[5] Glanville, l. 1, c. 4; Assis. de Jerusalem, c. 99; Cout. de Beauv. c. 58, 61.

to cause the relation, instead of the grant to be in consequence of the relation, and homage was considered as the acknowledgment of tenure. As the relation between the lord and the vassal continued to be formed on the same principles as the personal engagement of general and soldier, so the duties and consequences, which result from the relation as above, partook of a similar military nature; and they were either moral or material duties. Of the first sort: as a general is entitled to all the advice and information his followers can give, so the lord was entitled to the Counsel of his vassals; and the greatest breach of duty was to counsel, conspire, or plot against the superior; and the vassal was bound not merely not to do, but also not to permit or consent to have done, any act to the detriment of the lord, without endeavouring to prevent, or informing the lord of it.[1] Again, as a general is of more importance to the conduct of an army and the direction of a war than any of his followers, so it was the duty of the vassals to become Hostage[2] for the lord in case he was taken prisoner. Such were some of the moral duties due from the vassal to the lord, in return for which the lord was called upon to protect the person of his vassal.

Moral duties arising out of the feudal relation.

During the anarchy which devastated the French kingdom under the latter Carlovingian princes, the possessors of allodial property,[3] who stood unconnected with any great chief, harassed and oppressed on every side by the neighbouring feudal lords, were eager to surrender their lands, and take them again as fiefs or benefices encumbered with all the feudal appendages, in order to secure protection; and few if any allodial lands survived the second dynasty.

Services.

The other or material kind of duties are usually called

[1] Assis. de Jerusalem, c. 205. [2] Ib.

[3] Bernardi, de l'Origine, &c. p. 103; Montesquieu, Spirit of Laws, b. 31, c. 8. Sir F. Palgrave says, p. 22, "The Capitularies testify the manner in which the poor and needy were harassed and vexed by the bishop, the abbot, the earl, the

services. The first of these is Military service.[1] This military duty, called knight's service (service du chevalerie), was the original cause of the relation, and was therefore essential to the constitution of the true feud; and accordingly this was a duty of all proper feuds or fees (fiefs d'haubert); and where any duty not of military nature, as to plough the land, &c., was substituted, it was considered as base or servile, and the benefice called a base feud, socage and villeinage (fiefs de roturier). It was also the duty of the vassal to contribute "Aid" to pay a ransom[2] to redeem his military leader or feudal lord from captivity, and to pay various other expenses of a military dignity or connection, as to make the lord's son a knight. Attempts were also made to establish on the part of the lord numerous other calls for pecuniary contributions, for miscellaneous as well as military purposes, under the name of aids; but the only one which seems to have been obtained generally as compulsory, besides those of ransoming the person of the lord and of making his son a knight, was to assist him when he married his daughter.

Other consequences of the feudal relation.

Other consequences, though not originally inherent, resulted from the nature of the relation. Thus, as the heir was not entitled to succeed as a matter of course to the fief of his ancestor, the lord demanded a sum of money on renewing the grant, called a Relief (relevium, or relevatum). Again, neither party was at liberty to substitute a person in his stead without the consent of the other. Hence, when this principle relaxed, the lord demanded a Fine on every alienation for his consent;[3] and it was necessary the tenant should by attornment express his consent to the lord disposing of his seignory.[4]

---

judge, and the centenary, until they surrendered their allodial property as the price of tranquillity," Cap. de Causes Regni Italiæ, A.D. 793, s. 13; Cap. Quartum, A.D. 803, s. 17; Cap. Tertium, A.D. 811, s. 2, 3.

[1] Bernardi, de l'Origine, &c. p. 190.

[2] Liber Feudorum, l. 2, t. 24.

[3] Fines of alienation were established throughout France.

[4] 2 Bl. Com. 71, 2.

When the blood of a tenant of a fief in perpetuity became extinct, the land reverted to the lord: hence the doctrine of Escheats;[1] and if the tenant or vassal refused to perform the duties of his station, a Forfeiture (forisfactura) ensued, and he was put out of possession. Before fiefs became universally hereditary, and while some continued to be granted for life or other shorter period, and the feudal theory was not reduced to exact system, it seems that if the heir of a deceased vassal, who had held in perpetuity, was unable, from youth or other cause, to perform the military service or other duty, the lord made a new grant to some person competent. When, however, feuds became generally hereditary, and the system became more perfect, the lord respected the right of the heir, but claimed the Guardianship of his person (garde noble), in order to see that he was duly educated and prepared for the duties he had to perform, and in the meanwhile took possession of the profits of the fief, on the plea of supplying a substitute in the place of his ward.[2] There was also another right, called the Marriage of the ward. According to the military theory of feuds, it seems but just that the lord after the land created the relation, instead of the relation causing the grant, that the female heir should not be allowed by marriage to place her feud in the hands of an enemy of the lord; hence his right of bestowing her in marriage (maritagium), or at least the necessity of his consent;[3] and thence the origin of fines on the marriage of a female;[4] but the origin of fines on the marriage of a male ward, as was afterwards introduced, is not so obvious.[5]

In Germany, courts had been held and justice rendered by an assembly of all the freemen of the tribe,

---

1 Glanville, l. 7, c. 17; Lib. Feud. l. 2, tit. 86.

2 Montesquieu, Spirit of Law, b. 31, c. 33; Glanville, l. 9, c. 8.

3 Montesquieu, Spirit of Law, b. 31, c. 34; Assis. de Jer. c. 242.

4 Glanville, l. 9, c. 9, 12; Gr. Coust. de Norm. 95.

5 Bracton, l. 2, c. 38, s. 1.

presided over by the grav or calderman. When settled in their new countries the same system was continued; and the lord, whether he originally derived his superiority as chief of the tribe or as leader of the voluntarily formed band, held the courts, and it was the duty of all the vassals to do Suit to his courts (justitia). They formed the court of peers for the trial of the suits between his followers.

Feudal subordination.

Besides the connection of the actual occupier of the soil with his lord, there was in the feudal theory a relation of the possessors of fiefs among themselves. The immediate occupier of the land was called the tenant paravail: his lord was perhaps vassal to some greater lord, and held his lordship of this superior lord upon terms of military services, &c., similar to those on which the tenant paravail held his fief. In such case he was called the mesne lord, and his fief was called an arriere fief.[1] He of whom others held fiefs, and who held his domains of no superior, was called the lord paramount. Thus, the possessors of fiefs, in theory, formed a regular system of organization for legislative, judicial, and military purposes, from the superior, or suzerain of the state, down to the lowest class of fief-holders.

The mesne lords who held of a superior constituted his council, court, and army, and they formed the court of peers by whom themselves were judged. Thus, the English kings, as dukes of Normandy, Anjou, Guienne, and other provinces, held their continental territories (like the other great vassals) of the king of France; their great nobles held their domains in those duchies under them; and under these were lesser barons, of whom the simple knight and castellan were the tenants, and connected the lord paramount with the actual occupiers of the soil. The knight or castellan was judged by his peers or fellow knights, who held of the same lord;

---

[1] Bernardi, de l'Origine, &c. p. 189.

and in like manner the great vassals by the peers of the court of the lord paramount. Such was in principle the association of the possessors of fiefs; but in effect this organization never was very efficacious on the Continent. The association of holders of fiefs was very little compacted; they were constantly in a state of incoherence and war: no superior had power to maintain peace and justice among them. In England this theory was more fully carried into effect; and, from the great power of the crown, was really more than the mere speculation of the learned, though a greater degree of symmetry has been attributed to it than it really possessed.

We must not omit here to observe that, besides the holders of fiefs, and villeins who held at the will of the feudatory or lord, and who, having their grants entered on the court rolls of the fief or manor, subsequently became the English copyholders (holding at the will of the lord by copy of court-roll, according to the custom of the manor), there were in early times (at least in France) another class of men who held in precarium (something like leaseholders). Under the Roman law, precarium signified the gratuitous grant of the usufruct of property for a limited and generally very short time. After the fall of the empire, the clergy, who retained the Roman law, often farmed out their property at a fixed rent by a contract, also called precarium, of which the term usually was one year.[1] As early as the time of Pepin this mode of holding lands in precarium was known.[2] The term was afterwards usually entered into for five years.[3]

Peculiarities of the feudal system in France.

These were the main features of the feudal system, common to the west of Europe; but there were others peculiar to each country. In France, in consequence of

[1] Guizot, Histoire de la Civilization en France, vol. iv. lect. 2.

[2] Bernardi, de l'Origine, &c. p. 132.

[3] Guizot, ib.; Bernardi, ib.; Guizot, Essais sur l'Histoire de France, Ess. 4, c. 1, s. 2, Des Benefices Temporaire.

the anarchy which had succeeded the death of Charlemagne, the absence of any central administration, and the usurpations of the great vassals and the officers of the crown, a great number of the fiefs had been erected into little sovereign states, which neither acknowledged any external authority, nor required any commerce beyond their limits. Hence, one of the characteristic features of the feudal system in France was an union of the rights of sovereignty with the ownership of the soil, which placed almost all the rights and authorities, now vested in the national government, in the proprietor of the soil over all the inhabitants of his domains: so that not only the military and executive powers of making war and peace, coining money, &c., but the legislative and judicial authority of rendering justice, and decreeing and levying taxes, belonged to him.[1]

It is not difficult to trace the source of the power thus exercised by the French feudal seignors. The delegation of the royal authority to the great vassals of the crown, and chiefs of the nation, to be exercised in the name of the sovereign, has been already noticed, and the fact, that the officers of the crown, after the anarchy which commenced in the time of Louis le Debonnaire, claimed to exercise these powers in their own right, or at most as only nominally subjected to the royal interference. Originally, there was a material difference between their authority over their Teutonic countrymen and fellow-conquerors, and that over the vanquished Gauls. In settling in France, the Germans carried with them and established judicial institutions, similar to those of their father-land; and the lord merely presided over the Frankish court of peers, in person, or by the gerefa, as the chief of the freemen had done in the gau. Over the vanquished Gauls he assumed the right of appointing the Roman judge. At first, by

[1] Bernardi, de l'Origine, &c. p. 193.

the side and above this sovereignty, was, on the one hand, the power of the Frankish kings, who affected to continue the imperial royalty of the Roman administration;[1] on the other, the assemblies and jurisdiction of the freemen: but as the central government declined, and the assemblies of the freemen disappeared, the authority of the feudal lord became nearly sovereign, or paramount. From the first, the German chief in Gaul had found himself surrounded by an inimical population, different in race, language, and manners, and against whom he must constantly be on the watch. Romanized Gauls were the inhabitants and cultivators of his domains. Over them[2] he exercised the authority of a conqueror; and the powers he possessed in the Court of Peers became more and more of a similar nature: the patriarchal system of the tribe diminished, and that of conquest, on the contrary, took a greater development, and became, if not the sole, at least a very dominant principle, and constituted one of the grand characters of the French feodal system. There existed, at the time of the invasion, a very large number of slaves in Gaul; and the whole population was imbued with a servile spirit.[3]

---

[1] See ante, p. 33.

[2] The term "vassal" is supposed to be of Celtic origin (from gwâs).—Palgrave, Rise and Progress, part 2, p. ccclxxxviii.

[3] M. Guizot, in his admirable lectures, Sur l'Histoire de la Civilization en France, remarks, "It is an opinion generally entertained, and sustained by a multitude of writings, that the deplorable condition of the agricultural population in our territory (France), its servitude, its misery, date from the invasion of the barbarians; that the conquest, and the progressive development of the feudal system, completely changed its condition. In my opinion, the invasions and the conquest of the barbarians caused the agricultural population to suffer cruel evils, renewed without ceasing, evils much more pregnant than those it had to support under the Roman administration; but at the bottom its social condition was, I think, little enough changed. It was before the invasion, and under the empire, nearly the same as it appears to us in the following centuries."

To the same effect Sir F. Palgrave says, "Cæsar bears testimony that the policy and institutions so generally ascribed to the Franks, the powers of the clergy, the pride and power of the feudal nobility, and the oppression and almost total annihilation of the third estate existed in Gaul, and were established before the Merovingians crossed the Rhine; that subsisting in effect, though exercised by other hands, they continued undisturbed during the sway of the Romans, and

As to the personally free Gallic cultivators of the soil, the coloni, it is easy to imagine that the German master would not be very careful to distinguish them and their privileges from slaves, and such they soon became; nor, after a time, were the free but poorer classes of their German countrymen treated with more consideration. The capitularies often speak of the oppression of the poor but free men, who were thus compelled to resign their independence; and, eventually, the jurisdiction over slaves was extended over Germanic freemen as well as the Gallic coloni.

When the owner of the fief had excluded the royal authority from his domains, he claimed and exercised for himself all the other rights, besides that of the administration of justice, which the Frankish sovereigns, affecting to carry on the government of the Roman emperors, had derived from them. Of this nature were the powers of legislation and taxation which he possessed: he fixed and regulated the tailles due to him; (the tailles had succeeded to the capitation of the Roman empire.) Under the empire, the rent due to the owner had been fixed, while the capitation, a personal impost due to the government, had been augmented according to the arbitrary regulations of the state. Hence, when the government of the inhabitants of his domains was united to the ownership of the fief, and the lord or possessor of the fief claimed the rent and the capitation, the rent still remained fixed, while he possessed, in the place of the

---

that they were merely renewed and confirmed under the sceptre of the barbarian dynasties."—Rise and Progress, part 1, p. 34. "The French peasantry, oppressed in the days of Divitiacus and Vercingetoria, bore the same burden when they tilled the ground as coloni (under the Romans). The peculiar pride and haughtiness of the French feudality in the middle ages is perhaps to be deduced from the usages prevailing in Gaul before the Roman conquest."—Ib. p. 500.

Deplorable state of the peasantry of France at the time of Fortescue, c. 35, and absolute and limited monarchy (passim); the tyrannical nature of their government, c. 55; Comines; Aylmer's Harborowe for Faithful Subjects (the marginal references, "how the French pezantes be handled"); Heyward's Life of Henry IV., p. 250; D'Ewes. p. 169; Harl. Misc. vol. v. p. 259.

imperial authority, the power of imposing the capitation or taille, and augmented it at pleasure.[1]

Feudal abuses.

But, besides these authorities, the lord or seignor of a French fief had numerous other vexatious rights. Almost every thing was given in fief, to the prejudice of the community at large. Thus, the jurisdiction over woods and forests (gruerie); the rights of chace; the tolls[2] (peage, travers, rouage, barrage); the escort or conduct of merchants coming to fairs; the judicature in the hall of the prince, or of the lord; places of change in the cities; where money was coined; the houses and stands of fairs; the exclusive or bannal ovens, mills, and wine-presses of the town or neighbourhood; public stews; the wine ban, and other similar prohibitions; the rights of purveyance of (geste) provision (paste), quarters (logement), and supplying provisions or tackle (fourniture); service in the fields, or on the roads (corvées); watch and guard; the right for the seignor to place his leg and thigh in the bed of his vassals newly married (cuissage et jambage), which was substituted for the right of prelibation and markette;[3] and even the swarms of bees which could be found in the forest, were thus granted as fiefs, or rights claimed by the feudal lord.[4]

Peculiarities of the feudal system in England.

When William the Conqueror introduced the feudal system into England, he did it chiefly as a system of military organization,[5] for the benefit of the crown; and he does not appear to have wished to meddle with the Anglo-Saxon customs and franchises in this respect, further than was necessary to derive all the benefits and

---

[1] Guizot, Histoire de la Civilization en France, lect. 8, cours de 1830.

[2] The ecclesiastical power interfered to endeavour to prevent the exaction of new tolls.—Decretal, lib. 3, tit. 39; de Censib. cap. 10.

[3] See Botrius, Decis. 297, No. 17; Ducange et Lauriere verbo Marquette, Bracton, l. 2, c. 8.

[4] See Examen de l'Usage general des Fiefs aux 11, 12, 13 et 14 siecles, par Brussel, t. i. p. 42. See L'Abbé Fleury, Precis Historique du Droit Français, s. 16; Guizot, Lecture sur l'Historie de la Civilization en France, l. 2, cours 1830; Dict. de l'Anc. Regime et des Abus Feodal.

[5] Saxon Chron. A.D. 1085, 6.

fruits to the crown; and during the period immediately after the Conquest, we constantly find his followers appealing to the Anglo-Saxon county court, or a jury, to testify what rights their Anglo-Saxon predecessors had enjoyed, and what they were entitled to in consequence of the grant from the conqueror of the forfeited rights and estates of the Saxon nobles. So that when the change was effected by consent throughout the whole country, at first it was except as regards the king, more in name than in substance: but that king himself introduced the forest laws, and the Norman nobles were not backward in making known and claiming the rights to tailler haut et bas, and the other fruits of tenure, as they had learned them in France. By the time of Henry II. perhaps some consequences were added which were unknown on the Continent; but the chief distinction arose from the greater power of the king, and the comparative insignificance of the English noble. One of the burthens unknown in France imposed on the English feud, arose from this source, namely, the right of Primer Seizin,[1] which, in the nature of an additional relief or sum of money, the crown was entitled to receive, when one of his tenants in capite died seised, from the heirs if he were of full age. With regard to the amount of the sum, it was settled that the king should receive one whole year's profit of the land on this account. The lords also assumed the right of interfering with the marriage of their male as well as female wards, or receiving the price of the marriage, a practice not known in other countries; but on the whole, though they claimed the rights of venery, and other privileges known on the Continent, their power was much more circumscribed than that of the French noble. "The paramount authority of the king's court," says Mr. Hallam,[2] "and those excellent tribunals of the county and hundred, kept within very

[1] Blackstone, Com. v. i. p. 66. [2] Hallam, Middle Ages, v. ii. pp. 432, 4.

narrow limits that great support of the feudal aristocracy, the right of territorial jurisdiction."[3] Except in the counties palatine, the feudal courts possessed a very trifling degree of jurisdiction over civil, and not a very extensive one over criminal cases.

The consequences of the feudal habits of the personal relations.

When the original Germanic relation of leader and follower had thus become completely converted into the feudal one of lord and vassal, the general basis of the law was altered, inasmuch as territorial possessions now became the sole standard of importance, and gave the owner or occupier his rank and character in society, instead of the rank and character of the person giving a characteristic quality to the land: thus, for example, we now find the English freeholder, or tenant of freehold property, in place of the Anglo-Saxon freeman.[4] This alteration necessarily affected, to a considerable extent, all the personal relations of life; but while it chiefly tended to depress those not possessed of lands, it was not in the power of this or any other system of law to convert a free people into slaves; and it recognized the rights of the freeholder, however poor. In France, the distinction between the various ranks became, under the feudal system, more marked than ever. The lord, possessor of the fief, during the period of anarchy which had devastated the country, had, in exacting the services due to him from the tenant or roturier, acquired a more elevated character; while the follower, formerly his companion, became, when possessed of an arriere fief, his vavassor, or else descended into a subject or slave; and the personal distinctions of Frank, Ripuarian, Visigoth, and Roman had disappeared. In England, the Anglo-Saxon ealdorman had been exchanged for the Norman baron, who, even when he retained the old title of eorl, estimated his own rights over his newly-acquired lands by the standards of

[1] See also ante, p. 43; and Palgrave, Rise and Progress, part 1, p. 119.

[2] Bract. l. 4, fo. 224.

his continental domains; and he had some opportunities, while might was right, during the early period of Anglo-Norman history, especially in the reign of Stephen, of acting on his own theory of dominion. But, though from this time we find villeinage introduced, and the villeins sold alone or with the land (regardant, or in gross), yet the freeman preserved his right to be tried (like the baron) by his peers or fellow-freeholders of the county-court; and this, even though his freehold did not exceed forty shillings in annual value. Some traces also continued to exist in France of the ancient judicial polity, and the suitor or subject of the lord's court still claimed to be judged by his peers (pares).[1]

As to females.

The spirit of the domestic relations was also affected by the feudal system. If the Germans, in their forests, highly esteemed the weaker sex, the chivalrous manners introduced and encouraged in the feudal ages tended to increase this feeling. From the voluntary deference paid by the stronger sex to the weaker, which still characterizes the gentleman, the wife and daughters of the owners of the fief were placed in a more elevated and more happy situation than under any other state of manners;[2] and though in the more strictly feudal parts possessors of fiefs only were entitled to become knights,[3] and to pretend to chivalry, yet in the south of France, and elsewhere, the citizen or burgess also often assumed the character, and the condition of his wife could not but be affected by it. Besides this, there was another mode in which the system operated: the German freeman, independent and solitary in his habits, had been accustomed to live in his native forests, separated from society, he had therefore sought more earnestly domestic

---

[1] Bernardi, de l'Origine, &c. pp. 188, 9; Guizot, Histoire de la Civilization en France, vol. iv. lect. 10.

[2] Guizot, Histoire de la Civilization en France, vol. iv. lect. 5; Article on Chivalry, in the Encyclopœdia Britannica, by Sir Walter Scott.

[3] Guizot, Histoire de la Civilization en France, vol. iv. lect. 6.

intercourse in the bosom of his family;[1] and although the Gauls loved to congregate in cities, yet feudalism drove the noble of his castle, or excluded him from the society of his inferiors. Thus separated from the world in general, the only equal nearer to him than the domains of the neighbouring lord was his wife. The value of her society, in his isolated state, became greatly enhanced, and the domestic relations of life perfected. It is only in society formed after the feudal fashion, that we find the wife, possessed of the genuine feminine qualities proper to her sex, capable or permitted to represent her husband in his absence, defend his fortress, or command his soldiers, in preference to a seneschal or servant.

As to children.

The rights of the children were also modified by the feudal principles. The duties to be rendered, the services to be performed, were indivisible:[2] the fief therefore could only devolve on one person; and the eldest son, to whom it did pass on the death of the ancestor, became of increased importance. In France the right of primogeniture (droit d'ainesse et preciput) had long been introduced: it seems, however, not to have prevailed under the first race, nor under the second, until the feudal habits were fully established.[3] Among the Anglo-Saxons, it is said that all the sons succeeded equally to the land. The inconvenience of this system was felt after the Conquest, as soon as the feudal law was established; and the law of primogeniture was perhaps introduced by William I.[4] In the laws of Henry,[5] we find an enactment, that the eldest son should have the father's chief fief.[6]

After this general view of feudalism, the extant docu-

[1] M. Hullmann traces the origin of both the civil and political order of modern times to our ancestors being essentially rural in their habits. — Geschichte, des Ursprungs der Stænde in Deutschland.

[2] Bernardi, de l'Origine, &c. p. 194.

[3] Montesquieu, Spirit of Laws, b. 31, c. 33.

[4] See Mr. Butler's Note to Co. Lit. 191 a. n. vi. 4.

[5] Leg. Hen. I. c. 70.

[6] Sir M. Hale, History of the Common Law, c. 11.

Feudal and customary law reduced to writing.

ments which record that system demand our notice. Happily for us, about the time when its doctrines were in the fullest force, an effort was made in each country to give a degree of certainty to its custom, by attempting to give them a written, though in most cases not an authoritative, form. One of the earliest of these attempts seems to have been that of Count Raymond Berenger the elder, who, in 1060, reduced the customs of Barcelona to a written form; and at least as early were those of Bearn. But the first document of importance that throws light upon the early customary laws of France and England, are the Assizes of Jerusalem; which, holding up to us a perfect mirror of the usages of this age, form one of the most interesting documents in the whole range of legal history. The crusade had gathered an immense number of French and other western people in the Holy Land; and having effected its conquest, the Duc de Bouillon had been elected king: the Assizes of Jerusalem are the laws, statutes, and customs granted to the kingdom of Jerusalem by Godefroy Duc de Bouillon, in the year 1099, by the advice of the patriarch and the barons, after he had been chosen king. They were called assizes, because made in the assize, or assembly, of the great ones of the kingdom.[1] It is evident that they were chiefly drawn from the customs and usages of France; and they have usually been regarded as among the official works on the ancient jurisprudence of France.[2]

In this code we find two courts existing in Jerusalem, as in most parts of Western Europe. The first, the High Court (Haute Cour), formed of the barons, knights, and

---

[1] Assises et Bons Usages du Royaume de Jerusalem. Advertissement, par Gaspard Thaumas de la Thaumassiere. The Assizes of Jerusalem were arranged in their present order by J. d'Ibelin, Count of Jaffa and Ascalon, about 1250.

[2] Notices Historiques, Critiques et Bibliographiques sur plusieurs Livres de Jurisprudence Française, remarkables par leur Antiquité ou leur Originalité, par M. Dupin, Avocat, 1820.

peers, in which, like the aula regia of the Anglo-Norman monarch, the king presided, and the nobles and knights were judged; and secondly, the Sheriff's Court (Cour des Borges, or Cour du Visconte), in which the bailli or sheriff presided, to render justice to the people. This code contains a clear and extensive system of law on feudal matters; the forms of procedure in courts;[1] the duty of judges and counsel; appeals,[2] champions, wager of battle, and duels;[3] the law of contracts, warranty,[4] debt,[5] pledges,[6] and sale of animals[7] and slaves,[8] and such like matters;[9] and wills, marriage, forbidden degrees, bastards,[10] guardianship.[11] Other feodal duties, especially services due by the vassals in war, in justice, and in marriages,[12] are admirably treated of. The assizes then go on to consider the rights of the crown and the great officers;[13] the succession to the crown and the bailliage:[14] and lastly, it speaks of the duties and services due to the king from the bishops, nobles, and commonalties.[15] If we were to select a single chapter to characterize this most interesting record of that age, it would be one which, while it displayed the knightly faith we expect to find among the crusaders, would at the same time afford an insight into the nature of the feudal system, and the complication of its relations, namely, the chapter entitled, "How a man, who has several lords, can bear arms against his lord without forfeiting his faith."[16] In every respect (besides the light they throw on feudal manners) the Assizes of Jerusalem display a system of law so connected, so perfected, and

---

[1] Ass. de Jer. c. 1 to 81.

[2] Apeau de Homicide, c. 82.—See the English law of appeal for murder.

[3] Ass. de Jer. c. 82 to 112.

[4] Ib. c. 114; Ass. des Bestes Restives.

[5] Ass. de Jer. c. 118.

[6] Ib. c. 120 to 134.

[7] See note 4.

[8] Ass. de Jer. c. 137.

[9] Ib. c. 112 to 137.

[10] Ib. c. 136 to 171.

[11] Ib. c. 176 to 181.

[12] Ib. 182 to 282.

[13] Ib. c. 282 to 292.

[14] Ib. c. 293 to 308.

[15] Ib. c. 314 to 386.

[16] Coment un home qui a plusieurs seigneurs peut porter armes contre son seigneur sans mesprendre de sa foy, c. 222.

so extensive, as it would be difficult to account for in that age, except for the then existing knowledge of the Roman law.[1]

Two other works of the same nature, but not possessed of an official stamp, were undertaken about half a century later, viz., the Liber Feudorum, in 1150, a work formerly considered of great authority in feudal law; and the Tractatus de Legibus et Consuetudinibus Angliæ of Ranulph de Glanville, the neat and perspicuous Glanville, who was chief justiciary of the English king, Henry II.; and who seems to have caused this work to be composed at the command, and with the authority, of the king. If we examine the contents of this work, which must be considered as the earliest in the series of English common law authorities, with reference to the four heads mentioned in the commencement of this sketch, it is evident that the laws in it relating to persons, though modified by the feudal principles, are formed from those of the Anglo-Saxons,[2] mixed with the laws of Normandy.

The laws of property, as stated in the preceding page,[3] had undergone a great alteration, and become of a more refined and subtle technicality. The rational part of the law is evidently drawn from the Roman code, of which the author seems to have made great use;[4] and in the

---

[1] See Bernardi, de l'Origine, &c., p. 214.

[2] A very great difference has been stated to exist between the language of this work of Glanville, who is the earliest Anglo-Norman legal writer, and that of the Anglo-Saxon laws (see Reeve's History of English Law); and it has been concluded, that the substance of the law was entirely changed by the Anglo-Normands, because of the difference of the language in which it was thus embodied: but a comparison of the early statutes of the Anglo-Normand kings with those of the Anglo-Saxons, proves this opinion to be erroneous. The difference between Glanville with his successors, and the Anglo-Saxon laws, is scarcely greater than between that of statute law of Henry III. and Bracton, and consisted chiefly in the more classic phraseology and the scientific form which, in consequence of the revival of the study of the Roman law, the writers on the customary law attempted to give to their works.

[3] See page 64.

[4] The whole book on this part of the law in Glanville is little more than a repetition of the Roman law, the same in phraseology and in effect, lib. 10. De

formal part,[1] the French origin of the chancellor and clerks, who framed the writs, and of those who enacted and administered the laws, had become apparent; and the imperial mandate of the Cæsars, and the forms of the canon law, are seen adapted to the Anglo-Saxon system.[2]

Relaxation of feudal doctrines in England, and Magna Charta.

Scarcely had the feudal doctrines had time to develop and establish themselves in England, when limits were put to their most obnoxious doctrines, and their strictness began to relax. During the time of Henry II. military service, the very essence of feudality, began to be exchanged for a pecuniary compensation—scutage, or escuage. Under Richard Cœur de Lion little legal progress was made: the crusades and the continental wars absorbed the attention of the brave monarch and his nobility. But the feudal system did not produce in the mass of the people of England those habits of military life which are still so conspicuous throughout France.

The Normans and Saxons, both equally anxious to curtail the power of the crown, and to enjoy the ancient Anglo-Saxon franchises, wrung, in 1215, from the pusillanimous John, the immortalized Magna Charta,

---

debitis laicorum quæ debentur ex diversis contractibus, viz. ex venditione, emptione, donatione, mutuo, commodato, locato, conducto, et de plegiis et vadiis, sive mobilibus sive immobilibus et de cartis debita continentibus. Bishop Nicholson accuses Glanville of having in his book servilely copied Justinian.

[1] It is somewhat singular that Glanville's work, like the Assizes of Jerusalem, commences with the procedure and the distinctions of the superior and inferior courts. The coincidence is probably purely accidental.

[2] M. Houard, Anciennes Loix, says, "There is not perhaps one writ preserved in Glanville of which the model cannot be discovered in the French and Norman system. The precipe quod reddat answers to the 28th formula of the first book of Marculphus; the pone to the 23rd; and the quod posuit to the 21st formula of the same book."

Marculphus was a French monk, who published a collection of the forms used in his days, i. e. either the 7th or 8th century, but it is not satisfactorily decided which. Savigny says, the formulæ of Paris were collected by Marculphus about the year 660.—Hist. Rom. Law in the Middle Ages, v. ii. c. 2.

They exhibit strong traces of the Roman law. A great number of them are, in their very terms, the ancient forms of the Roman jurisprudence.

which, while it affixed limits to the feudal burthens, restored the ancient usages so cherished by the Anglo-Saxons. This charter, so often violated during the reign of John and his son Henry III., and confirmed—violated again and cancelled, and again confirmed with increased solemnity, and with awful imprecations and excommunications on the heads of all violators of it—cannot be considered to have been really observed as law until the reign of King Edward I. (1272 to 1307.)

From the time of the Norman Conquest to this reign every king, except perhaps William II., nominally confirmed the Anglo-Saxon laws, or granted new charters to a similar effect. The charter of Henry I. bears a close resemblance to the Magna Charta. The principal articles of the latter are—first,[1] for establishing the rights of the church;[2] secondly, for relieving the vassals in respect of various feudal fruits and burdens, by making them fixed in quantity instead of arbitrary: thus, it fixed the amount of the relief,[3] regulated the rights of wardship,[4] and the marriage of feudal wards;[5] it abolished the rights of purveyance for castleward without paying for the articles taken,[6] regulated castleward,[7] and restrained other grievous exactions begun to be made without payment of the old price;[8] it also regulated the law of forfeiture for felony, and limited the king's right to the felon's land, as against his lord, to a year and a day:[9] the king's tenants in socage and by petit serjeanty[10] are also protected; and the rights of tenants who held under any barony escheated to the king are provided for.[11] The importance of these various regulations will be evident by reference to the nature of feudal burthens, and a con-

---

[1] We take the chapters of this charter, as confirmed by King Edward.
[2] Magna Charta, c. 1. [3] C. 2.—See ante, as to Reliefs, &c., p. 70.
[4] C. 3, 4, & 5, as to Wardships, p. 71.
[5] C. 6 & 7, as to Marriage, p. 71. [6] C. 19. [7] C. 20. [8] C. 21.
[9] C. 22.—See Forfeiture, p. 71; and see Ass. de Jerusalem, c. 29 & 61, un et jour.
[10] C. 27. [11] C. 31.

sideration of how oppressive each of them, being acknowleged as due to the lord, might have been made by the sovereign or great nobles possessed of power, and unlimited by any rule except their own will. There were, thirdly, enactments which either restored and regulated the old Anglo-Saxon law, or admitted principles of justice that have not yet lost their force or estimation. Of the one of these kinds are those on the law of wager;[1] appeal of murder;[2] the holding county courts and leets:[3] of the other, the putting down illegal wears throughout England, except on the sea coast;[4] the establishment of uniform weights and measures throughout the realm;[5] the abolition of fees for writs of inquisition of life or member;[6] protection to merchant strangers coming into the realm.[7]

There are several other important articles, of which the three chief, in a political point of view, are the ninth, which confirmed the liberties of London and other cities; the fourteenth, which regulated fines and amercements for inferior crimes; and the twenty-ninth, which is the most celebrated of all the chapters of this celebrated charter. It says, in the words of the king, "No freeman shall be taken or imprisoned, or disseised of his freehold, or liberties, or free customs, or be outlawed, or exiled, or otherwise destroyed, nor will we pass upon him or condemn him, but by the lawful judgment of his peers, or by the law of the land. To no man will we sell, deny, or defer right or justice."

Perhaps the eleventh, twelfth, and thirty-sixth chapters had the greatest direct effect upon the civil laws of England. The royal court (aula regia), composed of his great officers, accompanied the sovereign when he moved from place to place. By the first of these chapters it was provided, that the Common Pleas should be held in a fixed

---

[1] C. 28. [2] C. 29. [3] C. 35. [4] C. 23. [5] C. 25. [6] C. 26. [7] C. 30.

place; and in consequence, a committee of the aula regia, called the Court of Common Pleas, has been from this period stationary at Westminster. The king's court still continued to move about; but as its progress had been necessarily irregular, and the justices in eyre (barones errantes) had usually gone at long intervals, a provision was made by the twelfth article for justices of assize to go a circuit once every year. In these circuits, afterwards directed to be three times a-year, the modern assizes originated; and the form of directing trials to be before the King's Bench at a certain day, "unless" the justices should "before" then come to the assizes, introduced the modern practice of trials at "nisi prius." The judicial iters of the sovereign, in which they exercised all the functions committed at other times to the justices in eyre, were not entirely discontinued until the accession of Edward III.[1] The thirty-sixth chapter of the Charter directed that no lands should be given (in mortmain) to any religious house.

One of the doctrines introduced into European polity by the feudal system was, not only that "no land was without a lord, but no lord without land."[2] This doctrine seems to have been brought into England by the Normans; but it did not long remain: and the old principle of the Anglo-Saxon times was early revived—that nobility might be conferred on persons without regard to territory.[3]

Progress of legislation in France.

While in England all these changes were taking place, in France, from before the time when Hugh Capet ascended the throne, and the feudal system was fully established to the 12th century, little change was formally made in the laws and customs, or in the judicial establishments. The French statute book is totally silent

---

[1] Palgrave, Rise and Progress of the English Commonwealth, part I, p. 292.

[2] Bernardi, de l'Origine, &c., 185; Guizot, Essais sur l'Histoire, Ess. 4.

[3] See Butler's Note to Co. Lit. 191 a. v. iv.

from the last capitulary of Charles the Simple, in 921, until an ordonnance of Henry I., in 1057,[1] respecting the city of Orleans, appears, after an interval of 136 years, to recommence the task of legislation in France. However, the feudal authority of the French monarch had become more firmly established. Hugh Capet, Robert, Henry I., and Philippe I. reigned only in their domains,[2] the duchy of France and the county of Paris.[3] Under Louis le Gros, who reigned from 1108 to 1137, the royal authority began to raise itself.[4] Among other institutions of this reign was the establishment of the right to appeal, in many cases, from decrees given by the officers of the various seignories to the royal judges. The sovereign, become thus first judge, did not fail soon to assume equally extensive legislative authority; for Philippe Auguste, the second succeeding sovereign, who, by his victories over the English king, John, added Normandy, Maine, Touraine, and Poitou to the Ile de France, part of Orleans and Picardy, of which he was sovereign by birth,[5] continuing the design of raising and concentrating[6] the royal power, required the lords and seigneurs to cause his own laws to be executed in their domains, and he made them swear to observe his ordonnances. Under St. Louis (1226 to 1270), who also added to the royal domains, the jurisdiction of the royal courts was still further extended. Before his time, by a law of the reign of Louis le Jeune,[7] who succeeded to the throne in 1137, trial by combat, allowed previously, it would seem, in all cases, had been prohibited for a debt which did not exceed five French sous. St. Louis, in 1260, notwithstanding the detriment to his revenue, abolished judicial

---

1 Bernardi, de l'Origine, &c., p. 173.

2 Guizot, Ess. 6, c. 2, s. 2.

3 Bernardi, de l'Origine, &c., p. 249.

4 Ib. p. 264; Guizot, Histoire, &c. v. iv. lect. 12.

5 Millot, Elemens de l'Histoire de France, v. i. p. 287; Hume, History of England.

6 Guizot, Histoire, &c., vol. v. lect. 13.

7 Recueil des Ordonnances, t. i. p. 15.

duels in all the courts of his demesnes, as Henry II. had previously done partially and indirectly in England; and although he could not suppress it in the courts of the barons,[1] yet by ordaining that the appeal[2] of false judgment from the court of a lord might be made without a judicial combat,[3] and extending the royal cases,[4] by determining the circumstances and occasions where the laws of his duchy of France became the law of the other fiefs, he greatly increased the jurisdiction of his courts.

Previously to the time of St. Louis, legal proceedings were carried on with little ceremony, and questions of fact or custom decided by the lord and the (prud'hommes) peers, or freemen of the court. St. Louis ordered translations, and endeavoured to bring the Justinian code into repute. The consequent study of the Roman law produced a great change in the legal process and judicial institutions of France.[5] Artificial methods of procedure, infinity of processes, and delays were introduced; a science of jurisprudence began to be formed, and legal practitioners arose. The mode of trial, instead of being a simple proceeding, agreeable to the notions of a tribunal composed of a warlike noble and his followers, became a course of pleading, which they neither understood or cared to learn: the peers, no longer capable of judging, began to withdraw from the lords' tribunal; baillies, seneschals, and other judges of the long robe took their places and functions; and the custom of trying by peers began to be less used, and was finally abolished.[6]

---

1 Montesquieu, Spirit of Laws, b. 28, c. 29; Guizot, Histoire de la Civilization en France, vol. v. lect. 14.

2 Henrion de Pensey, de l'Auctorité Judiciaire dans les Etats Monarchiques, pp. 27, 36, 50, 54; Guizot, Histoire de la Civilization en France, vol. v. lect. 14.

3 Recueil des Ordonnances, t. i. p. 91.

4 Bernardi, de l'Origine, &c., p. 247.

5 As to the preservation of the Roman forms of law by the functionaries, called tabelliones and notarii, see Savigny, History, v. i. c. 6; Precis Historique, &c., de l'Abbé Fleury, s. 21.

6 Montesquieu, Spirit of Laws, b. 28, c. 42; and Fleury, s. 21

The institutions of St. Louis, in which great use was made of the civil laws, contributed to hasten that event; the change was, however, gradual. We are told of that virtuous monarch's administration of justice in person: and even as late as about the 15th century, we meet with trial by peers in France; yet nothing but feodal matters were any longer tried by peers. In process of time, in France, a secret form of proceeding was introduced; everything before had been public; everything now became secret: the interrogatories, the informations, the re-examinations, the confronting of witnesses, the opinion of the attorney-general; and this was the practice down to the revolution.[1]

Consequences of the studies of this period on the law.

All the sciences are so intimately connected, and the progress of each so greatly effected by that of the others, that we may be sure the century following the revival of the Roman law, the age of Averroes, Thomas Aquinas, Roger Bacon, Duns Scotus, was not wanting in acute and learned lawyers and legal writers,[2] whose valuable treatises exhibit to us the aid they had derived from the popular legal, and dialectical studies of the times, in matter and method.

It is astonishing how rapidly the technical part of the law had been worked out in England since the Norman conquest. This must be partly ascribed to the example of close coherent reasoning afforded in the Roman law, but still more to the logical studies of the age. Sir W. Blackstone observes, that "as soon as the feudal system came to be considered in the light of a civil establishment, rather than as a military plan, the ingenuity of the same ages, which perplexed all theology with the subtlety of scholastic disquisitions, and bewildered philosophy in the mazes of metaphysical jargon, began

---

[1] Montesquieu, Spirit of Laws, &c., b. 28, c. 34.

[2] See Bernardi, de l'Origine, &c., b. 5, c. 1. Du renouvellement des etudes et comment il s'opéra.

also to exert its influence on this copious and fruitful subject."[1] And, by the time of the Edwards, we find the notions of most legal subjects almost as completely formed, and their relations almost as clearly and precisely settled, as they were two centuries afterwards, or are even now: and, making allowance for the alterations in the rules of law which have been produced in the course of six centuries, the same notions would still have the same relation; and the same questions, if brought before the tribunals of to-day, would be decided in the same way as in the earlier period of our reports of decided cases.[2]

Defontaines.

Of the legal authors of this period that have come down to us, three demand our especial notice. Pierre Defontaines,[3] contemporary with St. Louis, must be regarded as the most ancient writer on the French law.[4] In 1253, at the request of a nobleman, who wished his son to be acquainted with the laws, that he might know how to render justice to his subjects, and how to hold his land according to the laws of his country, and also that he should know how to advise his friends, when occasion required, the work called "The Counsel Pierre Defontaines gave to his Friend and to all others," was written. Like that of the justiciary of Henry, it was the production of a practical lawyer; for Defontaines was master of requests to St. Louis, and often called upon by that prince to assist him, with Messire Geoffrey de Villette, in rendering justice to his subjects.[5] This work

[1] Commentaries, s. 2, p. 58.

[2] Take, for example, the very first case contained in our venerable Year Books, in the first year of the reign of King Edward II., between Peter, son of Peter de Malo Lacu, and others, and Johanna Driby.—Maynard, Report, p. 1. We might there almost fancy ourselves perusing a page of Fearn's Contingent Remainders, or discussing the effect of a judgment recovered, or recovery suffered.

[3] Dupin, Biographie Abrégée des Principaux Auteurs de Droit.

[4] Montesquieu, Spirit of Laws, b. 28, c. 38; c. 23, 27; Bernardi, de l'Origine, &c., pp. 236, 329.

[5] For a tradition of the justice of St. Louis rendered under the trees of Vincennes, see Millot, Elemens de l'Histoire de France, v. i. p. 342.

is said to be, in a manner, the result of the ancient French jurisprudence, the laws or establishment of St. Lewis, and the Roman law.

The next in point of time is an elegant, methodical, and almost classical writer on the law of England, Henry de Bracton.[1] Of his personal history we know but little; he was probably a native of Devonshire. In 1244, he was appointed by Henry III. one of the justices in eyre, and ten years afterwards he became Lord Chief Justice of England, and is said to have filled that important office with reputation for twenty years. In 1262, or 1268, he published his work "De Legibus et Consuetudinibus Angliæ." He studied at Oxford, where, since the time of Vacarius, lectures on the digests of Justinian had been given, and he took the degree of doctor of civil law; and there seems no good reason to doubt that he was also professor of civil law in that university.[2] His work shows an intimate acquaintance with the imperial code; and not only his method, but chapter after chapter is evidently drawn from that source. The offices which he held, the length of time he held them, and his high reputation, gave a weight and authority to his work, which, considering how much he derives from the civil law, and the view taken by subsequent English lawyers of that code, it perhaps would not otherwise have obtained. As it, however, is a more extensive work than that of Glanville, it must be considered as the most copious fountain of the common law, from whence succeeding lawyers, and Coke himself, drew their maxims and fundamental notions.[3] Bracton.

[1] Reeve, History of the English Law, v. ii. p. 86; Pref. to 8 Coke Rep.

[2] Duck, de Usu et Auth. Juris Civilis Romanorum, l. 2, c. 8, 328; Bale, Scriptor Britan., cent. 3.

[3] The author of this work had formed the design of tracing to their source the principles of the English law. From the time of Bracton the English law, written and unwritten, flows on in an unbroken stream, and the origin of the new principles introduced since then is sufficiently obvious. The author had therefore taken Bracton, and intended to have compared the principles of the law as displayed by him, with the remains of the Anglo-Saxon laws still accessible, to have

Until the time of Glanville, the English common law was almost wholly derived either from the Anglo-Saxon customs, considerably modified by the judicial institutions and executive administration of the Normans, or from the feudal law. The Saxon origin of the fundamental laws of persons, &c., as set forth by Bracton, cannot be disputed. Both the feudal system and the Saxon laws were totally defective in provisions on the rational part of the law. Glanville had set the example of an attempt to remedy the evil; but his work was intended for the use of the justices of the supreme court; and after having briefly treated of some such matters, he says, "But the above-mentioned contracts, which arise from the consent of private individuals, we treat of briefly; because, as is before observed, the court of our lord the king is not accustomed to assist private agreements." In Bracton's time, a larger original jurisdiction had been obtained by the king's courts; and having adopted the method and arrangement of Justinian, in composing his treatise, where the feudal and Anglo-Saxon law were deficient, he seems to have filled up the outline, left vacant in his treatise by them, from the imperial code.[1] Shortly after the time when this treatise

discovered how much is truly to be traced to that source. A comparison with the Assizes of Jerusalem, and the liber feudorum, would have shown how much was the result of the general principles of feuds, and the grand Coutumier of Normandy how much was peculiarly derived from Normandy, and what was due to the Roman law would then have been more clear. The author had made some progress in collating passages of Bracton with the texts of the Roman code; but a change of prospects renders it improbable he will ever be able to pursue a design (to him at least) so highly interesting.

[1] This agrees with the opinion of the learned Selden, who says, "Tum ubi deest nostri juris præscriptum expressius, ad rationem juris etiam Cæsarei ratione suffultam recurreretur, tum ubi jus utrumque consonum, etiam Cæsarei quasi firmatur explicareturve res verbis."—Seld. Diss. ad Flet. c. 3, s. 4.

As to the adoption of the Roman law at this period in England, see Seld. Diss. ad Flet. c. 3, s. 1. Librorum Juris Cæsarei usus prisci apud Juris Anglicani consultos, qua tales vestigia manifesta tam in Thorntonio et Fletæ autore quam in Bractonio.

Mr. Spence, however, imagines that the rational part of the law (relating to to contracts) had been preserved by tradition in London, and the other trading was written, from circumstances which will be presently noticed, the connection of the English lawyers with the civil law was cut off, and the affection hitherto manifested for it turned into hatred. From that time, the new sources of legal knowledge became almost exclusively of English origin. The fact of much of this fountain of common law being derived from the civil law, instead[1] of detracting from its merit, as some English writers have appeared to think, greatly adds to its real value;[2] as is evident, when we compare with the ample materials, and the highly finished intellectual system of the imperial code, anything which those times could have produced as a substitute to supply the deficiency.[3]

About this time, at least after the fourteenth year of Henry III., 1230, the Coutumier de Normandy was compiled.[4]

The third author of the same period, though a little later, is Philip de Beaumanoir, characterised as one of the most learned men of his age in civil and canon law, but especially in the customary law of France, who was successively steward (bailly) of Clermont en Beauvoisis, of Senlis and Verman, and counsellor of Robert, Count Beaumanoir.

towns throughout the kingdom; and when Bracton reduced them to writing, "so little had they departed from their Roman originals, even after a lapse of centuries, that he found they might, with trifling variations, be expressed in the very terms of the Institutes and Digests of Justinian."—Inquiry, p. 540.

We may mention, at the same time, what seems to be equally founded in error, viz. Mr. Spence's opinion, that, following each of the leading doctrines of the common law, there are few which can be traced to a much earlier period than the reign of Edward I.; and what can be so traced, are chiefly found to be the remnants of the ancient Roman law handed down by tradition.—See Inquiry, p. 553.

[1] Bracton, considered as to the authority of his work.—Plowden, Com. 357; Reeve, History Henry III.

[2] "In questions of rational law, no cause can be assigned why we should not shorten our labour by resorting occasionally to the wisdom of the ancient jurists, many of whom were the most ingenious and sagacious of men."—Sir W. Jones on Bailments.

[3] As to the effect of the use of the Roman law from the time of Stephen to Edward III., more than 150 years, on the English law, see Seld. Diss. ad Flet. c. 9, s. 1; Effectus usus qualiscunque Juris Cæsarei per Intervallum.

[4] Hale, Hist. Com. Law, c. 6.

of Clermont, son of the king, St. Louis.[1] His "Coutumes de Beauvoisis," published in 1285, which Montesquieu[2] calls an admirable work, and frequently cites, may be studied not only for the particular local customs of which it treats, but from the great similarity of the institutions then existing, for a general view of the customary law of the whole kingdom of France, and for the light it also throws on the law of England as it then stood, and on the manners of the age.[3] From this highly-esteemed work the very chief of succeeding French lawyers derived their purest lights, and drew the maxims of the French customary law. Beaumanoir makes comparatively but little use of the Roman code;

[1] See Coutumes de Beauvoisis, par Messire Philippes de Beaumanoir, Bailly de Clermont en Beauvoisis: avec Notes, par Gaspard de Thaumas de Thaumassière; and particularly the introductory observations of M. de Thaumas for information respecting this writer.

[2] Spirit of Laws, b. 26, c. 15.

[3] "This treatise," says Mr. Barrington, "is so systematical and complete, and throws so much light upon our ancient common law, that it cannot be too much recommended to the perusal of the English antiquary, historian, or lawyer. He kept the courts of the Comte de Clermont, and gives an account of the customary laws of Beauvoisis (which is a district about forty miles to the northward of Paris) as they prevailed in the year 1283. He is consequently a more ancient writer than Littleton; and, to speak with all due reverence of this father of our law, perhaps a better writer. It need hardly be said that the customs of the two countries were at this time very similar, especially of the more northern parts of France. If we wanted other proof, the commentators on the oldest French law books cite Littleton as illustrating their customs." With all deference to Mr. Barrington, affection or prejudice for a father of our law induces the author to think that Littleton's tenures being confined to but one branch of law, scarcely admits of a comparison with the work of Beaumanoir, which includes a whole body of then existing law and the practice of the courts; and in those parts where any comparison can be instituted, Littleton certainly does not appear to disadvantage. Ducange seems exactly to hit the mark when he says, "Among all the treatises which have been written on the French ancient law, *the most curious* is that of Philippes de Beaumanoir;" and the historian and legal antiquary will scarcely find any book which will convey more general information on the manners of that age, or so well repay his attention; but it is of so different a nature from Littleton as scarcely to admit of any comparison being made between the two. A more fair comparison would have been with a contemporary of Beaumanoir, namely, Bracton, whose method is undoubtedly more scientific, and who, as a lawyer, would be no loser by comparison with any author of his age, though he would not be so amusing to the antiquary for a record of the manners of that age, as the curious work now under consideration.

and he appears to have undertaken the task of bringing the ancient jurisprudence into agreement with the regulations of St. Louis.[1]

Other writers.

During the reign of Edward I., who has been called the English Justinian,[2] several English treatises of law were published, of which our space will not admit a lengthened notice; nor — as most of them are little more than epitomes of Bracton, whom we have sufficiently characterised, so much was he respected—does our design require it. Among these the first is Fleta—seu Commentarius Juris Anglicani—written about the thirteenth year of Edward's reign (1285). Then Breton, which (as sometimes Bracton was thus named, and from the great similarity of the contents), though written in the person of the king, is regarded as an abridgement of Bracton's work interspersed with new matter.[3] Ranulph de Hingham and Gilbert de Thorton, both chief justices, also wrote in that reign. The Summa of the latter is an abridgement of Bracton.[4] Most of these writers, from Glanville, not only adopt much of the matter and method of Justinian, but also seem to have been singularly taken with a fancy for the introductory idea of his Proëmium.[5]

---

1 Montesquieu, b. 28, c. 38.

2 For a succinct account of the laws of Edward, see Blackstone's Com. vol. iv. p. 425.

3 See Seld. Diss. ad Flet. c. 2, s. 1. De Compendio juris Gallicano, Briton dicto. Johannes Breton, Episcopus Herefordensis.

4 Ib. c. 2, s. 1. Thorntonius Bractonii Epitomator.

5 Justinian says, "Imperatoriam majestatem non solum armis decoratam, sed etiam legibus oportet esse armatam, ut utrumque tempus, et bellorum, et pacis, recte possit gubernari: et Princeps Romanus non solum in hostilibus prœliis victor existat, sed etiam per legitimos tramites calumniantium iniquitates expellat; et fiat tam juris religiossimus, quam victis hostibus, triumphator (magnificus)."

Glanville says, "Regiam Protestatem, non solum armis contra rebellis et gentes sibi regnoque insurgentes, oportet esse decoratam, sed et legibus, ad subditos et populos pacificè regendos, decet esse ornatam; ut utraque tempora, pacis et belli, gloriosus rex noster ita feliciter transigat, ut effrænatorum et indomitorum, dextra fortitudinis, elidendo superbiam, et humilium et mansuetorum

It is a very curious coincidence that most of the Germanic nations had their Mirror of Justice. In Germany, about the year 1220 A.D., appeared the Speculum Saxonicum, or Sachs Senspiegel. In France, about 1280, Guillaume Durant published his Speculum Juris. Of the same period, or a little later, in England is the Miroir des Justices. This latter book is supposed to have been formed, by Andrew Horne, on the basis of an older law tract, called the Speculum Justitiariorum, which is said to have been written in the time of the Saxons.

Separation of the judicial and legislative functions of the High Court of Peers in England.

During this period, the legislative powers and the ordinary administration of justice began in England to be permanently separated from each other, and to be exercised in conjunction with the royal authority by two distinct bodies—namely, the parliament and the courts of justice. Our object does not permit the discussion of parliamentary history, except so far as regards the administration of civil justice, and civil, as distinguished from political, legislation.

Much discussion has taken place as to the early history of Parliament; and the exact period when it assumed its present form may be questionable. But the origin of the parliaments (or parlements) of both England and France can scarcely, we think, be doubted. Among all the Teutonic nations who settled in Europe,[1] there existed a general assembly of freemen in each country, under the title of Witangemot or Mahl, Champs de

æquitatis virgâ, moderando justitiam, tam in hostibus debellandis semper victoriosus existat, quam in subditis tractandis æqualis jugitŭr appareat."

Bracton says, "In rege qui rectè regit, necessaria sunt duo hæc, arma videlicet et leges, quibus utrumque tempus, bellorum et pacis, rectè possit gubernari: utrumque enim istorum alterius indiget auxilio, quo tam res militaris possit esse in tuto, quâm ipsæ leges usa armorum et prœsidio possint esse servatæ. Si autem arma defecerint contra hostes, rebelles et indomitos, sic erit regnum indefensum: si autem leges, sic extirminabitur justitia, nec erit qui justum faciat judicium."

Fleta says, "Regiam potestatem non solem armis contra rebelles et gentes sibi regnoque insurgentes oportet esse decoratam sed legibus ad subditos populosque pacificos regendos decentur ornatum esse," &c. Proëmium.

[1] See ante, pp. 10, 42, 43, 46.

Mars or Mai, (Commune Concilium, Concilium Magnum, Curia de More, Placitum Generale, Conventus Generalis or Synodus.)[1] In these assemblies both in France[2] and England,[3] it seems indisputable that all the freemen were originally entitled to attend and take part. But even under the Anglo-Saxon Heptarchy, so large an assembly as they formed in each kingdom must have been felt to be inconvenient, and accordingly we find, at a very early period, the courts attended by the four men of the township and the priest, together with the landlords. Similar causes produced similar results in France; and the count and twelve scabini of his county attended the Placitum Generale.[4] The precise nature of the constitution of the witangemots under the Anglo-Saxon kings, after the union of the Heptarchy in one kingdom, does not very clearly appear. They seem, however, to have consisted of a convocation of the freemen in general, or of such of the nobles and freemen (sapientiores et nobiliores) as the sovereign selected. We find this assembly, however, attending the king, and, like the Frankish general assembly, called Mahl (Mallum, Champs de Mars, Placitum Generale),[5] forming the court of peers of the realm, and assisting him not only in enacting new laws, but also in administering justice. We have seen that shortly after the death of Charlemagne these general assemblies of the whole kingdom disappeared; but, under the feudal system all the tenants (the place of the freeman being, in almost all things, taken by the freeholder), all who

---

[1] Millot, Elemens de l'Histoire de France; Bernardi, de l'Origine, b. 1, c. 35; Guizot, Essais sur l'Histoire de France, Ess. 4, c. 3, s. 2; des Assemblées Nationales; Reeve's History of the Common Law; Hume, History of England; Mackintosh, History of England, v. i. p. 74.

[2] Guizot, ubi supra; Bernardi, de l'Origine, pp. 38, 9.

[3] Palgrave, Rise and Progress, part 1, p. 19; and see the part taken by the ceorls of Kent in laws of Æthelstan, 5.

[4] Cap. Lud. P. a. 819, s. 2; Bernardi, de l'Origine, p. 39; Guizot, Ess. 4, c. 3, s. 2; des Assemblées Nationales.

[5] Guizot, Ess. 4, c. 3, s. 2; des Assemblées Générales.

held freehold lands of a prince[1] or noble were entitled and even bound to attend his courts and assist him, as the court of peers in administering justice and in matters of legislation, with their counsel and advice.

In France, only the great nobles and those of the royal duchies held their lands immediately of the crown, and the former only[2] were bound or entitled to attend his royal councils—the aula regia, or "cours pleniere." The inferior nobles and freeholders attended the courts of the chief vassals in like manner.[3] When William took possession of the country, he and the Norman barons introduced the feudal form of the aula regia or supreme court of peers in the place of the witanegemot;[4] and it would seem that all those who held lands of him immediately (tenants in capite or barons)[5] were entitled or bound to attend his courts, and formed the court of peers. But there were from the first at least six hundred tenants in capite, and afterwards a still larger number. We find a distinction between the great and lesser barons in the reigns of his successors—barones majores et minores.

Besides the ordinary aula regia or curia regia, we find in his reign, as already mentioned, a general council formed on a new plan, in which twelve men were selected from each county to testify their customs.[6] From this time to the reign of Edward II., there appear continually to have been assembled a general council of the kingdom (called Curia de More, Curia Regis, Commune Concilium), the constitution of which varied according to cir-

---

1 Bernardi, de l'Origine, p. 254, b. 4, c. 3; des Cour Royale.

2 Bernardi (p. 255) says, tradition reduces to twelve the number of peers of the "Cour Royale:"—the Dukes of Burgundy, Normandy, and Guyenne; the Counts of Flanders, Toulouse, and Champagne; the Archbishop of Rheims, and the Bishops of Langues, Laon, Soisson, Beauvais, and Noyou.

3 Bernardi.

4 See ante, pp. 57, 58, 63, 64.

5 Concil. Clarend., art. ii. Universæ personæ regni qui tenent in capite, debent interesse judiciis curiæ regis.—Wilkins, Anglo-Sax. Ll. p. 322.

6 See ante, p. 58, note 5.

cumstances each time it assembled.[1] Sometimes we find it directed to consist of only a few of the nobles; sometimes of a large number of tenants in capite and barons; at other times of certain great barons with knights elected from each county;[2] and sometimes, as late even as Henry III., of all the tenants in capite (omnes qui regi servicium debent).[3]

These great assemblies are called constantly curia regia as well as commune concilium:[4] we may therefore presume that the supreme judicial as well as legislative functions were nominally still exercised by the tenants in capite.[5] But for the regular administration of the supreme jurisdiction of the realm, the collection of a large body of the tenants in capite would have been inconvenient, and the ordinary aula regis, or curia regia, consisted of only such nobles and other persons as the sovereign chose to select or appoint. During the reigns of John and Henry III., we find that the great barons were expressly summoned (or it was agreed between the barons and the king that they should be assembled in parliament), with knights chosen from each county. The latter seem to have been called together either under a design of the king to use them as a counterbalance to the nobles, or on the stipulation of the barons to make inquiry into all grievances.[6]

In the reign of the latter monarch, we find a new

---

1 Edinburgh Review, No. 69, March, 1821, pp. 4—15.

2 Hallam's Middle Ages, v. iii. p. 20.

3 Report of the Lords' Committees, appointed in 1820 to search the journals of the House, &c., touching the dignity of a peer, p. 90. John, in his Magna Charta, art. 14, promises to summon the archbishops, bishops, abbots, earls, and great barons individually, and, by the sheriffs, all his tenants in capite, omnes illos qui in capite de nobis tenent.—Wilk., p. 369.

4 See, however, the Report from the Lords' Committees, p. 20.

5 Edinburgh Review, No. 69, March, 1821.

6 Henry III. agreed, at the colloquium held at London in eight days of the Epiphany, 1223, that evil customs, &c., should be inquired into by twelve sworn knights in each shire, the verdict to be returned to him on the morrow of the clause of Easter, the time when the great council or curia regia usually assembled. By the provisions of *Oxford*, due to the memorable parliament of 1258, it was ordained that four knights should be elected in every county, who should

constituent[1] called into being to support the government of Simon de Montfort, Earl of Leicester. He, it seems, from being leader of the barons, had, by attempting to establish himself over his fellow barons, lost their support, and was thus compelled[2] to have recourse, in 1264, to a power then just rising into importance—namely, the burghers or citizens.[3] From this time we find the burgesses summoned to parliament; and they appear to have sat together with the knights of the shire originally in one chamber with the great barons. The two former afterwards sat in a separate assembly, and having acquired the exclusive right to grant extraordinary aids and taxes to the crown, formed the House of Commons, as now constituted, possessing a legislative voice only. The superior nobles still formed the House or court of Peers of the realm, and consisted of such tenants in capite as the crown summoned. They possessed, jointly with crown and commons, not only a legislative voice, but they still retained the supreme appellate and extraordinary jurisdiction of the ancient Anglo-Saxon witangemote.

---

make inquiry, by the jurors of the hundred, of all grievances to which the people were subjected, and that three parliaments should be held every year.—42 H. III.

18 Ed. I., 1290, two or three knights to be elected from each county, to advise upon, and consent for themselves and the county, what should be ordained by the earls, barons, and proceres, forms an epoch in our constitutional history. The relation between remedial representation, whether in the guise of echevins or jurors, and the station of the commons, is so evident, that it would probably have been long since acknowledged by our constitutional writers, had they not been determined on considering parliament merely as a political congress.—Palgrave, p. 315.

[1] Selden, however, says that the borough of St. Alban's, in the eighth year of Edward II., claimed to send two burgesses to parliament *by prescription*. — Selden, tit. Honor, 709.

[2] Rymer, Fœdera, v. i. p. 802. See the Writ to Sandwich Report of the Lords' Committees, p. 149.

[3] The " parliament" held at Pamiers by Simon de Montfort, 1212, is the first of these assemblies of which we possess any distinct account; and it is singularly interesting to an English reader to observe the " Tiers Etat" in an assembly convened by him who is supposed to have first summoned the citizens and burgesses to appear in the parliament of England.

Council or parliament of Toulouse, A.D. 1229. — Palgrave, Rise and Progress, p. 548.

At what precise period this House of Peers came to be entirely distinct from the king's court, which lost the name curia regia and aula regia,[1] cannot be traced; but from the time of the Edwards, the ordinary supreme jurisdiction of the aula regis and the other courts became practically entirely distinct from the house of peers, or the full and extraordinary court. It was, as before stated,[2] divided into the several Courts of Chancery, King's Bench, Common Pleas, and Exchequer. These courts, however, still form a part of the High Court of Peers; and though the members of the several courts (when not summoned by writ or created by patents) are not entitled to take part in that assembly as lords or peers of the realm, the House of Lords is still entitled to call for the counsel and advice of all who exercise the divided jurisdiction of the original aula regis or curia regia,[3] and for the attendance of the Masters in Chancery.[4]

With regard to the French "Cour Plenière," "Cour Royale," or Court of Peers, in which, in early times, then called the aula regis, the French monarchs, in person, dispensed justice, it was separated from legislative authority; and its fate was nearly similar to that of the English Supreme Court of Justice.[5] The authority of the kings of France continued to be very small out of their own dukedom; within it, they had the same power as other sovereigns, with a domanial court and privy council.[6] At an early period of the third race the great vassals had a repugnance to attend the royal court; and by their default the same officers who sat in the domanial court became members of the royal court.[7] The great vassals only attended when any feudal matter interested them, the courts became confounded together, and the peers of France with those of the duchy.[8]

French parliaments.

[1] See Blackstone, Commentaries, v. iii. c. 4, s. 5.
[2] Ante, p. 64.
[3] Blackstone, p. 168.
[4] Ib., and ante p. 44.
[5] See Butler, Note to Co. Lit. 191 a. V.
[6] Bernardi, de l'Origine, &c. p. 250.
[7] Ib. 257.
[8] Ib. p. 256.

With the States-General (Etats Généraux), our object does not lead us to meddle. About the year 1150, under Louis VII., the term "parliament" seems to have been first introduced, in France.[1] The French writers are not agreed whether the parliament of Paris arose out of the states-general or the king's private council.[2] It seems to have resembled our aula regis closely, and was originally ambulatory. In 1302, Philippe le Bel made the parliaments of Paris and other provinces[3] stationary. In rendering them sedentary, Philippe le Bel did not alter their constitution, during all the time they had the same ministry, the same duties, the same rights. The king was still presumed to be present in them. The first function of these august tribunals was, to give to the laws and edicts of the king the necessary sanction, by enregistering them, which seems to have been taken as their consenting to them or enacting them. They also appear as the court of peers, and judged the vassals; and they possessed the appellate jurisdiction which had been so greatly enlarged by Louis le Gros and St. Louis. In 1319, Philip V., the Long, ordained that the prelates should no longer be admissible into parliament.[4]

Reports of judicial decision.

The commencement, at about the same period, of a system of reporting notes of adjudged cases, in both England and France, is a curious coincidence. As to the latter country, Montesquieu says, no sooner had the

[1] Matthew de Paris uses the term parliament for the first time in the year 1246, and applies it to the English general council.—See also notes 1 and 3, Butler, Co. Lit. 110 a.

[2] Meyer, l'Origine et les Progrès des Institutions Judiciaires, t. ii. p. 503; Henrion de Pansey, p. 47, n.

[3] Philip III. the Bold, after the reunion to the crown of Languedoc and its dependencies, established the parliament of Toulouse, a tribunal without appeal, in 1280.—Vaissette, Hist. de Languedoc, t. iv. pp. 60, 71, 524.

Sovereign courts or parliaments were established at Grenoble for Dauphine, by Charles VII., at Bordeaux and Dijon, by Louis XI. for Guienne and Burgundy.

[4] Probably from jealousy of the clergy and canon law.—See the separation by the clergy from the civil tribunals in England, ante, p. 59; and the consequence, ib., note 1.

parliament become a fixed body, than they began to compile its decisions. John de Montluc, during the reign of Philippe le Bel, made a collection, which at present is known by the name of the Olim Registers. They are generally supposed to have been made about A.D. 1312; but it seems doubtful whether they are not as old as the 28th year of the reign of St. Louis, 1254. In England, we have printed reports of cases decided as early as the 4th year of the reign of Henry III., 1228, but those of that reign printed are only occasional ones; and though a series of reports of cases, decided in the reign of Edward I., exists in manuscript, they have never been printed. However, from 1307, the first year of the reign of Edward II., the printed reports of cases determined in the superior courts have been continued down, almost without interruption, to the present day. The earlier of the reports are styled the Year Books; and the first volume, which contains some cases of the reign of Edward I., is also called Maynard Report. In these volumes the common law was worked into a system; and the relation of the legal notions respecting real property acutely discussed and definitively fixed.

Rise of municipal corporations and enfranchisement of the commons.

The introduction of burgesses into parliament naturally draws attention to the rise and the state of cities, and the important part they performed, not only in the general civilization of society, but also in the emancipation of villeins, both in France and England. It has been already stated, that many of the municipal corporations of France traced their origin to, and retained the institutions of, the Roman polity.[1] In England, under the Anglo-Saxons, the cities, though organized in a similar manner to the open country, attained a very considerable importance. Though an agricultural or rural people, the Anglo-Saxons encouraged commerce. A freeman, not noble, was raised to the rank of a thane by making three

[1] See ante, p. 24; also see Guizot, Histoire de la Civilization en France, vol. iv. lect. 15, 16, 17.

voyages at sea; and many of the cities were rich, populous, and influential, especially London, which acted an important part on many occasions under the Anglo-Saxon kings.

The feodal system was still more inimical to the cities than the agricultural habits of German life; but, in France, several of the cities had already wrested from the feudal nobles many important privileges. The insurrections[1] which had taken place in Laon, Beauvais, Cambrai, Rheims, and Vezelay, had obtained for several cities advantages, charters, and privileges. It has been remarked,[2] that more charters were granted to the cities in the north than in the south of France. This seems to have arisen from the latter standing less in need of them, as having more generally retained the Roman institutions. Henry I. of France (who reigned 1031 to 1061) granted a charter to his ducal city of Orleans.[3] Paris, another of the king's cities, had always retained its importance; and the sovereigns turned their attention to the establishment of their own courts (prevotés) and the suppression of the nobles.[4] In England, after the Norman conquest, there was a great falling off in the cities. Commerce was greatly impeded by the disorders of the times; and the cities, in losing their importance, lost many of their rights, which feodal habits were little calculated to respect. In London, though William I. granted charters, we find Baynard and Montfichet castles erected in addition to the Tower. Under Henry I. the prosperity of the cities began to revive; and London received a charter from him, with additional immunities. Its liberties were, as we have seen, expressly secured, with those of the other cities, by Magna Charta;[5] and under its Lord Mayor, who had

---

[1] Bernardi, de l'Origine, &c., l. 3, c. 4; de l'Etablissement des Communes, &c., c. 6, p. 239.
[2] Guizot, Histoire, &c., vol. v. lect. 17.

[3] See Charter to the City of Orleans, in Appendix to 5th vol. of Guizot's Histoire, &c.

[4] Robertson, Charles V., vol. i. lect. 1, 4, and notes.
[5] Ante, p. 86.

succeeded the Anglo-Saxon portreeve and the bailiff of John, it has gone on ever since in increasing wealth and prosperity. Already, in the time of the barons' wars, we find London sending out a large army to support its liberties. The cities of the north of France[1] and Flanders, about this time, enjoyed an equal degree of prosperity; and, in the reign of Edward III., the cities of Belgium were almost the arbiters of peace and war.

Much of the prosperity of the cities is to be traced to their trading guilds, or companies, which, by admitting persons as members, conferred on them freedom, at least within the city walls. It would seem that these trading guilds[2] owe their origin to the colleges of operatives (collegia artificum et opificum), which had existed among the Romans from the earliest period[3] down to the fall of the empire; and which continued to exist in England, as well as France, through the Anglo-Saxon and feudal periods, and now played so important a part.

This will not appear improbable, when we recollect, not only that the right of property, called borough English,[4] has survived the Roman, Saxon, and Norman invasions, but also that the peculiar customs of London and York[5] can be traced to no other period than the time of the Romans. But even if the city guilds[6] cannot trace their existence (through the Anglo-Saxon period) directly

---

[1] Guizot, Histoire, &c., vol. v. lect. 19, for the History of the "Tiers Etats," from the 11th to the 14th centuries, and as to the rapid decline of the Commons in France.

[2] Palgrave, Rise and Progress, part 1, pp. 103, 628.

[3] Numa Pompilius, we are told, divided the Romans according to their arts or trades, of musicians, goldsmiths, masons, dyers, shoemakers, tanners, braziers, and potters. He collected the other artificers into companies, who had their respective halls, courts, &c., that each might consult the interests of his college or trade.—Plut. Numa, translated by Langhorne.

[4] See ante, p. 16, n. 2.

[5] A true history of the Lodge of Antiquity at York would, perhaps, throw a light on this point.

[6] Maddox thinks they were hardly known to the Anglo-Saxons, Firma Burgi, c. 1, s. 9; and that they might have been brought into England by the Normans, and that the French and Normans borrowed them from the cities of Italy. If this be the case, they undoubtedly there sprung from the Roman institutions.

to the time of the Romans, they were already of importance in this period;[1] and as the Anglo-Norman monarchs no doubt imitated the continental system, which certainly was derived from Rome; and, moreover, as the king's chancellors, who drew up and sealed the charters, were always ecclesiastics, and devoted to the Roman law, they undoubtedly correspond with the Roman colleges of operatives. Each of these colleges had distinct meeting places (like the halls of the city companies), a treasury and common chest, a register (like the lists of freemen), a person to represent them upon public occasions and in acts of government (like the clerks to the various companies). They had the power to manumit slaves[2] (like conferring the freedom of the city); and they had the right to make bye-laws, provided they were not inconsistent with those of the government; and certain exemptions and other privileges.[3] This close resemblance almost establishes their identity; and although, during the Anglo-Saxon period, the cities were divided into hundreds and tithings, which latter are also called guilds, as well as borghs (from guildane, to pay), yet there is no reason why, though the colleges of operatives took the same name (guild, because they were liable to pay the fine or 'were' for their members), they should not have been entirely distinct from, and independent of, the local organization. At any rate, about the period[4] our history has now brought us to, these guilds, or trading companies, played an important part in the enfranchisement of the Commons.[5] A villein, admitted into one of them, became a freeman, and he might through it acquire riches and importance.[6]

[1] Several of the city companies have charters of this date, particularly the Goldsmiths' Company.—1180.

[2] Dig. 2, tit. 4, l. 10, s. 4.

[3] Dig. 27, tit. 1, l. 17; Dig. 2, tit. 4, l. 1; Dig. 8, tit. 6, l. 5.

[4] Merchant guilds, or fraternities, afterwards styled companies, came into general use about the 11th century.—Anderson, History of Commerce, v. i. p. 70.

[5] Ante, p. 31, n. 3.

[6] We know of no better illustration than the following, taken from our

The origin of the first and second popular and technical portions of the laws of England and France have now been traced. We have seen how the latter partly arose out of the former, and how it affected it, and also how the remedial laws partook of the character of the popular, and were also modified by the principles of the technical, part. The feudal system has been traced from its origin to the commencement of its decline, which, in England, was owing partly to the power, and in furtherance of the designs, of the crown; but chiefly to the existence of habits and institutions (as the county courts) opposed to its principles, and the numerous middle class of knights, yeomen, and freeholders, and the enfranchisement and rising importance of the lower orders and villeinage. In France, the decline of the feudal system may have been slightly accelerated by the rise of the cities: that, however, was but temporary; and the royal power was almost the sole cause operating to lessen the force of the feudal system.

Third period of legal history.

We must here leave the popular and technical laws. Our space will not permit us to follow the variations and alterations which the doctrines of either of those portions of law underwent in the more modern period, though it would be highly interesting to follow up the parallel courses their leading doctrines took in each country—to remark the consequences of the English law of entails under the statute De Donis Conditionalibus, and its counterpart, the French law of substitutions; the English law of mortmain, and the French on amortissement;

---

earliest published reports of decided cases; than which there are few, if any, extant documents which so perfectly and intimately exhibit to us the state of society at that time. In the reign of Edward II. we find the case of one Symon de Paris, who was born the villein of Sir R. Tonney; and while his mother and his brothers remained villeins he had become a free citizen of London, an alderman of the city, and he had even been the king's sheriff in that city, and had rendered his accounts in the Exchequer. He was seized by the bailiff within the demesne of Sir R. Tonney; and it seems his freedom was held not to have extended beyond the city.—Maynard, Rep. 4.

and the numerous other points of resemblance which in countries so similarly circumstanced as France and England might be pointed out, and which it would be both curious and interesting to trace. Our attention must be chiefly directed to that part of the law (the rational) which scarcely, and only incidentally, existed during the two first periods, and therefore which remained to be almost entirely called into being in the third or more recent period; and we shall chiefly confine ourselves to two things—1st, the development of the rational portion, and its effect on the previously formed law; and, 2ndly (what will scarcely be thought irrelevant to that subject), the labours of some of the eminent men who have given, either as to matter or form, the existing laws their highly scientific character; and under the latter the attempts made in France to give the customary law a written and authoritative form class themselves.

Roman law the source of rational and scientific law.

The Roman law must be considered not only as the great storehouse of rational jurisprudence, but also as the only example in the early period of a scientific form of law; and even now its classification of the subjects of law, its precision and definiteness in legal notions, and the consequent closeness and accuracy of thought which it displays, still remain unrivalled in most modern systems of jurisprudence. We may consequently expect that the degree of study that system received must have operated on the law of this period; and it is necessary to state the very different connections which existed between it and the English and the French law, in order to account for the different state of each of these.

Separation of the English common law from the Roman.

During the greater part of the third period of our legal history in England, the Roman law was seldom or never resorted to as an acknowledged guide. We have already stated[1] how greatly Glanville, Bracton, and the authors of his period, drew on the Roman code; and

[1] Ante, p. 94.

they informed us that, where an express rule was wanting in our law, recourse might be had to the rule of the civil law;[1]—and not only in theory, but also in practice, this seems to have been admitted, and in the reports of the cases decided during the reigns of Edward I. and Edward II., the rules of the imperial law are quoted, and are apparently relied upon as good authority.[2] The theory and practice of the common lawyers of this period seem to have met the approbation of the sovereign as well as of the ecclesiastics; and we find Edward I. countenancing and encouraging the study of the civil law. He invited to England Francis, the son of the celebrated Accursius,[3] to lecture at Oxford. The early formation of the English law into the scientific state (as before mentioned) in which we now find it is, no doubt, partly to be attributed to the pattern thus copied. But a highly scientific state, however desirable, may be acquired at too great a cost; and though the English lawyers of the above-mentioned reigns, probably enamoured with the scientific form and the coherent reasoning of the Roman law, which so well accorded with the scholastic philosophy, in some respects so profound, were carried away by the enthusiasm which prevailed as to this study,[4] yet

---

1 Seld. Diss. ad. Flet. c. 8, s. 5.

2 Case of John de B. and the Abbot of Abingdon, Maynard, Rep. fo. 368; Hil. 12 Ed. II., where almost the words of Celsus, Dig. 1, tit. 3, l. 39, are quoted. Mr. Selden, Diss. ad Flet. c. 8, s. 3, says, l. 11 of the Dig. 4, tit. 5, and the 16th tit. of the Institute, are referred to in the case of the Prior of Walingford.—Maynard, Rep. fo. 351; Mich. 12 Ed. II.

3 Seld. Diss. ad. Flet. c. 8, s. 1. How long he stayed in England, or indeed whether he came at all, though invited and offered a pension, seems doubtful.

4 Dugald Stewart says, "The study of the Roman law, which from a variety of causes, natural as well as accidental, became, in the course of the 12th century, an object of general pursuit, shot a strong and auspicious ray of intellectual light across the surrounding darkness. No study could then have been presented to the curiosity of men more happily adapted to improve their taste, to enlarge their views, or to invigorate their reasoning powers; and although, in the first instance, prosecuted merely as the object of a weak and undistinguishing idolatry, it nevertheless conducted the student to the very confines of ethical as well as of political speculation; and served, in the meantime, as a substitute of no inconsiderable value for both these sciences. Accordingly we find that, while in its *immediate*

the English nation, from the very first, and even during the time of Bracton himself, were exceedingly tenacious of their own customs, the common law of England, and jealous of all other systems, especially the canon and civil laws; and the lawyers joined in this feeling.[1] And justly so; for undoubtedly they neither of them contained those guarantees for the freedom of the private individual which the so-cherished Anglo-Saxon and English common law does.[2] And the nobles of the realm had as little reason to wish for the introduction of the imperial law; for one part would not have been

---

effects it powerfully contributed, wherever it struck its roots, by ameliorating and systematizing the administration of justice, to accelerate the progress of order and civilization, it afterwards furnished, in the further career of human advancement, the parent stock on which were grafted the first rudiments of pure ethics and of liberal politics taught in modern times."—Preliminary Dissertation to the Encyc. Brit.

[1] Glanville, who led the way in the study of the Roman law, Tractatus de Legibus et Consuetudinibus regni Angliæ, in the Prologue says, "Leges Anglicanas licet non scriptas leges appellari non videtur absurdum (cum hoc ipsum Lex sit quod principi placet et legis habet vigorem) eas scilicet, quas super dubiis in consilio definiendis. Procerum quidem consilio et principis accedente authoritate constat esse promulgatas." See also Bracton, quoted subsequent.—Flet.

[2] To deal fairly, with regard to the supposed tendency of the civil law to despotism, we must allow both sides to be heard: Dr. Millar, in his Historical View of the English Government, v. ii. p. 331, says, "The compilations of Justinian relate almost entirely to the private, and touch very slightly upon the public law of the empire. But with respect to property, and the rights of private persons, the opinions and decisions of the Roman lawyers do not seem to have been at all perverted by the nature of their government. Perhaps it will be difficult to point out any modern system of law, in which the rules of justice among individuals appear to be so little warped by the interest of the crown, and in which the natural rights of mankind are investigated and enforced with greater impartiality."

Professor Savigny, whose authority respecting the Roman law will be admitted as unquestionable, says, "The advocates of the Roman law frequently place its principal value in its containing the eternal elements of justice in peculiar purity, a law of nature, sanctioned as positive law: on looking closer, the larger part will appear little better than narrowness and subtilty, and our admiration is almost entirely confined to its theory of contracts: deduct the stipulations, and some other superstitious forms, and the excellence of the remainder of this law is beyond measure great; nay, it may well be termed l'expression des sentimens mis par Dieu même dans le cœur des hommes (Motifs de la Loi, du 3 Sept. 1807, by Bigot Preameneu). But this very remainder of the Roman law, so cited for its real excellence, is of so general a nature, that it might have been discovered by plain good sense, without judicial cultivation."—Beruf.

introduced without the others, and they as well as the common people would have been rendered cyphers before the crown by the lex regia,[1] which manifestly stripped the Roman people of all share in enacting laws,[2] and gave to the will of the emperor the force of law.[3] The sense of this passage was totally opposed to the system of English government,[4] and indeed to that of the whole Germanic races which settled in the Western Empire;[5] and we cannot but conceive, that a perception of this contrariety made the Visigothic legislators, when they first came in contact with the imperial system and adopted it,—as well as Bracton and the other English authors, when, in the enthusiasm of the study, they adopted some of its rules,—lay down those extraordinary assertions which have but very recently been admitted as containing truth and being of real validity.

We cannot avoid quoting the particular passages alluded to:—"The king (says the Visigothic law) is called king (rex), because he governs justly (recte). If he act rightly (recte), he possesses lawfully the name of king; if he act with injustice, he loses it miserably. Our ancestors said with reason—Rex ejus eris si recta facis; si autem non facis, non eris. The two principal royal virtues are, justice and truth."[6]

Bracton, after having spoken of the coronation oath,

---

[1] According to the construction of the lex regia, in the 12th century (see Littleton's History of Henry II.), the emperor (then Frederick Barbarossa) was the absolute master of his people, and might dispose of their property as he pleased (see also Fleury, Precis Historique, s. 21); and this only corresponds with the words of Theophilus in the days of Justinian, quoted in Gibbon, c. 44. "What interest or passion can reach the calm and sublime elevation of the monarch? He is already master of the lives and fortunes of his subjects; and those who have incurred his displeasure are already numbered with the dead."

[2] Seld. Diss. ad Flet. c. 8, s. 1.

[3] Digest, l. 1, tit. 4. Quod principi placet, legis habet vigorem: utpote cum lege regia, quæ de imperio ejus lata est, populus ei in eum omne suum imperium et potestatem conferat.

[4] Seld. Diss. ad Flet. c. 8, s. 5.

[5] Ante, p. 10, n. 1.

[6] Forum Judicum, tit. 1, s. 1.

says, " the king can do only what the law allows; notwithstanding, it is said, according to the lex regia, what pleases the prince has the force of law; for not just what is rashly willed by the king, even though with the intention of enacting justly, but what in the assembly of his officers shall be defined to be right. His power is, therefore, to do justice, and not injustice. The king ought to exercise the power of the law as the vicar and minister of the Deity, because that power is of God alone. The power of injustice is of the devil, and not of God; and the works of which of these the king shall do, his minister he will be whose works he shall do. While, therefore, he does justice, he is the vicar of the Eternal King; but when he falls into injustice, he is the minister of the devil: for he is called king (rex) from well-governing, not from reigning (à bene regendo et non à regnando); for he is king while he governs rightly—a tyrant when he oppress the people entrusted to him."[1]

This was strong language for the chief justice of a feudal prince; and, probably, no continental sovereign of that period, except St. Louis, would have permitted it. As this passage arises out of a consideration of the lex regia, there can be no doubt that the Roman law was, in that age, believed to be founded on arbitrary principles, and fully accounts for the hatred with which the whole system came to be regarded; and, from shortly after the time of Bracton, the Roman law seems to have ceased to have been studied, and to have been discountenanced and disliked by common lawyers. No footsteps can be traced of the use of this law in the common law courts, as an authority, after the reign of Edward II.;[2] and the lawyers

---

[1] We have here given a free translation of some of the passages in the 9th chapter of the first tract of the 3rd book of Bracton, De Legibus et Consuetudinibus Angliæ. The whole chapter is to the same purport, but is too long for insertion.

[2] Seld. Diss. ad Flet. c. 8. s. 4, 5. Usus Justiniani juris qualiscunque olim fuerit tum in tribunalibus regis tum in jurisperitorum nostratium studiis scriptisque, quà talium evanuit sub Edw. tertii initia, sub Edw. sec. paucis culta.

of that system, in the reign of Edward III., made no scruple to acknowledge their ignorance of even its very terms.[1]

To the period of the reign of John or Henry III. is to be referred the commencement of this separation of the common and civil law, and of the feeling of hatred between the professors of the two systems, which has hardly yet subsided. Some have attributed this separation and hatred to the jealousy entertained against the clergy, who were the chief promoters of the civil law; but whatever may have been the motive, when an attempt was made to introduce a doctrine which the canon, had adopted from the civil, law, and which differed from the common law respecting the legitimation of bastards by the subsequent marriage of the parents, we are informed that the earls and barons in parliament, with one voice replied, "Nolumus leges Angliæ mutari."[2] The civil law continued to be taught to the clergy in the universities, and practised in the ecclesiastical courts. Its professors made no scruple of asserting their ignorance and contempt for the common law, upbraiding it as barbarous and uncouth.

The fixing the Court of Common Pleas at Westminster, as before mentioned, brought together the professors of the common law, who, excluded from studying their own science at Oxford and Cambridge, where the civil and canon laws only were taught, formed themselves into a society, purchased houses (since called hostels, or inns of court and chancery), and raised a legal university, in which the common law was taught to the nobility and gentry; and the hatred of the partisans of the two systems of law greatly increased.[3]

In France, the fate of the civil law was totally different.

---

[1] See the Year Book, 22 Edward III., Michaelmas Term, p. 14, n. 37; and the same case quoted, Blackstone, Commentaries, v. i. p. 22, n.

[2] Stat. Mert. 20 Hen. III., c. 9.

[3] See Fortescue, De Laudibus Legum Angliæ, c. 48.

We have seen that St. Louis caused its volumes to be translated, and made great use of it. Philippe le Bel ordered the laws of Justinian to be taught as written reason in those provinces of France that were governed by customs; and they have been adopted as law in those provinces where the Roman law had been received.[1] It was held indispensable for all the officers of justice; who all, down to the procurators and notaries, studied and graduated in it.[2] At first the study was chiefly confined there, as in England, to the clergy; but it was found that the clerical judges, when guilty of any delinquency, claimed the benefit of the immunities of the church: it was therefore ordered, that the bailiffs and judicial officers of the lords should be taken from the laity.

The rational part of the law, and the distinction between it and the popular and technical parts.

From what has been already said,[3] it will be pretty well understood what subjects are included in the rational part of the law. It must not, however, be supposed that the popular and technical portions are not also based upon reasons or causes, as valid in their kinds as those of the law of contracts. The principal distinction between them arises from the source from whence their fundamental principles are drawn.[4] We are not going here to enter into a discussion of the efficient and final, material and formal reasons or causes of the scholastic philosophy, or even the distinction between the material and formal reasonings of sound logic; but we may ob-

[1] Whether or not the Roman law was the common law in the pays coutumier, for the cases which were not expressed in the customs, was a question agitated by the French lawyers of the 16th century. The president Liset held the affirmative, the president De Thou the negative.—See Recherches pour servir à l'Histoire de Droit Français.

[2] These persons changed the forms of all the public acts. Until then they had been simple, and not superfluous, though sometimes with bad preambles; but from about the year 1250, a practice began of surcharging the documents with an infinity of clauses, conditions, restrictions, renunciations, and protestations expressing that which would have been better understood without mention.—Fleury, Precis Historique.

[3] Ante, pp. 3, 38, 39, 84, n. 4, 94.

[4] Ante, pp. 1, 2, 3.

serve, that the fundamental principles of the popular and technical portions of law, arise out of what may perhaps be called material, or extrinsic causes; while the principles of rational law are based upon an internal and intrinsic cause, a kind of formal reason, consisting in the relation of notions purely the creations of the mind. Thus, we find the reason of a law belonging to the popular portion (as, for example, a law of matrimonial relation) in the feelings and passions of the human heart. In technical law, we look for the reason of a law in the circumstances of the times, the polity of the commonwealth at the time when it came into action; and when the effects of these causes, the consequences of these reasons, have once produced a fundamental rule of law, the process by which the consequences of that rule are deduced, and its relations with other rules settled, and by which it is made coherent with the general notions of the law, is as strictly the operation of the reasoning powers, a rational act, as any part of the law of contracts, or, indeed, of any the most abstract process of logical or mathematical science. The origin of the fundamental rules of the rational portion of the law, differs entirely from either of these: we neither look to the feelings of the heart, nor to the circumstances of time or place. The theory of contracts arises entirely from the perception of the relation, actual or presumed, of mental acts and ideas. A contract is purely an intellectual act, (viz., the consent of the mind, or rather of two or more minds,) either expressed by signs symbolical or verbal, or collected and implied from circumstances. The interpretation of signs and symbols is simply a dialectic process. The rules relating to implied or presumed contracts, founded on the principle of adequate mutual compensation—actus contra actum—which distinguishes them from gifts, are for the most part based on fictions created by the mind. These fictitious notions, like all those of purely intellectual creations, contain within themselves all their qualities: and they have only to be understood, when the mind immediately perceives all the relations which can be pointed out respecting them. The rules, therefore, respecting implied contracts, are merely the expression of the relation of preconceived notions. While, therefore, the causes and reasons of the popular and technical parts of the law must be painfully sought after in the passions of the human breast, or the history of past ages, and admit only of limited application and but partial expression; those of contracts are to be sought in the relation of notions, or, in other words, in the nature of reason, and they admit of expression in broad general principles of unlimited application. The conception of formal relations, when perfect, is the same in all ages and all places. Hence, the difference between these various portions of law. But, after the principles are once laid down, the same apodictic process is applicable to all three portions of the law; and the law of contracts, except as to the origin of its principles, is not more a rational system than the other two; indeed, we doubt whether, in the precision and coherency of its notions, and the strictness of the logical deduction of consequences, the boasted Roman law, in any way, surpasses the English law of real property.

In a rude state of society, the wants and desires of man are simple; a simple symbol is sufficient to express the unqualified assent of each party to a contract; and the theory of contracts, as a rational science, has scarcely any existence: but when society becomes complicated, and a man's desires are modified, not only by the numerous relations of his situation, but also by the fluctuating nature of the value or estimation of property, the consents or intentions of the parties to a contract are modified accordingly; and it is found that neither signs or words will adequately express all their intentions, and the science of the lawyer is called in to decide what is fair, to estimate and apportion the actus contra actum, between the parties; and, as society advances, the theory of contracts, as a rational science, is daily called into action.

State of the law of contracts in France and England.

From the continued existence of the Roman law in France from the time of its first establishment, and from the adoption of the study of the Justinian codes by the practising lawyers of that country, we are led to expect to find the law of contracts in general in a more advanced state than in England; and, if we may really credit the assertion that De Beaumanoir made no use of the Roman law in his compilation of the customs of Beauvoisin, such no doubt was the case: for though that portion of law is in Bracton treated more scientifically, it is evident that he, as well as Glanville, adopted not only the ideas but the very words of Justinian, and therefore he does not fairly exemplify the English law on that portion as it existed before his time.

Effects of the Roman law on that of England.

But the Roman law, though its doctrines were excluded from the English courts of common law, was not without its operation on them, through the forms of their proceedings, as we shall presently show. It is necessary, however, here to remark that the Anglo-Norman, like the Roman lawyers,[1] reduced the several kinds of rights and injuries to certain classes, and an express form of action or remedy was provided for each class: except in these forms, which were rigorously adhered[2] to, no action could be instituted.[3] This had the effect of giving to the Court of Chancery part of the extensive and exclusive jurisdiction it now exercises.

[1] Inst. lib. 4, tit. 6; Voet. ad Pandect, l. 2, tit. 13, s. 9; Dig. l. 1, tit. 2; Cic. pro Rosc. Com. c. 8; Quinctil. lib. 7, c. 3; Brisson, de Formul. lib. 5, 40.

[2] Sunt quadam brevia formata super certis casibus, de cursu, et de communi consilio totius regni concessa et approbata, qua quidem nullatenus mutari poterint absque consensu et voluntate eorum, Brac. f. 413, b: and this strictness seems to have arisen partly from political motives; for the barons in 1258 insisted that the chancellor should issue no writs but those de cursu, without the commandment of the king and the council, Gale, v. i. p. 413.

[3] Non potest quis sine brevi agere.—Brac. f. 413, b.

But, previous to this innovation of the Court of Chancery, principles and practices affecting a very large portion of law of property were introduced through the instrumentality of the clergy, who continued to adhere to the Roman and canon law.

Devices to evade the statutes of mortmain.

In England and in France attempts were made to prevent the accumulation of landed property in the hands of the ecclesiastical corporations. St. Louis (1226) and his successor established what is called the right of amortissement, to prevent the church and others of main morte (dead hand) from making acquisitions, to to the damages of the rights of the lords to fines on alienation (lods), redemption, &c. In England, during the Saxon period,[1] such acquisitions of property required the king's license; but even then, and after the introduction of the feudal law, notwithstanding the forfeiture which in those days took place on alienation, the church continued to receive gifts: for a person gave his land to a religious house to take it back again, to hold of that house, and so prevented forfeiture. The Magna Charta (9 Hen. III. c. 36), as already stated, expressly provided against mortmain, and it was thereby ordained that such surrenders and regrants should not be lawful. This only put the ecclesiastics of the day to new shifts: among others, they took lands on leases,[2] which, we have already seen, were not totally unknown even in the first period of the invasion, among the Romanized clergy on the continent under the name of "precaria," though now they were of very long duration; from which arose those extensive terms for 99, 1000, or more years, now in use. This produced the statute De Religiosis,[3] with still stronger provisions forbidding mortmain. The clergy, however, set up fictitious titles to the land[4] intended to be given to them, and brought

---

[1] Seld. Jan. Angl. l. 2, s. 45. [2] Coke, 2 Inst. 75. [3] 7 Ed. I.
[4] Coke, 2 Inst. 75.

actions, in which, by collusion, no defence was made, and thereby judgment was given for the religious houses, who by these feigned recoveries[1] eluded the statute of mortmain. Another statute[2] was, therefore, passed, to prevent this, and the astuteness of the clergy was immediately called into action to evade it. Driven from all their former holds, they found another device by which the freehold was not given directly to them, but nominally to an individual and his heirs for the use of the church;[3] which answers to the fidei commissa of the Romans: hence the origin of uses.

Uses.

Court of Chancery.

This brings us to the period when one of the features peculiar to the present English system of law took its origin. In France, from the time of Clovis—about 500 to 1302—the dignitaries who were the supreme chiefs of the law (called by the different Roman titles of grand referendaries,[4] apocryssiary, sovereign chancellor, arch chancellor,[5] grand chancellor, arch notary, and then chancellor,[6]) were generally taken from the ecclesiastical ranks, who governed then in civil and political affairs. Since then, after the fixed establishment of the parliaments, the dignity of chancellor has followed the progress of the magistracy, and eventually was conferred only on men of the long robe (en robe), jurisconsults, or magistrates.[7]

We have seen the chancellor and his clerks were originally the scribes of the Anglo-Saxon king[8] when

---

[1] Recoveries, as a legal remedy, of course were long before in use, even under the Anglo-Saxons; but this, no doubt extended their use as a species of conveyance.

[2] 13 Ed. I., c. 32.

[3] Coke, 2 Inst. 75.

[4] The Referendarius of the Frankish monarch may be traced back to the reign of Clovis.—Du Cange, vol. v., p. 1227.

[5] The Frankish arch-chaplain and the chancellor were the same offices.—Du Cange, p. 227.

[6] Dupin, Chronologie Historique des Chanceliers de France.

[7] Ib.

[8] Ante, p. 44. We find a charter witnessed by the Referendarius of Ethelbert, King of Kent, A.D. 561, 616, in Somner, History of Canterbury.

he administered justice in person, and they indited his mandates, and that the Conqueror constituted his aula regia on the model of the French. After the revival of the Roman law, the English, like the French, chancellor was usually an ecclesiastic, and he followed the forms and principles of the civil law, though he consulted the common law judges in cases of doubt. His jurisdiction was, and still is, ordinary and extraordinary. The extraordinary, or equitable jurisdiction of chancery—supposed to be suggested by the practice of the Roman prætor[1]—appears to have been assumed to afford relief to suitors for every species of hardship or injury where there was either fraud or breach of trust, for which there was no redress, no action, at common law.[2]

On the introduction of uses into England, there was no form of action adapted to them, the common law would not recognise them, and the person for whose benefit the use was created was entirely dependent on the good faith of the party to whom the estate was conveyed. The equitable jurisdiction of chancery interfered, and furnished a remedy—the subpœna—whereby the person to whom an estate was given for the use of another (technically called the feoffee to uses) was compelled to answer in this court in respect of his trust.[3] The first use of the writ of subpœna in chancery is generally ascribed to John Waltham, Bishop of Salisbury, who was chancellor or keeper of the seals about the fifth

[1] The duty of the prætor seems partly to have been to moderate and obviate injustice from the actiones stricti juris: this he accomplished by invalidating the actions made, by supposing imaginary circumstances (fictiones), or declaring them absolutely void (restitutiones); thus, for example, an insolvent sold his goods in fraud of his creditors. The sale and tradition, according to the old law, was sacred; but the prætor, to prevent the fraud, declared that there had been no tradition at all.

[2] Sir F. Palgrave says, "The alleviation of heavy laws is the primary source of the authority delegated by the king to his council, and afterwards assumed by his chancery and chancellor, whence are derived courts of equity."—Rise and Progress, part 1, p. 284.

[3] Sanders on Uses and Trusts, v. i. p. 16.

year of Richard II.; but it seems probable that a writ of a similar nature was previously used by the king's council. However, the application of it to aid the devices of the clergy in evading the statutes against mortmain, revived the jealousy of the laity against the civil law; and in the thirteenth of Richard II. the commons[1] prayed the king that the chancellor might make no order against the common law; and, on another occasion, that no one should appear before the chancellor where recovery was given by the common law. In course of time the skill and constancy of the chancellor, however, prevailed in acquiring an extensive jurisdiction; and in matters of trust and confidence, accident and mistake, &c., there sprung up a jurisdiction in chancery independent of the common law courts, and governed by different forms of proceeding. The business of the court, in its extraordinary jurisdiction, became extensive; and those who had been, in the Saxon times, the king's chaplains, became the modern masters in chancery.

From the ordinary or legal Court of Chancery,[3] writs to be prosecuted in the king's courts of common law were to be issued; and, an act[2] having been passed, providing that when in one case a writ existed in the chancery register of writs, and in a like case (in consimili casu) no writ was to be found, the clerks of the Chancery should frame one, new ones were there invented, to meet the demands of justice. This court was therefore called officina brevium. From this it is sufficiently evident, that the simple citation, pleadings, trial, and judgment of the Anglo-Saxon period, had been entirely displaced in the king's superior courts, by a train of formal proceedings, commenced by a mandate, or writ of the sovereign.

---

[1] Rot. Parl. 13 Rich. II.

[2] The Frankish chancellor wrote the royal writs.—Hincmari, Ep. de Ordine Palatii, s. 10.

[3] Westm. 2nd, 13 Ed. I., c. 24.

Roman origin of the original writs of the English common law.

The origin of these mandates, which were called original writs, has been a matter of some uncertainty. One learned English lawyer[1] has asserted, that they were known and used by the Anglo-Saxons:[2] other writers, English[3] and foreign,[4] have said that they trace their source to the forms of the Roman law; and an eminent English antiquary,[5] a man of deep research, has said, that in the register of these writs not a word is derived from the Roman law.

The correspondence between the forms of Marculphus and the writs of Glanville has been already mentioned. It seems certain, that at Rome, after the ancient forms were abolished by Constantine,[6] there were certain carefully framed formulæ to be used in each kind of action.[7] The sovereigns who led the Germanic invaders of France and Italy continued, to the extent of their power, the imperial government; and the Roman forms of judicial proceedings, transcribed by the tabelliones and notaries,[8] were retained in some of the courts. The formulæ of the Frankish monarch, preserved in Marculphus, and among those published by Mabillon, are often in the very words of those of the ancient Roman law. The proceedings of the ecclesiastical tribunals were those of the Roman law.[9] These, afterwards modified, but only slightly, by the canon law,[10] were adopted by the civil

[1] Lord Coke, Preface to 10th Rep.; in reply to which see Hickes, Diss. Ep. 3; Dugdale, Orig. Jur. 34. Spelman, Gloss. verb Breve.

[2] As to "gewrits," see Palgrave, Rise and Progress, part 1, p. 551.

[3] Duck. & Noy.

[4] M. Houard, ante, p. 85, n. 2.

[5] Seld. (Diss. ad Flet. c. 9), says, "Neque aut locutionis, scriptionis aut agendi formulam aliquam in tabulas publicas et Cæsareo, quantum observarerim, desumi admittive vellent," p. 535. He also says, "Uti et rescriptorum promptuarium quod registrum Brevium vocitamus quæ exitima Anglis vetustate ad posteros transmissa vix vocabulum habent ex jure Cæsareo sibi admixtum," ib.

[6] Cod. lib. 3, tit. 58, de formulis et impetrationibus actionum sublata.

[7] Voet. ad Pandect, lib. 2, tit. 13, s. 9.

[8] Ante, p. 90, n. 5.

[9] Bernardi, de l'Origine, &c., p. 91.

[10] Ib. Pref. x.; Meyer, Institutiones Judiciares, t. i. p. 278.

tribunals;[1] and from the Romans is to be deduced the course of judicial proceedings in France.[2]

The Normans, on settling in Normandy, adopted many forms similar to those used by the French;[3] and after their establishment they introduced, or at least undoubtedly employed, them in England:[4] and the opinion of Duck,[5] whose eminence as a civilian is admitted on all hands, and of the attorney-general, Noy,[6] is, that the writs of the English register[7] (registrum brevium) must have been settled by great civil lawyers; and as the chancellors, by whom the new writs were framed and issued, had a decided partiality for the civil law, there seems no more reason to doubt the origin of all such as were framed in England, than of those which were introduced from abroad.[8]

Scientific cultivation of the law in England.

From the reign of Edward III. to that of Henry VIII. in England, 1377 to 1509, the French and civil wars, and the disputed titles to the crown, gave no leisure for scientific cultivation and juridical improvements; though numerous enactments were made on the part of the legislature, they were rather in practical details than in general principles, and but little affected the law as a science. There were, however, two English lawyers, who flourished while the credit of the common law schools was at its height, that must not be passed over. Sir

[1] Bernardi, de l'Origine, &c., p. 447.

[2] Ib. pp. 79, 445. See also Montesquieu, Spirit of Law, b. 28, c. 34.

[3] Sir F. Palgrave remarks, "To the precept framed by Cassiodorus the general similarity of the writ of King John is sufficiently evident."—Rise and Progress, part 1, p. 502, n. "All the monks of Latin Europe were virtually bred in the same college. A good precedent, carefully settled at Monte Casino, was rapidly transmitted to the 'Scriptorium' of Worcester or Canterbury."—Ib. part 2, p. 204.

[4] As early as Henry I. we find contemptus brevium.—Leg. H. I., c. 14.

[5] He says, "The book of original writs (Registrum Brevium Originalium), which is deservedly called the foundation of the laws of England and the register of the High Court of Chancery, resembles the Book of Actions, published for the benefit of the Roman people by Cneius Flavius."—Duck. l. 2, c. 8, pp. 329, 30.

[6] Duck, de Auth. Jur. Civ., pp. 54, 58.

[7] Concerning the Register Brevium, see Nichols, English Historical Library, 215.

[8] The pactum constitutæ pecuniæ bears a striking conformity to the English indebitatus assumpsit.—Evans' Pothier, note, p. 306.

John Fortescue, distinguished for his knowledge of the civil as well as the common law, was chief justice of the King's Bench in 1442, and afterwards chancellor to Henry VI. He is said to have written his principal work, the treatise De laudibus Legum Angliæ, during his exile in France with the Lancastrian party, for the benefit of Prince Edward. To show the excellence of the law of England, he takes a comparative view of the common and civil laws.[1] He was afterwards reconciled to Edward IV. Sir Thomas Littleton[2] was one of the judges in the reign of Henry VI., and also of Edward IV. His work on "tenures" has been, from its first appearance to the present time, most highly esteemed as an institute of jurisprudence; and, from the depth of the author's learning, the simplicity of his style, the comprehensiveness of his thoughts, and the precision and accuracy with which he sets out the notions, then fully formed, of the laws of property, it has obtained more notice than any other book in the law. At its first appearance, it was the text-book for students; and even now, notwithstanding the abolition of feudal burthens and tenures in chivalry, it continues the highest authority for those parts (and they still constitute a very large portion) of the law not obsolete. A very competent judge on such matters[3] says, " The merit of Littleton's

[1] As the English lawyers of after ages derived many of their notions respecting the civil law from this source, it may be as well to point out one of the errors, on the question of guardianship (see Blackstone, Commentaries, v. i. pp. 461, 2), into which, from the then imperfect knowledge of the law of Rome, Fortescue fell, and has led subsequent English authors. The Roman law, it is said, committed the care of the minor to him who was next to succeed to the inheritance; which, say Lord Coke and Blackstone, is " quasi agnum committere lupo, ad devorandum." This error (which even until very recent times was partaken in by the French lawyers) arose from not understanding the meaning of the Roman term "person" (see post, Preliminary Observations to Book I), which differed from the individual. The Roman tutor, who exercised the minors' legal capacities, and the curator, differ almost as much as the committee of the estate of a lunatic differs from the committee of his person.—Savigny, Beruf.

[2] See Preface to Coke's Commentary upon Littleton's Tenure.

[3] Mr. Charles Butler, in his Reminiscences.

tenures is great; neither England nor the Continent can produce any contemporaneous work on the subject of law, of equal or even approximating merit."

During part of the period, in both countries a knowledge of law was only to be learned in the schools and inns of court. In both countries the schools declined; and private teaching and private study were the only means of acquiring a legal knowledge.

Reduction of the French customs to writing, and their numbers.

We have noticed the numerous subdivisions of the territory, and the consequent great variety of different customary laws existing in France. This want of uniformity was early felt.[1] Charles VII., having freed the country from the English, undertook a reform of all the parts of the state; and, among others, by an ordonnance, dated 1453, he directed that all the customs in each district should be written and settled by the practical lawyers, and then examined and authenticated by the grand conseil and by the parlement; and that no customs should be allowed[2] unless contained in the digest so formed. It is said that the design was afterwards to make one general law out of these digests for the whole kingdom.[3] This design, if it really existed, was not at that time carried into execution. His successor, Louis XI., expressed a desire to have throughout his kingdom but one weight, one measure, and the same law;[4] but he was too much occupied with his political schemes for aggrandizing the crown, and the consequences of his tyrannical practices, to give the subject his attention; and the reduction of the customs to writing proceeded very slowly, and was not completed for more than a century after the death of Charles VII.[5]

Design of having one uniform law in France.

[1] It has been said that Charlemagne felt the need of a general code in place of the numerous laws of his empire. This assertion, however, seems to be unfounded.—Bernardi, de l'Origine, &c., p. 107. But it bears evidence how early the necessity is supposed to have been felt.

[2] Fleury, Precis Historique du Droit Français, s. 23; Bernardi, de l'Origine, &c., p. 367.

[3] Dumoulin.

[4] Fleury, ib.; Bernardi, ib.

[5] Ib.

Indeed, it can hardly be considered to have been finished until about the year 1609, just before the reign of Louis XIII. (1610.)

"If these customs are counted (says Fleury),[1] we find at least as many as 285, including the local customs and those of the neighbouring countries, as the Low Countries, where, in imitation of France, they were reduced to writing; and, counting even the principal customs of the kingdom only, we find at least sixty for the most part greatly differing from each other."[2]

Scientific cultivation of the Roman law in France.

But, while in France the customary law occupied so much of the attention of the government, law, as an abstract science, was making a rapid progress, and the study and practice of the civil law had, in the south and other parts of France, attained a great degree of method and excellence. In Italy, glosses[3] or interpretation of one word, at first simply by another, afterwards by expository sentences, had been the mode of teaching the civil law; and the school of Irnerius, though meriting high admiration, had so overburthened the text of the civil law, that a new method became indispensable. Francis Accursius (born 1182, died 1260) accomplished this. Instead of an entirely new glossary, he undertook and executed a union and arrangement, in his work called the Great Gloss (Corpus Juris Glossatum, Glossa Ordinaria) of all the best Glosses, and thus brought into one body the endless comments of the glossators, which had previously involved the subject in obscurity and contradiction.[4]

The universal addiction to the study of scholastic

---

[1] Precis Historique, s. 23.

[2] In France it was said, you changed the system of law which affected you as often in travelling through the country as you changed horses.

[3] Alcuin defined glossa, unius verbi vel nominis interpretatio.—Du Cange, Præfat in Glossar. p. 38.

[4] Gravina, Origines Juris, p. 184. Savigny, however, thinks Accursius has not done justice to his predecessors.—Geschichte, vol. v. pp. 258, 267; Bayle, art. Accursius.

philosophy which took place, did not fail to exercise its influence on this part of jurisprudence. The new school, which succeeded during the fourteenth and fifteenth centuries, no longer confined themselves to a mere explanation of word for word,[1] but they applied the prevailing dialectic method to their own science,[2] and attempted new arrangements and general commentaries. In the beginning of the sixteenth century, Alciat[3] (born at Milan in 1492) opened a new era in the study of the Roman law in France. At a very early age he taught in the schools at Avignon; from whence, in 1529, on the invitation of Francis I., he went to Bourges, and in five years he succeeded in producing an entire change in the mode of studying the civil law, and founded a new school. The overthrow of the Eastern Empire had spread the learning of Constantinople through Europe; and, besides a profound knowledge of jurisprudence, the numerous works of Alciat on other subjects, exhibit him as well versed in the Greek and Latin classical literature;[4] and by the aid of those studies he happily succeeded in giving a more elegant phraseology to his explications of the law; and from his time, the barbarity of language which had hitherto reigned in the lectures and writings of the lawyers began to disappear.

Shortly after Alciat went to Bourges, about 1547, the celebrated James Cujas,[5] at twenty-five years of age, commenced a course of lectures, on the Institutes of Justinian, at Toulouse. But, opposed by the old school then in vogue at that place, and not finding his talents and the method he had adopted duly appreciated there, he removed to Cahors; and afterwards (having successively taught at Bourges, at the instance of Michel de Cujas.

[1] Bartolus even said, de verbis non curat jurisconsultus.

[2] Savigny, 5, 330; 6, 6.

[3] Dupin, Biographie Abrégée des Principaux Autours du Droit, &c.; Bernardi, de l'Origine, &c., p. 464.

[4] Lerminier, Introduction Générale à l'Histoire du Droit, c. 5.

[5] Cujas was born 1522, and died 1590, aged sixty-eight.

l'Hopital, Valence, Paris, and Turin) he returned in 1577 to Bourges, where he finished his days,[1] lecturing and encouraging the study of the Roman law in that city, where the science of law was fully appreciated and cultivated with success. Pupils flocked to him from all parts of Europe, and returned to spread his fame; and his memory has continued highly revered to this day; so much so, that the house inhabited by Cujas is still shown to strangers at Bourges.

On the merit of Cujas it is useless to enlarge. All the jurisconsults of Europe are agreed in considering him as the first and greatest of expositors on the civil law, and his method a model for instructors. One of his labours was this:—The Pandects of Justinian consist of a series of extracts from the Roman jurisconsults, arranged sometimes without a due regard to method: Cujas conceived that each jurisconsult, of whom Justinian offers fragments, represented an entire system, a coherent whole, which was only to be fully comprehended by getting into the author's train of thought and reasoning, by replacing the fragments of each lost author dispersed through the code, in the same relative situations in which they were originally written.[2] He therefore undertook the task of restoring the extracts of each author to its original place, and thus re-creating what the minister of Justinian had abolished, and resuscitating the jurisconsults of ancient Rome. He was a good classic, and under his hand the Roman jurisprudence became, it is said, elegantior; and this jurisprudence, better cultivated and more polished, was called jurisprudentia Cujaciana. Contemporary with Cujas was Hugo Doneau,[3] whose antipathy to Cujas was partly the result of the different method in which the two proceeded. He is said to be a model of the dogmatic method. In France,

---

[1] Dupin, Biographie Abrégée, Cujas; Bernardi, de l'Origine, &c., p. 465; Lerminier, Introduction Générale à l'Histoire, c. 5.

[2] Lerminier, ib.

[3] Dupin, Biographie Abrégée; Lerminier, c. 5.

he is now almost unknown; in Germany, he has recently been reprinted, admired, and studied.

Shortly prior to Cujas was "the French Papinian," "the prince of the French customary law," Charles Dumoulin (in Latin called Molinæus[1]), who gave himself up with incredible ardour to that system.[2] By his commentary under the title of "fiefs" on the custom of Paris, he established the principal rules of the French customary law, and effected for the French law what Cujas had done for the Roman.[3] His commentary is a masterpiece, for the sound logic and profound learning it displays. It has, however, those defects of want of method which can scarcely be avoided in commentaries.[4] In his treatises, de Dividuo et Individuo, Dumoulin is considered to have carried to its highest pitch the spirit of analysis and the metaphysics of laws.

Customary law. Dumoulin.

The professors of the civil law were rather scientific discussers and expositors than practical men, actually engaged in the courts or in actual business. It was otherwise with the leaders of the customary law: Dumoulin originally practised as a pleader; and an anecdote related of him shows that the profound respect due from the profession to the bench and magistracy never prevented the French advocates from estimating their prerogatives, and maintaining their rights with vigour, when violated or misunderstood. The following instance of their interference exhibits the high esteem in

[1] Caroli Molinæi, Commentarius in consuetudines Parisiensis, consists of Glosses on the Custom.

[2] Bernardi, de l'Origine, &c., p. 466; Lerminier, c. 5; Dupin, Biographie Abrégée.

[3] M. Le Trosne, in his Eloge on Pothier, says, "Dumoulin applied the wisdom and intelligence of the Roman law to the application of our own (French) municipal usages."

[4] "Of the foreign writers on law whose works have fallen under the eye of the Reminiscent, those who have appeared to him to resemble Lord Coke most, and to approach nearest to him in depth of learning and profound thought, are Dumoulin and Lord Stair: the latter has the additional merit of arrangement."—Butler, Reminiscences.

which Dumoulin was held even early in life, and the dignified modesty of a celebrated French judge, as well as their tenacity. Dumoulin's manner of pleading was very disagreeable; so much so, that in the year 1522, shortly after he was called to the bar, the first president (De Thou), fatigued at hearing him, said to him one day, "Hold your tongue, M. Dumoulin, you are a dunce (un ignorant)." The order of advocates felt a most lively resentment at this injury; and it was decided that the batonnier of the advocates, with a deputation of the ancients, should go and make complaints to the first president. When they were admitted to his audience, the batonnier, with all the gravity the occasion required, said, "Læsisti hominem doctiorem quam unquam eris." "That is true," said M. De Thou, with as much frankness as modesty; "I was wrong; I did not know all the merit of M. Charles Dumoulin."[1]

He died at the age of sixty-six, with the glory and

---

[1] This anecdote is related by M. Dupin, in a note to a published discourse pronounced by him at the Bibliotheque des Avocats, on 1st Dec. 1829.

Dumoulin was remarkable not only for his profound logic and immense erudition, but also for the elevation and force of his character. He struggled, with invincible constancy, in favour of civil and political order against the enterprises of the Ultramontains, in union with l'Hopital, defending the king and the kingdom against the invasion of the Council of Trent; and resisting (as to an illegal tax) the tarifs and exactions of the court of Rome. He was much superior in this respect to the timid Cujas, who eluded answering on these weighty matters, by prudently saying to those who consulted him on the subject, "Nil hoc ad edictum Prætoris."

Dumoulin's glory, bought even at the price of calumny and persecution, still lives untarnished in the eyes of posterity; and even during his life he was thought to merit the eulogium made of him by the constable, Ann de Montmorency. The Pope, Julius III. had denounced war against the king, Henry II., and carried himself with such animosity and fury that he could not be overcome by prayers, gold, or the force of arms. In the meanwhile, in 1552, Dumoulin published his Commentary on the Edict des Petites Dates, which (though it raised against him the fury of all who were neither parliamentary or Gallican, and obliged him to leave France) it is said so troubled and frightened the Pontiff, that he was constrained not only to put down his arms, but also, as acknowledging himself conquered, to give a carte blanche, demand peace, and agree to all the conditions, &c. The constable, De Montmorenci, in presenting him to King Henry II., said, "Sire, what your majesty was not able to do and execute with 30,000 men, this little man (Dumoulin was of short stature) has achieved with his little pamphlet."

renown of the first French jurisconsults. The feebleness of his health and the ill condition of his voice prevented him from being a great pleader; but in his chambers, by his numerous consultations, he animated the whole bar with his learning.[1]

Contemporary with Dumoulin was the celebrated Michel de l'Hospital[2] (born 1505, died 1573), chancellor of France, under Charles IX., from 1560 to 1568. Notwithstanding the anarchy of the times consequent on the struggles between the Catholics and Hugonots, he effected many reforms in the judicial system: he had planned many more, which were never carried into effect. His ordonnance of Orleans, 1560,[3] his edict respecting second marriages, and ordonnance of Moulins, 1566[4] (which, among other things, excluded parol evidence in cases exceeding 100 livres, and has been styled the civil code of the 16th century), have rendered his name famous in the history of French legislation. By the ordonnonce of Rousillon, 1554, he fixed the commencement of the year on the 1st of January,[5] which was not effected in England till a century and a half later. His eulogist has characterized him as an indefatigable magistrate, in court before day, in court after night; a courageous minister, resisting with an inflexible firmness the violence of the men of war, the ambition of the churchmen, the greediness of the courtiers;[6] a profound legislator, carrying light into the L'Hospital.

---

[1] Dumoulin born 1500, died 1566.

[2] Dupin, Biographie Abrégée; Lerminier, Introduction à l'Histoire du Droit, c. 5; Bernardi, de l'Origine, &c., p. 468.

[3] Bernardi, p. 473. [4] Ib. p. 475. [5] Art. 39.

[6] The following is an instance of the high conduct of L'Hospital, which, resembling that of our own Coke, we are glad to quote. It was the duty of the French chancellor, or keeper of the seals, not to suffer to pass any surprise on the prince, or any act which would be contrary to the laws. After the dissolution of the conference of Poissy, the Pope sent into France Hippolyto d'Este, Cardinal of Ferrara, in the quality of legate; the chancellor, L'Hospital, refused him the letters patent, which he demanded to confirm his powers: L'Hospital alleged, as ground of refusal, that these letters were contrary to the liberties of the Gallican church. Menaces, prayers, seduction, and every means was employed by the legate to conquer the chancellor, but he remained firm. By intrigues the legate obtained

feudal chaos of the 16th century, and preparing with patience, amid the ruptures of civil war, and publishing, notwithstanding the obstinate resistance of the parliaments, the great works of the legislation, the inheritance of which the age of Louis XIV. ought to receive with respect.

The age of Cujas, Dumoulin, and L'Hospital, seems to have been the golden era of French law writers. There are so many brilliant characters of that class and age, that our space will not admit of any adequate notice of them;[1] the greater part, like L'Hospital and Dumoulin,

---

from the king what he had vainly demanded from the chancellor, on condition that he should not use the letters. The chancellor, however, still refused to put the seal of state. The legate produced the king's order, and the chancellor obeyed, putting under the seal the protestation which he used to employ on such occasion—me non consentiente.—Essai sur L'Hospital, at the head of his works, by M. Dufey de l'Yonne.

[1] We may be allowed to introduce some of them in a note to the English reader:—Jean Bodin à Angers, born 1530, died 1590, is known to the English reader by the notice he has received from Dugald Stewart and Sir James Mackintosh; not as an advocate and jurisconsult, in which he was but malhabile; but all know something of his De Republica, which gave the first impulse of the political science of modern Europe, and which has been characterized as between theory à priori and observation. His work, Juris Distributio, is also worthy of notice. He was independent deputy to the estates of Blois, and sacrificed the favour he enjoyed at the court of Henry II. to his duty.

Guy Coquille, sieur de Romenai, born 1523, died 1603, Deputy for Nevernois to the States of Orleans, 1560, and of Blois, united in friendship with his colleague Bodin—animated with the same love of his country—jurisconsult exact and profound—an intimate correspondent with Lord Bacon, and one whom D'Aguesseau never mentions but as the judicious Coquille. In his Institutes Coutumiers, his Commentary on the Customs of Nevernois, he explains the origin of the French customs. In a treatise, ex professo, he exposes the "Liberties of the Gallican Church," which he defended in the midst of the rages of the League. His annotations and comments on the "Edits and Ordonnances," given at the command of the estate-general, at which he had assisted, are equally remarkable.

Loyseau holds a distinguished rank among the small number of good jurisconsults,—profound and clear in treating the most abstruse matters of the law in his treatise of offices and seignuries—historian as well as jurisconsult—a writer of a style so piquant, that the little work in which he attacks with ridicule the crying abuses of the "justices de villege," and the "juges guêtrès" of the lords of that day, with a warmth and liberty of expression, was not to be tolerated in the times of old French local tribunals.

Pierre Pithou (Pithœus), born 1539, died 1596, pupil of Cujas. He reduced into one code the articles of the Gallican church; and though this collection of maxims was the work of an individual, it receives an honour almost unparalleled in took a zealous interest in the ecclesiastical broils of their day. Of them all, perhaps the most unfortunate was the president, Barnabé Brisson,[1] of whom Henry III. said, "No prince in the world can boast of having a man so learned as my Brisson." He was well versed in the antiquities of the Roman law; and contemplated a reform of the French law. By the order of Henry III. he composed the collection known under the title of the Code de Henry III., published in 1587, and spoken of by D'Aguesseau as a model to be followed in a general reformation of the laws. It professed to be a compilation of the ordonnances of the French kings; but D'Aguesseau says of this work, that Brisson acted rather as a legislator than a compiler.[2] Living, unfortunately, in the days of the League, he suffered himself to be seduced by

Attempts to reduce the French statute law to form.

these days, in being quoted as of the force of law. This work, said M. D'Aguesseau, is so estimated, and in truth so estimable, that it has been regarded as the palladium of France; and that it has acquired a sort of authority more flattering to its author than that of the laws themselves, because it is founded only on the merit and the perfection of the work. The President Henault also attests that "the maxims of Pithou have to a certain extent the force of law, although they have no authenticity." His other works are Corpus Juris Canonici, Codex Canonum, Observations on the Code and Novelles.

Francis Pithou, born 1543, died 1621, pupil of Cujas. A Treatise on the Grandeur of the Rights, Pre-eminence, and Prerogatives of the Kings and Kingdom of France, and another on Excommunication and Interdiction.

Antoine Loisel, born 1536, died 1617, a pupil of the celebrated Ramus and of Cujas. He left many works, all remarkable; among others, Institutes Coutumieres, Pasquier, or Dialogue of the Advocates of the Parliament of Paris.

Etienne Pasquier, considered as one of the classics of the French law, born 1529, died 1615: received lessons of Cujas. In 1564 the bold mode of his attack on the Jesuits put him at once in the first ranks of his profession. His Researches on France gave him the first reputation as a writer.

Pierre Seguier, born 1504, died 1580.

Antoine Seguier, born 1552, died 1625.

Christophe de Thou, President of the Parliament of Paris, died 1582.

Jacque Augusté de Thou; his son, the historian, born 1553, died 1617.

Achille de Harley, born 1536, died 1616.

René Chopin, born 1537, died 1606, who published several good works. Commentary on the Custom of Paris.

Charles Loyseau, born 1566, died 1627.

Omer Talon, born 1595, died 1652.

1 Dupin, Biographie Abrégée; Bernardi, de l'Origine, &c., p. 492.

2 Bibliotheque choisie d'un Avocat, dans les Lettres sur le Profession, &c. Title, Code Henri.

one of the parties who then troubled France. Suspected by them, on the morning of the 15th of November, 1591, in going to the court, at 9 o'clock he was seized, shrived at 10, and hanged at 11, to one of the beams of the council chamber.

The Code de Henry IV., also professedly a general collection of ordonnances, was compiled by T. Cornier.

State of commercial law in France.

The labours of Cujas and Dumoulin brought the customary and civil laws in France almost to their very highest degree of scientific cultivation; and even in their time the above-mentioned attempts were already made to reduce the French statute book or collection of ordonnances to form and orderly arrangement, as well as the unwritten customary law. But these labours had been applied to the law in general, and not peculiarly to the rational portion. Indeed, from having adopted the almost perfect system of the Roman law of contracts, that portion was more in advance and required less cultivation in France than in England.

In England.

The adoption of some of the principles of Roman law on this subject into the law of England, through the works of Glanville and Bracton, has been already noticed; and that from the reign of Edward III. the imperial code had been entirely discountenanced in the common law courts. It still continued to be so.[1] The law of landed property occupied the court until the time of Henry VIII. almost exclusively; and from that time, when commerce was daily rendering the commercial law of more and more importance, this branch had to be wrought out from the principles derived from the civil

[1] In the time of Richard II. the Lords and Commons protested, and the king assented, that the civil laws had no force in England.

In the reign of Henry VI. attempts were made to bring in the civil law.—See Coke, 3 Inst. 35.

The partiality of James I. for the civil law is well known.

Laud obtained of Charles I. that the masters of the requests should be all doctors of the civil law, and also eight masters in chancery.—Straff. Let. & Disp. v. i. p. 176; Clarendon's History, lib. 4.

law, thus admitted into the system, and from the feudal and Anglo-Saxon customs. The principles of the latter (for even Bracton only adopted the Roman law when the other was silent) still continued unaltered. To give an instance:—We have already noticed that, by the Anglo-Saxon law, on a sale of goods the seller was not bound to take them back, on the discovery of a defect in them, unless he was acquainted with it before he sold them.[1] The civil law is precisely the reverse of this, and implies a warranty of the quality and soundness of the goods;[2] but it was not allowed to alter the Anglo-Saxon principle, which we find recognized at this middle period;[3] and to this day the rule is, that the vendor is not bound to answer for the goodness of his wares, unless he expressly warrants them or knew them to be defective or misrepresented them.[4]

To attempt to trace out the development of the doctrines, or even of only a few of the leading ones, from the first principles derived from those sources, through the year books, would be an interesting but too extended a task for our present object, especially as they, being cut off from the Roman law, and based on so scanty a supply of principles, were any thing but stable until the time of Plowden's Commentaries and Coke's Reports.

In the reign of Edward III. commerce and manufactures were in a thriving state; and from that period the system of commercial law of this country may be considered to have commenced,[5] and to have required working out, as commerce, notwithstanding civil and foreign war, continued to prosper and extend itself from time to time, necessarily giving rise to all species of contracts and bringing them in litigation before the courts. In a rude state, where all rights relating to contracts are

---

[1] Ante, p. 39, and n. 4.

[2] Pothier's Obligations.

[3] Fitz. N. B. 94 A.

[4] 2 Blackstone, Com. p. 451.

[5] See Year Books, 21 Ed. III. 11; 27 Ed. III. 84; 17 Ed. IV. 1; 18 Ed. IV. 5; 37 H. VI. 8; 9 H. V. 14.

expressed by formal acts or visible signs, the remedies for injury to them easily resolve themselves into an action for a debt, on a covenant, for an unlawful detainer, a trespass, or the like; and such were, together with real actions, the chief forms provided and strictly adhered to, and in which all actions must have commenced. They were found to be inadequate to meet the new shades of verbal or implied contracts, and the more indirect rights and injuries which the altered state of the times created; and the barbarous modes of trial by battle and wager of law (compurgation), were more clearly seen to be unjust when they came to be applied to decide questions which in their very nature depend upon principles of abstract reason. Accordingly, we find a new species of action introduced, under the authority of the statute of Westminster 2, founded upon the particular circumstances of the case, called an action of trespass on the case,[1] to meet the demands of the more artificial system of society. The use of this form of action was greatly extended in the reign of Henry VI., and out of it had previously grown two new forms of action—the one called trover; the other, the form of action most used of any in modern times, called assumpsit, founded on a promise implied or verbal, or written, but not amounting to a formal covenant. And to these latter actions neither the trial by wager of law or by battle was applied;[2] and accordingly — partially from as early as the time of Henry IV.,[3] and fully[4] from the time of Queen Elizabeth[5]—until the recent abolition of wager of law, the form of the action of assumpsit, for debt even though on an express contract, when it was not a formal docu-

[1] The first example of this kind of action seems to occur in the reign of Edward III., 22 Ass. 41.—See Reeve, History of the Law, v. iii. pp. 243, 391.

[2] See note 1, p. 49.

[3] 2 Hen. IV. 3.

[4] Previous to which this action had not acquired certainty.—Fitz.N.B. 94 A.

[5] Slade's Case, 9 Rep. 91.

ment under seal, was adopted in lieu of that of an action of debt.[1]

From that period the commercial spirit of the country has greatly increased, particularly in the reign of Queen Elizabeth, and called into existence an extensive system of new law on kinds of contracts which were scarcely, if at all, known to the lawyers of Rome.

State of other portions of law in England.

While this new portion of law was being called into existence, the other parts[2] were receiving considerable scientific culture. Although, in the fourteenth century, we find the office of chancellor of France filled by a layman, in England it remained, long after that period, in the hands of ecclesiastics. In the reign of Henry VIII.[3] his favourite, Cardinal Wolsey, was lord-chancellor. In that office he gave great dissatisfaction. He was charged with interfering with matters not within the cognizance of that court; with deciding them without regard to the principles of common law, and endeavouring to substitute the civil law in its place.[4]

His successor, Sir Thomas More, was the first layman who held that office in England. The author of the Utopia, notwithstanding his industry and an inflexible integrity, which cost him his life, could not succeed in

---

[1] Blackstone, Com. p. 347.

[2] The modern system of law (of real property) may be supposed to have taken its rise at the end of the reign of Henry VII., and to have assumed something of a regular form about the end of the reign of Charles II. The principal features of this alteration are the introduction of recoveries, conveyances to uses, the testamentary disposition by wills, the abolition of military tenures, the statute of frauds and perjuries, the establishment of a regular system of equitable jurisdiction, the discontinuance of real actions, and the mode of trying titles to landed property by ejectment. They have been effected not so much by superseding, as by giving a new direction to the principles of the old law, and applying them to new subjects. Hence a knowledge of the ancient legal learning is absolutely necessary to a modern lawyer.—Butler, Reminiscences.

[3] The Natura Brevium of Sir A. Fitzherbert, who died 1533, has rendered that author popular with his profession. His grand Abridgement was also a highly useful book in his day. St. Germain's Doctor and Student is also popular.

[4] One of the articles prepared against Wolsey was, that he endeavoured to subvert antiquissimas leges hujus regni, universumque hoc regnum legibus imperialibus subjicere.

giving satisfaction to the common law judges, who declaimed against the improper interference of the Court of Chancery. The jurisdiction and doctrines of that court, at that time, seem to have been so little settled, that the wonder would have been if any person could have given satisfaction.[1]

The year books, which, from being at first almost exclusively occupied with real property law, now contain many commercial cases,[2] about this time were discontinued, and reporting cases was left to private individuals. The first results of the new system were the Reports of Sir James Dyer, who died in 1581. Those about this period, of Edmund Plowden, who died 1584, called his Commentaries, are of eminent authority: he has been considered the most correct of all reporters. In his Commentaries we find some few points of commercial law discussed and definitively settled.[3]

The common law as a science.

With regard to the fate of the law of England as a science, it was never cultivated in the abstract—never otherwise than for practical purposes. During the period since the time of Edward III., excluding all help from the civil law, it had proceeded in a steady course of self-development. But, intent upon actual decisions, and buried under an immense accumulation of cases, the common lawyers of that day do not appear to have kept in view the grand leading principles which alone can give order and arrangement to a chaotic mass of materials, originating in ancient customs, in more recent

[1] Much of the modern jurisdiction of Chancery is due to the law of uses. The statute of Uses, 27 H. VIII., which was passed to abolish uses, followed up by the statute of Elizabeth of Charitable Uses, laid the foundation of part of that broad and comprehensive judicature in which equity administers, through its searching interrogatories addressed to the consciences of men, the most beneficent and wholesome principles of justice. The whole modern structure of trusts, infinitely diversified as it is by marriage settlements, terms to raise portions or to pay debts, contingent and springing appointments, resulting uses, and implied trusts, grew out of this statute, and the construction put upon it.—Story.

[2] Year Book, 14 H. VIII. 19; 7 H. VII. 4; 14 H. VII.

[3] See Sharrington and Stratton, Reniger and Fogassa.—Plow. Com.

statutory amendment, or in decisions begotten as the altering relations of life had called for legal intervention, and which had been therefore produced entirely without regard to method. There was no adequate power capable of altering this state of things. Great care seems to have been bestowed on education for the profession; and the philosophy of Aristotle was held in the highest esteem by the lawyers of that day. But, from the perversion it had undergone in the hands of the schoolmen, the dialectic skill of the common lawyers, as well as of the schoolmen, seems rather to have consisted in the subtle distinctions and minute subdivisions of the parts of individual cases, than in those general views of right classification which sound logic inculcates.

And it must be admitted, that the common law, with its unarranged materials, its apparent want of those extensive general principles (or rather their non-expression, —for as to real property they existed), which form the foundation of science, and with its mixed dialect wears an uncouth and almost deformed appearance, by the side of the comparatively perfect arrangement, the comprehensive notions, the broad general principles, and the classical phraseology of the civil law. But it must be borne in mind, that the common law originated in custom, the reasons of which are remote, and, not like those of the rational law, admitting the expression of extensive general principles in the first instance. Yet, though difficult, and at first sight repulsive, the works of the common law authors of that age are like a rich mine, which will, both for acquiring clear legal notions and closeness of thought, repay the toils of labour. Such at least are the works of the celebrated Sir Edward Coke, who, born in 1550, was successively attorney and solicitor, speaker of the House of Commons, lord chief justice of the Common Pleas, and lord chief justice of the King's Bench. His independent

Sir E. Coke.

spirit[1] and high character, and his patriotic struggles for the laws and liberties of his country, would have endeared him to his country, and immortalized his name, even had he not ranked so highly in his profession; but, as a lawyer, he stands unparalleled in the annals of his country. His chief works are, his Institutes of the Laws of England, and his Reports of Cases decided in the Courts of Westminster. The latter work, which commences in 1572, is the fourth in the series of English Law Reports; the Year Books, the Reports of Sir James Dyer, and Plowden's Commentaries, being the only prior ones. While all others were called by the names of their authors, these reports of Sir Edward Coke were so higly esteemed, that they were quoted pre-eminently as the "Reports." They, undoubtedly, are the first copious source of English rational law; and they connect the old and modern legal systems.

His great rival and opponent, Lord Bacon, says of them: "To give every man his due, had it not been for Sir Edward Coke's Reports (which, though they may have errors, and some peremptory and extra-judicial resolutions more than waranted, yet they contain infinite good decisions and ruling over of cases), the law, by this time, had been almost as a ship without ballast." The first part of his Institutes, consisting of his commentary on Littleton's tenures, usually called Coke upon Littleton, is, however, his most important work. As the greatest of French lawyers, Dumoulin, was styled the Prince of the French Law, so the high esteem entertained for this production of his great English counterpart, Sir E. Coke,

[1] In the case of the Commendams, the conduct of Lord Coke was even more noble than that of the French chancellor L'Hospital, already mentioned. The king having threatened the judges, asked them "whether, in a case where the king believed his prerogative or interest concerned, and required the judges to attend him for their advice, they ought not to stay proceedings till the king had consulted them?" Coke answered, "When that case should be, he would do that which should be fit for a judge to do."

has been manifested by having the title of the Bible of the English Lawyer bestowed upon it.[1] Objections of obsoleteness, defect of method, pedantry, and quaintness, have been raised against this work; but the three latter are the universal defects of the age in which it was written, the result of the system of study then pursued. It must be admitted that considerable portions of the law is different from what it was in Coke's time. We do not think any one who has seen the foundation of our personal laws laid in Germany; the technical at the Conquest, if not before; and even some portions of our rational or commercial law in the Anglo-Saxon period, will consider any part really obsolete. Out of the doctrines contained in the parts of Coke's work apparently most obsolete, new law has grown; and as to the work in general, a slight reference to the writings of any modern author who has obtained legal celebrity, will show that the countenance and authority of this work are eagerly sought, and will refute the charge of obsoleteness.

A recent author, one of the most likely of any persons competent to judge to be unprejudiced, affirms, in speaking of Lord Coke's Commentary on Littleton's Tenures, "The profound and extensive learning to be found in this work, the numerous points and illustrative examples, the many cases propounded and solved, with their nice, acute, and well founded doctrines; the carefulness of the author to maintain his positions by most apt and approved authorities; and to trace the great principles of the law under all its modifications, must for ever recommend this work to the student's special regard."[2] He is

---

[1] The Commentary of Sir Edward Coke is an extraordinary work: the language of it everywhere is most clear; but the doctrines and illustrations are often so subtle and abstruse as to require the utmost stretch, even of the strongest understanding, to comprehend them. A profound algebraist once mentioned to the writer, that he had never found in that science a problem, the solution of which required greater mental exertion, than passages occurring in almost every page of this celebrated Commentary.—Butler, Reminiscences.

[2] Hoffman, L. S. p. 225.

the best lawyer, and will succeed best in his profession, who best understands Coke upon Littleton.[1]

During the time of Sir E. Coke, a memorable struggle took place between the courts of common law and the chancellor, Lord Ellesmere, arising out of the question, whether a court of equity could give relief against a judgment in the common law? Sir E. Coke, it would appear, was wrong; and King James I., to whom the matter was referred, on the opinion and advice of his learned counsel, gave a decision in favour of the chancellor's rights. Lord Ellesmere was succeeded by Lord Bacon, who reduced the practice of the court into a more regular system; and his ordinance still continues to be the polestar of the practice of the court. He did not sit long enough to effect any considerable revolution in the science of chancery law.

Lord Bacon.

Francis Bacon, Lord Verulam, is better known in his own country, and even in his own profession, as the father of experimental philosophy, than as a lawyer: this, of course, is still more the case on the Continent. While yet only in the seventeenth year of his age (1577), he was removed from Cambridge to Paris, where it is not to be doubted, that the novelty of the literary scene must have largely contributed to cherish the natural liberality and independence of his mind.[2] He was appointed, in 1607, by Elizabeth, solicitor-general; and he became keeper of the great seal in 1617, and lord chancellor in 1619. His knowledge of the common law seems to have been equally extensive with that of the generality of lawyers in his day; and he had evidently made the civil law a study. As a practical lawyer, he did comparatively little to the formation of the science of English law; and he has left but few, and those not very important works, on practical jurisprudence. His common law tracts contain them all: the reading on the Statute of Uses, Elements of the Common Law of England,

[1] Butler, Reminiscences, p. 62.

[2] Dugald Stewart.

and Ordinances in Chancery, form the chief of his practical works. In them, his genius is evidently fettered, and he does not find room to display the compass of his mind; but, in his views on universal jurisprudence, the legum leges, tractatus de fontibus universi juris, contained in his grand work, De Dignitate et Augmentis Scientiarum, he exhibits the masterly efforts of a mind formed to excel in every thing to which it applied itself, and which could conceive a Novum Organon Scientiarum, a new instrument for the use of the students of nature, that has given a new direction to the pursuits of succeeding philosophers.

It is, perhaps, to be lamented, for the common law as a science, that more of the attention of this great man was not given to the practical jurisprudence of his country. We might then have had a classification and orderly arrangement of details—a successful generalization, and a development of leading principles, which, combined with the profound erudition and vast accumulation of cases of Coke's Institutes, would have carried the English system of law to a higher degree of perfection than has even yet been attained in any country. But the task was less congenial to his taste than rooting up prejudices and laying down principles of inductive science; besides which, he probably felt that unless they received an express authority from the state, his works on higher jurisprudence would be little valued or regarded by practical lawyers, and therefore he wanted encouragement to undertake the task. An uniform system of law, contained in one fair volume, had been long felt as a want, and almost a necessity, for France, with its hundreds of local customs. Dumoulin had cherished the idea: Brisson shortly afterwards produced a specimen; and Bacon, while studying at Paris, could scarcely have failed in becoming acquainted with the project. To this source are probably to be attributed the first notions of the plan he embodied in his proposition for an amendment of our laws, and his offer of a digest of the laws.

Other English authors.

We cannot pass by Dr. Cowell,[1] because the persecution he met with shows the hatred of the common lawyers of this period for the civil law. He compiled his Institutiones Juris Anglicani, an arrangement of the common law in the form of the Institutes of Justinian, with the professed view that in the Universities, where the civil law was studied, the transition might be rendered more easy to an acquaintance with the municipal law; and his work was so highly esteemed, that during the commonwealth it was translated into English by order of the parliament.[2] But his most celebrated work was a Law Dictionary, or Interpreter, in which he was accused of introducing the principles of the civil law, and which gave the common lawyers an opportunity of venting their feeling against that system on his head. He was stigmatized as a betrayer of the rights of the people: he himself was committed to custody, and his works were ordered to be publicly burnt: a violence of proceeding which sufficiently marks the public revolution then fast approaching.

Of this period are Sir Henry Spelman, the antiquary, born 1562, died 1641, whose Glossary, illustrated with comments, Concilia, and other works, have secured his fame; and John Selden, "the arch antiquary," whom Grotius called the Glory of England. His high conduct enabled him to preserve himself firm and unspotted during the excesses of parties. The Dutch had claimed the rights of navigation to the East Indies, and Hugo Grotius, the celebrated author of the book De Jure Belli et Pacis, wrote a work on the liberty of the sea, entitled Mare Liberum, to which Selden replied by a refutation, entitled Mare Clausum, which was highly approved by

---

[1] See a Memorial of the Life of Dr. Cowell, prefixed to his Interpreter, by Manby.

[2] Translated by G. W., and printed by Roycroft in 1651.

the Court of Admiralty, under James I., and it was ordered to be published by Charles I. in his disputes with Holland. His learned dissertation to Fleta, Judicature in Parliament, History of Tithes, Office of Chancellor, Jani Anglorum-Epinomis, and other smaller law tracts, are the best known of his works to the English lawyers, as his Mare Clausum, his De Jure Naturali et Gentium Juxta Disciplinam Hebrœorum, and works on Jewish Antiquities, with the Dissertation to Fleta, form the foundation of his reputation on the Continent. Mr. Selden was a person whom no character can flatter or transmit in any expressions equal to his merit and virtue. He was of so stupendous learning in all kinds and in all languages, that a man would have thought he had been entirely conversant amongst books, and had never spent an hour but in reading and writing.

Comparative view of England and France in the 11th and 17th centuries.

While in England, the course of events had by this time led to democratic revolution, the energy and ability of one great man, the Cardinal Richelieu, had humbled all parties in France before the throne, and brought the government to an absolute despotism. It is curious to compare the very opposite conditions of the French and English monarchies, at the periods of the latter end of the eleventh and the seventeenth centuries, during which time, their situation had precisely changed positions. At the former period, the English monarch was possessed of ample domains and vast revenues; the French sovereigns were little more than feudal superiors, with scarcely a shadow of power beyond their own patrimonial duchy. But the situation of their subjects was widely different: the one had a rude, but free, Germanic population; the lower classes of the other were a more polished, but a more servile Celtic race, without free institutions or guarantees for their personal independence; and from these differences had gradually resulted such a change, that the situations of the two monarchs had become totally the reverse. The English monarch had laid his head on the block before his rebellious subjects, assuming to sit in judgment over him; the French monarch had acquired a despotic power, and the nobles, the descendants of the Frankish conquerors, as the oppressed Celtic serfs had bowed before them, now couched before the throne.

Despotic power of the French king.

We have seen how Philippe Auguste, St. Louis, and Philippe le Bel extended the authority of the French crown. The whole policy of the crafty, unscrupulous, Louis XI. had been directed to the humbling of the nobles and the exaltation of the royal power. The seizure of the English provinces of Normandy, Maine, and Anjou, Poitou and Guienne, the acquisition of Auvergne and Saintonge, Toulouse, Angouleme, and La Marche, and the Lyonnois, by forfeiture, escheat, or conquest; the inheritance of Navarre and Champagne; the fall of Charles the Bold, and the seizure of the duchy of Burgundy; the acquisition of Dauphine[1] and Provence under wills; and lastly, of Brittany, by the marriage of the heiress with Charles VIII., had vested in the crown the territories and the power long held by the great vassals, and established the royal authority.

Still, however, the power of the lesser feudal nobles was very great. The religious wars of the League and the Hugonots in France, had tended, like the wars of the Roses in England, to destroy the nobility, and Richelieu, the minister of Louis XIII., reduced them almost to a cypher. And when Louis le Grand, the XIV., ascended the throne, he found himself one of the most absolute princes of Europe. The victories of that prince have made him an object of affection to the French nation, and the brilliant age of Louis le Grand is still a favourite theme. It is not, however, entitled to any very great legal celebrity. Before he came to the throne, jurisprudence and the magistracy had produced their greatest men. Cujas and Dumoulin had enriched the Roman

Age of Louis XIV.

[1] On condition that the king's eldest son should be called Dauphin.

and the French law with their learned works. The parliament had seen at its head Arnaud de Corbie, Jean de Vacquerie, Christophe de Thou, Achille de Harlay; L'Hospital had been Chancellor.[1]

Domat.

There is but one legal writer of the age of Louis XIV. whose merit demands a notice in this brief sketch. Jean Domat,[2] born 1625, died 1695, the friend and almost the pupil of the celebrated Pascal. In France as well as in England, the study of the law in public schools had rapidly declined, and at the commencement of the seventeenth century, individuals were left to penetrate the profoundest depths of the legal science, chiefly by the light of private study. The controversy between the Jesuits and Jansenists had formed the latter into the society of Port Royal, which Gibbon says, contributed so much to establish in France a taste for just reasoning, simplicity of style, and philosophical method. They not only consecrated themselves to God, and opposed a more strict morality to the doctrine of the Jesuits, but devoting themselves to study and meditation, they gave to the world some of the most profound as well as the most charming works of the age. The school which produced the art of thinking, "L'Art de Penser," was likely to form its pupils into close and systematic reasoners, as well as virtuous characters; and such we find Domat. The celebrated Boileau speaks of Domat as the restorer of reason in jurisprudence. Like Pascal in philosophy, Domat in jurisprudence was a Christian. He discovered a very close and surprising agreement between the maxims and doctrines of the Gospel, and the highest wisdom of the Roman jurisprudence. In his work on Civil Laws,[3] he took for fundamental axioms the simple

[1] M. Dupin, Continuation du Precis Historique du Droit Français, Premiere Partie, s. 1.

[2] Dupin, Biographie Abrégée.—Bernardi, de l'Origine, &c., p. 516; Lerminier, Introduction à l'Histoire du Droit, c. 12.

[3] Translated by Dr. Strahan; with Notes and Remarks on the Difference between the Common and Civil Law.

and profound doctrines of the Bible, that man was made by God, and for God, and that men ought, therefore, to love one another. Based on these principles, he framed his system of civil law from the Roman laws with the ordonnances of the French kings and the maxims of French jurisprudence. He showed that the highest and soundest exercise of one gift of the Creator, reason, led to the same consequences, respecting the duty of man to man, as might be deduced from the disclosures of Revelation. That the principles and maxims of the Roman law might be treated as the natural consequences of the sacred principles of Christianity. From these ideas, with the skill of one schooled in the logic of the Port Royal, he formed a closely united and coherent system of civil law. Notwithstanding his talents, he remained in comparatively obscure practice as an advocate at Clermont, and would not listen to any proposal for his advancement. "No one better understood," says an admirable judge, the celebrated D'Aguesseau,[1] "the true principles of legislation. He descends from them to the true consequences; he developes them in an order almost geometrical; all the different species of laws are detailed, with the characters which distinguish them. It is the best formed and most complete general plan of civil society which has ever appeared." He also says, "whoever shall thoroughly make himself master of Domat's work, will not, perhaps, be the most learned of jurisconsults, but he will be the most solid and sure of all judges."

Interference of the French parliaments in legislation.

The origin of the French parliaments has been already mentioned. In the absence of the states general, which, during these centuries, constituted the only assembly truly national, the parliaments had acquired, about the end of the sixteenth century, a sort of power of opposition to the legislative authority of the crown. It was their office to register the royal ordonnances,[2] they could

[1] Tom. i. p. 396.

[2] Bernardi, de l'Origine, &c., p. 548.

examine the edicts addressed to them, and remonstrate before they registered and published them; and in consequence of the custom of remonstrances, they possessed a power of temporary opposition.[1] The parliament owed the gradual increase of its power principally to the great men who had communicated the force of their character, and had spread over this illustrious body the eclât of their virtues.

The design of producing a uniformity of laws in France continued.

Notwithstanding the labours of Cujas, Dumoulin, and other celebrated men on the legal science, though they had prepared the way, a complete and regular system of law had not been created. The principles were explained in a great number of good works; the customs had been reduced to writing; a long course of decisions had fixed the law on great part of the points of controversy, and there only remained to give method and a compact form to the laws.[2] Dumoulin had conceived the design of recasting all the local customs in one sole code,[3] which should form the common law of France. At the epoch when he lived, the difficulty was, not so much to form a code, as to cause it to be received uniformly through the kingdom. As early as 1315, an attempt had been made to reduce to order the ordonnances of the French monarchs, by G. Du Breuil, whose compilation of them forms the third part of his Ancien Style du Parlement de Paris. The Code Henri III., already mentioned, professed to have this object solely in view, but it contains new enactments, which Corbin[4] says, it was hoped to get verified by the parliament: which, however, could not be accomplished. He adds that the code of Henri IV. contains not only the text of the ordonnances, but a new composition and mix-

---

[1] Dupin, Continuation du Precis Historique, part 1, s. 2; Bernardi, de l'Origine, &c., pp. 85, 86.

[2] Dupin, Continuation, &c., part 1, s. 1.

[3] Ib.

[4] See Corbin, in the avertissement at the beginning of the Code Louis XIII.

ture of laws from the Roman jurisprudence with the French ordonnances. Under Louis XIII., another compilation, called the Code de Louis XIII., was formed,[1] and about the same period, an attempt was made, which demonstrated the difficulty of giving a uniformity to the law throughout France. A grand ordonnance of 1629 was drawn up under Michel de Marillac, Keeper of the Seals of Louis XIII., and formed a sort of code, composed of four hundred and sixty-one articles.[2] It had been prepared on the complaints made by the deputies of the states of the kingdom, convoked and assembled in the city of Paris, in 1614, and on the advice given to his Majesty by the assemblies of Notables at Rouen in 1617, and at Paris in 1626. This ordonnance contained a great number of useful dispositions: Pothier, in citing it, always calls it la belle ordonnance. But many of its enactments displeased the French nobles, and it was not adopted by the parliaments. Some refused it altogether; others only admitted when compelled by a bed of justice, or registered it with modifications, and, in short, it remained without execution as a law.[3] It was called in derison, the Code Michau.

The grand ordonnance of Marillac, or Code Michau.

Ordonnances of Louis XIV.

The celebrated Colbert[4] adopted the design of reforming the French law, and Louis XIV., having become more absolute than his predecessors, found means of surmounting all effective resistance. With the assistance of Pussort, a very learned man, the minister formed many general ordonnances, which, by their wisdom, and the great care bestowed on them, merit attention; and notwithstanding the opposition of the president, Guillaume de Lamoignon, to the despotic principles of Pussort and Colbert, the parliaments were obliged to adopt the

[1] Le Code de Louis XIII. Contenant les Ordonnances et Arrêts des Courts Soveraines, Commentés et Confirmées avec Ceux de Henri IV. et des Rois ses Predecesseurs, par J. Corbin.—Par. 1628.

[2] Bernardi, de l'Origine, &c., p. 500; Dupin, Continuation, &c., part 1, s. 1,

[3] Dupin, ib. [4] Ib.

ordonnances of the ministers.[1] These ordonnances have been quoted in the English courts, and they have received the highest encomiums from the English bench and bar, particularly the ordonnance sur la Marine.[2]

The progress of the law of England, and its scientific development to the present period.

In order that we may not break in on the progress of French law again, we here conclude our notice of the few alterations, and the scientific cultivation and enlargement which the English law has undergone. The restoration of Charles II. in 1660, rendered invalid the legal alterations of the Commonwealth; but the spirit of liberality and fairness in the administration of justice, which had greatly increased during that period, has remained undiminished, except during the short reign of James II., to this day. The burthens of the feudal system, long nearly obsolete, during the Commonwealth became quite so: and one of the first acts of the Restoration was to sweep away, by an act of parliament for the abolition of military tenures and of the courts of Wards and Liveries, all the antiquated claims, and place the property laws of this country on the footing on which it now stands: in which the technical theory and consequences of the feudal doctrines are retained as a system, while the obnoxious burthens and fruits to the superior lord have ceased.

We have already alluded to the habeas corpus act, which was passed in this reign, and we have now only to notice the great English lawyers who lead the way in forming the rational system of commercial law, and the refined science of equity, or chancery law.

---

[1] Of which the chief are—

The Ordonnance of 1667 on Civil Process (Procedure Civile).

The Ordonnance of 1669 on Waters and Forests (Eaux et Forêts).

The Ordonnance of 1670 on Criminal Process (Procedure Criminelle).

The Ordonnance de la Ville on the Jurisdiction of the Prêvots, &c. in 1672.

The Ordonnance on Shipping, sur la Marine, in 1681.

The Ordonnance on Colonial Slavery, called le Code Noir, in 1685.

Dupin, ib.; Bernardi, de l'Origine, &c., l. 8, c. 8; Lerminier, Introduction à l'Histoire du Droit, c. 12.

[2] Luke v. Lyde, 2 Bur. 882; 1 W. Bl. 190, respecting freight.

Commercial law.

Previous to the time of Henry VIII., the law had been almost wholly occupied by the details of the feudal system, which, holding moveable property in little esteem, contained few provisions respecting it. During that and the three or four succeeding reigns, the amount of moveable property had been so greatly increased by commerce, as almost daily to come under the consideration of the courts, and the defective state of the law in part became evident.

Study of the civil law by English lawyers.

Perhaps to this cause is due the attention given to the civil law in this period, by the common lawyers, who, in the preceding half century, had persecuted Dr. Cowell. No attempts had for many centuries been made to force it on the nation. First and foremost among those who studied it in this age, is Sir Matthew Hale, born 1609, chief baron, and afterwards lord chief justice, during the reign of Charles II., who, to the greatest integrity of character, and profound knowledge of the common law, added an acquaintance with the civil law; and though be preferred the guarantees offered by the common law for the protection of the subject, yet often affirmed that "the principles of jurisprudence were so well delivered in the digests, that the law could not be understood as a science, without first resorting to them for information," an assertion, however, which experience has shown, must be taken with limitation, even as to commercial law.

Sir M. Hale.

Sir John Holt.

Sir M. Hale died in 1676, full of honour. His example in the study and estimation of the civil law, was followed by Sir John Holt, born 1642, and lord chief justice of the king's bench under William III., from 1689 to 1709. With great sagacity and boldness, he led the way to the establishment of some of the doctrines of commercial law on the rational principles of the civil law, out of which he considered the laws of all modern nations were raised.[1] By his celebrated judgment in the case of Coggs v. Bernard, he expounded the law of bailments with precision and fulness, and laid the whole foundation

[1] Lane v. Cotton, 12 Mod. Rep. 482.

of this important branch of English law in almost entire accordance with the Roman law on the subject. He was succeeded by several eminent common lawyers, whom we must pass over until we come to Lord Mansfield, lord chief justice of the king's bench, from 1756 to 1788, whose long occupation of that important office, at a period when the doctrines of commercial law were still unsettled, and when the rapidly increasing wealth of the country brought numerous cases before the tribunals for legal decision, entitles him to hold a very high eminence among the learned men who wrought out the rational part of our law. He had maturely studied the civil law, and he was deeply indebted to that source for his profound views and the high authority his decisions have attained. It was for his continual allusions to the imperial law, that the celebrated anonymous author of Junius launched his anathemas against him.[1]

Lord Mansfield.

During the reign of Charles II., the Roman law respecting the succession to the personal estates of an intestate, was introduced into the common law. Sir Leoline Jenkins,[2] a judge of the admiralty, and a professed civilian, in framing the statute for the distribution of the personal estate of an intestate, had in view the 118th novel of Justinian.

Statute of Distributions.

In that court, where the forms of the Roman law still prevail, and which in early times professed to have adopted the doctrines of that code, as well as vague notions of natural equity, in 1673, Sir Heneage Finch, Lord Nottingham, took his seat as Lord Chan-

Chancery.

Lord Nottingham.

[1] In his letter to Lord Mansfield, Nov. 1770, Junius says, "The Roman code, the law of nations, and the opinion of foreign civilians, are your perpetual theme; but who ever heard you mention Magna Charta or the Bill of Rights with approbation and respect?" and again, "No learned man, even among your own tribe, thinks you qualified to preside in a court of common law; yet it is confessed that under Justinian you might have made an incomparable Prætor. It is remarkable enough, but I hope not ominous, that the laws you understand best, and the judges you affect to admire most, flourished in the decline of a great empire, and are supposed to have contributed to its fall."

[2] Wynne's Life of Sir L. Jenkins.

cellor; under him the doctrines of the courts of equity began to be definitely fixed. To adopt the language of the brief but correct and elegant history of a recent author,[1] "Lord Nottingham brought to the subject a strong and cultivated mind, and pronounced his decrees after the most cautious and painstaking study. Lord Cowper and Lord Talbot pursued the same career with the genuine spirit of jurists. But it was reserved for Lord Hardwicke, by his deep learning, his extensive researches, and his powerful genius, to combine the scattered fragments into a scientific system; to define with a broader line the boundaries between the departments of the common law and chancery; and to give certainty and vigour to the principles, as well as the jurisdiction of the latter. Henceforth equity began to acquire the same exactness as the common law; and at this moment there is scarcely a branch of its jurisprudence that is not reduced to method, and does not, in the harmony of its parts, rival the best examples of the common law. Our own age has witnessed, in the labours of Lord Eldon, through a series of more than twenty-five volumes of reports, a diligence, sagacity, caution, and force of judgment, which have seldom been equalled, and can scarcely be surpassed; which have given dignity, as well as finish, to that curious moral machinery, which, dealing in an artificial system, yet contrives to administer the most perfect of human inventions,—the doctrines of conscience, ex æquo et bono."

Lord Hardwicke.

Lord Eldon.

In France the law commenced with two systems of administration, the one consisting of the Teutonic institutions, the other the Roman; both applied to persons, and which grew into one. In England, beginning with one system of Teutonic law, and one system of administration, a second, originating with the ecclesiastical Chancellor, who studied the civil law and adopted its forms of

[1] Mr. Justice Story, on the Past History, Present State, and Future Prospects of the Law.

administration, has grown on it and formed the one into two.

We need not mention Sir W. Jones, the only lawyer equally conversant with the Year Books of Westminster, the Commentaries of Ulpian, the Attic pleadings of Isæus, and the sentences of Arabian and Persian Cadhis; the classic commentator, Sir W Blackstone; nor Hargrave, Romilly, Butler, Ellenborough, Kenyon, Erskine, Gifford, Grant, Tenterden. But we cannot omit drawing attention to the work of Mr. Fearne on contingent remainders, as a specimen of the systematic arrangement, the close coherent reasoning, of which the English law of property is susceptible.

Recent English lawyers.

To return to the French legal history at the commencement of the 18th century, we find a man who would have been an honour to any country taking the lead in French jurisprudence, namely, Henri François D'Aguesseau,[1] born 1668, advocate in 1690. Though menaced with disgrace during the life of Louis XIV. on account of his resistance to the Bull Unigenitas, in 1717, two years after the death of that monarch, he became Chancellor, and filled that important office until 1750, having however been exiled during ten years of that time; when he retired, leaving behind him an unrivalled reputation. Like many other great men, he owed his after fame greatly to the training he received from his father, who had filled several important public situations. He also had the advantage of the instructions of Domat and Lamoignon. D'Aguesseau made his first appearance with so much eclat, that the president a mortier, Denis Talen, declared he should wish to finish as that young man had begun. To the most brilliant eloquence,[2] he

Further attempts to give France uniform laws.

D'Aguesseau.

[1] See Charles Butler, Memoir of D'Aguesseau; Dupin, Biographie Abrégée; Lerminier, Introduction à l'Histoire du Droit, c. 12; Evans, Pothier on Contracts.

[2] The English reader may see a specimen of D'Aguesseau's eloquence, in his pleadings in the cause of the Sieur de la Puardiere—referred to by Mr. Butler: also in Selections from the Pleadings of D'Aguesseau, translated and contained in the Appendix to Evans' Pothier on Contracts; case of Sieur Brouillerot de Vindutes,

administration of D'Aguesseau. During the leisure of one of his exiles at his country-house at Fresnes, he wrote a treatise on the general views which ought to be observed in the reformation of justice; and his subsequent return to power, enabled him to carry them partly into execution in the above ordonnances.[1]

D'Aguesseau had not that rude energy and that force of character, which made L'Hospital the first of French chancellors, but he was without contradiction the most lettered of French magistrates, the one whose style is the most pure and most graceful: he is the Massillon of the French bar.[2] For christian piety and integrity of character, legal erudition, and universal knowledge, embracing a wide range of subjects, he bears a striking resemblance to Sir M. Hale.[3]

D'Aguesseau is justly celebrated for the encouragement he gave to the talented men of his profession: Domat and Pothier were distinguished and honoured by his friendship and advice.

Pothier.

The latter, whom we have now to introduce to the reader, was the last French lawyer we are called upon to notice before the Revolution. Robert Joseph Pothier[4] was born in 1699, at Orleans, at the university of which place he completed his education, and at the age of twenty-one he was admitted a counsellor of the court of his native town. From an early age the study of the Roman law was almost a passion with Pothier.[5] It is said, he no sooner began to study the Digests, than he perceived invincible attractions in it. He felt it his vocation, and followed it; and he gave it a more scientific method than it had yet received. It has often been lamented, that so

[1] Dupin, Continuation, &c., part 1, s. 1.

[2] Dupin, Biographie des Principaux Auteurs de Droit, &c.

[3] Butler, Reminiscences.

[4] Eloge of Pothier, pronounced upon his decease, in the University of Orleans, by M. Le Trosne, translated and prefixed to Evans' Translation of Pothier on Contracts.

[5] Dupin, Biographie Abrégée; Lerminier, Introduction à l'Histoire du Droit, c. 12.

important a work as the Digests of the Roman Law had not been executed in a more learned and enlightened age, instead of being deferred to the sixth century, and undertaken by the order of Justinian at a time when taste had degenerated, and barbarism had begun to disfigure the Roman empire. In this celebrated code, among other faults, texts and extracts from former Roman jurisconsults are often placed in titles to which they have no relation; and incredible labours have been bestowed to repair the defects occasioned by the inaccuracy, the incapacity, and the infidelity of the compilers. Among those who gave themselves to this task are a Cujas and a Pothier.

It is curious to observe that these two great men, who of all Frenchmen have best understood the Roman law, followed methods diametrically opposed. Cujas, as we have seen, reunited all the extracts of each jurisconsult which are dispersed through the digest.[1] In explaining the laws in the schools, it was not (to speak properly) the Digests that he read, but the works of Papinian, Paulus, Ulpian, &c.: on the contrary, Pothier, in his New Model of the Pandects, has multiplied the divisions. He has preserved the same distribution, and the same order of books and titles; but he has changed the order of the laws placed under each title: he has often divided that which is only one law in the Digest, and distributed the different parts under several titles. The method of Cujas is more fit to explain the true sense of the jurisconsults; that of Pothier unites, under one point of view, all that relates to the same question.

Prevot de la Janés, the professor of law at Orleans, to whom Pothier communicated the design he had formed of thus reducing the Roman law to a more perfect order, apprised D'Aguesseau of it; and from that time, Pothier received the encouragement and advice of the chancellor

[1] Bibliotheque Choisi des Livres de Droit, &c., par MM. Camus et Dupin; Pothier.

in the execution of the plan, which redound equally to the credit of the learning and the good feeling of that great lawyer.

This new arrangement of the Pandects[1] was completed and published in 1748. Pothier also published a Commentary on the Customs of Orleans, and numerous treatises on the French law. But his most celebrated work, at least the one best known and most esteemed in England, is the Treatise on Contracts (Obligations), published in 1761. It displays his profound and extensive knowledge and acute reasoning powers. Pothier has been considered as the greatest jurist who had appeared in France since the time of Dumoulin. His principal studies were the Pandects, the Code of Justinian, and the works of Cujas and Dumoulin: from the latter he appears to have chiefly drawn the principles of the French customary law. The principles and substance of his Treatise on Contracts are collected from the Pandects, intermixed with discussions of the various customary laws of France, and set forth with a regard to order and logical sequence which it were to be wished could be more often met with among legal writers. On the death of Prevot de la Janés, he was chosen professor of law at Orleans. His writings were so highly esteemed, that even during his life they obtained a great weight of authority. He retained a great simplicity in his manners to the last, and died in 1772 unmarried, for he used to say he had neither time nor courage to marry.[2]

We need not mention the author of the Persian Letters, and of the Spirit of Laws, the well-known Charles de Secondat, Baron de Montesquieu. His own countrymen do not consider him as a lawyer.

Events which led to the French Revolution.

Although, during the last century, the French nobility had been stripped by Richelieu of many of their ancient prerogatives, and, no longer the leaders of the national

[1] Pandectæ Justinianeæ in novum ordinem digestæ.

[2] Dupin, Lerminier, Evans (ubi supra).

army, were reduced to comparative insignificance before the throne, yet the only benefit resulting from their abasement had accrued to the crown; the people not obtaining any share in it. The king had been rendered absolute; so that a lettre-de-cachet, or order for imprisonment from the king or his minister, could immure the most unoffending subject in a dungeon for life, without power of redress, or even of complaint; but the old feudal burthens which oppressed the people remained undiminished;[1] and the apparent absolute power of the monarch induced him to permit a lavish expenditure, to meet which the people were to be further taxed.

Opposition of the parliaments.

There was, however, one body, and only one body, of the state, capable of resisting the royal pleasure; that was, the French Court of Justice, or Parliament,[2] which, in the exercise of the power of remonstrance, and refusal to register the royal edicts (without which they had not the force of law), could, at some risk to the members, check the power of the monarch. Louis XIV. had attempted to abolish this impediment to his arbitrary legislation; and, in 1657, he ordained that the parliament should never remonstrate until eight days after having obediently registered the ordonnances.[3] In 1673, the right was re-established; though the monarch was too powerful to render it of any avail. Scarcely was Louis XIV. dead, when the parliaments retook the exercise of their prerogatives, annulled his testament, and gave the regency to the Duke of Orleans. The Regent Orleans had need of their support, and in return recognized their

[1] The social state of the middle ages was, especially in France, odious and insupportable. The cradle of a nation never before inspired it with such an antipathy. The feudal system, its institutions and principles, never obtained that unreflecting adhesion, generally the consequence of habit, which nations have often given to the worst system of social organization. France constantly essayed to escape them, to abolish them. Whoever gave it a blow—kings, lawyers, church—was approved and popular: even despotism, when it appeared a means of deliverance, was accepted as a benefit.—Guizot, Histoire, &c.

[2] There were twelve parliaments in France; Paris, Toulouse, Grenoble, Bordeaux, Dijon, Rouen, Aix, Rheims, Pau, Metz, Douai, and Besançon.

[3] Fleury, Precis Historique, s. 24.

prerogatives.[1] Towards the end of the reign of Louis XV. they offered opposition to his measures, and attempts were made to abolish them entirely.[2] At first, each party had recourse to the arms most familiar to it: the crown to beds of justice, forced registrations, and commands (lettres de jussion); the parliament to reiterated remonstrances, permanent assemblies of the chambers, union of the parliaments under the title of classes,[3] cessation of judicial functions, and combined resignations of the members. The minister then had recourse to extreme means: lettres-de-cachet, exiles, and imprisonments. In 1753, the parliament being exiled to Pontoise, a chambre-royal was created to replace it in the administration of justice. Public opinion went to the aid of the parliament, and it was recalled; but with soured spirit, to find new causes of discord.[4] The high nobility had suffered with impatience the judicial and legislative functions to be shared by the bourgeois en robes, and therefore sided against the parliament. In 1770, a new edict being refused by the parliament, its members were exiled; and the chancellor Maupeou, in 1771, substituted a sort of temporary tribunal, which he soon replaced by the superior councils, among which he divided out the immense extent of the ancient parliamentary duties. Such was the Parlement Maupeou. Several advocates refused to accept places in the new judicature, or to plead before it.[5]

The parliaments were restored, with the right of remonstrance, as a popular measure at the beginning of the reign of Louis XVI. At his accession, that prince found the finances in a most disastrous condition; and, notwithstanding all the retrenchment he could effect, the deficit increased, and new taxes became necessary.[6] The plan of administration of Turgot, then comptroller-

---

1 Dupin, Continuation, &c., part 1, s. 3.

2 Bernardi, de l'Origine, &c., b. 9, c. 2.

3 Dupin, Continuation, &c., part 1, s. 3. 4 Ib. 5 Ib.

6 Histoire de France; Scott, Life of Napoleon, vol. i.

general, was directed against the privileged classes. He wished to make them subject to the charges of the state. The privileged classes hastened to form a league to defend their menaced immunities, and united with the parliaments which refused to register Louis XVI.'s edicts for the suppression of the corvees, jurandes, and communities. Malesherbes and Turgot retired discouraged; Calonne was appointed, and wished to raise money: the parliament resisted. Calonne, to avenge himself on this body, convoked in 1787 the assembly of notables, which had not been called together since 1626. Having passed the proposed edicts, and made several other useful laws, they separated.[1]

Assembly of Notables.

New disputes between the crown and the parliaments.

After the separation of the notables, new sources of discord between the minister and the parliament arose. The embarrassments of the crown, in the meanwhile, daily increased. The parliament refused obstinately to register some proposed edicts, which, by taxing the privileged classes, while they ameliorated the condition of the people, would have increased the revenues of the state. Several of the members went so far as to assert the necessity of convoking the states-general, as having alone the power of granting taxes. Thus, the court having called the notables as auxiliaries to overcome the parliament, the parliament in its turn, at the risk of what might happen to itself, made an appeal to the states-general to frighten the court. A bed of justice was held; the edicts registered by virtue of absolute command; and the parliament exiled to Troyes. It was soon recalled, the new edicts withdrawn, and the old tax of a twentieth imposed. Two new edicts, one giving rights to the Protestants, the other concerning new imposts, having been refused, the minister exiled some, and arrested others of the members of the parliament.[2] To quiet the public mind, on the 18th of December, 1787, the king an-

[1] Dupin, Continuation, &c.; Bernardi, de l'Origine, &c., b. 9, c. 2.

[2] Dupin, Continuation, &c., part 1, s. 3.

States-General.

nounced the convocation of the states-general in five years: but circumstances so pressed as not to permit this delay; and on the 23rd of September, 1788, appeared the royal edict for the convocation of the states-general. They had not assembled for one hundred and seventy-five years: and the usages and traditions had so died away, that a prior meeting of the notables was necessary in order to settle the proportion the representatives of the tiers-état should bear to the other two orders (clergy and nobility). On the 5th of May, 1789, the states-general were opened at Versailles: they soon took the name of National Assembly.[1]

Took the name of National Assembly.

The French Revolution; state of France, and causes of irritation.

The events which followed this assembly present a spectacle at once astonishing and appalling: a people, hitherto loyal and contented, and almost idolizing the most arbitrary of their monarchs, suddenly became excited to fury, and vented its rage upon one of the best intentioned kings that ever swayed its destinies; whose only fault was a vacillation arising from weakness of character: a population, which had long quietly submitted to the most oppressive slavery, was seen occupied with the most visionary schemes of freedom: a nation, brave, humane, and polished, became in an instant, to an unparalleled degree, ferocious, sanguinary, and brutal; and, though at that time the most civilized of the world, allowed its leaders to enact a series of barbarities unheard of in the annals of civilization.

It is not difficult to point out numerous causes, each of which, in themselves, was sufficient to account for a very great revulsion of feeling, and which now almost excite our wonder that it had not occurred sooner. The servile state of the Celtic population at the fall of the Roman empire, had enticed the Germanic invaders to assume a despotic power throughout the country, and the nobles

[1] Scott, Life of Napoleon. These facts are so well known, that we can only refer to every history of France, and almost every history of any European country in that period.

established themselves as petty feudal tyrants during the middle ages.[1] They made peace and war with each other, coined money, and exercised the most absolute jurisdiction over their vassals or subjects, whom they bought and sold like slaves. But the whole population were naturally warlike; and while the noble could assemble his vassals and put himself at their head, and they considered themselves as forming a little army round their chief, and could rejoice or lament with him in the glory of victory or in the disgrace of defeat, their restraints and burthens were not felt or thought of. When, however, the measures of Richelieu had drawn the nobility from their ancient castles to become the courtiers of the throne, dependant for their importance on their intrigues at court, the bond which united the vassal to his lord was broken, and their connections and feelings severed. The nobility, crowding round the court, and plunged in sensuality and intrigue, required increased incomes to support them in their splendour, and enable them to vie with each other. Each anxious not to be outdone in the capital, they became greedy landlords: the management of their estates naturally fell into the hands of a class of middle men, who acquired the influence properly belonging to the noble. In the meanwhile, the local burthens and feudal rights and services, due by the tenantry to their feudal superiors, remained undiminished, and to the last degree vexatious and oppressive. As was to be expected, the rural population, neglected by their landlords, harassed by the agents who supplied their places, and reduced to the most abject misery, became discontented and ripe for any change.

Possessed of the organization derived from Rome, under the protection of the kings, who beheld in them a powerful counterbalance to the nobility, the cities of France had gradually acquired a great degree of importance. From commerce the inhabitants of the cities had become

[1] Ante, pp. 15, 16, 19, 20, 73 to 77.

wealthy, and naturally felt galled by the contempt with which they were treated by a proud nobility, who regarded the useful and commercial arts, and even the liberal professions of law and physic, as beneath their dignity, and who disdained intermarrying with the classes who followed these pursuits. We have seen how the feudal superior of the French nobles, or sovereign, gradually acquired unlimited power, by the union of the domains and authority of the great vassals, and by the abasement of the lesser nobility; and that the people had not been raised proportionably, and had gained little or nothing by the change. The nobles had retained their feudal privileges; and, although the possessions of some of them were immense, they were exempt from taxation. The clergy claimed and enjoyed the same exemption. So that, on the plebeian population of the cities and the peasantry, devolved the burthen of supplying the extravagance of the crown and defraying the national expenditure. These causes made the wealthy citizen as desirous of change as the peasantry.

Added to the discontent arising in the rural and urban population from these causes, the unlimited spirit of inquiry, which had become the fashion of the age, had in France taken a decidedly wrong direction. Naturally inclined to devotion, the French people had long adhered to the religion of Rome, without any doubt or hesitation, and without inquiry. But when the searching spirit turned to investigate the doctrines and practice of the papal form of worship, so much of mere ceremonial, mummery, and absurdity, and such practical immorality were found, that the whole system became a subject of ridicule. The higher orders of clergy enjoyed immense revenues, and were selected almost exclusively from the younger branches of the nobility; and, with a few high and honourable exceptions, passing their lives in the intrigues of the court or the dissipation of the capital, were but little fitted to meet and parry the overwhelming raillery of Voltaire and his fellow-sceptics, either by the simple force of a character for piety and morality, or by the powerful reasoning which may be adduced, not only from indirect arguments, such as the necessity and consequent certainty of a revelation, but also from the direct evidence of history, which more fully supports each of the whole train of facts on which man's highest hopes are fixed, than any other event, past or present.[1] The lower orders of clergy had either not the inclination or not the ability for the task. Hence a spirit of infidelity spread amongst all classes; the most hallowed associations being destroyed, institutions, formerly the most revered, were become objects of contempt or hatred. The whole nation, rendered discontented, and all classes exasperated, started into violent commotion, without the mild humanity of the Christian feeling to soften its ferocity, or the self-respect of the ancient pagan to restrain its excesses.

With a spirit thus unrestrained by any of the higher or more amiable feelings, it is scarcely to be wondered, that a people, galled by the privileges of the clergy and nobility, exasperated by feudal and other burdens, looked on in silence, and even complacency, while the democratic orators led the rabble to exercise its power and vent its wrath on its oppressors.

Character and conduct of Louis XVI.

The virtuous but weak monarch, before the meeting of the states-general, had shown his inclination to reform abuses, by abolishing the use of torture, and emancipating those who still remained of the ancient serfs, by ordering the destruction of the dungeons under ground, and by the suppression of the corvées. He had also curtailed his personal expenditure, and dismissed some of his body guards, and he seemed inclined to follow the advice of the National Assembly. From weakness of character, his actions and policy seem to have vacillated as he was urged by the various parties, and left an

[1] See the principles of the sceptical school applied to the events of the present day, in Dr. Whateley's "Historic Doubts relative to Napoleon Buonaparte."

impression of insincerity in the public mind. During the sitting of the National Assembly, the tranquillity of the city of Paris became daily more disturbed.

The night of sacrifices.

On the night of the 4th of August, 1789, called the "night of sacrifices," one of the most unparalleled scenes of the Revolution took place; it was, perhaps, of the most importance of any to the civil laws of the state. A nobleman, the Viscount de Noailles, seconded by the Duc de Aguillon, proposed to do justice as the shortest way of restoring tranquillity; and for this purpose, to decree, that henceforth every tax should be imposed in proportion to the wealth of the contributors, and that no order of the state should be exempted from the public burthens; that feudal claims should be redeemed at a fair valuation; but that such claims as consisted of personal services on the part of the vassals, should be abolished without compensation, as contrary to the imprescriptible rights of man.[1] The extensive possessions of the noblemen with whom these proposals originated, added lustre to the disinterested sacrifices which they had made: the speeches delivered on the occasion were received with the most enthusiastic applauses by the assembly and the galleries, and their proposals were decreed by acclamation. The patriotic contagion spread with inconceivable rapidity, and a contest of generosity ensued. The hereditary jurisdictions possessed by the nobles within their own territories were unconditionally sacrificed. The game laws, having always been numbered amongst the most severe grievances of the French peasantry, were renounced,

[1] In 1776 appeared a pamphlet, entitled, Inconveniences of the Feudal Law, in which, among others, was the assertion that the king could enfranchise the serfs even without the consent of the lords in their fiefs; and that if he used this power, liberty would adore its author, and their independence would be the perpetual homage and the first title of vassallage. The aristocracy could not let this insolence pass with impunity; an indictment followed, in which the passage was quoted, and a decision of the parliament condemned the writing to be torn, and burnt at the foot of the gallows.

That which in 1776 was not permitted with impunity to be called an "inconvenience," in 1789 was suppressed as an usurpation, an abuse.

along with the exclusive rights of rabbit-warrens, fisheries, and dove-cots. The sale of offices was abolished, and the fees exacted from the poor, together with the privilege of holding a plurality of livings, were relinquished by the clergy. The deputies of the Pais d'Etat, or privileged provinces, with the deputies of Dauphiné at their heads, next came forward, and offered to surrender their ancient privileges, requesting that the kingdom might no longer remain parcelled out amongst Dauphinois, Bretons, Provençaux, and others, but that they should form one great mass of French citizens. They were followed by the representatives of Paris, Marseilles, Lyons, Bordeaux, Strasbourg, and other places, who requested leave to renounce all their separate privileges as incorporations, for the sake of placing every man and every village in the nation upon a footing of equality. And thus the assembly proceeded, until every member exhausted his imagination upon the subject of reform. To close the whole, the Duc de Liancourt proposed that a solemn *Te Deum* should be performed, and a medal struck in commemoration of the events of that night of sacrifices; and that the title of Restorer of Gallic Liberty should be bestowed upon the reigning monarch. Several days were necessary to form into laws the decrees of the 4th of August, and committees were appointed to make out reports for that purpose.

The Parliaments suppressed. The parliament now conceived regrets, and wished to prevent its own fall;[1] but in November, 1789, it was adjourned (mis en vacance); and by the decree of August, 1790, it was definitively suppressed, with the other tribunals of ancient creation.

The Legislative Assembly. The States-General, or National Assembly, became constitutional; and, having published their declaration of rights, passed numerous laws urgently required, formed a new constitution, and made provisions for the meeting of a new assembly, dissolved; and were succeeded by the

---

[1] Dupin, Continuation, &c., p. 1. s. 3.

Legislative Assembly. Our plan does not require us to dwell on the invasion of the French territory, the massacres of September, the formation of the National Convention, the mock trial and murder of the unfortunate Louis, the anarchy and dreadful horrors of the Reign of Terror which followed, and the fall of the moderate but powerless Directory before the genius of Napoleon: suffice it to say, a revolution had been completed, the old laws had been swept away, the old institutions had been rooted up.

The National Convention.

Napoleon Buonaparte.

Opportunity now presented of making one uniform law for the whole of France.

Up to this period, the opportunity of giving uniformity to the law of France, like that which the supreme courts of Westminster, and the circuits of the judges through the country, had long produced in England, and which must have resulted from the centralization of the government and the circuits of Missi Dominici in France, had the plans of Charlemagne been executed, had never been recovered since the abandonment of those plans. Each province continued to hold its separate usages and customs. The Loire had divided the Franks from the Visigothic and Burgundian settlers, and the northern parts chiefly formed pays coutumier, and the southern the pays du droit écrit.

We have seen the projects originating with Charles VII. carried on by his successors, until all the customs of the different districts were reduced to writing; the reformations of the customary law, the futile attempts of the Codes Henri III. and IV., and the Code Michau, the partial uniformity effected in details by the ordonnances of Louis XIV. and Louis XV., and the unexecuted desires of Dumoulin and D'Aguesseau for a general code. The time had now at length come when a code could be formed; all impediments had been swept away; and it was necessary to supply the place of the feudal and other laws and legal institutions which had been abolished.

It was not, however, until Napoleon had obtained the

direction of affairs, that any sensible progress was made towards the completion of the undertaking. The first National Assembly, or Constituent Assembly, gave their attention to political rights and criminal legislation. Engrossed in the formation of the new constitution and the declaration of rights, and in providing for the immediate necessities of the times, it left to its successors the task of making a code of civil law common to all the kingdom. The Legislative Assembly was too short-lived to effect this; but during the Convention, notwithstanding the anarchy and horrors of the period, the outline of the civil code was laid.[1]

Legislation of the National Assembly.

Legislation of the National Convention.

In 1793, Cambacères[2] presented a report to the committee of legislation on the project of a code, which was to consist of four books: viz. on the State of Persons, on Contracts, on Things, and on Actions. It was clear and precise; it embodied the political principles of the epoch, and submitted the regulation of civil and domestic life to their influence with a rigorous unity: the Convention, however, was not satisfied. At this period it seems to have been the leading idea in legislation, on civil as well as political matters, to tolerate nothing of antiquity which reason did not respect; to shrink from no novelty to which reason might seem to point,[3] in the hope, under the guidance of reason, of discovering principles of legislation, which, while they rendered justice simple, should at the same time make provisions capable of regulating all the details of life: so that the proposed code should require no study to comprehend it, that it should be so clear and precise, that persons of ordinary capacity might understand its principles and details, and be able to refer to it, in the same manner as

The four first projects for a Code.

Cambacères' first projet.

[1] As to the formation of the codes, see Recueil Complet des Travaux Preparatoires du Code Civil, par P. A. Fenet, Introduction, v. i.; Dupin, Continuation, &c., part 2; Lerminier, Introduction à l'Histoire du Droit, c. 20; Bernardi, de l'Origine, &c., b. 9, c. 4.

[2] See the 1st Project of Cambacères in the above collection, by Fenet, v. i. p. 16.

[3] Butler.

they would to a dictionary, when occasion required. The project of Cambacères did not meet these views; the Convention required more brevity and more innovation. Another and more succinct scheme[1] was, therefore, prepared and presented by Cambacères in September, 1794, some articles of which were being discussed when the convention separated, 27th of October, 1795. Under the Directory two years afterwards, in 1796, a third project[2] was presented by Cambacères, which differed from the two others almost as greatly as the principles of the then ruling party differed from those of their predecessors, inasmuch as many of the principles of the ancient French jurisprudence reappeared. But the reign of the Directory was not energetic enough to execute with success a measure of such importance, and this scheme was not proceeded with: a legislative commission of the Council of Five Hundred also presented another project.[3]

Cambacères' second projet.

Cambacères' third projet.

Projet of the Legislative Commission.

Napoleon. His commission for drawing up a code.

As soon, however, as Buonaparte became master, he and his fellow consuls issued a new commission, in August, 1800, to Messrs. Tronchet, Bigot-Preameneau, and Portalis, with M. Maleville for their secretary, directing them to hold conferences on the formation of a civil code, to compare the projects published up to that time, and to determine the plan which should appear most suitable.

Mode of executing the task.

Aware of the glory the execution of a code of laws must throw round his administration, Napoleon caused the work to be proceeded with most rapidly. The new commission hastened to fulfil his wishes, and immediately commenced their labours; the order of the titles was soon agreed upon, and the subjects distributed; "and by dint of exertion," says one of the members, "we were enabled to frame a civil code in four months." The rapidity in

---

[1] See the 2nd Project of Cambacères in the above collection, by Fenet, p. 110. The first project occupies 82 pages of this collection, the second 39 pages only.

[2] See the 3rd Project of Cambacères, ib. p. 178.

[3] See the project presented by M. Jacqueminot, in the name of the Section of Legislation, ib. p. 333.

which the Roman Pandects were compiled by the seventeen lawyers, under the direction of Tribonian, in three instead of ten years, has been considered a subject of deep regret; and it must be admitted that the project of the French code was executed in too great haste.

In the selection of the subjects of the books and titles of the new code, the Institutes of Justinian appear to have been taken as a model, and many important heads were omitted, or but partially treated in the project, because they do not occur at all, or only incidentally, in the works of the Roman emperor.

In filling up the outline thus drawn, two plans presented themselves. For centuries, schemes of universal jurisprudence and abstract justice had been a constant theme of discussion, and the commissioners might have adopted the plan which prevailed in the early days of the Revolution; and which, by starting from some certain theory or given principles, proposed to work out a rational system, and bring all the parts into coherence. But in this plan, in rendering the new system consistent, many of its parts must have been ill suited to the inconsistent habits which arise out of the customs and feelings of a nation; and even in France, notwithstanding the very great want of any fixed principle, and the rupture of ancient habits which had resulted from the anarchy of the Revolution, this course must have been displeasing to the sober part of the nation. The other plan was, to fill up the outline with the remaining fragments of the ancient jurisprudence, and with new enactments to supply the place of the feudal and other part of the ancient law which had been swept away. Under the altered state of the nation, this plan appeared to the commissioners to be the most advisable; and Napoleon, from the first establishment of his power, was desirous to check the revolutionary mania, and to strengthen himself, by bringing back the ancient manners and system as much as possible. The Code civil.
commissioners, therefore, applied themselves to the old

law, which we have seen consisted of the Roman jurisprudence, modified by customary law (droit écrit), and the customary law, tinctured by the Roman system, which supplied its deficiencies. Various treatises of Pothier were rapidly dissected, and, with morsels from Domat and the ancient ordonnances, formed into the articles of the projected code. The titles relative to contracts are merely an analysis of the treatises of Pothier[1] on these matters; and at least three-fourths of the whole civil code consists of extracts from his works.[2]

After the projet was thus formed, a plan similar to that of D'Aguesseau, in forming his ordonnances, was pursued. The projet was printed in the future tense, and sent to each of the courts of appeal for their observations; the projet, with their observations, was then discussed in the Conseil d'Etat and at the tribunate; after which, under the guidance of the government orators, who explained their principles, the different titles of the code were presented to the legislative body, and passed into laws. They were then promulgated, and official editions published.[3] The reports and discourses pronounced before the tribunate were also published, to serve as a commentary to explain the intent of the articles of the new code.[4]

All these discussions, however, had little more than the effect of giving the government clearer views on the different parts of the subject, by placing them in a

---

1 Lerminier, Introduction, &c., c. 20.

2 Dupin, Life of Pothier, affixed to an edition of his works.

3 In the three forms of quarto, octavo, and duodecimo. The edition of the codes published by the Imperial government ceased to be official after the Restoration; and the only edition of them which can now be cited, and appealed to in pleadings, consultations, and public acts, is that printed at the royal press (imprimée à l'Imprimerie Royale), in execution of the ordonnances of the 30th August, 1816, and inserted in the bulletin, 7 serie, No. 109, bis.

4 Whoever will properly understand the codes, ought to have in his library, 1. The Projet; 2. The Observations of the Courts on this Projet; 3. The Discussions of the Conseil d'Etat; 4. The Exposé of the Motives; 5. The Reports and Discourse; 6. The Official Discussion. These are all contained in the above-mentioned collection, by Fenet, in 15 volumes.

variety of lights; and notwithstanding the parade made in taking the advice of the superior courts of justice, and submitting the whole to the Legislative Assembly, all the important questions of the code must be considered rather as decreed by the government than the result of the legislation of the nation; for Napoleon's principles were too arbitrary to permit opposition to his schemes. While there can be but little doubt that there was much of faction in the decided opposition and rejection, which the three first titles submitted to the tribunate met with from the majority, none but honorable intentions can be attributed to such men as Guignené, Andrieux, Chenier, Daunou, Constant, Say, &c., who are found among the opposition. Napoleon however was highly incensed: he could not or would not appreciate their grounds of opposition; and he considered them as metaphysicians only fit to be ducked in a pond (metaphysiciens bons à jéter a l'eau). The members obnoxious to him were therefore expelled from the tribunate.

The other codes.

After the civil code others were formed, discussed, and enacted in a similar manner for the other portions of the law, namely, a commercial code and a code of civil procedure,[1] a penal code and a code of criminal instruction. The codes of rural law (code forestier and code de la peche fluvial) were not published until after the restoration of the Bourbons.

The general character of the French codes.

The codes were avowedly a composition between the principles of the old customary laws of the French and the Roman law. Pothier, from whom the greater part was drawn, had derived his loi coutumiere from Dumoulin, his droit écrit from Cujas. To revert to the distinctions laid down in our first pages, the Rational portion of the law admitted of little or no dispute which reason could not decide. The feudal law had been abolished; there

[1] This code is said almost to have nullified its predecessors. M. Bernardi says, "It is embarrassed with numerous complicated forms, and far beyond the management of the half-instructed judges who people the tribunals."

remained, therefore, only the droit écrit out of which to form the Technical part of the law: and the principles of the law of property are drawn almost wholly from the Roman jurisprudence: but on the Popular part of the law, there was considerable difference of opinion between the legislators from the pays coutumier and pays du droit écrit. One of the fundamental sources of this portion of law, namely, that which regulates the contraction and dissolution of marriage, had, during the revolutionary period, from the rupture of religious and social principles, fallen into a state almost as depraved, especially among the lower classes, as it had been in at the time of Charlemagne.[1] It was the wish of all sober-minded men to remedy this evil; and the unsettled state of popular feeling on the subject left it almost entirely to the discretion of the legislator. On the subjects of paternal power, guardianship, minority, succession to the property of deceased persons, and the rights of husband and wife, arising from the contract of marriage when made, the framers of the code had to make a decision. On this last subject, which formed a striking example of the contrast of the droit écrit and the loi coutumiere, the question arose, whether the community of goods (a sort of partnership), as before stated of Celtic origin,[2] which prevailed in the pays coutumier, or the dotal system introduced with the Roman law, should be adopted as the marriage law of the new code. After reiterated discussions a compromise took place, which leaves it to the married couple to choose whichever system they prefer; and if they make no declaration before marriage, which they prefer, community of goods prevails.

In the discussion of some titles of the projet by the Conseil d'Etat, Napoleon took a lively interest. He frequently took a part in them, and entered the lists with the members; and notwithstanding the council was composed of lawyers and magistrates, possessed unquestion-

---

[1] Ante, pp. 26, 7, 8, 9.

[2] Ante, p. 28.

ably of great talents, he appears to considerable advantage among them. The peculiar state of his family plans and prospects rendered the subjects of divorce and adoption of very great interest to him individually. Notwithstanding his presence, the discussions of the Conseil d'Etat were conducted with great freedom, and sometimes with animated warmth.

The absurd notion, that a code could be formed so simple and complete that nothing more should be required than mere reference to its contents, and literal application of them, to decide all legal disputes, does not seem to have been entertained by the eminent men who framed the code. M. Portalis says, "We have guarded against the dangerous ambition of wishing to regulate and to foresee everything. The wants of society are so varied, the intercourse between men is so active, their interests so multifarious, and their relations so extended, that it is impossible for the legislator to provide for every emergency. We know that never, or scarcely ever in any case, can a text of law be cited so clear and precise that good sense and equity will alone suffice to decide it. A question springs up: then what is to decide it? To this it is replied, that the office of the law is to fix, by enlarged views, the general maxims of right and wrong; to establish principles fruitful in consequences, and not to descend to the details of all questions which may arise upon each particular topic. It is for the magistrate and jurisconsult, penetrated with the general spirit of the law, to direct their application." Still, however, in those cases where there was no precise regulation, and the general spirit would not apply, other aids must be resorted to. Those indefinite principles, equity, natural law, were talked of: but it seems that the code only abrogated the old law, so far as it was inconsistent with the new; and where the new law is silent, each judge is to decide according to the law which formerly prevailed in the vicinity: so that a knowledge of the old

N 2

loi coutumiere and droit écrit is still partially necessary for the French lawyer.

The promulgation of the codes commences a new era in the French judicial literature. The greater part of ancient law books were rendered useless. At first, in the enthusiasm of the moment, it was imagined that the French law had arrived at a definitive perfection; that there remained nothing more than to apply literally, isolated from its origin and sources, a text of the new laws. However, this was soon found not to be the case, and that the labours of modern jurisconsults were required to explain and illustrate the new codes, and numerous commentators sprung up. Some confined themselves to enrich and overcharge it with notes and comparisons; others have commented at length, compiling, with painful care, on each article the lights of the ancient jurisconsults, or the decisions of the modern tribunals. Some few have taken a particular subject, and treated it with more or less depth. Napoleon, it is said, at the sight of the first Commentary on the Civil Code, exclaimed, "My code is lost."

Napoleon's fears from the labours of commentators.

General merits of the codes.

An unqualified assertion, of the immense utility of this great work of legislation for France, is due to it, in one point of view, without a moment's hesitation or doubt. It has accomplished the desires of some of the greatest men France or the whole world ever produced, by giving to a great nation an uniform system of law, and substituting to a certain extent one science of law in the room of hundreds of conflicting and contradictory local customs. But a collection of rules, without relation and systematic coherency, does not constitute the science of jurisprudence; and of the merit of its execution there is more room to doubt. It has numerous defects, some evidently resulting from the haste in which it was compiled, and the not having taken a wider range in the choice of subjects; others, and by far the most to be lamented (as want of scientific coherence), seem to arise from the difficulties which must inevitably present themselves in the execution of a task like this, and which peculiarly pressed on France. But it is both difficult and invidious for a foreigner to criticize a national work: we will, therefore, give the summary, furnished by a native of France, whose intelligence aud capacity have been highly estimated in his country. Speaking of the formation of the code, he says,—" It is this legislation which we now enjoy, and which forms our civil and positive life: our codes are embosomed in our manners; we love them as a conquest and a patrimony. The political element predominates; and science only appears in them as a subaltern condition. This was inevitable, since our codes were produced as the consequence, and by means of a political revolution. That Pothier, almost alone, furnished the materials of the code civil, is rather a source of congratulation than regret. It was a most happy circumstance that the framers, in their hasty creation, had Pothier to avail themselves of. Our forefathers, who so rapidly raised the codes between the tribune of the convention and the imperial throne, and who by their energetic promptitude obeyed marvellously their political calling, were neither speculative philosophers nor profound historians: thence the defects of their performances. The civil code is full of misconceptions of the dogmas of history; the code of procedure is an elegant resurrection of the practice of the Châtelet,[1] and has but little of what is rational about it, except in the first book, on the justices of the peace: our criminal procedure calls for reform, and above all in the correctional jurisdiction: lastly, the penal code offers a striking anarchy of principles the most contrary. At the same time, the civil code, notwithstanding its imperfections, is by far superior to the other four: it has inherited the riches of the ancient French law, the wisdom of our old customs, the labours of Dumoulin, Cujas, d'Aguesseau, and Pothier."[2]

[1] A court of justice at Paris.

[2] Lerminier, Introduction, &c., c. 20.

Napoleon's commission for revising the codes.

The experience of ten years served to render clear some of the errors and defects of the codes; and a revision of them was ordered by an imperial decree, dated 7th January, 1813. From the whole body of the laws published in the official bulletin, those which were still in force were to be taken and separated from those abrogated or grown into desuetude; 1. The obsolete laws were to be omitted; 2. Similar ones brought together; 3. Contradictory ones (antinomia) pointed out and resolved; 4. Questions proposed; 5. The laws of each sort collected from the others; 6. Full indices were to be made. This revision was never accomplished.

Restoration of the Bourbons.

By the charter of Louis XVIII., the restored monarch provided, that the courts of justice then actually existing should be maintained, and the civil code and the existing laws should retain their full force, except where they contradicted any provision of the charter. On the accession of Napoleon to the imperial dignity, the title of the "Code Civil of the French," as it was then called, was altered to that of the "Code Napoleon." On the restoration, it was again changed back to the old title; and titles suitable to the royal government were given to the public functionaries.

Revolution of 1830.

The fatal ordonnances of the 25th July, 1830, brought about a new revolution, which, without producing any material changes in the civil law, placed the younger branch of the Bourbons on the throne.

AN

ARRANGEMENT OF ENGLISH LAW,

IN THE FORM OF

THE CODE NAPOLEON.

PRELIMINARY TITLE.

Of the Laws in general; their Publication, Effect, and Application.

Parallel Articles of the French Code.

LAW,[1] in its most general and comprehensive sense, signifies a rule of action.[2] As applied to human actions, a law is a rule established by an authority which we are bound to obey.

If a man is contemplated by himself, as a being unconnected with other men, it is immediately seen that he has a right to follow, without restraint, his own natural desires in accordance with the will of his Creator; but when he is considered in relation to other men, it is evident, that as their desires are entitled to equal action with his own, some limit must be imposed, in order to give each their due share of action. The principle which decides how far the actions and desires of one man are to be restrained, in order not to infringe on those of others, so as to leave room for their equal action, is called justice.[3] In living in society then, in order to be just,

---

[1] The word "law" is derived from the Anglo-Saxon laga, laghe, lah; from the root lecgan, legan. As to the meaning of this word, and application in Anglo-Saxon times, see ante, p. 23, n. 2, and p. 20, n. 1.

[2] Blackstone, Com. v. i. p. 38.

[3] The Roman law accurately defines it as it is outwardly exhibited to us: Justitia est constans et perpetua voluntas, jus suum cuique tribuendi.—Inst. l. 1. tit. 1. in pr. But the Grecian philosopher gives us a more perfect notion of its

Parallel Articles of the French Code.

man is compelled to forego some of his desires, and his claim to unlimited appropriation of the natural productions of the earth. Now, supposing him inclined to be just, and willing to give the desires of others a fair action with his own, it is sometimes (unless directed by a rule) difficult, or even impossible, to decide on the proportion in which he ought to allow his neighbours' desires to restrain his own. Hence, it becomes necessary to predetermine the rights of all parties by fixed rules, founded, as far as possible, on the principles of right or abstract justice (the ars boni et æqui). The science which directs us in this object is called jurisprudence.[1] Every possible conflict of the desires of men with each other should be considered, their respective claims weighed, and some rules laid down to determine the rights of each before their desires come actually into conflict. Each such rule constitutes a law; and the whole system of rules, by which the mutual action of each is thus made consistent with the freedom of others, is called law.[2] When these rules are founded on an evident reason, that is to say, when it is evident (on attentive consideration, or after laborious investigation) in what proportion the desires of one man, or of one class of men, should be restrained, in order to allow the action of those of another, they are called Natural Laws; but as it is often impossible to discover this rule or proportion, in this case an Arbitrary rule (the will of the legislature) must be laid down, in order to decide between the conflicting desires of men. This is

---

essential nature. Justice, says Aristotle, is a medium between excess and defect; η δικαιοσυνη μεσοτης τις αν ειη υπερβολης και ελλειψεως.—Mag. Mor. l. 1, c. 34.

It is called just (δικαιον), from διχα, in two parts, as if it were a division into two parts (διχαιον); and the judge is called δικαστης, for διχαστης, a divider into two parts.—De Mor. Nic. l. 5, c. 7; see also c. 9.

[1] The principles of jurisprudence are the eternal laws of truth engraved on man's mind, and the constitution of nature: it may, therefore, well be defined in the same terms as philosophy, humanarum atque divinarum rerum notitia.

[2] It will be obvious that the word law (lex) is here used as synonymous with right (jus). They both signify the norma recti, and correspond with the old law maxim, lex est norma recti, and jus est norma recti. Et quicquid est contra normam recti est injuria.—3 Buls. 313.

especially the case as to rights which relate to objects purely the creation of society.

Parallel Articles of the French Code.

In this point of view, whether the reason be evident or not, the object being to lay down a rule for regulating the intercourse of man with man, so that the desires and free will of one may not be unfairly disturbed or interfered with by others, the law may be defined as the "rule of right;"[1] which, by defining their mutual relationships, enables us to decide when one or the other ought to give way:[2] and, from the necessity of decision between individuals, or between an individual and the state or community, whether the reason of a rule of right be apparent or not—whether it be what is called a natural law, or an arbitrary one—it is obligatory on the conscience, without regard to compulsion.[3]

In the foregoing observations, the law has been considered, in regard to its essential nature, as furnishing the rule which might enable persons desirous of doing justly, to determine on the proportion in which their natural rights to the unrestrained use of the bounties of Providence, or their artificial rights, arising purely from social advantages, ought to be limited by those of others; and it will have been perceived, that it differs but little

---

1 It is thus the law expressing, or being supposed to express, the rule of right for governing intercourse between man and man, (and if taken unrestrictedly in this point of view only), that the following legal maxims are to be understood:

Æquum et bonum est lex legum.—Hob. 224.

Ratio est anima legis.

Lex semper intendit quod convenit rationi.—Co. Lit. 78.

Nihil quod est contra rationem est licitum.—Ib. 97.

Lex est dictamen rationi.—Jenk. Cent. 117.

The law is the perfection of reason.

Lex deficere non potest in justitia exhibenda.—Co. Lit. 197; Jenk. Cent. 51.

Lex est ab æterno.—Jenk. Cent. 36.

Lex appetit perfectum.

Lex est ratio summa quæ jubet quæ sunt utilia et necessaria et contraria probibet.—Co. Lit. 319 b.

Contra veritatem lex nunquam aliquod permittit.—2 Inst. 252.

2 Quid sit jus et in quo consistit injuria, legis est definire.—Co. Lit. 158 b.

3 Non omnis quod licet oportet, sed quod non licet non oportet.

Parallel Articles of the French Code.

in that respect from the moral code.[1] This, though the most essential character of the nature of law, is not the only one; there are others which, in the existing state of things, are necessary to it; for men are not always willing[2] to control their desires from a regard to others; indeed the contrary, that men are generally prompted to pursue their own desires, regardless of the rights and interests of others, is notoriously the case; hence, voluntary submission not being to be expected, unless the relative strength of the parties is to decide between them when their desires are in conflict, it becomes necessary that the law should be not only the rule of right, but it must have a power of coercion. It must not only enable those inclined to act justly, to decide upon what is just, but it must be able to compel those not so inclined.

This power of coercion, arising out of the necessity of the case, may be vested (by consent, or derived, as in the earliest times, from a patriarchal authority) in one person; or it may be vested in a definite number or the whole community.

It need scarcely be here remarked, that in a barbarous state, the abstract science of law would be inappreciable; and the dictates of the judge, influenced greatly by his feelings and prejudices, would take the place of the rule of right. Customs would arise out of the circumstances of the times, or from a popular but indefinite conception of the rule of right, blinded more or less by national feelings, habits, and prepossessions. When civilization advances, the legislator seeks to discover the more abstract rule of right, and to make the habits of the people conform to it.

Much has been said about mutual compact and the

---

[1] A judicial law differs from a moral one only inasmuch as the former is applied to external actions, the latter to internal.

[2] At cum jus æquabile ab uno viro homines non consequerentur, inventæ sunt leges.—Cic. de Off. l. 2.

Parallel Articles of the French Code.

social contract, as being the original source of the authority of laws; but such notions, as to the primitive or barbarous state of society, are totally inapplicable, and the records of civilized nations do not inform us that such a contract ever had any real existence. These notions, therefore, are merely the creatures of fancy. The necessity of imposing some limit on the desires of men in the early state of society, was sufficient of itself to create an authority.

The legislative power may be vested in the whole body of the community, actually or virtually; or it may be placed in the hands of a person over whom society may have no direct control. If the rule of right is fairly sought, it does not signify greatly which of the two are clothed with authority. Perhaps, in the latter case, the knowledge of having public attention fixed on him, would make the legislation of a wise prince, in a highly civilized kingdom, even more strictly just, and less biassed by prejudice or interest, than in the former state of a community, or the majority of a community, legislating for itself: but in this case the law would be the common opinion of the community as to what is right.[1]

But by whomsoever the law is made, it is necessary it should be laid down before the parties are called upon to submit to it. The parties ought to have been made aware of it before it came into operation, that they might have regulated their conduct accordingly. It is more for the interest of society, that some known rule should be prescribed to prevent uncertainty, even though not strictly in accordance with the principles of reason or natural justice, than that it should be left for decision at the moment of action, or for litigation afterwards. The certainty of the legal rule is of more consequence to the well-being of society, than its exact correspondence with the norma recti—the perfection of reason.

---

[1] Lex est communis republicæ sponsio.
Lex est commune præceptum.—Papinian.

Parallel Articles of the French Code.

Municipal law may, therefore, be defined "a rule of civil conduct, prescribed by the supreme power in a state commanding what is right and prohibiting what is wrong."[1]

All municipal laws must be divided into three classes, namely:—constitutional, regulating the organization of government, judicial administration, and judicial proceedings:—civil, establishing and governing the rights and interests, personal capacities, and property of individuals:—and penal or criminal, for the punishment of infractions of the other laws.

Another division must also be made of the municipal law of England, into two kinds: which have been termed, the lex non scripta, the unwritten or common law; and the lex scripta, the written or statute law:[2] these terms are not strictly accurate. The common law, though it originated in the oral customary traditions of the people, is almost as much a lex scripta (written law) as the statutes. The main difference between the two is, that, in administering the common law, the judge has to commence his reasoning from the principles contained in the reports of decided cases and precedents, and to draw conclusions as to the particular law which is to govern the cases brought before him, so as to declare what that law is. In administering the statute law, he has to commence with a positive enactment in place of general principles, and to draw conclusions as to it, by way of interpretation, and to declare what it means.[3] The terms "scientific law and positive law" would perhaps more correctly distinguish the common and statute law from each other, than the terms "written and unwritten law."

The common law is the general customary law of the realm, and as such must be distinguished from the local and particular customs of certain districts or classes of

[1] 1 Bl. Com. 44. [2] Ib. 63.

[3] We say interpret and declare the meaning; for if it can be applied directly without doubt, the judge's office is not called into action.

Parallel Articles of the French Code.

persons. Originally the general customs of the country were verified by the evidence of the jurors who composed the court;[1] and particular customs must be proved.[2]

The scientific law must be again divided into two kinds: viz. common law and chancery law or equity. Chancery law or equity is very frequently confounded with natural equity; and even among English lawyers, a great many rules and definitions have been handed down from times, when the principles of chancery law were almost as uncertain as the ideas different persons have of natural equity are. Common law is often represented as being strictly bound by precedent, while equity is left almost entirely to the judge's notions of natural justice, which would for the most part be his arbitrary discretion; but these are totally erroneous views: for, on the one hand, the common law, as well as chancery, seeks to do natural equity;[3] and on the other, the principles of chancery law, or equity as it is called, are as much fixed by decided cases as those of common law.

The chief difference between the two arises, either out of the objects over which they have jurisdiction, from the forms of their procedure, or from the nature of the relief they give. The proceedings at law differ from their very first commencement from those in equity. Specific forms of complaint, applicable alike to whole classes of injuries, are adhered to at common law,[4] but not in chancery. In the latter, the defendant answers specifically on his oath the allegations of the plaintiff: a practice not known at law. The evidence in the latter is given vivâ voce, whereas in chancery it is written down in the form of depositions. At common law, the jury give their verdict on the points of fact at issue between the parties:

---

1 See ante, p. 50.

2 See ante, p. 46, n. 7.

3 Lex æquitate guadet.—Jenk. Cent. 36.

Equity is part of the law of England.

Jus sequitur æquitatem.—Co. Lit. 246; Hob. 224; Bract. b. 4, f. 186.

Bonus judex secundem æquum et bonum judicat et æquitatem stricto jure præfert.—Ib.

4 See ante, p. 119, and n. 2 and 3.

Parallel Articles of the French Code.

in chancery, the judge gives directions on facts admitted or proved. A judgment at common law is general, as that the party is entitled to a certain sum of money: a decree in chancery is specific, varying according to each circumstance of the case.

The rules and principles of law and equity are the same in almost every respect, as to those objects over which they have concurrent jurisdictions.[1] There are however, on the one hand, certain kinds of rights which the common law courts do not recognize, and over which the courts of equity have therefore exclusive jurisdiction, such as trusts and some others.[2] On the other hand it is a maxim, that equity cannot interfere where there is a remedy at law. Hence there may be two sets of interests or estates in the same property: the one recognized by the courts of law, and called legal; the other termed equitable; because exclusively administered in courts of equity or chancery. The courts of equity recognize legal interests and estates, though they consider them as subordinate to the equitable. And the same view is taken of a legal estate, and the same rules govern it in equity, as at common law. But there are also certain rules applicable to an equitable estate, in some respects different from those of a legal estate; these the common law does not recognize. Besides this, there are some few other points where the rules of law and equity differ: equity granting relief where justice cannot be obtained at common law.[3] But in such cases the two systems are not long in opposition, the law in effect giving way: and those rules of law which[4] are in plain opposition to the rules of "equity," are like obsolete statutes,—not expressly repealed; but incapable, practically, of being acted upon. The English common law, and equity or chancery law, therefore, do not constitute two distinct systems, applicable to the same interests and rights, but

[1] Æquitas sequitur legem.—Gilb. 136.

[2] Historical Introduction, ante, p. 122, 123. [3] Ib. ante, p. 144.

[4] Lex fingit ubi subsistit æquitas.—11 Rep. 90.

Parallel Articles of the French Code.

only one system of law; different parts of which are administered in two distinct courts, each having jurisdiction of different interests; and thus, the distinction between law and equity, as administered in the courts of chancery, is in some cases rather a difference of subject matter within their respective jurisdictions, and in others a difference in form of procedure and relief: than one which regards courts of equity as deciding merely by what is equitable between the parties, while common law is considered the more strict and severe application of the letter.

The common law has grown out of the general customs of the nation; and is now a highly wrought scientific system, governed by principles which are contained in, or illustrated by, precedent decisions. Out of it, with the aid of principles adopted from various sources, has grown chancery. The local and special customs[1] are what the old common law was, but of a more confined application.

The statute law has arisen as the deficiency or abuses of the common law have required an addition of new laws, or the correction of the old. The authority of parliament alone can change an established law, or make a new one[2] by act of parliament or statute. Whatever was at common law, and is not taken away by statute, still remains.[3] Where common law and statute law concur, the common law shall be preferred.[4] Statutes in the affirmative do not derogate from the common

---

[1] Consuetudo est altera lex.—4 Rep. 21.

Consuetudo præscripta et legitima vincet legem.—Co. Lit. 119.

Custome est un reasonable act, iterated, multiplied, and continued by the people de temps dont memory ne court.—Da. 32.

Consuetudo debet esse certa: nam incerta pro nullis habentur.—Ib. 33.

Ratio est formalis causa consuetudinis.

Customs and prescriptions against reason are void.—Co. Lit. 140.

In consuetudinis non diuturnitas temporis sed soliditas rationis est consideranda.—Ib. 141.

[2] Lex Angliæ nunquam sine parliamento mutare non potest.—2 Inst. 618.

[3] Co. Lit. 115. [4] 4 Rep. 71.

Parallel Articles of the French Code.

law.[1] Statutes, introductory of new law, made in the affirmative, imply a negative of all that is not in the purview.[2]

1. The mode of promulgating or making known these various kinds of laws, necessarily differs greatly. Laws may be prescribed and notified by universal tradition and long practice; and this is the case of the common law of England,[3] or general customs of the realm, which has acquired the force of law by a long and immemorial usage, and by the strength of custom and reception in this kingdom,[4] and therefore can require no new promulgation, and will be taken notice of by the judges of their own accord; but all private or local customs, except gavelkind and borough English, must be specially pleaded and proved.[5]

New laws may be notified, *vivâ voce*, by officers appointed for that purpose, as is done with regard to proclamations, and such acts of parliament as are appointed to be read in public assemblies;[6] or they may be notified by writing, printing, or the like, which is the general course taken with all our acts of parliament.[7]

An act of parliament, after having passed the Houses of Lords and Commons, as soon as it receives the Royal Assent becomes immediately the law of the land, without any thing further being required to give it sanction or executory force. It needs no formal promulgation, because every man in England is, in judgment of law, party to the making of an act of parliament, being present thereat by his representatives.[8] However, 5,500 copies of every public general statute, and 300 of every public, local, and personal statute, are printed by the king's printer for distribution.[9]

---

[1] Jenk. Cent. 24. [2] Hob. 298. [3] 1 Bl. Com. 45.

[4] Hale, History of the Law. [5] 1 Bl. Com. 76; ante, p. 189. and n. 2.

[6] Ib. 45. [7] Ib. 46. [8] Ib. 185.

[9] See address of the Lords and Commons, and answer of the King, 1 June, 1801. To devise any mode of publication that shall personally reach every individual is

Parallel Articles of the French Code.

The courts of law are bound to take notice of a general or public act ex officio, without its being particularly pleaded, or formally set forth, by the party who claims an advantage under it; but special or private acts, like particular customs, the judges are not bound to notice, unless they be formally shown and pleaded.[1] Copies of the statutes, printed and published by the king's printer, are conclusive evidence.[2]

Acts of parliament usually specify the time from which, according to the discretion of the legislature, they are to take effect; when, however, they do not do so, they become operative from the day on which they receive the Royal Assent[3] throughout the realm at all distances.

All laws should be made to commence in futuro, and 2.
be notified before their commencement;[4] and it is a rule and law of parliament, that regularly, nova constitutio futuris formam imponere debet, non præteritis.[5] Many instances, however, formerly occurred, of acts of parliament taking effect prior to their passing by legal relation to the first day of the session;[6] and a statute may have a retrospective action expressly given it by parliament,[7] whose authority is uncontrollable;[8] and such it often has, as in cases of private acts for divorces, bills of attainder, bills of pains and penalties for crimes.[9]

The common law is founded on past immemorial usage, or deduced from it as a consequence, and therefore is held to be always in being, although it may have to be

---

plainly impossible. Public exhibition, or reading of a new law, is disregarded (by those not immediately interested). Through the medium of the press new laws are most effectually promulgated to those concerned in their administration, or affected by them.

[1] 1 Bl. Com. 86.

[2] Extended to Irish statutes, 41 G. III. c. 90, s. 9.

[3] 33 Geo. III. c. 13.

[4] 1 Bl. Com. 46.

[5] 2 Inst. 292; 1 Bl. Com. 46; 2 Bing. 257.

[6] 1 Lev. 91; 4 T.R. 660.

[7] See Home v. Haig, 8 Bro. P. C. 196; 10 Rep. 55, Chancellor of Oxford's case; and cites Pl. C. 227 a, Stradling v. Morgan.

[8] 1 Bl. Com. 160.

[9] 1 Bl. Com. 46; 4 Bl. Com. 259.

Parallel Articles of the French Code.

declared or expounded by the judge, and applied to a past transaction; in the same manner as a statute, doubtfully worded, is held to mean what the judge interprets; and though this may seem a hardship, in both cases it is unavoidable.

3. Having now stated the nature, the mode of promulgation, and the time of commencing operation of the law, it remains to consider to what persons and things it is applied, and in what places;[1] and here we find,[2]

1. Laws applicable to all persons within the realm.
2. Laws applicable to property within the realm.
3. Laws attaching to the person of the subject wherever he is.

As a general principle it may be laid down, that the laws of every state bind all persons who are resident within it, whether natural-born subjects or aliens.[3]

As to matters of police, the common law considers crimes as altogether local, and cognizable and punishable exclusively in the country where they are committed.[4] No person shall be excused from punishment for crime, unless on the ground of infancy, idiotcy, mistake, chance, compulsion, &c.[5] And an alien coming into the kingdom, is bound by the laws and statutes of the realm;[6] for our law considers a foreigner to owe allegiance to the crown of England, and a submission to its laws, during his residence within the realm, in return for that protection to his person, his family, and his effects, which his residence ensures to him; and if he violate that

---

1 Extra territorium jus dicenti non paretur impune.—10 Co. 77.

2 Foreign jurists divide laws into *real* and *personal*. Personal laws are such as affect primarily the person, and which go with him wherever he goes, and into every country. Real laws are those which affect property: they are confined to a particular territory, and regulate the property with it.—See Story's admirable work on the Conflict of Laws.

3 Story, Conflict of Laws, 19.

4 Folliott v. Ogden, 1 H. Bl. 135; in error Ogden v. Folliott, 3 T. R. 733; Wolffe v. Oxholm, 6 M. & S. 99.

5 4 Bl. Com. 2.

6 32 Hen. VIII. c. 16, s. 9.

Parallel Articles of the French Code.

temporary allegiance by any act amounting to treason, or is otherwise guilty of any infraction of those laws,[1] he becomes thereby liable to the same penalty as a natural-born subject of the realm.[2]

All the authorities recognize the principle in its fullest import, that real estate within the realm is exclusively subject to the laws of this country.[3] Aliens cannot hold real property, otherwise than for a term of years,[4] if a merchant, but not otherwise;[5] though no officer of the crown would advise the king to seize the lease of an alien.

Where personalty is immoveable, as stock and other public funds; and wherever the subject-matter relates locally to England, the law of England must govern.[6] Moveable personalty follows the law of the country where the party was domiciled.[7]

To a certain extent the capacities or incapacities of an English-born subject follow him into every country; thus his incapacity for marriage by the law of England

---

[1] If a foreign ambassador, being pro rex, committeth here any crime which is contra jus gentium, as treason, felony, or other crime which is against the law of nations, he loseth the privilege and dignity of an ambassador, and may be punished here as any other private alien, and not be remanded to his sovereign but of courtesy. And so of contracts, that be good jure gentium, he must answer here. But if anything be malum prohibitum, by an act of parliament, private law, or custom of this realm, which is not malum in se jure gentium, or contra jus gentium, an ambassador residing here shall not be bound by any of them.—Coke, 4 Inst. 153; 1 Hale, P. C. 85, 100; Foster, C. L. Diss. 1, s. 7; 1 Bl. Com. 253; 4 Bl. Com. 70; Don Pantaléon Sa, 5 How. State Trials, 462.

The privilege of exemption of the servants of an ambassador in civil suits, under 7 Anne, c. 12, extends only to what is necessary to the personal convenience, the dignity, and the religion of the ambassador himself.—Novello v. Toogood, 2 D. & R. 833.

[2] Foster, C. L. 185.

[3] Robinson v. Bland, 2 Burr. R. 1079; 1 W. Bl. 234, 246, 259; Doe dem. Birtwhistle v. Vardill, 5 Barn. & Cress. 438.

Our courts have disclaimed all right to interfere with the legal course of devolution not only of land, but even of any right or charge affecting lands situated out of the limits of their territorial jurisdiction.—Elliot v. Lord Minto, 6 Mad. 16; Jerningham v. Herbert, 1 Taml. 103; Lansdown v. Lansdown, 2 Bligh, 60.

Actor sequitur forum rei.—Homes, L. T. 232.

[4] 2 Bl. Com. 249.

[5] Co. Lit. 2.

[6] Robinson v. Bland.

[7] Munroe v. Douglas, 5 Mad. 379.

Parallel Articles of the French Code.

is not removed by foreign residence.[1] But he may, by violation of law, forfeit many of the advantages of a natural-born subject, and place himself in the situation of an alien.[2]

4. Having stated the nature of law, the mode of giving a new enactment force, and the time and commencement of its operation, and the persons and things affected by it, we pass to the consideration of the office of the persons by whom it is administered; and their powers and duties in carrying it into execution.

The statute-book, notwithstanding its bulk,[3] must obviously be frequently silent, or insufficient to furnish rules for deciding the infinite variety of cases which come before the judges for determination; but where the statute law does not apply, the common law does; the latter cannot be presumed to be insufficient. Its first principle is, to apply the law decided in any previous analogous cases to the new ones. And there being no solemn, well-considered decision, the judge must resort to principles;[4] and when such a new case occurs, we have no right to consider it as one for which the law has not already provided.[5]

The judges are to decide according to the settled and established rules and ancient customs of the realm, approved for many succession of ages. Every judge at his creation takes an oath that he will not deny right to any man, though the king or others command the contrary.[6] The judges are, however, in consideration of

[1] Scrimshire v. Scrimshire, 2 Hag. C. 407; Doe v. Vardel, 5 Barn. & Cres. 438; Conway v. Beazley, 3 Hag. E. 639.—See, as to the capacity and incapacity of British subjects from Minority, Male v. Roberts, 3 Esp. N. P. 163; Legitimacy, 5 Barn. & Cres. 444, 3 Hag. E. 652; Lunacy, exparte Lewis, 1 Ves. 298.

[2] 1 Bl. c. 374, n. 8; 14 and 15 Hen. VIII. c. 4.

[3] Though its bulk appears to diminish by the side of the 104 volumes of French statutes (Bulletin des lois), since the Revolution up to 1835, and the three or four volumes probably added since then.

[4] Eaton v. Jaques, Dougl. 457; Roe v. Galliers, 2 T. R. 133.

[5] Mirehouse v. Rennel, 8 Bing. 515; 1 Moore & S. 683. Ratio potest esse allegari deficiente lege, sed ratio vera et legalis et non apparens. Law Max. Co. Lit. 191.

[6] 18 Ed. III. st. 4; 20 Ed. III. c. 1, 2.

Parallel Articles of the French Code.

their high character and difficult office, freed from all prosecutions for anything done by them in court which appears to have been an error of their judgment.[1] Nor is a judge of record liable to an action for anything done within his jurisdiction, in his judicial capacity.[2] If an action be brought against a judge of record, for an act done in his judicial capacity, he may plead that he did it as a judge of record, and that will be a sufficient justification.[3] The protection existing by law under our constitution, against judicial delinquency in the supreme judicatures of the kingdom, consists in the superintending power of parliament to address the crown to remove any judge.[4] If an inferior court misdemean itself, the Court of Queen's Bench has a superintending authority, and a mandamus will issue from that court to compel an inferior court to give judgment;[5] and where any subordinate court delays to do justice, a writ of procedendo ad judicium[6] may issue out of chancery commanding them in the Queen's name to proceed to judgment.[7]

In ancient days the jurors of the court used to testify or declare the law or custom, as well as decide the facts of the cases:[8] gradually, the law becoming too complex, and science superseding custom, the jury were confined to deciding on the facts of the case: and the judges declared the law in the place of allowing the jury to testify it. Hence the origin of the power of our judges, whose office, recognized by distinct enactments, 5.

---

[1] 2 Bac. Abr. 388. Whoever is clothed with a judicial character, in every kind of forum, when called upon in judicial capacity to decide in his respective forum, upon cases brought before him, is, although his decisions be illegal, and his judgments founded in error, protected from action.—Taafe v. Downes, Chief Justice of King's Bench in Ireland, by Hatchell.

[2] 1 Mod. 184; 2 Mod. 218; Hamond v. Howell; Garratt v. Ferrand, 4 Barn. & Cres. 625.

[3] Mostyn v. Fabrigas, Cowp. 172.

[4] 13 W. III. c. 5; Trial of Earl of Macclesfield, 16 Howell's State Trials, 767.

[5] 3 Bl. Com. 110; Brook v. Evans, 1 Stra. 113; Exparte Amherst, T. Raym. 214; Exparte Morgan, 2 Chitty, 250.

[6] Fitzherbert says, of the writ de procedendo ad judicium, that it appears from the writ that it lies as well against judges of record as other justices.—Nat. Brev.

[7] 3 Bl. Com. 109.

[8] Ante, p. 50.

Parallel Articles of the French Code.

increased in consequence and difficulty as the relations of society became more complex; and the maxim of our law now defines the province of the judge still to be, jus dicere non jus dare.

Every judge is sworn to determine not according to his own judgment, but according to the known laws and customs of the land; he is not delegated to pronounce a new law, but to maintain and expound the old one.[1] It is generally laid down, that if a case occurred, not within any general principle, or if any alteration of the law is necessary, recourse must be had to Parliament;[2] but, practically, some rule of law, principle, or analogy, applies. "Our common law system consists," says Mr. Justice Park, "in applying to new combinations of circumstances those rules of law which we derive from legal principles and judicial precedents: and for the sake of attaining uniformity, consistency, and certainty, we must apply those rules where they are not plainly unreasonable and inconvenient to all cases which arise; and we are not at liberty to reject them, and to abandon all analogy to them, in those to which they have not yet been judicially applied, because we think that the rules are not as convenient as we ourselves could devise."[3]

6. The law being made for the benefit of all the individuals of a community, though single individuals may by agreement waive their rights, they cannot be allowed to abrogate the law to the injury of the community; and therefore contracts which are opposed to the national policy and institutions,[4] and contracts which in their

---

[1] 1 Bl. Com. 69; 7 Durn. & E. 696; 1 Bro. & B. 563; 1 Atkins, 353; 4 Ves. 332; 4 Bro. C. C. 458; 1 Milne & K. 2904; Hale, Hist. C. L., c. 4.

[2] See Lord Kenyon, Durn. & East, 682. Ante, p. 191.

[3] Bing. 515.

[4] Procuring loans for the prosecution of war against a country at peace with us.—De Weitz v. Hendricks, 9 Moore, 586; 2 Bing. 314.

Contracts with a government not acknowledged by ours.—Thompson v. Powles, 2 Sim. 194; Jones v. Garcia del Rio, 1 Turn. & Russ. 299.

Contracts in violation of a monopoly granted.—Pattison v. Mills, 1 Dow. & Clarke, 342.

nature are founded in moral turpitude, and are inconsistent with good order and the interests of society, cannot be enforced.[1]

Parallel Articles of the French Code.

[1] Future illicit cohabitation and prostitution.—1 Selw. N. P. 59, 60; Walker v. Perkins, 3 Burr. 1568; 4 Barn. & Ald. 650; Lloyd v. Johnson, 1 Bos. & Pull. 340; Jones v. Randall, Cowp. 37; Appleton v. Campbell, 2 Carr. & P. 347.

Printing and circulation of irreligious publications; to promote or reward the commission of crimes; to corrupt or evade the administration of justice, see Com. Dig. Assumpsit, p. 7; Smith v. Stotesbury, 1 W. Bl. 204; 2 Burr. 924; Foxes v. Johnes, 4 Esp. 97; Willis v. Baldwin, Doug. 450; Walcot v. Walker, 7 Ves. 1; Southey v. Sherwood, 2 Meriv. 435; Lawrence v. Smith, Jacob, 471.

BOOK I.—OF PERSONS.

PRELIMINARY TITLE.

On the Subjects and Source of Civil Rights, and the causes affecting them in general.

Parallel Articles of the French Code.

A person in law is defined to be a man,[1] considered according to his state or condition. To constitute a person, two things are requisite: the one is a human nature,[2] the other is a legal state. The state (status) of a person is the condition, capacity, or incapacity, with which a human being is by law invested;—and it forms

[1] Persona, est civile nomen; homo, naturale.—Cuj. in Papin.

The word "person" is originally a Latin word (persona), signifying primarily a mask which actors wore on the stage, which being painted suitably to a character to be represented, and worn by every one who acted the part, the word came to signify the character itself which the actor played, and afterwards any character proper or assumed which any one sustained. It does not properly signify a man (so that another person must needs imply another man), for then the word "homo" would have served, and they needed not have taken in the word "persona," but rather it means one so circumstanced: and the same man, if considered in other circumstances (considerably different), is reputed another person; thus the same man may at once sustain the person of a king and a father, guardian; or, on the other hand, two or more individuals may constitute only one person in law. Husband and wife, having only one capacity or status, are one person, Co. Lit. 112 a., 1 Bl. Com. 442; and an incorporate society, for the same reason, are one person.

[2] Co. Lit. 7 b. 29 b. 2 a.; Brac. lib. 5, c. 30, s. 10.

Homo et persona in jure maxime differunt. Homo est cuicumque mens ratione prædita in corpore humano contingit. Persona est homo, cum statu quodam consideratus, s. 75.

Status est qualitas, cujus ratione homines diverso jure utuntur: isque est vel Naturalis vel Civilis, qui iterum in statum libertatis, civitatis, et familia dispescitur. L. ult de ff. cap. minut. Certissimum ergo juris axioma est: quicunque nullo statu gaudet, jure Romano non persona, sed res habetur, s. 76.

Servus itaque est homo: est etiam *persona*, quatenus cum statu *naturali* consideratur: L. 22 pr. ff. de leg. jur.: sed ratione status civilis est *απροσωπος*. L. 32, s. 2, de legat 2 sine capite, s. 4; Inst. de cap. demin: immo pro nullo et mortuo habendus. L. 2 & 209 ff. de reg. jur. quia nec statu familiæ, nec civitatis nec libertatis quabet, s. 77.

Elementa juris civilis secundum ordinem institutionem, a. Jo. Gottl. Heineccio, I. C.; lib. i. tit. 3, de jure personarum.

Parallel Articles of the French Code.

the qualification by virtue of which he exercises his rights.[1]

In the English law we scarcely know the distinction between the person and the man; and it is only where some portion of the human race are deprived of all capacity, in a state of slavery, that there are any individuals who are not, civilly, persons.[2] For many centuries, if not from the earliest period of English legal history, every human being has had some rights and capacities,[3] and therefore has been regarded as a person; so that we have come to consider the term "person" as quite synonymous with human being. To a certain extent it really is so: but the municipal civil law can only recognize the acts of the persons, that is, the acts of men in respect of the capacities or incapacities with which they are clothed; and it is obvious that the condition or state (status) of an individual person may vary very much in a civil view, and still more in a penal or political one (as from civil death, outlawry, or the place of his residence, or other circumstances), while his natural state and his capacity, as a man, remains unaltered; and therefore it is evident, that there is a real distinction between the person and the man.[4]

---

[1] It is not necessary to make any apology for using these terms (which may sound strange to the English lawyer), seeing that they have been, in recent times, used by Lord Eldon.—In Head v. Head, 1 Turner, 138, where he employs the words *status et conditio;* and in the period of the Norman lawyers, after the revival of the study of the civil law, the terms *status personæ* is frequently used by them. See Glanville, lib. 5; Brac. lib. 1, c. 6, et seq.; and probably the use of the word, though not its precise meaning, was derived from the Roman law.

The maxim, mulieres ad probationem *status* hominis admitti non debent, is quoted by our great common law luminary, Coke.—Co. Lit. 6.

[2] Among the Romans slavery existed, and the distinction between such as were and such as were not civil persons is strongly marked.—See Heineccius, quoted in the preceding page, note 2.

[3] See, respecting slaves as to the status of persons, Glanville, lib. 5, and Brac. l. 1, c. 6 (who copies the words of the civil law, prima divisio personarum hæc et brevissima quod omnes homines aut liberi aut servi: the very words of Justinian, Inst. l. 31, tit. 3), and particularly Brac. lib. 1, c. 11, s. 3, servi sub potestatem dominorum sunt.

[4] The distinction between the natural man and the civil person has been clearly and nicely appreciated by the English law.—See a curious consequence mentioned in 7 Rep. 13 b. 14 a. arising from this distinction.

Parallel Articles of the French Code.

The civil condition of a British subject is derived from a mixture of the Germanic law of the Anglo-Saxons and the feudal law of the Normans[1] (the laghe and the ligeance); and as the lawyers of the latter race were more learned and acute than those of the former, the English theory of personal rights, as well as property, owes its consistency to the feudal doctrines, while its practical operation is in spirit Saxon.[2]

The first principle of the feudal law is that of dependance;[3] and the same forms a fundamental element of the English law of persons; and from it the British subject derives the peculiarities of his civil state. The sovereign, as we have already stated, is the source from whence justice and privileges[4] are supposed to flow (the fons justitiæ); and though this is, if taken by itself, a somewhat harsh maxim, it bears a different character when it is remembered that social rights are the offspring of society, and when the sovereign is considered as the representative, or a personification of the state,[5] and as

---

1 At the same time as the person was made a lawful man (see Spelm. Gloss. Legamannus, a lagaman, or lahman), or freeman, on which all his rights depended, by being sworn into the Anglo-Saxon frankpledge, or burgh (see ante, pp. 20, 21, 22, 23, and notes, ib.); he was also made a subject, or liegeman. This easily accounts for the one being, to a certain extent, identical with the other. The individual must be a liegeman to be a lagheman, or lahman, and entitled to the privileges thence derived.

2 See b. 1, title 1.

3 Ante, pp. 65, 6, 7; Glanville, l. 9, c. 4.

4 Le Roy est l'original de touts franchises.—Law Max.; Keilw. 138; but on the other hand, plus valet vulgaris consuetudo quam regalis concessio, Co. Cop. s. 31.

5 As the rights of the crown often affect the civil rights of individuals, it is necessary to state the nature of those rights. We have already stated that the Anglo-Saxon and Anglo-Norman monarchs, following the Frankish example, ante, p. 33 & n. 1, affected to continue the government of the Roman emperors. By the lex regia, ante, p. 113, n. 3, the imperial royalty was the personification of the Republic; and as Louis XIV., in the plenitude of his despotism, said "L'Etat c'est moi," so the successor of Augustus might have said "I am the Roman people." Part of this theory was admitted, and continues (for conveniency sake) still to form part of the law of England, though, as we have seen, governed by the principles of freedom, ante, pp. 113, 114: and the crown is still, besides its political capacity, regarded, for the purposes of civil law, as the state embodied or personified, as the following law maxims show.—Rex, est caput et salus Reipublicæ, 4 Rep. 124; Rex, est major singulis, minor universis, Bract. l. 1, c. 8; Rex, est lex vivens, Jenk. Cent. 17; Rex, tuetur legem, et lex tuetur jus, Co. Lit. 130. The king is the head

Parallel Articles of the French Code.

the parent of the people (parens patriæ).[1] And such the law considers the crown; so that the interests and rights of the public are entirely represented by the interests and rights of the crown:[2] and, instead of considering persons as citizens or foreigners, our law regards them according to the definite rule of the feudal law, namely, as subjects or not subjects, considering whether the individual is entitled on the one hand to protection from the crown, and rights and privileges, in return for the allegiance or subjection which is due on the other hand. Protection means the securing to the person the full enjoyment of his state and condition, or the rights with which the law invests him against all persons, friends or enemies. For our purpose, it is unnecessary to define subjection; but, according to the feudal law, every subject owed certain duties to his lord when he entered his allegiance, and professed himself his liege man; and this subjection bore with it in return the duty of protection on the part of the sovereign:[3] and, according to the English law, which still presumes the subject to have taken the oath of allegiance, allegiance is the source from whence the British subject derives his peculiar rights and privileges—it is the essence of the law,[4] which invests him with his civil state.

Allegiance, or ligeance (à ligando), is the mutual bond and obligation between the king and his subjects,

---

of the law and the fountain of justice. Lex est anima regis et Rex est anima legis. Potestas regis est facere justitiam, 2 Inst. 374. In ambiguis casibus semper præsumitur pro rege. Rex nunquam moritur. Nec tempus nec locus occurrit regi.—Jenk. Cent. 190, 83; 2 Inst. 273. Quando jus domini regis et subditi concurrunt, jus regis præferri debet, 9 Rep. 129.

[1] Bonus rex nihil a bono patre differt et patria dicitur à patre, quia habet communum patrem, qui est pater patriæ. Law Max.—7 Rep. 13 b.

[2] See 7 Rep. 10, 11, 12.

[3] Ante, pp. 68, 69, and p. 35, n. 2. Protectio trahit subjectionem et subjectio protectionem.—Co. Lit. 65.

Sicut subditus Regi tenetur ad obedientiam, ita Rex tenetur ad protectionem, merito igitur ligeantia dicitur à ligando, quia continet in se duplex ligamen.—7 Rep. 5.

[4] Ligeantia est quasi legis essentia.—Co. Lit. 129 a.

Parallel Articles of the French Code.

whereby subjects are called his liege subjects (liegemen), because they are bound to obey and serve him, and he is called their liege lord, because he is bound to maintain and defend them;[1] and it is either natural and perpetual (alta ligeantia), when founded on the relation in which every man stands to the crown, as the head of that society whereof he is born a member: it is then an incident inseparable from him.[2] Or, allegiance is local and temporary (ligeantia infima), founded on the protection a foreigner enjoys for his person, his family, and his effects, during his residence here; and it ceases whenever he withdraws with his family and effects.[3]

Persons thus, by the law of England, deriving their legal state from their allegiance, are divided in several classes, in consequence of the nature of the beings invested with a legal condition, and according to how that legal state is modified by various causes. According to the nature of the objects invested with capacity, persons are, by the law of England, divided into natural and artificial.[4] Natural persons are such as the God of nature formed men, as each individual; artificial persons are such as are created and devised by human laws for the purposes of society and government, as incorporate bodies.[5] The state and civil condition of individuals is modified (and, therefore, persons are to be distinguished) according to the following circumstances:—their allegiance; hence, they are divided into natural born subjects, alien enemies, friends, denizens, naturalized persons:[6] as they have forfeited their privileges, and become aliens for certain purposes or periods, civilly dead, attainted, and outlawed:[7] by their being able to prove their condition:[8]

[1] Skene, de expos. verb, quoted in 7 Rep. 5.—Co. Lit. 129 a.

[2] Ligeantia naturalis nullis claustris coercetur, nullis metis refrænatur, nullis finibus premitur.—7 Rep. 10.

Nemo patriam, in quâ natus est, exuere, nec ligeantiæ debitum ejurare possit. Co. Lit. 129 a.

[3] Forst. C. L. 183.

[4] Co. Lit. 2, a.; 1 Bl. Com. 123.

[5] The French civil code contains no chapter on this subject.

[6] B. 1, tit. 1, c. 1.

[7] Ib. c. 2.

[8] Ib. tit. 2.

Parallel Articles of the French Code.

the place of their abode, hence the home is to be distinguished from a mere residence:[1] by their absence, permanent or fraudulent, from home:[2] by their sex, marriage,[3] and divorce,[4] and the consequences as to legitimate or illegitimate issue:[5] and to a certain extent by adoption:[6] by their age as minors and majors:[7] by being in their own right or by another, guardian, ward, committee, lunatic;[8] and by numerous other causes.[9]

TITLE I.

OF THE ENJOYMENT AND PRIVATION OF CIVIL RIGHTS.

CHAPTER I.

Of the Mode of acquiring the Enjoyment of Civil Rights.

The rights of a person are either political, arising from his relation with the government of the society to which he belongs; or civil, from his relations with individuals. We are here considering the latter: and it may be laid 7.
down as a general rule, that in the law of England the enjoyment of civil rights is independent of political rights or privileges; and though many persons do not possess the qualification for exercising political privileges, as for example women and children, yet as a general rule their civil condition is unaffected by it, and they are entitled to the enjoyment of the same private civil rights, given by the general law of the land, as they would have been if possessed of those political qualifications. But in some particular cases the civil state[10] of natural born subjects

---

[1] B. 1, tit. 3. [2] Ib. tit. 4. [3] Ib. tit. 5.
[4] Ib. tit. 6. [5] Ib. tit. 7, 9. [6] Ib. tit. 8.
[7] Ib. tit. 10. [8] Ib. tit. 11.

[9] Infamy, nobility, excommunication, and a few others, are omitted in the French civil code.

[10] If it were not for the abstract principle, recognized equally by the English and the Roman law, (omne jus personarum causa constitutum est. Inst.),

Parallel Articles of the French Code.

is slightly affected by the local customs and privileges, closely connected with the ancient political privileges of certain boroughs and districts: thus the right and condition, capacities and incapacities of the freemen and burgesses, their wives and children, of certain boroughs, differ from that of other persons as to some civil acts which they have power to do; for example: in some boroughs a married woman has a capacity to convey her property without the same formalities as are in general requisite. But such variations are so rare, and so strictly local, as not to call for our further notice.

We have now to consider how the civil condition (status) is acquired, or its enjoyment affected, according to the law of England, by the parentage of a person, and the allegiance or protection under which he is supposed to live at the time of birth. Of the persons deriving the civil rights from the English law, and affected by birth, place, or parentage, there are three
8. classes. The first class are natural born subjects, all of whom are equal before the law, and entitled to the full enjoyment of civil rights; and for them the rights, privileges, and duties, are, by the law of the land, generally created: special exception only conferring on others those rights and privileges. The second class are aliens; and the third are those who, though born aliens, have been admitted partially or entirely to the civil condition of a natural born subject by naturalization or denization.[1]

9. Of the first class, or natural born subjects, are all such as are born within the allegiance or protection of the Crown of England;[2] and the children of aliens, born here in England, are, generally speaking, natural born subjects, and entitled to all the privileges of such,[3] pro-

---

these variations might perhaps in some cases be considered as attached to the things rather than as affecting the civil status of the parties.—Onslow v. Onslow, 1 Sim. 18, Honorary Freemen.

[1] See 1 Bl. C. c. 10.

[2] Ib.; 2 Bl. Com. 250, and the celebrated case of Calvin, 7 Rep. 1.

[3] 1 Bl. Com. 374; Co. Lit. 8 a.

vided such aliens be at the time under the protection or temporary allegiance of the English crown.[1]

Parallel Articles of the French Code.

And as a natural born subject cannot divest himself of his allegiance (and where there is allegiance there is also protection), a natural born subject, though not within the dominions of the crown, is still under allegiance, and entitled to protection; consequently all persons, though born out of the dominions of the crown of England, whose fathers or grandfathers, by the father's side, were natural born subjects under the allegiance of the crown, are held to be natural born subjects.[2] But if such ancestor were out of protection, as a traitor or outlawed felon, or in the service of an enemy,[3] his children would not be natural born subjects. And they whose more remote ancestor than a grandfather was the last actually to enjoy the rights of an English subject, are presumed not to have retained their allegiance. A woman however is supposed, by the law of England, to be under the same protection and allegiance as her husband; and therefore the issue of an English woman, by an alien born abroad, is not a natural born subject;[4] but otherwise, if the issue were born in England.[5] 10.

An alien is one born out of the ligeance of the crown.[6] 11.

There is no reference to any reciprocal internal regulation of the alien's country, nor any distinction among aliens, except those of friends and enemies.

An alien enemy is a subject to one that is an enemy[7]

1 Calvin's case, 7 Rep. 6.

2 7 Anne, c. 5; 4 Geo. II., c. 21; 13 Geo. III., c. 2, s. 1.

3 4 Geo. II. c. 21, s. 2; Co. Lit. 8 a. n. 1, 129 a.

4 Collingwood v. Pace, 1 Vent. 422; Doe dem. Duroure v. Jones, 4 T. R. 300; 25 Edw. III.

5 Collingwood v. Pace, 1 Vent. 422. It is nec cœlum, nec solum (neither the climate or the soil), but ligeantia and obedientia that makes the subject born.—7 Rep. 6.

6 7 Rep. 18. Alienigena est alienæ gentis seu alienæ ligeantiæ, qui etiam dicitur Peregrinus, Alienus, Exoticus, Extraneus, &c.—7 Rep. 10.

Extraneus est subditus qui extra terram, i. e. potestatem regis natus est.—7 Rep. 16.

7 Hostes sunt qui nobis, vel quibus nos bellum decernimus, cœteri proditores prædones.—7 Rep.

Parallel Articles of the French Code.

to the king,[1] or under the allegiance of a state at war with England:[2] all others are friends.

As to the rights and capacities bestowed by our law on aliens, alien enemies have no rights, no privileges, unless by the king's special favour, during the time of war;[3] but the king, by the proclamation of war, usually qualifies it by permitting the subjects of the enemy resident here to continue so long as they peaceably demean themselves; and such are to be deemed alien friends in effect.[4]

Alien friends are under the king's protection.[5] They may acquire personal property, or hire leasehold property; but they cannot hold real property[6] except with the king's licence. They may sue, and be sued; and may make a will of personalty.[7] They may trade, subject to certain restrictions and higher duties.

A person suing in this country cannot, by virtue of any regulations in his own country, enjoy greater advantage than other suitors here; and he ought not therefore to be deprived of any superior advantage which the law of this country may confer.[8]

The privilege of trial, per medietate linguæ (that is, by a jury half composed of aliens), is conceded by the law of England to foreigners on trials for felony. By statute 28 Edward IV. c. 13, half the jury shall be aliens,

---

1 Co. Lit. 129 b.

2 Sparenburg v. Bannatyne, 1 Bos. & Pul. 163.

3 1 B. C. 373. A contract made with an alien enemy in time of war, and of such a nature that it endangers the security, or is against the polity of the country, is void: such are policies of insurance to protect an enemy's trade. And however valid a contract originally may be, if the party become an alien enemy, he cannot sue; but if the crown do not, during the war, lay hands on the debt and recover it, then on the return of peace the rights of the contracting alien are restored, and he may himself sue.—Antoine v. Morshead, 6 Taunt. 267.

A prisoner of war may sue and be sued in our courts, upon contracts entered into by him whilst a prisoner, or upon engagements to which he may have been previously liable, just as other aliens may.—Sparenburgh v. Bannatyne, 1 Bos. & Pul. 163.

4 Co. Lit. 129, n. 3.

5 Magna Charta, c. 30; 1 Bl. Com. 260.

6 7 Rep. 17; ante, p, 195.

7 1 Bl. C. c. 10, p. 372.

8 De la Vega v. Vianna, 1 B. & Ad. 284.

Parallel Articles of the French Code.

except in case of felony by Egyptians, within 1 and 2 Philip and Mary, c. 4; or in case of treason.[1]

An alien woman, married to a natural born subject, still remains an alien,[2] though she is entitled to dower 12.
if she marries with the licence of the king;[3] and her children[4] by such husband would not be aliens, she being sub potestate viri et quasi, under the allegiance of the British crown.[5]

An alien, by the common law, may come into this 13.
country in time of peace without a safe conduct; and an alien friend, having taken up a residence here,[6] and being tacitly permitted to remain,[7] is entitled to all the civil benefits an alien can enjoy without any express permission.

There are two methods by which the civil condition (status) of persons born out of the legiance of the crown, may, by the law of England, be made more similar to that of natural born subjects; namely, by naturalization or by denization.

By naturalization (which can only be by act of parliament), an alien is put in exactly the same state (ligeantia acquisita) as if he had been born in the king's legiance except only that he is incapable of being a member of of the privy council, or parliament, holding offices, grants, &c.

By denization (which is by the king's letters patent),[8]

[1] Hale, P.C. 271. [2] Co. Lit. 31 b; 3 Bl. Com. 131. [3] Ib. 31, n. 9; 129 b. n. 4.

[4] Ante, p. 29. Lex Angliæ nunquam matris sed semper patris conditionem imitari partum judicat.—Co. Lit. 123. [5] See Cro. Car. 602.

[6] We do not consider ourselves called upon to consider passports, 1 Bl.Com. 259, or the regulations of the Alien Registration Act, 6 & 7 Wm. IV. c. 11, repealing 7 Geo. IV. c. 54, because they relate rather to the political or penal law, than affect the civil condition. Any subject, being in league, may come into this realm without licence: though a monarch cannot, 7 Rep. 21; and see this principle recognized, Wells v. Williams, Ld. Raym. 282, 3. The only case in which the want of licence can be taken advantage of in civil matters, is that of an alien enemy. See Chitty's Pleading; Stevens' Pleading.

[7] The king can, at any time, by proclamation, order aliens to leave the kingdom.

[8] Taking the oath of allegiance sworn in the leet is no denization.—14 H. IV. fol. 6; 7 Rep. 5.

Parallel Articles of the French Code.

an alien acquires a kind of middle state. He may take lands by devise or purchase, and his issue born *after*, not those before denization, may inherit from him.[1] He is not excused from the alien's duty, and other mercantile burthens, and he is incapable of holding office, being member of parliament, or privy council.[2]

14. Protection being consequent upon allegiance and sub-
15. jection, and subjection co-extensive with protection; a question naturally arises how far the jurisdiction of the courts of the English crown extends, over persons or things done, out of the legiance or realm.

In an international point of view, jurisdiction, to be rightfully exercised, must be founded either upon the person or the thing being within the territory;[3] and at common law, until there is some one within the jurisdiction of the court whom he can sue, no one has a complete right to prosecute an action with effect. If a party owing a debt in this country be absent from the kingdom, his goods may be distrained, if there be any in the jurisdiction of the court, or seized by foreign attachment, according to the custom of London, or his person, if a subject, may be outlawed. In the Court of Admiralty there is a personal citation of non-resident subjects and foreigners, by posting them upon the Royal Exchange in London.

Contracts respecting personal property have no situs, no locality; they follow the person of the creditor,[4] though the remedy must be according to the law of the place where they are sought to be enforced.[5] A party, whether a natural born subject or an alien, upon becoming amenable to the process of our superior courts, by presence

---

[1] Kinds of denization, as in tail, for life, &c.—7 Rep. 6—18.

[2] 1 Bl. Com. 374; 7 Rep. 7.

[3] Extra territorium jus dicenti impune non paretur, 10 Rep. 77; Story, 450.

[4] Thorne v. Watkins, 2 Ves. 35.

[5] An obligation made beyond the seas may be sued here in England, in what place (venue) the plaintiff will.—Co. Lit. 261 b.

Parallel Articles of the French Code.

within the realm, will be held judicially answerable for contracts entered into by him, whether at home or abroad; and whether with foreigners or natural born subjects of Great Britain; and will be liable to all remedies for the enforcement of such contracts allowed by our law, even though such remedies may exceed those to which the party would be liable in his own country.[1] In construing contracts, the law of the country in which they were made must govern, but the remedy upon them must be pursued by such means as the law points out where the parties reside.[2]

When persons resident abroad sue in this country (as 16.
the court in which they sue can have no authority over their persons, and they may remove their property), in order to compel them to pay the defendant the costs he sustains if awarded to him, the courts (on the application of the defendant) will not allow the party residing abroad to proceed and put the defendant to expense, until there is sufficient under the subjection of the court to do equal justice to either party, in whose favour the judgment may be given.

In cases where the plaintiff is permanently resident abroad (domiciled), whether a native or an alien, he may, both at law and in equity, be compelled to give security for costs of suit, and all legal proceedings may be stayed in the meanwhile.[3] The fact of his possessing estates in land in this country, of whatever value, affords no reason why he should not give security for costs:[4] but it will not be ordered by the courts in cases of mere temporary absence;[5] nor where the plaintiff is in the

---

[1] Antoine v. Morshead, 6 Taunt. 267; Flack v. Holm. 1 Jac. & W. 405; De la Vega v. Vianna, 1 B. & Ad. 284.

[2] Melan v. D. of Fitzjames.

[3] Seilaz v. Hanson, 15 Ves. 26; Cole v. Beale, 7 Moore, 613; Weeks v. Cole, 14 Ves. 518.

[4] Ld. Lucan v. Latouche, 1 Hogan, Irish Rep. 448.

[5] Hoby v. Hitchcock, 5 Ves. 698; 2 Dick. 775.—See Tidd, 9 ed. 534, Archb.

Parallel Articles of the French Code.

king's service,[1] nor against an ambassador or judge.[2] But an officer in the military service of the East India Company has been held liable to give security for costs, on the ground that he is by his duty compelled to reside in a foreign settlement, and his intention of returning home cannot be presumed.[3]

CHAPTER II.

OF THE LOSS OF CIVIL RIGHTS.

SECTION 1.

Of the Loss of Rights and Privileges by Forfeiting the Condition of a Natural born Subject.

17. A natural born subject may lose the rights which he derives either from being in the legiance, or the law (laghe).

Natural born subjects have a great variety of rights which they acquire by being born within the king's legiance, and which they cannot forfeit by any distance of place or time, but only by their own misbehaviour;[4] and, on the other hand, a natural born British subject cannot at his own will and pleasure divest himself of his native duties. He may go into other countries, and acquire privileges there, but still his native rights and duties adhere to him;[5] and so sacred is this birthright of an Englishman, that no alteration in it can he effect but by act of parliament: not even by the sole act

---

1 2 M. & R. 404; 2 Dowl. 578.—See Domicil.

2 Colebrook v. Jones, 1 Dickens, 154; Stanley v. Hume, 1 Hogan's Rep. 12.

3 Powel v. Bernard, 1 Hogan's Rep. 144.

4 1 B. C. 371.

5 Sir John Nicholls, in Stanley v. Bernes, 3 Hag. 374.

Parallel Articles of the French Code.

of the king, much less by any act of his own, without the concurrence of the crown.[1]

But though a natural born subject cannot voluntarily emancipate himself from his natural allegiance, so as to exempt him from the duties incident hereto,[2] yet he may, by his violation of law, forfeit many of the advantages. Thus, as the being in allegiance and subjection to the king is the cause of the extension of the protection of the law and civil rights and privileges to a subject, when he attempts to throw off that allegiance, or violates it by acting in a manner contrary to that allegiance and subjection, or disobeys the commands of his liege lord, he forfeits his right to that protection, and to those rights and privileges.

There are two ways in which, by his own act, the right and privileges of a natural born subject of the British crown may be forfeited or suspended for a time: 1st, By becoming the sworn servant of a foreign prince or state; 2nd, By residence, whether naturalized or not, in the territory of a country at war with Great Britain without licence from the crown, or in the territory of a country at peace after proclamation to return.

Any engagement with a foreign state, which subjects the party to an influence or control inconsistent with the allegiance due to the crown of these realms, is a contempt against the prerogative, and a high misdemeanor at common law. Therefore, if a subject enter into the service of a foreign potentate, or receive a pension from

---

[1] Pp. 203, 4, 5. It should seem, however, that with the consent of the crown, especially if ratified by parliament (as in the treaty recognizing the independence of the United States), that a natural born subject may become, to all intents and purposes, an alien.—Wood, Lect. v. i. p. 382; 22 Geo. III. c. 46; Doe dem. Thomas v. Acklam, 2 B. & C. 779.

Persons who adhered to Great Britain, at the time of the recognition of the independence of the United States, would not have been allowed afterwards, of their own accord, to throw off their allegiance.—Auchmuty v. Mulcaster, 5 B. & C. 74, and vice versa; Doe v. Acklam, 2 B. & C. 779.

[2] See the cases of Dr. Storey, 1 Hale, P. C. 96; of Townley, Fost. 71; of Æneas Macdonald, 18 Howell's State Trials, 858; Fost. 59.

Parallel Articles of the French Code.

a foreign state, without the licence of the king, it is an indictable offence.[1]

By 14 and 15 Henry VIII. c. 54, a native born subject going abroad, and becoming the *sworn* subject to any foreign prince or state, shall, while abroad, pay such impositions as aliens do.

The 3 Jac. I. c. 4, makes it felony for any person whatever to go out of the realm to serve any foreign prince or state, without having first taken the oath of allegiance.

All trading with an alien enemy is unlawful, unless by the king's licence;[2] and, by doing so, the natural born subject puts his goods in the situation of those of an enemy, and liable to seizure:[3] and a contract made in time of war with an alien enemy, cannot be enforced here, even by a native.[4] Where a natural born subject resides under the allegiance and protection of a hostile state for commercial objects, he is to be considered to all civil purposes as much an alien enemy as if he were born there;[5] but if his residence in an enemy's country be for the purposes of trade, licensed by the government of this country, it does not constitute a disability.

A natural born subject may also be a citizen of another country (as America), and entitled to all the advantages of that character.[6] Where there can be no conflict of duties in claiming and exercising the privileges which belong to the character of a citizen of another country, one natural born subject may have those privileges

---

[1] 1 Hawk. c. 22, s. 3; 4 Bl. Com. 122; 1 East, P. C. 81.

[2] Potts v. Bell, 8 T. R. 54.

[3] The Jonge Klassina, 5 Rob. 297; The Hoop, 1 Rob. 216.

[4] Willison v. Pattison, 7 Taunt. 439.—See ante, p. 208, n. 3, & p. 198, & n. 4, ib.

[5] O'Mealey v. Wilson, 1 Camp. 482; M'Cound v. Hector, 3 B. & P. 113; Pearce v. Cowie, Holt, N. P. 69. See also De Metton v. De Maltis, 12 East; Kennington v. Inglis, 8 East; Mariav. v. Hall, 1 Taunt. 33 n.; Antoine v. Morshead, 1 Marsh, 558; 6 Taunt. 558.

[6] The circumstances of his coming over here for a temporary purpose does not deprive him of those advantages. Wilson v. Marryatt, 8 T. R. 31; in error, 1 B. & P. 430; Scott q. t. v. Schwartz, Com. Rep. 677; Reeve's L. of Shipping, 252.

Parallel Articles of the French Code.

which another of the king's subjects has not. A native born subject may be entitled to the privileges of a neutral country, as well as those of a British subject, while he resides in a neutral country.[1] It was considered that a person naturalized abroad, could not avail himself of his privilege of trading, as an Englishman, without returning to this country to reside, or fixing his domicil here.[2]

By naturalization in a foreign country, a subject may entangle himself in difficulties and a conflict of duties,[3] but he is still a native born subject;[4] and, notwithstanding his naturalization, when in this country he may be restrained from going out of the kingdom by ne exeat regno; and when abroad he might be recalled by the king's proclamation.[5] It is a high misprision and contempt, if a subject neglect to return from beyond the seas when commanded by the king so to do; and his lands may be seized until he does return.[6]

As the law sets its face against depriving a subject of 18.
his birthright, so it allows him easily to recover it; insomuch so, that a native born British subject, who may have become liable to alien duties, or have lost any of his native privileges, reacquires them by a return to this country;[7] and even while returning (in itinere) to his native country.[8] All the authorities seem recon-

---

[1] Bell v. Reid, & Bell v. Buller, 1 M. & S. 726; Marryat v. Wilson, 1 B. & P. 430.

[2] Com. 690. For some purposes, in the Court of Admiralty, it has been laid down that, an Englishman residing and trading abroad (as in Holland) is just as much a foreign (Dutch) merchant as the native of any other state (as a Dane or Swede) would be.—See Domicil.

[3] Hale, v. i. p. 6.

[4] Nemo patriam, in quâ natus est, exuere, nec ligeantiæ debitum ejurare possit. Co. Lit. 129 a.

A foreign prince was about to appoint, as minister to our court, a native born subject (Sir Benjamin Thompson, Count Rumford)—the British government signified that he could not be received in that station.

[5] Dy. 296 a.

[6] 1 Hawk. c. 22, s. 4; 4 Bl. Com. 122.

[7] 14 & 15 Hen. VIII. c. 4, s. 3.

[8] The Snelle Zeylder, cited 3 Rob. 21. See also La Virginie, 5 Rob. 99.

Parallel Articles of the French Code.

cileable on this point, that immediately on his return all his rights and duties revive.[1]

An Englishwoman, by marrying an alien, does not
19. lose the privileges of a natural subject;[2] though the issue born out of the realm cannot inherit.[3]

21. Formerly, by act of parliament,[4] enlisting in foreign service was felony, without benefit of clergy; but these acts have been repealed; and now, by 59 Geo. III. c. 69, the entering into, or agreeing to enter into, the aid of a foreign prince or state in any warlike capacity whatever, or going abroad with that intent, or attempting to get others to do so, without licence, is a misdemeanor, and punished by fine or imprisonment, or both; and a penalty of 50*l.* for each person is imposed on masters of ships assisting in this offence.

Section 2.

Of the Deprivation of Civil Rights in consequence of Judicial Proceedings.

22. An individual may be deprived not only of the privileges he derives from being a liegeman, or in the legiance, but also of the civil rights and capacities (status et conditio) which he derives from being a lawful man (lahman), or in the law (laghe), which formerly signified in the frankpledge, or friborgh.[5] This deprivation is called civil death.[6]

This deprivation may result from the individual becoming so corrupt (attaint) as to be totally incapable of being invested with a legal condition, or from the law

---

[1] 8 T. R. 41.
[2] Doe v. Jones, 4 T. R. 300; ante, p. 209.
[3] Id. ante, p. 207 and 29, note 8, ib.; and Collingwood v. Pace, 1 Vent. 422.
[4] 9 Geo. II, c. 30, and 29 Geo. II. c. 17.
[5] Ante, pp. 20, 21, 22, 23; Co. Lit. 122 b.; Co. Lit. 128 a; Brac. l. 3, tr. 2, c. 12, 13, f. 125.
[6] Extra legem positus est civiliter mortuus.—Co. Lit. 130.

Parallel Articles of the French Code.

withdrawing its protection from him. When an individual, in his conduct to others, has violated or contemned the law under which he lives, and from which he claims protection for himself, it is but just to deprive him of some, or all, of the privileges which that law confers. In England, we have no sentence simply depriving a man of his status, or civil rights, as a punishment in itself; but such a consequence follows from certain judicial sentences, or from contumacy in not appearing to the process or command of a court of law, which it is supposed the person has contemned and disobeyed. Sometimes, in these cases, the party is deprived of only some of his rights and capacities; sometimes, of all indiscriminately. Such deprivation of all civil rights, when perpetual, is as much a civil death, as depriving a man of the sources of animal existence is a natural death: the one being dead in law, the other dead in fact. When, however, it is only partial, or only temporary, it rather suspends than extirpates the civil life. The subject naturally divides itself into two heads, viz., civil death, in consequence of attainder on judgment pronounced in the presence of the party condemned, and civil death in consequence of outlawry for contumacy on a party not appearing to obey the process of the law; and the latter is again divided into outlawry in civil, and outlawry in criminal cases. Civil death, strictly speaking, is the deprivation of all participation in civil rights.

It was formerly accounted that there might be a civil death, not being the consequence of judicial condemnation, as where a man was banished, or abjured the realm,[1] or went into a monastery.[2] But it seems this

---

[1] Exilium est patriæ privatio, natalis soli mutatio, legum nativorum amissio.—7 Rep. 20.

Qui abjurat regnum amittit regnum sed non Regem, patriam sed non patrem patriæ.—7 Rep. 9.

[2] 1 Bl. Com. 132; Co. Lit. 133.

Parallel Articles of the French Code.

doctrine is obsolete, for there is no longer any legal establishment for professed persons in England; and our law takes no notice of foreign profession.[1] And the disability of banishment consequent upon abjuration is also abolished by 21 Jac. I. c. 28.

By law, no subject can be exiled, or banished his country, whereby he shall perdere patriam, but by authority of parliament;[2] but civil death is implied as the consequence of some sentences of punishment thus: If, by act of parliament, a person is attainted of treason or felony, and saving his life is banished for ever, this is civil death;[3] and where a man receives judgment of death, and afterwards leaves the kingdom for life upon a conditional pardon, this seems also to amount to a civil death.[4]

23. In the ordinary course of law, when sentence of death is pronounced, the immediate inseparable consequence from the common law is attainder;[5] and by attainder he is dead in law.[6] After judgment pronounced (not merely after conviction), he is, by an anticipation of his punishment, already dead in law.[7]

24. A person also incurs the consequences of attainder for felonies,[8] even such as are not punishable with death; and in cases of a continued corporeal punishment, as by transportation, the party may, during the continuance of the punishment, be deprived of his civil rights: for though transportation has the effect of a pardon under

---

[1] Co. Lit. 318, n. 7, and the references therein.

[2] Co. Lit. 133 a. [3] Ib. [4] Ib. [5] 4 Bl. Com. 380.

[6] 3 Inst. 213. Every person that is attainted of high treason, petit treason, or felony, is extra legem positus, and is accounted in law civiliter mortuus.—Co. Lit. 130 a.

[7] 4 Bl. Com. 380.

[8] We usually attach the idea of capital punishment with that of felony; but properly a felony is defined "an offence which occasions a total forfeiture of either lands or goods, or both, at the common law, and to which capital or other punishments may be superadded, according to the degree of guilt."—4 Bl. Com. 94.

Spelman, in verb. felon, derives the word from *fee* (feud or fief) and *lon* (price or value). According to this derivation, felony is the same as pretium feudi, the consideration for which a man gives up his fief, or estate.—Tomlin's Law Dic.

Parallel Articles of the French Code.

the great seal,[1] yet a felon attainted is not by mere transportation restored, under that statute, to his civil rights; but he still remains in the situation of an attainted felon till after the termination of the period for which he was transported;[2] and personal property accruing in the meanwhile is forfeited.[3]

The following are the principal effects of attainder on the civil state and capacities (status) of a person; and a man attaint (attinctus) is so corrupted, that not only can he no longer perform any of the functions he was before permitted to discharge for himself, but he is unable to be invested with certain capacities or a civil condition for another man, though it seems some others he may take.[4] 25.

1st. As to real property.—By attainder, in high treason, a man forfeits[5] to the king all his lands, for the whole of his interest, from the time the treason was committed; but it does not avoid prior incumbrances.[6] For murder, also, the whole interest escheats to the lord.[7] But escheat by forfeiture, on attainder of felony or præmunire (except for treason and murder, and procuring, abetting, and counselling the same), extends only to the offender's interest for life.[8]

2nd. As to personal property.—Goods and chattels are forfeited by conviction of treason, felony, felo de se, petit larceny.[9] There must be office found (on inquisition)[10] as to real property;[11] but all personal property is

[1] 8 Geo. III. c. 15. Transportation, 5 Geo. IV. c. 84; 11 Geo. IV. & 1 Wm. IV. c. 39; 1 Vict.

Imprisonment in Penitentiary, 5 Geo. IV. c. 84, repealing 43rd section of 56 Geo. III. c. 68.

Confinement on board hulks. 16 Geo. III. c. 43.

[2] Bullock v. Dodds, 2 B. & A. 258.

[3] 1 Russ. & M. 752, and cases there cited.

[4] 3 Inst. 213; 4 Bl. Com. 380.

[5] Forfeiture for crimes is of such estates only as might have been alienated by consent.—Law Max.

[6] 4 Bl. Com. 381.

[7] Excepted out of 54 Geo. III. c. 145.

[8] 54 Geo. III. c. 145; Chitty, General Practice, 1, 279.

[9] 4 Bl. Com. 387; 1 C. G. P. 103.

[10] Ante, p. 58.

[11] 5 B. & C. 587.

Parallel Articles of the French Code.

vested in the crown without office found.[1] The crown takes the property of a convict, free from liability to the previous debts of the convict; though in some cases the crown will allow the creditors to reap benefit from them.[2]

3rd. Another immediate consequence of attainder for treason is corruption of blood, upwards and downwards; so that an attainted person can neither inherit lands from his ancestors, nor retain those he is already possessed of, nor transmit them by descent to any heir.[3] But no attainder for felony (except treason and murder) extends to disinherit the heir, nor to prejudice the right or title of any person, except the offender.[4]

As to his condition (or status), the property of a person attaint is no longer at his own disposal, so that he is incapable of making a gift or will.[5] He may have lands conveyed to him, but he cannot retain them;[6] nor is he capable of taking them by descent.[7] Attainder, it seems, is no disqualification to an executor;[8] but a person attaint cannot be a guardian under certain rights; and though appointed, he becomes incapable;[9] but when derived from other sources, attainder is no forfeiture of this office.[10]

Persons convicted of treason, felony, or any species of the crimen falsi, as forgery, perjury, subornation of perjury, &c., are incompetent to be witnesses.[11] Every person attainted of treason or felony, is disabled to bring any action.[12] Persons attainted may be sued, but cannot sue.[13]

---

1 Bullock v. Dodds, 2 B. & A. 258.

2 Chitty, Com. Law, 1, p. 737.

3 4 Bl. Com. 388; 39 Geo. III. c. 93. He who commits treason can have neither ancestor nor heir.—Law Max.

Non valebit felonis generatio, nec ad hæreditatem paternam vel maternam; si autem ante feloniam generationem fecerit, talis generatio succedit in hæreditate patris vel matris à quo non fuerit felonia perpetrata.—3 Rep. 41.

4 54 Geo. III. c. 145.

5 2 Hale, P. C. 205; Toller on Executor, p. 11.

6 Co. Lit. 2 b.

7 Cro. Car. 477.

8 3 Bac. Abr. 5.

9 Vin. in Ab. Guard (N. 6), 4.

10 See post tit. 10, c. 2, s. 7.

11 Com. Dig. Testim. a. 3, 4; Co. Lit. 6 a. b.

12 Co. Lit. 130 a; Bisse v. Harcourt, 1 Show, 155.

13 Co. Lit.; Ramsay v. Macdonald, 1 Blac. Rep. 30.

Parallel Articles of the French Code.

Though all relationships grounded in consanguinity are dissolved, yet the relation founded on the matrimonial contract continues until natural death.[1]

26. No man can be attainted of treason or felony but on judgment by express sentence, or by outlawry:[2] and judgment cannot be given for a corporal punishment in the absence of the party.[3] After judgment pronounced (and not upon mere conviction,[4] though chattels are forfeited from conviction only), and not before, the attainder of a criminal for felony commences;[4] and till then he is not deprived of his property or rights. And it is clear that a party indicted may sell any of his goods for his own support in prison, or that of his family, or to assist him in preparing his defence on the trial;[6] but if he sold them fraudulently they might be seized.[7] But in case of attainder for treason, the forfeiture relates backwards to the time of the treason committed, so as to avoid all intermediate sales and incumbrances, but not those before the fact.[8]

27. Outlawry is the being put out of the law (utlagatus), extra legem positus,[9] which in ancient time amounted to the loss of the king's protection, and the benefits of a subject; but protection was afterwards extended to the outlaw's life, though the rest of the punishment still attaches; and it is the penalty inflicted, both in civil and criminal cases, for a contumacy or contempt in avoiding the process of the king's courts. But in criminal cases, the law distinguishes between outlawry in capital offences and those of an inferior nature; and in civil cases, and for inferior crimes, a distinction must be made, whether the outlawry is either upon mesne or final process; but out-

[1] Foster, C. L. 62, 3; see ante, p. 201, and n. 4.
[2] 2 Hawk. P. C. c. 48, s. 25. [3] 1 Salk. 400. [4] See 2 Bl. 421.
[5] Ib. 384. [6] 1 Ch. Cr. S. 730. [7] 13 Eliz. c. 5.
[8] 3 Inst. 211; Co. Lit. 392; 3 Inst. 19; 1 Hal. P. C. 240.
[9] Co. Lit. 122 b. Utlagatus est quasi extra legem positus: caput gerit lupinum.—7 Rep. 14.

Nemo inauditus nec summonitus condemnari debit, si non sit contumax.—Jenk. Cent. 8.

Parallel Articles of the French Code.

lawry, or commission of a capital felony, produces the same consequences as an express sentence.[1] The attainder of a criminal commences, or takes place, on a judgment of outlawry on a capital crime, pronounced for absconding or fleeing from justice, which is held tacitly to confess the guilt.[2] But outlawry for inferior crimes, or in personal actions, does not occasion the party to be looked upon as guilty of the fact.[3] In civil action, it is rather in the nature of a process to compel the defendant to submit to the jurisdiction of the court.

The law does not allow the consequences of outlawry to be inflicted, without what is presumed to be sufficient notice.[4] A person, before he can be outlawed, must be proclaimed, and required to surrender at five county courts, and at the quarter sessions, and the church-door of his parish; but if he does not appear at the fifth exaction or requisition, then he is adjudged to be outlawed by the coroner;[5] and a writ, capias utlagatum, general or special, issues, to take his body, or his goods and land. It being then presumed he has heard of the proceedings, he is outlawed for his contumacious disrespect of the legal process of the court.[6]

28. The consequences of outlawry differ materially from those of attainder, in the manner of being terminated, but the civil disabilities are almost as great while they last: thus, in civil cases,[7] and upon indictments for misdemeanors,[8] outlawry brings with it forfeiture[9] of goods and chattels, personal and real, the loss of the profits of all real estate, and restraint of liberty.[10] The outlaw is incapacitated from suing in any action in his own right,[11] or of serving on a jury: he may, however, be a witness.[12]

---

1 Co. Lit. 390 b.
2 4 Bl. Com. 381.
3 Plow. 541; 9 Hen. VI. 206.
4 Co. Lit. 128.
5 Ib. 288.
6 Rex v. Tippin, Salk. 494.
7 3 Bl. Com. 283, 4.
8 4 Bl. Com. 319.
9 Rex v. Wilks, 4 Bur. 2333.
10 Chitty, Crim. Law, v. i. p. 366.
11 Lit. sec. 197.
12 Chitty, Crim. Law, v. i. pp. 366, 7.

Parallel Articles of the French Code.

He cannot be an auditor of accounts, or execute an office in a corporation; but he is not disabled from suing or acting in right of another, auter droit, as an executor or administrator.[1] Formerly, if a man had a ward by reason of seignory, and was outlawed, he forfeited the wardship to the king; but wardship by seignory is abolished. If a man hath the wardship of his own son or daughter, who is his heir apparent, he does not forfeit his wardship; nor are certain other kinds of wardship forfeited.[2] By a special writ of capias utlagatum (in a civil action), the sheriff is commanded not only to take the outlaw, but to summon a jury to appraise the chattels and value the lands (not trust or copyhold), &c. the outlaw had on the day of outlawry or afterwards; upon this an inquiry is executed. After inquiry the sheriff is to take possession of the goods and chattels, real and personal, but he must not disturb the possession of the tenants; and he only takes the profits of freehold. A transcript of the inquisition is sent into the Exchequer, whence there issues a writ called venditioni exponas to sell the goods; a scire facias to recover the debts due to the outlaw; and a levari facias to levy the issues of the outlaw's lands.[3] The money raised under the writ belongs to the crown,[4] though, upon motion or petition in the Exchequer, the plaintiff may have it paid to him.[5]

After outlawry, and before inquisition, a lease made bonâ fide, and upon good consideration, will prevent the king's title;[6] and in a penal action, after outlawry and before seizure the party outlawed may alien.[7]

An outlaw in criminal cases may be apprehended by any person; and when apprehended, he is not to be subjected to any severer punishment than he would have suffered upon a regular conviction.[8]

---

1 Co. Lit. 128 a.
2 33 Hen. VI. 55; 7 Rep. 13 b.
3 Tidd's Practice.
4 Co. Lit. 288 b.
5 Tidd, 4 Bur. 9549.
6 Attorney-General v. Freeman, Hard. 101.
7 Windsor v. Seymell, T. Raym. 17; 1 Lev. 33.
8 Hawk. b. 1, c. 33.

Parallel Articles of the French Code.

Outlawry is reversed on any plausible ground, however slight, whether error in law or fact:[1] in civil cases by writ of error or even motion, upon terms, when it is
29. on mesne process, of his appearing to a new action, and paying the costs; or on final process, paying the debt and costs.[2] An appearance in non-bailable actions, and bail in bailable actions, must be put in and perfected before supersedeas.[3]

The effect of falsifying or reversing an outlawry is, that the party shall be restored to his law,[4] and be in the same plight as if the outlawry had never taken place.[5] The defendant may have his property restored by writ of amoveas manus;[6] and the plaintiff proceeds on the merits in the new action.

Upon reversal of the outlawry in criminal cases, the party accused is admitted to plead[7] to and defend himself against the indictment,[8] as if he had appeared upon the capias;[9] and of course a new forfeiture only takes effect from the time judgment of attainder is pronounced. As outlawry in capital cases is equivalent to being found guilty by the verdict of a jury, the party's goods are forfeited absolutely: but if he appear (or is apprehended) within a year and traverse the indictment, on being acquitted he shall be discharged of the outlawry.[10]

30. As in case of the reversal of an outlawry, the effects are the same as if the outlawry had never been. If the king has granted over the lands of a person outlawed for treason or felony, when afterwards the outlawry is reversed the party may enter on the patentee, and need neither sue a petition to the king nor a scire facias against the patentee.[11] If the goods of a person outlawed

---

1 Co. Lit. 259 b.; Rex. v. Wilks, 4 Bur. 2527; 4 & 5 Wm. and Mary, c. 18.

2 Tidd, 4 Bur. 2549. 3 Ib. 4 Co. Lit. 280 b.

5 President of St. John's College v. Murcott, 7 T. R. 259.

6 Tidd.

7 Utlagatus pro contumacia vel fuga, non propter hoc convictus est de facto principali.—Fleta, 42; 2 Salk. 494. 8 4 Bl. Com. 320.

9 Ib. 392. 10 5 & 6 Ed. VI. c. 11, s. 8. 11 Bac. Abr. v. . p. 99.

Parallel Articles of the French Code.

are sold by the sheriff upon a capias utlagatum, and after the outlawry is reversed on writ of error, he shall have the goods restored, because the sheriff was not compelled to sell the goods, but only to keep them for the king's use.[1] It is said, however, that if a man be outlawed in the King's Bench, and the party's goods seized into the king's hands, and then the outlawry be reversed, there can be no restitution.[2] And the goods and chattels are forfeited by flight in treason or felony, even though the party be acquitted of the fact.[3]

A person dying an outlaw may make a will and 31.
appoint an executor, by whom the outlawry may be reversed.[4] Every outlawry determines upon the death of the party; and if he was outlawed in a civil suit, his reprsentatives shall have restitution of the real and personal effects, if they remain in the hands of the sheriff undisposed of: but in the above criminal cases the forfeiture is absolute of personalty.[5] Before an amoveas is issued, the death must be pleaded, and judgment entered thereupon on a plea confessed by the attorney-general in the Exchequer.[6]

Transportation of an attainted person, after the expira- 32.
ration of the period sentenced, has the effect of a pardon under the great seal, which puts the offender in the same situation as he stood in before he committed the offence, and frees him from penalties and disabilities;[7] but till then he is under attainder, and, as an attainted person,
is under disability, and cannot acquire property. If 33.
any personal property accrue to him before the expiration of his term of punishment, it would be forfeited, together with the profits of realty, to the crown,[8] like what he had at the time of sentence; and only after the expiration of the period of his punishment would he be entitled to subsequently accruing rights and pro-

[1] Bac. Abr. p. 91. [2] Ib. [3] 2 Bl. Com. 421.
[4] Chitty, Crim. Law, v. i. p. 366. [5] Tidd, 144. [6] Id.
[7] 4 Bl. Com. 482. [8] 1 Russ. & M. 752.

Parallel Articles of the French Civil.

perty. As to property accruing during outlawry, like that possessed by the party at the time of the outlawry, in civil cases, the outlawry being reversed, it is restored to him, or after his death to his representatives;[1] but in criminal cases, as above, all his personalty is forfeited.[2]

It is the prerogative of the crown to grant pardons and restitution,[3] and to deal with forfeited estates and property as it thinks proper, so that it can allow the widow, children, or relations some part of the property or not, as it thinks proper; but a pardon does not restore the blood to its former purity:[4] and when the offender's property and civil rights have once become vested in the crown, they cannot be restored to the offender, nor are they diverted from her Majesty by a mere pardon, without a clause of restitution.[5]

TITLE II.

OF THE PROOFS OR EVIDENCES OF THE CIVIL CONDITION OF PERSONS.

CHAPTER I.

General Regulations.

We have now to consider the mode in which the civil condition and rights (status) claimed by any individual, are to be established, as rightly belonging to him. In order to prove that a person is entitled to the condition and privileges of a native, it is necessary to show that he was born in the king's legiance:—to establish kin or relationship, he must prove his birth and parentage:—to show his title as an heir, it is necessary he should prove his legitimacy, or the lawful marriage of the parents, and also the death of the ancestor he is to suc-

---

[1] Tidd. [2] Ib. [3] 1 Bl. Com.; 4 Bl. Com.

[4] Plow. 558.

[5] 1 Saund. 362, 3; 1 Lev. 120; 2 Mod. 53; 3 Mod. 104.

Parallel Articles of the French Code.

ceed. To assist him in proving these and other points of a similar nature, which constitute his civil state, relationship, or position in society, certain public registers are established in most countries. Our parish registers, though not originally intended for the purposes of evidence, have long served as such. They do not, however, constitute the only evidence of the facts they record. Until very recently, the parochial registers[1] of the religious ceremonies of baptism, marriage, and burial by the clergy of the Church of England, were the only records publicly kept of the births, marriages, and deaths of private individuals; but by the new acts of parliament, registers have been established for those events, independent of the parochial clergy, and independent of religious institutions.[2]

The register entries of births, deaths, and marriages contain the date of the year and day of the month when they are entered; the name and surname, age, profession, and residence of the persons registered (except infants as to the two last, then of the parents); and the signature of the official person making the registry, and of the witnesses.[3] 34.

The registrars and other public officers are carefully to learn the particulars, which it is their duty to register, touching all births, deaths, and marriages.[4] If any officer 35.

[1] Parish registers, wherein baptisms, marriages, and burials are registered, were first instituted in 1538, 13 Hen. VIII., by Lord Cromwell. As to the method of keeping the parish registers, see Canon 70 for the government of the Church of England, passed in convocation 1603. The evidences of the civil state, in early times, were not only from enrolment in frankpledges, but from numerous other sources, much more numerous than in later periods. A family that can trace its pedigree to the time when Lord Cromwell's registration commenced, may generally continue it for many centuries beyond.—See Grimaldi, Origines Genealogicæ.

[2] On the subject of registration of births, deaths, and marriages, see the acts of parliament passed 6 & 7 Wm. III. c. 6; 9 & 10 Wm. III. c. 35, s. 4; 52 Geo. III. c. 146, partly repealed by 6 & 7 Wm. IV. c. 84, 85, 86, and 1 Vict. c. 22; also the Rules and Orders, Notices and Letters of Instructions issued from the General Registrar's Office, under the two latter acts.

[3] See Schedules to 6 & 7 Wm. IV. c. 86; B. & C.

[4] 6 & 7 Wm. IV. c. 86, s. 18—40.

Parallel Articles of the French Code.

registered information which it was not within the scope of his duty to register, according to the general principles of the law, it would have no more weight as evidence than the hearsay evidence of a common unofficial person.[1]

Every person who wilfully makes any false statement, for the purpose of having it inserted in any register of birth, death, or marriage, is liable to the same pains and penalties as if guilty of perjury.[2]

37. Witnesses brought to attest the registers or giving information must, as in other cases, be credible persons of either sex, and an age to understand.

39. The register entries are to be signed by the registering person.[3] Every person, by whom the information contained in any register of birth or death shall have been given, must sign his name, description, and place of abode in the register, otherwise such register shall not be given as evidence.[4] Every register entry of a marriage shall be signed by the person by or before whom the marriage has been solemnized, and by the registrar (if under the new act), and also by the parties married, and attested by two witnesses.[5]

40. The entries are to be made in proper register books,[6] furnished to the registrars by the General Register Office.[7] Marriage registers to be in duplicate.[8]

41. The register books are to be of durable materials, and every page is to be numbered progressively from the beginning to the end, beginning with number one; and every place of entry must be also numbered progressively in like manner, and every entry be divided from the following entry by a printed line.[9]

42. Every entry must be made in order from the beginning to the end of the book.[10]

---

[1] See on this point Wihon v. Law, 3 Stark. N. P. C.; Phil. Ev. 415.

[2] 6 & 7 Wm. IV. c. 86, s. 41.

[3] 6 & 7 Wm. IV. c. 86, and schedules.

[4] Ib. c. 86, s. 28.

[5] 4 Geo. IV. c. 76, s. 28; 6 & 7 Wm. IV. 85, s. 23.

[6] Costs of register books, 1 Vict. c. 22, s. 25.

[7] 6 & 7 Wm. IV. c. 86, s. 17—30.

[8] Ib. s. 31.

[9] Ib. s. 17.

[10] Ib. s. 18—31.

Parallel Articles of the French Code.

Certified copies of the registers of births and deaths are to be sent quarterly,[1] and the register books themselves when filled, to the superintendant registrar.[2] Marriage registers are to be made and kept in duplicate, 43. and each must be signed.[3] And the duplicates and certified copies of the registers of marriage must be sent to the superintendant registrar,[4] who is to send the certified copies of the registers of births, deaths, and marriages to the General Register Office.[5]

Every rector, vicar, or curate, and every registrar, 45. registering officer, and secretary, who has the keeping for the time being of any register book of births, deaths, or marriages, must at all reasonable times allow searches to be made of any register book in his keeping; and must give a copy, certified under his hand, of any entry or entries in the same, on payment of 2*s.* 6*d.* for each certificate, and 1*s.* for the first year's search, and 6*d.* for every subsequent year.[6]

Indexes are to be kept at the Superintendant Registrar's Office, and at the General Register Office, and searches allowed. The certified copies of entries given at the General Register Office are to be under the seal of the office;[7] and the certificate under the seal of the office will be received as evidence of the birth, death, or marriage to which the same relates, without any further proof of the entry.

For legal purposes, registers of births, deaths, and 46. marriages are not essential in trial,[8] and important only to assist in evidence. When any document has been accidentally lost, evidence may be given of its contents.

---

[1] The last days of March, June, September, and December are the periods of making up quarterly returns.—1 Vict. c. 22, s. 26. Penalty for not making return of certified copy, s. 28.

[2] 6 & 7 Wm. IV. c. 83, s. 32.

[3] Ib. c. 86, s. 31.

[4] Ib. s. 33.

[5] Ib. s. 34.

[6] Ib. s. 35.

[7] Ib. s. 38.

[8] 1 Chitty, G. P. 62; Reed v. Passer, Peake, 231; 1 Esp. N. P. C. 213; and see same case as to the general reputation of the family respecting the marriage, Bul. N. P.; 2 Phil. on Evid. 207.

Parallel Articles of the French Code.

If a marriage is proved by a person who was present, it is not necessary to prove the registration, or licence, or banns;[1] and so as to births and deaths. Entries in a family Bible, when made by the parent at or about the time of the occurrence, are generally received as genuine evidence;[2] as are also wills, declarations, and monumental inscriptions.[3]

47. Although a marriage celebrated in a foreign country is valid, if solemnized according to the law of that country, yet an examined copy of the register of the marriage, or a baptism, is not admissible as evidence.[4]

48. A marriage of English subjects in the chapel of the English ambassador abroad, according to the forms of the law of England, is valid.[5]

The notorial certificate and seal, verified by the British consul, whose hand-writing is sworn to, is not sufficient evidence of the due execution of a document without the affidavit of the subscribing witness;[6] nor will such certificate of vice-consul be admitted as evidence of the facts stated in it.[7]

50. Every person who ought to register any birth, death, or marriage, refusing, or without reasonable cause omitting to do so, or carelessly losing any register book, shall forfeit 50*l.* for every offence.[8]

Every person who shall knowingly register the birth of any child after forty-two days (except on the required solemn declaration, and in the presence of the superintendant registrar), or after six months (except in births at sea), shall forfeit for every such offence a sum not exceeding 50*l.*

---

1 Alliston's case, R. & R., C.C.R. 109.

2 3 Phil. Ec. Ca. 42.

3 Per Lord Eldon; Whitelock v. Baker, 13 Ves. 514; Higham v. Ridgway, 10 East, 120.

4 Leader v. Barry, 1 Esp. 353; Huet v. Le Mesurier, 1 Cox's Ca. 275.

5 4 Geo. IV. c. 91.

6 Exparte Church, 1 D. & R. 324.

7 Waldron v. Coombe, 3 Taunt. 162.

8 6 & 7 Wm. IV. c. 86, s. 42.

Parallel Articles of the French Code.

Every person destroying any register book, or any part or certified copy of any part, or falsely making or counterfeiting any part of any such register or certified copy, or wilfully inserting any false entry, or giving any false certificate, or forging the seal of the General Register Office, is guilty of felony.[1] The registrars would, no 51.
doubt, be liable to an action on the case, if by their 52.
gross negligence an alteration was made in the entries so as to injure any party.

The penalties upon offences against the registration 53.
may be recovered before two justices of peace for the county, city, or place where the offence happened, upon the information or complaint of any person.[2]

In all cases, where the sum adjudged on any summary 54.
conviction shall exceed 5*l.*, the party convicted may appeal to the next general or quarter sessions.[3]

CHAPTER II.

Registration of Births.

Every registrar is required to inform himself carefully 55.
of every birth which happens within his district, and to 56.
learn and register, as soon after the event as conveniently may be done, in one of the books, the particulars required to be registered respecting every such birth.[4] The father or mother of every child born in England, or in case of the death, illness, absence, or inability of the father and mother, the occupier of the house or tenement in which such child is born, must, within forty-two days next after the day of such birth, give notice, and must within that

---

[1] 6 & 7 Wm. IV. c. 86, s. 43. Offences punishable upon summary conviction must be prosecuted within three months.—1 Vict. c. 22, s. 31.

[2] Committal to the county gaol, 1 Vict. c. 22, s. 4.

[3] 6 & 7 Wm. IV. c. 86, s. 46.

[4] Ib. s. 18.

Parallel Articles of the French Code.

time, upon being requested so to do, furnish information to the registrar, according to the best of his or her knowledge and belief, of the several particulars required to be registered touching the birth of such child.[1]

After forty-two days, it shall not be lawful for the registrar to register any birth, unless some person present at the birth, or the father or guardian, within six months after the birth, make a solemn declaration of the particulars required to be known touching the birth of such child, according to the best of his or her knowledge and belief; and then the registrar, in the presence of the superintendant registrar, may register it according to such declaration, and the superintendant registrar must sign it as well as the registrar.[2] No register of births entered after the forty-two days can be given in evidence to prove a birth, unless the entry shall have been signed by the superintendant registrar.[3] After six months, no entry at all may be made (except in births at sea), or if made, it cannot be given in evidence to prove the birth.[4]

57. The register entries of births must contain—the date of the year; the name of the district and county; the day and month; the name (if any) and sex of the child;[5] the name and surname of the father and his rank or profession; the name and maiden surname of the mother; the signature, description, and residence of the informant; the date when registered, and the signature of the registrar.[6]

When a name is given to a child in baptism within six months after it was registered, such name, on delivering to the registrar[7] a proper certificate of baptism, on payment of one shilling, shall be forthwith entered, and the registrar shall certify on such certificate of baptism the

[1] 6 & 7 Wm. IV. c. 86, s. 19, 20.

[2] Fee to the superintendant registrar 2s. 6d., to the registrar 5s., unless occasioned by his default.

[3] 6 & 7 Wm. IV. c. 85, s. 22.

[4] Ib. c. 86, s. 23.

[5] The registrar-general may direct the place of birth to be added.—1 Vict. c. 22, s. 8.

[6] See Schedule to 6 & 7 Wm. IV. c. 86.

[7] Or superintendant registrar.—1 Vict. c. 22, s. 2.

Parallel Articles of the French Code.

registration of the name, and he shall forthwith send the certificate to the registrar-general.[1] The register of birth or baptism is not admissible to prove the actual time of birth, although it contain a declaration respecting it.[2]

58. In case any new-born child shall be found exposed, the overseers of the poor shall forthwith give notice and information thereof, and of the place where such child was found, to the registrar of that district.[3]

59. If any child of an English parent shall be born at sea on board of a British vessel, the captain or commanding officer of the vessel shall[4] forthwith make a minute of the several particulars required to be inserted in the register touching the birth of such child, as far as the same may be known, and the name of the vessel wherein the birth took place.[5]

60. 61. The captain or commanding officer of any British vessel, on board of which a child shall have been born, shall, on the arrival of such vessel in any port of the United Kingdom, or by any other sooner opportunity, send a certificate of the said minute through the post-office to the registrar-general, who shall file the same, and enter a copy thereof under his hand, in a book to be kept for that purpose in the General Register Office, to be called the "Marine Register Book," and shall keep the said book with the other registers.[6]

---

[1] 6 & 7 Wm. IV. c. 86, s. 24.

[2] Wihon v. Law, 3 Stark. N. P. C.

[3] 6 & 7 Wm. IV. c. 86, s. 19.

[4] After the 30th June, 1837.—1 Vict. c. 22, s. 6.

[5] 6 & 7 Wm. IV. c. 86, s. 21.

[6] Ib.

Parallel Articles of the French Code.

CHAPTER III.

Registration of Marriages.

Marriages may be solemnized, either according to the rites of the Church of England, by banns or licence, or without the rites of any sect or religious denomination, before the registrar, by the registrar's certificate of publication or licence.[1]

63. If a marriage is intended to be solemnized by banns, a
64. notice, correctly dated, of the day it is delivered, and stating the true Christian and surnames of both parties, and of the houses of their respective abodes within the parish or chapelry, and of the time during which they have dwelt, inhabited, or lodged there, must be given to the minister of the Church of England, seven days at least before the time required for the first publication of such banns.[2] All banns of matrimony must be published in the parish churches or chapels of the parishes where each of the parties dwell, upon three Sundays preceding the marriage;[3] or in a chapel licensed by the bishop:[4] but the banns in that case, where they reside in different parishes or districts, must also be published in the district in which each of the parties is resident.[5]

Where by any law or canon in force, it is provided that any marriage may be solemnized after publication of banns, such marriage may be solemnized in like manner, on production of the registrar's certificate.[6] In every case of marriage solemnized after 1st of March, 1837

[1] Canon 62, as to penalty for non-publication of banns.—Wiltshire v. Prince, otherwise Wiltshire, 3 Hag. 332, as to the construction of s. 22 of 4 Geo. IV. c. 76.

1 Vict. c. 22, declares that the word directed to be given to the registrar, shall be construed to include the superintendant-registrar, s. 1.

[2] 1 Chitty, G. P. 53; 4 Geo. IV. c. 76, s. 7. [3] Ib. c. 76, s. 1.

[4] 1 Vict. c. 23, s. 33. [5] Ib. s. 24. [6] 6 & 7 Wm. IV. c. 85, s. 1.

Parallel Articles of the French Code.

(except by banns or licence), one of the parties shall give a notice under his or her hand, to the superintendant registrar of the district, within which each of the parties shall have dwelt seven days at least, next preceding, and shall state therein the name and surname, and the profession or condition of each of the parties, the dwelling-place of each, and the time not being less than seven days, during which each has dwelt therein, and the church or other building in which the marriage is to be solemnized,[1] the superintendant registrar must file such notice, and enter a true copy into "the Marriage Notice Book," which shall be open at all reasonable times, to all persons desirous of inspecting it.[2]

The clerk to the guardians of the poor-law union, parish, or place, shall read such notice immediately after the minutes of the proceedings of the guardians' last meeting, three several times in three successive weeks, at the weekly meetings of such guardians (unless notice of licence be given to the clerk).[3] Or if the guardians shall not meet, such notice may be read at any meeting of such guardians, which shall be held within twenty-one days after the day such notice was entered.[4]

A marriage may be solemnized without publication by a licence from the spiritual officer for the church of England, or when the marriage is not to be had in a church, from the registrar.[5] But before a licence can be obtained, one of the parties must make oath that he believes there is no impediment, that one of the parties has had his or her abode within the parish or district for fifteen days immediately preceding, and if either of the parties are under age (not being a widower or widow), that a consent has been duly obtained, or that there is no person

[1] 6 & 7 Wm. IV. c. 85, s. 4. [2] Ib. s. 5.

[3] Where there is no board of guardians, the notice is to be suspended in some conspicuous place in the office of the registrar.—1 Vict. c. 22, s. 24.

[4] 6 & 7 Wm. 4, c. 85, s. 6. Such publication to stand to all intents and purposes, instead of publication of banns.—1 Vict. c. 22, s. 36.

[5] 6 & 7 Wm. IV. c. 58, s. 11.

Parallel Articles of the French Code.

authorised to give such consent.[1] No marriage without licence or notice to the registrar shall be solemnized or registered until twenty-one days, nor by licence until
65. seven days, after the entry of the notice.[2]

A new licence must be obtained if the parties be not married within three months;[3] and there must, in case of marriage by banns or registrar's certificate, be a new notice and re-publication, if the parties are not married within three months.[4]

66. A marriage may be opposed by any person authorized
67. in that behalf, publicly forbidding the banns, or entering the word "forbidden," in the marriage notice book, or a caveat against the granting a licence. Any person authorized may forbid the issue of the registrar's certificate, by putting the word "forbidden," opposite the notice in the marriage notice book, and by subscribing the name, place of abode, and character, which authorized such person to interfere.

68. If dissent be publicly declared by a duly authorized person forbidding the banns, the banns are void.[5] If a caveat be entered against granting a licence, no licences shall be issued until the caveat is withdrawn, or the ecclesiastical judge or the registrar is satisfied that the objection on which the caveat is founded ought not to obstruct the licence.[6] Every person who shall enter a caveat against licence or certificate, which the registrar shall declare to be frivolous, shall be liable to the costs of the proceedings, and a special action for damages.[7] Every

---

[1] 4 Geo. IV. c. 76, and 6 & 7 Wm. IV. c. 85, s. 12.

[2] 6 & 7 Wm. IV. c. 85, s. 14.

[3] 4 Geo. IV. c. 76, s. 19.

[4] Ib. c. 76, s. 9; 6 & 7 Wm. IV. c. 85, s. 15. A superintendant-registrar who issues licence three months after the notice, or solemnizes any marriage, declared void by the Act of the previous session, is guilty of felony.—1 Vict. c. 22, s. 3.

[5] 4 Geo. IV. c. 76, s. 8.

[6] Ib. c. 76, s. 11; 6 & 7 Wm. IV. c. 85, s. 13.

[7] Ib. c. 85, s. 37. The registrar-general's certificate, under seal, is evidence that he declared "the caveat to be frivolous."

Parallel Articles of the French Code.

registrar is guilty of felony who issues knowingly and wilfully a certificate for a marriage, which has been duly forbidden by an authorized person, or after three months, or before the seven or twenty-one days provided by the act, or who shall register a marriage declared void by the act.[1]

If the marriage is not forbidden, or no objection shown to the satisfaction of the registrar after the expiration of seven days if the marriage is to be by licence, or after twenty-one days if without licence, after the entry of the notice, he shall, on request, issue a certificate, stating the particulars set forth in the notice, the day on which the notice was entered, and that the seven or twenty-one days have elapsed, and it has not been forbidden by any person authorized.[2] In order to distinguish the certificate for marriage by licence from those without licence, a watermark of the word "Licence" shall be manufactured in the paper on which the certificates for marriage by licence shall be written, and the printing of certificates for marriage by licence shall be in red ink, those without licence in black.[3] 69.

The certificate of the registrar shall be delivered to the officiating minister, and the certificate or licence of Quakers shall be delivered to the registering officer, and of Jews to the officer of the synagogue. And in all other cases the certificate shall be delivered to the registrar present at the marriage.[4]

Consent to the marriage of any person under twenty- 73.
one year of age, (not being a widower or widow,) must be obtained from the father, or if he be dead, from one of the guardians, or if no guardian, from the mother if unmarried; and if the party authorized to give consent be non compos mentis, or beyond the seas, or unduly refuse, an application may be made to the Chancellor,

[1] 6 & 7 Wm. IV. c. 85, s. 40.

[2] Ib. s. 7.

[3] Ib. s. 8.

[4] Ib. s. 6.

Parallel Articles of the French Code.

Vice-Chancellor, or Master of the Rolls, who, if he approve the marriage, may direct it to take place.[1]

74. No licence from the spiritual judge is to be granted for marriage in any other place than the church or chapel of the parish, wherein one of the parties shall have resided fifteen days before the granting of such licence.[2] If persons wilfully intermarry[3] in any place other than the church or chapel where banns may be published, or the registered building or office, or other place specified in the registrar's notice and certificate, or without banns or such notice and certificate, or without licence where necessary, or either by a person not in holy orders, or in the absence of the proper registrar, the marriage of such persons shall be null and void.[4]

75. All the rubrics concerning the solemnization of marriages, shall continue to be duly observed by every person in holy orders of the Church of England, who shall solemnize any marriage in England.[5] Quakers and Jews may continue to solemnize marriage according to the usages of their societies, where both parties are of one religion, on giving the proper notice to, and obtaining the certificate of, the registrar.[6] After expiration of the proper periods of seven or twenty-one days, the marriage may be solemnized at the office of the registrar, or in the registered building stated in the notice of marriage, according to such form and ceremony as the parties may see fit to adopt, being in the presence of the registrar and two or more credible witnesses: provided that in some part of the ceremony, and in the presence of the registrar and the witnesses, each party shall declare, "I do solemnly declare, that I know not of any lawful impedi-

[1] 4 Geo. IV. c. 76, s. 16 & 18. The like consent is required by the new Act, as before, 6 & 7 Wm. IV. c. 85, s. 10.

[2] 4 Geo. IV. c. 76, s. 10.

[3] Ib. c. 76, or 6 & 7 Wm. IV. c. 85.

[4] Ib. c. 85, s. 42; 4 Geo. IV. c. 76, s. 22. A marriage on board a king's ship by a captain, duly entered in the log-book, is considered as valid as if the ceremony were performed by the Archbishop of Canterbury.

[5] 6 & 7 Wm. IV. c. 85, s. 1.

[6] Ib. s. 2.

Parallel Articles of the French Code.

ment why I, A B, may not join in matrimony to C D," and each of the parties shall say to the other, "I call upon these persons here present to witness, that I, A B, do take thee, C D, to be my lawful wedded wife, (or husband),"[1] Every marriage must be solemnized with open doors, between the hours of eight and twelve in the forenoon, and in the presence of two or more credible witnesses.[2]

The Registry Entry of Marriage shall set forth:[3] 76.

1. The date of the year.
2. The church, chapel, office, or other building in which it is solemnized.
3. The name of the parish or district, and county.
4. The day of the month.
5. The names and surnames, conditions, and residences of the parties married.
6. The ages of both, whether of full age or minors.
7. The ranks or professions.
8. The names and surnames, and the ranks or professions of the fathers of both the persons married.
9. Whether by licence, certificate, or banns.
10. The signatures of the persons married.
11. The signature of the person by or before whom the marriage was solemnized.
12. The signatures of two or more witnesses.

CHAPTER IV.

Registration of Deaths.

Every person who shall bury, or perform any funeral 77.
or any religious service for the burial of any dead body, for which he has received no certificate duly made by the

---

[1] 6 & 7 Wm. IV. c. 85, s. 20, 21.

[2] 4 Geo. IV. c. 76, s. 21, 26; 6 & 7 Wm. IV. c. 85, s. 20.

[3] See Schedule to 6 & 7 Wm. IV. c. 86 (C.)

Parallel Articles of the French Code.

registrar or the coroner, and who shall not, within seven days, give notice thereof to the registrar, shall forfeit a sum not exceeding ten pounds for every offence.

78. The occupier of every house or tenement in which any death happens, may, within five days after the day of such death, give notice of it to the registrar of the district.[1] Every registrar is required to inform himself carefully of every death which happens within his district, and to learn and register, as soon after the event as conveniently may be done, in one of the register books, the particulars required to be registered respecting every such death.[2] Some person present at the death, or in attendance during the last illness, of every person dying in England, or, in case of the illness, death, inability, or default of all such persons, the occupier of the house or tenement, or if the occupier be the person dead, some inmate of the house or tenement in which such death happens, must, within eight days after such death, give information, upon being requested so to do, to the registrar, of the several particulars required to be registered touching the death.[3] Every registrar, immediately upon registering any death, or as soon after as he may be required so to do, must, without fee or reward, deliver to the undertaker, or other person having charge of the funeral, a certificate under his hand that such death has been duly registered, and such certificate must be delivered to the minister or officiating person who shall be required to bury or perform any religious service for the burial of the dead body; and if any dead body be buried without such certificate, the person burying or performing any funeral or religious service for the burial, shall forthwith give notice thereof to the registrar. In case any dead body shall be found exposed, the coroner shall forthwith give notice and information thereof, and of the place where the dead body was found, to the registrar of the district.[4]

---

[1] See Schedule to 6 & 7 Wm. IV. c. 86, s. 19.

[2] 6 & 7 Wm. IV. c. 86, s. 18. [3] Ib. s. 25. [4] Ib. s. 19.

Parallel Articles of the French Code.

The register entry of every death shall contain the date of the year, the name of the district and county, the day of the month of the death, the name and surname, sex, age, profession, or rank of the deceased,[1] the cause 79.
of death, the signature, description, and residence of the informant, the time when registered, and the signature of the registrar.

The registrar is to learn particulars, and to register 80.
all deaths within his district;[2] and the master or keeper of every gaol, prison, or house of correction or workhouse, hospital, or lunatic asylum, or public or charitable institution, is deemed the occupier of the tenement, and must, when requested, furnish information to the registrar.[3]

When any person is slain, or dies suddenly, the body 81.
must not be interred until a coroner's inquest has been 82.
held on it, to inquire the manner of death.[4] The townships are bound to give notice to the coroner, under pain of amercement.[5] The inquiry is to be made by the coroner with a jury from the neighbouring towns, on view of the body.[6] The coroner, upon holding any inquest, may, if he thinks fit, order the body to be buried before registry of the death, and, in such case, is to give a certificate of his order in writing, under his hand, to the undertaker or other person having the charge of the funeral, which must be delivered like the registrar's certificate.[7] In every case in which an inquest is held on any dead body, the jury are to inquire the particulars required to be registered concerning the death, and the coroner must inform the registrar of the finding of the jury, and the registrar must make the entry accordingly.

The coroner is to hold an inquest, when any person 84.
dies in prison, touching the manner of his death.[8] In 85.

---

[1] The Registrar-General may direct the place of death to be added.—1 Vict. c. 22. s. 9.
[2] 6 & 7 Wm. IV. c. 86, s. 18.
[3] s. 19, 20.
[4] 4 Ed. I. c. 2; 1 Bl. Com. 348.
[5] 1 Burn's Justice, 786.
[6] 1 Bl. Com. 348.
[7] 6 & 7 Wm. IV. c. 86, s. 27.
[8] Umfreville's Coron. 212; 2 Hale, 61; 4 Ed. I. s. 2.

Parallel Articles of the French Code.

the cases of violent death, there is no provision that the registrar shall enter the death otherwise than in the usual form.

86. If any of her Majesty's English subjects die at sea on board a British vessel, the captain or commanding officer of the vessel on board which such death happens, must[1] forthwith make a minute of the several particulars, to be inserted in the register, touching such death, so far as the same can be known, and the name of the vessel.[2]

87. On the arrival of a vessel wherein a death occurred at any port of the United Kingdom, or by any other sooner opportunity, the captain or commanding officer shall send a certificate of the minute of the death, through the Post-office, to the registrar-general, who must file the same, and enter a copy thereof under his hand in the marine register-book.[3]

CHAPTER V.

Registers of the Civil State of the Military.

88. In military service, both within the kingdom and abroad, although the registration acts do not extend to places beyond the seas, there are two kinds of records kept, from one or other of which the birth, death, or marriage, of persons attached to the army may be learned, namely, the muster-rolls and the regimental register.

89. With regard to the first, it is the duty (imposed by act of parliament) of the adjutant of each regiment to prepare a monthly list, containing the names of every man in his regiment (whether officer, non-commissioned officer, private, drummer, or trumpeter), in alphabetical order, or by troops or companies, which lists are called

[1] After 30th June, 1837.—1 Vict. c. 22, s. 6.
[2] 6 & 7 Wm. IV. c. 86, s. 20.
[3] Ib. c. 86, s. 26.

muster-rolls, or adjutant rolls; and a copy of this monthly list is transmitted to the secretary at war. The original, or another copy, is understood to be kept at regimental head-quarters.[1] Parallel Articles of the French Code.

The other document, or regimental register, applies only, or chiefly, to the non-commissioned officers and privates; but when in foreign service, as no other kind of record may be at hand, the officers are recommended (by the commander-in-chief) to avail themselves of this regimental register. The present system of keeping this register appears to have commenced in 1816, when the adjutant-general, by order of the commander-in-chief (the Duke of York), "with a view of ascertaining the marriages of soldiers, and the age and baptism of their legitimate children," issued (on July 1, 1816) a General Order, requiring that a book of registry should be kept in every regiment or battalion, in which "the marriage of every non-commissioned officer and private, and the baptism and age of every legitimate child born of parents belonging to such regiment or battalion, shall be recorded; and the said registry shall be certified by the signature of the adjutant."[2] 89. 90.

In all cases of baptism of the children of non-commissioned officers and soldiers, the parties are commanded to bring without delay, to the adjutants of their respective corps, for the purpose of being registered, an account containing— 92.

1. The date of the child's birth.
2. The place and date of its baptism.
3. The Christian name of the child.
4. The Christian and surnames of the parents.
5. The rank of the father.
6. The name of the chaplain, or other clergyman, by whom the ceremony was performed.[3]

[1] Grimaldi, Origines Genealogicæ, p. 324. See War-office Circular, dated April, 1803, as to troops serving in the East Indies.

[2] General Order, 1 July, 1816.

[3] Ib. 1 July 1816.—Grimaldi, Origines Genealogicæ, 326.

Parallel Articles of the French Code.

Marriages solemnized within the British lines by any chaplain, or officer, or other person, officiating under the orders of the commanding officer of a British army
94. serving abroad, are as valid as if the same had been
95. solemnized within his majesty's dominions with a due observance of all forms required by law.[1]

The regimental register of marriages is to contain the following particulars, viz.[2]:—

1. The rank, and Christian and surname of the soldier, specifying whether bachelor or widower.

2. The Christian and surname of the woman, specifying whether spinster or widow.

3. The date of the marriage.

4. The signature of the parties married.

5. The signatures of two witnesses present at the ceremony.

6. The signature of the chaplain, or officiating clergyman, by whom the marriage was solemnized.

7. The certificate of the adjutant that the registry is correct.

96. In the returns made of the muster-rolls, it is the
97. duty of the adjutant to notice all casualties which have occurred since his last return, which is done by an entry against the party's name, thus, "died, 15 Jan.;" or thus, "killed in action, 15 Jan.;" or thus, "died in hospital, 15 Jan."

All deaths in a military hospital are duly reported to the proper officer, and entered on the muster-rolls in the return made by the adjutant.

---

1 4 Geo. IV. c. 91. Marriages beyond the sea being excepted out of the Marriage Act. A marriage in a foreign country, by British subjects attached to the British army, having military possession of the place, solemnized by a priest in holy orders, would, it seems, be as good by the law of England as a marriage contract would have been, per verba de presenti, before that Act.—Rex v. Brampton, 10 East, 288.

As to the presumption that a marriage was duly celebrated in a foreign country, ib.

2 General Order, 1st July, 1816.

Parallel Articles of the French Code.

CHAPTER VI.

Amendment of Accidental Errors.

No person charged with the duty of registering any 99.
birth, death, or marriage, who discovers any error to 100.
have been committed in any entry, is liable to the 101.
penalties, if, within one month after the discovery of such error, in the presence of the parents of the child, or the parties married, or two persons attending the decease where death shall have been so registered; or, in case of the death or absence of the superintendant registrar, two other credible witnesses who attest the same, he corrects the erroneous entry according to the truth of the case, by entry in the margin without any alteration of the original entry, and signs the marginal entry with the day of the month and year when such correction is made; such correction to be made in the duplicate marriage register, or the certified copies, or the other registers, or a separate certificate.[1]

TITLE III.

OF LEGAL HOME OR DOMICIL.[2]

The rights and condition (status) of a person may be greatly affected by the particular rules and local customs of the place of his general residence or home; and hence it becomes necessary, in many cases, to determine what constitutes a person's home or domicil, and how a new one may be acquired. A person's domicil, or home, is in

---

[1] 6 & 7 Wm. IV. c. 86, s. 44.

[2] Not only the term domicil, but also the subject, being somewhat foreign to our jurisprudence, the importance of considering it has been dwelt upon with more length than has been thought necessary for any other legal topic.

Parallel Articles of the French Code.

ordinary acceptation the place where he lives or has his general residence. With the great majority of persons, as they have but one residence, no question can arise as to the domicil: but where a person occupies alternately a town house and a country house, or carries on trade at several places, or travels about from country to country, and seems to have no fixed residence, it may often be doubtful where he is domiciled.[1]

The consideration of this subject is of very great importance, in a country governed by numerous local customs and with numerous local courts of justice, both in order to decide what persons and property are subject to those customs, and who is within the jurisdiction of those courts. In England, where one system of common law pervades the whole kingdom (with but insignificant exceptions), and where all its inhabitants[2] are subject to the same superior courts of law, and there are few or no local inferior courts of any importance,[3] this question has been of comparatively little consequence, and has received but little attention from English lawyers.[4]

It is, however, very important, considering how the

---

[1] In one case (the Harmony, 1 Rob. 322), Lord Stowell remarked, "a question of residence or domicil is in itself often a question of great difficulty, depending on a great variety of circumstances, hardly capable of being defined by any general precise rules."

[2] The most casual temporary residence in England or Ireland is sufficient to make persons amenable to the process of the superior courts, De la Vega v. Vianna, 1 B. and Ad. 284. Consequently questions of domicil can seldom arise on that score.—Mackenna.

[3] It is always open for the parties to show that the subject matter of a suit is not properly cognizable by a particular court, Com. Dig. tit. Courts, p. 15; Redesd. Treatise, p. 151. It is not generally the residence or locality of the parties but the subject matter of a suit which gives an inferior court exclusive jurisdiction, except courts of request, which usually require the defendant to be resident within the district.

[4] In the case of Potinger v. Wightman, the master of the rolls said, "On the subject of domicil there is so little to be found in our own law, that we are obliged to resort to the writings of foreign jurists."—See Definitions and Maxims in Story's Conflict of Laws; Burge's Commentaries on Colonial and Foreign Laws; the Roman Law, D. 50, tit. 1, ad municipilem et de incolis; Voet. Pothier, Denizant, Cochin, Bynkershoek. Questions of settlements under the poor laws, however, bear a close analogy.

Parallel Articles of the French Code.

English traverse the world for pleasure or traffic, to determine where, by the law of England, is to be considered a person's domicil, not only for public political purposes, relating to the various parochial, municipal, and parliamentary elective franchises, eligibility to office, &c., but also for private civil objects; for example, it is necessary to determine the domicil, in order to regulate the succession to the moveable property of an intestate, as that is governed in the law of all countries by the lex domicilii, and not by the lex loci rei sitæ, or by the law of the place at which a party may happen to die.[1] And the construction, execution, and proof of a will or testament must be (in whatever court or country considered), regulated according to the law of the party's domicil[2] unless a clear intention is shown to the contrary.[3] In general the whole moveables of an intestate or testate are governed by the law of his domicil (lex domicilii), and not by the law of the place in which they may happen to be (lex loci rei sitæ), for otherwise, as they might be situate in many different countries, the succession to them would have to be ruled by as many different local laws. And again, the accidental place of death of a person ought not to affect the succession to his property: for a person whose whole property was situated in London, might die within the limits affected by the custom of York, or he might die in France, or in Italy; or a Scotchman, or foreigner, merely travelling or visiting, might die in England.

In regard to certain personal legal incapacities, it is also necessary to determine the domicil: thus the law

---

[1] See Balfour v. Scott, 6 Bro. P. C. 550; Hog v. Lashley, 6 Bro. P. C. 577; Drummond v. Drummond, 6 Bro. P. C. 601; Somerville v. Somerville, 5 Ves. 750.

[2] See, as to the validity of the will of a British subject dying in foreign parts, where it is not valid by the law of the place where it was made, Curling v. Thornton, 2 Add. 6. A will to be valid here need not be valid according to the foreign law where a conflict of domiciles exists; and, as to the validity of the will of a British subject dying out of England, but within the British dominions, as in Scotland, see Hare v. Nasmyth, 2 Add. 25.

[3] Anstruther v. Chalmers, 2 Sim. 1; Stanley v. Bernes, 3 Hag. Eccles. R. 373.

Parallel Articles of the French Code.

of the place where a contract is made (lex loci contractus) as to a marriage will not prevail, when either of the contracting parties is under legal incapacity, by the law of the domicil.[1] The domicil of a merchant is in time of war a matter of great importance, for on it his national character, and the detention or restitution in case of capture of his goods, often depends.[2] No position is more strongly established than that, if a person goes into another country and engages in trade there, he is by the law of nations to be considered as a merchant of that country.[3] An Englishman, domiciled (residing) and trading in Holland, is just as much a Dutch merchant as a Swede or Dane would be.[4] Though in the east (China, Turkey) foreigners, not being admitted into the general body and mass of society, have been held to derive their national character from the association, or factory, under whose protection they live and carry on their trade.[5]

Besides which, the rules of the English courts, both of law and equity, often direct their notices and processes to be left at the residence of the parties; but in such cases, the object being to secure that the parties receive the notice, it is generally determined by mere residence; and for the most part the temporary actual abode is sufficient, without any question whether it be domicil or home.[6] The residence required for matrimony is also so clearly defined, as to leave but little question respecting it as a domicil. But although such questions may not turn upon the actual home of the parties, yet

[1] Conway, otherwise Beazley v. Beazley, 3 Hag. Eccl. R. 639; Scrimshire v. Scrimshire, 2 Hag. Cons. R. 405.

[2] The Indian Chief, 3 Rob. 12; La Virginie, 5 Rob. 99.

[3] The Indian Chief. [4] The Citto, 3 Rob. 41. [5] 3 Rob. 29.

[6] Different lengths of time are allowed in a town and country cause, for service of notice of trial, &c.; and a cause is a town or country one, according to the defendant's residence.—See Spence v. Hall, 1 East, 688; Douglas v. Ray, 4 T. R. 552; 2 Price, 279. Where defendant had town and country residences, see Leicester, E. v. Perry, Hinde, Pr. 92; Wy. Pr. Reg. 405; Bound v. Wells, 3 Madd. 434.

Parallel Articles of the French Code.

residence is a very indefinite term in the English law, and may acquire a greater degree of fixedness from a consideration of legal home.[1]

The first source from which domicil arises, is the place of birth and connections, or rather the parent's domicil at the time of the child's birth. Domicil thence derived attaches to every child born, and is called domicilium originis, or domicil of nativity. The mere accident of birth at any place cannot alone affect the domicil; for the domicil of a legitimate child born on a journey, would follow that of the father at the moment of its birth.[2] This domicil if once lost is re-acquired, according to the English law, more easily than that gained subsequently by any other means.

The second source of domicil is that acquired by the act of the party voluntarily (proprio marte); this must be judged of from circumstances. To constitute domicil, there must be a residence in fact and intention (facto et animo). The place of residence is primâ facie evidence of the domicil;[3] it lies on those who say otherwise to rebut it.[4]

A person may for some purposes have two domicils, 102.
but for other purposes he can have but one; and then the domicil of origin will generally prevail, unless that has been clearly abandoned.[5] Of two domicils acquired voluntarily (proprio marte), the principal establishment will prevail; and this distinction takes place, that a person not under obligation to live in the capital in a permanent manner, as a nobleman or gentleman having a mansion his residence in the country, and resorting to

---

[1] It is obvious that the question of residence, domicil, home, must have borne a very different character in the times of the Anglo-Saxon laws, when every man belonged to a local frankpledge; and also in after times, when the resiant rolls made out by the steward of the court-leet still clearly held the parties to local duties and privileges.

[2] Scrimshire v. Scrimshire, 2 Hag. Cons. R. 405; Somerville v. Somerville, 5 Ves. 750.

[3] Bempde v. Johnstone, 3 Ves. 19.

[4] Bruce v. Bruce, cited 2 Bos. & Pul. 229.

[5] Somerville v. Somerville, 5 Ves. 786.

Parallel Articles of the French Code.

the metropolis for any particular business, or for the general purpose of residence, shall be considered domiciled in the country; on the other hand, a merchant, whose business lies in the metropolis, shall be considered as having his domicil there, and not at his country residence.[1]

103. A domicil may be changed by change of abode. The status, character, or condition, gained by residence no longer adheres to a person the moment he puts himself in motion, bonâ fide, to quit the place or country without intention of returning there, (sine animo revertendi,) to resume a former domicil:[2] but the mere intention of leaving, without some act done,[3] is not sufficient. A British subject settled as a merchant abroad, and enjoying the privileges of the place, may mean to return when he has made his fortune; but if he die in the interval, it cannot be maintained that he had his domicil here.[4]

A person is only said to have changed his domicil, quando quis re et facto animum manendi declarat, and domicilium non procedit si ille habetet animum revertendi.[5] An acquired domicil is not lost by mere abandonment, unless to resume a former one, but continues until a subsequent domicil is acquired, which can only be in fact and intention (in animo et facto).[6]

105. The native character easily reverts; and it requires fewer circumstances to constitute a domicil in the case of a native subject, than to impress the national character on one who is originally of another country.[7] A British born subject, who, having been resident abroad, left with intention of returning to this country, was held to have re-acquired his domicil of origin while on the road (in itinere).[8] Actual abandonment of the acquired domicil must be proved (animo et facto).

[1] Somerville v. Somerville, 5 Ves. 789.
[2] The Indian Chief, 3 Rob. 12.
[3] Stanley v. Bernes, 3 Hag. Eccl. R. 373.
[4] Bruce v. Bruce.
[5] Scrimshire v. Scrimshire.
[6] Munroe v. Douglas, 3 Madd. 379.
[7] La Virginie, 5 Rob. 99.
[8] The Snell Zeylder, cited 3 Rob. 21.

The domicil of origin is to prevail until the party has not only acquired another, but manifested and carried into execution an intention of abandoning his former domicil, and taking another as his sole domicil.[1] Parallel Articles of the French Code.

To change the domicil of nativity (domicilium originis), residence must be without intention of returning (sine animo revertendi). The force of residence, as a proof of intention of remaining, is much increased by the length of time during which it continues:[2] so that time is one of the grand ingredients in domicil; and mere length of time of residence must, in many cases, be taken to constitute a domicil.[3]

In some cases, as specially privileged, change of abode, 106.
and even length of residence, will raise no presumption 107.
of intention to abandon the domicil of origin. Thus, an ambassador, being in the king's service, retains his native domicil; and a soldier ordered abroad, though detained there for some time in the king's service, retains his former domicil.[4] A distinction has been adopted between the king's service and the service of the East India Company. If a person went out in a king's regiment and died in the king's service, his domicil would not be changed; but in the Company's service it would be changed.[5]

And it is a point fully established, that the character of consul does not protect that of merchant united in the same person; and his domicil (of origin) would be changed.[6] Entering into foreign service is also an abandonment of the domicil of origin.[7]

A third source of domicil is, as to individuals not sui 108.
juris consequential on that of other persons, as that of the wife arising from marriage; and a minor is domi-

[1] Somerville v. Somerville, 5 Ves. 786.

[2] Stanley v. Bernes, 3 Hag. 373.

[3] Per Sir W. Scott, in the Harmony, 2 Rob. 322.

[4] Bruce v. Bruce.

[5] Per Lord Thurlow, in Bruce v. Bruce.

[6] 3 Rob. 27.

[7] Ommaney v. Bingham, cited 3 Ves. 202, and 5 Ves. 750.

Parallel Articles of the French Code.

ciled where his father was domiciled until the child comes of age and acquires another domicil. During the state of pupilage a person cannot acquire any domicil of his own. No domicil can be acquired until the party is sui juris;[1] therefore a lunatic cannot gain a domicil. Domicil of birth is presumed to continue until the contrary is proved. Minors, with a mother or guardian in another country, without being able to have an intention of their own to change their domicil, may gain a new one;[2] for the domicil of children follows not only that of their father, but also the domicil of the surviving mother during widowhood, or the guardian.[3]

109. The residence of a person in the service of another, as a domestic or in other capacity, may afford a presumption that he has abandoned his former domicil. The place where such servant usually slept is the principal point.[4]

110. The jurisdiction, by which probate of a will or letters of administration are granted, depends, according to the law of England, on the place where the personal estate (being bona notabilia) is situated;[5] but the succession to the personal estate of an intestate is regulated by the law of that place which was his domicil at the time of his death, being supposed to follow his person;[6] and though

---

[1] Somerville v. Somerville.

[2] Scrimshire v. Scrimshire, 2 Hag. Cons. R.

[3] Potinger v. Wightman, 3 Mer. 67.. Thus the moveable property of a minor, sent abroad to study at a foreign university, would be distributed according to the domicil of his parents or guardian, and not that of his residence.

[4] See the cases under the poor law, Rex v. Hedsor, Cald. 51; Rex v. Mildenhall, 1 B. & A. 374.

[5] 1 William, Law of Executor, 167, 175. Administration granted in two countries (England and Jamaica), Burn v. Cole, Amb. 415. See a case of a foreign married woman possessed of property here, as to granting administration according to the law of this country or her own; in the goods of Maraver, 1 Hag. 498. See, as to person to whom administration granted, in case the residue of personal estate be undisposed of, according to a foreign law (the French), and the deceased was domicil in a foreign country (a French island), in the goods of Anne Dormoy, 3 Hag. 767.

[6] Pipon v. Pipon, Ambl. 23; Ridgw. Ca. Temp., Hardw. 172; 9 Mod. 431; see ante, p. 195, 247. See a query whether a British subject can select a foreign domicil in so complete derogation of his British, as to subject his property here to any foreign law, even in case of intestacy, Curling v. Thornton, 2 Add. 8.

a man may have two domicils for some purposes, he can have only one for the purpose of succession.[1]

We know no reason why the parties to an agreement may not create a kind of forensic domicil for themselves, by stipulating that, in case of proceedings at law, notices or process, otherwise required to be left at the residence, may be served at any other particular place instead of such residence. 111.

TITLE IV.

OF ABSENT PERSONS.

By absence must be understood, not the mere temporary departure from home, but an unaccounted for and total disappearance of a person under such circumstances as to leave his existence uncertain. When a person has disappeared, without there being any certainty of his death, there are three classes of interests to be considered:—1st, If he be still alive, the interest of the party himself for the preservation of his rights and property; 2nd, Whether he be dead or alive, the claims of those to whom he owes debts or duties, as his creditors, his landlord, the lord of a manor; and 3rd, If he be dead, the interests of the relatives entitled in such case to his property. As the regulations of the English law on this subject do not admit of being arranged exactly in the order of the French code, we adopt this division as the basis of our arrangement. 112 to 144.

As to the first, it is so rare an occurrence—so much so, that it might almost be said never to happen in England—for a person possessed of property to disappear

[1] Somerville v. Somerville. An English subject resident and dying in England, having debts and choses in action in Scotland, they would be distributed as the rest of his estate.—Thorne v. Watkins, 2 Ves. Sen. 35.

Parallel Articles of the French Code.

without his relations, or friends, or neighbours knowing something about him, and some person being authorized to act for him, that there is no public officer, or other person, authorized to interfere with the property of the absentee on account of the mere fact of absence; and there are but few cases or decisions to be found in the English law books relating to the subject. And though it is true that Bracton,[1] in treating of the obligations which arise quasi ex contractu, mentions the actio negotiorum gestorum with others from the civil law, yet the English common law does not recognize any right to interfere, much less any claim for interfering, with another's goods without authority.[2]

Our law considers, that to permit interference with the property of another without his permission, on the plea of benefit to him, would only afford a pretext for intermeddling, fraud, and oppression; and it leaves to the gratitude of the party, from the sense of the benefit, any recompense to the party interfering; and, according to analogy, it would appear that persons not authorized, interfering with the estate of an absentee, though ostensibly with a view of preserving it for him, must do so at their own hazard; and they would be liable to an action of trespass for intermeddling, whether any injury accrued or not, or to an action on the case for any damage the absentee might sustain by such interference.[3] But a distinction exists herein as to an action of trover and

---

1 Br. l. 3, tr. 1, c. 2, n. 10; Flet. l. 2, c. 60, in pr.

2 Dr. Cowell, in his Institutiones Juris Anglicani, says, "Quod tamen ad negotiorum gestionem attinet, operæ absentium causâ sine mandato præstitiæ, conscientiæ ejus cujus negotium geritur et integritati potius relinguntur, quam actione aliquâ sustinetur."—Tit. de Oblig. quæ Quasi ex Cont.

As somewhat analogous to this point, however, it is said, in Doctor and Student, Dial. 2, c. 11, "Though a man waive the possession of his goods, and saith he forsaketh them, yet by the law of the realm the property remaineth still in him, and he may have them after when he will. And if any man in the meantime put the goods in safeguard to the use of the owner, I think he doth it lawfully, and that he shall be allowed for his reasonable expenses in that behalf."

3 Dyer, fo. 36, n. 38, 39; Year Book, 21 Hen. VII. 27 B, 28 A; Year Book, 12 Hen. VIII. 2, 3.

Parallel Articles of the French Code.

conversion, which will not in general lie where an injury has been done to a chattel, in endeavouring to do a service to the owner out of charity, or to prevent mischief from the act of other persons.[1] And in trespass or case a jury would probably refuse to give more than nominal damages, where the interference was intended bonâ fide for the benefit of the absentee.

The various statutes and limitations provide for the protection of the interests of persons absent beyond the seas, and for a reasonable time prevent their being barred by lapse of time; but to obviate uncertainty of possession, after a definite period, though absent, they are totally barred.[2]

Where the heir of a person dead, leaving landed property, cannot be found, it has been decided that the Court of Chancery will not declare a will (affecting such property) proved;[3] but, though not proved, it may be established for some purposes;[4] and a sale of land, directed by such will for payment of debts, will be decreed.[5]

By 36 Geo. III. c. 52, s. 32, an executor is enabled to discharge himself, by paying legacies bequeathed to persons absent beyond the sea into the Bank of England, with the privity of the Accountant-General of the Court of Chancery, to be placed to the account of the legatee; who on summary application may have it paid over.

As to the second class of interests, absence, except for illegal purposes, is so extremely rare, that it is for the 112.

[1] Drake v. Shorte, 4 Esp. 165.

[2] See tit. As to the excuses for not making claim or entry, see Bract. 437, si in prisona detentus, and si ultra mare quacunque occasione; 163, si in perigrinatione extra regnum, and si in terra sancta; and see Co. Lit., Blackstone, Entry and Claim.

[3] French v. Barron, 2 Atk. 120; 1 Dick. 138.

[4] Stokes v. Taylor, 1 Dick. 349.

[5] Cator v. Butler, 2 Dick. 438; Braithwaite v. Robinson, 2 Dick. 439 n.; Williams v. Whinyates, 2 Bro. 399.

In one case, Bannister v. Way, 2 Dick. 599, though the heir could not be found, Lord Thurlow declared the will proved; and said the heir, when he should appear, must get rid of it as he could.

Parallel Articles of the French Code.

most part considered and treated as voluntary and fraudulent; and the law will not allow a party, by absconding, to avoid the just demands of his creditors, or the duties he owes to others. There are as to traders two courses, when it is necessary to interfere with the goods of absent persons, in order to obtain the satisfaction of debts or claims; by the one, a specific debt may be recovered, by the other, the whole of an absent person's creditors may recover their debts, or a rateable proportion, as far as his property will extend. In the first case, the parties interested may either proceed to outlaw the absentee for want of appearance[1] to the process of the causes; and then his goods may be seized by the sheriff, and the claim satisfied on motion or petition out of the effects in the sheriff's hands:[2] but if the plaintiff or his attorney knows the defendant's attorney, he must apply to the defendant's attorney, or the outlawry will be set aside with costs.[3] Or, the parties may commence an action and distrain 40*s.* of the absentee's goods, and then cause an appearance to be entered for him, and proceed to judgment and execution.[4]

As to the other course, where a person departs from his dwelling-house, or otherwise absents himself to defraud or delay his creditors, he may be made a bankrupt, and his goods sequestered.[5] If the party absconding be not a trader, the first is in general the only course that can be pursued.

There are other remedies provided for some of the cases, where persons who have duties to perform are not forthcoming: thus, where copyholds are descendible, the

---

[1] Ante, p. 222.

[2] Ante, p. 223, Tidd's Practice. To give the Court of Chancery as effectual a remedy as the proceeding to outlawry affords, 5 Geo. II. c. 25, an act for making process in courts of equity effectual against persons who abscond, &c., was passed, see 11 Geo. IV. and 1 Wm. IV. c. 36.

[3] Pigou v. Drummond, 1 Bing. N. C. 354.

[4] 2 Wm. IV. c. 39, and sched. 3; Johnson v. Smealy, 1 Dowl. 526.

[5] 6 Geo. IV, c. 16, and the works on bankrupt law.

Parallel Articles of the French Code.

heir is bound on the death of his ancestor, and the devisee on the death of his testator, to come to the lord's court, and require to be admitted, on paying the customary fine and fees. If he neglects to appear within the time prescribed by the custom of the manor, proclamations are made for him to come in and be admitted; and on default of doing so, the lord may seize the copyhold as forfeited, quousque, &c.[1]

Where the party absent is a trustee, executor, or other person, only legally interested, and appears to have absconded to avoid service of subpœna, at the suit of the party equitably interested, the Court of Chancery will appoint a receiver over the estates:[2] and an administrator, durante absentia, may be appointed on the prolonged absence of an executor.

In order to prevent abuse of the process of the court, where the defendant cannot be met with, the court requires an affidavit of the facts, or the return of the sheriff that the party cannot be found, either to entitle the plaintiff to enter an appearance on distringas, and to proceed to judgment and execution, or to outlaw the defendant:[3] and before outlawry can issue, the party is to be called, exacted, or proclaimed, to appear at five several county courts or hustings. One proclamation must be made near the door of the church of the parish wherein the party most usually dwelt.[4] 116.

If a defendant be in prison or beyond the sea, at the time of the exigent awarded, the outlawry will be reversed.[5]

---

1 Cruise, tit. 10, c. 5.

2 Maguire v. Allen, 1 Ball & B. 75; Montgomery v. Clarke, 2 Atkins, 378; Huguenin v. Basely, 13 Ves. 105; Middleton v. Dodswell, 13 Ves. 266.

3 Books of Com. Law Practice.

4 See p. 222, art. 27 to 31. The whole system of Anglo-Saxon law having been founded on the frankpledge, in which every person was a member of some tithing, and in which all the members were pledge (borh) for each other, persons not forthcoming in their tithings were outlawed; and out of this system the present law, governing the cases of persons who are not to be found by their creditors, has grown.

5 Pp. 224, 5; 5 Rep. 111 a; 4 Skin. 116; Barnes, 228.

Some analogy existed between the causes which prevented the necessity of

Parallel Articles of the French Code.

If the outlawry is reversed, the party outlawed is entitled to be put in the same situation as if an outlawry had not taken place; for a strict construction is put, in
114. favour of a person absent, on acts done by the sheriff or others during the outlawry.
127. With regard to the third class of interests, namely, those which would arise from the death of the person supposed to be absent, although the general rule is that the presumption of law in all cases is, that the party
129. continues alive until the contrary is shown,[1] yet the proof of unaccountable absence for a given time will
120. raise a contrary presumption. In general, the judge will not proceed to grant probate of the will, or letters of
130. administration of the effects, in case of doubt whether the person be dead or not: but recourse may be had to the presumption of law to prove the death of an absentee, and the probate or administration will be granted, especially if his goods are bonâ heritura.[2] The presumption of the duration of the life of persons of whom no account can be given, ends at the expiration of seven years from the time when they were last known to be living;[3] and a ship not heard of for two or three years is presumed to be lost: but at what exact time a person on board perished is a question to be judged by the jury on the peculiar circumstances of the case;[4] and strong circumstances would even induce a presumption of death at a still earlier

---

claims or entry to avoid a disseizin, and now postpone the operation of statutes of limitation and those which prevented outlawry, or the essoins or excuses formerly allowed for not immediately obeying the process of the court; and therefore see Glanville; Bracton, lib. 5; Britton, c. 22; Fleta, l. 6, as to essoins; especially essoin de ultra mare, de terra sancta, de servitio regis, allowed in the cases of absence. In the pilgrimages to the Holy Land, and in the wars between France and England, there must have been frequent cases of total absence, without anything certain as to the death of the party.—See Assise de Mort d'Ancètor, where a man dies on pilgrimage beyond the sea, Fitz. N.B. 195, 6.

[1] 2 Stark. Ev. 457. Bishop of Salisbury's case, 10 Rep. 59. Webster v. Birchmore, 13 Ves. 362.

[2] Swinb. part 6, s. 13, pl. 2; Godolph. part 1, c. 20, s. 3.

[3] 1 Jac. I. c. 11; 19 Car. II. c. 6; Doe d. Lloyd v. Deakins, 4 B. & A. 433; Doe d. George v. Jesson, 6 East, 84.

[4] Watson v. King, 1 Stark. 12.

Parallel Articles of the French Code.

period. From the time when the death is to be presumed, the parties entitled by death enter immediately into possession of the deceased's property, though it seems security to refund might be ordered.[1] In general, a 121.
power of attorney terminates with the death of either 122.
party; and if a person absent left a power of attorney with another, and afterwards a presumption arose of the death of the absentee, the power would be determined, it should seem from analogy, from the time of the supposed death; and the attorney would have from that time to account to the respective parties interested in the absentee's real or personal property; and his ignorance of the absentee's death would not delay their rights.[2]

The will of a person presumed to be dead would be 123.
operative, like that of any other person. As to the time at which the estates would be considered to have vested, in general it may be laid down, that the death would be presumed to have taken place at the end of seven years from the time the absent person was last heard of;[3] and the parties then entitled would be con- 130.
sidered to have taken the estates at that time. This is, however, properly a subject for inquiry, and for the determination of a jury in a court of law,[4] or for inquiry before a master in chancery.[5]

---

[1] There is a case stated in Vin. Ab. iv. 235, B 2, as follows:—B, about five years since, went beyond sea, leaving a note that he would not return in seven years, but it is not known if he be living or not. C, as next of kin, suggesting B to be dead, takes out administration, and brings a bill for a legacy bequeathed to B. The legacy and interest since B went were decreed to be paid to C, he giving security to repay it to B if he should ever return, which security is to stand for three years and no longer, but the plaintiff's own security to stand for ever.

[2] Lepard v. Vernon, 2 Ves. & B. 51: Welles, 105; 5 Esp. 118; 6 East, 356.

[3] Doe d. George v. Jesson, 6 East, 84; 2 Smith, 236. Doe v. Nepean, 2 N.&M. 219.

[4] In Doe d. George v. Jesson, the judge left it to the jury to say when and where a party not heard of for many years died; and it was said to be incumbent on the jury to find the fact as well as they could, under the doubt and difficulty of the case. Park, Insur. 433.

[5] See Hudson v. Twining, 1 Taml. 315, where, on a bill filed by the representatives of A, who had been unheard of for many years, for payment of a legacy given to him if he attained twenty-one, an inquiry was directed as to whether he attained that age.

Parallel Articles of the French Code.

As to rights and property accruing by descent or distribution to an absent person, who should not re-appear, the question as to whether they vested in him, would
135. turn upon the period when the death was to be pre-
136. sumed to have taken place according to the foregoing principles, and according to whether he was presumed to have died before or after the right accrued: and in the latter case his representatives, or the representatives of those entitled in default, would take.

128. At common law, possession taken on the disappearance
131. of a person would render the person liable to the party
132. in case he re-appeared, according to the principles already laid down; and where under a statute a person is to be presumed to be dead if he is unheard of for seven years, yet if he re-appear, or be proved to be alive, he shall recover his property; and he may recover, in an action at law, the rents and profits, interests and damages, of his real estate.[1] And there does not appear to be any period put to the time of regaining his property on re-appearance, unless the statutes of limitation of actions could be construed to apply to it; but as a possession in right of representation of the absent party could scarcely be considered as adverse to him, they would probably be held not to bar his right.[2]

139. The husband or wife of a person absent, without the one knowing the other to be living, may presume the absentee to be dead, and may marry again.[3] And a wife may sue, as if single, after seven years since the husband was last heard of.[4]

141. If the father or guardian of an infant be absent, application might be made to the Court of Chancery; and where the minor has property to make the child a ward of the court, so as to get its interference and protection, it is sufficient to file a bill.[5]

---

[1] 19 Car. II. c. 6, s. 25; 6 Anne, c. 18, s. 3. It was said he might recover of the lessor of the plaintiff, Doe d. Lloyd v. Deakin, 4 B. & A. 433.

[2] But see 3 & 4 Wm. IV. c. 27, s. 7, 8.

[3] 1 Jac. I. c. 11, s. 2.

[4] Hopewell v. De Pinna, 2 Campb. 113.

[5] Butler v. Freeman, Amb. 301.

TITLE V.

OF MARRIAGE.[1]

Its General Nature.

Parallel Articles of the French Code.

Difference of sex greatly affects the civil state of persons, but chiefly that of females in marriage, or under coverture, as the English law calls it. Marriage is legally defined to be the natural union[2] of two individuals of different sexes, in a contract formed, by mutual consent, with the observance of due forms, in the presence of a properly constituted authority, and entered into with a view of one undivided state of society for life,[3] for the purposes of procreating and bringing up children. For the most part it may be considered as a civil contract: but, besides the important end for which marriage was instituted, in most civilized countries, acting under a sense of the force of sacred obligations, it has had the sanction of religion superadded;[4] and in the Catholic church, marriage has been elevated to the dignity of a sacrament. The relation of marriage is in England considered as a subject of so much higher a nature than ordinary contracts, that it is seldom referred to as having any analogy with them.[5]

As a general rule, all persons arrived at puberty are legally competent to marry; there are, however, besides mere legal forms to be observed, certain conditions which are requisite to prevent a marriage from being totally void or voidable: these are chiefly arising from the parties' ages, want of consent of either party, impediments from prior marriage, or from relationship. The

[1] As to marriage in the Anglo-Saxon period, see ante, pp. 25 to 29.

[2] Maris et fœminæ conjunctio est de jure naturæ.—7 Rep. 13.

[3] Consortium omnis vitæ.

[4] See ante, p. 27.

[5] Sir W. Scott, in Dalrymple v. Dalrymple.

Parallel Articles of the French Code.

want of the consent of the parents of minors does not, in the English law, affect the validity of a marriage once contracted,[1] though it may prove an impediment to its being contracted. By the law of England, definite public forms are established, without which the relation of husband and wife cannot be contracted;[2] and, in order that a marriage may be valid, it is essential that it should be celebrated in due form of law, by a proper person, in a proper place, and at a lawful time, and after due notice or licence.

CHAPTER I.

Of the Qualities and Conditions required, in order to be able to contract Marriage.

144. With regard to the age at which a marriage may be contracted, as it is necessary the parties should be capable of consenting, which is the very essence of the contract, if either of the parties be under seven years of age, the marriage is absolutely void.[3] And if a boy under fourteen or a girl under twelve years of age, marries, this marriage is inchoate and imperfect; and when either of them comes to that age, they may disagree, and declare the marriage void.[4]

145. And though the Archbishop of Canterbury can grant dispensations not contrary to the Scriptures, for whatever the court of Rome could formerly have granted;[5] yet he cannot supply the want of consent which a party under the above age is incapable of giving, so as to

---

1 Rex v. Birmingham.

2 Dalrymple v. Dalrymple.

3 Swin. Mat. Cont. They cannot even contract sponsalia.—Burn. Eccl. L. Mar. Sponsalia dicuntur futurarum nuptiarum conventio et repromissio.—Co. Lit. 34. Sponsalia inter minores contracta, ante 7 annos nulla sunt.—Jenk. Cent. 95.

4 1 Bl. Com. 436; Co. Lit. 79 a; 1 Jac. I. c. 11, s. 3; M'Neill v. Macgregor, 2 Bligh & R. Their contract would only amount to sponsalia.—Burn, Eccl. L. Mar.; Sir G. Arthur's case, Vin. Ab. Mar. D. 2.

5 25 Hen. VIII. c. 21, s. 4, 8.

prevent the parties disagreeing when of age to do so.[1] Parallel Articles of the French Code.
But the marriages of princes made by the state in their behalf, at any age, are held good.[2]

Where there is not the consent of both, there is no marriage.[3] The consent[4] of the parties being the very essence of the contract, the presence of proper and lawfully constituted authorities is generally sufficient to ensure that such consent is given in marriages lawfully contracted; and a rational agent (having attained the above age[5]) shall not be at liberty to allege a secret dissent of the mind from an act avowedly done in the face of God and man, under all the sanctions of religion and law, with apparently complete consent:[6] it would be otherwise[7] in cases of open or actual violence;[8] and want of reason would invalidate the consent. A deliberate and serious consent of a free and rational agent, is essential to the validity of the marriage contract.[9] 146.

As to the next impediment: if a first marriage subsist, a second marriage is to all intents and purposes void; it is a mere nullity.[10] 147.

With regard to the consent of parents,[11] as publication 148.

---

[1] Co. Lit. 33 a, 79 a.

[2] Swinb. Mat. Cont.; Swinb. Spons.

[3] Ubi non est consensus utriusque, non est conjugium.—Constitutions of Edmund, Archbishop of Canterbury, from Lyndwood. See Poynter, Law of Marriage and Divorce, p. 30.

[4] Consensus, non concubitus facit matrimonium, 1 Bl. Com. 436; et consentire non possunt ante annos nubiles.—6 Rep. 23.

[5] The law allows the minor to marry, and attributes to him, in a way which cannot be legally averred against upon the mere ground of youth and inexperience, a competent discretion to dispose of himself in marriage. He is arrived at years of discretion, quo ad hoc, whatever he may be with other transactions of life; and he cannot be heard to plead the indiscretion of minority.—Dalrymple v. Dalrymple.

[6] Dalrymple v. Dalrymple, 2 Hag. 106.

[7] 1 Rolls Abr. 840; Harford v. Morris, 2 Hag. 436. But subsequent voluntary cohabitation will give validity to the marriage.—Wakefield v. M'Kay, 1 Phill. 134.

[8] Vani timores sunt æstimandi, qui non cadunt in constantem virum.—7 Rep. 27.

[9] Portsmouth v. Portsmouth, 1 Hag. 372.

[10] Dalrymple v. Dalrymple, 2 Hag. 129.

[11] By the 100th canon, no persons under the age of twenty-one years shall contract themselves in marriage without the consent of their parents or guardians.

Parallel Articles of the French Code.

of banns, or registrar's notice, is supposed to give the parents and guardians notice sufficient to enable them to oppose the proposed marriage, except in case of frauds, the marriage of an infant after such publication is binding;[1] but if the parents or guardians of a party under twenty-one years openly declare or cause to be declared, at the time of publication of banns, their dissent to the marriage, the publication becomes absolutely void.[2] And all marriages by licence, where either of the parties is under twenty-one years of age, (not being a widow or widower), must be with the consent of the father, or, if he be not living, of the mother or guardians.[3]

149. 150. If the father be dead, the guardian, or if there be no guardian, then the mother if unmarried, or if there be no mother unmarried, then the guardian appointed by the Court of Chancery, if any, shall have authority to give consent to the marriage; and such consent is required for the marriage, unless there be no person authorized to give such consent.[4] But the section of the marriage act requiring the consent has been held only to be directory, and the want of such consent will not invalidate the marriage of a minor by licence, after it has been solemnized.[5]

151 to 157. When both parties have attained the age of twenty-one years, they may lawfully marry without consulting any person, however unadvisable such a course may often be.

156. If any person solemnize matrimony without due publication of the banns, or due notice to the registrar (unless by licence), he shall be guilty of felony, and transported for fourteen years.[6]

---

1 2 Phil. Ecc. C. 363.

2 4 Geo. IV. c. 76, s. 8.

3 See Canon 100, 103, 104; 1 Bl. Com. 437; 4 Geo. IV. c. 76, s. 16; 6 & 7 Wm. IV. c. 85, s. 10.—Ante, p. 235, 6; and Rex v. Birmingham, 8 B. & C. 29. As to obtaining licence, see ante, p. 235.

4 4 Geo. IV. c. 76, s. 16. And then the party is required by the ordinary to make oath to that effect.

5 Rex v. Birmingham, 8 B. & C. 29.

6 4 Geo. IV. c. 76, s. 21; or felony, 6 & 7 Wm. IV. c. 85, s. 39; and a clergyman would be liable to be suspended per triennium, 63rd canon.

Parallel Articles of the French Code.

The only methods by which the marriage of a natural child can be legally solemnized, while a minor, are either after publication of banns, or registrar's notice, or after the appointment of a guardian for the child, by the 158. Court of Chancery,[1] and then the marriage may be per- 159. formed under a licence, with the consent of such guardian.[2]

Where there is no father, guardian, or mother, a minor 160. may be married by licence without consent, but he is required to make oath of such being the fact; and in case the father of the party under age be non compos mentis, or the guardian, or mother, or any of them whose consent is necessary, be non compos mentis, or in parts beyond the seas, or shall unreasonably, or from undue motives, withold consent to a proper marriage, the Court of Chancery may, if they think proper, declare the same to be so, which shall be as effectual as a consent.[3]

We now come to impediments arising from relation- 161. ship, either of consanguinity by blood, or affinity by marriage;[4] in the direct ascending and descending line all marriages are prohibited.[5] But persons may marry their consanguinei, if beyond the fourth degree of the civil law: thus a man may marry his grandmother's sister.[6]

The English law takes the Levitical law for its 162. standard,[7] and in the collateral line marriage is prohibited between brother and sister, and their widow or widower, and between all who are in the fourth degree of consanguinity. But the consanguinei of the husband are not at all related to the consanguinei of the wife: hence two brothers may marry two sisters, and

[1] The words father and mother have been held to mean legitimate parents only.—Priestly v. Hughes, 11 East, 1; Horner v. Liddiard.

[2] 1 Roper, 340.

[3] 4 Geo. IV. c. 76, s. 17; ante, pp. 237, 8.

[4] Consanguineus est quasi eodem sanguine natus.—Co. Lit. 157 a.

Affinitas dicitur cum duæ cognationes, inter se divisæ, per nuptias copulantur et altera ad alterius fines accedit.—Co. Lit. 157 a.

[5] Burn, Eccl. L.

[6] Gibs. Cod. 413.

[7] Canon 99; 32 Hen. VIII. c. 38, s. 2; Harrison v. Burwell, Vaugh. 219.

Parallel Articles of the French Code.

a brother's widow and a sister's widower may marry. Between collaterals, all who were in the fourth degree of the civil law or higher, are permitted to marry; affinity arises between the consanguinei of each party, and the other party.[1]

163. Uncle and niece, aunt and nephew, are within the fourth degree, and cannot contract marriage.[2]

164. These impediments cannot be removed, as the Archbishop or other person has no power to grant dispensation contrary to the Levitical law.[3]

CHAPTER II.

Of the Formalities to be observed in the Celebration of Marriage.

165. To make a legal marriage, the parties must not only be willing and able to contract, but they must do so in due form of law.[4] A marriage must be celebrated either in some parish church or chapel, by a person in holy orders,[5] or before the registrar or his deputy, in a public place, with open doors, between the hours of eight and twelve in the forenoon, in the presence of two or more credible witnesses.[6] And a marriage so solemnized in fact, is presumed to be valid to all intents and purposes, until the contrary is proved.[7]

166. The publications mentioned in (parallel) article 63, must have been duly made in the parish or poor law district, in which each of the contracting parties reside,[8]

---

[1] Jones v. Bean, 1 Mod. 25.

[2] Harrison v. Burnell, 2 Vent. 17; Murgatroyd v. Rotham, Jones, 191.

[3] 25 Hen. VIII. c. 21; 32 Hen. VIII. c. 38.

[4] Dalrymple v. Dalrymple; and see ante, p. 238.

[5] Ante, p. 27.

[6] 4 Geo. IV. c. 76, s. 21—26; 6 & 7 Wm. IV. c. 83, s. 20.

[7] Poynter, p. 50

[8] See par. art. 63, pp. 234, 5, 6.

unless the marriage be by licence; otherwise it is absolutely null and void.[1]

Parallel Articles of the French Code.

And the parties must give seven days' notice before the publication, and they must have resided in the district,[2] at least seven days' previously; but there need be no publication in any other places than where the parties have resided the last fourteen days;[3] and the residence of the parties cannot be enquired into after the marriage has been solemnized.[4]

167.
168.

When licence of the surrogate is obtained, marriage may be forthwith solemnized without any such publication or notice.[5] 169.

As to the celebration of marriages out of the realm, it is a rule of the English law, that a foreign marriage, whether of natives or foreigners, valid according to the laws of the place where it is celebrated, is (as far as the ceremony is concerned) good every where.[6] And even a marriage, invalid by the laws of the place where it was celebrated, may be good according to the law of England.[7] 170.

---

[1] 4 Geo. IV. c. 76, s. 22.

[2] By 6 & 7 Wm. IV. c. 85.

[3] There is no provision for publication in any other place.

[4] 4 Geo. IV. c. 76, s. 26; 6 & 7 Wm. IV. c. 85, s. 25; Tree v. Quin, 2 Phil. Eccl. C. 14; and see marriage by banns held legal, though only one of the parties resided in the parish, 18 Ves. 289; or, though neither resident, 16 Ves. 259.

[5] 4 Geo. IV. c. 76, s. 14; 6 & 7 Wm. IV. c. 85, s. 12. As to seven days' notice for registrar's licence, see ante, p. 236.

[6] Ante, p. 230. Ryan v. Ryan, 2 Phil. Eccl. R. 332; Herbert v. Herbert, 3 Phil. Eccl. R. 58; Lacon v. Higgins, 3 Stark. 178; 1 D. & R. N. P. C. 42; Latour v. Teesdale, 2 Marsh, 243; Dalrymple v. Dalrymple, 2 Hag. 59; Scrimshire v. Scrimshire, 2 Hag. 402.

[7] Ruding v. Smith, 2 Hag. Con. R. 390; Harford v. Higgins, 2 Hag. Con. R. 423. Marriage is to be determined by the law of that country where it was contracted.—Law Maxim. Marriage contracts made in all countries to be performed.—Ib.

Parallel Articles of the French Code.

CHAPTER III.

Of Opposition to a Marriage.

172. In general, those only whose consent is necessary to
173. a marriage have any absolute power to oppose, for want
174. of age;[1] but it may also be objected to by a person on
175. the grounds of prior marriage, want of reason in either party, or incest;[2] and any person duly authorized in that behalf may oppose a marriage, by openly dissenting at the publication of the banns, or by writing "forbidden," with the name and address, in the registrar's notice-book, or by entering a caveat against licence.[3]

176. In publicly opposing a marriage by banns, the party must attend when required (usually, immediately after the service is concluded), and give the particulars of name, &c., and the grounds of opposition, to the clergyman.[4] A person writing "forbidden" in the registrar's notice-book, must sign his or her name, place of abode, and character;[5] and a caveat to a licence in the registrar's books must be duly signed by the person entering it, with the place of residence, and the ground of objection:[6] or a caveat may likewise be entered by a proctor in the Spiritual Court.[7]

177. In marriages, according to the church of England, when the banns of a minor are forbidden by the parent or guar-

[1] 26 Geo. II. c. 33, s. 3; and see ante, p. 236.

[2] The Rubrick says, "If any man do allege and declare any impediment why they may not be coupled together in matrimony, by God's law, or the law of the realm, and will be bound and sufficient sureties with him to the parties, or else put in a caution (to the full value of such charges as the parties to be married do thereby sustain) to prove his allegation; then the solemnization must be deferred until such time as the truth is tried."

[3] 4 Geo. IV. c. 76, s. 8; 6 & 7 Wm. IV. c. 85, s. 9—13.

[4] Ante, p. 236; Burn, Eccl. Law.

[5] 6 & 7 Wm. IV. c. 85, s. 9.

[6] Ib. s. 13.

[7] 4 Geo. IV. c. 76, s. 11; 6 & 7 Wm. IV. c. 85, s. 13.

dian, the publication is void, and in other cases the parties must appeal to the spiritual judge; and when a caveat is entered, licence shall not be granted until the matter has been examined by the judge whose office it is to issue it.[1] In marriages under the new system,[2] no certificate or licence under the act can be issued or granted until the superintendant registrar is satisfied that the marriage ought not to be obstructed.[3]

If the superintendant registrar is doubtful, or decide 178.
against the marriage, an appeal may be made to the registrar-general.[4]

Persons vexatiously entering a caveat forbidding a 179.
marriage are liable to costs, and also to damages, in an action on the special case.[5]

CHAPTER IV.

Of Suits for Nullity of Marriage.

According to the law of England, some kinds of impediments incapacitate the parties from contracting marriage at all; such as prior marriage, want of due notice, and knowingly marrying without due publication, or after banns of a minor forbidden; and unions formed in opposition to them are not matrimonial, but meretricious only: they are illegal and void ab initio. Sentence declaring the fact of marriage to be a nullity may in such case be obtained at any time.[6] Other kinds of impediments render it voidable after it has been solemnized, if sentence of the court be obtained, which makes it void ab initio, but until sentence the marriage subsists for all civil purposes: of this kind are consanguinity, affinity, and certain infirmities In these cases, a sentence of the court is necessary to decide whether the

---

[1] 4 Geo. IV. c. 76, s. 11; 6 & 7 Wm. IV. c. 85, s. 13. [2] Ante, p. 234.
[3] 6 & 7 Wm. IV. c. 85, s. 13. [4] Ib. [5] Ib. s. 37. [6] Poynter, 49.

Parallel Articles of the French Code.

marriage be valid or null: and others are obstacles to its being solemnized, but do not avoid it afterwards, as want of the parents' consent, if not expressed, when the party is a minor.

Suits for nullity of marriage may be brought on account of force, or fraud, or incest, or too near relationship, or incapacity to consent, or want of actual consent as in case of lunacy, or great mental weakness imposed on by fraud, or for want of due form as misnomer in banns, or on account of impotency or sterility.[1]

The law of England has made provisions[2] for preventing, as far as possible, parties from being forced into a marriage against their wills, or even without consent; and the ceremony having been performed, and consent expressed, according to the prescribed forms, neither party capable of giving a consent is at liberty to pretend want of consent, except in the cases of force or fraud. There are but few cases of forcible marriages in England, and they would be void, though not without the suit.[3]

180. It must be laid down as a general rule, that to entitle any third person to institute proceedings for annulling a marriage, it is necessary that such third person should be proved to have a sufficient interest in the matter on which to ground their right of interference;[4] and any party interested, though a third person, and even a committee of a lunatic, or a person claiming an estate in remainder on failure of issue, may institute a suit for nullity of marriage in the Consistory Court,[5] or may intervene in a court of appeal.[6]

---

1 2 Chit. Gen. Prac. 458; Poynter's Law of Marriage and Divorce, p. 140.

2 See par. art. 165.

3 Brown's case, 1 Vent. 243; Roll. Ab. 340, p. 5; and Vin. Ab. B. & F. A. 5, and margin; Harford v. Morris, 2 Hag. 436.

4 Poynter, p. 120. A father of a minor has a right to institute and prosecute a suit for nullity of marriage even against the will of the minor.—Bowyer v. Ricketts, 1 Hag. Cons. 214, 5.

5 Donegal v. Chichester, 3 Phil. Ecc. Rep. 590; 1 Add. R. 16 S. C.; Parnell v. Parnell, 2 Hag. Cons. R. 169; Portsmouth v. Portsmouth, 1 Hag. Ecc. R. 355.

6 Exparte Turning, 1 Ves. & B. 140; Donegal v. Chichester, 3 Phil. R. 593, n.

Parallel Articles of the French Code.

In suits for nullity for fraud on a third person, the act of alleged fraud must be proved to have been knowingly committed.[1] As to the effect of fraud between the parties, mistake or error as to person, if it could possibly occur, might avoid a marriage; but error or misrepresentation about the family or fortune of the person, would not at all affect the validity of the marriage.[2] The law will not allow a person to take advantage of his own wrong; and where one party has acted fraudulently, or married under disqualifications of which the other party was ignorant,[3] it shall not avoid the marriage if the other party be innocent.[4]

Where a marriage in fact is consummated without 181.
the consent of either of the parties, and therefore void or voidable, such consent may be subsequently given expressly or impliedly, and establish the marriage. Thus when parties are married before the age competent to consent, they may disagree when they attain that age, and the marriage is void; but if after the age of consent the parties continue to live together, the marriage is good:[5] and the same principle applies to cases of marriages originally contracted by fraud or force, continued after the period when the fraud was discovered, or the force withdrawn.[6] And in all cases the non-consent must be proved: and perhaps only actual dissent would in most cases be allowed to set aside the presumption of consent.[7]

Where the parties are of age competent to consent, 182.
we have seen the want of the consent of the parent or guardian does not avoid a marriage, whether by banns

[1] Allen v. Wood, 1 Bing. N. C. 11; Rex v. Wroxton, 4 B. & Ad. 640; Periget v. Tomkins, 2 Hag. Cons. 142; Wyatt v. Henry, ib. 215; Sullivan v. Sullivan, ib. 238.

[2] Wilson v. Brockley, 1 Phil. E. C. 173; Wakefield v. McKay, 1 Phil. 134; ante, p. 263, n. 7.

[3] King v. Wroxton; 4 B. & Ad. 640; 3 Man. & Sel. 230; 1 Phil. 47; 2 Phil. 12; but see 1 B. & Ad. 144.

[4] Norton v. Seton, 3 Phil. 147.

[5] 1 Bl. Com. 436; Co. Lit. 79.

[6] Wakefield v. M'Kay, 1 Phil. 134.

[7] See Poynter, pp. 31, 2.

Parallel Articles of the French Code.

or licence; though expressed dissent, when the party is a minor, avoids it entirely. A marriage by licence, where one party is a minor, without the consent of parent or guardian, although obtained by false swearing that the party was of age, is not void; though the husband, when a party to the violation of the law, is to be deprived of all right to the property of the wife:[1] and a court of equity has no discretion to mitigate that penalty, but must settle and secure all the property of the wife, present and future, for the benefit of herself or the issue of the marriage.[2] Where either of the parties is under the age competent to consent (ætas nubilis), though the consent of the parent have been obtained, although one be above that age, either of them may, when the one under that age attains that age, disagree; for the rule is, that in contracts of matrimony both must be bound, or the election of disagreement must be given to both.[3] This rule, however true may be its application to actual marriages, or to marriages per verba de præsenti, must not be taken as extending to contracts of marriage per verba de futuro, for in them the person of full age may be bound at all events, and liable to damages for breach of promise; and yet as to the infant, the contract may be voidable.[4] Where the parties continue to cohabit after the marriageable age is attained, they cannot afterwards avoid their marriage by disagreeing.[5] The fact of the female who had not attained that marriageable age having conceived before the disagreement, would not affect the power of disagreeing, and would bastardize the issue.[6]

---

[1] 4 Geo. IV. c. 76, s. 23; Rex v. Inhabitants of Birmingham.

[2] Attorney-General v. Mully, 4 Russ. 329; see Russell & R. Cro. C. 459.

[3] Co. Lit. 79 b.

[4] Note to Co. Lit. Hag. & But. 79; Holt v. Ward, 3 New Ab. 314; Vin. Ab. Marr. C. 4.

[5] Co. Lit. 79 b.

[6] See Kenne's case, 7 Rep. 42. And it has been decided that if the wife, being marriageable, of an infant under fourteen has issue it is a bastard.—Vin. Ab. Enfant (I. 2) 1, and Vin. Ab. Bast. (A. 2) 9, (H.) 3, 4.

Parallel Articles of the French Code.

Every marriage contrary to the regulations in the parallel articles 144 (when under seven years of age), 147, 161, 162, 163, is either in itself, or after sentence, absolutely void ab initio; and a suit for nullity may 184.
be instituted by those interested therein.

Any person having an interest to avoid a marriage, 187.
may institute a suit for that purpose in cases of incest.[1]
A second marriage, during the existence of the first, is 188.
absolutely void; but in cases where a question arises as 189.
to the validity of the second, on the ground of the invalidity of the first, that will be first considered.[2] Every marriage not celebrated before the proper person, or in an improper place (except by special licence), is 191.
absolutely void, besides subjecting all the parties to criminal prosecution.[3]

Clandestine marriages are punishable, under the old 192.
common law, by fine and imprisonment; and by statute 193.
a marriage by banns, not truly stating the christian and surnames of each party, is invalid when the mis-statement is knowingly made;[4] though if one party did not know of the misnomer till after the solemnization of the marriage, it will be valid.[5]

If any persons wilfully intermarry under the new marriage act (which does not interfere with 4 Geo. IV. c. 76), without due notice to the superintendant-registrar, the marriage is null and void.[6] Persons wilfully making false declarations, or signing false notices, are liable to the penalties of perjury.[7] Every minister who celebrates marriage contrary to the canons, as to banns and licence, is liable to be suspended, per triennium.[8]

---

[1] 1 Phil. 355.
[2] Kenne's case; Dalrymple v. Dalrymple.
[3] 4 Geo. IV. c. 76, s. 22.
[4] Ib.; Rex v. Inhabitants of Tibshelf, 1 B. & Ad. 194; Rex. v. Inhabitants of Billinghurst, 3 M. & S. 257; Allen v. Wood, 1 Bing., New Cases, 11; 1 Phil. Ecc. C. 133, 224, 230, 298, 375; 2 Phil. Ecc. C. 14, 104, 367.
[5] Ante, p. 271; Rex v. Wroxton, 4 B. & Ad. 640.
[6] 6 & 7 Wm. IV. c. 85, s. 42.
[7] 6 & 7 Wm. IV. c. 85, s. 38. See 165.
[8] Can. 63.

Parallel Articles of the French Code.

The registration of a marriage is not absolutely necessary to make it valid;[1] and all the legitimate consequences of marriage may be enjoyed without it.

194. 195. A marriage may be proved by the testimony of persons who were present and witnessed the ceremony, or by general reputation;[2] but in case of adultery, proof of cohabitation and general reputation is not sufficient.[3]

196. A marriage register is primâ facie evidence that a marriage was celebrated at the time, place, &c. mentioned in it; but strong circumstances might be allowed to rebut it, and it is not positive evidence unless the identity of the parties be proved.[4]

197. A marriage not void of itself is not voidable by the ecclesiastical law after the death of either of the parties;[5] but no length of time establishes a marriage void in itself, and the death of either or both parties does not prevent sentence declaratory of the nullity of the fact of the marriage being given.[6]

Where the actual marriage can be proved, the mere absence of the register would not affect it at all. And where the actual marriage cannot be proved, the usual presumptive proof of marriage is not taken away by the acts of parliament, which require every marriage to be registered in case of a question respecting the legitimacy of children.[7] A distinction, however, exists as to the sufficiency of presumptive proof: that to establish a legal right to real property, an actual marriage must in general be proved by such evidence as will satisfy a jury; but a marriage in possession is always sufficient in personal things.[8]

---

1 Reed v. Passer, 1 Peake, 231; ante, p. 229.

2 Evans v. Morgan, 2 C. & I. 453; Hervey v. Hervey, 2 W. Black. 877; Birt v. Barlow, Dougl. 162; Allison's case, B. & R. 109.

3 Morris v. Miller, 4 Burr. 2057.

4 Draycot v. Talbot, Vin. Ab. Mar. D. 6.

5 1 Bl. Com. 440; Cro. Jac. 186; Brownsward v. Edwards, 2 Ves. 245; Elliot v. Gurr, 2 Phil. R. 19.

6 Poynter, pp. 49, 50.

7 St. Devereux v. Much Dew Church, 1 Blac. Rep. 367; Rex v. Allison; Russ. & Ry. 109.

8 Leigh v. Hanmer, 1 Le. 53.

Parallel Articles of the French Code.

In those cases where the marriage is declared null, as being absolutely unlawful ab initio, the issue are bastards,[1] and the wife shall receive all again that she brought with her, unless the goods are spent or given away without collusion.[2] A second marriage is so absolutely void, that the second wife, however innocent, is not entitled to the rights consequent of marriages as dower.[3] But, as already stated, in the case of false publication of banns, if one party be innocent, the marriage shall be established for the benefit of the innocent party.[4] 201. 202.

CHAPTER V.

Of the Obligations to third Persons arising from Marriage.

One of the principal objects of marriage is the procreation and bringing up of children; and there is a legal as well as natural obligation on every man to provide for those descended from his loins;[5] and not only the father and mother, but also the grandfather and grandmother of poor impotent persons, must maintain them at their own charges, if of sufficient ability.[6] Beyond this the law leaves it to the natural feeling: and no person is bound to provide maintenance for his issue unless the children are impotent and unable to work, either through infancy, or disease, or accident;[7] and, therefore, of course a child has no action against his parents for an establishment in marriage, in business, or otherwise. 203. 204.

1 Co. Lit. 235.
2 Dyer, 62.
3 Moore, 226; 1 Roper, 332.
4 See ante, 271, 3.
5 1 Bl. Com. 448.
6 43 Eliz. c. 2; 1 Bl. Com. c. 448. It is an indictable offence to neglect to provide sufficient food and necessaries for infants of tender years.—R. v. Friend, 1 R. & R. 20; and Rex v. Squires, 1 Russ. C. & M. 16; Hughes v. Hughes, 1 Bro. C. C. 386.
7 1 Bl. Com. 449; Raym. 669.

Parallel Articles of the French Code.

Where an infant orders necessary and suitable articles, it is a question for a jury whether they can infer authority from the father;[1] and the father is not liable to pay for clothes furnished to his infant son, unless by express or implied contract on his part.[2] The only method of compelling the maintenance of children is under the poor law.[3]

205. On the other hand, children may be compelled to maintain and provide for their fathers and mothers, grandfathers and grandmothers.[4]

206. 207. The legal obligation of furnishing maintenance, however, extends only to natural or blood relations, and not to such as are acquired by marriage: hence, sons and daughters-in-law are not bound to support their fathers and mothers-in-law;[5] and reciprocally, the father or mother-in-law is not bound to maintain the son or daughter-in-law,[6] even though the husband had an estate with his wife.[7]

208. 209. In order to compel a maintenance, it must appear that the party applying for it is unable to work, sick, aged, or impotent;[8] and that the party by whom it is to be made, is of sufficient ability.[9] The amount of maintenance, or rate of relief, is to be assessed at the discretion of the magistrates,[10] who of course will judge of the circumstances of both parties. And it would seem that the order of the General Quarter Session is final.[11]

210. No order can be made to compel the party to re-

---

1 Baker v. Keen, 2 Stark. 501.

2 Blackburn v. Mackay, 1 Car. & P. 1; Flack v. Tollemache, id. 5. See recent case.

3 43 Eliz. c. 2; 4 East, 84. Alimentorum appelatione venit victus, vestitus et habitatio.—2 Inst. 17.

4 43 Eliz. c. 2.

5 Tubb v. Harrison, 4 T. R. 118; 1 Stra. 190.

6 Rex v. Munday, 1 Stra. 190.

7 Cooper v. Martin, 4 East, 76; Rex v. Kemp, 2 Stra. 755.

8 Rex v. Gully, 10 Mod. 307; 1 Bot. 366; St. Andrew Undershaf v. Jacob, 1 Ld. Raym. 699.

9 Rex v. Hallifax, 1 B. & A. 366; 10 Mod. 221.

10 43 Eliz. c. 2, s. 7; 59 Geo. III. c. 12, s. 26.

11 Ib.; Rex v. Robinson, 2 Burr. 799.

ceive his relation into his house. The only authority there is for interference between these relations, is founded on 43 Eliz. c. 2, and other statutes, which provide for nothing further than an allowance for maintenance. Parallel Articles of the French Code. 211.

CHAPTER VI.

Of the Consequences of Marriage, and the respective Rights and Duties of Married Persons between themselves.

The first consequence of the natural union under legal sanction, of persons of different sex, capable of performing their respective duties in marriage, affecting the condition (status), capacity, and incapacity of the woman, is, according to the law of England,[1] that husband and wife are, in law, but one person.[2] And they owe to each other conjugal affection and conjugal treatment.[3] 212.

Another consequence of marriage, which must be mentioned here as fundamental, affecting the property of the woman, is, that by the marriage the husband acquires a freehold interest, during the joint lives of himself and wife (and after her decease, if he survive, as tenant by the courtesy), in all such freehold property of inheritance as she was seized of at the time, or may become seized of during coverture. And as to chattels personal, marriage is an absolute gift to the husband of all the personal chattels she possesses; and to her chattels real and choses in action, if he reduce them into possession, or dispose of them, he becomes absolutely entitled.[4]

On the other hand, the wife becomes entitled[5] by marriage to be provided with necessaries (during his life),

[1] See the origin of this maxim, ante, p. 25 and n. 6.

[2] Lit. s. 291, s. 168. Vir et uxor sunt quasi unica persona quia caro una et sanguis unus.—Brac. l. 5, f. 416.

[3] See suits for restitution of conjugal affection.

[4] Omnia quæ sunt uxoris sunt ipsius viri; non habet uxor potestatemsui sed viri.—Co. Lit. 112.

[5] Ante, p. 27.

Parallel Articles of the French Code.

and (after his decease) to dower out of her husband's real property, and thirds out of his personalty.

213. Being in law only one person, the husband may protect his wife as if he were protecting his own person,[1] it is morally his duty so to do, and he would be entitled to damages against the aggressor; but she cannot by law compel him to bring an action if she be beaten, or slandered.[2] The wife is bound to obey her husband.[3]

214. They are bound to live together; and though the duties of matrimonial intercourse cannot be compelled by the courts, either the husband[4] or wife[5] can compel the other to cohabit; she must reside where he prescribes.[6] The husband, it is said, may confine his wife;[7] he may compel any person detaining her against her will to give her up;[8] or he may sue any person for enticing her away, or harbouring her after demand, in an action on the case.[9] The husband is bound to supply her with necessaries[10] suitable to his means and station in life.[11]

215. At law the very existence of the civil state, or person of the wife, being incorporated in that of her husband[12] in civil matters, a married woman cannot in any case at common law, sue or be sued alone, while the relation of marriage subsists, notwithstanding she lives separate from him, and has a separate maintenance secured

1 3 Bl. Com. 3; 2 Rol. Ab. 456.

2 Manby v. Scott, 1 Lev. 4; Bridg. Rep. 232.

3 1 Bl. Com. 444, 5; 1 Hale, 629; ante, see note 12 infra.

4 Barlee v. Barlee, 1 Add. 301; Swift v. Swift, 4 Hag. Con. R. 139.

5 Dalrymple v. Dalrymple, 2 Hag. Con. R. 54.

6 Ozard v. Darnford, 1 Selw. N. P. 273: Montague v. Benedick, 3 B. & C. 637; 1 Carr. 356.

7 1 Bl. Com. 445; Stra. 478, 875.

8 Rex v. Wiseman, 2 Smith, 617.

9 Winsmore v. Greenbank; Willes, 578; 6 T. R. 321; 3 Bl. Com. 139.

10 Scott v. Manby, 1 Lev. 4; 1 Sid. 109; Harris v. Morris, 4 Esp. 41; Bolton v. Prentice, 1 Selw. N. P. 249; 2 Stra. 1214; except in cases of her misconduct, as adultery, Ham v. Toovey, 1 Selw. N. P. 278; leaving him, Horwood v. Heffer, 3 Taunt. 421.

11 Montague v. Benedict, 3 B. & C. 631; Seaton v. Benedict, 5 Bing. 28; Hunt v. Blaquire, 5 Bing. 550.

12 Uxor non est sui juris, sed sub potestate viri.—3 Inst. 108. Cui in vitæ contradicere non potest.

Parallel Articles of the French Code.

to her.[1] There are, however, cases in equity where the wife may set up a claim adverse to her husband, and then she may prosecute a suit in the name of her prochein amy, or next friend, and even sue her husband:[2] but a stranger cannot sue her alone.[3] In our ecclesiastical courts, a woman may sue and be sued, without her husband.[4]

In the defence of her person from unlawful violence, 216.
a married woman has the same rights and remedies, in the criminal law, as a single person; and on the other hand, in criminal prosecutions, the wife may be indicted and punished separately.[5] And in all such cases where the wife offends alone, she is responsible, and may be prosecuted as if she were not married.[6] The law, however, protects the wife in all felonies committed by her in company with her husband, and where she can be considered as under the coercion of her husband, except murder and manslaughter.[7]

As a general rule, a married woman is incapable of 217.
contracting, in any way, without her husband; and all deeds executed, and acts done even with her husband, by the wife during her coverture, are void,[8] except formerly by fine or matter of record,[9] and now under the act for the abolition for fines and recoveries, or under a power.

At common law, every agreement of any nature en- 220.
tered into by a married woman, without the express or implied consent of her husband,[10] is absolutely void;[11] but

---

[1] Marshall v. Rutton, 8 T. R. 545.

[2] 1 Fonb. 94; Mitford, 22, 83; 1 Ves. Jun. 21; Griffith v. Hood, 2 Ves. 452; Lady Elibank v. Montoliew, 5 Ves. 757.

[3] Co. Lit. 133 a; 1 Fonb. 109; 3 P. W. 37.

[4] 2 Rol. Ab. 298; 1 Bl. Com. 444.

[5] 1 Bl. Com. 443.

[6] 4 Bl. Com. 29.

[7] Ib. 24; Hal. P. C. 47; 1 Hawk. c. 1, s. 9.

[8] Feme covert can be bound only by fine, or consent in court.—Law Maxim.

[9] 1 Bl. Com. 444.

[10] Except under the custom of London,—and arrangements may be made before marriage by the intervention of trustees, for the wife to carry on a separate trade.

[11] Marshall v. Rutton, 8 T. R. 545; 1 Taunt. 217.

Parallel Articles of the French Code.

where the wife is accustomed to transact business for her husband, she is, quoad hoc, his servant or agent, and his assent is implied; and he is answerable for her contracts, if within the scope of her accustomed transactions.[1] If, however, the wife sell or dispose of the husband's money or goods without his assent, express or implied, the sale is void, and the husband may recover his goods; and if she loses money at cards, the husband may bring an action for the money.[2] We have seen the husband is bound to provide necessaries for his wife, and if she contracts debts for them, he is obliged to pay them.[3]

In equity, however, if a married woman, having separate property, give a bond or bill for a debt, she would be liable to pay it out of her separate estate.[4]

221. Where the husband is civilly dead, the wife may sue,
222. alone.[5] But unless he be civilly dead, she cannot, either on account of his imprisonment or other punishment, or on account of his absence,[6] unless a presumption arises of his death, or he be a foreigner or alien enemy.[7]

223. By the intervention of a trustee, the husband may give his wife a general authority to contract and sue in his name, or do any other act.[8] In such case, she is in law considered as the agent of the trustee; and the same general or special authority that might be vested in him, may be exercised by her, as agent or servant;[9] but she should use her husband's name, and not her own.[10]

---

1 1 Bl. Com. 430; Tracy v. Dutton, Palm. 206; Seaborne v. Blackston, 2 Freem. 178.

2 Com. Dig. Bar. & Feme.

3 1 Sid. 120; 2 Esp. 637; 4 Camp. 215; 2 Stra. 1214; 3 B. & C. 631.

4 Heatley v. Thomas, 15 Ves. J. 596; Bullpin v. Clarke, 17 Ves. J. 366; Hulme v. Tennant, 1 Bro. C. C. 16; Stuart v. Kirkwall, 3 Madd. 387; 4 Russ. 112.

5 Co. Lit. 132 b, 133; 1 Rol. Rep. 400.

6 11 East, 301; ante, p. 260.

7 Derry v. Duchess of Mazarine, 1 Ld. Raym. 147; Walford v. Duchess of Pienne, 2 Esp. 554; Franks v. id. 2 Esp. 587; Marsh v. Hutchinson, 2 B. & P. 226.

8 Pawlet v. Delaval, 2 Ves. 663; Hulme v. Tenant, 1 Bro. C. C. 16; 2 Dick, 560; 4 Chit. Pl. 696, n. e; Jane v. Matilda, 1 Hag. R. 187.

9 Jarman v. Woolloton, 3 T. R. 618.

10 Barlow v. Bishop, 1 East, 432; Cotes v. Davis, 1 Camp. 485; 2 Roper, Husband and Wife, 140.

Parallel Articles of the French Code.

The wife of a minor cannot sue, or be sued, alone.

A contract made by a married woman, without the express or implied authority of her husband, being absolutely void, can be treated as void by any person.[1] 224.

At common law, a married woman cannot make a will 225.
of lands[2] or of chattels without her husband's licence;[3] 226.
but before marriage the husband may, and frequently does, covenant with her trustees to allow her to make a will;[4] and where personal property is given for her sole and separate use, she may dispose of it by will without her husband's assent.[5]

CHAPTER VII.

Of the Dissolution of Marriage.

Marriages may be dissolved—1st, By the natural 227.
death of one of the parties; 2nd, By a divorce.

Civil death does not dissolve the natural union of husband and wife,[6] though it does to a certain extent the civil connection, and she may sue alone.

CHAPTER VIII.

Of Second Marriages.

A woman is not restrained by the law from contracting 228.
a new marriage immediately after the death of her first husband,[7] or after the divorce à vinculo matrimonii, unless expressly so by act of parliament.

---

1 Smith v. Plomer and another, 15 East, 607; Rex v. Inhabitants of Ashton-under-Lyne, 4 M. & S. 357.

2 34 & 35 Hen. VIII. c. 5.

3 4 Rep. 51.

4 2 Bl. C. 497.

5 3 Bro. C. C. 8; 1 Ves. J. 46; 2 Vern. 535.

6 See ante, p. 201, n. 4, and p. 221.

7 Co. Lit. 8 a; Cro. Jac. 686.

Parallel Articles of the French Code.

TITLE VI.

OF DIVORCE.

Its Nature and Kinds.

Divorce is the separation of two individuals, de facto married together. There are two kinds: the one total, from the bonds of marriage, à vinculo matrimonii; the other partial, from bed and board, a mensa et thoro. The divorce à vinculo matrimonii must be for some cause of impediment existing before the marriage, and preventing it from being a lawful marriage; and not for anything supervenient, or arising afterwards,[1] unless by act of parliament. In cases of this kind of divorce, the fact of marriage is merely declared a nullity, and void as being unlawful ab initio, and the issue are bastards. Divorce a mensa et thoro, is when the marriage is just and lawful ab initio, but for some supervenient cause it has become improper or impossible for the parties to live together.

The causes for which a divorce à vinculo matrimonii can be pronounced by the English courts, must be precedent the marriage, as existing prior marriage, consanguinity, or affinity within the forbidden degrees, previous and continuing impotency, impuberty. Conformably to the arrangement of the French code, suits for nullity of marriage have already been considered. The nullity pronounced in consequence of those suits, constitutes the only divorce à vinculo matrimonii recognized by the English law as resulting from the sentence of our courts. The legislature, however, sometimes interferes, and dissolves a marriage by a kind of sentence of divorce à vinculo matrimonii, for a cause arising subsequently to the marriage. This title of the French code

[1] 1 Bl. Com. 440.

does not relate to suits for nullity on the ground of pre-existing cause, and we are therefore chiefly confined to divorce a mensa et thoro.

Parallel Articles of the French Code.

CHAPTER I.

Of the Causes of Divorce.

Adultery is a cause only of separation from bed and board, divorce a mensa et thoro;[1] but divorces à vinculo matrimonii have frequently been granted by act of parliament for this offence.[2] Either party, husband or wife, may apply for a divorce a mensa et thoro, on the ground of the adultery of the other;[3] or the committee of a lunatic.[4] 229. 230.

Either of the married parties may demand a divorce for intolerable cruelty on the part of the other, amounting to legal sevitiæ.[5] The courts have declined to define what degree, or what instance of cruelty, will amount to legal cruelty or sevitiæ.[6] In suing for divorce on this or the preceding ground, it will not be granted if it appear that the party applying is equally guilty, or equally in fault.[7] 231.

The public infamy of the husband, arising from a judicial conviction of an attempt to commit an unnatural crime, is a sufficient cause to decree a divorce a mensa et thoro.[8] 232.

[1] 3 Salk. 138; 1 Bl. Com. 441; ante, 29.

[2] 1 Bl. Com. 441.

[3] 1 Ought. 317; 11 Ves. J. 536.

[4] Parnell v. Parnell, 2 Hag. C. R. 169.

[5] Poynter, p. 84.

[6] See Evans v. Evans, 1 Hag. R. 36; Oliver v. Oliver, id. 364; Kirkman v. Kirkman, id. 409; Holden v. Holden, id. 458; Harris v. Harris, 2 Hag. 148; Waring v. Waring, id. 154; 2 Phil. Ecc. C. 132; Neeld v. Neeld, 4 Hag. Ecc. C. 264.

[7] Waring v. Waring, 2 Hag. C. 159; Beeby v. Beeby, 1 Hag. 790; Astley v. Astley, 1 Hag. 714.

[8] 3 Bl. Com. 94; Mr. Christian's note; Burn's Eccl. L. 496 n.

Parallel Articles of the French Code.

233. The mere mutual desire of the parties is no ground whatever for a divorce, even a mensa et thoro; and though it was formerly held that the husband and wife may live separate by agreement between themselves and a trustee, it seems doubtful how far a deed of separation between man and wife is valid.[1] The House of Lords have decided, that a prospective deed of separation is invalid, and may be set aside, or treated as void;[2] but the Court of King's Bench considered that this only applied to a prospective separation, and not to immediate separations.[3]

CHAPTER II.

OF DIVORCE FOR DETERMINATE[4] CAUSE.

Section 1.

Of the Forms of Proceeding for Divorce.

234 to 259. Suits for divorce are brought in the ecclesiastical courts on whatever ground such divorce is demanded. They must be plenary, or full and formal suits. Their form is sufficient to protect the parties from violence or hasty decision, and to prevent collusion. The proceedings differ in such case very little from those in any other plenary proceedings in these courts for other causes. There are no especial enactments applicable only to divorce in England; and, therefore, this chapter is scarcely so appropriate here as in the French code: and it will be necessary here only to consider

---

1 Elsworth v. Bird, 2 Sin. & Stra. 372; Jee v. Thurlow, 2 Barn. & Cres. 547.

2 Westmeath v. Westmeath, 1 Dow. R. New S. 519; Jacob, R. 141, S. C.; Hendley v. Westmeath, 6 B. & C. 200; Durant v. Titley, 7 Price, 577.

3 Wilson v. Murfett, 3 Bar. & Adol. 713. See the arguments, 1 Jacob, 141, 187.

4 This term is here adopted, because used in the French code in contradiction to mutual consent (Chapter III.) where there is no definite cause.

Parallel Articles of the French Code.

the general course of proceeding in such suits. And first, with regard to the court in which the suit should be instituted. The Consistory Court, or Court of the Diocesan Bishop, is usually the court in which the proceedings for the trial of all ecclesiastical causes (including divorce) arising within his diocese[1] should be instituted. Sometimes the Archdeacon's Court is in concurrence with, and sometimes in exclusion of, the Consistory Court. The Court of Peculiars has jurisdiction over certain parishes exempt from the ordinary or the bishop's authority.[2] 234.

Where a right of civil suit arises out of a crime amounting to felony, legally punishable, it is a general rule, for the interest of public justice, that the felony suspends the civil remedy; and, before conviction of the crime, there is no remedy against the offender;[3] but for inferior crimes, as assault and battery, the party injured may institute both civil and criminal proceedings.[4] In the ecclesiastical courts, a suit for divorce, on the ground of a felony (as an infamous crime) would require probably a criminal conviction of the offence.[5] 235.

As to the form: in proceeding for a divorce, a citation or decree issues for the other party, to appear and show cause why the parties should not be divorced; and on this being complied with, by entering an appearance, a statement of the complaint called a libel is brought in, and on its admission by the judge, and the averments being denied by the defendant's answer upon oath, witnesses are examined, and their depositions are taken down in writing by the officer of the court.[6] If the defendant has any circumstances to offer in his defence, he must propound them in his defensive allegation, to which he is entitled to have the plaintiff's answer upon oath. 236. 259.

[1] Laws, Oughton, 2.
[2] 3 Bl. Com. 61.
[3] Styles, 346; 17 Ves. 331.
[4] 1 Bos. & Pul. 191.
[5] See Mr. Christian's note, 3 Bl. Com. 94.
[6] 2 Burns, Ecc. L. tit. Courts; 3 Bl. Com. 100; 2 Chit. G. P. 482, 489.

Parallel Articles of the French Civil.

With regard to delay for the purpose of reconciliation,[1] none is requisite according to the English law: for a divorce a mensa et thoro, is merely a sentence for separation of the parties, until they are reconciled;[2] but in suit for divorce on the ground of impotency (except in palpable irremediable cases), three years' cohabitation for trial is required before the suit can be entertained.[3]

The mere confession of the other party cannot be received as evidence of adultery, or other fact, on which the suit is founded: to prevent connivance, there must be depositions of witnesses, inspection, or other proof.[4] But confession may be received as collateral proof in support of presumptive evidence.[5] The parties on each side name their witnesses previous to examination, so that the other party may have an opportunity of impeaching their evidence, or cross-examining them. Examination may be secret if necessary: the examinations are taken by a practitioner, who represents the judge, and remains quite alone with the witnesses.[6] After the witnesses are examined, and after the publication of the evidence, if there be no allegation excepting to them, or any of their testimony; or if the averments of the libel be admitted, the judge proceeds to hear the cause argued by advocates, and then gives sentence. Every ecclesiastical sentence must be reduced to writing, and then pronounced in the presence of the parties.[7] And sentence of divorce, or separation, must be pronounced in open court.[8]

259. Alimony is frequently directed to be paid to the wife during the pendance of the suit, according to the discretion of the court, on consideration of the fortune of the husband.[9] As soon as the fact of marriage is shown, the court can order alimony.[10]

---

1 But see as to the duty of the spiritual judge as to advising reconciliation, and also as to private examination, lest the arcana familiæ should be made public.

2 Poynter, p. 69. 3 Ib. 60. 4 Ib. 71, 2. 5 Ib. 73.

6 Per Lord Stowell, 2 Hag. R. 267.

7 Gibs. 1046, c. 2, 1, 8, c. 3, 9, 11. 8 7 Can. 106.

9 Poynter, p. 91. 10 Ib. 92.

Parallel Articles of the French Code.

The appellant jurisdiction of the Court of Arches extends to all causes or suits, relative to marriages.[1] And the judicial committee of the Privy Council, is the ultimate court of appeal. 262.

If the sentence of the court be not appealed from in fifteen days, it is final by the statute.[2] 263.

SECTION 2.

Of the Rights of the Parties pending the Suit for Divorce.

The father of an infant legitimate child is entitled to the custody of it;[3] and the ecclesiastical courts have no power to deprive him of it, whatever may be its age. 267.

The wife may leave the residence of the husband, and if he attempt to confine her, she may have an habeas corpus;[4] and the husband cannot prevent her from residing where she likes, as the court would not decree restitution of conjugal rights, pending suit for divorce; nor would an habeas corpus be granted to the husband.[5] 268.

All her personal property is, by a valid marriage, absolutely her husband's, and her real property is his for life;[6] but the court will grant alimony at discretion in divorce a mensa et thoro;[7] and in divorce à vinculo matrimonii, for adultery, parliament will make such directions as appear proper. 270. 271.

---

[1] Burn, Ecc. L. tit. Arches.

[2] 25 Hen. VIII. c. 19; 3 Bl. Com. 101.

[3] 5 East, 221; 1 Bos. & Pul. 148; 7 East, 579. But as to the Court of Chancery changing the custody of the children on the ground of the father's gross immorality, see Shelley v. Westbrooke, Jac. 266; Wellesley v. Duke of Beaufort, 2 Russ. 1; 1 Dow. 154; 2 Bligh, 124. On the pecuniary grounds, Jackson v. Hankey, Jac. 264, n. See also Lyons v. Blenkin, Jac. 251.

[4] Lady Vane's case, 13 East, 173; Rex v. Middleton, 1 Chit. 654; Middleton v. Middleton, 1 Jac. & W. 94.

[5] Rex v. Wiseman, 2 Smith, R. 617.

[6] See ante, p. 277.

[7] See ante, p. 286.

Parallel Articles of the French Code.

Section 3.

Of waiving the Right to sue for Divorce.

272. The right to sue for a divorce may be waived by the conduct of the parties, either before suit commenced or after. By the rules of the canon law, followed by the law of our ecclesiastical courts, divorce for adultery is not to be admitted in any of the following cases: where both parties are equally criminal;[1] where the husband prostitutes his own wife, or connives at her doing so:[2] where the adultery is unaccompanied by guilt, having happened through mistake, or by force, or by ravishment; when a reconciliation or condonation has taken place between the husband and wife, after knowledge of her criminality.[3]

274. A suit may, however, be instituted for subsequent cause, and the former causes of suit brought forward in it.

Condonation may be direct or implied; direct, when expresssed by words in writing; implied, when the husband (for instance), after reasonable knowledge of the infidelity of his wife, continues to admit her as the partner of his bed.[4]

CHAPTER III.

Mutual Consent no ground for Divorce.

275. 295. When the parties have not attained the age of consent at the time of marriage, they may, on attaining that age, by the dissent of either of them, dissolve the marriage. But when both parties are of sufficient age,

---

1 Ante, p. 283. 2 Timmings v. Timmings, 3 Hag. 82.

3 Poynter, p. 77 to 84; Corvin. Jus. Can. l. 2, tit. 17; Proctor v. Proctor, 2 Hag. 292. Mackenna.

4 Poynter, Marriage and Divorce, p. 82; Betcher v. Betcher, 2 Phil. 155, cited Best v. Best, 2 Phil. 161; Kirkwall v. Kirkwall, 2 Hag. 277.

the mutual consent of both married parties is in no case a ground for divorce; and separation by mutual consent is of so little avail, that the parties shall be presumed to have had access, and to have exercised matrimonial functions, until the contrary be proved.[1] It is not uncommon for husband and wife to enter into agreement to live separate, by a covenant between themselves and a trustee.[2]

Parallel Articles of the French Code.

CHAPTER IV.

Of the Effects of Divorce.

The distinction between the three kinds of divorce, viz., a declaration of the nullity of a marriage ab initio, or divorce à vinculo matrimonii by the ecclesiastical courts; a dissolution of a marriage not originally void, or divorce à vinculo matrimonii by authority of parliament; and a separation from bed and board, or divorce a mensa et thoro, must be kept in mind in considering their effects. As to marrying again, in divorce of the 295.
first kind, while the same impediments exist which rendered the marriage unlawful ab initio, the parties of course cannot, after sentence, contract a lawful marriage between themselves any more than they could before sentence. If those impediments were removed, they might then be lawfully united. After a divorce à vinculo matrimonii by authority of parliament, the parties can do all acts as if they had never been married; and, except when restricted by acts of parliament, can marry each other again.[3] Divorce a mensa et thoro is no dissolution

---

[1] The case of the parishes of St. George and St. Margaret, 1 Salk. 123.

[2] Jee v. Thurlow, 2 Barn. & Cres. 547.

[3] 1 Jac. I. c. 11; Com. Dig. Bar. & Feme, C. 1 & C. 7; Moore, R. 666, Ca. 9, 10; 1 Salk. 115; Cro. Eliz. 908; 3 Mod. 71.

Parallel Articles of the French Code.

of the marriage, but a separation only from bed and board; the marriage still continues.[1]

In cases of divorce à vinculo matrimonii, the parties
296. may immediately marry other persons.[2]

297. In divorce a mensa et thoro, the parties being still bound to each other as man and wife cannot marry again: and separation by mutual consent is no divorce.[3]

298. After divorce à vinculo matrimonii by parliament for adultery, the party guilty may marry his or her accomplice; and it is considered dishonourable, after having seduced a married woman, and caused her to be divorced, not to make her amends by marriage. Adultery is not punishable criminally.[4]

299. As to property, on divorce à vinculo matrimonii by the
300. ecclesiastical courts, the property is restored on both sides,[5] and the parties are restored to their former condition. In the dissolution of a marriage by act of parliament, the property remains vested in the husband, unless parliament otherwise direct; and in divorces a mensa et thoro, the husband retains the wife's property. For adultery[6] the wife loses her dower;[7] but it is no bar to a claim for arrears of annuity by her trustee under a separation deed;[8] and a jointure is not forfeited.[9]

301. In divorce a mensa et thoro, the husband retaining the property, the ecclesiastical court will order him to make her a suitable permanent maintenance, called alimony.[10] The quantum is in the discretion of the court, and may be increased or decreased by it according to the state of the husband's fortune.[11] In cases of divorce for the adultery of the wife, the legislature always makes her an allowance out of the husband's estate, that

---

1 Porter's case, Cro. Car. 462.

2 2 Jac. I. c. 11, s. 3; Co. Lit. 8 a.

3 Porter's case, Cro. Car. 462.

4 3 Bl. Com. 139.

5 Dyer, 62, 3.

6 Sponte virum fugiens mulier et adultera facta, dote sua careat, nisi sponsi sponte retracta.—Co. Lit. 32.

7 1 Bl. Com. 440; 2 ib. 136.

8 Jee v. Thurlow, 2 Barn. & Cres. 547; 4 D. & R. 11, S. C.

9 2 Bl. Com. 138, n. 35.

10 3 ib. 94; Poynter, 91.

11 Poynter, 93, 8.

Parallel Articles of the French Code.

she may not be driven by want to continue in a course of vice.[1]

With regard to the children after divorce à vinculo matrimonii, they are illegitimate; and, as a general 302.
rule, the mother is entitled to the custody of an ille- 303.
gitimate child in preference to the father;[2] but parliament may interfere to legitimatize the children, and direct as to the custody of them. And after a divorce a mensa et thoro, the father is entitled to the custody of a legitimate child; and a court of common law, or a spiritual court, cannot control this custody.[3] But a court of equity will interfere, and if necessary take the child out of the father's custody, where his conduct is very bad, or he attempts to mislead him.[4] The right of custody draws with it the right to direct the education, and the duty of maintaining the children.

Divorce a mensa et thoro does not affect the rights of 304.
the children, either as to legitimacy or as to property;[5] 305.
but divorce à vinculo matrimonii, making them illegitimate, unless parliament otherwise provide,[6] of course deprives them of the rights legitimate children would have.

CHAPTER V.

Of the Separation of Persons.

This division is almost superfluous here, since, as 306.
has already been remarked, divorce in the ecclesiastical courts a mensa et thoro, is merely a separation of person from bed and board.[7] It may, however, be as well to observe, that for those causes rendering a mar-

---

1 Per Best, 4 D. & R. 17.
2 Bos. & Pul. 148; 7 East, 579.
3 5 East, 221.
4 10 Ves. J. 58.
5 1 Bl. Com. 441.
6 Ib. 440.
7 Ib. and 3 ib. 94.

Parallel Articles of the French Code.

riage void ab initio, for which divorce à vinculo matrimonii can be decreed by the ecclesiastical court, divorce a mensa et thoro would not be applicable; and for adultery or other cause, arising after marriage, for which divorce a mensa et thoro is provided, it is only by special grace that parliament allows divorce à vinculo matrimonii.

307. It has been already stated, that the suit for divorce
308. a mensa et thoro is entered, carried, and determined, in
309. very nearly the same way as other suits in the ecclesias-
311. tical courts:[1] and that adultery is not punishable criminally:[2] and that the separation of persons does not affect the husband's right to retain the wife's property.

TITLE VII.

OF PATERNITY AND FILIATION.

CHAPTER I.

Of Children born during Marriage.

The next important circumstance affecting the legal condition (status) of a person is, legitimacy or illegitimacy. This is dependant on the preceding laws relating to marriage. Legitimacy is a civil state or condition, derived from being the lawful issue of a marriage sanctioned by the law. In one point of view, it depends on the lawful marriage of the alleged parents of the person; and in the other, on his being the fruit of such marriage. Whether a child be born in lawful matrimony or not, there can be no dispute as to its mother;[3] and the law establishes the lawful marriage of

[1] Ordo Judicorum; Oughton, 59; Burn's Eccl. Law, tit. Courts; 3 Bl. Com. 100.
[2] 3 Bl. Com. 139.
[3] The maxim of the civil law is, Semper certa est mater, etiam si vulgo conceperit.

Parallel Articles of the French Code.

the parents as the criterion (and almost the only test admitted by English law) for ascertaining paternity; and every child born in lawful wedlock is presumed to have the husband for its father:[1] and it seems but just and right that every presumption should be taken in favour of the fidelity of the wife;[2] so that nothing but strict proof should be allowed to deprive a person of his condition of legitimacy,[3] his right to which it would be absolutely impossible strictly to prove. 312.

The father, however, or any other person interested to do so, is allowed to prove a child illegitimate. It seems formerly to have been held, that it was necessary to establish that he was beyond the four seas[4] to rebut the presumption of legitimacy; and still the law respects and protects the legitimacy of a person, and will not suffer his state and condition to be overturned on slight grounds:[5] there must be evidence which excludes all doubt, amounting to a moral or physical impossibility—either from absence, or proved non-access, during the period of gestation.[6] With regard to the latter point, whether the birth be alleged to have taken place either too soon or too long after access, the law does not prescribe any exact time,[7] but leaves it as a question for a jury to decide on medical evidence, coupled with other

[1] 1 Bl. Com. 446. Pater est quem nuptiæ demonstrant.—Law Maxim, Co. Lit. 123, 4, recognized King v. Luffe, 8 East, 193; Banbury Peerage case, 1 Sim. & Stu. 153.

Hæres legitimus est quem nuptiæ demonstrant.—Law Maxim, Co. Lit. 7.

[2] Partus ex legitimo thoro non certius noscit matrem quam genitorem suum.—Law Maxim, Fort. c. 42.

[3] Semper presumitur pro legitimatione puerorum, et filiatio non potest probari.—Law Maxim, Co. Lit. 126; Lord Redesdale, in Banbury Peerage case.

[4] 1 Bl. Com. 457; 4 T. R. 356, 251, Foxcroft's case.

[5] In Head v. Head, 1 Turn. 138, 1 Sim. & Stu. 150, Lord Eldon said, "The law respects and protects legitimacy, and does not admit any alteration of the status et conditio of any person, except upon the most clear and satisfactory evidence."

[6] Banbury Peerage case, opinion of the judges.

[7] Gardner Peerage case, Le Marchant's Report; and Hargrave and Butler's Notes to Co. Lit. 123.

Parallel Articles of the French Code.

facts.[1] Until such proof,[2] the mere disavowal of the father would not affect the child's claims to maintenance, or to any advantages of which the father could not deprive a child acknowledged to be legitimate.

313. The impotency of the husband, when clearly proved, illegitimatizes a child; and there seems no rule for restraining the husband from alleging his own impotency; though, when natural and irremediable, it would be ground for annulling a marriage:[3] and on a question of legitimacy, evidence that the husband was of such a habit of body, as to make his having children an impossibility, may always be given by any persons interested.[4] Adultery illegitimatizes the children, where the wife is living separate from her husband in open and notorious adultery;[5] but where there is access on the part of the husband, he cannot illegitimatize the child for the wife's adultery, except by divorce à vinculo matrimonii. And there will always be presumed to have been access, until the contrary is shown beyond all doubt.[6] Sentence of divorce, however, bars the presumption of access;[7] but a voluntary separation does not.[8]

314. Where the parents have married so recently before the birth of the child, that it could not have been gotten in wedlock, as within a day,[9] the child is legitimatized by

---

[1] The jury may not only take into consideration proofs tending to show the physical impossibility of the child born in wedlock being legitimate, but they may decide the question of paternity, by attending to the relative situation of the parties, their habits of life, the evidence of conduct and of declarations connected with conduct, and to every induction which reason suggests for determining upon the probabilities of the case.—Phillips on Evidence, ii. 288.

[2] See art. 319.

[3] A suit might be instituted for that purpose; but if the husband knew of his own impotence at the time of marriage, it would bar his right to a sentence of nullity.—Poynter, 60, 1, 2, 3.

[4] Foxcroft's case, 10 Ed. I. Roll. Ab. 358; Lomax v. Holenden, 2 Stra. 940; 1 Salk. 123; Co. Lit. 224 a.

[5] Goodright v. Saul, 4 T. R. 356.

[6] Co. Lit.; 3 P. W. 275; Pendrel v. Pendrel, 2 Stra. 925; Corvin, Jus. Can. l. 2, tit. 13.

[7] 1 Salk. 123.

[8] Ib. 125.

[9] 1 Roll. Ab. 729.

Parallel Articles of the French Code.

the husband's recognition of it by the marriage;[1] but this presumption may be repelled.[2]

Children born so long after the death of the husband, that, by the course of gestation, they could not be begotten by him, are illegitimate:[3] but the course of nature is a question for the court and jury on medical evidence.[4] 315.

There is no definite limit to the time for contesting the legitimacy of a person:[5] the illegitimacy of any person may at any time be tried;[6] but of course, length of acquiescence would afford strong presumption in favour of legitimacy; and a limit is practically put to it in most cases, in the limitation of the time for bringing the actions in which the question can arise. 316. 317. 318.

CHAPTER II.

Of the Proofs of the Filiation of Legitimate Children.

Marriage being the presumptive proof of the parentage of a child, every child born during the marriage, or within a competent time after, is presumed to be the issue of the mother's lawful husband; and it rests with those who dispute the legitimacy to disprove the fact.[7] Judicial proceedings cannot be instituted on the part of the supposed father, or of any other person, for the mere purpose of disproving the presumptive filiation arising from birth during marriage; or by a person representing himself as the child of any individual, to establish his claim of paternity, unless the decision of some claim of

---

1 Co. Lit. 244 a; Rex v. Luffe, 8 East, 193.

2 Foxcroft's case.

3 1 Bl. Com. 455.

4 Stark v. Bird.

5 Banbury Peerage case.

6 Co. Lit. 245 b; 1 Salk. 120.

7 Head v. Head, 1 Sim. & Stu. 152; 1 Turner, 139; Banbury Peerage, 1 Sim. & Stu. 153; Morris v. Davies, 3 C. & P. 218, 427.

Parallel Articles of the French Code.

right depends on the ascertainment of the fact.[1] The entry of birth or baptism in the register is not conclusive, but only primâ facie proof of legitimacy, and
319. may be rebutted;[2] or it may be proved without such
320. register.[3] Where other proof cannot be obtained, the
321. facts of an individual having always borne the alleged father's name,—having been treated by him as such, and educated, maintained, and established in life,—having been uniformly received in society as such, and having been acknowledged by the family, are presumptive proof of that individual being a legitimate child of the person whose name he bears; but it may be rebutted by proving the contrary.[4] Inscriptions on tombstones and engravings on rings, and tradition, are also admissible in evidence of pedigree.[5]

322. There is no restriction to a person claiming his birth and proving he is not the child of the person supposed to be his father, but of some other person.[6] He would, however, by establishing another parentage, lose the advantages conferred upon him by the law in consequence of his previous supposed right. And any person interested may contest another's legitimacy, and claim property he holds possession of.[7]

323. Recource may always be had to witnesses to prove legitimacy; and in default of better evidence, even hearsay evidence may be resorted to, where it is the natural effusion of a party, who must know the truth, and who, at the time, has no temptation to exceed or

---

[1] Angell v. Angell, 1 Sim. & Stu. 83; Lord Dursley v. Berkeley, 6 Ves. J. 251; Allan v. Allan, 15 Ves. J. 130.

[2] 3 Stark. R. 63: 5 B. & C. 508; Rex v. North Pemberton, 8 D. & R. 325.

[3] Higham v. Ridgway, 10 East, 109.

[4] The recognition of the parents is the only evidence that the child is their child, or even the child of the woman, except the evidence of persons present at the birth can be produced.—Per Lord Redesdale, in the Banbury case.

[5] Vowles v. Young, 13 Ves. 147; Whitelocke v. Baker, 13 Ves. 514.

[6] See a case mentioned by Lord Redesdale, on the authority of Lord Erskine, in the Gardner Peerage case.

[7] As to rebutting the claim, see the Douglas case.

Parallel Articles of the French Code.

fall short of the truth;[1] but such is not conclusive, and may be rebutted: and the possession of a recognized state and registry of birth or baptism, though strong evidence, is not conclusive.[2]

Declarations in a family, descriptions in a will, in- 324.
scriptions on monument, in bibles and registry books, public and private, are admissible, to prove births and points of pedigree, or a pedigree hung up in the family mansion.[3]

Proof may be made, that the claimant is not the 325.
person he pretends, or the child of the mother he pretends, and the register is no proof of identity;[4] or, the maternity being proved, that he is not the child of the husband of such mother.[5]

Legitimacy is a question for a jury in a court of 326.
common law; and a court of equity will refer it to one on a feigned issue where it is doubtful.[6]

As soon as a party is in possession of sufficient proof 327.
to support his own claims, he may proceed to indict any person guilty of a conspiracy to defraud him.[7]

The claim of legitimacy is imprescriptible for the 328.
person and his heirs;[8] but after the period limited by 329.
the various statutes, the party could not recover back 330.
property held adversely by others as in their own rights during that time.[9]

---

1 Whitelock v. Baker, 13 Ves. 514; Higham v. Ridgway, 10 East, 120; B. N. P. 233.

2 Berkeley case.

3 Herbert v. Tuchal, T. Raym. 84; 7 East, 290; Taylor v. Cole, 7 T. R. 3 (n.) Doe v. Pembroke, 11 East, 504.

4 Birt v. Barlow, Dougl. 162.

5 Rex v. Luffe, 8 East, 206; Goodright v. Saul, 4 T. R. 356.

6 Har. Chan. 508; Gr. 240.

7 False certificate, Rex v. Mawbey, 6 T. R. 619.

8 See Claims of Peerage.

9 3 Bl. Com. c. 10; 3 & 4 Wm. IV. c. 27.

Parallel Articles of the French Code.

CHAPTER III.

Of Natural Children.

Section 1.

Of the Legitimation of Natural Children.

331 to 334. Children born out of wedlock cannot be legitimated by the subsequent marriage[1] of their father and mother.[2] The only way in which a bastard may be made legitimate, and capable of inheriting, is by act of parliament.[3]

Section 2.

Of the Recognition of Natural Children.

334 to 342. No recognition of an illegitimate child confers any civil right beyond that of a reputed name.[4] The law does not recognize the relation between the putative father and illegitimate child.[5] A bastard is quasi nullius filius.[6] The nomination of guardians to illegitimate children takes no effect as a legal devise of their custody and tuition under the statute, though it would be attended to as a recommendation of great weight in a Court of Chancery.[7]

[1] Matrimonium subsequens legitimos facit quoad sacerdotium, non quoad successionem, propter consuetudinem regni quæ se habet in contrarium.—Co. Lit. 245 a.

[2] 1 Bl. Com. 455; Doe d. Birtwhistle v. Vardell, 5 B. & C. 438; ante, p. 115.

[3] Co. Lit. 244 a, 245 a; 1 Bl. Com. 455, 9; Fortesc. de Land. L. A. c. 39.

[4] Lit. s. 188; Co. Lit. 123 a; 4 Inst. 36.

[5] Pye exparte, Dubost exparte, 18 Ves. 152; Snelham v. Bayley, in note to Cartwright v. Vawdry, 5 Ves. 534; Beckford v. Tobin, 1 Ves. J. 310; ante, p. 265.

[6] Co. Lit. 3 b, & Harg. n.

[7] Ward v. Paul, 2 Bro. C. C. 583; Peckham v. Peckham, 2 Cox, 46; Chatteris v. Young, 1 Jac. & W. 106; Barry v. Barry, Molloy's R. 210.

Parallel Articles of the French Code.

TITLE VIII.

OF ADOPTION.

Adoption, as an act affecting the civil capacity or incapacity (status) of an individual, is totally unknown to the laws of England.[1] It is true, in Bracton we find the mention of adoption;[2] but in England there are now no laws in use concerning it, as a formal act affecting the personal capacity. It is, however, an institution to a certain extent, practically though not formally, existing, as in the instance of persons undertaking to take care and provide for orphans or others, or devising or settling property on condition of the party's assuming their name and arms: but laws respecting it are unnecessary, because every man is at liberty to dispose of the whole of his property in any way he may think proper, by deed or will. Lord Coke says,[3] "We remember not to have read in any book of the legitimation or adoption of an heir, but only in Bracton, and that to little purpose; but the surest adoption is to make good assurance of land by learned advice." The courts, however, will recognize adoption as a matter of feeling and affection; and in case of the seduction of a female who had been adopted and bred up by a stranger in blood, they will allow the feelings of such a person so standing, in loco parentis, to be taken into consideration, and a compensation to be given not only for mere loss of services, but also for the aggravated injury done to the object of affection.[4] 343 to 370.

---

[1] See Harris's Justinian, p. 85.

[2] Brac. l. 2, c. 29, n. 4 & 5.

[3] 2 Inst. 97.

[4] Edmonson v. Machell, 11 East, 23; Irwin v. Dearman, Selw. N. P. 1075.

Parallel Articles of the French Code.

TITLE IX.

OF PATERNAL POWER.

371. 372. It is a rule of morals, as well as of the municipal law of all civilized nations, that a child at every age owes honour and respect to his father and mother.[1] With regard to the duration of parental authority, according to the law of England the power of the father continues over his children until they attain the age of twenty-one
373, 381. years,[2] or are emancipated: and as to the parent by whom it is to be exercised, the father alone has legal power over his children;[3] and the mother, as such, is
374. entitled to no power over her legitimate child.[4] As to the extent of this authority in the custody of the person, a child may not quit his father's residence, or the place he prescribes, without permission; and the father may repossess himself of his child by recaption,[5] by habeas corpus,[6] or by assistance of a court of equity;[7] which, however, will not be granted in case of gross misconduct on the part of the father.[8] The court will not, on habeas corpus, order a child to be delivered to its father if he has ill used it;[9] and in such a case the Court of Chancery has appointed a guardian to the child, and ordered a proper allowance for maintenance.[10]

375 to 380 and 382. A parent may lawfully correct his child under age, either corporally or by confinement in his house, if in moderation;[11] but he has no power to consign him to a

[1] 1 Bl. Com. 453; Exparte Hopkins, 3 P. W. 153; anonymous case mentioned in note to Lyons v. Blenkin, Jac. Rep. 264.

[2] 1 Bl. Com. 453. [3] Ib. [4] Ib.

[5] 3 Bl. Com. 3, 4. [6] 4 Moore, 366; 7 East, 579.

[7] 1 Stra. 167; 3 Atk. 721; 3 P. W. 51; 1 P. W. 702; 2 P. W. 117; 4 Bro. C. C. 101. [8] Blenkin v. Lyon, Jac. 245.

[9] R. v. P. Smith, 2 Str. 9821; R. v. Sir F. Flake Delaval, 3 Burr. 1436.

[10] Whitfield v. Hales, 12 Ves. 492; Shelley v. Westbrooke, 1 Jac. 266.

[11] 1 Bl. Com. 452; 1 Hawk. P. C. 130; 1 Ves. J. 58, 61.

Parallel Articles of the French Code.

public prison unless he commit some crime of which the public magistrate can take cognizance; and the courts of law and equity will interfere in gross cases of cruelty or ill usage, but generally not otherwise.[1]

The putative father of a bastard is (though no legal relationship subsists between them) considered so far its natural guardian as to be entitled to the custody of it for its maintenance and education;[2] and while not likely to be chargeable, the poor law officers have no concern with it, or the putative father's care and protection.[3] The mother, however, has a prior and legal claim to the custody and care of her bastard child; and if the putative father take the child from her, the court will restore it to her.[4] 383.

In repect of the child's property, a parent has no other power over or interest in his child's estate than as his trustee or guardian;[5] and though he may receive the profits during the child's minority, yet he must account for them when he comes of age.[6] The father cannot, as guardian, receive a legacy given to his child;[7] neither can he charge his child for maintenance, as he is bound to find that himself: but where the parent is not of sufficient property suitably to maintain the child, an adequate income out of the child's property will be allowed by the Court of Chancery;[8] or where the child's expectancies and the expenses of his establishment are very great.[9] The mother, however, is not bound to find maintenance, and would be entitled to an allowance, although of sufficient ability without. 384. 385. 386.

---

[1] 1 Jac. R. 254 n. (6); Wellesley v. Wellesley, and Wellesley v. D. Beaufort, 1 Dow. R. N. S. 154; 2 Bligh, 124; 2 Russ. 1; De Manneville v. De Manneville, 10 Ves. 62. [2] 2 Stra. 1162. [3] 1 Mod. 43; 1 Sid. 444.

[4] Rex v. Moses Soper, 5 T. R. 278; Exparte Ann Knee, 1 N. R. 148; 5 East, 224 n.; sed quere, Strangways v. Robinson, 4 Taunt. 498.

[5] 1 Bl. Com. 453; Wood's Inst. 63; 1 P. W. 702; 2 P. W. 117; 4 Bro. C. C. 101; 2 Bligh, N. S. 124. [6] 1 Bl. Com. 453.

[7] 1 P. W. 285.

[8] Roach v. Garvan, 1 Ves. 160; Hughes v. Hughes, 1 Bro. C. C. 387; 6 Ves. J. 454. [9] Jervois v. Silk, Coop. 53.

Parallel Articles of the French Code.

387. The father is entitled to the benefit of his children's labour and earnings while they live with him and are maintained by him.[1]

TITLE X.

OF MINORITY, GUARDIANSHIP, AND EMANCIPATION.

CHAPTER I.

Of Minority.

388. A minor (or in legal phraseology an infant) is an individual of either sex, who has not yet attained the age[2] of twenty-one years;[3] who is therefore not fully[4] invested with a legal capacity,[5] and cannot bind himself, except in marriage,[6] or for necessaries[7] supplied to himself or wife.

CHAPTER II.

Of Guardianship.

A guardian is a person to whom the care of a minor is committed, and who exercises, under certain restrictions, the powers and capacities (status) of the minor; and he has, in general, an interest in the body and lands of the minor.[8] There are in the English law several kinds of guardians, differing from each other, from the mode in which the duty devolves on them, in the extent of their powers and the duration of their office. Thus

[1] 1 Bl. Com. 453; 2 Car. & P. 578; 3 B. & Ald. 548.

[2] Additio probat minoritatem.—Law Maxim; 4 Inst. 80; Wing. 211.

[3] 1 Bl. Com. 463; Lit. s. 104, 259; and Co. Lit. 171 b.

[4] Meliorem conditionem suam facere potest minor, deteriorem nequaquam.—Law Maxim; Co. Lit. 337 b.

[5] As to the various degrees of capacity of infants, male and female, at various ages, see Co. Lit. 78 b.

[6] Ante, p. 263, n. 5.

[7] 10 Hen. VI. 14; Roll. Abr. 729; Co. Lit. 172; Hands v. Slaney, 8 T. R. 578; Mackerell v. Bachelor, Goulsb. 168.

[8] Tomlin, Law Dic.

Parallel Articles of the French Code.

persons may become guardians, either under the statute[1] or at common law. Of the latter kind[2] are guardians: 1st, by nature; 2nd, by nurture; 3rd, in socage; 4th, by election of the infant; 5th, by the appointment of a court of justice (ecclesiastical or chancery), for general purposes or ad litem; 6th, according to the custom of London, and some other cities and boroughs, or of a manor. Guardians under the statute are usually called testamentary guardians.

At first sight it may be imagined that there must be confusion, arising from so many kinds of guardianship; but, as their priorities and natures are definitively settled, such is not the case. In general, one takes in default of another; or one relates to the body, and the other to the lands of the ward. A guardian appointed under the statute excludes all the others, except those by the custom of London, or other cities, and may last until the ward attains twenty-one years of age.[3] The guardian in socage is the next in priority; but it can only arise when the infant is seized of lands in socage tenure by descent, and not by purchase;[4] and it only continues until the infant attains the age of fourteen years.[5] The guardian in socage is the next in blood to the heir to whom the inheritance cannot descend.[6] The next is guardianship by nature, which, strictly speaking, applies only to heirs apparent, and continues until they attain twenty-one years of age.[7] Where there are none of these kinds, the next is guardian by nurture, which, however, extends merely to the custody of the infant's body; and it applies to the other children as well as heirs apparent, until they attain the age of four-

[1] 12 Car. II. c. 24.

[2] The ancient common law guardian in chivalry (ante, p. 71; Co. Lit. book 2, c. 4) was of course abolished with that tenure, ante, p. 153.

[3] Co. Lit. 88 b, 9, and n. 15; 12 Car. II.; 1 Sid. 363; 3 Salk. 177.

[4] 2 Mod. 172; Lit. s. 123.

[5] Harg. note 13 to Co. Lit. 87 b; Vin. Ab. tit. Guard. 1.

[6] Co. Lit. 87.

[7] Harg. n. 12, Co. Lit. 88 b.

Parallel Articles of the French Code.

teen years: none can have this guardianship but the father and mother.[1] In the absence of any of these, and of a guardian under any local custom,[2] the Ecclesiastical Court, or the Lord Chancellor, appoints one;[3] or the infant may elect one.[4]

Section 1.

Of the Guardianship of the Father and Mother.

389. The father is guardian of his legitimate children,[5] either in socage, by nature, or by nurture. When all these rights of guardianship concur together, that in socage takes precedence, as being most for the benefit of the ward.[6] The father is exclusively entitled, in respect of nature, to the wardship of his son's body, being his heir apparent; and this though another, as during the existence of tenure in chivalry, might have been entitled to the wardship of the lands:[7] except on gross misconduct, when the Court of Chancery has power to appoint another guardian in his stead.[8] As regards the property of the ward, the father is accountable for the profits of his child's estate, like other guardians.[9]

390. A father may by his will, or by deed, appoint a guar-
391. dian,[10] to the exclusion of or jointly with the mother, but if he assign none, the mother has the second title to be

---

[1] Harg. n. 13, Co. Lit. 88 b. [2] Co. Lit. 88 b, n. 16.

[3] Ib. [4] Ib.; Hall v. Hall, 3 Atk. 721; 2 Ves. 374; 10 Ves. 52.

For further information respecting these different kinds of guardians, the reader must refer to Co. Lit., where cited in the previous notes; to Viner's Abridgment, title Guardian; or to Petersdoff's Abridgment, title Guardian. Mr. Mackenna points out the resemblances between these various kinds of guardians and the testamentary, legitimate, and dative guardians of the civil law.

[5] 1 Bl. Com. 460. [6] Co. Lit. 88 b, and n. 9.

[7] Lit. s. 114; Co. Lit. 84 a, 88 b.

[8] Hard. 96; Wellesley v. Beaufort, 2 Russ. 4; Pennington v. Alvin, 1 Sim. & Stu. 269; Beaufort v. Bertie, 1 P. W. 705.

[9] Co. Lit. 88 b; 1 Bl. Com. 460.

[10] 1 Bl. Com. 453; 12 Car. II. c. 24.

Parallel Articles of the French Code.

guardian.[1] The mother is guardian by nature, in the strict legal meaning of the term, of her heir apparent only, and as such, has the custody of his person till he attain the age of twenty-one years.[2] And the mother is guardian by nurture, as it is called, of such of her infant children as have no other guardian, and is entitled to the custody and government of the infant till the age of fourteen years, males and females.[3] Where the infant, under fourteen years of age, is entitled to lands in socage by descent, the guardianship devolves on the next of kin to whom the inheritance cannot possibly descend, who is called the Guardian in Socage;[4] thus, if the land descended to the heir on the part of the father, the mother, if living, shall have the wardship of the land, and of the heir as guardian in socage.[5] As the father 392.
could exclude the mother, of course he can limit her authority, like that of any other guardian; and if he thinks right, make her abide by the advice of any person or persons he may name.

Posthumous children are now considered as actually 393.
born to all purposes, except in the case of a descent at common law;[6] and in that case the heir presumptive may enter, but he gives place to the heir when born.[7] An infant in ventre sa mere may have a guardian assigned to it, like any other person.[8] And a father may appoint a person guardian to his children to be born after the appointment, including those of a second wife:[9] and if none were so appointed, the same person would be guardian as to a child not posthumous. The children 394.
have a natural right to the care of their mother.[10] But

[1] 1 Bl. Com. 460; Co. Lit. 88, n. 12, 13.

[2] Hargrave's note, Co. Lit. 88 b.

[3] Harg. n. 13, Co. Lit. 88 b.

[4] 1 Bl. Com. 461.

[5] Lit. s. 123.

[6] 10 & 11 Wm. III. c. 16.

[7] Thelluson v. Woodford, 4 Ves. 334, 5; Doe v. Clark, 2 H. Blac. 399.

[8] 12 Car. II. c. 24.

[9] Exparte the Earl of Ilchester, 7 Ves. 348.

[10] Per Lord Hardwick; Mellish v. Da Costa, 2 Atk. 15; Eyre v. the Countess of Shaftesbury, 2 P. W. 102.

Parallel Articles of the French Code.

of course she is not bound to undertake the guardianship without power of refusal. The second marriage of the mother does not alone furnish a presumption, that
395. she will neglect her duties as guardian to the children of her first marriage, and she is not deprived of her ward-
396. ship.[1] If she were a testamentary guardian, the guardianship is not thereby transferred to her second husband,[2] nor is it in socage on her death.[3]

Section 2.

Of the Right of appointing a Guardian.

397. The right of appointing a guardian belongs only to the father, the mother has no power to do so;[4] nor have the grandfather or grandmother.[5]

398. This right may be exercised by deed or will, executed in the presence of two or more witnesses;[6] and no particular form of appointment is required, provided the father's intention be apparent.[7]

401. The guardian appointed by the father may refuse the office, and then the chancellor will appoint one.[8]

Section 3.

Of the Guardianship of other Ancestors or Relations.

402. Where the father and mother are both dead, and no
403. guardian is appointed by the father, the grandfather and

---

1 Villareal v. Mellish, 2 Swanst. 533; Corbel v. Tottenham, 1 Ball & B. 60; Dillon v. Mountcashel, 4 Bro. P. C. 305.

2 Com. Dight. Guard. E. 2.

3 Co. Lit. 89 a.

4 12 Car. II.; Bedell v. Constable, Vaugh. 180; Exparte Edwards, 3 Atk. 5, 19; Lord Shaftesbury's case, 2 P. W. 102.

5 Roome v. Roome, 3 Atk. 183; Blake v. Leigh, Amb. 306.

6 12 Car. II. c. 24; Exparte Jordan, 1 Dick. 294; De Bathe v. Fingal, 16 Ves. 167; Reddell v. Liddiard, 3 Phill. 256.

7 Storke v. Storke, 3 P. W. 51.

8 1 Eq. Ca. Ab. 260, pl. 1; 1 P. W. 703; Selby v. Selby, 2 Eq. Ca. Ab. 488. Revocation of appointment, Ilchester exparte, 7 Ves. 367; Lord Shaftesbury v. Hannan, Finch R. 323.

Parallel Articles of the French Code.

other ancestors are guardians by nature of their heirs apparent.[1] If an infant happen to be heir apparent to two, as both a paternal and maternal grandfather, in this equality of rights, it has been contended priority of possession of the infant's person may decide;[2] though, in general, the law prefers the male, or paternal ancestor.[3] 404.

A grandfather,[4] or brother,[5] or other person, may leave property to a minor upon condition that a certain person shall be guardian; and if the father tacitly, by accepting the property, or expressly consent, he entirely waives his own right.

Section 4.

Of the Appointment of a Guardian by Judicial Authority.

The crown, as pater patriæ, is the universal guardian of infants;[6] and delegates this function to the lord chancellor, who may appoint guardians to such infants as are without them;[7] and the lord chancellor has power to remove a ward from the custody and control of a guardian (even though the father) who misconducts himself.[8] The Court of Chancery, in the exercise of its jurisdiction upon the affairs of minors, invites the assistance of their nearest relatives; and will be governed by their representations in the course to be pursued as 405 to 416.

[1] Ratcliffe's case, 3 Rep. 38 a; Co. Lit. 88 a, n. 12. Quere, if the mother renounce, whether the grandfather has any legal right to the guardianship.—Villareal v. Mellish, 2 Swans. 537.

[2] Harg. n. 12 to Co. Lit. 88 a. In æquali jure melior est conditio possidentis.—Law Maxim.

[3] Harg, n. 13 ib.

[4] Blake v. Leigh, Amb. 306.

[5] Potts v. Norton, Bridg. Dig. 2, p. 26.

[6] 2 Inst. 14; Beverley's case, 4 Rep. 126; and ante, p. 202.

[7] Co. Lit. 88 b, n. 16; Bac. Ab. Guard.; Lady Teynham v. Lennard, 1 Bro. C. C. 500; 1 Bro. P. C. 544; 2 Fonbl. 255; Exparte Watkins, 2 Ves. 470.

[8] Duke of Beaufort v. Berty, 1 P. W. 705; O'Keefe v. Casey, 1 Sch. & Lef. 106; Ingham v. Bickerside, 6 Madd. 275; Dillon v. Mountcashel, 4 Bro. P. C.

Parallel Articles of the French Code.

regards the person or property of the minor.[1] The ecclesiastical courts also exercise a power of appointing a guardian as to the personal estate of minors;[2] and all the courts have a power of assigning a guardian ad litem.[3]

417. The law of England (though the statute gives all the ward's property to the testamentary guardian) does not pretend to give a guardian any power to exercise the office over the immoveable property of the minor situated out of the realm, unless the office is conferred on him by the tribunals of the country in which such property is situated. The Court of Chancery, however, exercises the jurisdiction of appointing receivers and managers of lands situate in our colonies. If there be a second party appointed by the colonial courts, the functions of the two are quite distinct.[4]

418. The authority of the guardian appointed by the Court of Chancery commences from the date of the order appointing him, or confirming the master's appointment; with such authority, as to arrears and past matters, as the court directs.

419. The testamentary guardian can neither assign over the guardianship during his lifetime, or demise it by will,[5] unless authorized to do so by the father's will,[6] nor can guardian in socage:[7] and the guardianship does not pass to their executors or administrators;[8] but they would be liable as his representatives for his defaults.[9]

The Court of Chancery is not precluded from appointing a guardian by the circumstance of the infant having by deed appointed one himself.[10]

---

[1] Spencer v. Chesterfield, Amb. 146; Wellesley v. Duke of Beaufort, 2 Russ. 1; Drake v. Fortune, Molloy's R. 201. The marriage of a ward in chancery, without its leave, is a high contempt.

[2] Co. Lit. 88 b, n. 16.

[3] See Tidd's Practice; Smith's Chancery Practice.

[4] 15 Ves. 91; Hibbert v. Hibbert, 3 Mer. 681.

[5] Vaugh. 181; Da Costa v. Mellish, 2 Atk. 14.

[6] Darcy v. Holderness, in note to Duke of Beaufort v. Berty, 1 P.W. 703.

[7] Co. Lit. 90, and n. 1.

[8] Bedell v. Constable, Vaugh. 181; Lit. 125.

[9] 4 Anne, c. 16, s. 27.

[10] 4 Mad. 462.

Parallel Articles of the French Code.

Section 5.

Of a Conflict of the Interest of the Guardian and Ward.

The Court of Chancery will always interfere where there is such a conflict between the interests of guardian and ward, as to cause those of the latter to be neglected; and the infant may sue his guardian by his next friend (prochein ami),[1] who, however, does not supersede the guardian, except by the express direction of the court, and who is liable for costs. Or the father may nominate as guardians any number of persons he thinks proper; either jointly, for the general purposes of the guardianship, or severally, with particular duties assigned to each;[2] or he may appoint any person, or number of persons, whose advice the guardian shall be bound to follow.[3] 420 to 426.

Section 6.

Of Refusing to undertake Guardianship.

According to the law of England, guardianship is not a public office or duty, and nobody is forced to be guardian, but may refuse the office;[4] but if he accept the trust, and act upon it, the court will compel him to continue his office, and will not permit him to be discharged except upon very strong grounds, and with the approbation of the nearest relatives of the minor.[5] It has, however, been said, that where the law appoints who shall be trusted, as in the several guardianships at common law, the trust cannot be refused; but where the 427 to 442.

[1] 2 Vern. 362; 2 P. W. 119; 1 Ves. 91.
[2] Swinb. on Wills.
[3] Duke of Beaufort v. Berty, 1 P. W. 703; Smith v. Smith, 3 Atk. 304.
[4] Eq. Ca. Ab. 260, pl. 2; 1 P. W. 703; O'Keeffe v. Casey, 1 Scho. & Lef. 106.
[5] Spencer v. Earl of Chesterfield, 1 Amb. 146.

Parallel Articles of the French Code.

party names the trustee, as under the statute, it may be refused.[1] When a proper person cannot be found to undertake the office gratuitously, the Court of Chancery will appoint a receiver at a salary, or with a poundage on the income.[2]

Section 7.

Of Incapacity for, or Deprivation of, Guardianship.

442. Any person whatsoever may be appointed guardian by the father, and is qualified to act as such until removed or controlled by judicial authority;[3] but an infant within age,[4] an idiot, a man non compos mentis, a lunatic, a man cæcus et mutus, or surdus et mutus, cannot be[5] guardian in socage.[6]

443. Guardians at common law may be removed if there appear danger of their abusing the person or property of the ward.[7] If he become lunatic he may be removed,[8] or bankrupt.[9] A guardian under the statute cannot be wholly removed;[10] but the Court of Chancery will appoint a proper person to superintend the maintenance and education of the infant;[11] and if a testamentary guardian be attainted of treason, or felony, or outlawed, the guardianship is not thereby forfeited; but he may

---

1 Bedel v. Constable, Vaugh. 182.

2 Davis v. Denby, 3 Mad. 170; Potts v. Leighton, 15 Ves. 276.

3 Harg. n. 15, Co. Lit. 88 b.

4 Minor minorem custodire non debet.—Law Maxim, Co. Lit. 88 b. If, however, such infant have himself a guardian, he shall be guardian of both, per causa de ward.

5 Alium regere non potest, qui seipsum regere non novit.—Law Maxim, ib.

6 Co. Lit. 88 b.

7 Si quis custos fraudem pupillo fecerit, à tutela removendus est.—Jenk. Cent. 39, pl. 75; Foster v. Denny, 2 Cha. Ca. 237; Style, 456; Hard. 96; Bla. 424; 3 Salk. 177.

8 Exparte Brydges, H. T. 1791.

9 1 Bl. Com. 463, n. 11.

10 Hide's ca. 3 Salk. 178; Davis's ca. 1 P.W. 698; 2 P.W. 112; 2 Fonbl. 232; Ingham v. Bickerdike, Madd. & Geld. 275.

11 Ingham v. Bickerdike, Madd. & Geld. 275.

continue to exercise the office until removed by the Court of Chancery.[1] A guardian in socage shall not forfeit his interest by outlawry, or attainder of felony, or treason.[2]

Parallel Articles of the French Code.

Section 8.

Of the Guardian's Powers and Administration.

The reciprocal power and duty of a guardian and ward, are the same, pro tempore, as that of a father and child.[3] The office of a testamentary guardian appointed by the father, is a continuation of the paternal authority, until the ward attain the age of twenty-one years, or until an earlier period of emancipation appointed by the father.[4] The office of guardian is a trust, to be exercised solely for the benefit of the minor and the good and honour of the family.[5] It implies two general obligations; one relating to the government and education of the minor (the wardship of his body), the other the administration and care of the infant's estate (the wardship of the estate). It must be remembered, that the management of the personal estate of the father devolves on his personal representative, *i. e.* executor or administrator, and not on the guardians of the infant, persons beneficially interested. The executor or administrator is a trustee for the infant, until the age of twenty-one years. 450.

The law invests the guardian with such an interest in the person and estate of the ward, as is necessary for the due execution of those obligations.[6] As to the first of these duties, he must supply his ward with the necessaries of life,[7] protect,[8] and educate him.[9] And

---

[1] 1 Wood, Lect. 46. [2] Co. Lit. 88 b. [3] 1 Bl. Com. 463.

[4] Eyre v. Countess of Shaftesbury, 2 P. W. 115.

[5] Co. Lit.; 2 P. W. 123; Bedell v. Constable, Vaugh. 181.

[6] Brac. l. 2, c. 3, f. 87.

[7] 2 Salk. 175; Dormer v. Dormer, Finch R. 435.

[8] Burfort v. Reynolds, 2 Stra. 954; 1 Burn's Just. 270.

[9] 2 Inst. 12; Eyre v. Shaftesbury, 2 P. W. 115: Tremaine's ca. 1 Stra. 168; Hall v. Hall, 3 Atk. 721; Storke v. Storke, 3 P. W. 51.

Parallel Articles of the French Code.

as to marriage,[1] his consent to the marriage of his ward is required, as that of the father's, if living, would have been.[2]

The guardian, testamentary or other, is in general entitled to the possession and custody of his ward, in preference to the claims of any other person whatsoever:[3] and he is entitled to direct and enforce the place of the ward's residence.[4] If he be deprived of his ward, he may have a writ of ravishment, or an action of trespass,[5] or a writ of habeas corpus;[6] but recourse is more frequently had to the Court of Chancery.

450. With regard to the administration of his estate, it is
467. a general rule, that whoever will stand forward in the character of next friend, on behalf of infants, is to be encouraged to every possible extent, while he can be
455. supposed to intend the infant's benefit.[7] The guardian must use his discretion in dealing with the minor's property; and he is in the nature of a bailiff or servant to the infant, and undertakes no otherwise than for his diligence and fidelity;[8] but he must act carefully, and he will be answerable for all losses, arising from his wilful default or negligence.[9] But if he entrusts his ward's property to his attorney, or co-guardian, and à fortiori to a stranger, he will be responsible for any loss occasioned thereby.[10] Most kinds of guardians are trustees of the property of the minor of every description.[11]
450. Though the guardian represents the ward in the exercise

---

1 2 Inst. 12; 1 Cruise, Dig. 36; Goodall v. Harris, 2 P. W. 561.

2 Ante, pp. 237 and 264.

3 Eyre v. Earl of Shaftesbury, 2 P. W. 102; Exparte Hopkins, 3 P. W. 155; Wright v. Naylor, 5 Madd. 77.

4 Tremaine's case, 1 Stra. 167; Hall v. Hall, 3 Atk. 721.

5 Lord Anglesey v. Lord Ossory, 3 Kebb. 528; 2 Inst. 9.

6 Rex v. Johnson, 1 Stra. 579; Rex v. Delaval, 3 Burr. 1434.

7 Whittaker v. Morlar, 1 Cox, 286.

8 Co. Lit. 89 a, 172.

9 1 Bl. Com. 463.

10 Chambers v. Minchin, 7 Ves. 196; Langford v. Gascoyne, 11 Ves. 333; Davis v. Spurling, 1 Russ. & M. 66; Kilbee v. Molloy, 2 Moll. 199.

11 Wood, Lect. 158.

of his civil capacity in most acts,[1] he derives his authority, not from the infant, but from the law; and he may make leases[2] during his ward's minority,[3] or for a longer period;[4] and grant copies of court-roll;[5] or he may 453.
occupy the estate of the ward.[6] He may also distrain for rent of the infant's lands,[7] and transact all affairs in his own name, and not in the name of the ward.[8] Guardian 464.
ad litem, or prochein ami, represents him in all cases of judicial proceedings, for or against him,[9] as actions of covenant or debt,[10] ejectment,[11] trespass.[12] With respect 450.
to purchasing the ward's property, the guardian stands in the same light as a trustee; and purchases of trust property by trustees for their own benefit will be set aside.[13]

Parallel Articles of the French Code.

It has been the practice for many guardians, to prevent 450.
disagreeable contests with their wards, to indemnify 454.
themselves, by applying to the Court of Chancery, acting 455.
under its discretion, and accounting annually before the 457.
officers of that court.[15] When any particular measure proposed is doubtful in its tendency, the more prudent course for the guardians to pursue, is to seek the indemnity of a court of equity, which will direct one of its officers to enquire and report, whether the measure be or be not, in its probable tendency, beneficial to the infant.[15]

The guardian should be prepared with such inventory 451.

---

[1] Cro. Jac. 98; Co. Lit. 135 b; 2 Inst. 261; 2 Strat. 734.

[2] But see 2 Wils. 129; Cro. Eliz. 678, 734.

[3] Shaw v. Shaw, Vern. & Scri. 607; 2 Roll. Ab. 41, p. 3.

[4] 1 Wm. IV. c. 65, s. 17.

[5] Shopland v. Ryoler, Cro. Jac. 55, 99.

[6] Rex v. the Inhabitants of Oakley, 10 East, 494. Copyholds, Shopland v. Ryoler, 2 Cro. 55, 98.

[7] Bradby on Distresses, 91.

[8] Bac. Abr. tit. Guard. (G), Leases (A) 9.

[9] Co. Lit. 135 b, & n. 1; Sid. 424; Taylor v. Attwood, 2 P. W. 643.

[10] Shaw v. Shaw, V. & S. 607; Shopland v. Ryoler, 2 Cro. 55, 98; Eyre v. Shaftesbury, 2 P. W. 115.

[11] Adams on Eject. 66.

[12] Wade v. Baker, 1 Lord Raym. 131.

[13] The law will not permit a trustee to purchase of himself.—2 Sug. Vend. & Pur. 109; Fox v. Mackreth, 2 Bro. C. C. 483; Attorney-General v. Lord Dudley, Coop. 146; Whitmore v. Lawrence, 2 Ves. 741; Exparte Lacy, 6 Ves. 128.

[14] 1 Bl. Com. 463.

[15] 2 Vern. 224; Burgh. 155.

Parallel Articles of the French Code.

and accounts of the ward's property, as to be able to account to his ward, though no exact time or kind of schedule is fixed by the law; and debts due from the ward to him have no peculiarities.

452. A guardian ought, in a reasonable time, to sell all moveables at the best prices that can be reasonably obtained, but no peculiar mode of sale is required; and he should invest the produce at interest: but if the minor is nearly of age, and may require them himself,[1] the goods
453. should not be sold. He is answerable to the ward for whatever goods are not sold; and if any are lost by his wilful default or negligence, he must pay their value.

454. The guardian is to appropriate such a sum as a judi-
455. cious parent would, for the maintenance and education of the minor, suitably to his age, fortune, and condition in life.[2] The Court of Chancery will, on petition, make an order of maintenance out of the infant's property,[3] according to the circumstances of the family, and the expectations of the minor.[4]

456. He should invest all surplus income, on security bearing interest. He is liable for interest for money in his hands, which might have been put out at interest:[5] but it is breach of trust to lend it on private security;[6] it should be invested in government security.[7]

457. The guardian has no power to change the nature of
467. the infant's estate, as realty into personalty, or personalty into realty,[8] so as to change the order of succession;[9] and

[1] 3 Salk. 177.

[2] Dormer v. Dormer, Finch R. 435; Chaplin v. Chaplin, 3 P. W. 368.

[3] 3 Bro. C. C. 88; 12 Ves. 492.

[4] 2 P. W. 21; 1 Ves. 60.

[5] 3 Salk. 177.

[6] Pocock v. Reddington, 5 Ves. 779; Piety v. Stace, 4 Ves. 620; Flanagan v. Nolan, 1 Molloy, 85; Walker v. Symmonds, 3 Swanst. 638.

[7] Holme v. Dring, 2 Cox's ca. 1.

[8] 1 Ves. 461.

[9] As to the produce retaining its original character after sale of timber, Amb. 322; Exparte Bromfield, 1 Ves. J. 454; 3 Bro. C. C. 516; Tullet v. Tullet, 1 Dick. 370; Exparte Phillips, 19 Ves. 124; Saville's ca. temp. Talb. 16; Pocock v. Reddington, 5 Ves. 799. But see where the infant is tenant in tail, Mason v. Mason, Amb. 371. Repairs, Brac. l. 2, c. 37, n. 3; Exparte Grimston; in re Redington, 1 Molloy's R. 256. Interest of a mortgage, Jennings v. Looks, 2 P. W.

Parallel Articles of the French Code.

he has no power to sell real estate.[1] It should seem he might change the nature of the estate, by an act manifestly for the infant's advantage.[2] A guardian, under the sanction of the Court of Chancery, may purchase real property for his ward, and the real property so purchased would retain the character of personalty, for the purpose of testamentary disposition, during the infant's minority.[3] A guardian may borrow money to pay off an incumbrance on an infant's estate, but he must complete his security; or if he die, the court would not decree satisfaction out of the infant's estate[4]: and if he employ the infant's money in paying off a charge or redeeming a mortgage, the sum so invested would be looked upon as personalty.[5] If a guardian takes a bond for arrears of rent he thereby makes it his own debt, and shall be charged with it.[6]

Guardians have no power to receive a legacy left to 463.
an infant.[7] It is said, a partition made by the guardian 465.
shall bind the infant, if it be equal.[8] The infant cannot 466.
by deed make partition;[9] but under the jurisdiction of the Court of Chancery it seems he can.[10] He has, however, a day given him to show cause, after he comes of age;[11] but the only way in which he can be absolutely bound, is by act of parliament.[12]

Guardians, like executors, may compound a debt[13] or

267. Principal, Dennis v. Badd, 1 Ca. in Cha. 156; Palmer v. Danby, 1 Eq. Ca. Ab. 261. Trade, Brown v. De Tastet, 15 Ves. 225; Heathcote v. Heathcote, 1 Jac. & Walk. 130. Employing agents, and defraying the expense out of the minor's income, 2 Eq. Ca. Ab. 489; Brocksopp v. Barnes, 5 Mad. 90.

1 Burton, Compend. 74; Earl of Winchilsea v. Norcliffe, 1 Vern. 437.

2 See cases cited, Bridg. Dig. v. ii. p. 29; Guard. & Ward, pl. 38.

3 Pierson v. Shore, 1 Atk. 480; Ashburton v. Ashburton, 6 Ves. 6.

4 Hooper v. Eyles, 2 Vern. 480.

5 Exparte Bromfield, 3 Bro. C. C. 516; Tullet v. Tullet, 1 Dick. 323.

6 2 Cha. Rep. 97.

7 See ante, p. 301 and n. 7, and Dagley v. Tolferry, 1 P.W. 283; 1 Eq. Ca. Ab. 300, pl. 2; Cooper v. Thornton, 3 Bro. C. C. 96; Whopham v. Wingfield, 4 Ves. 630.

8 2 Rol. Ab. 256; Bac. Abr. tit. Guard. G.; Lit. s. 255.

9 Co. Lit. 57 b, n. 3.

10 Ib. 169 a, n. 2, vii.

11 Tuckfield v. Buller, Amb. 197; 1 Dick. 240.

12 Coventry's note b to Walk. on Conv. p. 155; and see post, b. 1, tit. 1, c. 6.

13 Roberts v. Newbold, Cumb. 318.

Parallel Articles of the French Code.

rent, if absolutely necessary,[1] as where the debtor is insolvent, but they do it at their own risk.[2] He may even release rent, or give money to get rid of a bad tenant.[3]

467. Articles by a guardian for a sale of timber have been executed in equity.[4]

If an infant be joint owner with another person of real property, neither he nor his guardian can sell his interest: the other owner may sell his interest separately.[5]

Section 9.

Of the Accounts of Guardianship.

469. Every guardian[6] is accountable for his management at the close of it,[7] and may be compelled, by bill in equity, to furnish his accounts.[8]

470. Even during the minority and guardianship, every guardian may be required to account before the Court of Chancery, at the suit of the infant's next friend (prochein ami);[9] but at common law no action of account would lie, until the guardianship determined.[10] In equity the guardians are bound by recognizance to account regularly, or when called upon.[11] A father must account[12] like other guardians.

471. The guardian in his account shall be allowed all reasonable costs and expenses in all things;[13] so in socage,[14] and of course those of rendering accounts included; and if the estate should fail, a trustee or a guardian may recover the amount against the party beneficially interested, personally.[15]

---

1 See Goring v. Goring, Yelv. 10; Norden v. Sevit, 2 Lev. 189.

2 Ib. Barker v. Talcot, 1 Vern. 474.

3 Blue v, Marshall, 3 P. W. 381.

4 Clavering v. Clavering, Mos. 224.

5 Co. Lit. 337 a, b.

6 Guardian in chivalry, while it existed (see ante, p. 71), was not, but guardian in socage is at the heir's age of fourteen years.—Lit. 123.

7 1 Bl. Com. 465; Co. Lit. 88 b, n. 9.

8 Morgan v. Morgan, 1 Atk. 489; Eyre v. Shaftesbury.

9 2 Vern. 342; 2 P. W. 119; 1 Ves. 91; Mitf. Pl. 25.

10 Co. Lit. 89 a, and n. 2.

11 Re Burke, 1 Ball & B. 74.

12 Wood, Inst. 64.

13 Co. Lit. 89 a, and notes.

14 Lit. 123.

15 Balsh v. Higham, 2 P.W. 453.

Parallel Articles of the French Code.

A ward may, on attaining his majority, dispense with the accounts of his guardian, or release him without examining them; and any agreement on good consideration between guardian and ward, after the ward has attained his majority, is binding on him; except in case of fraud, or where he is non compos mentis, &c.[1] It is, however, a rule that a trustee, guardian, or other, cannot buy from himself his ward's estate; and, in considering any agreement between guardian and ward, the Court of Chancery would take into consideration how far this principle applied to it, and how far the ward was in need, or entitled to its protection. And where any transaction originates in the influence arising from the relation of guardian and ward, it will be set aside, though all the accounts have been settled, and such relation is at an end.[2] 472.

A bill in Chancery for an account, or an action of account, may be brought when there is any dispute. 473.

Interest will be ordered, on repayment of a balance of money in the guardian's hands.[3] 474.

If an infant neglect to bring his action or suit for six years, he is bound, by the statute of limitation, from bringing a bill for an account, as well as an action at common law.[4] 475.

Where a guardian, after his ward attains full age, continues to manage the property of the ward, and before the accounts of his receipts and payments during the minority are settled, it is in effect a continuance of the guardianship, and he must account on the same principle, as if they were transactions during the minority;[5] and the guardian in socage, occupying after the heir attains the age of fourteen, shall be charged as bailiff.[6]

---

[1] 2 Ves. 260; Revett v. Harvey, 1 Sim. & Stu. 502; Wych v. Packington, 3 Bro. P. C. 46; Dawson v. Massey, 1 B. & B. 219.

[2] Wright v. Proud, 13 Ves. 138.

[3] See note 1.

[4] Prec. Ch. 518; 1 Scho. & Lef. 352; 2 Fonb. 235; Earl of Pomfret v. Lord Windsor, 2 Ves. S. 482.

[5] Mellish v. Mellish, 1 Sim. & Stu. 138.

[6] Lit. s. 124; Co. Lit. 90; 2 Inst. 380.

Parallel Articles of the French Code.

CHAPTER III.

Of Emancipation.

476 to 487. The term "emancipation" is sometimes used in the English law; but the notion, at least as affecting the whole civil capacity of a minor, is not known to it. As regards contracting a second marriage, the minor is considered as emancipated by the first marriage,[1] so as not to require the parent's consent;[2] but the marriage of a male infant, before he is twenty-one years of age, does not determine the guardianship, though the marriage of a female does.[3] The most common application of this word is in the system of the poor laws, where it signifies a child so separated from its parent, as to be able to gain a settlement, or pauper domicil, in a new parish. It was in a case of this kind laid down, that "no emancipation is effected during minority, unless by marriage, becoming the head of another family, or contracting some such other relation, as wholly and permanently to exclude parental control."[4]

TITLE XI.

OF MAJORITY, LUNATICS, AND UNTHRIFTS.

CHAPTER I.

Of Majority.

488. Majority, or full age, in male and female, is twenty-one years, which age is completed on the day preceding the anniversary of the person's birth:[5] the person then becomes capable of exercising all the civil rights of his condition.

---

[1] 1 Bl. Com. 437, 8.

[2] See ante.

[3] Mendes v. Mendes, 3 Atk. 625; 1 Ves. 91; Roach v. Garvan, 1 Ves. 160.

[4] Rex v. Wilmington, 1 D. & R. 140; 5 B. & Ald. 525.

[5] 1 Bl. Com. 463.

Parallel Articles of the French Code.

CHAPTER II.

Of Lunacy.

The law of England, like that of every other civilized nation, divests of capacity individuals deprived of their reason, and provides for the care of their person and the exercise of their rights. A distinction is in theory made with respect to such persons, between those that are idiots and those that are lunatics.[1] An idiot, or natural fool, is one that hath no understanding from his nativity, or is born deaf, dumb, and blind; and the custody of him and his lands is vested in the crown, as the general conservator of the people,[2] taking the profits to the royal use without waste or destruction, and finding him necessaries.[3] A lunatic, or non compos mentis, is he who had understanding, but by disease, grief, or other accident, hath lost the use of his reason; or who has become deaf, dumb, and blind, not being born so. To these the crown is a trustee, to protect their property, and to account to them if they recover, or to their representative after their decease.[4] From the time a person is found non compos mentis, or a natural fool (purus idiota), he is not allowed to interfere with his property, unless in a lucid interval.[5] 489.

Any person (relative, friend, creditor, or stranger)[6] is competent to petition for a commission, or to sue out a writ de idiota inquirenda,[7] to inquire into the party's state of mind.[8] In order that the property may not vest in the crown, a person is seldom found an idiot a 490.

---

1 Co. Lit. 247 a. 2 1 Bl. Com. 302, 3. 3 Ib. 4 Ib. 304.

5 As to insanity in general, and particularly what constitutes a sound and disposing mind and memory, see the Marquis of Winchester's case, Rep.; Burrows v. Burrows, 1 Hag. 109; Brounker v. Brounker, 2 Phil. 57; Evans v. Knight, 1 Add. 239; M'Adam v. Walker, 1 Dow. 172; Griffiths v. Robins, 3 Mad. 162.

6 Exparte Ogle, 15 Ves. 112; Exparte Ward, 6 Ves. 579.

7 F. N. B. 232. 8 15 Ves. 115.

Parallel Articles of the French Code.

nativitate, but only non compos from some particular time.

492. As to the mode of proceeding for this purpose, application by petition, or information for a commission to inquire into a party's state of mind, is made to the Court of Chancery.[1] It must be supported by affidavit, and must seem to the chancellor to be proper; and then a commission is issued to certain commissioners to summon a jury, who make inquisition whether the party be of sound mind or not.[2]

496. The lunatic, or his friends, may enter a caveat, and oppose the issuing of a commission, and if issued he may defend himself by attorney and counsel; and he may traverse the inquisition:[3] or he may apply to have the commission superseded.[4] When, upon the return of the inquisition, the party is found a lunatic, and such finding is not traversed, or the commission superseded, the appointment of committees of the person and estate of the lunatic is the next proceeding.[5]

500. When the return is traversed by any person, a new inquisition may be issued if the chancellor think proper; or the chancellor may inquire by inspection.[6]

502. The return of the inquisition states how long the person has been lunatic; and it should state whether he has lucid intervals. All past acts, subsequent to the time from which the lunatic is declared such, unless done during lucid intervals, are void.[7]

504. The acts of a lunatic may be, and frequently are, contested after his decease on the ground of insanity, even though no commission of lunacy was issued.[8]

505. The care of the lunatic's person is committed to some friend, who is called the committee of his person; and a suitable allowance for his maintenance is made. This

---

1 1 Bl. Com. 305.

2 Grant or Mad. Cha. Prac.

3 34 E. 3, c. 14; 2 E. 6, c. 8.

4 Cha. Prac.

5 In re Smith, 1 Russ. 348.

6 Cha. Prac.

7 Ib.

8 See Lit. s. 406.

Parallel Articles of the French Code.

committee is usually the next of kin, or the person who is nearest of blood, and entitled to the administration;[1] regard being had to the inclinations and aversions of the lunatic, as well as to the consideration of combining interest with duty in the appointment.[2] The wife and a relative have been appointed jointly, on account of her afflicting situation.[3]

The committee of the estate is usually the heir at law, 506.
or person entitled to the property of the lunatic, in the 507.
event of his dying intestate, as being the party most interested in the care of it.[4]

In the management of a lunatic's estate, the benefit 510.
and comfort of a lunatic is the great object; and his accommodation is consulted before other considerations in connexion with the amount of his property,[5] except where there are claims of creditors, which are first considered. Where the father of an infant is non compos, 511.
the Chancellor is guardian to give consent to the marriage of such infant.[6]

The commission of lunacy is superseded when the 512.
lunatic recovers;[7] and the committee is called upon to account and transfer the estates and balances to the party.

CHAPTER III.

Of Spendthrifts.

Sic utere tuo et alienum non lædas, is the only re- 513 to 515.
striction our laws have given with regard to economical prudence; and when on an inquest of idiotcy a man has been returned an unthrift, and not an idiot, no further proceedings can be had.[8] The commission of lunacy is

---

[1] 2 Fonb. Eq. 247.
[2] 2 P. W. 637; 6 Ves. 427.
[3] Exparte Le Heup. 18 Ves. 221.
[4] 1 Bl. Com. 305; 1 Coll. 250.
[5] 1 Ves. J. 297.
[6] See ante, p. 265.
[7] Cha. Prac.
[8] Bro. Ab. tit. Idiot.

Parallel Articles of the French Code.

not, however, confined to strict insanity, but is applicable to cases of imbecility of mind, to the extent of incapacity from any cause, as disease, age, or habitual intoxication;[1] and courts of equity watch narrowly contracts made with young persons engaged in a course of dissipation, in order to obtain their property or expectancies at an inferior value.[2]

---

[1] Ridgway v. Darwin, 8 Ves. 65; Exparte Persse, 1 Molloy, 219; Exparte Barnsley, 3 Atk. 175.

[2] Evans, Pothier, n. p. 30. Lord Coke, Co. Lit. 247 a. As for a drunkard who is voluntarius dæmon, he hath no privilege thereby, but what hurt or ill soever he doth, his drunkenness doth aggravate it.—Plo. Com. 19.

Parallel Articles of the French Code.

BOOK II.

PROPERTY.

TITLE I.

OF THE DISTINCTIONS OF PROPERTY.

From the consideration of the state and condition of persons, the French code passes to that of property; and here (as of persons), we find a twofold division of the subject, namely, 1st, The objects of property, and their legal natures, kinds, and distinctions; 2nd, The right to the objects of property, that is, the estate or condition (status) therein, and its various degrees and modifications.

With respect to the objects of property, it may be laid down as a general rule, that every inanimate thing or irrational creature, natural or civil, which has an exchangeable value, may be the object of property.

With regard to its kinds, all property is necessarily moveable or immoveable; but as the whole system of 516.
the English law of property is based upon the feudal principles,[1] the leading distinction of property by the law of England is not into moveable and immoveable, but into real and personal. Real property is such as is permanent, fixed, and immoveable,[2] and held for a period of not less in consideration of law than the life of the owner, or of another person or persons.[3] Personal property consists of all moveables, and also of certain interests connected with, and issuing out of real property, but which are temporary or only for years.[4] Thus, a lease of land for one thousand years, or renewable perpetually, is only personalty;[5] for real property is only such as

[1] Ante, p. 57. [2] 2 Bl. Com. 16. [3] Ib. 386.
[4] Ib. 16, 144, 386; Co. Lit. 182, 19, 20.
[5] 2 Bl. Com. 144, 386; Waldron v. Howell, 3 Russ. R. 376.

Parallel Articles of the French Code.

might have constituted a fief, while personal property, set by the law in contradistinction to realty, is all theat could not constitute a fief. Whatever wanted the two qualities of a fief, duration as to time and immoveability as to place, was by the Norman feudal law,[1] and still is by the English law, held to be personalty, and called a chattel. Chattels are either real or personal. Chattels real are all such interests in immoveable property as are not possessed of the other of the above requisites of a fief; and chattels personal are all kinds of moveables, and all rights wanting the immoveability, as well as the duration of realty.[2] Chattels are again divided into choses, or things in possession, and things or choses in action, of which the possession is to be recovered by action.

The objects of property, whether real or personal, moveable or immoveable, are either corporeal, such as are objects of sense, and can be touched (quæ tangi possunt), or they are incorporeal, existing in contemplation only, and not objects of sense (quæ tangi non possunt sed in jure consistunt).[3]

CHAPTER I.

Of Real Property.

517. Property may be immoveable, and constitute realty, either from its nature, or from being permanently annexed to, or issuing out of that which is in itself immoveable and real;[4] or under peculiar circumstances from an intention of having it converted into reality, it may be invested by the law with qualities of real property.[5]

518. The kind of property by nature really immoveable, or

---

[1] Gr. Coust. 87, 85; 2 Bl. Com. c. 2.

[2] 2 Bl. Com. 385, 6, 44; Mr. Christian's note; 1 Prest. on Est. 1 vol. 200.

[3] Co. Lit. 9 a; Bract. l. 2, f. 53, 366.

[4] 2 Bl. Com. 18, 428.

[5] Wheldale v. Partridge, 5 Ves. 396; Fletcher v. Ashburner, 1 Bro. C. C. 497.

Parallel Articles of the French Code.

incapable of being removed from place to place, requires little illustration. Thus lands, and the soil of the earth, houses, and such-like buildings erected thereon, are necessarily immoveable, and constitute realty.[1] Things, not in themselves immoveable, are sometimes so fixed to immoveable property that it may be doubtful whether they do not form part of that to which they are attached, and form fixtures.[2] And in examining this question, it must be always borne in mind, that there are three kinds of conflicting interests as to which they are considered, and with respect to which a somewhat different rule of strictness of construction is applied, namely, as between, 1st, executor and heir; 2nd, tenant for life and remainder-man; and 3rd, landlord and tenant.

The rule obtains with the most rigour, as between heir and executor representing the same ancestor, in favour of the inheritance, that things annexed to the land thereby become immoveable and part of the real estate. Between the executors of the tenant for life or in tail, and the remainder-man or revertioner, the right to disannex such things is considered more favourably for the executors than when against the heir. And the greatest latitude and indulgence have been allowed, to the claim to have any particular articles considered as personalty and moveable, in favour of a tenant against a landlord.[3] The general rule is,[4] that whatever is affixed to the freehold (whether annexed by nails, screws, mortar, &c., or let into the soil), forms part of it, and is not moveable. The first question, therefore, as to such things, including some kinds of buildings, is whether
they are fixed to, or let into the soil, or not. Thus though 519.
wind or water mills, barns, granaries, and other erections et into the soil, or attached by nails, screws, mortar, or she like, are in general immoveable; yet such buildings, when of wood, and only resting on pillars or a brick

[1] 2 Bl. Com. 18.

[2] The legal maxim is, Quicquid plantatur solo, solo cedit.

[3] Elwes v. Mawe, 3 East, 38.

[4] Co. Lit. 53 a.; Herlakenden's case, 4 Rep. 64; Lord Darby v. Asquith, Hob. 234.

Parallel Articles of the French Code.

foundation by their own weight, and not connected, are not part of the immoveable or real property over which they rest, but mere chattels.[1]

On this subject, however, even where the things are actually annexed to real estate, there are several distinctions affecting the right to disannex them. From a very early period in the history of English law, almost as soon as the first printed reports of cases commence,[2] we find a distinction made in favour of trade.[3] Others have been admitted, where the things affixed were annexed merely for the purpose of ornament, and others where they were for mere domestic convenience: and also, whether the fixture can be removed without damage to the estate.[4] The principle governing these distinctions, appears to depend on whether such things are accessory[5] or incident[6] to the freehold, or accessory to something else: in other words, whether they are necessary to complete the estate, and for its full enjoyment, as hearths, doors, &c., to a house, or whether they are put there for a purpose disconnected with the estate, as a trade or manufactory not dependent on the estate. This seems to be the basis of the difference of construction between a tenant in agriculture and one in trade, and why a tenant in agriculture is not permitted to remove a beast house, carpenter's shop, fuel house, &c., let into the ground,[7] while a tenant in trade has been allowed to remove a varnish house, though let into the ground;[8] or an engine-house, built to cover an engine. But in consequence of these various distinctions, the different degrees of strictness with which the right of disannexion is considered, and the mixture

---

1 Penton v. Roberts, 2 East, 88; Rex v. Otley, 1 Bar. & Ad. 161; 1 Brod. & B. 506; 4 Moore, 284; Rex v. Londonthorpe, 6 T. R. 377; 4 Leon, 241; 3 East, 55; Dean v. Allaley, 3 Esp. N. P. 11; Taylor v. Collinge, 1 Taunt. 19; 11 Vin. Ab. 154; Bul. N. P. 34; 9 East, 215. As to Machinery, 2 B. & Ald. 165; 1 Taunt. 19.

2 See ante, p. 105.

3 Year Book, 42 Ed. III. f. 6, pl. 19.

4 The principal thing shall not be destroyed by the accessory.—Per Lord Hardwick, in Lawton v. Lawton, 3 Atk. 13.

5 Accessorius sequitur naturam sui principalis.—Law Max.

6 Shepherd's Touchstone, 469, 470.

7 Elwes v. Mawe, 3 East, 38.

8 Penton v. Roberts, 2 East, 88.

of express agreement, or local and particular custom, with general law in most of the cases which have come before the courts, it is no easy task to discover the ruling principle in the apparently conflicting decisions. And the space allowable here will only permit us to state what has been decided, without further comment on the grounds of the decision, and without stating between what class of interests the question arose.[1]

Parallel Articles of the French Code.

Trees or shrubs, growing or planted in the soil, are in general (at least as between the heir and executor), realty: fruits while hanging on the trees, and crops uncut, are also in general real property, as part of the immoveable object to which they are attached. As soon as grain is cut and fruits plucked, although not carried away, they become personalty. If one part only of the crop is cut, such part alone is personalty; and a distinction is made in certain cases, between artificial and natural produce, even while standing attached to the immoveable object.[2] Where an estate or right of possession of land terminates unexpectedly, without the fault of the tenant or occupier, the growing crops of *artificial* produce (fructus industrialis), termed in law emblements, are considered as moveables and personalty.[3] But *natural* produce, as meadow-grass (though manured), and fruit growing on trees, are realty.[4] Though trees and shrubs are in general immoveable, yet when they are planted in the course of trade and for the purpose of sale, they are considered as moveable personal property.[5] And a nursery-man or gardener may, at the end of his tenancy, remove trees, shrubs, &c., which he has planted for the purpose of sale.[6] But unless planted by such a person for the purpose of 520.

[1] For more definite information the reader must refer to the cases cited, or to some work on the law of fixtures, as that of Messrs. Amos and Ferrard.

[2] Evans v. Roberts, 5 Bar. & Cress. 132; Scovell v. Boxall, 1 Young & Jerv. 398; Co. Lit. 56 a.; Com. Dig. Biens. G. 1, 2; Lawton v. Lawton, 3 Atk. 16.

[3] Co. Lit. 55 b, n. 1; 2 Bl. Com. 122; Swinb. pt. 7, s. 10, pl. 8; Williams' Executors, 453; Wentw., Office of Executor, 147; Latham v. Attwood, Cro. Car. 515; 9 Vin. Abr. 378; Lawton v. Lawton, 3 Atk. 15.

[4] Swinb. 934; Toller, Ex. 194; 9 B. & C. 577; 10 B. & C. 446; Gow. R. 109.

[5] 3 East, 38; 7 Taunt. 191; 4 ib. 316.

[6] 3 East, 38; 7 Taunt. 191.

Parallel Articles of the French Code.

sale, they may not be removed;[1] nor otherwise may any roots except annual ones.[2]

521. The cuttings of underwood as they are cut, and trees felled, become personalty;[3] and underwood sold to be cut, or trees to be felled by the purchaser, are personalty.

522. Animals (feræ natura) in a state of natural liberty (naturalis laxitatis) are attached to the soil, and when they are objects of property, would pass with the real estate. But tame animals, or wild ones in confinement or dead, are personal property; and beasts of the plough, and the live stock on a farm, are moveables and personalty, whether belonging to the landlord or tenant.[4]

523. Pipes which serve to conduct water into a house, as between the heir and executor, are part of the estate and realty; as between the landlord and tenant, who erected them, when only slightly attached, and removeable without much damage to the property, are moveable and personalty.[5]

524. Moveable property which the proprietor has thereto placed on a farm or estate, but not fixed in the soil, or attached, though for its service and management, does not thereby become immoveable, but remains personalty; for in general, only such things as can become actually immoveable, by being annexed to the soil or buildings thereon, or being actually part thereof, are capable of becoming real property;[6] and not only beasts of the plough, but also all tame animals, and implements of husbandry, seed unsown, &c., are personal property and moveable. In wild animals, unless good for food or beasts of burthen, a man can have no absolute property; but animals good for food, when in actual custody and confinement, are personalty.[7] When only confined, as conies in a warren, deer in a park, doves in a dove-cote, or the like, they are part of the realty.[8] Fixtures

---

1 4 Taunt. 316. 2 1 Camp. N. P. 227.

3 4 Moore, 547; 6 Moore, 114; 3 Bing. 3.

4 Shep. Touch. 469; Bract. l. 2, c. 1, n. 2, 3; Noy's Max. 230, 239; Vin. Ab. tit. Ex. L.; Davies v. Powell, Willes' Rep. 46. 5 Amos on Fixtures.

6 Lifford's ca. 11 Rep. 506; Rex v. Crosse, 1 Sid. 207; Com. Dig. tit. Biens. B.

7 2 Bl. Com. 403. 8 Shep. Touch. 469; Case of Swans, 7 Rep. 90.

Parallel Articles of the French Code.

annexed to the freehold for the purposes of agriculture, belong to the landlord.[1] It seems a nurseryman cannot take down hot-houses, green-houses, forcing-pits, &c., which he has built during his tenancy, and much less another person.[2] The fixtures annexed for purposes of manufacture, as in a distillery or brewery, have been held as part of the realty in favour of the heir.[3] But the tenant, for the purposes of trade or manufacture, is permitted, during his tenancy,[4] to remove his trade fixtures, vessels, and utensils, such as furnaces, coppers, brewing vessels and fixed vats, salt pans;[5] and machinery, as in breweries, collieries, mills, steam-engines, cider-mills, and the like.[6] Manure is not deemed part of a farm if it be in a heap: it becomes so only when it is scattered on the ground.[7]

The rule being that whatever is in any way, by plaster, 525.
lime, cement, nails, or screws, fixed to the property by the owner, or which cannot be taken away without injuring the freehold, belongs to the heir as realty,[8] as between heir and executor, glasses fixed instead of wainscots, cannot be removed;[9] but, as between landlord and tenant, articles set up at the expense of the tenant for ornament or furniture, are removeable by him, as hangings, tapestry, and pier glasses, nailed to the walls or pannels of a house, and, as it is said, though they are put up in lieu of wainscot.[10] They must, however, be so connected with

---

1 Elwes v. Mawe; 3 East, 38.

2 2 East, 90; 3 ib. 45, 56; 2 Brod. & Bing. 58.

3 1 B. & C. 76. 9 East, 215; 3 Barn. & Cres. 368; 5 Dow. & R. 240; Clark v. Crownshaw, 3 Bar. & Adol. 804.

4 But if not removed during the tenancy they are the landlord's.—Lyde v. Russell, 1 B. & Ad. 394.

5 Poole's ca. 1 Salk. 368; Lawton v. Lawton, 3 Atk. 13; Amb. 119; Lawton v. Salmon, 1 H. Bl. 259; 3 East, 56; Culling v. Tuffnall, Bul. N. P. 34.

6 Ib.; 2 Bar. & Ald. 165; 5 Esp. 11.

7 Yearworth v. Pierce, Aleyn's Rep. 32; Sty. 66.

8 2 Bl. Com. 427.

9 2 Com. Dig. 280, 5th ed.; H. Chitty on Desc., 257.

10 Moseley, 113; Beck v. Rebow. 1 P. W. 94; Stra. 1141; 3 Atk. 12; Dudley v. Ward, Amb. 113; 2 Saund. 259, n. 11; Buckland v. Butterfield, 2 Bro. & B. 25; 2 B. & C. 77.

Parallel Articles of the French Code.

the premises, as to occasion but little or no damage in their removal, or the tenant will not be at liberty to take them away.[1]

526. An estate for life in immoveable property is realty; as also are easements, and other incorporeal rights, arising out of immoveables, if held for sufficient duration; and actions for recovery of real property are called real actions.

CHAPTER II.

Of Personal Property.

527. It has already been said, personal property is either what is moveable in its nature, or not of sufficient permanency and legal estimation to make it realty. Real property may also be regarded and treated by the law as possessing the qualities of personalty, by the determination of law, as in certain cases where the intention of converting it into such has been manifested, though not accomplished.[2]

528. Moveables which are called personal chattels, are bodies which may be transported from place to place, whether animate or inanimate.[3] All interests in realty for a less period than that of life are called chattels real, and constitute personalty.[4]

529. Perpetual and life annuities charge the person of the grantor, and being payable out of personal estate are purely personal;[5] though the regular payment may be secured by charge on real property.[6] But they must not be confounded with rents and rent charges, which issue out of real estate, and constitute realty; or with annuities, which charge the land only, and not the person

[1] See note 10, preceding page.

[2] Audley v. Audley, 2 Vern. 192; Wheldale v. Partridge, 5 Ves. 396; Lord Winchelsea v. Norcliffe, 1 Vern. 434; 1 Eq. Ab. 262, pl. 4; Banks v. Scott, 5 Mad. 495; Atcherley v. Vernon, 10 Mod. 518. As to election, to take it in its actual state, Stead v. Newdigate, 2 Meriv. 531; Lingen v. Sowray, 1 P.W. 172.

[3] 2 Bl. Com. 16, 387.

[4] Ib. 386.

[5] Co. Lit. 144 b; 1 Williams' Executors, 522.

[6] 1 Chit. G. P. 225.

Parallel Articles of the French Code.

of the grantor.[1] Money secured on mortgage of real estate continues personalty; but a distinction is taken between a mortgage and an absolute conveyance with a collateral agreement to reconvey upon repayment of the purchase-money.[2] Rights primarily affecting the person only, or arising out of moveable property, and which are to be discharged by payment of money, are personalty.[3] Bonds for a sum of money, bills of exchange, bank-notes, and rights to sums demandable of commercial, insurance, and other companies or public funds, are called choses in action, and are personal property.[4]

An annuity or perpetual rent charge is not redeemable, without the consent of the owner of it, unless by express stipulation, which is construed strictly, being considered as an agreement for a new purchase, and therein differing from a mortgage.[5] 530.

Ships,[6] boats, and vessels, floating-mills, and floating-baths, and all machinery not fixed to the freehold, are moveable and personal property.[7] There are, however, certain peculiarities respecting ships, and their transfer and ownership, under the register acts, which affect them, and make a difference between them and other moveable property. 531.

Materials temporarily severed from the freehold still remain realty;[8] but when they arise from the demolition of an edifice,[9] and those collected for the construction of 532.

[1] Buckeridge v. Ingram, 2 Ves. J. 652; Drybutter v. Bartholomew, 2 P. W. 127; Howse v. Chapman, 4 Ves. 543.

[2] 2 Powell on Mortgages, 664; 1 ib. 130, 138 n.

[3] 1 ib. 144, v. ii. p. 662; Duffield v. Elwes, 1 Blight, Ap. C. 497.

[4] 2 Bl. Com. 396.

[5] Lawley v. Hooper, 3 Atk. 278; Murray v. Harding, 2 W. Bl. 859; Irnham v. Child, 1 Bro. C. C. 92; 1 Pow. Morg. 139 n, 5th ed.

[6] Stephens v. Sole, 1 Ves. 352; Atkinson v. Maling, 2 T. R. 462.

[7] 2 Bl. Com. 386.

[8] Wistow's ca., cited 11 Co. 50; Farrant v. Thompson, 5 B. & A. 826.

[9] 11 Rep. 84 a; Vin. Ab. v. xxii. pl. 31. But the pulling down houses for the purposes of converting the materials into chattels is waste, and a tenant for life will be restrained.—Vane v. Bernard, Pre. Cha. 454; 2 Vern. 738; Bp. of London v. Webb, 1 P. W. 528.

Parallel Articles of the French Code.

a new one, are moveable and personal property, until they are employed in the building.[1]

When a general term, such as that of "moveables,"
533. "personal property," occurs in a public[2] or private docu-
534. ment, the context or general spirit of the whole document
535. is generally sufficient for raising an adequate presumption as to the extent of signification which such words are intended to have, by the party who used them. But such presumption may often be unfounded; and it is extremely desirable to make known the signification which the law has attached to certain words from decided cases. The term relating to moveable property, of most extensive signification, is personalty. The expressions "personalty," or "personal property," or "chattels," comprehend all that is not realty. They, and especially "chattels," will include a chattel real;[3] and they are therefore of larger signification than goods. "Goods and chattles" are sometimes used together, and these technical terms will include, for some purposes, money, valuable securities, and all other personal effects;[4] also choses in action.[5] The term "goods,"[6] in common parlance, does not signify the whole personal estate.[7] "Goods" will not include fixtures, but the word "effects" would embrace them.[8] Where the terms "goods and chattels" follow the word "furniture," they will be restrained to things, "ejusdem generis;"[9] and so the words "and other effects," or "other things,"[10] following particulars enumerated, will be restricted by those specified.[11] The terms "household fur-

[1] Like manure in a heap, or trees felled, ante, p. 329.

[2] Goods, bona et catella.—Bullock v. Dodds, 2 B. & Cr. 276; Horn v. Baker, 9 East, 215.

[3] Co. Lit. 118; 3 Russ. R. 376.

[4] 3 Bl. Com. 384, 7; 7 Taunt. 188; 4 Moore, 73; 4 B. & Ald. 206.

[5] 12 Coke 1; 1 Atk. 182.

[6] See as to the construction of the term "goods and moveable effects," Sutton v. Sharp, 1 Russ. 146.

[7] Crichton v. Symes, 3 Atk. 63.

[8] Clark v. Crownshaw, 3 B. & Ald. 804; Coombes v. Beaumont, 5 B. & Ad. 72.

[9] Stuart v. Bute, 11 Ves. 666.

[10] Res generalem habet significationem, quia tam corporea quam incorporea, cujuscunque sunt generis, naturæ sive speciei comprehenditur.—3 Inst. 182.

[11] Rawlings v. Jennings, 13 Ves. 39; Hotham v. Sutton, 15 Ves. 326; Stuart v. Bute, 1 Dow. P. C. 87.

Parallel Articles of the French Code.

niture, and household effects," in a dwelling-house, comprise all property therein kept for use, or consumption, or for ornament.[1] The word "furniture"[2] will include china,[3] plate, pictures hung up, and linen, but not books.[4] If the party using the words be a shopkeeper,[5] or in trade, a distinction will be made in the construction of the terms "goods," &c. according to the presumed intention between his stock in trade and other goods.[6] Stock will pass under the term "moneys," or "goods and chattels," unless the context is opposed to such a construction.[7]

By a bequest of a man's house at a certain place, with all that shall be in it at his death, bank-notes and cash were held to pass as well as other things;[8] but not promissory notes, bonds,[9] and securities, which it was said[10] were not things, but only evidences of title[11] to things.[12] 536.

CHAPTER III.

Common, Public, and Private Property.

In considering property with reference to possessing it, a division necessarily arises into such as can be only common to all individuals; such as can only belong to the state; and such as can belong to one or more individuals to the exclusion of all others. All private persons in possession of property, real[13] or personal,[14] are capable of disposing of their estates, or interests therein, unless the 537.

[1] Cole v. Fitzgerald, 1 Sim. & Stu. 189; and 3 Russ. 301.

[2] By a bequest of the use for life of a house, with all the furniture, stock of carriages, live and dead stock, plate passed, but not wine and books.—Porter v. Torney, 3 Ves. 311.

[3] Hele v. Gilbert, 2 Ves. 430.

[4] Kelly, Knt. v. Powlet, Amb. 605.

[5] Hele v. Gilbert, 2 Ves. 430.

[6] Le Farrant v. Spencer, 1 Ves. 97; Pratt v. Jackson, 2 P. W. 302.

[7] Kendal v. Kendal, 4 Russ. 360.

[8] Popham v. Lady Aylesbury, Amb. 68, s. 11, Ves. 657.

[9] Moore v. Moore, 1 Bro. C. C. 127; Sander v. Earle, 2 Ch. Rep. 188.

[10] Sed quære per Lord Eldon, whether the same reason would not affect bank-notes.—11 Ves. 657.

[11] A chose in action, right of entry, title cannot be granted over, Co. Lit. 214 a; yet the parchment, paper, and wax may be assigned, ib. 232 b, n. 1.

[12] Miller v. Race, 1 Bur. 452.

[13] 2 Bl. Com. 290.

[14] Ib.

Parallel Articles of the French Code.

law has laid them under any particular disabilities arising from their personal state or condition. Where property belongs to public bodies, or the crown, it can only be administered or alienated under seal; or in such other form as the peculiar constitution and laws affecting such corporate person permit.[1]

538. The right of way through a highway, road, or street, at the public or parish charge of repair, is vested in the public, though the soil, mines, and trees remain in the private owner.[2] Navigable rivers[3] and streams, the sea shore,[4] creeks, ports,[5] harbours, roads for ships, &c.,[6] belong to the crown.[7]

539. The property of persons who died intestate without any relations escheats to the crown.[8] Moveable property, unclaimed by any owner, belongs to the first occupant or finder, unless they fall within the description of waifs or estrays, or wrecks, or hidden treasure,[9] which belong to
540. the crown,[10] or to the lord of the manor. Gates, moats,
541. ramparts of places of war, and fortresses, belong to the crown.[11]

542. By the word "common" is understood a right which one person has of taking some part of the produce of land while the whole property is vested in another.[12] In almost all manors there are certain lands called commons, over

---

1 Watkins on Conveyancing, b. 3, c. 6.

2 Selw. N. P. 1280; Burn's Highway; Dovaston v. Payne, 2 H. Bl. 527.

3 Lord Raym. 725, 1174; R. v. Hammond, 10 Mod. 382. Publica vero sunt omnia flumina et portus. Ideoque jus piscandi omnibus commune est, in portu et fluminibus. Riparum etiam usus publicus est de jure gentium sicut ipsius fluminis.—Br. l. 1, c. 12, n. 6; Brit. 83.

4 2 Bl. Com. 262.

5 Flumina et portus publica sunt. As to restrictions, see Da. Rep. 55.

6 Naturali vero jure communia sunt omnia hæc, aqua perfluens, aër et mare et littora maris quasi maris accessoria. Nemo enim ad littora maris accedere prohibetur, dum tamen à villis et ædificiis abstineat.—Br. l. 1, c. 12, n. 5.

7 Schultes on Aquatic Rights; Rex v. Smith, 2 Dougl. 411; 4 Burr. 2163.

8 2 Bl. Com. 246.

9 Thesaurus competit Domino Regi, et non domino libertatis nisi sit per verba specialia.—Fitz. Coro. 281, 436.

Thesaurus non competit Regi, nisi quando nemo scit qui abscondit thesaurum. —3 Inst. 132.

10 2 Bl. Com. 403.

11 Ib. 263; Com. Dig. Prerog. C. 4; 4 T. R. 796.

12 Burt. Comp. 375,

Parallel Articles of the French Code.

which the tenants have a right to depasture their cattle, subservient to tillage and manurance.[1] This somewhat differs from corporate property, which is that to the ownership of which one or more corporations, sole or aggregate, or townships or parishes, have acquired right.[2] Corporations cannot acquire a right to real property, in contravention of the laws of mortmain.[3]

A person may have over an object of property either a right of ownership or a simple right of possession and enjoyment,[4] or only claims for incorporeal rights or easements therein.[5] 543.

TITLE II.

OF THE RIGHT OF PROPERTY AND ESTATES IN FEE.

Having considered property with regard to its objects, their nature and kinds, there remains now to consider the right of property, its various degrees and qualifications. Property (or dominium) is the right of using and abusing any object of property.[6] The law of England recognizes three kinds of such right: 1, Absolute property (dominium directum); 2, Qualified property (dominium utile); and 3, A property in trust for another (dominium fiduciarium). The law of England respecting property having been formed almost entirely out of feudal principles,[7] does not, theoretically speaking, recognize the absolute right of property in the land, or other object of a fief, to exist in any subject. And though in moveable 544.

[1] See Co. Lit. 122 a, b; 2 Bl. Com. [2] 1 Bl. Com. c. 18.

[3] Watk. Conv. b. 3, c. 6. [4] 2 Bl. Com. c. 13. [5] Ib. c. 2.

[6] Property is the highest right or title a man has or can have to anything, and in no ways depending upon another man's courtesy.—Bailey's Dic.

Property, or the right of property, consists in the free use, enjoyment, and disposition of all a man's acquisitions, without any control or diminution, save only by the laws of the land.—1 Bl. Com. 138.

Sometimes the word "property" means the things themselves, and in this sense it has received various constructions.—Hardw. 53; 9 East, 48.

[7] Ante, pp. 35, 57, 64, et seq.

Parallel Articles of the French Code.

things a subject may have an absolute property, yet, theoretically, the king only can have real estates in absolute property.[1] It is a received and fundamental principle in law, that all the lands in England are holden mediately or immediately of the king: the king, therefore, only hath absolutum et directum dominium. All subjects' lands are in the nature of a feodum or fee, whether derived to them by descent from their ancestors, or purchased for a valuable consideration.[2]

The king is styled the lord paramount.[3] All lands being held of him, such persons as held immediately of him were formerly called tenants in capite,[4] and they are now said to be the freeholders. In copyholds and customary freeholds, the lord of the manor is the tenant (in capite) to the king, and the copyholders hold of the lord of the manor, who is the mesne or intermediate lord.[5] The mesne lord is both tenant to the king and lord, and the lowest tenant is called tenant paravail.[6]

As to that which in legal theory is considered as qualified property, the highest right the subject can have is a fee.[7] The term fee (feudum) is used in contradistinction to what in feudal language is called allodium, which is defined to be a man's own land, which he possesses merely in his own right, without any rent or service to any superior.[8] This allodial property no subject in England can have.[9]

But although, in a theoretical sense, the king is the only proprietor, and the tenant in fee is an usufructuary, yet in a practical view the tenant in fee is the proprietor; and he could not have a more absolute dominion if the doctrine of tenure were abolished.[10] The right of the English subject in his landed property is fully as ample as that of the subjects of any state; and the chief distinc-

---

[1] Ante, p. 36, n. 1, and p. 202. [2] 2 Bl. Com. 105, 6.
[3] Ib. 59. [4] Ib. 60. [5] Ib. 59, 90, 148. [6] Ib. 59, 60.
[7] See the various definitions of a fee or feudum, ante, p. 67, and n. 2.
[8] 2 Bl. Com. 105. [9] Ib. [10] Co. Lit. 10.

Parallel Articles of the French Code.

tion between the English and most foreign systems of jurisprudence is, that the English possesses a more perfect nomenclature, in which almost every distinction of right is designated by a technical name.

Some few of the distinctions respecting real estates owe their origin entirely to the feudal law, and almost all the others are more or less tinctured with it, though they arise out of the nature of things, and exist necessarily in the laws of all civilized countries Thus the law distinguishes between estates or interests of freehold, customary freehold, copyhold, and leasehold; fees simple, fees base, qualified or conditional, and fees tail, special or general, male or female; estates in frankmarriage, estates for life, of various kinds, as, estate for life after possibility of issue extinct to an estate tail, by courtesy, in dower, by lease, gift, or devise; chattels real and personal; estates in severalty, joint tenancy, coparcenary, tenancy in common, reversions, vested remainders, contingent remainders; uses, trusts, and executory devises. A whole treatise would not suffice to explain fully these various interests, and the others recognized and distinguished with a technical name by the law of England, as to their natures, peculiarities, and relations with each other, and as affected by the varying condition (status) of their owners or possessors. We must, however, attempt to give sufficient explanations of some of them, to render intelligible what is to be stated as parallel to the articles of the French code.

An estate (status), technically[1] speaking, is any interest, if sufficiently perfect, in an object of property, whether in possession or to be in possession after a given event or period. This interest may be held immediately or mediately of the crown, and may be a freehold, copyhold, or customary freehold estate. Freehold[2] arises from free

[1] This word is often used, by lawyers as well as laymen, to signify the land or object of property, as well as the right to it.

[2] The term "freehold" is often used in contradistinction to inheritance, in which case it signifies an estate for life.—Co. Lit. 266 b, n. 1.

Parallel Articles of the French Code.

tenure:[1] and the feudal possession or seisin[2] is vested in the freeholder. The only kinds of estate existing, in which the actual tenants do not hold immediately from the crown, are copyhold and customary freehold. Copyhold is an estate held of the lord of the manor, at the will of the lord, according to the custom of the manor:[3] the freehold, or feudal seisin, is theoretically vested in the lord; but practically, whatever may have been the original nature of this tenure, the right of the tenant is as certain as the right of the lord, whose will, as it is called, is only such as is agreeable to and regulated by the custom of the manor.[4] The tenant holds of the lord by suit of court, &c. Their estates are distinct, and the copyhold tenant derives his estate from custom, and not out of the estate of the lord. Customary freeholds are held of the lord of the manor; but they are not said to be held at the will of the lord, but only according to the custom of the manor.[5]

Each of these kinds of tenure, according to the time for which they are held, may be held in fee or for life. An estate in fee,[6] or a fee, signifies an estate of inheritance; being the highest and most extensive interest a subject can have in a feud: and fees are either fees simple, conditional, qualified, or tail. When the term "fee" is used simply, without any adjunct, or has the adjunct of simple annexed to it (a fee or a fee-simple), it is used in contradistinction to a fee-conditional at the common law, or a fee-tail by the statute, importing an absolute inheritance,

---

[1] 2 Bl. Com. 104.

[2] Freehold in deed is called naturalis possessio seu seisina, and freehold in law is called civilis possessio seu seisina.—Co. Lit. 266 b.

[3] Ante, p. 73.

[4] Co. Lit. 60; 2 Bl. Com. 95, 147.

[5] Copyholds must be immemorial. Copyhold descents are guided by the rules of the common law; but customary inheritances have not the collateral qualities of freehold. Nor doth a descent bar an entry, copyh. 15, s. 50. Copyholder is in by him who surrendered, and not by the lord.

[6] The estates of all subjects being held as fiefs or fees, the term "fee," like that of freehold, has come to signify the duration of the estate rather than the nature of the interest; that is, in fee, in feudum, as contradistinguished from absolutely in allodium.—Ante, pp. 335, 6.

Parallel Articles of the French Code.

clear of any condition or limitation to a particular heir (which distinguishes a fee-tail), but descendible to the heirs generally, whether male or female, lineal or collateral,[1] and alienable at the uncontrolled option of the owner or tenant of the fee-simple.[2] Tenant in fee-tail is clogged with certain conditions and impediments on alienation from the heirs, to whom the fee is specially limited.[3]

Estates for life are created either by the acts of the parties or by the operation of law. They correspond most nearly with the usufructuary interests of the French and civil laws, and therefore they belong to the next title of this book.

Property may be held by one person only, in severalty; or by several persons, whose interests may be joint, or both joint and several. When they take by purchase, they may be joint tenants, or tenants in common; when they take by descent, they are coparceners.

The interest may be an estate in possession, entitling the party to the immediate enjoyment of the legal seisin (possessio civilis), or actual occupation (possessio naturalis), of the object of property;[4] or the right to possession may be future, and either vested now, or to become vested only after a certain event or contingency: such are reversions, remainders, contingent remainders, springing or shifting uses, and executory devises. Or the party may have no estate, vested or contingent, but only a possibility or expectancy of an estate, or a power of disposing of an estate, either coupled with an interest or without. And lastly, these several kinds of interests or estates are either legal or equitable, that is, such as are recognized both at law and in equity, or such as are recognized only in equity: thus, for example, one may have the legal estate or feudal seisin, holding the property for the use or in

[1] 2 Bl. Com. 106. [2] 1 G. Ch. P. 242. [3] 2 Bl. Com. 110.

[4] Aliud est possidere, aliud esse in possessione: is the maxim of the English as well as civil law.

Parallel Articles of the French Civil.

trust for another, who has the equitablee state or beneficial interest.[1]

In having the most absolute interest which the law allows in land (an estate in fee-simple), the tenant has the exercise of the most perfect rights of property. His power of alienation, or disposing of it to any other person within the rules against perpetuities, is not only unrestrained, but, provided he do no injury to his neighbours, his power to use or abuse it is equally extensive, permitting him to destroy, burn, or desolate it in any way he may choose.[2]

545. But whatever may be the amount of his interest in real or personal estate, no man can be legally compelled to give up his property, except for a just compensation;[3] or except, in certain cases, by authority of parliament, or for public necessity.[4]

546. As a general rule, property in things personal confers a right over all which it produces, and over all naturally connected with it by accession;[5] and so it does in things real, to the extent of the tenant's interest therein, except in the case of a large dereliction of land by the sea or a navigable river.[6] It also gives all the artificial increase of personal property, except where the nature of the thing has been so changed by the new operation, that the former owner cannot identify it; and then he has, in general, a right to compensation.[7] The annual productions of the object of real property are called rents and profits, and of personal property, interest and annual proceeds: only that which is added to the substance of the thing is claimed by the right of accession.

---

1 Ante, p. 121.
2 Chitty, Gen. Prac. v. i. pp. 230, 258.
3 Magna Charta, c. 20; 1 Bl. Com. 138, 9; 8 Rep. 92.
4 4 T. R. 794, 6, 7; 3 Wils. 461; 6 Taunt. 29.
5 2 Bl. Com. 404.
6 Ib. 260; Schultes on Aquatic Rights, 115.
7 2 Bl. Com. 404; 2 Campb. 576; Poph. 38.

Parallel Articles of the French Code.

CHAPTER I.

Of Rights to the Produce of Property.

The natural and artificial produce of the earth,[1] the civil produce, the rents and profits of land, dividends, and interest of money or stock,[2] belong to the party entitled to the estate or property in possession; and as to real estate, the tenant of the freehold is, in general, entitled to the whole produce, and others only acquire any right thereto by agreement. The increase or growth of animals belongs to the proprietor;[3] of tame animals, the brood belongs to the owner of the dam, with the exception of swans.[4] 547.

As a general rule, if a person employs his work and labour upon materials which belong to another, without express or implied contract, he is not entitled to any compensation.[5] And if a man build on, or plough and sow another man's ground, it is considered as a gift, and he is entitled to no compensation.[6] 548.

In case of a disseisin, or where anything is wrongfully taken and held by another, the mesne profits and the fruits produced by it belong to the proprietor,[7] without his being liable to reimburse the expenses of the labour or outlay incurred by such person.[8]

1 2 Bl. Com. 404.

2 Ib. 40, 453 to 468; 3 & 4 Wm. IV. c. 42, s. 28.

3 2 Bl. Com. 404.

4 Ib. 390; 7 Rep. 17.

5 Hayes v. Warren, 2 Barn. 55.

6 Br. l. 2, c. 2, n. 4, 5.

7 The mesne profits may be recovered in an action of ejectment or an action of trespass.—Selw. N. P. Eject. s. 15; 2 Bl. Com. 205; Statute of Gloucester, 6 Ed. I. c. 1.

8 In an action for mesne profits, it seems the owner would only be entitled to recover the value at which the estate might have been leased, and not the crops growing from manurance.—Vin. vol. xv. p. 397, H. pl. 2. And in taking an account of the rents and profits, if the plaintiff will not accept the account, according to the value of the estate when the purchaser (bonâ fide possessor) entered, but insists to have the account taken according to the present value, the court will compel him to make an allowance for repairs and improvements.—Thomlinson v. Smith, Finch 378.

Parallel Articles of the French Code.

A party in possession of property, without title to it, is bound to render the produce or pay for the use and occupation, according to the value, to the real proprietor,
549. whether he supposed himself entitled[1] as owner or not:[2] the right to recover for such use and occupation, or the mesne profits, would be limited to six years.

550. A person may be in possession, under a defective title, of the viciousness of which he was ignorant; but the rule of law is caveat emptor, and his possession does not convey a right to the property or its produce: but if the rightful owner knew the party so bonâ fide in possession was making improvements, and did not set him right, he would not be permitted to have the benefit of those improvements without reimbursing the other.[3]

And where the title is fradulent, equity in giving relief will reimburse the party in possession for permanent improvements.[4]

CHAPTER II.

Of Right of Accession over that which is united to and incorporated with the substance of Property.

551. Whatever is united and incorporated with a thing belongs to the proprietor, according to the following rules:

[1] Bonæ fidei possessor, in id tantum quod ad pervenerit, tenetur.—2 Inst. 285.

[2] 3 Bl. Com. 205; Dr. & Stu. Dial. 2, c. 47.

[3] See cases, East India Company v. Vincent, 2 Atk. 83; Stiles v. Cowper, 3 Atk. 692; Jackson v. Cator, 5 Ves. 689; Pilling v. Armitage, 12 Ves. 85; Rex v. Inhabitants of Butterton, 6 T. R. 554.

[4] Shine v. Gough, 1 Ball & B. 444; and see where lasting improvements allowed, Savage v. Taylor, For. 234; where quieted in possession for a term, Hanning v. Ferrers, 1 Eq. Ab. 356.

Parallel Articles of the French Code.

SECTION 1.

Of the Right to Improvements of and Accession to Immoveable Property.

Cujus est solum ejus est usque ad cœlum, is the maxim of the law upwards; and downwards, whatever is in a direct line between the surface of any land and the centre of the earth belongs to the owner of the surface.[1] Provided he does not injure his neighbours, the proprietor may make above, all kinds of erections and buildings he may judge convenient;[2] he may make beneath, all buildings and excavations he may judge convenient; and draw from such excavations all the products which they are capable of furnishing.[3] 552.

All buildings, plantations, and works[4] fixed upon the soil or beneath the surface belong to the proprietor, whether made at his expense or not, unless it be shown that some other person has acquired, by agreement with the present or previous owner, by prescription or otherwise, a right of property, whether to a part above or below the surface.[5] 553.

When plantations, buildings, and works have been made by another party, and with his own materials, and fixed to the soil, unless for the purposes of trade, the proprietor of the soil has a right to retain them without making any compensation; or he may proceed to remove them, and sue the party for the damage and expense occasioned thereby.[6] 555.

The proprietor of the soil having made buildings, plantations, and works with materials which did not belong to him, must pay the value thereof; and he may also be compelled to pay the damages or compensation 554.

---

[1] 2 Bl. Com. 18; 1 Co. Lit. 4 a.
[2] 2 Bl. Com. 18.
[3] Lyddall v. Weston, 2 Atk. 19; 2 Bl. Com. 18.
[4] Co. Lit. 53 a, b; Herlakenden's case, 4 Rep. 64; and ante, par. art. 519.
[5] 2 Bl. Com.
[6] See ante, par.. art. 519.

Parallel Articles of the French Code.

to the owner of them. He may be compelled to return such as are not altered in their nature by an action of trover. The owner of such materials is not allowed to remove them after they have become part of the freehold,[1] and would be liable to an action of trespass for entering on the land to do so.

556. The accumulation and increase of mud, formed successively and imperceptibly on the soil bordering on a river or other stream, or the sea, is denominated "alluvion:" the sudden shrinking of the water is called "dereliction." Alluvion, or imperceptible increase, is for the benefit of the proprietor of the soil of the river, or of the owner of the adjoining land, whether in the case of the sea or of a navigable or unnavigable river.[2]

557. If a river running between two lordships by degrees gains upon one, and thereby leaves the other dry, the owner of the dry bank gains what is so left dry; and the owner, who loses his ground thus imperceptibly, has no remedy.[3] The derelictions of the sea belong to the crown.[4]

558. Alluvion does not take place with respect to lakes and ponds, the proprietor of which preserves always the land which was covered with water, though the volume of water should be diminished.[5] In like manner, the proprietor of a pond acquires no right over land bordering on his pond, which may happen to be covered by an extraordinary flood.

559. If the river suddenly had gained on the one's land and left the other's dry, he should have the land so derelict.[6]

560. All islands, relicted lands, and other increase arising in the sea and in navigable streams, except under certain local circumstances, or by imperceptible degrees, belong to the crown.[7]

---

1 Vin. Ab. Property E. pl. 6, n.

2 2 Bl. Com. 261; Callis on Sewers, 51; Schultes on Aquatic Rights, 115; Rex v. Lord Yarborough, 3 Barn. & Cres. 91.

3 2 Bl. Com. 262.

4 Ib.

5 Co. Lit. 4.

6 Callis, 51; Schultes, 136.

7 Schultes, 115.

Parallel Articles of the French Code.

Islands, relicted lands, and the soil of inland unnavigable rivers, belong to the proprietor of the estates to which such river acts as boundary.[1]

If a river or other stream, in forming itself a new arm, divide and surround land belonging to a person, and thereby form an island, he shall retain the ownership of his land, although the island be formed in a navigable river.[2] 561. 562.

If a navigable river form a new course, abandoning its ancient bed, the land so derelict belongs to the crown.[3] 563.

Deer in a park, hares and rabbits in an enclosed warren, doves in a dovehouse, and fish, are no longer the property of a man than while they are in his actual possession; and if at any time they regain their natural liberty, his property instantly ceases, unless they are animus revertendi, or in the habit of returning.[4] 564.

Section 2.

Of the Right of Accession over Moveable Property.

The doctrines of the Roman law on the subject of accession have been adopted by Bracton, and have since been confirmed by many resolutions of the courts.[5] 565.

When two objects belonging to different masters, and which have been united by consent, or without fault on either side, the proprietors have an interest in common in proportion to their respective shares.[6] As to things which cannot be distinguished and separated: if one wil- 566.

---

[1] Schultes on Aquatic Rights, 138. [2] Ib. 115.

[3] Ib. [4] 2 Bl. Com. 391.

[5] Ib. 404; Bro. Ab. Propertie, 23; Moor, 20; Poph. 38; 2 Camp. 576; Com. Dig. Pleader, 3 M. 28; Bac. Ab.; Tres. E. 2.

[6] 2 Bl. Com. 405; 1 Vern. 217. Bracton, following the civil law, says, "where two things become confused or united together, the smaller of the two shall belong to the owner of the larger or more valuable," Br. l. 2, c. 2, n. 3; but there appears to be no decision confirming this view. In the case of Ward v. Ayre, no reference was made to the quantities or values.

fully intermixes[1] his property with that of another man without his approbation or knowledge, our law gives the entire property, without any account, to him whose original dominions were invaded.[2] But when the things be such as are clearly separable, if one person mixes his goods, though for fraudulent purposes, with those of another, he retains his right to them.[3]

570. If any person has employed materials which do not
571. belong to him, whatever alteration of form the property has undergone, the owner may seize it in its new shape, if he can prove the identity of the original materials.[4] Thus, if one person embroiders cloth belonging to another, and converts the metal of the latter into vessels or utensils, the property still remain in the first.[5] But if the nature of the thing be changed, so that it can no longer be identified, he cannot take it, as if olives or grapes be converted into oil or wine; but he shall be entitled to compensation for his materials.[6]

If the workmanship were done by the desire of the owner of the materials, he of course must pay for the labour of the artisan;[7] but he cannot be compelled to part with his property.

572. When the material belongs to them both jointly, it remains in common; and the proportionate share of the workman would probably increase with the increase of its value.

575. A tenant in common may sell his share of the property, or he may compel a division of it.

577. Persons who shall have employed materials belonging to others, and without their knowledge, may be compelled to pay any damage they may have occasioned.

---

1 Nemo debet immiscere se rei alienæ, ad se nihil pertinenti.—Jenk. Cent. 18.

2 Ward v. Eyre, Cro. Jac. 366; 2 Buls. 823; 2 Bl. Com. 404.

3 Colwell v. Reeves, 2 Camp. 575.

4 Year Book, 5 Hen. VIII. f. 15; 12 ib. f. 19.

5 2 Camp. 577 n; Bro. Tres. pl. 23; sed vide Bract, l. 2, c. 2, n. 5.

6 2 Camp. 577 n. Mutata forma prope interimitur substantia rei.—Law Max.

7 See Action for Work and Labour.

Parallel Articles of the French Code.

TITLE III.

OF ESTATES FOR LIFE, AND OF USES AND TRUSTS.

(Usufruct, Use, and Habitation.)

CHAPTER I.

Estates for Life or Years.

Although the terms usufruct, use, and habitation, have been employed by the ancient English law writers, they are, in the sense in which they are used in the Roman and French codes, scarcely known to the English law. Usufruct is defined by the civil law to be the right of using and enjoying the things of another, preserving the substance of the things.[1] This kind of right undoubtedly might be created among us by express agreement or testament: it however belongs so entirely to a system of law totally dissimilar to that of England, that it would be a waste of time to occupy ourselves with the consideration of its exact nature. A right of this kind is so much in the nature of things, that we may be sure that something similar exists in the English system; and we find that in the English law, the fee or inheritance (nearly corresponding with the jus proprietatis) may remain in one person, while portions (as it were) are carved out of it for the benefit of others (as closely corresponding with the ususfructus). One person may be entitled to enjoy the property for life, and the fee or inheritance be in another person (who then has the nuda proprietas of the civil law). The person thus entitled to the immediate enjoyment is called the tenant for life;[2] or a person may be entitled to the possession and enjoyment of the property 578.

[1] Ususfructus est jus alienis rebus utendi, fruendi, salva rerum substantia.—Inst. lib. 2, tit. 4.

[2] 2 Bl. Com. c. 9.

Parallel Articles of the French Code.

for a number of years, the inheritance or fee remaining unchanged by his right of occupation; such a person is called the tenant for years, or termor.[1] Neither of these estates, though somewhat similar, entirely correspond with the usufruct. Estates for years are usually created
383. by lease or agreement, upon conditions which differ materially from the rights of a usufructuary. In the Scotch law, which has adopted the Roman along with the feudal system, what is called a life-rent constitutes a usufruct;[2] and in England, estates for life (especially when not created by lease, but by operation of law, or by testament) most fully correspond with the usufruct of the French and civil laws. They are almost of the same nature, except the English estate for life is a feudal estate, and constitutes a fief, or freehold interest.[3]

579. A tenancy for life may be created by the law, as in the case of dower (the right of the widow to enjoy a third of the property of the deceased husband for her life); and by the courtesy of England, the husband is entitled to the enjoyment of the real estates of his deceased wife for his life; or it may arise by agreement, or the last will, or the gift of any man under a lease for life, or a devise; or by accident, as the tenant in tail after the possibility of issue is extinct.[4] A tenancy for years is by agreement or will.

580. An estate for life may be established either simply or on condition;[5] and so may a tenancy for a term of years.

581. An estate for life, or years, may be established over every species of property, moveable or immoveable, real or personal, corporeal or incorporeal.[6]

---

[1] 2 Bl. Com. c. 10. [2] Bell, Dic. Erskine, b. 2, n. 19, s. 39 and 40.

[3] Wood's Inst. See Co. Lit. 191; a note by Mr. Butler. An usufruct is an estate for life, or other temporary easement.—Ev. Pot. n. p. 217.

[4] 2 Bl. Com. c. 9, A. [5] Ib. c. 9.

[6] Ib. But see as to personalty, post, par art. 587.

Parallel Articles of the French Code.

Section 1.

Of the Rights of the Tenant for Life.

A tenant for life has a right to the enjoyment of every species of annual profit and benefit, whether natural, or artificial, or civil, which the object of possession is capable of producing during his estate, without waste or injury to the inheritance, and sometimes without regard to injury to the inheritance, except malicious waste.[1] 582.

Natural fruits[2] are those which the earth produces spontaneously. 583. The production and increase of animals are also natural benefits. 584. The artificial fruits of the soil are those obtained by cultivation; and the rent of real property, interest of money, dividends, &c., may be called civil fruits.

Natural fruits, attached to the branches and roots at the commencement of the tenancy for life, belong to him; 585. but most artificial fruits constitute emblements, and go to the predecessor, or his executor where the tenancy of such predecessor terminated suddenly.[3] The natural fruits, which are in a similar state at the period when the tenancy for life closes, go to the succeeding tenant or owner of the fee; but if the tenancy closed suddenly, the emblements or artificial fruits go to the predecessor or his executor, unless the sudden determination were caused by his own wrong act.[4]

Rents, rent charges, annuities, are reputed to accrue periodically, according to the mode and terms of their reservation; 586. but various acts of parliament have been passed to direct an apportionment of rents, annuities,

---

[1] 2 Bl. Com. c. 8, p. 121, 281.

[2] Sol sine homine herbam generat.—Off. of Exec. 57.

[3] 2 Bl. Com. 122.

[4] Ib. 122, 403.

Parallel Articles of the French Code.

and other periodical payments,[1] up to the determination of the estate of the tenant.

587. Personal property may be limited for life or in tail, by means of trustees or by executory devise.[2] If any part of the property be of a wasting nature, it must be immediately sold, and converted into permanent property.[3] But things which perish in the using cannot be directly limited to one and after to another, but the whole interests in them vests in the first taker.[4]

588. The life-owner or holder of an annuity is entitled, during the period for which the annuity is held by him, to all arrearages of payments due during such period, but not to the arrears of payments accrued due prior to such period.[5]

589. Where the use of books, furniture, and goods is given to one for life, he is allowed the reasonable wear and tear of them: formerly he was compelled to give security that the goods should be forthcoming at his death, but now he is only required to sign an inventory, expressing that he is entitled to them for life, and that afterwards they belong to the person in remainder.[6]

590. The tenant may cut down underwood, if of sufficient growth, at any seasonable times, and in any quantities he pleases, provided he does not suffer the young germins to be destroyed or stubbed up.[7] Young fruit trees and shrubs in a garden or nursery of a person who uses them for the purposes of sale or trade, may be removed;[8] but no other person.

591. The tenant for life is entitled to what are called esto-

---

1 2 Bl. Com. 124; 10 Rep. 127; 11 Geo. II. c. 19; 4 Wm. IV. c. 22.

2 2 Roper on Legacies, 393; 2 Bl. Com. 398, n. 13.

3 Alcock v. Sloper, 2 Myl. & H. 699.

4 Co. Lit. 20 a, n. 5; Cooper v. Williams, Pre. Ch. 71; Randall v. Russell, 3 Merev. 190; Porter v. Tournay, 3 Ves. 311.

5 2 Bl. Com. 124; 4 Wm. IV. c. 22.

6 Bracken v. Bentley, 1 Ch. Rep. 110; Foley v. Burnel, 1 Bro. C. C. 279; Stanning v. Style, 3 P. W. 336; Hale v. Burrodale, 1 Eq. Ab 361, pl. 8.

7 Co. Lit. 53 a; 2 B. C. 282; 10 East, 319; 1 Barn. & Cres. 373; Strach. v. Francis, 2 Atk. 217; Brydges v. Stephens, Mad. & Geld. 279.

8 2 East, R. 88.

Parallel Articles of the French Code.

vers or botes,[1] viz. firebote, housebote, ploughbote, hedgebote, and other botes or allowances of wood and timber from off the estate, sufficient for the repair of the premises and to burn[2] in the house;[3] and to the loppings and trimmings of trees, provided he does not injure the timber; but he may not destroy or cut down ornamental timber.[4]

The tenant for life cannot cut down timber trees except for housebote, &c., unless he be tenant without waste, and dispunishable for waste;[5] and even then he cannot cut down ornamental timber.[6] 592.

In some places he may cut saplings and timber trees for other agricultural uses, besides ploughbote, &c., according to the custom of the country. 593.

Fruit trees growing in a garden or orchard, (but not young nursery plants), and trees blown down or torn down by accident, belong to the owner of the inheritance,[7] unless the tenant for life be without impeachment of waste. 594.

The tenant may occupy and enjoy, in his own person, or he may let on lease to another for his whole period of interest, or sell or otherwise dispose of his estate.[8] 595.

The tenant is entitled to the enjoyment of the augmentation accruing by alluvion to the object of his estate, where the tenant in fee would be. 596.

The tenant is entitled to enjoy all the appurtenances, rights of way, and generally to all the rights, necessary for the enjoyment of his interest, which the tenant in fee is capable of enjoying.[9] 597.

---

1 But he must not cut live trees for this purpose if there be sufficient dead wood.—Co. Lit. 53.

2 Ib. 41 b; 2 Bl. Com. 35.

3 Estoveria sunt ardendi, arandi, construendi, et claudendi: firebote, housebote, ploughbote, and hedgebote.—13 Rep. 68.

4 Co. Lit. 53 a; Lushington v. Boldero, Mad. & Geld. 149.

5 Co. Lit. 53 a.

6 O'Brien v. OBrien, Amb. 107; Chamberlain v. Dummer, 3 Bro. C. C. 549.

7 Co. Lit. 53 a; Mildmay v. Mildmay, 4 Bro. C. C. 76; Bewick v. Whitfield, 3 P. W. 266; Garth v. Cotton, 3 Atk. 755.

8 2 Bl. Com. c. 19, and p. 274.

9 Ib. 8.

Parallel Articles of the French Code.

The tenant may continue digging and working mines and quarries open at the commencement of his tenancy; but to open the land to search for new mines or pits is a
598. detriment to the inheritance and waste,[1] though he may open new pits to work the old veins.[2]

599. The tenant in fee cannot by his own acts, nor in any other way, be allowed to interfere with or injure the rights of the tenant for life,[3] provided he commit no forfeiture or injury to the inheritance. The tenant for life, or his executors, cannot, at the conclusion of his estate, claim any compensation for improvements he may have made, although the value of the thing[4] may have thereby increased,[5] unless they are trade fixtures. The tenant for life, or his executors, may not carry away mirrors, pictures, or other ornaments fixed to the freehold;[6] but he may such as are not let into the freehold.[7]

Section 2.

Of the Obligations of the Tenant for Life.

600. The tenant for life takes things in the state in which they are, and he can enter with livery of seisin, or more often without, immediately into possession and enjoyment of the real estate, without interference from any one.[8] But in personal property an inventory should be made.[9]

601. He is not bound to give any security (unless by express condition) even in the case of moveable articles.[10] But he is liable to the next tenant in remainder, or the reversioner if he commit waste.[11]

---

1 2 Bl. Com. 282.

2 Clavering v. Clavering, 2 P. W. 388. 3 2 Bl. Com. c. 8, 11.

4 See ante, par. art. 519. and Lawton v. Lawton, 3 Atk. 13; Dudley v. Ward. Amb. 113. 5 1 Sch. & Lef. 50.

6 2 Com. Dig. 280, 5th ed.; Co. Lit. 53 a; H. Chitty on Descents, 257. But see Harvey v. Harvey, Stra. 1141; Squier v. Mayer, 2 Freem. 249.

7 Beck v. Rebow, 1 P.W. 94. 8 Co. Lit. 49, 50, 1. 9 Par. art. 589.

10 Leeke v. Bennett, 1 Atk. 470. 11 Co. Lit. 53.

Parallel Articles of the French Code.

Specific legacies are to be given to the tenant for life without any security.[1] Sums of money given to one for life, with remainder over, are to be invested in the three per cent. Consols by the executors or administrators; and all commodities not specifically bequeathed, should be sold and invested in like manner:[2] the interest on such sums to be paid to the person entitled for life.[3] 602.

A tenant for life, it is said, is bound to repair;[4] but he will not be decreed to repair permissive waste or decay.[5] An account was decreed for equitable waste against the representatives of a deceased tenant for life.[6] 605.

Neither the tenant in fee or the tenant for life are bound to repair what is destroyed by mere accident;[7] but the tenant for life, it is apprehended, would be liable so to repair as to prevent any buildings from falling through age.[8] 607.

The tenant for life is bound, while his estate continues, to discharge all the annual charges on the property, whether interest on incumbrances, or parliamentary, parochial, and other taxes and rates.[9] 608.

A tenant for life is not subject to the payment of any principal sums charged upon the inheritance.[10] Where a tenant for life pays off an incumbrance charged on the inheritance, he becomes a creditor on the estate for the sum so paid.[11] Where he pays off a mortgage, he formerly paid one-third, the remainder man the other two-thirds.[12] 609.

---

[1] Sec 601.

[2] Toller, 427.

[3] Fearns v. Young, 9 Ves. 549.

[4] Co. Lit. 53.

[5] Wood v. Gaynon, Amb. 395.

[6] Lansdowne v. Lansdowne, 1 Madd. 116; Garth v. Cotton, 1 Dick. 183; Winchester, Bp. v. Knight, 1 P. W. 407; Williams v. Bolton, 2 P. W. 286; Co. Lit. 57, n. 1.

[7] And as to accidents, actus Dei nemini facit injuriam.—5 Co. 87; 2 Bl.Com. p. 282.

[8] Art. 605.

[9] Tracy v. Hereford, 2 Bro. R. 128; Penryn v. Hughes, 5 Ves. 99.

[10] White v. White, 4 Ves. 33, and 9 Ves. 554; Allen v. Backhouse, 6 & 7 Wm. IV. c. 115, s. 46, 47.

[11] Jones v. Morgan, 1 Bro. C. C. 206; Shrewsbury v. Shrewsbury, 1 Ves. J. 234.

[12] Ballett v. Sprainger, Pre. Ch. 62.

Parallel Articles of the French Code.

Whether an annuity given by will is chargeable upon the real or personal estate of the testator, depends on his intention as apparent in the words and form of the will.[1]

610. And whether the tenant for life or the tenant in fee is liable for a pecuniary legacy, or an annuity, depends upon the apparent intention of the testator.[2] In general, unless expressly otherwise directed by the testator, the general devise of real estates for life, already charged with an annual rent charge, would render the estate for life liable to the rent charge;[3] and it would not be redeemable without the consent of the party entitled to it.[4]

611. 612. A specific devise of land takes place of pecuniary legacies, and would not be liable for debts, whether on mortgage or not, until after the personal assets were exhausted;[5] and in default of assets, the tenant for life and in fee would have to contribute, the tenant for life being chargeable only with the interest of the money raised to pay the debt.[6]

613. In all real actions, a tenant for life may pray in aid, or call for the assistance of the person entitled to the inheritance, to defend his title.[7]

614. The usurpation, or adverse possession of an estate by a stranger, has no effect against the rights of the tenant in remainder, during the continuance of the tenancy for life.[8]

615. It should seem[9] if the life estate be in an animal, as by specific legacy, which perishes, without the fault of the person entitled for life, he would not be bound to find another, or to pay its value.

616. If the tenant of a dovehouse, warren, park, vivary, estangues, or the like (as a flock of sheep), take so many

---

[1] Elliott v. Hancock, 2 Vern. 143; Clowdsley v. Pelham, 1 Vern. 411.

[2] Sadd v. Carter, Pre. Ch. 27.

[3] Every land of fee-simple may be charged with a rent charge in fee-simple.—Lit. s 648.

[4] See ante, par. art. 530.

[5] Kightley v. Kightley, 2 Ves. J. 328; 3 Ves. 55.

[6] Ante, par. art. 609; post, art. 871.

[7] Booth's Real Act, 60.

[8] 3 & 4 Wm. IV. c. 27, s. 2; 2 Bl. Com. c. 9, and vol. iii. c. 10.

[9] See Bac. Ab. tit. Leases (A.)

that such sufficient store is not left as he found when he came in, he is liable for the waste;[1] but not if they are all killed by inevitable accident.[2]

Parallel Articles of the French Code.

SECTION 3.

Of the Determination of a Life Estate.

An estate for life is extinguished: 617.

By the natural or civil death of the tenant for life.[3]

By the happening of a contingency, on which it was made determinable.[4]

By merger, or the union in the same person of the two characters of tenant for life and tenant in fee.[5]

By the adverse possession of another person for twenty years.[6]

And in personal property, by the total destruction of the object in which the estate existed.[7]

A tenancy for life may cease by forfeiture; for any abuse the tenant is guilty in his use of the property by waste, either by committing spoliation upon, or by suffering it to fall to decay for want of repair;[8] by crimes and misdemeanors;[9] by breach of condition;[10] by alienation[11] and disclaimer.[12] 618.

The Court of Chancery will, in some cases, interfere to relieve against a forfeiture; and it particularly favours creditors.

All grants of lands to bodies corporate, for a longer term than twenty years, unless they have a proper licence to take lands in mortmain, or are for charitable uses executed with due form, are void.[13] 619.

The sale of the estate in remainder, makes no altera- 621.

1 Co. Lit. 53 a. 2 2 Bl. Com. 282. 3 Ib. 121. 4 Ib.
5 Ib. 177. 6 3 & 4 Wm. IV. c. 27.
7 Art. 615. 8 2 Bl. Com. 281; but see art. 605.
9 2 Bl. Com. 267. 10 Ib. 281.
11 Tenant for life, granting a greater estate than he hath, forfeits his estate.—Noy's Max. 12 2 Bl. Com. 274. 13 Ib. 268.

Parallel Articles of the French Code.

tion in the right of the tenant for life; and he continues to enjoy his life estate, unless he formally part with it.[1]

A conveyance in fraud of the creditors of a tenant for
622. life is void.[2]

624. If a house be destroyed by a fire, tempest, or inevitable accident, the tenant for life is not entitled to the use of the materials, except to rebuild.[3]

CHAPTER II.

Of Uses.

(Use and Habitation.)

625 to 636. The kind of right understood by the word "use" in the English law, differs totally from that of the civil and French laws.[4] With us, it signifies a right to the whole beneficial interest, or equitable estate, with a right to dispose of it:[5] the right of such use as existed among the Romans, and is mentioned in the French code; that is to say, the right of making of as much use as is needful of corporeal property belonging to another, without prejudice to the substance of the thing, may, by special agreement, or by the express direction of a testator, subsist in England: but the creation and forfeiture of such a right, and the mode and quantity of enjoyment, must depend entirely upon the covenants and conditions of the special agreement, or the directions of the will on which it is founded; for by the law of England, the gift or grant of the use without such explanation, and express provision to the contrary, gives the whole property: for, since 27 H. VIII. c. 10, he that hath the use, in the sense of the English law, hath the property; so that the demise of the use of a thing is the demise of the thing itself.[6]

---

[1] Co. Lit. 15 b.

[2] 2 Bl. Com. 296; 13 Eliz. c. 5.

[3] Co. Lit. 53 a; unless he be tenant without impeachment of waste.

[4] 2 Bl. Com. 327.

[5] Co. Lit. 272 b. Usus est dominium fiduciarum.—Bacon, Statute of Uses.

[6] Pomfret v. Ricroft, 1 Saund. 321. See the construction put in modern times by equity on a bequest of use, Porter v. Torney, 3 Ves. 311; and as to personalty, art. 589.

Parallel Articles of the French Code.

A right of habitation, which is defined to be a right of living in the house of another without prejudice to the substance of it, may also be acquired by special agreement, or under a will. An estate may be limited to a person, on condition of his inhabiting it: thus, in the case of a grant to A and his heirs, tenants of the manor of Dale, whenever A and his heirs cease to be tenants of the manor, the estate is determined and void.[1]

Before the above-mentioned statute,[2] the use was a trust or confidence[3] reposed in some person (called the terre tenant), that some other person (called the cestui que use) should take the profits, and he had a power of disposing of it.[4] This statute, which was intended to abolish all distinctions between the real and the nominal owner,[5] by converting the beneficial into the legal estates, did not effect that object. It was held that a use could not at law be limited upon a use; and, therefore, that on the limitation of an estate to A and his heirs, to the use of B and his heirs, in trust for C and his heirs, the statute executed (as it is technically called) the first use only; *i. e.* transferred the legal estate to B and his heirs; and the second use to C and his heirs was at law a nullity.[6] The court of equity, as it had originally interfered[7] to enforce the first use, now assumed a jurisdiction to enforce the second; and such have been called trusts in distinction from uses executed by the statute; and trusts are now almost exactly what uses were before the statute of uses.[8] For the most part, the same rules as govern legal estates extend to equitable ones, uses and trusts;[9] but from there being a legal owner (called the trustee)

[1] 2 Bl. Com. 109, 154; Yelv. 150; 1 Leon. 74.

[2] 27 Hen. VIII.

[3] Ante, p. 121.

[4] See the distinction as to uses before and since the statute, Sanders on Uses, v. i. p. 85, et seq.

[5] See the Preamble.

[6] See Sanders on Uses and Trusts.

[7] Ante, pp. 122, 190.

[8] Ante, p. 140, n. 1; Co. Lit. 272, 290; and Mr. Butler's note 1, ib.

Usus et status sive possessio potius differunt secundem rationem fori, quam secundem rationem rei.—Bac.; Reading on the Statute of Uses.

[9] 1 Sand. on Uses and Trusts, 269.

Parallel Articles of the French Code.

and an equitable owner (called the cestuique trust), there are, necessarily, an entirely distinct class of rules affecting their relationship; and these are recognized in equity and not at law. Besides which, in the rules governing the conveyance of the estate (the aid of the statute of uses being called in to execute the use), there are many differences between a conveyance at common law and a conveyance under the statute of uses.[1]

TITLE IV.

OF EASEMENTS AND INCORPOREAL HEREDITAMENTS.

637. Incorporeal property is a right issuing out of a thing corporeal (whether real or personal), or concerning or annexed to, or exerciseable on the same.[2] It is not the thing corporate itself, which may consist of land, houses, jewels, or the like; but something collateral thereto, as a rent issuing out of such land or houses, or an office relating to such jewels.[3] Incorporeal hereditaments are said to lie in grant, and cannot pass without deed; and are either annexed to, and essential or useful to the enjoyment of some particular corporeal property, as ways, windows, watercourses, commons, pews; or they are unconnected with, and independent of, the enjoyment of any such corporeal estate, as advowsons, tithes, offices, dignities, franchises, rents.[4] Such a right may be either a profit a prendre, or an easement.

An easement is a privilege that one neighbour has of another by charter or prescription:[5] the object of an easement is the convenience of one estate at the expense of another. Strictly speaking, they cannot be claimed in right of persons unconnected with any estate, and therein differ from personal rights claimed by custom; they can only arise in respect of an estate, and therefore

---

[1] 2 Bl. Com. p. 327; Watkins' Conveyancing; Burton's Compendium.

[2] 2 Bl. Com. 20; Co. Lit. 19, 20, ante, p. 324.

[3] Ib.

[4] Chitty, Gen. Prac. 1, p. 206.

[5] Term de la ley.

Parallel Articles of the French Code.

cannot be in gross, as a way over another's land, a gateway, a washing-place, a place to dry fishing-nets for the occupiers of other lands. A profit a prendre is a right to take some produce from off another's land (proficua capienda in alieno solo), as herbage, pawnage, &c.;[1] but there can be no custom to take the soil of another.[2] A right to fetch water, or to drive cattle to water over another's ground, is not a profit a prendre, but an easement,[3] for it is not part of the produce of the soil.

An incorporeal hereditament[4] does not establish any pre-eminence, lordship or seignory, honour, or manorial right over the estate out of which it issues.[5] 638.

Incorporeal hereditaments are derived from obligation, imposed by the law ex necessitate, as natural watercourses or ways; or they are created by grant under seal,[6] or by custom[7] or prescription, which supposed a grant.[8] 639.

CHAPTER I.

Of Easements and Burthens necessarily arising from Locality.

Running water is originally publici juris. There is no property in water; every proprietor has an equal right to the use[9] of water flowing on his land without diminution or alteration.[10] Lands which lie low are subject, 640.

---

[1] Hale, Analysis of the Law, 49; Fitch v. Rawlings, 2 H. Bl. 395; Vin. Ab. v. xvii. p. 547.

[2] Blewit Tregonning, 2 Ad. & El. 554; 1 Har. & Wal. 431.

[3] Manning v. Wasdale, 2 Har. & Wal. 431.

[4] Incorporeal hereditaments differ from the ancient services arising from feudal tenure, which were distinguished into personal and real, free and base, continual or annual, casual or accidental, intrinsic and extrinsic (Brac. l. 2, c. 16, n. 7, 8; Brit. c. 66; 4 Rep. 9); these latter had entirely disappeared when feudal tenures were abolished (ante, p. 153) by 12 Car. II. which expressly discharges services (ante, p. 70), the fruits and consequences of tenure.

[5] Perk, s. 702.

[6] Things lying in grant cannot pass without deed, 2 Roll. Ab.; and a deed is an instrument under seal.—Bryan v. Whistler, 8 B. & Cr. 298.

[7] Cro. Eliz. 362.

[8] Bealey v. Shaw.

[9] Williams v. Morland, 2 B. & C. 915.

[10] Bealey v. Shaw, 6 East, 214.

Parallel Articles of the French Code.

as regards those which lie higher, to receive such waters as flow naturally (without the interference of man) from the one to the other.[1] The proprietor of the lower ground cannot raise a bank, or cause any obstruction which shall prevent such flowing, or throw the stream back on the proprietor above;[2] and the proprietor of the higher lands cannot do anything to increase or diminish, by artificial means, the watercourse over the lower lands.[3]

641. Any person may use or divert a part of the water of a river or watercourse to his own use, so that he does not injure the works and rights of another.[4] As soon as water is appropriated by an individual, his right is co-extensive with the beneficial use to which he appropriates it in derogation of the right of the public; and a party complaining ought to show that he is prevented from having that which he has acquired a right to use for some beneficial purpose.[5] The mere obstruction of water which had used to flow through his lands does not give any right of action: there must be actual damage from want of water,[6] though it seems the smallest deprivation of actual benefit would be sufficient.[7] By prescription he may acquire a right to diminish it in quantity, or corrupt it in quality.[8]

642. Prescription in case of a watercourse, whether in acquiring or barring a right, secures the rights of the parties after an uninterrupted enjoyment during the space of twenty years.[9]

643. The proprietor or occupier of a spring or stream cannot change the course in which it has been accustomed naturally to flow, when it supplies other persons, whether the inhabitants of a district, village, hamlet, or

---

1 Canham v. Fisk, 2 Tyrw. 155; 2 Bl. Com. 14, 403; 3 ib. 218.

2 Saunders v. Newman, 1 B. & A. 258; Rex v. Smith, 445.

3 Wright v. Howard, 1 Sim. & Stu. 190; Mason v. Hill, 3 Bar. & Ad. 192; 1 Bar. & Ad. 874.

4 Bealey v. Shaw, 6 East, 207; Liggens v. Inge, 7 Bing. 694.

5 Williams v. Morland, 2 B. & Cer. 911.

6 Ib.

7 Mason v. Hill.

8 Bealey v. Shaw.

9 2 & 3 Wm. IV. c. 71, s. 2.

even a single individual, with water for their use, so as to deprive them of sufficient water for necessary purposes,[1] unless he does so by prescription.[2]

Parallel Articles of the French Code.

Every owner of land on the banks of a river or smaller watercourse, has primâ facie a right to the use of the water; and he may use it in any quantity, and manner, for irrigation or any other purpose, so that he leaves sufficient water untainted or defouled for the use of proprietors lower down the stream.[3] 644.

If a dispute arise between proprietors to whom the use of such waters may belong, the courts have no power to interfere with the strict rights of the parties; and a nuisance or obstruction must, on proof of right and injury, be abated, and the injury compensated,[4] whatever may be the supposed interests of agriculture. 645.

Every proprietor may compel his neighbour, either by a commission from the Court of Chancery, or by an ejectment or issue in a common law court, to determine the boundaries of their contiguous estates.[5] The expense of a commission for settling boundaries is to be borne equally by the parties interested;[6] but if the confusion were occasioned by himself, or those whom he represents, he is left to his remedy at law.[7] Either party may be specially bound by deed or prescription to repair the hedge:[8] and formerly the other party might have had a writ of curia claudenda;[9] and where neither party is bound to enclose,[10] either may have an action for damages in trespass or case, for injuries arising from intrusion of the cattle on one or the other.[11] Every man's land is sup- 646.

---

[1] Bealey v. Shaw, 6 East, 208; 2 Smith, 321; 7 East, 195; 1 Wils. 175.

[2] Cox v. Matthews, 1 Vent. 237; Wright v. Williams, 1 Mee & Wels. 77.

[3] 2 Bl. Com. c. 14, 403.

[4] 3 ib. 218.

[5] 1 Mad. Ch. Pr. 29, 30; Cramner v. Pennington, 5 Taunt. 167; Hetherington v. Vane, 1 B. & Ald. 428.

[6] Norris v. Le Neve, 3 Atk. 83.

[7] Godfrey v. Littel, 1 Russ. & M. 59; Raley v. Best, id. 659.

[8] Co. Lit. 283; and post, par. art. 653, 4, 5.

[9] Fitz. Nat. Brev. 182.

[10] Churchill v. Evans, 1 Taunt. 529; 3 Wils. 126.

[11] Starr v. Rookesby, 11 Mod. 163; 1 Salk. 335; Cheetham v. Hampsden, 4 T. R. 318.

Parallel Articles of the French Code.

posed in law to be enclosed; and every proprietor may enclose his separate estate,[1] but not a common, unless he be lord of the manor, and then he must leave enough for
647. the tenants,[2] and saving the rights mentioned in art. 682.

648. Where an owner has two distinct rights of common in different manors, an allotment in lieu of such right on one common will not lessen his claim on the other waste,[3] semble aliter, where the different wastes had appeared to have been originally holden under the same lord:[4] and after an allotment to one in lieu of common of pasture, of course he cannot send his cattle on the other portions of the common.

CHAPTER II.

Easements and Burthens not arising necessarily from mere Locality.

649. Some easements or burthens established by law are for the benefit of the public generally, as a right of way;[5] some for a particular parish or hamlet, or the inhabitants of it;[6] and others for private persons.

650. The public are not entitled at common law to tow on the banks of ancient navigable rivers;[7] but a right of that nature may exist by prescription or custom.[8] The construction of highways may fall on the estate of a private individual, but generally[9] it can only be done after compensating the party. The reparation of a highway primâ facie falls upon the inhabitants of a parish;[10] that

[1] 2 Wills. 269.
[2] 2 Bl. Com. 34.
[3] Barwick v. Matthews, 5 Taunt. 365; 1 Marsh, 50; Hollingshead v. Walton, 7 East, 485.
[4] 7 East, 485.
[5] Fitch v. Rawlings, 2 H. Bl. 393.
[6] Cro. Eliz. 441; 3 Mod. 293; Cro. Car. 419.
[7] Ball v. Herbert, 3 T. R. 253.
[8] Pierce v. Lord Fauconberge, 1 Burr. 292.
[9] Under 13 Geo. III. c. 78; 3 Geo. IV. c. 126.
[10] 1 Bl. Com. 358; Rex v. Broughton, 5 Burr. 2700.

Parallel Articles of the French Code.

of bridges on the county, unless by prescription[1] they can throw the onus on particular persons, by reason of their tenure.[2]

There are some burthens to which, from necessity, the law subjects proprietors, as respects each other, either as joint owners or in easement of their estates, independently of all agreement between them; but in general they only arise from grant, or prescription, or custom. 651.

Section 1.

Of Party Walls and Ditches.

If two tenants in severalty build a party wall, one half 653.
of thickness of which stands on the land of each, which is contributed by each under the building act,[3] the wall follows the nature of the land, and the owners of the land are not tenants in common.[4] In cases where the building act does not apply, the common use of a wall separating adjoining lands belonging to different owners, is primâ facie evidence that the wall and the land on which it stands belong to the owners of those adjoining lands, in equal moieties as tenants in common.[5] But this presumption only takes place in the absence of evidence. Thus the property of a wall is in him who is bound to repair it,[6] or in him who built it. Where there is no evidence as to these facts, or of the right to the soil, presump- 654.
tions may be drawn from circumstances. It would seem to be a sign that the wall is not in common, when from the summit it is straight and perpendicular on one side, and presents on the other an inclined plane; or when there is on one side only a coping, or ridges, and shouldering pieces of stone, which were placed there in building the wall. In such cases, the wall would seem to belong to the

[1] 22 Hen. VIII. c. 5.
[2] Rex v. Sheffield, 2 T. R. 106.
[3] 14 Geo. III. c. 78.
[4] Matts v. Hawkins, 5 Taunt. 20.
[5] Cubit v. Porter, 8 B. & Cres. 257.
[6] Duke of Newcastle v. Clarke, 8 Taunt. 602.

Parallel Articles of the French Code.

proprietor on whose side are the eaves, or the corbels, or ridges of stone. In all cases, the wall or hedge belongs to the owner of the soil on which it stands.[1]

655. Under the London Building Act, owners of adjoining houses may be compelled to join in building party walls. The reparation and rebuilding of the party wall are at the expenses of all those who have claim thereto, and in proportion to the claim of each, to be settled by a jury.[2] Independent of this act, there is no direct mode of compelling a party to build a party wall;[3] but where parties are joint tenants, or tenants in common of a house, wall, or ditch, each may compel the other to contribute to repairs, &c.[4]

657. If the party wall be in common, each party may make any proper use of it. The ends of girders, beams, and other timbers must have eight and a half inches of solid brickwork at their ends, except where such ends be opposite any timber of the adjoining building, in which case, no part of such timber must approach nearer than four inches to the centre of the wall.[5]

658. If one proprietor add to the height of the party wall, and the other pulls down the addition, the first may maintain trespass for pulling down so much as stood on the half of the wall which was erected on his soil.[6]

659. Fence walls are not to be built against, unless of sufficient thickness. But the owner of either side may take down a party fence wall and build a sufficient party wall at his own expense, making good all damage done to his neighbour.[7]

660. If the neighbour uses such new wall for building against, he must contribute his proportion of the expense.[8]

662. No recesses may be made in any party wall (except for

---

1 Par. Offic. 188.

2 14 Geo. III. c. 78, s. 40, 41. See a case independent of the Building Act, Stuart v. Smith, 2 Marsh, 435.

3 Par. art. 640.

4 Co. Lit. 200 b.

5 14 Geo. III. c. 78, s. 27.

6 Matts v. Hawkins, 5 Taunt. 20.

7 14 Geo. III. c. 78, s. 43.

8 Ib.

chimney-flues, girders, beams, and other timbers, and for the ends of piers and walls) so as to reduce the thickness required for party walls.[1] Parallel Articles of the French Code.

The ditch is deemed to belong exclusively to him on whose side the earth is thrown up.[2] 666. 668.

Where two adjacent fields are separated by a hedge and a ditch, the hedge primâ facie belongs to the owner of the field in which the ditch is not. If there are two ditches, one on each side the hedge, the ownership of the hedge must be proved by acts of ownership.[3] 670.

If the boughs of a tree standing in a neighbour's close grow over mine, I may cut them.[4] 671.

If a tree grow in a hedge which divides the land of A and B, and the roots take nourishment from both their lands, then they are tenants in common thereof.[5] 673.

Section 2.

Of the Intermediary Distance.

If a man had a house near to another's house, and suffered his house to be so ruinous that it was likely to fall upon the other's house, the latter might have had a writ de domo reparanda, and compelled him to repair his house;[6] and an action on the case will lie for the damage, arising from the neglect to repair.[7] One person has no right to sink a pit, undermine the ground, or dig on his own land near the foundations of another's ancient house or wall, so as to endanger it;[8] nor to cause any loss on the surface of the other's land, by making the 674.

1 14 Geo. III. c. 78, s. 26.

2 Vowles v. Miller, 3 Taunt. 138; Doe v. Pearsley, 7 B. & Cres. 307.

3 Vowles v. Miller, 3 Taunt. 137.

4 Norris v. Baker, 2 Roll. Rep. 394; 3 Bulst. n. 198.

5 Anon. 2 Roll. R. 255; Waterman v. Soper, 1 Lord Raymond, 737; Masters v. Pollie, 2 Roll. R. 141; Holder v. Coates, 1 Mood. & M. 112.

6 Co. Lit. 56 b; Fitz. N. B. 127; 4 E. 2.

7 Co. Lit. 56 b, n. 2.

8 Pomfret v. Rycroft, 1 Saund. 321; Dodd v. Holme, 1 Ad. & El. 493.

Parallel Articles of the French Code.

earth fall into his pit:[1] but in the case of a new house, he is not bound to sustain his neighbour's walls, if he choose to build at the edge of his own land.[2] If a person keeps his hogs or other noisome animals so near the house of another, that the stench of them incommodes him,[3] this is an injurious nuisance,[4] and actionable.

Section 3.

Of Ancient Lights and Windows.

675. Every man in his own land has a right to all the
676. light and air which will come to him, and may erect buildings with as many windows as he pleases. To appropriate to himself the use of the light, he does not require the consent of the owner of the adjoining land; but the neighbouring proprietor has a right to erect anything whatever on his own land and obstruct it,[5] unless there is a right to an ancient window;[6] and where the right to an ancient window-light exists, it entitles the party to a free access of light and air over the adjoining land, and restrains the owner of such adjoining land from such enjoyment of his land as would obstruct the window.[7] But where no such ancient right exists, one of two neighbours cannot claim any right, without the consent of the other, to form in the partition or other fence wall, any new window or aperture, overlooking the other's premises; and if he does, the owner of adjoining property may at any time obstruct it,[8] unless it has
678. been enjoyed for twenty years;[9] The distance does

---

1 2 Roll. Ab. pres. 1, pl. 1.

2 Peyton v. Mayor, &c. of London, 9 B. & Cr. 725.

3 Prohibetur ne quis faciat in suo quod nocere possit alieno: et, sic utere tuo ut alienum non lædas.—9 Rep. 59.

4 3 Bl. Com. 217.

5 Moore v. Rawson, 3 B. & Cr. 340.

6 But in London otherwise.—Wynstanley v. Lee, 2 Swans. 339; 4 C. & P. 333.

7 2 Bl. Com. 403.

8 Marsh. 140.

9 3 Camp. 82; 2 & 3 Wm. IV. c. 71, s. 3.—See where by a tacit agreement less time will suffice, 1 Price, 122; 1 R. & M. 24.

Parallel Articles of the French Code.

not signify; and if a new light is made, overlooking the adjoining property, the owner of such adjoining property may obstruct the view, by a wall or any erection on his own ground that he pleases, at any time within twenty years. And where an old house is pulled down, wherein are ancient lights, and a new one built, the lights in the new house must be in the same place, and of the same dimensions, and not more in number than the lights in the old house.[1] As to new windows, it is held, a party can only be bound not to obstruct light and air over his ground, by an instrument under seal;[2] and a licence may be revoked at any time,[3] unless it amounts to a lease for a definite period.

Section 4.

Of the Droppings of House Eaves.

No one has at common law a right to build[4] so near the land of another, that the eaves of his house drip on to the land of his neighbour: cujus est solum, ejus est usque ad cœlum; and overhanging eaves would be as much a trespass and nuisance as overhanging trees,[5] and may be abated;[6] but such a right may be acquired to an ancient house by prescription. 681.

Section 5.

Of Right of Way.

A private way[7] is a right which one or more persons have of going over the land of another. A man may 682.

---

[1] Blanchard v. Bridges, 5 N. & Man. 567; Cherrington v. Abney, 2 Vern. 646; Martin v. Goble, 1 Camp. 322; 1 B. & Ad. 164.

[2] Moore v. Rawson, 3 B. & Cr. 340.

[3] Bridges v. Blanchard, 1 Adol. & El. 536.

[4] Ædificare in tuo proprio solo non licet quod alteri noceat.—Law Max. 3 Inst. 201.

[5] 3 Bl. Com. 217.

[6] Penruddock's case, 5 Rep. 101; Roll. R. 394; Baten, 9 Rep. 54.

[7] As to the kinds of ways recognized by the English law, viz. a footway, a horseway, a cart or carriageway, and a driftway, see Co. Lit 56 a.

Parallel Articles of the French Code.

have a right of way by custom, or grant, or prescription, or of necessity. Of the latter kind is, where a man having a close surrounded by his own land grants the close to another, the grantee shall have a way to the close over the grantor's land.[1] But this way of necessity is limited by the necessity which creates it, and ceases with the necessity;[2] and it should be either the most direct and shortest, or the way least injurious to the owner of the land over which it passes. The right of way acquired by the three first modes, can only be used according to the mode permitted by the grant, custom, or established usage.[3]

CHAPTER III.

Of Incorporeal Rights established by the Act of Man.

Section 1.

Of the Different Kinds of Incorporeal Rights.

686. Incorporeal hereditaments may be imposed on real or personal property, and for the benefit of another property or of a person,[4] by express agreement or grant, or by prescription, or by custom. But an easement can, by its nature,[5] be only for the benefit of an estate. The mode of using, and the extent or quantum of incorporeal hereditaments, depend upon the grant, usage, or custom under which they are held.[6]

687. Easements, when established for the convenience of lands, have been styled rural; when the use of houses, urban;[7] but the English law founds no difference on this distinction.

[1] 2 Bl. Com. 36; 2 Roll. Ab. 60, pl. 17, 18; Owen, 122; 6 Mod. 3; Willes, 72, 3; 1 Saund. 323 a, note 6; Clark v. Cogge, Cro. Jac. 170; Howton v. Frearson, 8 T. R. 50; Buckley v. Coles, 5 Taunt. 311.

[2] 2 Bing. 76.

[3] Ballard v. Dryson, 1 Taunt. 279.

[4] 2 Bl. Com. c. 3.

[5] See ante, p. 357, 8.

[6] 3 Bl. Com. c. 3.

[7] Br. l. 2, c. 4, n. 3.

Parallel Articles of the French Code.

Incorporeal hereditaments may be such as are used constantly, or only at intervals: an advowson is of the first kind, and an ancient light of the second; and the law distinguishes these in allowing prescription to establish them. 689.

Section 2.

Of the Mode of establishing Incorporeal Hereditaments.

Incorporeal rights of whatever kind may be created or 690.
acquired by grant, or by prescription (of twenty or thirty 691.
years user[1] as to some, and sixty and one hundred as to others, par. art. 689), or by custom: except in the two latter cases, there must be grant under seal. But an easement may be enjoyed under a licence for years, or revocable at will: and a distinction has been made between a licence to do something on the land of the grantor, which otherwise would be a trespass, and a licence to do something on the land of the grantee, which otherwise the grantor might obstruct; and it has been urged that, in fact, the latter is only a relinquishment of the grantor's easement over the grantee's land, and might be effected without deed; but that the former can only be by deed under seal.[2] But it must be borne in mind, that a licence differs from a grant,[3] which can only be under seal. When an easement has been enjoyed for twenty years, the law of England presumes a grant from the mere length of enjoyment,[4] where such can be presumed; but not where no party had power to make any such grant.[5] Prescription cannot be for anything which cannot be raised by grant, for the law allows prescription

[1] 2 Bl. Com. c. 3.

[2] Leggins v. Inge, 7 Bing. 690; Hewlins v. Shippan, 5 B. & Cr. 221; 7 D. & R. 783.

[3] Ante, p. 359, n. 6.

[4] Darwin v. Upton, cited 3 T. R. 159; Campbell v. Wilson, 3 East, 294; Wright v. Howard, 1 Sim. & Stu. 203.

[5] Barker v. Richardson, 4 B. & Ald. 579.

Parallel Articles of the French Code.

only in supply of the loss of a grant. Thus, for this reason, the lord of a manor cannot prescribe to levy tolls of strangers.[1] A grant may enure as a confirmation of a prescription;[2] but many rights which could not be claimed by prescription, may by custom. Thus a multitude of persons cannot prescribe for an easement, but they may plead custom.[3]

694. If a person possessed of two adjoining estates, has used a new way or other convenience to the new estate, over his adjoining estate; and if he afterwards alienate the former, such new way or other convenience would not pass under a description of the estate, or even by the words, "all easements and appurtenances belonging thereto;" but it would under the words "easements and appurtenances used therewith."[4]

696. When a right corporeal or incorporeal is established, it is considered that everything is granted which is necessary in order to use it.[5] Thus the grant of a right of drawing water at the well of another person, necessarily implies a right of way over the land of the grantor to it.[6]

Section 3.

Of the Rights of the Owner of an Incorporeal Hereditament.

697. The mode of using an incorporeal hereditament must depend entirely on the terms of the grant, or the usage established by prescription or custom.

700. If an estate, to which a right of way or other incorporeal right of that nature is attached, be divided, the right belongs to each portion of the estate so divided. But an incorporeal hereditament shall not be increased

---

[1] 1 Vent. 387. [2] Moor, 818, 830. [3] Cro. Jac. 170.

[4] Cowlan v. Slack, 15 East, 108; Morris v. Edgington, 3 Taunt. 24.

[5] Co. Lit. 56.

[6] Cuicumque aliquis quid concedit, concedere videtur et id sine quo res ipsa esse non potuit.—11 Rep. 52.

Parallel Articles of the French Code.

by the division,[1] as a right of common, a rent, &c., but it may be proportionably divided.

The proprietor of an estate, from which an incorporeal right is derived, can do nothing which tends to diminish the right or obstruct it.[2] 701.

On the other hand, the owner of an incorporeal hereditament can only use it according to the grant, custom, or prescription, without power to increase it, or to change it, or burthen other property with it, without consent. 702.

SECTION 4.

Of the Mode of Extinguishing Incorporeal Hereditaments.

A prescriptive right may be lost by its exercise becoming impossible, by the destruction of the subject matter,[3] but not by an alteration of the thing to which it is annexed;[4] and if it becomes impossible for a time, the right revives when it again becomes possible. Where there is as high and durable an estate in lands out of which rent, common, or other profit issues, as the owner hath in the rent, common, &c., unity of possession extinguishes them.[5] Where the estate, for the benefit of which an incorporeal hereditament exists, and of the estate over which it subsists are united in the same person, the unity of possession and unity of seisin in general destroy it;[6] but not those of necessity.[7] 705.

An incorporeal right is extinguished by non user[8] during twenty years, in the case of ways, lights, &c.; during sixty years, in the case of a common;[9] but a title 706.

[1] Co. Lit. 164, 165.

[2] Terra transit cum onere.—Co. Lit. 231.

[3] 4 Rep. 88.

[4] Hob. 39; 4 Rep. 86 a.

[5] 4 Rep. 38.

[6] 2 Bl. Com. c. 3.

[7] A way of necessity revives when the unity of possession ceases.—Buckley v. Coles, 5 Taunt. 311; 1 Saund. 323 a.

[8] See non user, by building a blank wall, as implying abandonment of right to make windows.—Per Abbot, C. J. in Moore v. Rawson, 3 B. & Cr. 336.

[9] 2 & 3 Wm. IV. c. 71.

Parallel Articles of the French Code.

gained by prescription or custom is not lost by mere interruption of possession for ten or twenty years, unless there be an interruption of the right;[1] but if the right be discontinued for a day a custom is at an end.

709.
710. Where several persons are entitled to an incorporeal hereditament, the possession of one coparcener or joint tenant does not preserve the rights of the others;[2] but the rights of a minor to an incorporeal hereditament are not barred during his minority, nor until ten years afterwards.

[1] Co. Lit. 114.

[2] 3 & 4 Wm. IV. c. 27, s. 12.

Parallel Articles of the French Code.

BOOK III.

OF THE DIFFERENT MODES OF ACQUIRING PROPERTY.

General Dispositions.

The methods of acquiring on the one hand, and of 711.
losing on the other, a title to estates in things real, are 712
reduced by our law to two: descent, where the title is vested by the single operation of law; and purchase, where the title is vested by any other mode.[1] Purchase is of five sorts: escheat, occupancy, prescription, forfeiture, and alienation.[2] The methods of acquiring personal property are principally occupancy, prerogative, forfeiture, custom, succession, marriage, judgment, gift or grant, contract, bankruptcy, testament, and administration.[3]

The title to property is affected by three distinct classes of circumstances: the first, relating to the condition of those transmitting or acquiring it, both as to the nature of the person invested with a capacity to take or give; for example, whether in being or not, as a child not conceived, or conceived but not born (in ventre sa mere), or whether a natural or artificial body, a private individual, or a corporation sole or aggregate, and as to the degree and kind of capacity with which the object is invested, as that of minors, guardians, married women, lunatics. The second class of circumstances relate to the nature of the object of property, as moveable and immoveable, real or personal, corporeal and incorporeal; and also to the condition or estate in the object of property, as absolutely, in fee, for life, &c. And lastly, title is affected, 1st, by the mode in which it is acquired, either from the motive or

[1] 2 Bl. Com. 201, 241. [2] Ib. 244. [3] Ib. 400.

Parallel Articles of the French Code.

cause for which it is vested, as with or without a compensation or return; and when there is a compensation or return, whether it consist in money or a thing given, or an act to be performed; and 2ndly, by the form in which it is acquired, as by delivery, instrument in writing or under seal, expressed or implied.

713. As to the things to which a party can have title,[1] property which has no owner belongs to the first occupant or fortunate finder, by title of occupancy, unless it fall within the description of waifs, or estrays, or wreck, or hidden treasure.[2]

714. There are things, publici juris, common to all, as light, air, water, &c.[3] The benefit of these can only be appropriated by occupancy.

715. The property in game is incident to the ownership of the soil or ground on which it is found, and the right of shooting it depends on the consent of the owner of the soil, and the having a game certificate, which is obtained on payment of the government tax.[4]

The right of hunting noxious animals, as the fox, exists for the public good, but it must be done in the ordinary manner:[5] but it should seem not other animals.[6] The right of fishing in navigable rivers is in the public at large, except where there are old grants or charters to the contrary.[7]

716. Treasure-trove, *i. e.* money or bullion, or plate, found hidden, the owner thereof being unknown, belongs to the king;[8] but subjects, lords of manors, often hold grants.[9]

717. Wrecks, or property washed on shore, the owner being unknown, belong to the king, or his grantee; and so are goods found at sea, whether jetsam, flotsam, or ligan.[10]

---

1 Titulus est justa causa possidendi quod nostrum est.—8 Rep. 153.

2 2 Bl. Com. 402. 3 Ib. 14.

4 1 & 2 Wm. IV. c. 32. 5 3 Bl. Com. 213; 1 T. R. 338.

6 The Earl of Essex v. Capel, 2 Chitty, Game L. 1381; 1 Stark. 351.

7 Carter v. Teircott, 4 Burr. 2163; Magna Charta, c. 16.

8 2 Bl. Com. 39. 9 1 Ib. 295. 10 Ib. 290, 1, 2.

Parallel Articles of the French Code.

TITLE I.

OF THE DESCENT OF REAL PROPERTY, AND THE DISTRIBUTION OF PERSONAL PROPERTY OF INTESTATE PERSONS.

Succession in the English law is a term strictly applicable only to corporations aggregate of many, as mayor and commonalty, in which one set of men, by succeeding another set, acquire property.[1] A great distinction is made by the law of England in the disposition of the estate of a person dying intestate, as to real and personal property. The realty descends to the heir;[2] personalty goes to the administrator, to be distributed among the next of kin.[3]

CHAPTER I.

Of the Time of Descent and Distribution.

Descent and distribution may take place on a natural 718.
or a civil death;[4] though in cases of attainder, the 719.
property of a person civilly dead is forfeited.

Where several persons perish by one and the same 720.
event, it appears that abstract physical principles seldom 721.
afford sufficient grounds to decide on the presumption of 722.
survivorship.[5] The English law, therefore, has no express rules on the subject, but it leaves each case to be decided on the merits of its own peculiar circumstances of age, sex, health, &c. Thus where father and son were hanged in one cart, the son was presumed to have survived, because he struggled longest.

---

[1] 2 Bl. Com. 430.

[2] According to the civil law, Hæres est successor in universum jus quod defunctus habuit.—Heinec. l. 2, tit. 14, s. 534; 2 Bl. Com. c. 14.

[3] 2 Bl. Com. c. 32.

[4] Co. Lit. 132 a, b.

[5] See Dr. Beatty in the Cyclopœdia of Medicine, of Practical Medicine, art. Survivorship.

Parallel Articles of the French Code.

Where father and daughter perished in shipwreck, the court thought the presumption so doubtful that they recommended a compromise.

Where husband and wife perished in an accident to a steam-boat (the Rothsay Castle), the husband, as the strongest, was presumed to have survived.[1] The Court of Chancery will send a doubtful case of survivorship to a jury to decide.[2]

As between a party claiming under a will, and the heir or next of kin, the presumption of law as to survivorship is strongly in favour of the heir or next of kin; and the burthen of proof lies on those who would disturb the legal right of the heir or next of kin, and who must produce a presumption of fact sufficient to repel the presumption of law.[3] In one case it was contended by counsel, that the doctrines of the civil law were adopted by the law of the country as to presumption of survivorship.

723. A natural child can inherit nothing, being looked upon as filius nullius or filius populi.[4] In default of legitimate heir and next of kin, the property of an intestate escheats to the crown or mesne lord.[5]

724. The heirs of the real estate by mere descent, entry, and force of law,[6] and the personal representatives, by grant of the administration of the goods and chattels, are possessed of the same rights and claims with nearly as full authority as the deceased, subject to the charges thereon, except that the personal representative may be only legally entitled, and therefore equitably accountable to the next of kin.[7]

---

1 Rex v. Dr. Hay, 1 Black. R. 640; 6 East, 82; Fearne's Posthumous Works, 35; Taylor and others v. Diplock, 2 Phill. R. 261; In Re Selwyn, 3 Hag. Eccl. 748; Colvin v. King's Proctor, 1 Hag. 92; Broughton v. Randall.

2 Mason v. Mason, 1 Mer. 308.

3 1 Bl. Com. 450; 3 Atk. 680, 747; 11 Ves. 29; and particularly observations of Sir J. Nichol, in Taylor and others v. Diplock.

4 1 Bl. Com. 459.

5 2 Ib. 244.

6 Hæres est eadem persona cum antecessore.—Co. Lit. 22. Hæres est pars antecessoris.—Ib. 22.

7 2 Bl. Com. 244, c. 14, 32.

Natural children take nothing. The husband is in possession of his deceased wife's legal estates, and requires nothing further to vest in him her estate in possession, and only administration as to her choses in action. The widow must have her dower assigned,[1] and the crown is not possessed till office found.

Parallel Articles of the French Code.

CHAPTER II.

Of the Qualities requisite to take by Descent or Distribution.

To be able to take an inheritance, or be entitled to a distributive share of an intestate's property, at the moment at which the succession is opened, the party must be in existence, either actually born, or in ventre sa mere;[2] and in general, he who is not conceived cannot be heir, because, generally speaking, the person through whom he should claim must be alive to beget or conceive him, and would come before him, and therefore prevent his being heir: but as to posthumous children (in ventre sa mere at the death of the father), they are considered as born to all purposes, except in the case of a descent of lands at common law; and in that case the heir presumptive[3] may enter, but he gives place to the real heir when born.[4] But a person not even conceived may become subsequently entitled, and divest an inheritance once vested in another. Thus if a brother purchase land, which descends on his death without issue to his sister, she 725.

[1] 2 Bl. Com. 244, c. 14, 32.

[2] 1 Ib. 130; 2 ib. 169, 208; 1 Ves. 81; Co. Lit. 36; Goodtitle v. Newman, 3 Wils. 516.

[3] The heir presumptive would be entitled to the intermediate profits.—Co. Lit. 116 b, n. 4; 55 b, n. 8.

[4] Thelluson v. Woodford, 4 Ves. 334, 335; Doe v. Clark, 2 H. Bl. 399; 10 & 11 Wm. III. c. 16.— See how he is actually seized before entry, Lit. s. 448, 681; and as to transmitting the estate to his own heir, 3 & 4 Wm. IV. c. 106, s. 1.

Parallel Articles of the French Code.

can never be secure of the estate while both their father and mother are alive, for a brother may be born and become entitled to the estate.[1]

Those are incapable of taking the inheritance who are monsters, not having the human shape;[2] but children born alive, though incapable of living, may be heir;[3] those who are attaint and corrupt in blood cannot take.[4]

726. No person is capable of inheriting lands, unless he is a natural born subject, or naturalized, or made a denizen;[5] but aliens may take a distributive share of an intestate's estate, except chattels real.[6]

727 to 730. The having been the cause of the death of the ancestor, would not exclude the heir from his inheritance; though if it were done feloniously it would cause forfeiture;[7] nor would the having calumniated the ancestor, or neglected to prosecute one who had murdered him, affect the heir's right.

CHAPTER III.

Of the Line of Descent.

SECTION 1.

General Dispositions.

731. The heir and next of kin are the children and descendants of the deceased, his ancestors, and collateral relations, in the order and according to the rules hereafter considered.[8]

732. The law distinguishes between real and personal estate,[9]

---

[1] Co. Lit. 11 b. [2] Ib. 7 b. [3] 2 Bl. Com. 127, 8; Fisher v. Palmer.

[4] Co. Lit. 8 a; 391 b. If, but for his attainder, he would have been heir, he interrupts the descent, and there is no heir; and the land escheats.—1 P.W. 78.

[5] Co. Lit. 8 a; 1 Bl. Com. c. 10.

[6] 2 R. Rep. 93; Cro. Car. 8; Co. Lit. 2 b; 1 And. 25; N. Bend. 36.

[7] See ante, par. art. 23. [8] 2 Bl. Com. c. 14, 32. [9] Ib.

Parallel Articles of the French Code.

and it considers also the source from whence real property was derived,[1] in order to regulate the transmission of it; the descent is traced from the purchaser, and the person last seized[2] is deemed the purchaser until the contrary is shown.[3]

In the inheritance of real property among ancestors or collaterals, the paternal and male stocks shall be preferred to the maternal and female, unless where the lands have, in fact, descended from a female, and then it goes to her kin.[4]

Personal property is distributed among the next of kin 733.
in equal degree, maternal as well as paternal, and their representatives, when representation is admitted.[5] Half-blood (whether consanguine, *i. e.* of the same father, or uterine, of the same mother) is admitted to the personalty equally with germane or whole blood;[6] and to realty after the whole blood of the male ancestor, and if on the part of a female ancestor,[7] after the common ancestor.
There is no division of the personalty into two parts, for 734.
the paternal and maternal lines; and except where representation is allowed, each party takes an equal share.

In real estate,[8] and also in personal (except where the representation is allowed), the nearest in blood exclude

---

[1] 2 Bl. Com. 220.

[2] As to actual or virtual seisin, or possession, see ante, p. 338, 9; and Doe v. Keen, 7 T. R. 386; 3 & 4 Wm. IV. c. 106, s. 1. The old law maxims were Seizina facit stipitem, and that an heir claiming by descent in fee-simple must make himself heir to him who was last actually seized; but under 3 & 4 Wm. IV. c. 106, it is the persons last entitled, whether actually in possession or not.

[3] 3 & 4 Wm. IV. c. 106, s. 2.

[4] 2 Bl. Com. 222, 235; 3 & 4 Wm. IV. c. 106, s. 8.

[5] 2 Bl. Com. 515.

[6] Ib. 505.

[7] 3 & 4 Wm. IV. c. 106, s. 9. By the old law (altered by this act) half blood were excluded from real estate; and as to old titles, the former rule must be taken into account.

Possessio fratris de feodo simplici facit sororem esse hæredem.—3 Rep. 42.

Heir in fee-simple must have sanguine duplicatum.

Propter jus sanguinis duplicatum, tam ex parte patris, quam ex parte matris dicitur hæres propinquior soror, quam frater de alia uxore.—3 Rep. 41.

[8] Hæres est aut jure proprietatis aut jure representationis.—3 Rep. 40.

Parallel Articles of the French Code.

the more remote.[1] And in equal degree as to estates in fee-simple, the next worthiest of blood shall ever inherit, as the male and all descendants from him before the female; and the female on the part of the father before the male or female on the part of the mother;[2] and the eldest son[3] in preference to the younger.

735. The nearness, propinquity, proximity of relationship, is established by the number of generations; every generation is called a degree.[4] But in the descent of real property, the law respects the purchasing ancestor from whom the estate is derived, and calculates the proximity of relationship by the canonical degrees of consanguinity.[5]

736. The series of degrees form the line: lineal consanguinity is that which subsists between persons, of whom one is descended in the direct line from the other, and of course, from a common ancestor.[6] Collateral kindred agree with the lineal, in that they descend from the same stock or ancestor; but differ in this, that they do not descend the one from the other.[7] The direct line is distinguished into the direct descending and direct ascending line;[8] and the direct descending line has preference over the ascending.[9] Formerly the rule was, inheritances descend, but do not ascend.[10]

737. In the direct line are computed as many degrees as there are generations between the persons: thus the son is, with respect to his father, in the first degree; the grandson in the second; and in like manner, the father and the grandfather in respect of the son and grandson.[11]

738. In the collateral line, as to real property, our law has

---

[1] Propinquior excludit propinquum, propinquus remotum, remotus remotiorem.—Co. Lit. 10 b.

[2] Co. Lit. 14.

[3] Si quis plures filios habuerit jus proprietatis primo descendit ad primogenitum, eo quod inventus primus est in rerum naturæ.—Co. Lit. 14.

[4] 2 Bl. Com. 206, 224. [5] Ib. 224, 5. [6] Ib. 203.

[7] Ib. 204. [8] Ib. 203.

[9] 3 & 4 Wm. IV. c. 106, s. 6. [10] Lit. s. 3. [11] 2 Bl. Com. 203.

Parallel Articles of the French Code.

adopted the mode of computing in the canon law;[1] and in tracing the heirs, we begin at the common ancestor, and reckon downwards; and in whatsoever degree the two persons or the most remote of them is distant from the common ancestor, that is, the degree in which they are the most related to each other. Two brothers are in the first degree, nephews in the second, first cousins in the third.[2]

As to the distribution of personal estate, the next of kin are ascertained according to the computation of the civil law, including the relations on both the paternal and maternal sides,[3] which counts from the deceased up to the common ancestor inclusive, and down from him to the next relation; thus brothers are in the second degree.

Section 2.

Of the Right of Representation.

Representation, or taking per stirpes, is an intendment of law, by which the descendant represents the ancestor; that is, stands in the same place, degree, and rights, as the ancestor himself would have done had he been living.[4] 739.

As to real property,[5] the rights of representation of the parent by the issue, is allowed to prevail ad infinitum,[6] and so as to personal property in the direct descending line; but no representatives are admitted among collaterals, further than the children[7] of the intestate's brothers and sisters.[8] So that sometimes personal estates are divided, 740.

[1] Co. Lit. 23; 2 Bl. Com. 224.
[2] 2 Bl. Com. 206; Co. Lit. 23, 24.
[3] Toller, 382, 3; 2 Bl. Com. 504.
[4] 2 Bl. Com. 217.
[5] Hæredum appelatione veniunt hæredes hæredum in infinitum.—Co. Lit. 9 a.
[6] 2 Bl. Com. 225; H. Chit. Desc. 110.
[7] But not grandchildren of brother or sister.—Carter v. Crawley, T. Raym. 496; Caldicot v. Smith, 2 Show. 286.
[8] 2 Bl. Com. 515; Toller, 382, 3.

Parallel Articles of the French Code.

per capita, and sometimes per stirpes.[1] The doctrine and limits of representation seem to have been principally borrowed from the civil law.[2]

741. As to personal property, representation does not take place in favour of ancestors.[3]

742. In the collateral line, representation is admitted in favour of children of brothers and sisters of the deceased;[4] and a brother, or sister, or children, will exclude a grandfather, though in the same degree.[5] If all the brothers and sisters are dead, their lineal descendants take per capite; if any of the brothers and sisters are alive per
743. stirpes.[6] Among the descendants of the intestate, it goes by stock, per stirpes ad infinitum; but among collaterals, as to personalty, except as to the children of a brother's or sister's child, *i.e.* nephew's children,[7] the division is made by heads per capita.

744. There can be no representation of persons living, for it implies[8] the standing of a descendant in the same place as the ancestor would have stood if living.[9]

Section 3.

Of Descendants.

745. Where there are two or more male descendants[10] in equal degree, in persona vel in jure representationis, the eldest only shall inherit the real estate;[11] and the male issue excludes the females.[12] Where there are only females[13]

---

[1] 2 Bl. Com. 517.
[2] Ib. ante, p. 155.
[3] Blackborough v. Davis, 1 P. W. 51; Salk. 38, 351; Mod. 623; Woodroffe v. Woodroffe, Pre. Cha. 527.
[4] 2 Bl. Com. 515.
[5] Evelyn v. Evelyn, 3 Atk. 762; Amb. 191.
[6] 2 Bl. Com. 517.
[7] Pett v. Pett, 1 P.W. 25.
[8] See par. art. 739.
[9] Nemo est hæres viventis.
[10] Hæres est nomen juris; filius est nomen naturæ.—Bacon. Hæres est alter ipse, et filius est pars patris.—3 Rep. 12.
[11] 2 Bl. Com. 214.
[12] Ib. 212.
[13] Cohæredes una persona censentur, propter unitatem juris quod habent. —Co. Lit. 163 b. Omnes sorores sunt quasi unica hæres de una hæredite.—Ib. 67.

Parallel Articles of the French Code.

to inherit real property, they all take as coparceners; and in all cases as to personalty, children and their descendants succeed to their ancestors, without distinction of sex or primogeniture, and although they be the issue of different marriages.[1] They take by equal portions and by heads per capita, when they are all in the same degree, and take in their own right; and they take by stocks per stirpes, when part take by representation.

Section 4.

Of Ancestors.

If the deceased has left neither posterity, nor brother or sister, or their children, the personal estate goes to the next degree of kin equally per capita, whether father and mother, or either of them; or grandfathers and grandmothers, or great-grandfathers and great-grandmothers, without any distinction as to paternal and maternal lines. The ancestor in the nearest degree excludes all others more remote; thus, the father excludes the grandfather,[2] the grandfather would exclude the uncle or aunt, or great-grandfather.[3] The maternal ancestors of a person from whom a descent is traced, do not inherit any of the real property, until all his paternal ancestors and their descendants have failed.[4] 746.

When the father and mother, or only the father of an intestate without issue, survive him, the father is entitled to the whole of the personalty and realty, to the exclusion of the brothers or sisters, and other remote kindred.[5] But if there be a mother only surviving, with brothers and sisters of the deceased, they take equal shares of the personalty.[6] 748.

---

[1] 2 Bl. Com. 214, 5; 504, 515; Toller, 382, 3.

[2] Blackborough v. Davis, 1 P. W. 51.

[3] Mentney v. Petty, Pre. Ch. 393.

[4] Toller, 382; 3 & 4 Wm. IV. c. 106, s. 6.

[5] 3 & 4 Wm. IV. c. 106, s. 7.

[6] Toller, 382.

Parallel Articles of the French Code.

SECTION 5.

Of Collaterals.

750. In case of the previous decease of the father and mother of a person intestate without issue, the eldest brother surviving, or his issue if any, or sisters co-equally, inherit the realty; and the brothers and sisters and their children take the personalty, to the exclusion of ancestors or other collaterals,[1] either per capita or per stirpes, as regulated by the second section of this chapter.

751. 752. If the father survive, he takes the whole; but the mother only takes an equal share with the brothers and sisters,[2] without distinction of half blood.

753. Beyond the degrees of brother and sister, and their children, all in an equal and same degree, both on the father's and mother's side,[3] take per capita; and those who are beyond that degree neither take per capita or per stirpes, but are excluded.[4]

754. There is no limitation to the degree of consanguinity which, in default of nearer, shall take either realty or personalty; but while a legal relative[5] can be found there is no escheat.

CHAPTER IV.

Of the Rights of Bastards, and of Escheat.

SECTION 1.

Of the Right of Bastards, and their Property when Intestate without Issue.

756 to 766. Illegitimate persons take no interest in either the real or personal property of an intestate relative, unless they

---

[1] Evelyn v. Evelyn, 3 Atk. 762.
[2] Art. 748.
[3] 1 P. W. 5.
[4] Bower v. Littlewood, 1 P. W. 594.
[5] Parens est nomen generale ad omne genus cognitiones.—Co. Lit. 80 b.

Parallel Articles of the French Code.

are legitimatized by act of parliament; and then their interest therein depends more on the terms of the act than upon the general law of the land.[1]

If a bastard died intestate, and without issue, the whole of his property belongs to the crown, unless he left a wife, who would be entitled to her dower and thirds.

Section 2.

Of Escheat on Default of Heirs.

The husband is entitled to the whole of his deceased wife's property, the realty as tenant by courtesy for his life, and the personalty absolutely.[2] 767.

The wife is entitled to her dower, or thirds of her husband's estate in realty, for her life, and in personalty absolutely.[3]

In default of heir, subject to dower and courtesy, the real property escheats to the lord paramount;[4] and in default of next of kin, the personal estate vests in the crown.[5] When neither next of kin, or husband, or wife are found, the ordinary may grant letters ad colligendum bona defuncti to any person, whose only business is to keep the goods in safe custody, and to do other acts for the benefit of such as may be entitled to the property of the deceased.[6] 768.

---

[1] 1 Bl. Com. 458. A bastard is nullius filius, and cannot be heir to any one. —Lit. s. 188. Qui ex damnato coitu nascuntur inter liberos non computentur.— Co. Lit. 3.

[2] 2 Bl. Com. 126, 433.

[3] 2 Ib, 129; 3 & 4 Wm. IV. c. 105; 2 Bl. Com. 515.

[4] 2 Bl. Com. 244.

[5] Ib. 505; 1 Wood, 398.

[6] 2 Bl. Com. 505.

Parallel Articles of the French Code.

CHAPTER V.

Of the Mode in which the Inheritance is cast upon the Party, and of the undertaking or renouncing Administration of Personalty.

SECTION 1.

Of the Mode in which it is cast on the Party.

774. Of real property, the law casts the inheritance on the heir immediately on the death of the ancestor, without waiting for him to accept it, or leaving him an option;[1] and the heir of a fee-simple is bound, on failure of the personalty, to satisfy the debts of his ancestor as far as the property descended to him from such ancestor will extend, which property is called in law assets by descent.[2] But he is bound only to pay debts as far as the assets by descent[3] will extend; and when he has expended all that he has received as heir, he may refuse to pay more, and plead riens per descent.[4] The administration and distribution of the personal estate stands on a different
775. footing, in not being entirely for the benefit of the party undertaking it; and no person is compellable to undertake the administration of the personalty of a deceased.[5] An administrator of an intestate, or an executor of a testament, is not chargeable in any case (except by their own express or implied intention) beyond the value of the goods of the deceased that come to their hands.[6]

---

1 Co. Lit. 191 a; Butler's note, vi. 3; 2 Bl. Com. 201. The acceptance and renunciation of property stands on a totally different footing in the English and French law; inasmuch as in the latter the heir in taking undertakes to pay all the ancestor's debts: under the former only as far as the estates will extend.

2 Davy v. Pepys, Plowd. 439; Buckley v. Nightingale, 1 Stra. 665; 1 Wm. IV. c. 47; 3 & 4 Wm. IV. c. 104.

3 None can charge his heir but as part of himself.

4 4 Wm. IV. c. 47, s. 7.

5 2 Bl. Com. 505; Salk. 38; 11 Vin. Abr. 139; Brownl. 82; Roll. Ab. 907; Swin. p. 6.

6 2 Bl. Com. 511; Dr. & Stud. Dial. 1, c. 19.

An inventory of the property is directed to be made, and accounts are passed; but those that are actually made are not for the benefit of the administration, but in order to affix the amount of duty.[1] Parallel Articles of the French Code.

The law casts real property upon infants and femmes covert as upon other heirs; and a femme covert may be an administratrix, but not without the consent of her husband, expressed or presumed.[2] An infant cannot be administrator or executor, though his guardian may administer for him.[3] 776.

The heir succeeds to the realty the instant the ancestor is dead. Probate of a will has relation back to the time of the testator's death;[4] but it would seem that administration only relates to the time of the grant.[5] 777.

The administration of a deceased person's personal estate is undertaken by the express act of the party in obtaining letters of administration or probate. If a person, without any just authority, intermeddle with the goods of the deceased, he is called executor (de son tort) of his own wrong, and he is subject to all the liabilities of an executorship without the advantages.[6] 778.

The merely doing acts of necessity or humanity, as locking up the goods, or burying the corpse of the deceased, will not amount to such an intermeddling as will charge a man as executor of his own wrong.[7] 779.

The grant of administration, on application to the proper authority, or an officious intermeddling, alone renders party liable as administrator;[8] and the gift, sale, or conveyance of his distributive share of the personalty would in no way charge him as administrator. 780.

---

1 55 Geo. III. c. 184, s. 38.

2 S. C. 1 Sch. & Lef. 266; Vin. Ab. Bar. & Feme, 22; Com. Dig. B. & F.

3 38 Geo. III. c. 87, s. 6; Bac. Ab. Ex. & Ad.

4 2 Bl. Com. 507; Toller, 45.

5 2 Bl. Com. 507; Toller, 95; Winkford v. Winkford, Salk. 301; 2 Stra. Rep. 1106.

6 Wentw. Off. Ex. c. 14, p. 320; Stokes v. Porter.

7 2 Bl. Com. 507; Dyer, 166 b.

8 2 Bl. Com. 504, 5, 6, 7.

Parallel Articles of the French Code.

781\. When the heir, to whom real property has descended, dies before he has done any act of ownership, but has only been entitled thereto, it descends to his heir, and not to the heir of his ancestor from whom he had it.[1] Where an administrator dies before he has fully administered, the personal estate of the deceased administration is granted to some new person of the goods not administered, called administration de bonis non.[2]

783\. A person of full age having voluntarily undertaken the office of administrator, is bound to fulfil the duties he has taken upon himself, and cannot renounce;[3] but if a will is found appointing an executor, the grant of administration may be repealed.

Section 2.

Of the Renunciation of Administration.

784\. There is no renunciation of real property.[4] The renunciation of the next of kin of the administration of an intestate's goods and chattels, is made by the express act of the party, in person or by proxy, before the ordinary or surrogate.[5]

785\. The renunciation of administration does not affect the rights of the party renouncing, or his representatives, to a distributive share.

791\. At common law, expectancies may be barred by estoppel;[6] and in equity, every species of contingency may be bound for valuable considerations.[7]

792\. Conveying away, and concealing the goods of a deceased person, might amount to an officious inter-

---

1 3 & 4 Wm. IV. c. 106, s. 1.

2 2 Bl. Com. 506.

3 Roll. Ab. 917; Bac. Ab. Ex. & Ad. E. 10; Burn's Eccl. L. 198.

4 Art. 774.

5 Burn's Eccl. L.; Toller, Exors.

6 Helps v. Hereford, 3 Bar. & Ad. 342.

7 1 Ves. 409; 2 P. W. 132, 191; 3 Atk. 420 sed; vide an exception, 3 Meriv. 667.

meddling, sufficient to constitute the party an executor de son tort:[1] and the rightful executor or administrator could maintain an action of trover for the recovery of the goods, and for damages for the illegal conversion of them to the party's own use.[2]

Parallel Articles of the French Code.

Section 3.

Of the Extent of the Liability of an Heir or Administrator to the Payment of the Debts of the Deceased.

The administrator is only bound to pay the debts of the deceased to the amount of the property of the deceased come to his hands, which property is called assets; and to a demand by a creditor he may reply, that he has fully administered the goods of the deceased; and he may in an action put in a plea of plene administravit et issent riens inter mains;[3] and when the creditor has given primâ facie evidence of assets, he may prove that they have been exhausted in payment of other debts of the deceased.[4] On failure of the personal estate, the heir taking the realty is only liable for the debts of his ancestor to the amount of the property he received, called assets by descent, from that ancestor.[5] 793. to 810.

---

1 Dyer, 166 b, in marg.; 2 T. R. 99.

2 Rutland v. Rutland, Cro. Eliz. 377.

3 Selw. N. P.

4 Com. Dig. Adm. c. 2; Dyer, 32 a (margin), B. N. P.

5 See ante, par. art. 774. Formerly the maxims were, Hæres non tenetur in Anglia ad debita antecessoris reddenda, nisi per antecessorem ad hoc fuerit obligatus, præterquam debita regis tantum (Co. Lit. 38 b); and that the heir is not bound unless expressly named. But a practice had been long introduced of marshalling the assets of a deceased where the personalty was not sufficient to pay both simple and specialty debts, when the recent statute, 1 Wm. IV. c. 47, passed to extend the remedy against the heir or devisee; but the rule still is, that the personal estate is first liable in case of the heir; and legacies, &c. sink into the real estate to disburthen the heir.

Parallel Articles of the French Code.

Section 4.

Of Grant of Administration to Creditors, &c.

811 to 814. If none of the next of kin will take out administration, a creditor of the deceased may by custom do it;[1] and the court have a discretionary power, in default of next of kin, of granting administration to a discreet person, or of granting letters ad colligendum bona defuncti.[2]

CHAPTER IV.

Of Distribution and Hotchpot.

Section 1.

Of enforcing Partition and Distribution.

815. Where lands descend to females as co-heiresses, their estates in coparcenery may be dissolved by any one of them compelling a partition under a commission from the Court of Chancery.[3] A voluntary partition may also be effected.[4]

No distribution of the personal effects is to take place until after one year from the time of the intestate's decease.[5] But if the administrator detain the property after the expiration of the year, without reasonable grounds, it should seem that he is liable to pay interest.[6] Partition of real property, or distribution of personalty, may be suspended, or entirely prevented, by agreement among the parties.

816. The administrator takes the personal estate of an intestate under the express obligation of distributing it to the next of kin.[7] And the possession of one coparcener of

---

1 2 Bl. Com. 505. 2 Ib.

3 Co. Lit. 169 a, n. 2; 166 a; Mitford's Plead. 4 C. Lit. 166 a.

5 22 & 23 Car. II. c. 10, s. 8.

6 Kilvington v. Gray, 1 Sim. & Stu. 396; Turner v. Turner, 1 Jac. & Walker, 39; Cracklet v. Bethume, 1 Jac. & Walker, 586. 7 2 Bl. Com. 515.

part of the real estate does not affect the rights of the others to compel a partition, unless the possession of such coparcener were originally adverse to the rights of possession of the others, and had been confirmed by length of time.[1] Parallel Articles of the French Code.

The only mode of making an effectual partition of realty, where one of the parties is an infant, is by act of parliament.[2] The administrator may retain the distributive share in the personal estate of an infant, until he attains the age of twenty-one years, and must invest it in good securities; and with respect to absent persons, the administrator may retain possession of the distributive share till they appear, unless there be some person duly authorized to receive it, and to indemnify the administrator; or in either of these cases he may pay it into court.[3] As to coparceners absent at the death of the ancestor, their rights are preserved in full force until after they return,[4] or authorize some one to act for them. 817.

The husband is absolutely entitled to his wife's interest in the distributive share of the personal estate of an intestate, and may claim in the same manner as those who take in their own right.[5] The husband cannot make a voluntary partition of realty which shall bind the wife, or her heirs, after his death, if it be unequal;[6] but under legal authority, a partition might be made to bind a femme covert for ever.[7] 818.

No action at law lies for a distributive share of personalty.[8] A court of equity or an ecclesiastical court will decree an account and distribution by an administrator.[9] Now that the common law writ of partition is abolished,[10] the only remedy to compel partition of real property is a commission out of chancery.[11] 822.

---

[1] Co. Lit. 163 b, 164 a, 167 b, 174 a, b; 3 & 4 Wm. IV. c. 27.

[2] Wat. Pr. Con. 155 (n) b. [3] 36 Geo. III. c. 52, s. 32. [4] 3 & 4 Wm. IV. c. 27.

[5] 2 Bl. Com. 433; 2 Atk. 420. [6] Co. Lit. 170, b.

[7] Ib. 171 a. [8] 7 Bar. & Cres. 542.

[9] 22 & 23 Car. II. c. 10, s. 2; 2 Mad. Ch. Pr. 2; Bissett v. Axtell, 2 Vern. 47; Howard v. Howard, 1 Vern. 134.

[10] 3 & 4 Wm. IV. c. 27. [11] Co. Lit. 169 a, n. 2.

Parallel Articles of the French Code.

823. If any of the coparceners refuse to consent to a partition of realty, a commission issues out of chancery to make a division of the premises into as many equal parts as are required, and to allot the premises to the parties in severalty.[1]

824. The commission issued to make partition of real property, directs the commissioners chosen by the parties to survey the premises, and to divide and allot the parts to be held in severalty; and they may examine witnesses as to premises and their respective values.[2]

825. It is the duty of the administrator to sell the personalty of an estate, as speedily as possible, for the best possible price.

826. Each of the coparceners may demand her share of the premises in severalty.

827. Every part of the estate need not be divided, where the doing so (as in the case of houses) would spoil it; but recompense is to be made, in money or rent, for owelty of partition:[3] otherwise if one house only. Where there is a house and other lands which may make up the difference, there partition must be made.[4] By agreement among the parties, if of full age, the premises might be sold.

829. Every coparcener who has received lands in frankmarriage, and all the children of an intestate who have received portions from the deceased, must bring it into hotchpot, or into account, before they receive any further share of the intestate's estate.[5]

830. As to the personal estate, no actual restitution is directed; but the child so advanced is only to receive so much as, together with such advanced portion, is equivalent to the shares of the other children.[6] Only the lands given in frankmarriage are to be brought into hotchpot.[7]

831. The commissioners, under a bill for partition, divided

---

1 Ch. Pr. 2 2 Newl. 3rd ed. 484, 506; Seton on Decrees, 192.
3 1 P. W. 446; Lord Clarendon v. Hornsby. 4 11 Ves.
5 2 Bl. Com. 191, 516, 7. 6 Ib. 517. 7 Ib. 190.

Parallel Articles of the French Code.

the property into as many equal lots as there are co-heirs or stocks in coparcenery.[1]

The inequality of the lots in kind is balanced by an equivalent in money, or a rent called owelty of partition.[2] 833.

In a voluntary partition, if the eldest make partition, she shall choose last,[3] or they may agree mutually as to the lots, or get some friend to divide, and then choose in turn by priority of age;[4] or they may have the land divided by their appointee, or by a commission out of chancery, and draw lots for the shares.[5] 834.

The parties are heard by the commissioners, before they make division.[6] 835.

A bill for partition lies against or for infants;[7] and though, under 1 Wm. IV. c. 65, they are empowered to convey by the direction of the court, yet an act of parliament seems necessary absolutely to bind them.[8] Infants must sue and be sued by next friend (prochein ami) or guardian, and they must have guardians ad litem appointed.[9] A decree in Chancery will not be made, if a material party is, and has been throughout the suit, absent.[10] 838.

Voluntary or compulsory partitions, made by parties capable of entering into contracts, as they must be by deed,[11] are as conclusive as other deeds. The compulsory partition proceeds on the deeds, which, if the parties be not competent to execute, is not effectual.[12] 840.

Every person entitled as coparcener may sell her share of the property, without the consent of the other parceners, and without any power on the part of such other coparceners to interfere with such sale.[13] A distributive share of an intestate's personal estate, is only a chose in action, and not properly assignable at law;[14] 841.

---

1 Ch. Pr.
2 Co. Lit. 169 a, b.
3 Lit. 245. Cujus est divisio, alterius est electio.—Co. Lit. 166.
4 Ib. 244, 5; Co. Lit. 166. Eisnetia semper est preferenda propter privilegium ætatis.—Ib.
5 Co. Lit. 166 a; Ch. Pr.
6 Ch. Pr.
7 Ib.
8 Ante, p. 315.
9 Ch. Pr.
10 2 Bro. C. C. 276.
11 29 Car. II.
12 2 Sch. & Lef.
13 Lit. s. 309.
14 2 Bl. Com. 397, 442.

Parallel Articles of the French Code.

but in equity, an assignment of such distributive share for a valuable consideration, would be upheld as against the assignor.[1]

842. As to the title deeds, each coparcener shall have those belonging to her own moiety; and if the same deeds apply to all of their shares, the party entitled to the share of the greatest value is entitled to the custody of deeds upon entering into a covenant to produce them, and allow copies to be taken when required.[2]

Section 2.

Of Advancement and Hotchpot.

843 to 869. Property given by way of advancement, must be brought into account in the descent and distribution of the intestate estate of the ancestor by whom it was so given as advancement. An advancement is property given by way of portion in marriage, or to set up in the world, and not things given by way of emolument.[3]

If one of the daughters or coparceners had an estate given with her in frankmarriage by her ancestor (that is, land given as a species of estates' tail freely, by a relation, for advancement of his kinswoman in marriage), in this case, if lands descended from the same ancestor, to her and her sisters in fee-simple, she or her heirs could have no share in them, unless she would agree to divide the lands so given in frankmarriage, in equal portions with the rest of the land so descending.[4] This mode of division was called bringing lands into hotchpot. It was left to the choice of the donee in frankmarriage; and if she did not choose to put her lands into hotchpot, the rest of the inheritance was divided among the

---

[1] 2 Bl. Com. 442; Brace v. Marlborough, 2 P. W. 496; Tourville v. Naish, 3 P. W. 307.

[2] Seton on Decrees, n. 186.

[3] Hearne v. Barber, 3 Atk. 213; Hume v. Edwards, 3 Atk. 450; Edwards v. Freeman, 1 Eq. Ab. 249, pl. 10.

[4] 2 Bl. Com. 190, 115.

other sisters. No lands, but such as are given in frank-marriage, needed to be so brought in; and gifts in frank-marriage have fallen into disuse.[1]

Parallel Articles of the French Code.

No child of an intestate (except his heir at law), on whom he settled in his lifetime any estate in lands, or pecuniary portion equal to the distributive share of the other children, shall have any part of the surplusage with the brothers and sisters; but if the estates so given them by way of advancement are not equivalent to the other shares, the children so advanced shall have so much as will make them equal.[2]

SECTION 3.

Of the Payment of Debts.

The administrator has authority granted to him expressly, to collect the personal estate of the intestate, "to pay whatever debts the deceased at the time of his death did owe," so far as his personal estate will extend;[3] and not till after the payment of all the debts of the deceased, is any distribution to be made among the next of kin;[4] and then the residue of the personal estate of an intestate, deducting such payments and all the expenses of the administrator, is to be equally divided between the next of kin in the proportions already stated.[5] The debts must be paid in due order, according to the rules of priority.[6] The real estate is not liable to the payment of the debts of an intestate, until all the personalty has been applied and expended for that purpose, and is not sufficient to liquidate them all.[7] 870.

Where there are legatees under a will, the executor of 871.

---

[1] 2 Bl. Com. 191.
[2] Ib. 516. 7.
[3] Ib. 511; Burn's Eccl. Law; Toller, 258.
[4] 2 Bl. Com. 514.
[5] Ante, p. 378 to 384; 22 & 23 Car. II. c. 10.
[6] 2 Bl. Com. 511.
[7] Davy v. Pepys, Plowd. 439; 3 & 4 Wm. IV. c. 104.

Parallel Articles of the French Code.

the will is bound to pay the debts of the deceased, before he pays either general or specific legacies; or the residue or any part to the residuary legatee;[1] and he remains always liable to the extent of the assets, whether he has paid legacies or not, or whether or not he has taken security to refund in case of debts.[2] In case of a deficiency of assets, all the general legacies must abate proportionably in order to pay the debts; but a specific legacy is not to abate at all, unless there is not sufficiency without it.[3]

872. If a person borrows money on mortgage of his real property, and dies intestate, or without specific direction by will, his personal estate shall be applied, if sufficient, towards the payment thereof, for the benefit of the heir.[4] And a devisee of real property is entitled to have it exonerated of all mortgages on it out of the personal assets, and even out of real assets descended to the heir,[5] unless the testator otherwise direct; the mortgage money being in such case considered the personal debt of the testator, and the charge on the real estate as only collateral. But the rule is otherwise where the charge is primarily on the real estate, although there be a collateral personal security.[6] Thus a rent charge, issuing out of real corporeal estates, cannot be paid off without the consent of the person entitled to it; and it continues to charge the land, and all parts of it, into whose hands soever it passes; but on partition of the lands out of which the rent issues, the rent shall be apportioned.[7]

873. The administrator is liable to the debts and claims on the estate of the deceased, to the extent of the personal property of the intestate, which has devolved on him: but he is never liable personally beyond the assets, except

---

1 2 Bl. Com. 511, 4. 2 Co. Lit. 111; 4 Rep. 28. 3 2 Vern. 111.

4 Cope v. Cope, 1 Salk. 449; King v. King, 3 P. W. 359.

5 1 Vern. 37; 2 Atk. 430, 436. 6 2 Salk. 449.

7 Coventry v. Coventry, 2 P. W. 222; Freeman v. Edward, 2 P. W. 437; Wilson v. Darlington, 2 P. W. 664 n; Ward v. Dudley, 2 Bro. C. R. 316.

8 Dauv. Abr. 507. As to the apportionment of rent, see Co. Lit. 149, 150.

by his own express agreement or promise in writing.[1] After all the personal assets are exhausted, the real estate in the hands of the heir is liable for the intestate's debts; but specialty creditors shall be paid in full before simple contract.[2]

Parallel Articles of the French Code.

Any party, whether a devisee or heir, who pays off a mortgage, is entitled to stand precisely in the place of the previous mortgagee; besides the right which the devisee or heir has to take the estate, exonerated from the mortgage debt. 874.

If the administrator has not taken good security, and the residuary or other legatee, to whom he has paid any part of the assets, becomes insolvent, and cannot refund, the administrator would be liable to the creditor notwithstanding; but where there were several, he might go to the others for a rateable proportion. 875. 876.

Judgments against the deceased bind the lands which descend to his heir, when docketted;[3] and in the administration of the personal estate, a judgment against the deceased is considered as a debt.[4] If execution is already issued, it may be proceeded with;[5] but if execution be not issued, the judgment must be revived against the administrator before execution can issue. 877.

The claims of creditors against the real or personal estate of a deceased person, in the hands of the heir or administrator, have the same time to run after his decease as they had at the time of his death. 880.

The creditors of the next of kin, or of the heir, have no claim or remedy against the estate of the intestate, until it has vested in such heir or next of kin. The administrator is liable to debts to the extent of the personal assets; and when there is any doubt whether there are 881. 882.

---

[1] 29 Car. II. c. 3; Rann v. Hughes, 4 Bro. P. C.

[2] 3 & 4 Wm. IV. c. 104.

[3] Steel v. Rooke, 1 Bos. & Pul. 307; Hall v. Tapper, 3 B. & Ad. 655.

[4] Hickey v. Hayter, 6 T. R. 384; Landon v. Ferguson, 3 Russ. 349.

[5] Bragner v. Langmead, 7 T. R. 20; Waghorn v. Langmead, 1 B. & P. 571.

Parallel Articles of the French Code.

any debts outstanding, he should not pay over the residue or the legacies, without taking security from the parties to refund, in case he should be called upon to pay any debts for which he has not retained; the parties would, however, be liable to refund although he took no security.

Section 4.

Of the Effects of a Partition and Warranty.

883. Coparceners, though they have an unity, have not an entirety of interest. They are properly entitled each to the whole of a distinct moiety or part.[1] Between themselves they have in judgment of law several freeholds, though the unity of possession continues; and if the possession be once severed by partition, they are tenants in severalty.[2]

884. There is, after partition, a warranty annexed to each part, so that if either be impleaded, she may vouch her sister; and if she loses by a title paramount, she may recover one moiety of her loss in value against the other sister, and the party so evicted may enter on her sister's moiety, and avoid the partition of an undivided moiety of what is left.[3]

The next of kin are entitled to equal shares in the residue, and must refund proportionably.

Section 5.

Of setting aside a Partition, and of Suit against an Administrator by Next of Kin for Share of Residue.

887. A deed of partition, like any other conveyance, would be void on account of illegal violence or fraud. The

---

[1] 2 Bl. Com. 188. [2] Ib. [3] Co. Lit. 173 b.

Parallel Articles of the French Code.

mere ground of unequal division is not in itself sufficient to vitiate the partition.[1]

The administrator is bound to divide the residue equally, and if he fail to do so, he may be compelled to account in chancery by any of the next of kin who are entitled, and to pay to such next of kin a full proportion; and he would be liable for making a fraudulent division.

TITLE II.

DONATIONS DURING LIFE, AND WILLS.

CHAPTER I.

General Regulations.

A man may dispose of his real and personal property for the interest which he has therein, by gratuitous title (*i. e.* without valuable consideration), in any manner he pleases, by gift during life, donatio causa mortis, or will,[2] provided it be not in fraud of creditors[3] or purchasers.[4] 893.

A gift is properly a voluntary conveyance, not founded on the consideration of money or blood:[5] but conveyance (of real estate) by gift (donum, donatio) is, technically and strictly speaking, confined to the creation of an estate tail, as feoffment is to that of an estate in fee.[6] A gift of chattels personal is the act of transferring the right and the possession of them, whereby one man, the donor, renounces, and another man, the donee, immediately acquires, all title and interest therein, and must be either by deed or instrument of gift, or by an actual delivery of the thing to the donee.[7] Conveyances of chattels 894.

---

[1] Jones v. Totty, 1 Sim. 136; Dean of Hereford v. Hullock, 6 Price.

[2] 2 Bl. Com. 106, c. 20, 30, 32, 514; Tr. of Eq. b. 1, c. 3, s. 2; 7 T. R. 475.

[3] Debitor non præsumitur donare.—Law Max.

[4] 13 Eliz. c. 5; 27 Eliz. c. 4.

[5] Shep. Pr. 38; Touch, 227.

[6] 2 Bl. Com. 316.

[7] Ib. 440; 2 B. & Ald. 551.

Parallel Articles of the French Civil.

real seldom bear the outward appearance of a gift, however freely bestowed, being usually expressed to be made for nominal consideration.[1] A voluntary conveyance or a gift is good, both at law and in equity, against the party himself.[2]

A gift can hardly in this sense be considered as a species of conveyance, for it is rather the motive than the mode of this assurance which gives it its denomination; for a feoffment or grant are equally gifts when they are gratuitous.

895. A will is an act by which the testator legally declares his intention, and disposes of the whole or part of his property, to take effect after his death, and which he is at liberty to revoke or alter. A will of personalty is called a testament; of realty, a devise. These are founded on totally different principles, and governed by different rules.[3]

896. By the law of England, entails and limitations over after the death of one person to a second or other person, within the rules against perpetuities, are allowed.[4] Thus an estate of inheritance may be a fee-conditional or a fee-tail, as well as a fee-simple;[5] or an estate may be given to one for life, with a limitation over, on the death of the first donee or devisee, to another person in remainder for life, or in fee-simple or fee-tail.[6]

897. There is no distinction in favour of relationship as to the right of entailing property.

899. As what, strictly speaking, are estates-tail are easily barred,[7] when it is wished to entail an estate in a family, it is limited to the parent for life only, with remainder to his first and other sons[8] in fee-tail.

900. Conditions impossible, or contrary to law, are void;

---

[1] 2 Bl. Com. 440.
[2] Tr. of Eq. b. 1, c. 5, s. 2; 7 T. R. 475.
[3] 2 Bl. Com. c. 23 and 32.
[4] Ib. 111; 13 Ed. I. c. 1.
[5] See ante, p. 339.
[6] 2 Bl. Com. c. 11. As to barring after tail, see 2 Bl. Com. 117; 3 & 4 Wm. IV. c. 74.
[7] 2 Bl. Com. 117; 3 & 4 Wm. IV. c. 74.
[8] Watk. Con. 105.

and if they be conditions subsequent, the property becomes absolutely vested in the feoffee. If, however, they are conditions precedent, the grant is void.[1]

Parallel Articles of the French Code.

CHAPTER II.

Of the Capacity to make or receive Donations during Life, or by Will.

In order to make a gift, or valid deed, or a will, the party making it must be of sane mind.[2] 901.

All persons invested with their full rights in possession of property, are capable both of conveying the extent of their interests and of purchasing or taking by deed or will, unless the law has laid them under any particular disabilities.[3] 902.

A minor, or person under twenty-one years of age, cannot make a will of realty:[4] and he may waive any purchase or conveyance he has made when he comes to full age, or if he does not actually agree to it, his heirs may waive it after him.[5] Although formerly an infant might make a will at fourteen years of age of his personal estate,[6] by the recent statute no will by any person under twenty-one is valid.[7] 903. 904.

A married woman cannot convey or make donation during life without the assistance of her husband;[8] and as to realty, with such assistance only in conformity with the regulations of the recent statute.[9] A married woman cannot make a will, though by her husband's licence she may make an appointment in the nature of a testament.[10] 905.

It is an ancient rule of law, that an estate of freehold cannot be created to commence in futuro, and therefore could not be given to an infant not conceived: but, 906.

[1] 2 Bl. Com. 156, 7. [2] Ib. 291, 496. [3] Ib. 290, 496.
[4] Cruise, tit. 38, c. 2, s. 7. [5] 2 Bl. Com. 292. [6] 1 ib. 463.
[7] 1 Vict. c. 26, s. 7. [8] 2 Bl. Com. 292.
[9] 3 & 4 Wm. IV. c. 74, s. 77 to 91. [10] 2 Bl. Com. 497, 8.

Parallel Articles of the French Code.

under the statute of uses, by the intervention of trustees, or by way of executory devise, it may.[1] But a legitimate child in ventre sa mere is considered as born for all beneficial purposes; and it may take by deed or will.[2] Where a posthumous child takes by purchase, he is not only entitled to the estate itself, but also to the intermediate profits;[3] though it is otherwise where he takes by descent.[4]

907. Where a transaction appears to have originated in the influence arising from the relation of guardian and ward, the Court of Chancery will set it aside, though all accounts have been settled, and such relation is at an end.[5]

908. Natural children may receive by gift, deed, or will whatever the parents or other persons please to grant them.[6]

909. A voluntary deed or will, executed even by an old and infirm man, in favour of a person who attended him, as a surgeon or medical man, will not be set aside, if it appear that the nature and effect of it were explained to him by his solicitor, and that no undue influence had been exercised over him.[7]

910. No devise or gift by will of lands to a corporation is good, except for charitable uses; and a corporation, either ecclesiastical or lay, must have a licence from the king to purchase or take by gift from any living grantor;[8] but they may take personal chattels.[9]

911. Lands and tenements are forfeited by alienation contrary to law, either in mortmain or to an alien;[10] and

1 2 Bl. Com. c. 9; and ante, p. 357.

2 1 Bl. Com. 130; Co. Lit. 36; 1 P. W. 329; 2 Atk. 117; 1 Ves. 85; Thellusson v. Woodford, 4 Ves. 322.

3 H. Chit. Desc. 296, 7, 8; 3 Atk. 203.

4 2 Wills. 526; Miller v. Turner, 1 Ves. 85; Harg. Co. Lit. 11 b, n.

5 Wright v. Proud, 13 Ves. 138.

6 1 Bl. Com. 458, 9; 1 Atk. 410; 1 Ves. & B. 423; 2 Bl. Com. 247, 506.

7 Pratt v. Barker, 1 Sim. 1; 4 Russ. 507.

8 1 Bl. Com. 479; 2 ib. 268.

9 2 Burn, Eccl. L. 509.

10 2 Bl. Com. 268.

Parallel Articles of the French Code.

those of an attainted person vested in the lord or the crown.[1]

An alien may be grantee in a deed or will, though he cannot hold real property, for on office found the king shall have it;[2] but a denizen or naturalized person may take real as well as personal property.[3] 912.

CHAPTER III.

Of what a Person may Dispose of by Gift or Will.

913 to 930. All persons, whether or not they leave any descendants or parents living, may devise by will, or make gratuitous gift, of the whole of their real estates, and the whole of their goods and chattels, to any person not particularly incapacitated by law, for the whole of their estate and interest therein, unless in fraud of creditors, &c.[4]

CHAPTER IV.

Of Gifts or Donations during Life.

SECTION 1.

Of the Form of Donation.

Interests in land can only be conveyed by instrument 931.
in writing, signed by the party granting;[5] and therefore

[1] See ante, p. 219. [2] Co. Lit. 2 b; 5 Co. 52; 1 Lev. 47.

[3] 1 Bl. Com. 374.

[4] 2 Bl. Com. c. 19, 23, 30, 32; 34 Hen. VIII. c. 5; 1 Vict. c. 26, s. 3. This power of absolutely disposing of the whole of a man's property (allowed by the modern English law) was permitted in the Anglo-Saxon period (Wright, Tenures, 172; Lit. s. 167; Co. Lit. 111 b, and no. 1); though it does not seem to have originated in Germany. On the introduction of the personal relation of the military tenure of feuds, the power of alienation was incompatible with the new system (ante, p. 70); the right however was continued as a custom in some districts, and finally revived for the whole kingdom.

[5] 29 Car. II. c. 3.

Parallel Articles of the French Code.

all instruments intended to be donations of real property, or chattels real, must be in writing, duly signed, and should be sealed and delivered;[1] and in the transfer of chattels personal, there must be either a deed, or instrument of gift, or an actual delivery[2] of the thing to the donee.[3]

932 to 942. The gift, grant, or conveyance of property, immediately on the execution of the deed, divests the legal estate therein out of the grantor, and puts it in the grantee, though in his absence and without his notice; for a gift imports a benefit, and the law will not suppose that a man can be unwilling to that which is for his advantage, and therefore presumes his assent and acceptance until the contrary appear.[4] But a party is not bound to accept,[5] but may by deed disclaim a gift under a deed or will.[6]

943. At law, unvested rights to future property, as an executory or contingent interest, cannot be assigned;[7] but even at law, a vested remainder, or a reversion, may be conveyed to another person;[8] and a contingent remainder may be barred by estoppel, and sometimes passed in equity;[9] and a possibility may be released or or barred by estoppel, or assigned in equity, if accompanied by an interest; and an agreement to settle lands in possibility would be enforced if they afterwards descended.[10] A possibility coupled with an interest is held to be more than a possibility, it is a present interest:[11]

---

[1] Donatio alia perfecta, alia incepta et non perfecta; ut si donatio lecta fuit et concessa, ac traditio nondum fuerit subsecuta.—Co. Lit. 56, 57.

[2] Donatio perficitur possessione accipentis.—Jenk. Cent. 109. Formerly livery of seizin (delivery of possession) would have been sufficient to convey lands as well as goods without deed, but now a deed is essential.—29 Car. II. c. 3.

[3] Irons v. Smallpiece, 1 Bar. & Ald. 501.

[4] Gorton's case, 2 Rol. Ab. 787; Thompson v. Leach, 2 Vent. 201; 3 Mod. 296; 2 Salk. 618; Shower, Parl. Ca. 130.

[5] Donator nunquam desinit possidere, antequam donatorius incipiat possidere.—Dyer, 281.

[6] 3 B. & A. 31.

[7] 10 Rep. 50 a; Co. Lit. 264 b; 3 Ves. 391; 7 T. R. 589.

[8] Wat. Conv. 167, 190.

[9] Ib. 168, 9.

[10] Wat. Conv. b. 2, c. 18; Helps v. Hereford, 2 B. & A. 242.

[11] Perry v. Phillips, 17 Ves. 173, 182.

Parallel Articles of the French Code.

but in equity there should be a valuable consideration to bind a contingent interest.[1]

There seems to be no impediment to a grant upon conditions, the execution of which depends on the will of the grantor only,[2] subject, as to the performance, to the distinction between conditions precedent and subsequent, already stated.[3] 944.

A condition to keep a man without damage against all men is void;[4] and a condition to pay his future debts would probably also be void for uncertainty. Where a deed of trust is made for payment of debts, it shall extend only to debts contracted at the time of making the deed.[5] 945.

A donor may, under the statute, reserve to himself any right or any portion (as a fixed sum to be raised) out of the thing itself granted; or he may reserve a power of revocation and new appointment over the whole, or any part of it. There is a distinction between estates actually limited with a power of revocation, and estates limited in default of the exercise of a preceding power of appointment: in the first case the estates are vested, subject to be revoked or defeated by the exercise of the power;[6] and in the second case, it also seems, that the estates limited in default of appointment are vested, subject to be divested.[7] And a distinction is made between a mere power and a power in the nature of a trust.[8] A mere power, not executed, would leave the property over which it is reserved to the original donor or claimant in default; but a power, in the nature of a trust, would be executed by a Court of Chancery in default of execution by the donor.[9] 946.

A donor of an estate may reserve to himself a rent, or a particular estate, for his own benefit, or that of a 949.

[1] 1 Ves. 409; 2 P. W. 132, 191. [2] Co. Lit. 206 and 209.
[3] Article 900. Modus legem dat donationi.—Co. Lit. 19 a.
[4] Vin. 5, 171. [5] Purefoy v. Purefoy, 1 Vern. 28.
[6] Sug. on Pow. 150. [7] Ib. 158. [8] Ib. 396.
[9] Harding v. Glyn, 1 Atk. 469; 5 Ves. J. 501; Birch v. Wade, 3 Ves. & Bea. 198.

Parallel Articles of the French Code.

third person, for life or otherwise;[1] and he may exercise a power of revocation and appointment (reserved to himself at the time of the grant), for his own or for another person's benefit.[2]

950. A tenant in remainder, or reversioner, has an action of waste, covenant, or other remedy against the tenant of the particular estate,[3] according to the original nature of the grant to him.

951. A donor may limit real or personal property to one for life or years, or determinable on failure of the donee's issue or other contingency, retaining the reversion after the termination of that estate to himself, or granting a remainder over to third persons.[4]

952. The limitation over, as well as the right of reversion, comes in prior to any alienation or incumbrance whatsoever,[5] by the tenant of the particular estate after its determination; and all conveyances and charges of the first tenant, are either void against the reversioner and remainder man, or else they cause the forfeiture of his estate.[6]

Section 2.

Of Exceptions to the Irrevocability of Donations.

953 Donations, &c., of lands executed under the old common law, by livery, &c., cannot, by indenture of defeasance afterwards made, be defeated; but at the time of the feoffment, &c., the same may be defeated by indentures of defeasance,[7] upon events specially mentioned.[8] Uses, under the statute originally declared, may be re-

---

[1] Co. Lit. 143 b, 213 a and b. [2] 2 Bl. Com. 335.

[3] As to moveable, see ante, 350, 2, 3.

[4] 2 Bl. Com. 110; Co. Lit. 20 a, n. 5.

[5] He who claims paramount a thing shall neither have benefit or hurt thereby.—Law Max.

[6] 2 Bl. Com. c. 11, and p. 274; Cruise, v. i. p. 121.

[7] Co. Lit. 236 b; 2 Bl. Com. 327. [8] 2 Bl. Com. 335.

Parallel Articles of the French Code.

voked at any future time, and new uses be declared of the land, provided the grantor reserved to himself such a power at the creation of the estate.[1] Grants may become voidable, or absolutely void, by the non-performance of the conditions originally annexed to them.[2]

In case of revocation, or if on non-performance of conditions, the feoffor or donor enter for condition broken, he is in of the former estate, which he had at the time of the estate made upon condition;[3] and such entry defeats all rights and incidents annexed to that estate, as dower, &c., and all the mesne incumbrances of the feoffee or donee.[4] The revocation abridges or defeats the previous uses and estates,[5] and has the same effect as if the new appointment had been contained in the original donation. 954.

The power of actual entry on condition, broken or otherwise, is now very much curtailed, and a mere entry will not avail much. A right of entry may, under the present system, be defined to be a right to bring an action of ejectment:[6] and while ejectment is pending, a Court of Chancery will often relieve against the forfeiture and penalties, on condition broken, where it can be done with justice to both parties; and they can be put in statu quo, or compensated by payment of money.[7] 956.

But a gift is not revoked by implication, from the circumstance of the subsequent birth of a child to the donor, or of both the marriage of the donor as well as the birth of the child. 960.

---

1 2 Bl. Com. c. 335, 340; Co. Lit, 257 a.

2 2 Bl. Com. c. 10, p. 281.

3 Co. Lit. 202.

4 1 Roll. Ab. 474.

5 Co. Lit. 272 a; Butl. n. vii. 1.

6 2 Wood, s. 170; Co. Lit. 257 b; Milner v. M'Lean, 2 Car. & Payne, 17.

7 Newl. Cont. 307; Bracebridge v. Buckley, 2 Price, 200, p. 206, note; Green v. Bridges, 1 Clark & F. 106.

Parallel Articles of the French Code.

CHAPTER V.

Of Wills.

SECTION I.

Of the General Rules respecting the Forms of Wills.

967. Every person hath full power and liberty to dispose by will, that is not under some special prohibition by law or custom,[1] of the whole or part of his real estate by devise to strangers, who are called devisees and not heirs, and of the whole or part of his personal estate in like manner, by general or specific bequest, appointing executors or not.[2]

968. A mutual or conjoint will is an instrument unknown to the testamentary law of England, and disallowed.[3]

969 to 979. The law has not prescribed any particular form in which a will must be made; so that any writing (duly signed and attested), by which the intention of a person appears to give or dispose of his property after his decease, though in the form of a deed, will be considered as a good will.[4] As to wills made before the 1st of January, 1838, a testament of chattels, written in the testator's own hand, though it has neither his name or seal to it, nor witnesses present at its publication, is good, provided sufficient proof can be had that it is his handwriting; and though written in another man's hand, and never signed by the testator, yet, if proved to be according to his instructions, and approved by him, it is a good will of personal estate;[5] but all devises of lands

---

1 2 Bl. Com. 496. 2 Ib. c. 23, 32.

3 Hobson v. Blackburn, 1 Add. Prer. 274.

4 6 Cruise, 8; 2 Bl. Com. 501; Hickson v. Witham, Finch R. 195; Green v. Proude, 1 Mod. 117; Clymer v. Littler, 1 Black. R. 345; Habergham v. Vincent, 2 Ves. J. 228.

5 2 Bl. Com. 501, 2; 1 Phil. Ecc. C. 12, 22, 58; 2 ib. 122, 173, 213.

Parallel Articles of the French Code.

and tenements must be not only in writing, but signed by the testator or some other person in his presence, and by his express direction; and be published as his will, and subscribed in his presence, by three or more credible witnesses.[1] And now by the recent statute,[2] no will made since the 1st of January, 1838 is valid unless it be in writing,[3] signed on some part or the end thereof by the testator, or by some other person on his behalf, in his presence and by his direction; and such signature shall be acknowledged by him, in the presence of two or more witnesses present at the same time; and such witnesses shall attest and subscribe the will in the presence of the testator, but no particular form of attestation is necessary.[4] Observing this enactment, as to signature and two witnesses, any testamentary paper, in whatever form, whether in the hand-writing of the testator, or of his professional agent or other person, is valid.

With respect to the persons capable of being witnesses 980.
to a will, the statute of frauds only mentions the word "credible;"[5] and therefore all who are capable of being witnesses in any other matter, may also be witnesses to a will.[6] There is no restriction or exception against any credible person as a witness, on account of relationship, connection, or any other direct interest. A devise or 975.
legacy to any person, necessary to the attestation of a will, so far only as concerns such person, or any person claiming under him, is void; and such person shall be admitted as a witness to the execution.[7] Formerly, where there were three other witnesses to a devise, the attestation of one who was a legatee or devisee not being essential

---

[1] 29 Car. II. c. 2; 2 Bl. Com. 376; 3 Atk. 161; Peate v. Ongley, 1 Com. R. 196; 4 Burn, Eccl. L. 119.

[2] 1 Vict. c. 26.

[3] Exceptions as to the wills of seamen and soldiers, s. 12.

[4] Ib. s. 9.

[5] The question as to the credibility of a witness relates to the time of the attestation.—Doe v. Kersey, 4 Burn, Eccl. L. 97; Brograve v. Winder, 2 Ves. J. 636.

[6] 6 Cruise, 78.

[7] 25 Geo. II. c. 6, s. 1; 2 Bl. Com. 377; 1 Vict. c. 26, s. 15.

Parallel Articles of the French Code.

to the validity of the will, was considered null, and not the legacy or devise to him; but the latter statute declares it utterly null and void.[1]

Section 2.

Of Particular Rules relating to certain Kinds of Wills.

981 to 999. A nuncupative will is, when the testator, without any writing, declares his will before a sufficient number of witnesses.[2] Soldiers in actual military service, but not sailors,[3] may make nuncupative wills, and dispose of their goods, wages, and other personal chattels, without those forms which the law in other cases requires.[4] Many salutary regulations are prescribed,[5] as to the making and probate of the wills of petty officers and seamen in the king's service, and non-commissioned officers of marines, serving on board a ship in the king's service.

No nuncupative will is good, where the estate bequeathed exceeds 30*l.*, unless proved by three witnesses present at the making of it, and specially required to bear witness thereto by the testator himself; and in his last sickness in his own dwelling-house, or where he has been previously resident, ten days at least, unless he be surprised with sickness on a journey or from home, and dies without returning home.[6]

1000. As to real property, the law of the place where the property is locally situated regulates the forms and solemnities necessary to the execution and attestation of a will.[7] But it is now a well settled principle in the English law, though the question was for a great length of time much

[1] 1 Vict. c. 26, s. 15.

[2] Swinb. pl. 1, s. 12, and pl. 1, 6; Godolph. pl. 1, c. 4, s. 6, 7.

[3] Sed quere, as to merchantmen.—Morell v. Morell, 1 Hag. 51.

[4] 2 Bl. Com. 417, 500.

[5] 55 Geo. III. c. 60, which repeals various previous acts.

[6] 2 Bl. Com. 500, 1; Phillips v. St. Clement Danes, 1 Abr. Eq. 404; Bennett v. Jackson, 2 Phill. 190; Leman v. Bonsall, 1 Add. 389.

[7] Coppin v. Coppin, 2 P. W. 291; 2 Fonb. Eq. 440.

Parallel Articles of the French Code.

agitated, that a will of personal property, regularly made according to the law, of the testator's domicil, is sufficient to pass such property in every other country in which it is situated.[1] Probate of a foreign will must be obtained in those dioceses, or in that province where the bona notabilia are, in the same manner as other wills.

Section 3.

Of the Kinds of Testamentary Dispositions.

Testamentary dispositions are either devises of real property which would otherwise go to the heir;[2] or bequests of personal property by general or specific legacy, or by the appointment of general residuary legatee. An executor is essential to the completion of a will, whose duty it is to take possession of the personal property, and to carry into execution the intentions of the testator as to such property.[3] 1002.

Sections 4 and 5.

General Residuary Legacy and Devise.

A testator may devise and bequeath all his real and personal property to one person, or only his real or personal estate. A residuary legacy is the testamentary disposition by which the testator gives to one or more persons the residuum or surplus of the personal property, after the payment of his debts, and particular legacies 1003 and 1010.

---

[1] Brodie v. Barry, 2 Ves. & Bea. 127; Bempde v. Johnstone, 3 Ves. 192; Stanley v. Barnes, 3 Hag. Eccl. R. 373.

[2] Appointment of an heir. The word heir hath not, in the common law, altogether the same signification that it hath in the civil law; for the civilians call him hæredem, qui ex testamento succedit in universum jus testatoris. But by the common law he is only heir which succeedeth by right of blood.—Co. Lit. 237. Deus solus hæredem facere potest, non homo.—Br. l. 2, f. 62 b; Co. Lit. 7 b, 82.

[3] 2 Bl. Com. c. 23, 22.

Parallel Articles of the French Code.

which he leaves at his death. If the testator gives the whole of his real and personal estate to one or more persons, without any provision for his debts, and without any legacies to other persons, this general devise and bequest is subject to the testator's debts, and in effect makes him residuary legatee.[1]

The testator may bequeath his property or the residue to several persons, to take equally between them; or he may give an aliquot part or share to any one person, which constitutes such parties residuary legatees.

1004. On the death of the testator, his real estate, properly devised by his will, vests in the devisee, and his personal estate in his executor, without the intervention or interference of his heir or next of kin;[2] but a legacy does not vest in the legatee until the executor assents to it.

1007. The executor must prove the will of the deceased, whether all written in his own hand or in that of another person, either in the common form, upon his own oath (that it is the true and whole will of the deceased), before the ordinary or his surrogate, or in cases of dispute per testes by two witnesses. After the will is so proved, it is deposited or insinuated in the registry of the ordinary, and a copy on parchment, under the seal of the ordinary, with certificate of its having been proved, is delivered to the executor, and called the probate.[3]

1009. The devisee of real estate is not chargeable with any of the debts of his testator, until all the personalty and all the assets by descent in the hands of the heir are exhausted.[4]

Section 6.

Of General Pecuniary and Specific Legacies.

1014. A general legacy is the gift of a sum of money to a particular person, by which an inchoate property is trans-

[1] 2 Bl. Com. c. 32. [2] Ib. 212. [3] Ib. 508. [4] Ante, tit. 1, c. 6, s. 3.

Parallel Articles of the French Code.

ferred to the legatee, which is not perfected without the assent of the executor.[1]

A specific legacy is the bequest of a particular chattel, as a piece of plate, a horse, &c., to a person, which, like a general pecuniary legacy, only gives an inchoate right, and the object cannot be taken possession of without the assent of the executor being first obtained.[2] Every devise of real property is specific.[3]

In case of a deficiency of assets, all the general legacies are abated proportionably, in order to pay the debts.[4] A specific legacy is not abated at all, unless there is not sufficient to pay the testator's debts without it;[5] but except in case of deficiency, both the debts and legacies come out of the residue, although they may reduce the share of the residuary legatee to nothing.

If a legacy is given, and no time of payment specified, 1015.
the legatee shall have interest on his legacy from the expiration of one year after the testator's death;[6] but if any time be fixed, it bears interest from such time.[7] If an 1016.
executor wilfully neglect or refuse to pay a legacy after a year, when there are sufficient assets, he would be liable to pay the costs of a suit instituted to compel him.

The executor is the person to whom the legatee must 1017.
apply to obtain payment or transfer of his legacy to him; but an action at law will not be against him for a general pecuniary legacy:[8] a suit in chancery or in the ecclesiastical court is the proper remedy. But after the executor assents to a specific bequest, an action to recover it will lie against him.[9]

The appurtenances to real property are part of their 1018.
principal, and passed by a devise of the principal object.[10]

1 2 Bl. Com. 512; Deeks v. Strutt, 5 T. R. 690.

2 2 Bl. Com. 512; 3 East, 120.

3 Broom v. Monck, 10 Ves. 605; Hill v. Cock, 1 Ves. & B. 175.

4 2 Bl. Com. 512, 3.

5 Ib. 513; Toller, 339.

6 13 Ves. 333, 4.

7 3 Atk. 101, 2; 4 Ves. 1.

8 Deeks v. Strutt, 5 T. R. 690.

9 3 East, 120; 3 Atk. 223.

10 Carden v. Tulke, Cro. Eliz. 89; 5 B. & Al. 407; 2 Sim. 150.

Parallel Articles of the French Code.

Real property acquired after the execution of a will, did not formerly pass under a general or other devise in it;[1] but under the recent act it does.[2] Embellishments
1019. and new erections being part of the thing devised, would pass by the devise of the thing, though formed after the execution of the will.

1020. If before or after the will the real property devised has been mortgaged, unless otherwise directed, the personal estate in the hands of the executor is liable, if sufficient, after discharging the other debts, to the payment of the mortgage money for the benefit of the devisee.[3] The devisee can only take it, subject to all life or other estates vested before he comes into possession by the testator's death.

1021. If the testator bequeath any specific object to which he has no right,[4] but which belongs to some other person, the bequest is a mere nullity, and the legatee has no claim against the testator's estate for any compensation in lieu.[5]

1022. It rests with the executor to set out and give possession of a specific chattel; and he would have to determine an undetermined thing given by will, as a sheep out of a flock, unless the testator directed that the legatee or residuary legatee should have the choosing.

1023. A legacy to a creditor, equal to or greater than the amount of his debt, will be viewed as a satisfaction of his demand; though if it be less, or the will contain express directions for payment of debts, or if such appears to have been the intention of the testator, it will not be deemed in satisfaction of the fore-existing debt,[6] and in general not in satisfaction of the wages of a servant.[7]

---

[1] 2 Ves. J. 427. [2] 1 Vict. c. 26, s. 3. [3] 2 Cruise, 164, 5.

[4] Nemo plus juris ad alium transferre potest, quam ipse habet.—4 Rep. 24 b.

[5] Hinton v. Pinke, 1 P. W. 539.

[6] Fowler v. Fowler, 3 P. W. 353; Reech v. Hennigal, 1 Ves. 126; Atkinson v. Welb. 2 Vern. 478; Eastwood v. Vinke, 2 P. W. 616; Jeffs v. Wood, 2 P. W. 132.

[7] Chan. Ca. 1 P. W. 408; 10 Mod. 399.

Parallel Articles of the French Code.

Section 7.

Of the Appointment of an Executor and Devisees in Trust.

The appointment of one or more executors is necessary to the making of a complete will of personalty, and it may be performed by express words, or such as strongly imply the same;[1] and the testator may appoint such executors devisees in trust of his real estate. If the testator has not appointed an executor, or the executors named refuse to act, administration of the personalty cum testamento annexo is granted by the ordinary.[2] 1025.

The testator may appoint one or more executors, either over his whole property or over different kinds, as, one executor in respect of his trade, another in respect of the rest of his personalty, &c.; or he may so divide the duty where his property is in different countries.[3] In general, neither the legacies nor the residue ought to be paid over till a year after the death, and until then, the legatees cannot compel payment of their legacies, even though they offer security; and after the year the executor is not obliged to pay them without an indemnity, if there be reason to apprehend that there are debts or claims outstanding.[4] 1026. 1027.

All persons are capable of being executor that are capable of making wills, and many others besides; as femme coverts and infants, nay, even infants unborn, or in ventre sa mere, may be made executors: but no infant can act as such until the age of seventeen years, till which, administration is granted to some other durante minore ætate.[5] And a married woman cannot act as executor without her husband's consent or concurrence.[6] 1028. 1029. 1030.

---

[1] 2 Bl. Com. 503. [2] Ib. 503, 4. [3] Toller, 39.

[4] Angerstein v. Martin, 1 Turner & Russ. 241; Davis v. Blackwell, 9 Bing. 5.

[5] 2 Bl. Com. 503.

[6] 3 Bac. Ab. 9; Off. Ex. 203; Toller, 34; sed vide 1 Fonbl. 89.

Parallel Articles of the French Code.

1031. The executor is bound to make an inventory of all the goods and chattels, whether in possession or action, of the deceased, which he is to deliver in to the ordinary upon oath, if thereunto lawfully required;[1] but it is not usual to exhibit an inventory to the spiritual court, except upon citation.[2] It is the duty of an executor to reduce the personal assets, not specifically bequeathed, into money as speedily as possible, unless otherwise directed.[3] An executor ought at all times to be ready to account; but there is not any satisfactory way of calling an executor to account but by bill in chancery, which ought not to be filed without formal demand of an account, and refusal or unreasonable delay.[4]

1032. The powers and interest vested in the executor by the will of the deceased, may be continued by the will of the same executor, so that the executor of A's executor is to all intents and purposes the executor of A himself,[5] and so on ad infinitum; but the administrator of an executor is not the representative of the testator.

1033. Probate to one of several as executors operates, if granted to all, so as to enable each to sue until the other has formally renounced.[6] An executor, by merely proving a will, does not render himself liable to the consequences of a breach of faith by his co-executors:[7] but if he has concurred or assisted in getting possession of property, which was afterwards misapplied, he would in most cases be responsible.[8] It seems, that in general the liability of one executor for the conduct of the others depends on his acting.[9]

1034. The executor may pay before all other debts the funeral charges, and the expense of proving the will, and the like.[10] And he is allowed out of the estate all fair and

---

1 2 Bl. Com. 510. 2 Toller, 45, 247; 2 Williams, 642. 3 Toller, 247.
4 Pearce v. Green, 1 Jac. & W. 135; In mre Burke, 1 Ball. & B. 75.
5 2 Bl. Com. 503. 6 Wallens v. Pleil, 1 Mood. & M. 561.
7 2 Ves. J. 678; 4 Ves. 596; 11 Ves. 333; 1 Jac. R. 198.
8 1 P. W. 243; 2 Bro. C. C. 114; 1 Meric. 712.
9 3 Swanst. 64. 10 2 Bl. Com. 511.

reasonable expenses paid by him in the execution of his office;[1] but he is not allowed any remuneration for time or trouble.[2]

Parallel Articles of the French Code.

Section 8.

Of the Revocation of Wills.

Wills may be expressly revoked, wholly or in part, by a subsequent will, (which must be duly attested), by express declaration in writing; and by burning and cancelling: or they may be impliedly revoked by making another of a later date incompatible with the former; by subsequent marriage;[3] and formerly, a will of personalty might have been revoked by any act of the testators that showed that intention;[4] but now a will is not revoked by any presumption of intention on the ground of an alteration of circumstances.[5] 1036.

Where a second will does not expressly revoke all former wills, and does not make any disposition inconsistent with a former will, both are good together.[6] 1036.

Formerly, any alteration by the act of the devisor of the nature of the estate in lands devised, after the publication of his will, operated as an implied revocation.[7] An actual sale or disposition of the estate by the devisor after he had made his will, implied a revocation of the gift.[8] Even an agreement or contract to convey would have had that operation in equity, though not in law;[9] and an intended alteration of the estate, which failed of taking effect for want of some formality in the instrument, 1038.

[1] Wilkinson v. Wilkinson, 2 Sim. & Stu. 237; Henderson v. M'Iver, 3 Mad. 275; Macknamara v. Jones, Dick. 587.

[2] Robinson v. Pett, 3 P. W. 249.

[3] 2 Bl. Com. 502; Toller, 13, 14, 15; 6 Cruise, 92; 1 Vic. c. 26, s. 18, 20.

[4] Hyde v. Hyde, 1 Ab. Eq. 409.

[5] 1 Vict. c. 26, s. 19.

[6] Coward v. Marshall, Cro. Eliz. 721; Goodright v. Harwood, 7 Bro. P. Ca. 489.

[7] 6 Cruise, 118.

[8] 1 Roll. Ab. 615, 616; Sparrow v. Hardcastle, Ambl. 24; 3 Atk. 799; Arnold v. Arnold, 1 Bro. R. 401.

[9] Rider v. Wager, 2 P. W. 328; Cotten v. Layer, 2 P. W. 622; Vawson v. Jeffrey, 6 Ves. 519.

Parallel Articles of the French Code.

was held to be a revocation.[1] A mere alteration of the quality of the estate, without any intention of varying the quantity of the interest or the disposing power of the owner, would not operate as a revocation.[2]

1039. If either the devisee of real property or the legatee of personalty dies before the testator, the devise is void, and the legacy lapses, unless otherwise provided,[3] or it come within the saving of the new act.[4]

1040. If a devise or legacy be made to take effect on the happening of any contingency, if such contingency does not happen, or if the person in whose favour such devise or legacy were made, dies[5] before the happening of such contingency, it is lapsed or void.[6] When construing the devise or bequest to be contingent defeats a declared object of the testator, such construction will, if possible, be avoided.[7]

1041. Where it is evidently the intention of the testator, that the estate shall be vested now, though the possession thereof is suspended until the happening of a contingency, the death of the party in whose favour the devise or bequest is made, does not avoid or lapse it.[8]

1042. A bequest of a certain amount of stock, if the testator had it at the time, is specific: and any act destroying it proves an intention to revoke; if a ring, or picture, or other specific object bequeathed, cannot be found, that cannot be rectified.[9]

1043. A testamentary disposition of realty reverts to the heir of the donor, when the devisee disclaims or renounces it,[10] or where the party to take is too uncertain. The lands of of a traitor or felon are forfeited;[11] and of an alien vest in the king on office found.

[1] 1 Roll. Ab. 615; 3 Atk. 73, 803; Shove v. Pincke, 5 T. R. 124.

[2] 1 Roll. Ab. 616. pl. 3; 3 Atk. 749; Harmood v. Oglander, 6 Ves. 199; Roe v. Griffit, 4 Burr. 1952.

[3] Goodright v. Wright, 1 P. W. 397; 1 Stra. 25; Busby v. Greenslate, 1 Str. 445; Hodgson v. Ambrose, 1 Doug. 337; 2 Bl. Com. 513; 17 Ves. 347; 4 Ves. 418.

[4] 1 Vict. c. 26.

[5] See, however, the new Act, 1 Vict. 26, s. 32, 33.

[6] 2 Bl. Com. 168, 9; 513; Fearne, Cont. Rem.

[7] Bradford v. Foley, 1 Dougl. 63.

[8] 2 Bl. Com. 168, 513.

[9] Selwood v. Mildmay, 3 Ves. 310; Baugh v. Read, 1 Ves. J. 260.

[10] Co. Lit. 111 a; Townson v. Tickell, 2 B. & A. 31; Nicholson v. Wordsworth, 2 Swanst. 365; Crew v. Dicken 4 Ves. 97.

[11] Ante, p. 219.

Parallel Articles of the French Code.

In case of one of several tenants in common, to whom realty is devised, dying in the lifetime of the testator, his share goes to the heir;[1] and if personalty, for distri-
bution;[2] but if the devise be to two or more as joint 1044.
tenants, the whole will go to him who survives the tes- 1045.
tator.[3] And a similar result would follow, if the persons to whom an estate is given as tenant in common are described in general terms, and as constituting a class.[4]

If an estate be devised upon condition, and the con 1046.
dition be broken, the estate is forfeited, and reverts to the donor or his heir; though now, if there be a general devise, it goes to the general devisee.[5]

CHAPTER VI.

Of the Rule respecting Perpetuities.

Any person[6] may limit property to any number of per- 1048.
sons in succession, who are living at the time of the limi 1049.
tation, whether they are his descendants, relatives, or 1050.
strangers in blood; and for twenty-one years, (and in case of a posthumous child nine months longer,) after the death of the last of such persons in being at the time of the limitation;[7] and such limitation may be for the benefit of all of the children of a particular person, or any one or more of them, giving a preference to age, eldest or younger children, or sex, male or female.[8]

And under a settlement it would depend entirely on the terms of the limitation who would take, on the death of one of the tenants for life, leaving issue. In

---

[1] Goodright v. Opie, 8 Mod. 123; Wright v. Horne, 8 Mod. 224.

[2] Bagwell v. Dry, 1 P. W. 700; Page v. Page, 2 P. W. 489; Owen v. Owen, 1 Atk. 494; Peat v. Chapman, 1 Ves. 542.

[3] 3 B. & P. 22.

Doe v. Sheffield, 13 East, 526; Doe v. Over. 1 Tan. 26.

[5] 1 Vict. c. 26, s. 25.

[6] See Ante, par. art. 913 & 896.

[7] Fearne, Cont. Rem. 429, 435; 2 Ves. & B. 61; 5 Taunt. 393; 5 Barn. & Ald. 801; 4 Ves. 337.

[8] Voluntas donatoris secundum formam in charta doni sui manifeste expressam de cætero observetur: yet that will and intention must agree with the rule of law.—Co. Lit. 20, 21.

Parallel Articles of the French Civil.

the case of an estate tail the right of representation goes ad infinitum.[1]

1051. 1052. If a person gives an estate to one unconditionally, and afterwards offers another estate to such person, on condition that he shall settle the first on strict settlement, or hold it for his life only, the donee is not bound to accept the second estate; but if he does, he would be liable to perform the condition.

1053. The determination of the particular or prior estate by forfeiture or otherwise, before the estate can be vested in the remainder-man, defeats the remainder, unless there be trustees, or other provision, to preserve contingent remainders.[2]

Voluntary or fraudulent conveyances to the prejudice of creditors, are void.

1054. The wives of tenants for life, have no claim for dower on the remainder or reversion.[3]

1055. Trustees may be appointed to preserve the limitations, and to execute the intentions of the donor or testator. Minors in remainder have the same claim, the same remedies, against the tenants for life as other persons.

1058. After the death of the donor in tail, or settlor, the mode of proceeding, the respective rights of the parties, and the mode of enjoying and preserving the property in remainder, must depend upon the nature of the estate, (real or personal, general or specific), and upon the terms of the deed or will limiting the property. In default of dispositions and limitations over, in case of any of the appointments or limitations becoming incapable of taking effect, the property reverts to the donor's or testator's general estate: and the realty descends to the heir according to the common law, and the personalty is distributed among the next of kin. The estates so limited vest like any other, subject to an inventory of personalty by the executor of a will, before giving possession to a tenant for life;[4] and the executor would be a trustee for the

[1] See Ante, par. art. 740.

[2] 2 Bl. Com. 166, 7, 8.

[3] Wat. Conv. 84, 5.

[4] Ante, par. art. 589, 600.

Parallel Articles of the French Code.

remainder-man, and bound properly to secure the property.

The tenant for life may either be bound to sell moveables or not, or may use them according to the terms of the limitations;[1] and if he sells, the produce must be invested or employed according to the dispositions of the will or deed. 1062 to 1065.

The trustees are liable personally for the property committed to their charge, when they do not take the same care of it as they do of their own; and for all waste or misemployment of it.[2] 1073.

CHAPTER VII.

Of Divisions of Property by a Parent.

The English law places no restriction whatever on the mode and quantities in which a parent, or other person, directs the division and distribution of his property among his children, or among strangers, within the rules against perpetuities,[3] whether by deed or will. 1075 to 1080.

CHAPTER VIII.

Of Donations by Marriage Contracts, and the Limitations therein.

Marriage is as much a valuable consideration as money, which the law esteems an equivalent given for grant of property.[4] Gifts or grants in consideration of marriage to be had, but not already had, are therefore subject to the same general rules as other contracts made for valu- 1081.

---

[1] See Ante, par. art. 589, 600, 602.

[2] 1 Sand. 367, 8, 9.

[3] Ante, par. art. 1048.

[4] 2 Bl. Com. 297.

Parallel Articles of the French Code.

able considerations. A marriage contract may be made for the benefit of the children to be born, without any restrictions except as to perpetuities.[1]

1082. Any person may bind himself by contract, on a valuable consideration, to bequeath the whole of the residue of the estate of which he dies possessed for a specific purpose, as by marriage contract;[2] or he may settle a particular estate (or portion, or inventoried articles at the time), which becomes then vested, and excludes inter-
1083. mediate incumbrances; it would be irrevocable, and when once settled prevent alienation, except according to the terms of the settlement.

1084. But if a person is indebted to the extent of insolvency at the time of making a voluntary conveyance, it will be held fraudulent and void with respect to creditors;[3] and though a settlement made before marriage is a valuable consideration, yet if made of future property, with a view to avoid the payment of future debts, it would be void.[4]

1088. If after a marriage settlement is made no marriage follows, the donee would be held to be seized or possessed for the use of the donor.

1089. On failure of objects of limitation (as the donee and all issue), whether during the life of the donor or not, the estate reverts to the donor or his heirs.

1090. All donations in frank-marriage and advancement must be brought into account, before the parties who have received them can take any further share in the estate of the deceased intestate donor.[5]

---

[1] Ante, par. art. 1048.

[2] Bosvil v. Brander, 1 P.W. 460; Lord Warrington v. Langham, Pre. Ch. 89, cited in Collins v. Plummer, 1 P. W. 107; 2 Vern. 635; Gilb. C. R. 252; Perry v. Perry, 2 Vern. 505.; Eastwood v. Vincke, 2 P.W. 613; Broughton v. Errington, 7 Bro. P. C. 12; Haynes v. Micoe, 1 Bro. C. C. 129.

[3] Under 19 Eliz. c. 5, and 6 Geo. IV. c. 16.

[4] Stileman v. Ashdown, 2 Atk. 481; Fitzer v. Fitzer, ib. 511. [5] See Ante, p. 394.

Parallel Articles of the French Code.

CHAPTER IX.

Of Donations between the married Person by the Contract of Marriage.

In general, all compacts made between husband and wife when single, are rendered void by intermarriage;[1] but contracts and gifts by the intervention of trustees between man and woman before marriage, settlements before marriage, and jointures[2] are governed by the same rules as other contracts for valuable considerations. A covenant to leave a wife so much after decease is not destroyed by after marriage.[3] 1091.

We have seen the rights the husband acquires in the wife's property. After marriage, the husband cannot, by any conveyance at common law, give an estate to his wife;[4] but he may by the intervention of trustees.[5] And in equity, gifts between them are supported.[6] 1092. 1096. 1097.

Donations to trustees by either of the married parties, must depend upon the terms of the limitation as to their effect on the death of one or both of the married parties. The husband may by will leave all his estates, real and personal, to his wife. 1093.

An infant under twenty-one can make no deed which is not afterwards voidable,[7] and therefore cannot make a valid settlement. 1095.

On a second marriage, the whole of the parties' property, not previously tied up, may be settled on the newly married party, or the children of such party, to the prejudice of children by the first marriage. 1098.

---

[1] 1 Bl. Com. 442; Cro. Car. 551; 1 Ld. Raymond, 515.

[2] 2 Bl. Com. p. 137, 8.

[3] Hut. 17; Hob. 216; 2 Cro. 571; Cro. Car. 376; 1 Ch. Ca. 21; 1 Salk. 326; 5 T. R. 381.

[4] 1 Bl. Com. 442; Co. Lit. 112 a.

[5] Co. Lit. 30.

[6] 1 Atk. 270; 2 Ves. 666; 1 Fonb. Eq. 103; 3 P. W. 334.

[7] 1 Bl. Com. 466.

Parallel Articles of the French Code.

TITLE III.

OF CONTRACTS,[1] OR CONVENTIONAL OBLIGATIONS[2] IN GENERAL.

CHAPTER I.

Preliminary Regulations.

1101. A contract is an agreement[3] entered into by two or more persons, inducing by its own nature[4] a legal obligation,[5] whereby one party becomes bound to another to give a thing, or to perform or abstain from doing a particular act;[6] and the agreement of the parties, as far as it extends, supplies the rule of action (the law) of the transaction.[7]

Contracts, by the law of England, are distinguished into expressed and implied, written and verbal, simple, special, and of record, executed or executory.[8] The most important of these distinctions arises out of the degree of solemnity and consideration with which the contracts are

[1] The law of contracts has received, as compared with the law of real property, but little cultivation in England, until recent times; but it has since made rapid progress.—See ante, p. 136, 7, 8; 154, 5.

[2] The word obligation, in our law, usually means a penal bond.

[3] An agreement (conventio, in the Latin of the middle ages called agreamentum) has been defined to be a joining together of two or more minds in anything done or to be done.—Tomlin. Aggregatio mentium in re aliqua facta vel facienda.—Plow. C. 5 a. It is an engagement formed by the consent to two or more persons, who establish between them a rule or law for binding themselves to each other. Conventio est pactio duorum pluriumve in idem placitum consensus.—Ulpian. The word agreement is sometimes used in a loose incorrect sense, as synonymous to promise or undertaking: in its more proper sense, it signifies a mutual contract, on consideration, between two or more parties. Pactum est duorum consensus atque conventio: pollicitatio vero offerentis solius promissum.

[4] Contractus est quasi actus contra actum.—Co. Lit. 47 b; see ante, p. 117.

[5] Viner, Abr. Contract.

[6] 2 Bl. Com. 442; Powell, Newland, Comyn, Chitty, respectively on Contracts; Fonb. Equi.

[7] Modus et conventio vincunt legem.—Law Max.; Glanv.; Co. Lit. 19 a; 2 Rep. 73. Pacto aliquid licitum est quod sine pacto non admittitur.—Co. Lit. 166.

[8] Selw. N. P. Assump.

Parallel Articles of the French Code.

entered into, namely, that which divides them into simple contracts, specialty contracts, and contracts of record. Simple contracts are those not under seal; and they must be, in cases where the statute of frauds requires it, or to be negociable, written; otherwise they may be verbal. They are of as infinite variety as the transactions of life. Agreements to sell bills of exchange, promissory-notes, checks on bankers, policies of insurance, awards, contracts of loans, contracts to marry or perform works, contracts expressed or implied of bailees or agents, factors, wharfingers, carriers, agents, legal, general, and special, are among the most common sorts. All contracts relating to interests in land, and guarantees for third persons, must be written and signed by the party charged therewith. If agreements are merely written, and not specialties, they are called parol agreements.[1]

Contracts by specialty (specialties or special contracts) are deeds or other instruments under seal; and are legally regarded as having been entered into with so much consideration and solemnity, that they preclude the parties from making any averments contrary to them.[2] They are principally bonds in a penalty, conditioned to pay money, or give specific objects, or perform covenants, or do other acts: deeds relating to land (deeds of mortgages, leases, or conveyances,) usually containing many covenants and agreements; annuity deeds relating to personalty; charter parties; marine insurance policies; relating to lands, chattels, and persons; policies of insurance against fire, or on lives. Every contract that may be entered into by agreement not under seal, may, if the party think fit, be by deed under seal; and so have the properties and privileges of specialties.

Contracts of record are such as are acknowledged or recovered before a court, judge, or other official person; and they are treated as if originating with higher

[1] Rann v. Hughes, 7 T. R. 351 n.

[2] Nemo contra factum suum venire potest.—2 Inst. 66.

Parallel Articles of the French Code.

solemnity,[1] and are of still more conclusive force than deeds under seal:[2] they are chiefly judgments and recognizances.

Whether a contract be express or implied is to be proved by evidence of a promise, express or implied, written or not.[3] An express promise is where the terms of the agreement are distinctly stated or implied by intendment, and not raised from a mere casual speaking or discourse.[4] Implied promises are such as are not actually made by the parties, but are implied by the law.[5]

A contract may be executed where the possession and right are transferred together, which differs nothing from a grant. A contract may be executory where the right only vests, and the property is not in possession, but in action.[6]

Contracts under seal, are either deeds of conveyance or deeds of covenant.[7] A covenant is the agreement or consent of two or more persons by deed, in writing, sealed and delivered, whereby one of the parties doth promise to the other that something is done already, or shall be done afterwards.[8] Covenants are also clauses of agreements in a deed or contract,[9] whereby either party may stipulate for the truth of certain facts, or bind himself to perform or give something to the other.[10] A great variety of agreements of this kind have been introduced into modern deeds.[11]

---

[1] Quod per recordum probatum non debet esse negatum. Quod constat Curiæ opere testium non indiget.—2 Inst. 662. Quæ in Curia Regis acta sunt rite agi præsumuntur.—3 Buls. 43. Confessus in judicio pro judicato habetur, et quodammodo sua sententia damnatur.—11 Rep. 30. Confessio facta in judicio, omni probatione major est.—Law Max.; Jenk. Cent. 102.

[2] Nemo potest contra recordum verificare per patriam.—2 Inst. 380.

[3] Seward v. Baker, 1 T. R. 616.

[4] Roll. Ab. 6; Dutton v. Poole, 2 Lev. 211; Anon. 1 Lev. 88.

[5] 3 Bl. Com. 445; Bul. N. P. 147; Toussaint v. Martinnant, 2 T. R. 100; Lamb v. Bunce, 4 M. & S. 275.

[6] 2 Bl. Com. 443.

[7] Walk. Prin. of Conv.

[8] Shep. Touch. 160.

[9] In a strict sense covenants are only such as are in deeds under seal.

[10] 2 Bl. Com. 303, 4.

[11] Cru. Dig. tit. 32, c. 25, s. 1.

Parallel Articles of the French Code.

A covenant is distinguished from a conveyance, in that a covenant of itself neither passes an estate or raises an use.[1] It differs from the case where an agreement refers to a thing which is not to be done by a person of any, but to a thing to be executed in itself.[2] Where an agreement terminates in itself, it is not properly a covenant, but a defeasance.[3] Covenants are of two kinds: 1. Express; 2. Implied; *i. e.* covenants in law.[4] An express covenant, or covenant in deed, is an agreement entered into expressly by deed between the parties.[5] An implied covenant, or covenant in law, is an agreement raised by implication of law, from certain expressions used in the deed.[6]

There are three kinds of covenants: 1st, Such are called mutual and independent, where it is no excuse to 1102.
the one party to allege a breach of the covenant to be 1103.
performed on the part of the other. 2nd, There are covenants which are conditions, and dependant, in which the performance of one depends on the prior performance of another. 3dly, There is also a third sort of covenants, which are mutual conditions to be performed at the same time. The dependence or independence is to be collected from the evident sense and meaning of the parties; and that, however transposed in the deeds, their precedency must depend on the order of time in which the transaction requires the performance.[7]

Covenants are real or personal: real covenants are such as have for their object something connected with land or other real property; a personal covenant is one which does not affect the land demised, but is merely collateral to it.[8] Real either runs with the land or not,[9]

[1] Wigson v. Garrett, 2 Lev. 149; 1 Vent. 278; Rhodes v. Bullard, 7 East, 116; 3 Smith, 173. [2] Plow. 138. [3] Cru. tit. 32, c. 25, s. 2. [4] Shep. Touch. 160.

[5] Selw. N. P.; Shep. Touch. 160; Moor, 135; 1 Roll. Ab. 518 c, p. 2, 3, 5.

[6] Selw. N. P.; Shep. Touch. 160; Heddon v. Senate, 13 East, 63.

[7] Co. Lit. 203 b; Jones v. Barkley, 2 Doug. 689, and Kingston v. Preston, there cited; Anon., Lofft, 194; Lock v. Wright, 8 Mod. 40, 1 Stra. 569.

[8] Spencer's ca. 5 Co. 16.

[9] Wat. Com. 256 n. Rule in Spencer's ca. 5 Co. 16 a.

Parallel Articles of the French Code.

according to whether there is privity of estate or only a privity of contract. Covenants as to personalty are not binding on the assignee.[1]

1102. It is a general rule, that to constitute a complete valid contract, not under seal, both parties should be reciprocally bound.[2] But where a formal signature is required by the statute against frauds,[3] the party who has not signed may sue, both at law and in equity, the one who has signed;[4] but it seems doubtful whether the party, who has signed, is not at liberty to recede until the other party, who has not signed, has done some act to bind himself,[5] as commencing a suit.[6]

1103. But a contract under seal or a deed may be by
1104. indenture, inter partes, or by deed poll, de una partes.[7]

By deed-poll one party only may be bound without the other:[8] but as to contracts not under seal, or of record, the law of England simply divides them into nude agreements,[9] or those made without any reciprocal benefit, or upon an illegal consideration; and valid agreements, which are made either upon a good consideration, as natural love and affection (and binding on the donor, but not on creditors), or upon a valuable consideration, as money, marriage.[10] And an agreement, though morally binding, cannot be considered as a legal contract, unless there is a remedy furnished by the law to enforce it,[11] either at law or in equity. Hence the common lawyer, like

---

1 Selw. N. P. 484.

2 Cook v. Oxley, 3 T. R. 653; Payne v. Cave, 3 T. R. 148; M'Iver v. Richardson, 1 M. & S. 557; 2 Moore v. P. 86; 5 Bing. 34.

3 29 Car. II. c. 3.

4 Egerton v. Mathews, 6 East, 307; Wain v. Walters, 5 East; Allen v. Bennett, 3 Taunt. 169; 5 Taunt. 788; Hatton v. Gray, 2 Cha. Ca. 164; Seton v. Slade, 7 Ves. J. 265; Palmer v. Scott, 1 Russ. & M. 391; 2 Jac. & W. 426; Flight v. Bolland, 4 Russ. 301.

5 Remedies ought to be reciprocal.—Law Max.

6 See Lord Redesdale's Observations, Flight v. Bolland, 4 Russ. 301; 2 Jac. & W. 426.

7 Lit. 370, 2, and Coke's Com.

8 Lit. 370; Co. Lit. 55; Plow. 134, 121.

9 Nudum pactum est ubi nulla subest causa præter conventionem sed ubi subest causa fil obligatio et parit actionem.—Plow. 309.

10 2 Bl. Com. 296, 443.

11 See ante, p. 119, 124, 5.

Parallel Articles of the French Code.

the Roman, has been accustomed rather to consider agreements in their relation to the forms of action and pleading, than in their more abstract nature and qualities; but in equity they have been considered in a less classified view.

The same rules govern all valid agreements, except that those for a good, but not valuable, consideration, may be set aside in favour of creditors or bonâ fide purchasers.[1] 1107.

CHAPTER II.

Things Essential to the Validity of Agreements.

In every agreement by simple contract, there are four things essential[2] to its validity: 1108.

The consent of the parties, given with an intention of contracting.[3]

Their capacity to contract and be contracted with.

A certain object or subject matter forming the matter of the contract.

A lawful consideration or cause of obligation.

---

[1] 2 Bl. Com. 296.

[2] These are called "essential" (Pothier, Obligations, pt. 1, c. 1); other conditions are "of the nature" of a contract, and others only "accidental." Without the first no contract (civil, commercial, or other) can subsist (ib. art. 1). Things which are only of the nature of the contract form part of it without being particularly expressed, and may be excluded by the express agreement of the parties (c. 1, s. 1, art. 1; instance Warranty, &c.) Things accidental to a contract are only included in it by express agreement (c. 1, s. 1, art. 1); these several distinctions are illustrated, in a note of Mr. Evans' to his translation of Pothier, by the case of a lease. It is *essential* to a lease that the reversion should be in the lessor. This induces several *consequences*, as a right of action founded upon the privity of estate, a power to distrain, &c. If a person who makes a contract in the form of a lease does not retain a reversion, the essential character of a lease does not exist, and the *incidental consequences* do not attach; but still there is a valid contract of a different kind. It is of the nature of a lease for lives or years that it should be impeachable for waste; but the *contrary is specially every day* provided. A covenant that a tenant shall use a particular course of husbandry is *accidental*. Material question on things of the nature of, and those accidental to a contract, on 8 Anne, c. 9; R. v. Leighton, 4 T. R. 732.

[3] Animo contrahendæ obligationis.

Parallel Articles of the French Code.

Section 1.

Of Consent.

1109. The first essential of a contract is consent;[1] for an agreement is the consent of two or more persons, concerning the giving property or doing an act.[2] It may be said, there is no true consent when a party lies under mistake[3] as to any important matter. The law makes a distinction between mistake or ignorance of the law, and ignorance or mistake of facts.[4] Ignorance of law or of the parties' rights, is, in general, no excuse for the non-performance of a contract;[5] though sometimes in equity it is, as to the latter, otherwise.[6] Where there has been any wilful misrepresentation, or even concealment[7] of a material fact, the party to an agreement thus led into error may refuse to perform it, and equity will not compel him.[8] All contracts extorted by force, or entered into by persons under duress of illegal imprisonment, or duress per minas, are void.[9] It is an established maxim, that fraud will always avoid a contract.[10] An important alteration in a contract is an excuse for not performing the agreement.[11]

1110. Mistake, arising from a wilful, fraudulent mistake, as to

[1] Consentire est in unam sententiam concurrere. Consensus est voluntas multorum, ad quos res pertinet, simul juncta.—Dav. 48.

[2] 1 Bac. Ab. tit. Agr.

[3] See as to where mistake will be presumed, Lawrenson v. Butler, 1 Sho. & Lef. 13.

[4] 1 Rep. 177. Ignorantia facti excusat. Ignorantia juris non excusat. Ignorance of one's rights not to prejudice.—Law Max.

[5] Belbie v. Lumley, 2 East, 470; sed vide in Equity, Gibbons v. Caunt. 4 Ves. 849.

[6] Evans v. Llewellyn, 2 Bro. C. C. 150; 1 Cox, 333; Turner v. Harvey, Jac. 172; Stilwell v. Watkins, Jac. 282; Mason v. Armitage, 13 Ves. 25; Ramsden v. Hylton, 2 Ves. 304; Cole v. Green, 1 Ves. 306.

[7] Suggestio falsi, suppressio veri.—1 Vern. 20.

[8] Calman v. Horner, 18 Ves. 10; Clermont v. Tasburgh, 1 Jac. & W. 112; Beaumont v. Dukes, Jac. 422; Shurley v. Stratton, 1 Bro. C. C. 440; Newl. on Cont. 156.

[9] Perk. s. 16; 2 Bl. Com. 292.

[10] Sug. V. & P.; Mad. Ch. Pr. 404.

[11] 4 T. R. 329.

Parallel Articles of the French Code.

a small part of a contract, precludes the party guilty of a fraudulent misrepresentation[1] from being able to compel the performance of it:[2] but if the thing concealed be too trifling to work any injustice, or to affect the interests of the party, specific performance of the agreement might be compelled.[3] And if the misrepresentation were innocently made, then it must have been material, and to such an extent as to vary the spirit of the contract to excuse the non-performance, and it would be decreed to be specifically executed upon compensation being given.[4] In general, a patent defect,[5] or a mistake that might have been avoided by common prudence, is no ground of excuse for the nonperformance of an agreement.[6]

The person with whom the contract is made, his name or quality is in general immaterial;[7] but the character of the party with whom it is intended to contract, may be a material cause or consideration in the agreement;[8] and then a mistake or misconception on this point would vitiate the whole.[9]

Duress (or constraint,[10] durities) towards one of the contracting parties vacates a deed[11] or contract, although exercised by a person other than him for whose benefit it has been done.[12] 1111.

There may be duress by illegal imprisonment,[13] or duress per minas, which latter is the well-founded fear of death, 1121.

---

[1] As if a picture be sold as a painting of Poussin, when in truth it is not so.

[2] Cadman v. Horner, 18 Ves. 10; Clermont v. Tasburgh, 1 Jac. & Walk. 112; Harris v. Kemble, 2 Dow. & Clark. 463; overruling same case in 1 Sim. 111.

[3] Fellows v. Ld. Gwyder & Page, 1 Sym. 65; confirmed 1 Russ. & Mylne, 89.

[4] Halsey v. Grant, 13 Vess. 77; Stapleton v. Scott, 1 Ves. 426; Hearne v. Tenant, 13 Ves. 287.

[5] Non decipitur qui scit se decipi.—5 Rep. 60.

[6] Hob. 347; Wing. 672; 1 Sug. V. & P. 2.

[7] Nihil facet error nominis cum de corpore constat.—11 Rep. 21.

[8] See where a contract was set aside because there was reason to suppose that a person bidding at an auction was a puffer for the vendor, when in truth he was bidding for a bonâ fide purchaser.—Mason v. Armitage, 13 Ves. 25; Hill v. Buckley, 17 ib. 394; Twining v. Morris, 2 Bro. C. C. 326.

[9] Hill v. Gray, 1 Stra. 434.

[10] Voluntas coacta non est voluntas. (Puffend. and Grotius also.)

[11] Duress renders feoffments, leases, gifts, grants, &c. thereby made voidable. —Park, s. 16.

[12] Co. Lit. 253.

[13] Anon, 1 Salk. 68.

Parallel Articles of the French Code.

or mayhem, or loss of limb, by violence to the person of him who has entered into an agreement, which makes it void; but it is otherwise where the contract is executed for fear of battery, or of injury to his property only.[1] The condition, state of mind and body, age and sex, of the person towards whom the duress is exercised, would be taken into account in such a case; and infirmity of disposition would probably render slight impressions of fear sufficient to vacate a contract.[2]

1113. Duress is a ground for avoiding a deed not only when exercised towards the contracting party, but also when it has been the duress of the wife or of the descendant or ancestor of the party.[3]

1114. The exercise of parental authority in recommending a particular agreement, is no ground for setting it aside;[4] but a detrimental contract, obtained from a father by a son (or the like), &c. is always looked upon with very great jealousy in English courts of equity. If an undue advantage be taken of a person's situation, and money obtained from him by compulsion, such money may be recovered back again.[5]

1115. As to contracts which remain executory, it is not necessary in England for a person, whose consent is obtained by violence, to institute any proceedings[6] to set it aside: the force may be used as a defence in any suit founded on a contract. But the contract is not absolutely void; the party who has suffered the force may waive the exception by subsequent assent, and the party imposing the force can never allege it as a defence, if the contract be insisted on by the other side.[7]

---

1 2 Inst. 482; Strathmore v. Bowes, 2 Bro. 345; 1 Ves. J. 22; 6 Bro. P. C. 427; Sumner v. Ferryman, 11 Mod. 202; sed vide as to cattle, 2 Danv. 686.

2 Evans' note to Pothier, 18; but as to weakness and indiscretion, Willis v. Jernekan, 2 Atk. 251. Vani timores sunt æstimandi, qui non cadunt in constantem virum.—7 Rep. 27.

3 2 Danv. 686.

4 Kinchant v. Kinchant, 1 Bro. C. C. 369.

5 Analogous to the letters of rescission.

6 Astley v. Reynolds, Sh. 915; Fitzroy v. Gwillim, 1 T. R. 153; Smith v. Bromley, Dougl. 696.

7 Evans' Pothier, p. 15 (n.)

Parallel Articles of the French Code.

As to conveyances and contracts executed, proceedings must be instituted to recover back the object conveyed, or to obtain damages. Where a man under fear, enters into an engagement, and when at liberty does not immediately impeach it, or afterwards does any act expressly or impliedly confirming, or sanctioning[1] it, he will not be relieved.[2]

Fraud of every description is (as a general rule) always a ground for vacating an agreement, by the party on whom it has been practised.[3] An agreement entered into for a fraudulent purpose is considered in the same light as illegal contracts, and consequently an action cannot be maintained for breach of them.[4] The law will not define[5] what constitutes fraud; but as human ingenuity contrives new species of deceit, the courts will establish new principles to meet them.[6] Where both parties have concurred in a fraud on another person, the law will not assist even between themselves.[7] Fraud is not to be presumed.[8] Although a third person shall not be punished for the fraud of another, he shall not avail himself of it.[9] 1116.

Although an agreement contracted by mistake, duress, or fraud, is void at law and in equity,[10] either party may bring an action at law for damages against the other who refuses to perform his part, and leave it to a jury to decide whether there was fraud or not;[11] or he may file 1117.

---

[1] Confirmatio omnes supplet defectus, ubi id quod actum est ab initio non valuit.—Co. Lit. 295 b. Consensus tollit error.—Ib. 126; Wing. 481.

[2] Goodman v. Scuse, 2 Eq. Ab. 183, pl. 2; Gilb. Eq. R. 9; Anon. 3 P. W. 294 n. Fraud; Lloyd v. Tyms, Colles, P. C. 14.

[3] 1 Mad. Ch. Pr. 109; Cockshott v. Bennett, 2 T. R. 763; 3 T. R. 48; Jackson v. Duchaire, 3 T. R. 351; Middleton v. Ld. Onslow, 1 P.W. 768. Qui per fraudem agit, frustra agit.—2 Rol. Rep. 17.

[4] Jackson v. Lomas, 4 T. R. 166.

[5] Dolus est machinatio cum aliud dissimulat, aliud agit.—Lane, 47. Fraus est celare fraudem.—1 Vern. 240.

[6] Webb v. Rorke, 2 Scho. & Lef. 666.

[7] Fraus mereter fraudem.—Plow. 100.

[8] Fraus est odiosa et non præsumenda.—Cro. Car. 550; 3 Cha. Ca. 85; 3 Mod. 328.

[9] Robson v. Calzee, Dougl. 228; Ld. Mansfield.

[10] 1 Mod. Ch. Pr. 109; Cockshott v. Bennett, 2 T. R. 763; Edwards v. Browne, 1 Tyr. 196.

[11] By the Roman law the fraud must have been necessarily made the object

Parallel Articles of the French Code.

tors, administrators, and assigns,[1] or whom he properly represents, as one partner may bind his copartners; and a general agent, acting within the scope of his authority, binds the principal, though not named.[2]

A man may undertake for a third person, by agreement in writing, rendering himself bound, in case of the default or miscarriage of such third person.[3] If a contract be to be performed by a stranger, and he refuses it, it is no excuse for the non-performance of the agreement, because the contractor has undertaken that the stranger shall comply with his stipulation.[4] 1120.

Contracts made for the benefit of a third person, though without his privity and direction, may be rejected or affirmed at his election; but some degree of agency, however trifling, must always exist. By making the election he adopts the agent's contract.[5] 1121.

In all cases where a man contracts for himself, his executors and administrators are bound, though not named;[6] unless it be a mere personal act to be done by the party himself, though then they would be liable for the damages occasioned by the breach of his covenant.[7] 1122.

Section 2.

Of the Capacity of the Contracting Parties.

Every person, natural or artificial, may enter into a contract or agreement, who has no legal incapacity within the scope and according[8] to their capacity. 1123.

---

[1] But not always for his assigns; for no one is liable, on any contract, unless he is privy to it in fact or in contemplation of law. Express covenants which run with the land, entered into by a lessee for years for himself, his executors, administrators, and assigns, are binding on every person who takes the legal estate for the residue of the term by assignment; such person being affected by privity of estate.

[2] Pickering v. Buske, 15 East, 38.

[3] 29 Car. II. c. 2, s. 4; Worsley v. Wood, 6 T. R. 710; Routledge v. Burrell, 1 H. Bl. 254; Oldham v. Bewicke, 2 H. Bl. 577, n. (a); Co. Lit. 208 b, 209 a.

[4] 1 Roll. Ab. 452.

[5] 2 Stra. 859.

[6] Shep. Touch. 177.

[7] Touch. 180; 5 Rep. 21.

[8] Bodies corporate, by the common seal.—Ante, p. 334.

Parallel Articles of the French Code.

1124. The law incapacitates from contracting—minors;[1] married women without the authority of their husbands;[2] persons attainted of treason or felony;[3] idiots,[4] lunatics, and others[5] non compos mentis;[6] persons born deaf, dumb, and blind;[7] certain public bodies not corporations.[8]

1125. A minor on coming of age may confirm or avoid his contracts, except for necessaries.[9] A contract by a femme covert, is impliedly the act of her husband's agent, and good until he avoids it by his dissent. And if he does nothing to avoid it, or even actually consents to it, the femme covert herself may, after his death, disagree to it.[10] Contracts by persons attaint, are for the benefit of the crown.[11] Persons capable of binding themselves, cannot object the incapacity of the minor with whom they contract;[12] or of the attaint person, for the king would take;[13] or of the married woman, where her coverture is known, as her husband would be entitled to the benefit of her contract;[14] but otherwise, where her coverture is not known.[15]

---

[1] Zouch v. Parsons, 3 Bur. 1794; 2 H. Bl. 75; ante, p. 302.

[2] De Gaillon v. L'Aigle, 1 Bro. 357; ante, p. 279.

[3] Ante, p. 220.

[4] Infirmity of disposition would be an inadequate excuse for commission of an offence, or the omission of a duty. Weakness and indiscretion are not sufficient to set aside an agreement.—Willis v. Ternegan, 2 Atk. 257. Important observations, by Ld. Thurlow, on partial and general derangement, in Attorney-General v. Parnther, 3 Bro. C. 441.

[5] Drunkenness (Cory v. Cory, 1 Ves. 19; Bull, N. P. 192) alone will not afford ground for vacating a contract; but equity will not assist a person who has obtained a contract from another who was in a state of intoxication, Cooke v. Clayton, 18 Ves. 16; and if the party were intoxicated fraudulently, Johnson v. Medlicott, 3 P. W. 130, n. a; or if the party were dead drunk, Cooke v. Clayton, 18 Ves. 11.

[6] Ante, p. 320.

[7] Ib.

[8] Co. Lit. 3 Inst.; see Warner's ca. Cro. Jac. 532.

[9] 1 Bl. Com. 466; 2 ib. 292.

[10] Ib. 292, 3.

[11] Ib. 290.

[12] Holt v. Ward, Clarencieux, 2 Str. 937; Fitz. 175, 275; Bruce v. Warwick, 2 M. & S. 205; 6 Taunt. 118.

[13] 2 Bl. Com. 290; Bullock v. Dodds, 2 B. & A. 258.

[14] Barlow v. Bishop, 1 East, 132.

[15] Rex v. Inhab. of Ashton-under-Lyne, 4 M. & S. 357; ante, p. 281.

Parallel Articles of the French Code.

SECTION 3.

Of the Object and Matter of Contracts.

The object or subject matter of every contract must be either a thing[1] or an action. It may be a thing which one party binds himself to give, or an act which one party binds himself to do, or not to do.[2] 1126.

Or a contract relating to a thing may be for the simple use, custody, or possession of it, as in the case of a loan or deposit. 1127.

As to the subject matter of contracts, there is in general no restriction, provided the contract be not against the policy of the common law, or the provisions of some statute.[3] Certain kinds of property (res sacræ et res publicæ[4]) are in all states, from policy and morality, forbidden to be made objects of commerce.[5] Private property, real and personal, corporeal and incorporeal, and services in a private capacity, are the objects of contracts; but the sale of public offices[6] is prohibited.[7] A bare possibility of an interest, which is uncertain, choses in action, and things of that nature,[8] as causes of suits, rights, and titles of entry, animals feræ natura, are not at law properly the subject of contract.[9] In equity, every species of contingency[10] may be bound by contract for valuable consideration.[11] 1128.

---

[1] Charta de non ente non valet, Co. Lit. 36 a. Nomen non sufficit si res non sit de jure aut de facto, 4 Rep. 107.

[2] 2 Bl. Com. 296, 444, 5, 6.

[3] Com. Dig. Cov. A; 1 Plowd. 308.

[4] Ante, par. art. 538, 540.

[5] Barwicke v. Reade, 1 H. Bl. 627; Parsons v. Thompson, ib. 322; Garforth v. Fearon, 1 H. B. 330; Jones v. Randal, Cowp. 39; Baldwin v. Rochford, 1 Wils. 229; Stuart v. Tucker, 2 Bl. 1137; Lidderdale v. Montrose, D. 4 T. R. 248; Blachford v. Preston, 8 T. R. 89; Fores v. Johnes, 4 Esp. N. P. 97.

[6] Officia magistratus non debent esse venalia.—Co. Lit. 234.

[7] 2 Inst. 148; 5 & 6 Ed. VI. c. 16; 2 Bl. Com. 36; 49 Geo. III. c. 126.

[8] A chose in action, or a right of entry, cannot be granted or transferred to a stranger.—Co. Lit. 266.

[9] 2 Bl. Com. 442; Wood's Inst. 282.

[10] Licet dispositio interesse futuro sit inutilis, tamen potest fieri declaratio præcedens quæ sortiatur effectum, interveniente novo actu.—Bacon.

[11] 1 Ves. 409; 2 P. W. 142, 191; 2 Atk. 420, sed vide 3 Mer. 667.

Parallel Articles of the French Code.

1129. A contract is void unless it be sufficiently certain.[1] A party who seeks to enforce a contract must show that it is certain,[2] and clear in its material terms;[3] but the uncertainty of the object, quantity, or quality of a contract, does not vitiate it, if there are means provided, either within it or otherwise,[4] for determining them.[5]

1130. There is no limit to the stipulations that may be made by contracts; they may be for the past, the present, or the future:[6] whether the thing itself be future, as a mowing of grass not yet grown, or whether the interest in the thing be future: and though the expectancy of an heir apparent[7] or next of kin is a mere hope, yet his contract will bind him;[8] and a reversionary interest may be disposed of, though the reversioner is, like the heir, protected against fraud implied from inadequacy of price.[9]

---

1 Wheresoever there is a demand in law or equity, there must be a certainty of the thing demanded, 1 Cha. Ca. 309; Dav. 33: and if there be uncertainty as to the description or quantity of lands proposed to be conveyed, specific performance will not be decreed.—Bromley v. Jefferies, 2 Vern. 415; Newl. Cont. 151; Contr. ib. 152.

2 Incerta pro nullis habentur.—Dav. 33. *Incerta quantitas vitiat actum.*—1 Roll. Rep. 465.

3 Whaley v. Bagnall, 6 Bro. P. C. 48; Mosley v. Virgin, 3 Ves. 148; 1 Fonb. on Eq. 170; 5 B. & C. 583; 1 Russ. & M. 116.

4 Allen v. Harding, 2 Eq. Ab. 17.

5 Id certum est quod certum reddi potest; sed id magis certum est quod de semetipso est certum.—9 Rep. 47.

6 Com. Dig. Cov. A. 1; Plowd. 308; F. N. B. 145 a.

7 But a bargain with an heir for his expectancy is considered as pernicious in principle, from its obvious tendency to encourage extravagance, and induce him to shake off parental authority, besides the facilities it offers for taking undue advantage of the heir's necessitous circumstances, and it will be readily set aside for inadequacy of consideration.—Barnardiston v. Lingood, 2 Atk. 133; Gwynne v. Heaton, 1 Bro. C. C. 1; Nott v. Hill, 1 Vern. 167; 2 Vern. 27; Twisleton v. Griffith, 1 P. W. 310; Cole v. Gibbons, 3 P. W. 390; ante, par. art. 791.

8 Helps v. Hereford, 2 B. & Ald. 242.

9 Gowland v. De Faria, 17 Ves. 20.

Parallel Articles of the French Code.

SECTION 4.

Of the Consideration or Cause.

In every contract there must be a lawful and valuable cause or consideration,[1] a quid pro quo.[2] It is not, however, essential to the validity of a contract or deed under seal, to show a consideration or reciprocal benefit:[3] but a legal consideration is absolutely necessary to a contract[4] not under seal;[5] and unless by deed under seal, evidence of a consideration of some sort is so absolutely necessary to the forming of a contract, that an agreement to do or pay anything on one side without any compensation on the other, is totally void in law, and a man cannot be compelled to perform it.[6] But in general, no evidence of consideration is necessary to the validity of a deed or contract under seal, unless it be in fraud of creditors;[7] and if the consideration mentioned in a deed turn out afterwards to be void, yet the deed is good.[8] 1131.

As to the nature of the consideration, an action will not lie for a mere non-fearance, unless the promise is founded upon a consideration.[9] The consideration may be a benefit to the party promising;[10] or a benefit to a stranger,[11] or loss, damage,[12] or inconvenience[13] to the party promised at the request of the party promising: but it must be of some

---

1 Agreements must be on good consideration and mutual recompense. Ex nudo pacto non oritur actio.—Plow. 305.

2 Co. Lit. 47 b.

3 Harrington v. Stratton, Plowd. 308; 2 Atk. 150; 3 Burr. 1670; 7 T. R. 350.

4 2 Bl. Com. 445.

5 Cooke v. Oxley, 3 T. R. 653; 4 East, 455; 1 Taunt. 523.

6 2 Bl. Com. 445; Rann v. Hughes, 7 T. R. 350; Middleton v. Ld. Kenyon. 2 Ves. J. 188.

7 Fallowes v. Taylor, 7 T. R. 477; Plowd. 308; 2 Atk. 150; 3 Burr. 1670.

8 May v. Tree, Freem. 447; 3 Keb. 764, 780.

9 Elsee v. Gatward, 5 T. R. 143.

10 Per Buller, in Nerot v. Wallace, 3 T. R. 24; Cooke v. Oxley, ib. 653.

11 1 Roll. Ab. 27, pl. 49; Greenleaf v. Barker, Cro. Eliz. 194; 29 Car. II. c. 3, s. 4.

12 Bunn v. Guy, 4 East, 194.

13 Sturlyn v. Albany, Cro. Eliz. 67; Bailey v. Croft, 4 Taunt. 611.

Parallel Articles of the French Code.

value in law;[1] therefore the performance of an act which the party was by law bound to perform, is not a sufficient consideration;[2] nor natural affection, though sufficient to raise an use.[3] Moral obligation, it should seem, is sufficient for an express promise;[4] but it has been held not to raise an implied promise.[5] The consideration on which a promise is founded, must move from the party by whom it is to be enforced.[6] A consideration, past or executed, will not support a subsequent promise,[7] unless the act was done at the request of the party promising.[8] Debts barred by statute of limitations, bankruptcy, or infancy, are sufficient to support a subsequent promise to pay.[9]

1132. It is not in general necessary, though advisable, that the consideration should be expressed in the contract, except in the case of guarantees for third persons.

1133. As has already been stated,[10] contracts which are opposed to the national policy and institutions, or which are founded in moral turpitude,[11] or are inconsistent with good order and the interests of society, cannot be enforced; and this whether the consideration or the effect be so.[12]

---

1 1 Roll. Ab. 23, pl. 29.

2 Harris v. Watson, Peake, N.P. 72.

3 Bret. v. J. S. & Wife, Cro. Eliz. 755.

4 Lee v. Muggleridge and another, 5 Taunt. 36.

5 Atkins v. Banwell, 2 East, 505; Wennall v. Adney, 3 Bos. & Pul. 249, and note 249.

6 Bourne v. Mason, 1 Vent. 6; Crow v. Rogers, Str. 592.

7 Dyer, 272.

8 1 Roll. Ab. 112, pl. 6. See note by Serjeant Williams, Osborne v. Rogers, 1 Saund. 264, n. 1; Dy. 272; Hayes v. Warren, 2 Str. 933.

9 Hyleing v. Hastings, Ld. Raym. 389; Linbury v. Wightman, 5 Esp. 198; Trueman v. Fenton, Cowp. 544; Southerton v. Whitelock, 1 Stra. 690.

10 Par. art. 6. See ante, p. 198, and note 4; 199, and note 1; and see further.

11 Contractus ex turpi causa vel contra bonos mores nullus.—Hob. 167. Ex turpi causâ non oritur actio.

12 Illegality, as contravention of the general policy of the law, on account of perjury; in Collins v. Blantern, 2 Wils. 347, most ably discussed by Wilmot, Ld.C.J.—Public office; Parson v. Thompson, 1 H.B. 322; Holman v. Johnson, Cowp. 341.—Revenue smuggling; where both are equally in fault, potior est conditio defendentis; Waymell v. Reid, 5 T.R. 599.—Prostitution; Marchioness of Annandale v. Harris, 2 P. W. 339; Lady Cox's case, 3 P. W. 339; Walker v. Perkins, 3 Burr. 1568; Priest v. Parrot, 2 Ves. 160; Garforth v. Pearson, 2 H. B. 327; Blackford v. Preston, 8 T.R. 89; Wallis v. Baldwin, Doug. 450.—In fraud as to a bankrupt's

Parallel Articles of the French Code.

CHAPTER III.

Of the Effect of Obligations.

SECTION 1.

General Rules.

Contracts and agreements legally formed hold, as it were, the place of the law,[1] to a certain extent,[2] between the parties to them. They cannot be rescinded but by the mutual consent of the parties,[3] or by virtue of an agreement in the original contract, empowering one or both of them to abandon it.[4] At common law, lawfully formed agreements must either be performed, or the party refusing to execute his part must pay adequate compensation for any damage sustained by the other party by the non-performance.[5] Courts of equity, however, consider a party bound in conscience, not merely to make compensation for the breach when he cannot perform it, but actually to perform his agreement when it is in his power.[6] If, therefore, either party refuse to perform the contract, the other may bring an action at law for breach of contract, or file a bill in chancery for a specific performance:[7] unless the compensation in damages be necessarily commensurate with the injury, and 1134.

estate; Nerot v. Wallace, 3 T.R. 17.—In restraint of trade; Davis v. Mason, 5 T. R. 118.—In restraint of marriage; Low v. Peer, 4 Burr. 2224.—Illegal stock-jobbing; Faikney v. Renous, 4 Burr. 2069.

[1] Modus et conventio vincunt legem. Pacto aliquod licitum est, quod sine pacto non admittitur.—Co. Lit. 166 b.

[2] But it cannot deprive a court of equity of its right to interfere.—Fry v. Porter, Cha. Ca. 141.

[3] Nihil tam conveniens est naturali equitate quam unumquodque dissolvi eo ligamine quo ligatum est. — 2 Inst. 359. Eodem modo quo quid construitur, eodem modo dissolvitur, vel destruitur.—Law Max. 6 Rep. 53; Jenk. Cent. 66, 74; 2 Boll. Rep. 39.

[4] 1 T.R. 133.

[5] Lewis v. Ld. Lechmere, 10 Mod. 503.

[6] Alley v. Deschamps, 13 Ves. 228; O'Herlihy v. Hedges, 1 Sch. & Lef. 129; Moore v. Ball, 1 Ball & B. 69; History of this jurisdiction, Halsey v. Grant, 13 Ves. 76.

[7] Newl. or Cont. 88.

Parallel Articles of the French Code.

as beneficial as performance; for then the only remedy is an action for compensation.

Equity[2] looks upon things agreed to be done as actually performed.[3]

Morally speaking, contracts should be faithfully[4] performed according to the intention of the parties.

1135. In general agreements are binding, not only as to what is expressed in them, but further, in all the consequences which equity, usage, or law imply from the words used,[5] or the nature of the contract.

Section 2.

Obligations of Giving.

1136. One of the kinds of valuable considerations in contracts arising from the nature of things, and recognised by the law of England as well as that of Rome, is, do et des; as, when I give money or goods on a contract, that I shall be paid money or goods for them again. Of this kind are all loans of money upon bond or promise of repayment, and all sales of goods. Another species of consideration is facio ut des, when a man agrees to perform anything for a price or a specific object.[6] In either of these cases, one party is under an obligation of giving something to another, implying that of delivering at the time and place stipulated, primâ facie, the thing itself when a moveable; but delivery of a sample, or the keys of the warehouse containing the thing, is sufficient: and it binds to prove a title, and to execute a conveyance

---

[1] Errington v. Annesley, 2 Bro. C. C. 341; Flint v. Brandon, 8 Ves. J. 363; Whitby v. Cottle, 1 Sim. & Stu. 74.

[2] Adopting the maxim of the civil law, qui actionem habet ad rem recuperandam, ipsam rem habere videtur, D 50, tit. 17, 15.

[3] Francis' Maxims, max. 13; Callaway v. Ward, 1 Ves. 318.

[4] Fides est obligatio conscientiæ alicujus ad intentionem alterius.—Bacon.

[5] 1 H. Bl. 5; Dougl. 201; Holt, N. P. 197; 3 J. B. Moore, 536; Smith v. Wilson, 3 B. & Ad. 728; 5 B. & Ald. 918.

[6] 2 Bl. Com. 444, 5; Ross on Vend. & Pur.

Parallel Articles of the French Code.

either under the statute for transferring uses into possession, or by livery of seisin when an immoveable.

In general, a contract to give a thing in return for money or things is not a perfect contract until some earnest is paid, or there is some act of performance on the part of one or the other,[1] unless it be expressly agreed to be performed in futuro.[2] When the contract is completed, the party may proceed to compel delivery of the thing; and by bill in chancery, where only a deposit on a purchase has been paid, the party may be compelled to make delivery of real property in specie;[3] and where the whole price of a personal chattel, of a fixed and determinate nature, unmixed with others from which it has to be separated before delivery, has been paid, and the party to receive has peformed his part, the property in it becomes vested in him;[4] but in general, delivery in specie of a personal chattel will not be decreed: though where the breach of the delivery cannot be compensated for by damages at law, specific performance[5] would be decreed.[6] Damages may always be sued for at law, in case of non-delivery.[7] As equity looks upon things agreed to be done as actually performed, it consequently considers the vendor as a trustee for the purchaser of the real estate sold, and the purchaser as a trustee of the purchase money for the vendor.[8]

The vendee being equitable owner of the estate from 1137.

---

1 Noy's Max. 87; 2 Bl. Com. 447.

2 Tarling v. Baxter, 6 B. & C. 364.

3 Newl. on Cont.; 1 Mad. Ch. Pr. 360, 1.

4 Rugg v. Minett, 1 East, 210; 1 Taunt. 320.

5 As to the necessity of request to deliver, Bach. v. Owen, 5 T. R. 409.

6 Buxton v. Lister, 3 Atk. 383; Nutbrown v. Thornton, 10 Ves. 161; Painsett v. Humphreys.

7 3 Bl. Com. 154. In an action of detinue, it is at the defendant's election to deliver the goods in specie, or the value. In trover damages, only damages are recovered.—Selw. N. P.; Selw. N. P. Detinet.

8 Green v. Smith, 1 Atk. 572; Atcherley v. Vernon, 10 Mod. 518; Pallexfen v. Moore, 3 Atk. 272.

Pretium succedit in loco rei.—2 Buls. 312.

Solutio pretii, emptionis loco habetur.—Jenk. Cent. 56.

Parallel Articles of the French Code.

the time of the contract of sale, must bear any loss which may happen to the estate between the contract and the conveyance.[1] The same rule applies as to personalty.[2] And so at law, where the contract is complete, and nothing remains to be done on the part of the party delivering but to deliver the article, it remains at the risk of the other party; and if it be accidentally destroyed, the loss must fall upon him.[3] But it is said the same degree of care must be exercised, and the same responsibility is exacted from a seller as from a hirer of goods: and like any other such bailee or trustee, the party bound to deliver would be liable for fraud or gross negligence; and he must exercise at least the same degree of care as a man of ordinary prudence would bestow on his own property,[4] which would of course be regulated by the nature of the thing.

1138. It has been thought that any neglect[5] to deliver at the proper time or on demand, would render the party liable in case of accident to, or destruction of, the thing.[6]

1139. In the absence of stipulation, it is, however, the place of the party receiving to fetch the goods.[7] But if the other party is bound to deliver them, it has been thought that the liability to damages attaches without any demand, after a proper time has elapsed; that time may be either limited or collected from inference. Where there is no limitation of time, and no delay is implied

---

1 Paine v. Miller, 6 Ves. J. 349; Poole v. Shergold, 2 Bro. C. C. 118; Revel v. Hussey, 2 Ball & Bea. 280; Harford v. Parrier, 1 Mad. 532; Zagury v. Furnell, 2 Camp. 240.

2 Noy's Max. 88; Hind v. Whitehouse, 7 East, 571.

3 Tarling v. Baxter, 6 B. & C. 364.

4 Morley v. Morley, 2 Cha. C. 2; Jones v. Lewis, 2 Ves. 240; Mitton v. Cock, 2 Stra. 1099; Kettle v. Bromsall, Willes, 121; Coggs v. Bernard, 2 Ld. Raymond, 913; Foster v. Deacon, 3 Mad. 394.

5 Negligentia semper habet infortuniam comitem.—Co. Lit. 246 b; Wing. 669.

6 Evans' Pothier, p. 85; see however Rugg v. Minett, 11 East, 210.

7 Glazebrook v. Woodrow, 8 T. R. 366; Jones v. Berkeley, ib.

Parallel Articles of the French Code.

from the nature of the subject, the obligation attaches immediately.[1]

After earnest paid, the vendor cannot sell the goods to another person, without default in the vendee;[2] but where, by any mistake, two parties have a claim to a thing, the one who gets possession bonâ fide, is generally allowed to have the better right.[3] The general rule of law is, that all sales and contracts of any thing vendible in fairs or markets overt (that is, open), shall not only be good between the parties, but also binding on all those who have any right or property therein.[4] 1141.

Section 3.

Obligations to do, or not to do.

Another class of valuable considerations arising from the nature of things is facio ut facias, as when I agree with a man to do his work for him, if he will do mine for me: or if two persons agree to marry together, or to do any other positive acts on both sides. And a fourth species is do ut facias, as when I agree with a servant to give him wages on performing such work.[5] 1142.

Generally, an obligation to do or not to do resolves itself into damages, in case of non-performance on the part of the person bound to do or not to do the act, as promises to marry,[6] or to write a book.[7] But in some particular cases the parties may be compelled to perform their engagements, as an agreement to enter into partnership for a certain term of years, but not where there is

---

[1] Evans' Pothier, n. 85.

[2] Langford v. Administratrix of Tyler, Salk. 113.

[3] Vendens eandem rem duobus, falsarius est.—Jenk. Cent. 107. Qui prior est in tempore potior est in jure.—Co. Lit. 14. In æquale jure melior est conditio possidentis.—Plow. 296.

[4] 2 Inst. 713.

[5] 2 Bl. Com. 444, 5.

[6] 4 Geo. IV. c. 76, s. 27; 1 Stra. 34; Ld. Raym. 316.

[7] Clark v. Price, 2 Wils. Ch. R. 157.

Parallel Articles of the French Code.

no term fixed.[1] An agreement to build may be decreed, if sufficiently certain:[2] and a court of chancery will issue an injunction to restrain a party from doing certain acts, contrary to his contract, as to restrain an author from publishing;[3] to prevent the disclosure of a secret in a certain trade sold;[4] to restrain breaches of covenant,[5] as, to restrain a coach proprietor from running a coach in opposition.[6]

1143. And where damages cannot form adequate compensation for breach of a covenant not to do a thing, the party committing the breach may be compelled to demolish or remove what he has commenced.[7]

1144. If the party bound refuse or neglect to perform his agreement, the other party may cause it to be performed, and sue for the damages and expenses in an action on the case.

1145. If the obligation is not to do an act, the party who commits a breach is liable to an action at law for the breach by the simple act of committing the breach; but the amount of damages and the costs must depend on the nature of stipulation, as whether they are liquidated damages, or a penalty fixed;[8] or if neither one or the other, on the proof of the real damages. Repeated actions may be brought for successive breaches or a continued breach of a contract.[9]

---

1 Hercy v. Birch, 9 Ves. 357; Peacock v. Peacock, 16 Ves. 49; Newl. 92; 1 Mad. Ch. Pr. 411, n. (x).

2 Mosely v. Virgin, 3 Ves. 184; Franklyn v. Tuton, 5 Mad. 469.

3 Barfield v. Nicholson, 2 Sim. & Stu. 1; but see 2 Wils. Ch. R. 157.

4 Bryson v. Whitehead, 1 Sim. & Stu. 74.

5 Barrett v. Blagrave, 5 Ves. 555; 6 ib. 104; Ld. Grey de Wilton v. Saxon, ib. 106; Pratt v. Brett, 2 Mad. R. 62.

6 Williams v. Williams, 2 Swanst. 253; Harrison v. Gardner, 2 Mad. R. 198.

7 Rankin v. Huskisson, 1 Clark & P. 13.

8 Brigstock v. Stanton, 1 Ld. Raymond, 106.

9 13 East, 343; Holt, N. P. 46; 1 Camp. 78.

Parallel Articles of the French Code.

Section 4.

Of Damages resulting from the Non-performance of the Obligation.

To entitle one party to a contract to sue the other for damages for non-performance of it, it must be shown that the time of performance is past, and that there has been unreasonable delay on the part of the latter, and it should not have arisen from non-performance on the part of plaintiff. 1146.

Where no time for payment of debt or performance of an act is provided by the parties, or by custom of the trade, it impliedly accrues due immediately the consideration for it has attached without demand.

When the covenants are independent, or mutual and concurrent, immediately on breach, or after the party has been requested to perform it, where such request is necessary,[1] or if a specific time is fixed, and is material or necessary, the non-performance by such time vests a right of action for damages or penalties.[2] Time is the essence of the contract, where the subject matter is of a nature exposed to a daily variation in its value; and after delay, specific performance will not be decreed.[3]

If a person enter into an express and positive stipulation, though it may be hard, false, and absurd, yet he must abide by it.[4] And a fortuitous occurrence, though it arises from a foreign cause,[5] not imputable to him, does not discharge a party from liability for breach of the contract; but he must answer in damages.[6] 1147 to 1151.

---

[1] 1 Bos. & P. 59; 5 T. R. 409; Selw. N. P. [2] Per Holt, Salk. 113, 171.

[3] Doloret v. Rothschild, 1 Sim. and Stu. 590.

[4] Shubrick v. Salmond, 3 Burr. 1637.

[5] Accident is no excuse for non-performance of contract.—Brecknock Can. Co. v. Pritchard, 6 T. R. 750; Bullock v. Doromit, id. 650; Hadley v. Clarke, 8 T. R. 259: otherwise where the law creates a duty; Dyer, 33; Allen, 26.

[6] Chesterfield v. Bolton, 2 Comm. 626; Barker v. Hodgson, 3 M. & S. 267. See the old law, 1 Roll. Ab. 450, pl. 10.

Parallel Articles of the French Code.

In general, damages are assessed by a jury, and are given to the extent of the injury proved to be directly or indirectly sustained.[1]

1152. But when an agreement provides that any breach of it shall be compensated for by liquidated damages,[2] the exact sum, neither more nor less, becomes payable.[3]

1153. In case of an obligation conditioned for the payment of money, the payment of the principal sum due, with interest and costs, is a full satisfaction and discharge.[4]

1154. Compound interest may be payable by agreement, or after a written notice that it will be demanded; and in equity interest is sometimes allowed upon arrears of interest, by making annual rests in the account.[5]

Section 5.

Of the Interpretation of Agreements.

1156. Both at law and in equity[6] an agreement shall receive its interpretation from the reasonable sense and construction of the words, according to the intention[7] of the

---

1 Co. Lit. 257; Brigstock v. Stanion, 1 Ld. Raym. 106; Vivian v. Champion, 2 Ld. Raym. 1125; 11 Mod. 45; Shortridge v. Lamplugh, 2 Ld. Raym. 798; 7 Mod. 71.

2 Quod sub certa forma concessum vel reservatum est, non trahitur ad valorem seu compensationem.—Bacon.

3 See post, c. 4, s. 6.

4 4 & 5 Anne, c. 16

5 Howard v. Harriss, 1 Vern. 194; Walker v. Woodward, 1 Russ. 107; Donovan v. Tricker, Jacob, 165. See exparte Bevan, 9 Ves. 223; Ld. Clancarty v. Latouche, 1 Ball & B. 429.

6 "In construing contracts, I know no difference between a court of law and a court of equity. A court of equity cannot make an agreement for the parties, it can only explain what their true meaning was, and that is also the duty of a court of law."—Per Lord Mansfield, in Hotham v. East India Company, 278.

7 Every contract derives its effect from the intention of the parties, as expressed by their own words.—Law Max. Animus hominis est anima scripti.—Ib.; 3 Buls. 67. In Goodtitle v. Bailey, Lord Mansfield said, "The rules laid down in respect of deeds were founded in law, reason, and common sense, that they should operate according to the intention of the parties, if by law they might."—Cowp. 597.

Parallel Articles of the French Code.

parties,[1] and, if necessary, even contrary to the grammatical construction;[2] but where the words of a contract are so uncertain[3] that the intention of the parties cannot be discovered, the contract will be void.[4] Where any intention can be collected, it is a maxim of the highest antiquity in the law that all deeds shall be construed favourably, and as near the apparent intention of the parties as possible, consistently with the rules of law, ut res magis valeat quam pereat;[5] and where the intention is clear, too minute a stress is not to be laid on the precise and strict significance of the words;[6] and where a contract cannot act in the way intended by the parties, it will be construed in such a manner as to operate in some other way,[7] if for the benefit of the parties.[8]

When a disposition or agreement is referable to two things, or susceptible of two meanings, such that in one relation it is void, and according to the other good, then the relation is to be made to that which can give it effect.[9] 1157.

Where words are susceptible of two different senses, that sense shall be preferred which is most conformable to the intention of the parties.[10] 1158.

The words used are to be understood in their plain, ordinary, and popular sense, unless they have generally, 1159.

[1] Co. Lit. 219 b; Griffith v. Goodhand, T. Jon. 191; T. Raym. 464; D. of Northumberland v. Errington. 5 T. R. 522; Plowd. 329; Iggulden v. May, 7 East, 237; 3 Smith, 269; D. of St. Albans v. Ellis, 16 East, 352; Nind v. Marshall, 1 B. & B. 319.

[2] Fountain v. Guavers, 2 Show. 333; Comb. 59; Skin. 146.

[3] Divinatio, non interpretatio est, quæ omnino recedit à literâ.—3 Hen. VI. s. 20.

[4] Co. Lit. 20 b; Windsore v. Hobart, Hob. 313.

[5] 2 Bl. Com. 380; Co. Lit. 36 a; Plowd. 154, 160.

[6] 2 Bl, Com. 380; Wright v. Cartwright, 1 Burr. 282.

[7] Hob. 277; 11 Ves. 625; Pugh v. D. of Leeds, Cowp. 714.

[8] Constructions are to be according to what was the beginning, the cause, and subject matter.—Law Max. In verbis non verba sed res et ratio quærenda est.—Law Max.

[9] 6 Co. 76; 2 Bl. Com. 880; Co. Lit. 42 a, n. 6; 183 a; Wright v. Cartwright, 1 Burr. 282.

[10] Co. Lit. 42 a; 183 a & b, 225; Chapman v. Dalton, Plowd. 289; Parkhurst v. Smith, Willes, 332.

Parallel Articles of the French Code.

by the known usage of trade, acquired a peculiar distinct sense.[1] But no usage can contravene a clear express contract,[2] or a positive law.[3]

1160. An evident omission or mistake will be supplied in a deed or agreement;[4] and therefore, if it is clear that all the usual clauses were intended to be contained, those not expressed may in general be supplied.[5]

1161. The intention is to be taken from the whole instrument, not according to particular expressions; but the exposition shall be ex antecedentibus et consequentibus.[6] If there be two clauses in a deed so totally repugnant that they cannot stand together, the first shall be received and the latter rejected.[7]

1162. Where there is any ambiguity, the agreement is to be taken most strongly[8] against the party who had contracted the obligation;[9] provided a due regard be had to the intention of the parties, as collected from the whole instrument.[10]

1163. In support of the apparent intention of the parties, agreements in large and general terms[11] must be construed in a narrowed and confined sense.[12]

1164. The intention of the parties being the rule of con-

---

[1] Robertson v. French, 4 East, 135.

[2] Yeats v. Pim, Holt, 95; 2 Marsh, 141.

[3] Master, &c. of St. Cross v. Ld. Howard de Walden, 6 T. R. 343; Wigglesworth v. Dullison, Doug. 201.

[4] Lloyd v. Say & Sele, 1 Salk. 341; 4 Bro. P. C. 73; Wright v. Dickson, 1 Dow. 141.

[5] Campbell v. Beath, 2 Wilt. & Shaw, 37; Watson v. D. of Wellington, 1 Russ. & M. 602; 8 Bing. 231; 1 H. Bl. 5; Doug. 201; 2 Sim. & Stu. 420; 6 Ves. 34; 1 Meriv. 15; Freeman v. D. of Chandos, Cowp. 360.

[6] 2 Bl. Com. 330; Shep. Touch. 106; Plowd. 329; Moore, 58; Winch, 93; 5 T. R. 526; Butler v. Duncomb, 1 P.W. 457.

[7] 2 Bl. Com. 381.

[8] Verba chartarum fortius accipiuntur contra proferentem.—Law Max.

[9] 2 Bl. Com. 300; Co. Lit. 183 a; Browning v. Wright, 2 B. & P. 22; Dann v. Spurrier, 3 B. & P. 399; Love v. Pares, 13 East, 85; Fowle v. Welsh, 1 B. & C. 35. See the opinion of Sir J. Mansfield, Flint v. Brandon, 1 Bos. & Pul. 78.

[10] Browning v. Wright, 2 B. & P. 22.

[11] Verba generalia restringuntur ad habilitatem rei vel aptitudinem personæ.—Law Max.

[12] Cage v. Paxlin, 1 Leon, 16; Broughton v. Conway, Mo. 58.

struction, anything evidently introduced by way of example would not be held to restrain[1] the extent of the contract, beyond the intention which such example, coupled with the whole contract, indicated.

Section 6.

Of the Effect of Agreements as respects Third Persons.

In general, an agreement can only bind the contracting parties, their heirs, executors, and administrators; and in covenants real running with the land, their assigns, but not in covenants collateral;[2] and third persons, neither parties or privies, shall neither have benefit[3] or hurt[4] thereby; but it is a common thing for one person to covenant for another.[5] 1165.

And a creditor of one party has no claim against the other party, unless he obtain an assignment of the contract; or under a decree of the Court of Chancery in a case of fraud. 1166. 1167.

---

[1] Exempla illustrant non restringunt.—Co. Lit. 24 a.

[2] Mayor of Congleton v. Pattison, 10 East, 130; Cro. Jac. 438; 5 Rep. 16; 1 Ld. Raym. 322; Wilm. 341; 3 Wils. 25; 2 H. Bl. 133.

[3] One not to have the benefit of another's good bargain.—Law Max.

[4] Where a right is acquired to one person by the agreement (or act) of two other persons, such right cannot be afterwards defeated by the act of the parties originally contracting.—Evans' Pothier, n. p. 45; Smith v. Field, 5 T. R. 402.

Actus incœptus, cujus perfectio pendet voluntate partium revocari potest; si autem pendet ex voluntate tertiæ personæ vel ex contingenti revocari non potest. —Bac.

[5] Lilley v. Hedges, 1 Stra. 553; 8 Mod. 166.

Parallel Articles of the French Code.

CHAPTER IV.

Of the different Species of Obligations.

Section 1.

Conditional and Contingent Contracts.

Sub-section 1.

Of Conditions generally, and their different Kinds.

1168. Every species of contract may be upon condition,[1] *i. e.* it may depend upon some future uncertain event. A condition in such case signifies a contingency,[2] or some quality or qualification annexed to a contract or estate, by which, on the happening of such contingency, the estate, or the effect and obligation of a contract, may commence, be confirmed or defeated, enlarged or contracted.[3] The word "condition," considered in the sense in which estates are said to be held upon condition in the feudal sense[4] (being then limited to that which determines an estate), has a much more contracted meaning[5] than in the civil law, where it signifies, generally, all those pactions or agreements which regulate that which the contractors have a mind should be done, if a case, which they foresee, should come to pass.[6] Here, as applied to conditional contracts or agreements, it signifies every event, future and uncertain, on which they are made to depend.

A condition of an agreement, in general, differs from a

---

[1] 1 Roll. Ab. 413, l. 4.

[2] Conditio dicitur, cum quid in casum incertum, qui potest tendere ad esse aut non esse, confertur.—Co. Lit. 201 a.

[3] Co. Lit. 201 a; 2 B. & C. 154.

[4] 1 Pres. ed. Touch, 81.

[5] Conditio beneficialis quæ statum construit, benigne secundum verborum intentionem est interpretanda; odiosa, autem, quæ statum destruit, stricte, secundum verborum proprietatem, accipienda.—8 Rep. 90. Conditions which go to the defeasance of an estate ought to be taken strictly.

[6] This is the definition of Domat, lib. 1, tit. 1, 14; Co. Lit. 201 a, n. 1.

Parallel Articles of the French Code.

covenant or agreement;[1] for the latter may be mutual and independent,[2] only giving a right of action for breach of the covenant:[3] but the performance of a covenant may be a condition, and its nature is nearly the same, whether it suspends or defeats the obligation of a contract. Dependant and concurrent covenants are kinds of conditional obligations, the performance of one being conditional on the performance of the other.[4] If a promise or agreement is conditional, it is necessary the condition should be performed to vest a right of action.[5] When covenants are dependant, an action for damages lies for breach of covenant, only after performance of the conditions precedent.[6] Where there are mutual promises (or covenants), the mere promise and not the performance may be the consideration of the agreement;[7] but where covenants go to the whole consideration on both sides, the one is precedent to the other; but where they go only to part, such is not the case.[8]

There are various sorts of conditions, as conditions subsequent and precedent; conditions in deed, *i. e.* express; and conditions in law, *i. e.* implied; conditions inherent and collateral, affirmative and negative, single, copulative, and disjunctive. The distinction into conditions precedent, subsequent,[9] or concurrent,[10] is the most important. A condition precedent is such as ought to be performed, before the right or estate vests, or the grant or contract takes effect. The debt, estate, or obli-

1 See Mucklestone v. Thomas, Willes, 146.

2 Humlock v. Blacklow, 1 Mod. 54; Co. Lit. 208 a; Roll. Ab. 408; Co. Lit. 204; Winston and another v. Linn, 1 B. & C. 460; Terry and another v. Duntree, 2 H. Bl. 289.

3 Davidson v. Gwynne, 10 East, 355.

4 Thorpe v. Thorpe, 3 Ld. Raym. 662; Salk. 171; Glazebrook v. Woodrow, 8 T. R. 366; Goodisson v. Nunn, 4 T. R. 760; Hob. 41; 7 Mod. 236; 2 Bl. 1312; Willes, 496; 1 H. Bl. 573 n; 1 Saund. 320.

5 Besford v. Saunders, 2 H. Bl. 116.

6 Selw. N. P.; Thomas v. Cadwallader, Willes, 496; Griffith v. Mansell, Freem. 93; Wynne v. Fellowes, 1 Show. 334; Holt, 466.

7 Hob. 106; Martindale v. Fisher, 1 Wils. 88.

8 Boon v. Eyre, 1 H. Bl. 273; Campbell v. Jones, 6 T. R. 371.

9 Co. Lit. 201 a.

10 Morton v. Lamb, 7 T. R. 125.

Parallel Articles of the French Code.

gation to perform the contract, does not accrue until after the performance of the condition precedent.[1]

A condition subsequent is such as, on some subsequent act, defeats the right, estate, grant, or contract.[2] The question, whether a condition be precedent or subsequent, does not depend so much on the form of expression, as the apparent intention of the parties, and the nature of the contract. If a day be appointed for the payment of money, and the act for which the money is to be paid cannot be done before that day, then, though the agreement be to pay the money for the doing the thing, yet the action for the money may be brought before the thing done, because the agreement is positive, that the money shall be paid at the day named; and if a party will agree to pay his money before he has the thing for which he ought to pay, he must perform his agreement. But though a day certain be named for payment of the money, yet if the day is to incur after the time in which the consideration ought to be performed for which the money is to be paid, such consideration must be performed before action brought.[3]

1169. The event or contingency on which a condition de-
1170. pends, may be out of the power of either of the parties
1171. to the contract, one over which they have no control; or it may be within the power of the parties, or partly dependant on them, and partly on third persons. But these distinctions[4] are not of much importance in the English law; for if a person bind himself upon a con-

[1] Conditio præcedens adimpleri debet priusquam sequatur effectus.—Co. Lit. 201 a. Conditions precedent must be literally performed, but not so subsequent ones, where the court can make compensation. Equity will not vest an estate where, by reason of a condition precedent, it will not vest at law; but of conditions subsequent to divest an estate it is otherwise.

[2] D. of St. Albans v. Shore, 1 H. Bl. 270; Thorpe v. Thorpe, 1 Ld. Raym. 665.

[3] Thorpe v. Thorpe, 3 Ld. Raym. 662; Salk. 171.

[4] It must be observed that in the English law, there are numerous conditional interests, as estates to determine upon a condition; conditional estates to endure until the condition takes place; conditional remainders, springing uses, shifting uses, executory devises.

dition, it does not signify in whose power the performance of it may be; even though it may be absurd, the parties are not thereby relieved from their obligations. Parallel Articles of the French Code.

Conditions against law, and such as are repugnant or impossible, are void; whether they be impossible at the time of their creation, or afterwards become so by the act of God, or the act of the party to take advantage of the breach.[1] If the condition be a condition precedent, the obligation is void as well as the condition.[2] If it be a condition subsequent, and by contract under seal, the condition only is void, and the obligation is single;[3] but if the contract were not under seal, and the condition formed the whole consideration, it should seem the obligation would be void as well as the condition. An illegal condition must be distinguished from an illegal clause or covenant in an agreement. When an impossible condition is (in non faciendo), that the party shall not do a certain act, it does not render the obligation void; but the condition is of no effect, and the obligation single.[4] 1172. 1173.

A contract may, in general, depend upon a condition within the control of either of the parties, if there be a good consideration on the other side, or of a third party;[5] as a condition by a person, that he will pay portions to trustees for the children of a first marriage, in the event of his selling a certain estate; or if he agree to pay a certain sum, if he practise or trade within a certain distance of another person The most common form of obligation or bond is conditioned for making it void, if the obligee or party who binds himself does a certain act, as pay money; or for making it of no effect, until his default or misfeasance, or breach of covenant.[6] 1174.

---

[1] 2 Bl. Com. 156; 1 P.W. 189.

[2] 2 Bl. Com. 157.

[3] Ib.; Wall v. Grovet, 12 Mod. 418; Co. Lit. 206; Roll. Ab. 420; Say, 96; 2 Leon, 189.

[4] Co. Lit. 206; Ev. Pot. 114 n.

[5] Condition dependant, on the will of a third party. — Worsley v. Wood, 6 T. R. 750.

[6] Cru. tit. 32, c. 8.

Parallel Articles of the French Code.

Every condition must be performed in the manner in which the parties apparently intended it should be done, or as near as may be,[1] and bonâ fide, not colour-
1175. ably.[2]
1176. When an obligation is contracted under the condition, that an event or condition shall happen within a fixed time, and the time so fixed expires before the event happen, the condition fails and the obligation is discharged.[3] If a condition be to do a single personal act and no time is fixed, the obligor shall have the whole of his life to perform it;[4] it is sufficient that the act be performed at the last time limited:[5] and the same principle would apply to any such contract on condition, extending it to the time when it is rendered impossible;[6] as a condition, that if A be ejected from his possession B will indemnify
1177. him; and so, when an obligation is contracted under the condition that an event shall not happen within a fixed time, as in the case of insuring a life for one or more years, such condition is accomplished, and the obligation discharged when the time is expired without the event having occurred. It is equally so if, before the time limited, it is certain that the event will not occur: as, an agreement to pay money to the son of a man, if he have a son twenty-one years of age at a certain time, the obligation is discharged if that time arrive within twenty-one years before the son is born; and if there have been no determinate period, it is not accomplished until it is certain that the event will not happen.[7]

---

1 Co. Lit. 209 b; Roll. Ab. 426, l. 8; T. Raym. 464; D. of St Albans v. Shore, 1 H. Bl. 270.

2 Co. Lit. 219. Performance in effect.—Worsley v. Wood, 6 T. R. 750; 1 Roll. Ab. 426, 2, 4; Dorrington v. East, Yelv. 87.

3 Glazebrook v. Woodrow, 8 T. R. 366; Wils. 59; Careless v. Careless, 1 Mer. 384.

4 Co. Lit. 208, 9; Page v. Hayward, 2 Salk. 570; 3 ib. 90.

5 1 Roll. 442, l. 15.

6 A gift or devise on condition would be suspended until there is no possibility of the condition being performed.—Randal v. Payne, 1 Bro. 55.

7 Humlock v. Blacklow, 1 Mod. 64; 2 Saund. 155.

Parallel Articles of the French Code.

The performance of a condition is excused, when by an act of the obligee it is prevented or rendered impos sible.[1] And a discharge from a condition by the obligee is a sufficient performance; and if the obligee stop the obligor, it is not necessary he should do a nugatory act.[2] 1178.

The time to which the commencement of a contract on condition relates, would depend entirely upon the wording of it, and the apparent intention of the parties.[3] 1179.

Sub-section 2.

Of the Condition Precedent.

A condition precedent may depend on an event or contingency, not under the control of either party; or it may consist in some act to be done by one or other of them: thus, a party may add a condition to his agreement, suspending his liability until the happening of a contingency; as where the acceptor of a bill of exchange only subjects himself to the payment of the bill, upon the happening of a contingency, such a conditional acceptance becomes absolute as soon as the condition is fulfilled;[4] and if the event had happened before the contract it would take effect directly, and the debt would have been due from the date of the contract: if the event continue future the debt also continues future; and the distinction must be kept in mind, whether the condition suspend the right to a thing or only the time of its actual delivery, and whether there has or not been a virtual delivery, so as to vest the thing. Where the contract is perfectly complete, and the condition only suspends the possession, the article remains at the risk of the person 1181.

---

[1] Basset v. Basset, 1 Mod. 264; Co. Lit. 206; Roll. Ab. 453, 4; Hotham v. East India Company, 1 T. R. 638.

[2] Jones v. Barkeley, Doug. 684 (leading case), 1178.

[3] Hanson v. Graham, 6 Ves. 239.

[4] Milne v. Prest. 4 Camp. 393; Holt, 181; Smith v. Abbott, 2 Stra. 1152; 7 Mod. 426.

Parallel Articles of the French Code.

to receive it;[1] but where the right to possession is not perfect, and some act or condition precedent remains to be performed on the part of the person delivering, it remains at his risk.[2] If a condition precedent of a contract for services be the payment of a certain price, and the party afterwards refuse to give that price, the other may decline to perform the services, and sue for damages.[3]

1182. When the obligation has been contracted under a condition precedent, that something must previously be done by the contractors (as to fix the price, quality, or individuality of the commodity which forms the matter of the contract), a complete present right of property does not vest in the other party, and the thing remains at the risk of the debtor:[4] and if the thing perish by the act of God, the contract is at an end.

If an injury short of destruction happen to the thing while it remains in the custody of the party bound to deliver, the other party cannot refuse to take the things or to pay for the services performed, but he may sue at law for damages.[5]

Sub-section 3.

Of the Condition Subsequent, and Limitations.

1183. A condition subsequent determining the contract or estate is in the nature of a defeasance. A defeasance, however, is a collateral deed made at the same time with a feoffment, grant, bond, warrant of attorney, or other contract, containing certain conditions, upon the performance of which the contract is void, or the estate created by such feoffment or grant may be defeated. A defeasance differs

---

1 Tarling v. Baxter, 6 B. & C. 364.

2 Hanson v. Meyer, 6 East, 614; Zagury v. Furnell, 2 Camp. 240; Gillett v. Hill, 4 Tyrwh. 290.

3 Hyde v. Willes, 3 Camp. 202.

4 Hanson v. Meyer, 6 East, 614; Zagury v. Furnell, 2 Camp. 240.

5 Davidson v. Gwynne, 10 East, 355.

Parallel Articles of the French Code.

from a condition in this respect, that a condition is inserted in the deed, by which an estate, for instance, is defeated, whereas a defeasance is a separate deed created at the same time. The usual form of condition to a bond for performance of covenant is dissolutory, making the bond void on performance of such covenants.

By a condition subsequent the obligation may be defeated or made void ab initio, or only determined from the happening of the contingency. In the latter case, what had been paid or received by either party would not have to be refunded: in the former case it might be otherwise.[1]

Conditions subsequent must be distinguished into conditions in law, and conditions in deed. When an estate or the obligation of a contract is so expressly confined in words, that it cannot endure for any longer time than till the contingency happens, this is a limitation or condition in law;[2] as when land is given to a person while he continues unmarried, or until out of the rents and profits he shall have made 500*l.* But when an estate is expressly granted, upon condition to be void on payment of 40*l.* by the grantor, or so that he continues unmarried, this is a condition in deed, and the law permits it to endure beyond the time when such contingency happen, unless the grantor take advantage of the breach of the condition, and make either an entry or a claim.[3]

Where covenants are mutual, we have seen they are conditions precedent. Where either party refuses to perform his part of a contract, the other party is discharged from his part without suit,[4] and he may sue the other party for damages, or he may seek to compel specific performance;[5] and specific performance of a substantive 1184.

---

1 Towers v. Barrett, 1 T. R. 133.

2 Lit. s. 380; Co. Lit. 234; 10 Rep. 41.

3 Lit. s. 347; 3 Hen. VIII. c. 34; 10 Rep. 42.

4 Co. Lit. 208, 9; Shep. Touch. 134, 7.

5 Clayton v. Kynaston, 12 Mod. 221; 1 Ld. Raym. 419; Lacy v. Kynaston, ib. 688; 12 Mod. 415, 548.

Parallel Articles of the French Code.

part of an agreement will be decreed, although the plaintiff may have contravened a collateral covenant contained therein, leaving the defendant to his action at law for the breach of such covenant.[1]

Section 2.

Of Stipulations for Time[2] and Grace.

1185 to 1188. Grace (or what is called a term) differs from a condition, in that it does not suspend the engagement, but only delays the performance of it. This distinction is, in England, often very material with respect to cases affected by the bankrupt laws; a debt due at a future time (or, according to the phrase applied to that subject, debitum in præsenti solvendum in futuro), being entitled to the benefit of the commission, while a conditional (more frequently termed a contingent) debt is not.[3]

The law of England does not admit of any such term (as that of grace) for general purposes. The courts of equity often prescribe certain times within which acts are to be done, as for instance, the redeeming of mortgages; but the exercise of this discretion, or, more properly speaking, of this mode of adjudicating, has a very slight analogy to the term of grace referred to in the French law. By the special jurisdiction of courts of conscience, for the recovery of small debts, a payment is often awarded to be made by instalments, to which the effects of a term of grace may be fairly and naturally applied.[4]

It is manifest that if a husbandman engages to mow

1 Trant v. Dwyer, 2 Bligh, 11.

2 If an obligee covenant with the obligor who is bound to perform covenants not to molest or sue him before so many days, this is no suspension of the debt for the proper intent of the agreement is to have an action of covenant on it if he sue before the day, and not to make it a release,—1 Roll. Ab. 938, pl. 45; Dowse v. Jefferey, 3 Pro. 352; Hedges v. Smith, ib. 623.

3 Evans' Pothier, n. p. 131.

4 Ib. p. 131.

Parallel Articles of the French Code.

my meadow on the 1st of June, he does not discharge the obligation by mowing it on the first of May; neither can a person derive any collateral advantage from an anticipated payment; as if he is bound to pay money, with interest, on the 1st of June, he cannot discharge himself from the intermediate interest by offering to pay the principal on the 1st of May, against the will of the creditor, who, by express stipulation, was to have interest to a subsequent period. If there be a condition to re-enter on payment of 100*l.* on the 1st of May, though the grantor pays before, he cannot enter until the 1st of May.[1] Agreements sometimes contain both a condition and a term; in this case it is necessary to examine whether the term is applied only to the condition, or to the disposition also.[2]

Section 3.

Of Alternative Obligations.

When an obligation is disjunctive or alternative, the obligor shall have an election to do or give one or the other of the things to be given or done.[3] 1189.

The election belongs generally to the obligor,[4] for the condition is for the advantage of the obligor; but it may be given to the obligee, expressly or impliedly, as where the condition refers the matter to the request of the obligee, it gives the election to him;[5] and in default of per- 1190.

---

[1] Evans' Pothier, p. 132.

[2] Sidney v. Vaughan, 2 Bro. P. C. 254. Day, inclusive or exclusive.—Pugh v. D. of Leeds, Cowp. 714; Anon. 1 Ld. Raym. 180; R. v. Adderley, Doug. 463. Generally one day exclusive and one day inclusive. No fraction of day.—Herbert v. Tarbot, Keb. 589; Sid. 162; unless necessity, Combe v. Pitt, 3 Bur. 1423.

[3] Co. Lit. 145 a, 225. See distinctions taken, Eaton v. Monox, Cro. Eliz. 398; Baker v. Morecombe, ib. 864; Layton v. Pierce, Doug. 14.

[4] Br. Cond. pl. 161. It is however said, that a gift or grant made of uncertain things, the election belongs to him for whose benefit it was made.—Perk. s. 73.

[5] 1 Roll. 446, l. 35, 37; Wright v. Bull, 2 Mod. 304; 2 Danv. 79.

Parallel Articles of the French Code.

formance by the obligor before the time fixed, the obligee shall have the election,[1] and the obligor discharges himself by rendering one of the two things;[2] but part of one and part of the other is no performance.

1192. If one part was impossible at the time of the making, the obligor ought to do the other.[3]

1193. The alternative obligation becomes single, if one of the things promised perishes, or becomes impossible to be done:[4] though it is said, that if the condition consists of two parts in the disjunctive, in which the party hath an election that is to perform, and both were possible at the time of making the condition, and one becomes impossible by the act of God, this shall excuse the performance of that and the other also; for otherwise his election would be taken away by the act of God.[5]

There is a distinction between what is denominated disjunctive absolute and disjunctive contingent; as, if a man be bound to do one thing, or pay money if a certain event shall happen; if the event do not happen, the obligation is saved; but if it be to pay money, or to do an act before a certain time, if the act cannot be done accordingly the money must be paid.[6]

Section 4.

Of Obligations Joint and Several.

Sub-section 1

Of Creditors jointly and severally Interested.

1197. Where several persons enter into a covenant or agree-
1198. ment, they may bind themselves altogether, or else they

---

1 Br. Dette, pl. 159.

2 Shaw's case, Palm. 76.

3 1 Roll. 450, l. 40, 45; 1 B. & P. 244.

4 Topham v. Pannel, T. Raym. 373; Anon. 1 Salk. 170.

5 Laughton's case, 5 Rep. 22; Cro. Eliz. 398; Studholme v. Mandel, Ld. Raym. 279.

6 Per Popham, C. J. Goldsb. 192, pl. 141; Vin. Abr. 5, 210

Parallel Articles of the French Code.

may only bind each of themselves severally; from which arises a distinction between joint and several covenants.[1] A covenant of this kind may be both joint and several. Where a person covenants with two or more, and with each of them, and if each of the covenantees take a joint interest in the subject matter, it is a joint covenant. A man cannot bind himself to several and to each of them, to make it joint and several at the election of several persons for one and the same cause. The nature of the interest of the covenantees, whether joint or several, determines the covenant to be joint or several as to them.[2] 1199.

Where the legal interest of the covenantees is joint, the action must be brought in the name of all the covenantees;[3] and this rule holds even where the words of the covenant are joint and several; for the wording of the covenant cannot make that several which was before joint.[4] But joint words may be taken separately,[5] and an agreement may be joint in one part and several in another.[6] The legal interest may be joint, though the benefit be for one separately.[7]

Where the interest is several, although the wording of the covenant be joint, yet it shall be taken to be several.[8] And where the interest is several, each covenantee may bring an action for his particular damage, and the covenantor cannot make satisfaction to the one for the other.[9] Tenants in common may join in debt for a rent, or they may sue severally.[10]

When the covenants are several, they are as several deeds written on one piece of parchment.[11]

---

[1] Cru. pt. 32, c. 25.

[2] Slingsby's case, 5 Rep. 18; Jenk. 262; Eccleston v. Clipsham, 1 Saund. 153; Johnson v. Wilson, Willes, 248; Eccleston & Ux. executors, v. Clipsham, Saund. 153; 2 Keb. 338; Anderson, administrator, v. Martindale, 1 East, 497; James v. Emery and Clude, 8 Taunt. 245; Withers v. Bircham and another, 3 B. & C. 254.

[3] Rolls v. Yate, 1 Yelv. 177.

[4] Slingsby's case, 5 Rep. 18; Anderson v. Martindale, 1 East, 497.

[5] Windham's case, 5 Rep. 7.

[6] Eccleston v. Clipsham, 1 Saund. 153.

[7] Scott v. Goodwin, 1 Bos. & P. 67.

[8] Bull, N. P. 157.

[9] Wilkinson v. Lloyd, 2 Mod. 82.

[10] Martin v. Crompe, Ld. Raym. 340.

[11] Mathewson's case, 5 Rep. 23.

Parallel Articles of the French Code.

Sub-section 2.

Of Debtors jointly and severally Bound.

1200 to 1203. When there are several covenantors, they may either covenant for themselves altogether, and thus become, as it were, surety for each other, or severally and jointly, or severally only.[1]

Where the covenant is joint, and not several, all the covenantors must be joined in a suit to enforce the covenant.[2] But if they covenant jointly and severally, it is at the option of the covenantee to sue them jointly or severally.[3] But if there be more than two parties to a joint and several obligation, the obligee must proceed against them, either all jointly, or each separately.[4]

It is a principle, that if several persons stipulate for the performance of an act, they are impliedly bound jointly and not severally; and there must be express words creating a several liability in order to render them separately responsible.[5]

Where there are several parties to an implied contract, they are primâ facie jointly liable for the whole debt, and not merely each for his own share.[6]

At law, joint covenants survive in case of death;[7] but relief will sometimes be granted in equity to the survivor, against the estate of the deceased joint obligor.[8]

---

1 May v. Woodward, Freem. 248; Bolton v. Lee, 2 Lev. 56; Robinson v. Walker, 7 Mod. 153.

2 Com. Dig. Pleader (2 vol. ii.), Mathewson's case, 5 Rep. 23.

3 Lilly v. Hedges, 1 Stra. 553; 8 Mod. 166; Enys v. Dornithorne, 2 Burr. 1190; Exparte Vaughan, cited 3 P.W. 405.

4 Stratfield v. Halliday, 3 T. R. 782; Exparte Rowlandson, 3 P.W. 405.

5 Chit. on Cont.

6 2 Campb. 640; 3 ib. 51, 53, 168.

7 Rolls v. Yate, Yelv. 77; 1 Bulst. 25; Southcote, executrix, &c. v. Hoare, 3 Taunt. 87.

8 Primrose v. Bromley, 1 Atk. 89; Simpson v. Vaughan, 2 ib. 31; Bishop v. Church, 2 Ves. 100, 371; Burn v. Burn, 3 Ves. J. 573. See as to the creditors, rights against representatives, Hoare v. Contencin, 1 Bro. C. 27; Exparte Kendall, 17 Ves. 514; Paley v. Field, 12 Ves. 435.

Parallel Articles of the French Code.

Proceedings commenced against one of the parties jointly and severally bound, do not prevent the obligee from instituting the like against the others.

If a joint covenant be broken by the tort of one of the covenantors, the other shall not be charged with the breach of covenant.[1] 1204. 1205.

An acknowledgment by one of several joint contractors, does not revive the remedy for a debt barred by the statute of limitations as to the others;[2] but this statute does not affect the effect of a payment of any principal or interest by any person whatsoever; and payment of part by one of several co-contractors, takes the case out of the statute of limitations as to all of them.[3] But payment of part by an executor of a joint contractor, does not take the case out of the statute as to the survivor.[4] 1206.

If there be two or more obligors, a release by one will be a bar to all.[5] Where two are severally and jointly bound, a release to one will operate as a discharge of the other obligor.[6] A covenant not to sue is not a release.[7] 1208.

A court of common law expressed an opinion, that where one of several contractors had paid the whole he could not proceed against another for more than his aliquot part, although others were insolvent.[8] But in equity, the doctrine of contributions is the result of general equity, on the ground of equality of burthen and benefit, and the solvent obligors may be compelled to pay more than their aliquot parts.[9] 1214.

1 Coleman v. Sherwin, Show. 79; Carth. 97; 1 Salk. 137.

2 9 Geo. IV. c. 14.

3 Bealy v. Greenslade, 10 Law Journal, 1; Wyatt v. Hodson; Jackson v. Farebank, H. B. 340.

4 Slater v. Lawson, 1 B. & Ad. 396; Atkins v. Tredgold, 3 B. & C. 23; Whitcomb v. Whiting, Doug. 651.

5 8 Roll. Ab. 410, l. 47.

6 Co. Lit. 232 a; Lit. Rep. 191; 1 Keb. 936; Clayton v. Kynaston, 1 Ld. Raym. 420; Salk. 573. Admitted in Dean v. Newerall, 8 T. R. 168; Errington v. Evans, 2 Dick. 457.

7 Fitzgerald v. Trant, 11 Mod. 254; Dean v. Newall, 8 T. R. 168.

8 Cowell v. Edwards. 2 B. & P. 268; Turner v. Davies, 2 Esp. 478; 1 Roll. Ab. 20, pl. 15.

9 Peter v. Rich, 1 Ch. R. 19, 34; Hall v. Harrison, id. 240; Layer v. Wilson, 1 Vern. 456.

Parallel Articles of the French Civil.

Release to one is release to all.[1] A noli prosequi, or nonsuit, before judgment against one would discharge all.[2]

1215.

Section 5.

Of Obligations Divisible and Indivisible.

1217 to 1219. As the lands of an intestate descend to his heir, and the personal property goes to the executor or administrator, who are each in the eye of the law one person, viz. the representative of the deceased, and bound to perform his contracts (not strictly personal), there can be no divisibility of an obligation as to the persons who are to perform it, except among coparceners, who, although they are in general considered as only one, are sometimes necessarily regarded as several.[3]

Where rent is reserved upon condition, the condition is entire, and cannot by the act of the parties, as by a grant of part of the land out of which it is granted, be divided and apportioned.[4] By act in law, a condition may be apportioned.[5]

The legatees of a specific chattel, or the devisee of land, may be liable to an obligation in such manner as the deceased by will directed.

The mode of performance may be divisible or indivisible.[6] It is a general rule, that an entire contract cannot be apportioned; and if a party undertake to

---

[1] Art. 1208. [2] Parker v. Sir J. Lawrence, Co. Lit. Harg. n. 144.

[3] Of inheritances, some be entire and some be severall: again of entire, some be divisible and some indivisible.—Co. Lit. 164 b. Apportionments of rents, charge and service, rights of way and other easements, of service of a horse.—Lit. 222; Coke's Com.; Nightingale v. Lawson, 1 Bro. Ch. 440; Stone v. Theed, 2 Bro. C. 240; White v. White, 4 Ves. 24; Stevenson v. Lombard, 2 East, 575.

[4] Co. Lit. 215 a.

[5] Co. Lit. 215 a. Quæ in partes dividi nequeunt solida, à singulis præstantur.—6 Rep. 1. Annale, aut debitum, Judex nec separat ipsum.—3 Rep. 52.

[6] Agreement single and entire, consideration entire.—Chater v. Beckett, 7 T. R. 201; Bird v. Appleton, 8 ib. 562; Cro. Eliz. 200; Alexander v. Owen, 1 T. R. 225.

complete a certain act before his claim to remuneration is to accrue, he cannot recover for a partial performance, although the completion was prevented by accident, as fire, &c.,[1] unless the defendant disaffirm the entirety of the contract by receiving a partial benefit.[2]

Parallel Articles of the French Code.

If a promise be to do two or more acts, one of which is illegal, an action cannot be maintained for a breach of the agreement.[3]

If two things be sold by an agent in one lot, warranted at an entire price, the contract is entire; and on breach of the warranty as to one, the purchaser cannot maintain a separate action against the real owner of the thing which proves unsound.[4]

Sub-section 1.

Of the Effects of the Divisible Obligation.

When an obligation is capable of division, if part be illegal and part legal, the legal part must be performed.[5] 1220. 1221.

A distinction is made between contracts void at common law and such as are void by statute law; and it was said that in the one case, if it be bad or void in part, it is void in toto; but at common law it may be void in part and good in part.[6]

When that which is good and that which is void are put together, the common law makes such a construction, that the grant shall be good as to what is good, and void for that which is void.[7]

Where the contract is divisible, the consideration may be apportioned.[8]

---

1 Cutlar v. Powell, 6 T. R. 320; 2 East, 145; 8 id. 320; 3 Chit. Com. L. 129, 130.

2 Countess of Plymouth v. Throgmorton, 1 Salk. 65.

3 Morris v. Chapman, T. Jones, 24; Carter, 223.

4 Symonds v. Carr, 1 Campb. 361; Stort v. Dixon, Selw. 101.

5 Misdel v. Middleton, 1 Vent. 237; T. Raym. 222; Newman v. Newman, 4 M. & S. 66; Chesman v. Namby, 2 Ld. Raym. 1459; Laying v. Paine, Willes, 574.

6 Collins v. Blantern, 1 Mod. 35, 36.

7 Per Hutton Ley's Rep. 79, cited by Lawrence, J., 8 East, 236; Selw. N.P.

8 Stevenson v. Snow, 3 Burr, 1237; Rothwell v. Cooke, 1 B. & P. 172.

Parallel Articles of the French Code.

Where part of a contract arose upon a good consideration and part on a bad one, it was holden divisible, and that the party might recover on that which was good.[1]

Sub-section 2.

Of the Effects of an Indivisible Obligation.

1222 to 1225. When an obligation is indivisible, if part be legal and part illegal, if a party apply to a court of common law to have it rescinded, it must be done in toto.[2]

On an agreement to deliver a determinate quantity of goods at a fixed price by a certain time, it was held that as the contract was entire and could not be split, no action could be brought for the price until the whole quantity was delivered, or until the time for delivering the whole had arrived.[3]

Where a joint order is given for several articles at several prices, the contract is entire, and the purchaser may refuse to accept one unless the others are delivered.[4]

Where a party undertakes to do some particular and entire act, he cannot recover payment for a proportionable part of the work and labour bestowed in performance of such contract; but he must proceed for the whole, even though the work has been destroyed by accident, or he was prevented from finishing it.[5]

Section 6.

Of Obligations with Penal Causes.

1226. In criminal law a penalty is properly a fine imposed as a punishment, and it is viewed civilly in the same light.

[1] Robinson v. Bland, 2 Burr. 1077; 1 Blac. R. 234; 3 T. R. 418; 11 East, 165; 13 East, 87; 15 East, 440; 6 Taunt. 57, 105; Cro. Eliz. 143; Sid. 38; 4 Leon. 3; Yelv. 56; Cro. Eliz. 848, 199.

[2] Alexander v. Owen, 1 T. R. 225; Fitzroy v. Gwillim, ib. 154.

[3] Waddrington v. Oliver, 2 Bos. & Pul. 61; Walker v. Dixon, 2 Stark. 281.

[4] Champion v. Short, 1 Campb. 53; Baldey v. Parker, 2 B. & C. 47.

[5] Gandell v. Portyny, 4 Campb. 375; Gillett v. Mawman, 1 Taunt. 137.

Parallel Articles of the French Code.

If the bond or contract is void, as in the cases of illegality, the penal clause is also void.

With respect to penalties, there appear to be two classes of cases, the one of penalties in bonds conditioned 1227.
for the performance of one or more acts, and where the 1228.
obligee must proceed for the penalty; the other of penalties contained in other deeds or agreements, where the party is at liberty either to proceed for the penalty or for the damages which he has sustained by breach of the stipulation: the penalty being only in the nature of a further security for the due performance of the contract.

A bond with a penalty may in equity be considered as the evidence of an agreement, and the execution specifically enforced accordingly.[1] The condition of the bond is, the agreement of the party.[2]

Although where a penalty is provided in case of breach of a contract, the party is at liberty to proceed for the penalty or for the real damage he has sustained, yet in either case he is precluded from recovering more than the damages he really has sustained.[3] If he proceed for the penalty, it will stand as a security for future breaches; but then he cannot[4] recover in the whole more than the penalty.[5]

The statute 8 and 9 W. III. c. 11, s. 8, limits the execution to the damages assessed by the jury, and that assessment is definitive.[6]

There is a considerable difference between a penalty, and liquidated or stipulated damages. Thus for stipulated damages, the amount being fixed, the defendant

---

[1] Acton v. Pierce, 2 Vern. 280; Carmel v. Buckle, 2 P.W. 343; Watkins v. Watkins, 2 Atk. 97; Parks v. Wilson, 10 Mod. 518; Hodson v. Trevor, 2 P.W. 191.

[2] Collins v. Collins, 2 Burr. 820; Mackworth v. Thomas, 3 Ves. 329.

[3] 8 & 9 Wm. III. c. 11, s. 8.

[4] Equity may, on circumstances, carry the debt beyond the penalty.—Law Max.

[5] 6 T. R. 303; 2 Marsh, 226; M'Cluse v. Dunkin, 1 East, 136; sed Francis v Wilson, 1 R. & M. 103; Sloman v. Walter, 1 Bro. 418.

[6] Johnes v. Johnes, 5 Taunt. 656.

Parallel Articles of the French Code.

might have been holden to bail, but not for a penalty.[1]

It appears that, 1st, where a sum of money, whether in the name of a penalty or otherwise, is introduced into an agreement merely to secure the enjoyment of a collateral object, the enjoyment of that object is considered as the principal intent of the contract, and the penalty only as accessory, and therefore only to secure the damage really incurred.[2]

2nd. Where an agreement contains provisions for the performance of several things, and then a large sum is stated at the end of it to be paid upon the breach of performance, it will be considered a penalty.

3rd. Where the payment of a smaller sum is secured by a larger: and

4th. Where the word penalty is specifically used, it is merely as a security, and will effectually prevent the court from considering the sum mentioned as liquidated damages.[3]

5th. A court of equity will relieve against a penalty upon a compensation, and a court of law will not enforce it beyond the actual damage sustained; but where there is an agreement to pay a particular liquidated sum, neither a court of equity nor a court of law can make a new agreement for a party, nor is there any room for compensation or relief.[4]

6th. Where the precise sum, therefore, is not the essence of the contract, the quantity of damages may be assessed by a jury; but where the precise sum has been fixed and agreed upon by the parties, that very sum is the ascertained and liquidated damages; the jury are confined to it, and the plaintiff cannot recover beyond it.[5]

---

1 Wildey v. Thornton, 2 East, 410; Rolfe v. Peterson, 6 Bro. P. C. 460; Roy v. D. of Beaufort, 2 Atk. 190.

2 Astley v. Weldon, 2 B. & P. 346; Harrison v. Wright, 13 East, 343.

3 Smith v. Dickenson, 3 B. & P. 630; Orr v. Churchill, 1 H. Bl. 227.

4 See ante, par. art. 1152.

5 Love v. Peirs, 4 Burr. 2225; Farraut v. Olmius, 3 B. & A. 692.

A penalty is never held in equity to release parties from their contracts, which must be performed in equity though the penalty be incurred.[1]

Parallel Articles of the French Code.

In case of a bond conditioned for the performance of one or more acts, if there be a breach of condition, the obligee cannot in general recover at law or in equity, beyond the extent of the penalty, though the real damage should greatly exceed it.[2] But where the penalty is considered merely a further security for the performance of the contract, the party has his option either to proceed for the penalty or for the real damages, in which latter case more may be recovered than the amount of the penalty; if he bring an action for the penalty, he cannot afterwards resort to the covenant.[3]

If the obligation be to perform an act, or to deliver or remove a thing, though a time is fixed for so doing, if there is any condition precedent on the other part, or on the part of a third person, it must be performed before there can be a breach of the contract, and before the penalty or liquidated damages accrue.[4] 1230.

---

[1] Howard v. Hopkins, 2 Atk. 371.

[2] 6 T. R. 303; 1 Saund. 58; Newl. Cont. 330.

[3] Harrison v. Wright, 13 East, 343; Holt, C. N. P. 46; 1 Campb. 78; Benson v. Gibson, 3 Atk. 395; Hardy v. Martin, 1 Bro. C. 418, n.

[4] Co. Lit. 211.

Parallel Articles of the French Code.

CHAPTER V.

Of the Extinction of Obligations.

Contracts are merged, extinguished, discharged, or satisfied:—

1234. 1. By payment or performance.
2. By higher or better security given, accord and satisfaction.
3. By express release, or release in deed.
4. By set off.
5. By implied release, or release in deed.
6. By becoming impossible.
7. By nullity or insufficiency.
8. By non-performance of condition precedent.
9. And by the statutes of limitation or prescription.[1]

Section 1.

Of Payment and Performance.

Sub-section 1.

Of Payment[2] and Performance in General.

Payment (solutio) is every species of discharge of a debt or promise.[3] In a stricter sense payment has been defined "a delivery over of money, in discharge of an antecedent debt."[4]

1235. A payment necessarily supposes, and is considered to be in discharge of, a debt; but where money has been paid by mistake without being due, it may be recovered back again; but it must have been by mistake, and

---

[1] Chitty's Pleadings, v. i. c. 7.

[2] Qui tardius solvit minus solvit.—Jenk. Cent. 58.

[3] Bacon.

[4] Per Gaselee, J., Cannan v. Denew, 3 Mod. & S. 770.

Parallel Articles of the French Code.

not voluntary where the party knew he was not liable.[1] An action in such case only lies for money which, ex æquo et bono, ought to be refunded;[2] it does not lie where the money was payable in point of honour and honesty, although not recoverable by law.[3] And the party seeking to recover back money paid, must show that he has equity and conscience on his side;[4] and natural love or obligation is a sufficient consideration.

An obligation may be discharged by any of the persons interested to do so, such as a co-obligor, or a surety, or even a stranger. And if a stranger, in the name of the obligor (without his consent or privity), tender payment, and the obligee accepts it, it is a good satisfaction; but the obligor may disagree thereto if he will.[5] If a stranger of his own head, who hath not any interest, tender the payment, the party is not bound to receive it. 1236.

And where the obligation to do any act is entered into under personal considerations, and one party has an interest in having it performed by the other in person, there can be no valid performance by a third party. 1237.

Properly a party cannot discharge an obligation due from himself by delivery, as payment, of a thing which belongs to another;[6] for the owner cannot lose his property by the mere transfer of a person not entitled to dispose of it, except by sale in market overt.[7] But payment of money, or the transfer of bank-notes, or negociable instruments would, on account of their currency, give a valid indisputable property to the person receiving the payment (except in some particular cases resulting from the illegality of the contract). The delivery of articles of any other kind would not give any absolute right, and 1238.

---

[1] Brown v. M'Kinally, 1 Esp. 279.

[2] 1 Taunt. 263; 2 Moore, 240.

[3] Farmer v. Arundel, 2 Bl. 824.

[4] Stratton v. Rastall, 2 T. R. 370.

[5] Co. Lit. 206 b, 207 a.

[6] Nemo potest plus juris ad alium transferre quam ipse habet.—Co. Lit. 309; Wing. 56.

[7] 2 Bl. Com. 450.

Parallel Articles of the French Code.

the person who received them would be responsible for their value: the act of consumption would not, in either case, have any effect upon the nature of the right.[1]

1239. Payment should be made to the party to whom it is due, or to some person specially or generally authorized to receive it on his behalf. Payment to a plaintiff's attorney[2] is as good and effectual as payment to the plaintiff himself:[3] but payment to such attorney's agent has been held not to discharge the debtor:[4] but the correctness of this decision seems to be doubtful; and money paid into court by the debtor, and taken out by the attorney's agent, has been held to be conclusive against the creditor.[5] Payment to an agent,[6] in the ordinary course of business, is as effectual as to the principal, though known to be an agent, if made before the countermand by the principal;[7] and acts done by an agent under a power of attorney before he knew of its revocation, are good[8] against the principal, who, however, may consent to waive such as are for his benefit.[9] When payment is made to a person who has no authority to receive it, the debt is not thereby discharged, but it must be paid again to the creditor, leaving the debtor to his remedy against the person who so received the payment;[10] but if the money were accepted by the creditor, expressly or impliedly, the debtor would be discharged.

1240. Payment to the person, as a banker bonâ fide holding

---

1 Ev. Pot. n. p. 329.

2 As to a scrivener, Whitlock v. Waltham, 1 Salk. 157; Martyn v. Kingsly, Pre. Ch.—Payment to father; Dagley v. Tolferry, 1 P. W.; Cooper v. Thornton, 3 Bro. C. 96.

3 Coore v. Callaway, 1 Esp. 115; 1 Bl. R. 85; Powell v. Settle.

4 Yates v. Freckleton, Doug. 623.

5 Griffith v. Williams, 1 T. R. 710.

6 Where there is power to sell there must be a power to receive.—Anon. 12 Mod. 230.

7 Coates v. Lewis, 1 Camp. 444; Cowp. 251; 11 East, 36; 2 Camp. 24.

8 But see, where the power is terminated by the death of the principal, Wallace v. Cook, 5 Esp. 118; Watson v. King, 4 Camp. 272; Lepard v. Vernon, 2 V. & B. 51.

9 Per Buller, Salt v. Field, 5 T. R. 215.

10 Robson v. Eaton, 1 T. R. 62. Forgery; Cheap v. Harley, 3 T. R. 127.

Parallel Articles of the French Code.

a negociable security, though not the proprietor, is an effectual discharge of the debt; but where the person receiving is not bonâ fide the holder (as under a forged indorsement, or after an insufficient procuration), notwithstanding the payment to him, the debtor still remains liable to the real owner.[1] And if rent be paid to a person supposed to be landlord, who is afterwards evicted, the real landlord can recover the value of the use and occupation; and the tenant may recover in assumpsit[2] rents tortiously received.

In general, payment made to a creditor not competent to receive it is no discharge;[3] but when made to an infant, if beneficial to him, it might be good,[4] but in general it is otherwise;[5] and so of a married woman:[6] but payments to a bankrupt prior to the fiat of bankruptcy are specially protected.[7] 1241.

A debtor, not a trader, and not subject to the bankrupt laws, may pay one or more creditors in preference to others, and may assign not only part of, but all his property to satisfy one just debt in preference to another;[8] and an execution by a creditor against the estate or person of the debtor would not set aside or affect such preference.[9] If the debtor took the benefit of the insolvent act, any assignment of his property, though for the benefit of creditors, made within three months before the time when the insolvent went to prison, and in contemplation of insolvency, would be deemed fraudulent and 1242.

[1] Cheap v. Harley, 3 T. R. 127; East India Company v. Tritton, 3 B. & C. 280.

[2] 6 T. R. 683; Bul. N. P. 133; Cowp. 414.

[3] Payment to an executor having probate of a forged will, good against the rightful administrator.—Allen v. Dundas. If a legacy is bequeathed to a femme covert, payment of it to her alone is not good, the executor might have to pay it over again to her husband.—Palmer v. Trower, 1 Ver. 261.

[4] Bailey on Bills, p. 315; Marlow v. Pitfield, 1 P.W. 558.

[5] 1 Salk. 279, 386; Phillips v. Paget, 2 Atk. 80.

[6] Connor v. Martin, Str. 516; Miles v. Williams, 10 Mod. 246; M. Neilage v. Holloway, 1 B. & Ald. 218.

[7] 6 Geo. IV. c. 16, s. 82; 1 Jac. I. c. 15, s. 14.

[8] Cailland v. Estwick, 2 Anstr. 381; 5 T. R. 235, 420.

[9] Holbird v. Anderson, 5 T. R. 235.

Parallel Articles of the French Code.

void.[1] And in the case of a trader subject to the bankrupt law, a fraudulent preference would be an act of bankruptcy.[2]

1243. Where one party is under obligation to deliver a specific thing, he cannot compel the other to receive a different thing in lieu, though of equal or superior value.[3]

1244. A debtor cannot oblige his creditor to receive partial payment of a debt; and a judge at common law has no power to make an order on a plaintiff to take his debt by instalments.

1245. If chattels or real property contracted for be deteriorated in the hands of the party bound to deliver them, without his fault, after the property in them is vested in the other party, his obligation is discharged by delivery of them in their actual state, notwithstanding the deterioration.

1246. If the thing to be delivered be not specifically chosen by the party to whom it is to be delivered, it rests with the other party to set it out.

1247. Payment must be made at the place[4] appointed by the contract. Where a party is bound to pay a sum of money, and no place for payment is appointed, he is bound to seek the payee, and pay it if he can find him; and the mere readiness to pay is not sufficient.[5]

Sub-section 2.

Of the Assignment of Debts and Choses in Action.

1250. Debts are assigned either by agreement or by the act of the law. The cases in which the law assigns debts and choses in action are bankruptcy and insolvency. In strictness, choses in action (except bills and promissory

---

[1] 7 Geo. IV. c. 57, s. 32.

[2] 6 ib. c. 16, s. 3; vide s. 6.

[3] 9 Rep. 79.

[4] Locus pro solutione redditus aut pecuniæ secundum conditionem dimissionis aut obligationis est stricte observandus.—4 Rep. 73.

[5] Co. Lit. 340; Saward v. Palmer, 2 Moore, 276; Crawley v. Hillary, 2 M. & S. 120.

notes) cannot be assigned by agreement at common law;[1] yet in equity they may: and courts of law will permit the assignee to sue in the assignor's name.[2] And they have in some instances, though in a qualified manner, recognised the equitable interest of the assignee of a bond:[3] thus they would not permit the obligor of a bond to plead payment to the original obligee after notice of assignment.[4] If the debtor borrow money and pay off the original creditor, he may cause the securities held by such original creditor to be assigned to the person of whom he has borrowed the money, if such course would not prejudice the original creditor; or he may give his new creditor new securities, without the assent of the original creditor, whose power to interfere is in such case discharged by payment of his demand.

Parallel Articles of the French Code.

Where a person has laid out his own money for the use of another, either with the express or implied consent of such person, the law implies a promise of repayment, for breach of which an action may be maintained. As where a surety pays the debt for which he is bound, he may recover the money so paid from the principal debtor, even though not so paid by the desire of the principal:[5] but the consent of the debtor, express or implied, is essentially necessary.[6]

If a third mortgagee, who lent his money without 1251.
notice of the mesne incumbrance, obtains an assignment of the first mortgage he obtains a preference over the second mortgagee for the whole of his debt.[7] A party

[1] Co. Lit. 232 a.

[2] Delany v. Stoddart, 1 T. R. 26; Johnson v. Collings, 1 East, 123.

[3] Kingdom v. Jones, 2 Skin. 6; T. Jones, 150; Winch v. Keeley, 1 T. R. 619.

[4] Legh v. Legh, 1 B. & P. 417. Specific performance of a contract for sale of debts proved under a commission of bankruptcy (Adderley v. Dixon, 1 Sim. & Stu. 607), would be decreed.

[5] Ecall v. Partridge, 8 T. R. 108; Fisher v. Fellowes, 5 Esp. 171.

[6] Stokes & another v. Lewis & another, 1 T. R. 20.

[7] Bovey v. Shipwick, 1 Cha. Ca. 201; Churchill v. Grove, 1 Cha. Ca. 35; 2 Ves. 573; Hagshaw v. Yates, Stra. 240.

Parallel Articles of the French Code.

who has paid the debt of his principal is entitled to every remedy which the creditor has against the principal debtor; to enforce every security and all means of payment; to stand in the place of the creditor, not only through the medium of contract, but even by means of securities, entered into without the knowledge of the surety having a right to have these securities transferred to him, although there was no stipulation for it, and to avail himself of all these securities against the debtor.[1] A surety paying debt on a joint bond of himself and the principal, is only a simple contract creditor of the principal, although he would be entitled to stand in the place of a mortgagee.[2]

Sub-section 3.

Of the Application of Payments.

1253 to 1256. A person who is indebted to another on several accounts may, on paying him the money, ascribe it to which he[3] pleases;[4] and his election may be either expressed or inferred from the circumstances of the transaction: but if the payer does not specify a particular one, the receiver[5] may apply the payment to the discharge of either of the accounts as he pleases.[6]

Where a man pays money generally, and is indebted for principal and interest, it shall be applied first to reduce the interest; and where he is indebted in the two sums, the one bearing interest and the other not, the payment shall be applied to the credit of that which carries interest, or is the most penal upon the debtor, even

---

1 Craythorne v. Steinburne, 14 Ves. 162.

2 Cope v. Middleton, Turn. & Russ. 224.

3 Quicquid solvitur, solvitur secundum modum solventis.—2 Vern. 606.

4 Pinel's case, 5 Rep. 117; Anon. Cro. Eliz. 68; Colt v. Netterville, 2 P.W. 304; Peters v. Anderson, Marsh, 238; Bosanquet v. Wray, 5 Taunt. 594.

5 Campbell v. Hodgson, 1 Gow. 74.

6 Peters v. Anderson; Lechmere v. Hawkins, 2 Esp. 226; Preston v. Shutton, 1 Anst. 50.

Parallel Articles of the French Code.

though the creditor declares he receives it on the other account;[1] and it was decreed that the debt first contracted should be paid first.[2]

The debtor must at the time of payment declare, or do some act to indicate, on what account he pays the money, otherwise the creditor is at liberty to determine the application of it, and the creditor's acquittance would determine it if expressed in it.[3]

SUB-SECTION 4.

Of Tender of Payment.

Tender, in its ordinary and practical sense, means the formal offer of a debt to a person to whom it is due. It is also applicable to a duty to be performed, or a contract to be completed, as to deliver stock, goods, &c.[4]

A tender and refusal is equivalent to payment.[5] The 1257.
party must be ready to pay at any instant on demand.[6] A tender operates like the payment of money into court as an admission of the contract.[7]

In order that a tender should be valid, it must be for- 1258.
mally made and capable of proof; and therefore it is 1259.
necessary, that it should be made to the creditor or to a 1260.
person authorized to receive money for him;[8] that it should be made by or on behalf of the debtor, of a sum named; though it should seem it will be presumed to be

---

[1] Chase v. Box, 2 Freem. 261; Heyward v. Lomax, Vern. 24; Brett v. Marsh, Vern. 468.—Apply it to Bond before simple contract, Anon. 12 Mod. 559; ib. 8 Mod. 236; Goddard v. Cox, 2 Stra. 1194; Anon. Comb. 463.

[2] Wentworth v. Manning, 1 Eq. Ab. 261, pl. 1.

[3] Manning v. Westerne, 2606; Dawe v. Holdsworth, Peake, 64; Clayton's case, 1 Merr. 605.

[4] Rawson v. Johnson, 1 East, 201.

[5] Isaac v. Sedgingham, 1 Vent. 167. Reprobata pecunia liberat solventem.—9 Rep. 79.

[6] Paine v. Peploe, 8 East, 168.

[7] Cox v. Brain, 3 Taunt. 95.

[8] Goodland v. Blewith, 1 Camp. 477; Moffat v. Parsons, 5 Taunt. 307.

Parallel Articles of the French Code.

made on behalf of the person who owes the sum of money.[1]

Properly the exact amount of what is admitted to be recoverable should be produced and counted in English gold and silver (the latter not exceeding 40*s.*), or in foreign coin made current by proclamation, and the amount should be named to the party to whom the offer is made, and if possible, the money laid down and counted in his presence;[2] though if he, after being told that such a sum is about to be paid him, declare he will not take it because more is due, that dispenses with the actual production of the money.[3] It is also necessary that it should be made before action brought, unless upon payment of costs;[4] that it should be made at the time and place agreed upon for payment;[5] that it be an unconditional, unqualified offer to pay the specific sum due,[6] and not as a settlement of all demands;[7] that on action brought, the party plead the tender, and that he is still ready to pay, and pay the money into court when necessary.[8]

1261. If the party withdraw the offer, or is not at all times ready to pay, the tender amounts to nothing.[9] Money brought into court on a plea of tender cannot be taken out by the defendant, though he has a verdict.[10]

1264. If the contract be to deliver a specific object at the place where it is found, it is advisible to give notice to the party that it is ready for delivery, and to request it to be taken away;[11] but it seems that if the things be not taken away within reasonable time, although no notice or re-

---

[1] Clamount v. Thornton, 2 S. P. 50.

[2] Brady v. Jones, 2 Dow & Ry. 305.

[3] Thomas v. Evans, 10 East, 101; Douglas v. Patrick, 3 T. R. 683; Holland v. Phillips, 6 Esp. 46.

[4] Gibbon v. Copeman, 5 Taunt. 840.

[5] Hammond v. Ousen, 12 Mod. 421; D. of Rutland v. Hodgson, Stra. 177.

[6] Brady v. Jones, 2 D. & R. 305.

[7] Mitchell v. King, 6 Car. & P. 237.

[8] Bray v. Booth, 1 Barnes, 181; Rether v. Skelton, Stra. 638; Trevet v. Aggas, Willes, 111; 2 Saund. 48.

[9] Paine v. Peploe, 8 East, 168; Spybeg v. Hide, 1 Camp. 181.

[10] Cox v. Robinson, Stra. 1027.

[11] Langfort v. Administrators of Tiler, 1 Salk. 113.

quest is given, the other party may charge warehouse room, or bring an action for the special damage.[1]

Parallel Articles of the French Code.

Sub-section 5.

Of Assignments for the Benefit of Creditors in General.

The whole property of a person may be assigned and transferred to certain persons in trust, for the benefit of his creditors. Such assignments are voluntary or judicial. 1265. 1266.

An assignment may be voluntary on the part of the debtor, while the creditor's rights remain unchanged by it: thus, if a debtor voluntarily assign the whole of his property for the benefit of his creditors, this does not discharge him until the whole amount of the debts due from him is paid, unless his creditors agree to accept a composition, and give a release under seal; for an agreement not under seal, to take part in exchange for the whole, is a nudum pactum;[2] though it is otherwise where the guarantee of a third person is added,[3] or there is a mutual agreement among the creditors;[4] which, however, must be executed.[5] The common form of assignments, for the benefit of creditors, is a trust deed: and if no creditor is privy to it, it merely amounts to a power given to the trustees, who are as it were the agents of the debtor; and he may, before payment or communication to the creditors, revoke it: but it seems doubtful if he can revoke it after a communication to them.[6] And where an insolvent by a composition deed, conveyed to trustees to sell and apply the proceeds rateably in discharge of his debts amongst all his creditors, who should execute the deed, if the trustees or some of them being creditors execute or assented, the property becomes vested in those trustees.[7] 1267.

[1] Greave v. Ashlin, 3 Camp. 426.

[2] See ante, p. 439, 40; 3 Rep. 118; Heathcote v. Cruikshanks, 2 T. R. 27; Fitch v. Sutton, 5 East, 230.

[3] Co. Lit. 212 b; Steinman v. Magnus, 11 East, 390.

[4] Goode v. Cheesman, 1 B. & Ad. 328; Reay v. White, 3 Tyrw. 596.

[5] Reay v. Richardson, 2 C.M. & R. 422.

[6] Acton v. Woodgate, 2 M. & K. 495; Garrard v. Ld. Lauderdale, 3 Sim. 1.

[7] Small v. Marwood, 9 Bar. & Cres. 300; 4 Ves. 97.

Parallel Articles of the French Code.

1268 to 1270. The judicial assignment is either under the act for the relief of insolvent debtors, which only discharges the person, and not the future property of the debtor; or under the bankrupt acts, which discharge both person and future property. The assignment to the assignees under the insolvent or bankrupt act, vests the property of the bankrupt or insolvent in them.[1]

Section 2.

Of the Substitution of one Security for another.[2]

1271. A new contract by the same debtor cannot discharge an old one, unless it be a higher security, or otherwise better the creditor. Thus one contract not under seal cannot be extinguished by another similar contract not under seal;[3] nor can the delivery of one bond be pleaded in full discharge of another bond;[4] and even the bringing of an action on the new security does not operate to extinguish the old debt, if such new security was not sufficient otherwise without the action.[5] Where a new agreement by parol is substituted for the original one under seal, the plaintiff cannot maintain an action of covenant upon the first by showing a performance of his part of the last.[6]

Acceptance of a security for a lesser sum cannot be pleaded in satisfaction of a similar security for a greater.[7] An agreement to accept a less sum by instalments in lieu of the original debt, was held to discharge the original debt, when the nature of the claim was changed to

---

[1] 1 & 2 Wm. IV. c. 56, s. 25; 7 Geo. IV. c. 57, s. 11.

[2] A mere agreement to take a new security is void, unless carried into execution.—Lynn v. Bruce, 2 H. Bl. 317; James v. David, 8 T. R. 141.

[3] Brown v. Wade, 2 Keb. 851; Story v. Atkins, 2 Ld. Raym. 1430; Milward v. Ingram, 2 Mod. 43; Roades v. Barnes, 1 Bur. 9; Co. Lit. 212 b.

[4] Manhood v. Crick, Cro. Eliz. 716; Lobly v. Geldart, 3 Lev. 55; Pennel's case, 5 Rep. 117.

[5] Drake v. Mitchell, 3 East, 251.

[6] Heard v. Wadham, 1 East, 619.

[7] Cumber v. Wane, Str. 426.

Parallel Articles of the French Code.

the advantage of the creditor.[1] By the creditor accepting the security of a third party, the debtor may be discharged:[2] but if a negotiable security of a third party be dishonoured, the original debt is revived.[3] Indorsement of a negotiable security to a third party transfers the right of recovering on it to him, and in effect discharges the demand of the indorser until default. An assignment by the creditor would operate in equity and conscience as an extinguishment of his right to recover unless for the benefit of the assignee.

In some cases the debtor may be discharged by the creditor accepting the security of another in his stead:[4] but if a stranger give a bond for a simple contract due from another, this does not extinguish the simple contract debt; but if, upon making the contract, a stranger gives bond for it, or, being present, promises to give bond for it, and after does so, the debt by simple contract is extinguished, the obligation being made upon or pursuant to the contract.[5] And where two parties are indebted to a third, and one of the two to the other, the agreement of the third party, with the one so indebted to the other, to transfer the other's debt to such third party to the account of the one so indebted to the other, though it be executed, does not discharge the other's liability to pay the debt.[6]

A transfer to the account of the creditor, made according to agreement in the books of the mutual banker of the parties, will amount to payment, though the banker becomes bankrupt before any money actually passes, or even before notice of the transfer having been made reached the creditor, he having previously agreed to it.[7]

And a debtor is in effect discharged as to a particular creditor by the assignment of his debt to a third person,[8]

---

[1] Goring v. Goring, Yelv. 11, 11.

[2] Hearslake v. Morgan, 5 T. R. 513; King v. Dawson, Wightw. 32.

[3] 2 Ld. Raym. 928; Exparte Blackburne, 10 Ves. 204 b.

[4] Wade v. Wilson, 1 East, 195.

[5] 2 Leon. 110.

[6] Cuson v. Chadley, 5 D. & R. 417; 3 B. & C. 591; 1 Car. & P. 174.

[7] Eyles v. Ellis, 4 Bing. 112; Bolton v. Richards, 6 T. R. 139.

[8] As already stated, par art. 1249 to 1253.

Parallel Articles of the French Code.

unless the old creditor remain security to the new one, in which case he retains his remedy over against the debtor.

1273. This substitution, of one person or one kind of security for another, being a new contract, can in general only take place between persons capable of contracting.

1274. The assent of the debtor to have a debt due to him assigned to his creditor is essential, for he may have an account and set off against the creditor.[1]

1275. And the creditor is not bound to accept the security of a third person; and if he did, it would depend upon the nature of the assignment, whether the first debtor were discharged, or the new one merely accepted as a guarantee; in general, unless expressly provided otherwise, the latter would be held to be the case.

1278.
1279.
1280. The assignment of a mortgage debt or security, or of the equity of redemption, places the new debtor or creditor in precisely the same situation as the old one; but the effect of cancelling an old security and giving a new one would depend on the nature of the transaction, and would, when a mere negociable security not under seal, generally leave the creditor to resort back to the old one, in default of payment on the new. But if a judgment be obtained, or acknowledged, the creditor cannot afterwards sue on an inferior security.[2] The higher security would not, however, in general change any collateral con-
1281. current remedy.[3] And accord, with satisfaction by one debtor, would discharge all; and so to one creditor would operate as to all.[4] And time given to a principal, without the consent of the sureties, discharges the latter, and so of the alteration of the security.

---

[1] Surtees v. Hubbard, 4 Esp. 203.
[2] 6 Rep. 46.
[3] 3 East, 257.
[4] 5 Rep. 117 b; 9 Rep. 79 b.

Parallel Articles of the French Code.

SECTION 3.

Of the Release of a Debt.

A release is the gift or discharge[1] of a right of action 1282.
which one has, or claims, against another or his land.[2] An acquittance or receipt differs from a release, which intends a deed under seal; an acquittance is a discharge in writing of a sum of money paid, or other duty performed.[3] A release not under seal is inoperative for want of a consideration.[4]

A covenant not to sue operates as a release to avoid circuity of remedies.[5]

Releases are either in deed, that is express releases, or in law.[6] The latter are considered in section 5 of this chapter.

A promise before it is broken may be discharged by a parol agreement; but after it is broken, it cannot be discharged without deed by any new agreement without satisfaction.[7]

If a deed be delivered up to be cancelled to the party 1283.
who is bound by it, and it is accordingly cancelled by tearing off the seals or otherwise defacing it; or if the person who has the deed cancels it by agreement with the other party, it becomes void.[8]

A release to one of several debtors will operate as a 1284.
discharge to all.

Discharge of a surety does not necessarily imply dis- 1286.

---

[1] A release shall be made void when there is suppressio veri, or suggestio falsi.—1 Vern. 20.

[2] Termes de la ley.

[3] Shep. Touch. 348.

[4] Lodge v. Dicas, 3 B. & Ald. 611; 1 Leon. 283.

[5] Dean v. Newhall, 8 T. R. 268; Maure v. Harrison, 1 Eq. Ca. Ab. 93; Copis v. Middleton, 1 Turn. & Russ. 229.

[6] Co. Lit. 264 b.

[7] Per Holt, 12 Mod. 538; admitted in Edwards v. Weeks, 1 Mod. 262. Accord with satisfaction is a good plea in personal actions where damages only are to be recovered; but not so in real actions.—4 Rep. 1.

[8] Cruise, 497.

Parallel Articles of the French Code.

charge of his principal; but release to the principal generally releases the surety,[1] but not a release to one of several sureties, or if the rights against the others be
1287. reserved.[2]

1288. What a creditor receives from one of several sureties or from the principal, must go in discharge of such creditor's claim, the principal, and the other sureties.[3]

Section 4.

Of Set Off.

1289. Where there are mutual debts between the parties, one debt may be set off against and discharged by the
1290. other.[4] The common law did not allow this; and set off is made only by virtue of the statutes,[5] 2 Geo. II. c. 22, and 8 Geo. II. c. 24, which being passed for the benefit of a person sued by one against whom he has a debt, is not imperative, and may be waived by the party sued.[6]

1291. Set off is only allowed between two debts, and not in cases of uncertain unliquidated damages;[7] and the debt set off must be a legal, and not an equitable demand.[8] It is very clear that nothing can be the subject of set off which cannot be the subject of an action; one injury cannot be set off against another, or against a debt:[9] but stipulated liquidated damages may be set off.[10] The debts must be mutual and due in the same right, and not barred by the statutes of limitations.[11] A husband's debts cannot set off against debts due to wife, nor vice versâ.

---

[1] Capel v. Butler, 2 S & S. 457; Skip v. Edwards, 9 Mod. 438.

[2] Exparte Carstairs, Buck, 560; Exparte Glendinning, ib. 517; Boultbee v. Stubbs, 18.

[3] See ante, par. art. 1236.

[4] 2 Geo. II. c. 22, s. 13; 8 Geo. II. c. 24, s. 4.

[5] 3 East, R. 104.

[6] Howlett v. Strickland, Cowp. 56; Weyall v. Waters, 6 T. R. 488; Freeman v. Ryett, 1 Bl. R. 394.

[7] Wake v. Tinkler, 16 East, 36; 19 Ves. 467.

[8] Freeman v. Hyett, 1 Bl. R. 394.

[9] Fletcher v. Dyche, 2 T. R. 32.

[10] Remington v. Stevens, Sh. 1271.

Parallel Articles of the French Code.

Debts not due cannot be set off against those due; only such debts as are due at the commencement of the action[1] can be set off in it.

A surety for goods to be supplied, and not for a previous debt, was held to be entitled to the benefit of payments subsequently made by the principal.[2] A joint debt cannot be set off against a separate demand, nor a separate debt against a joint demand; but an originally joint demand, due to or from a single survivor, may be set off.[3] Under circumstances in a court of equity, a joint debt may be set off against a separate demand;[4] and where their obligation is joint and several, the debt of one of them may be set off.[5] 1292. 1294.

Section 5.

Of Release in Law.[6]

If a debtor makes a creditor his executor, and the creditor accepts the executorship, as he cannot maintain an action against himself, it is a release in law of the action, but not of the debt; and the executor may retain so much of thé goods of the testator as is sufficient to pay his debt.[7] If the creditor makes the debtor his executor, it is to be considered but as a specific legacy to the debtor to pay the debt; and, therefore, it is not to be paid or retained until the debts of the testator are satisfied.[8] If a femme obligee marry the obligor, this is a release in 1300 1301.

---

[1] Evans v. Prosser, 3 T. R. 186.

[2] Marryat v. White, 2 Stark, 101; Pemberton v. Oakes, 4 Russ. 154.

[3] French v. Andrade, 6 T. R. 582; Stupman v. Thompson, Willes, 103.

[4] 3 Mer. 618.

[5] Fletcher v. Dyche, 2 T. R. 32.

[6] See this subject fully discussed in Wankford v. Wankford, 1 Salk. 229; Carey v. Goodinge, 3 Bro. C. 110; Brown v. Selwin, Tem. Talb. 240, in the case of a bond due from the executor.

[7] Co. Lit. 264, n. 1.

[8] Co. Lit. 264, n. 1; Rawlinson v. Shaw, 3 T. R. 577.

Parallel Articles of the French Code.

law: the like is law if there be two femme obligees, and the one take the debtor to husband.[1]

Section 6.

Of the Loss of the Thing Due.

1302.
1303. After contract completed, for delivery of a specific object (as a sale), the property in the object becomes vested in the party to whom it is to be delivered. Thus, if a horse die in my stables between bargain and delivery, I may have an action of debt for my money, because by the bargain the property was in the buyer: so in the case of destruction by fire of an article, of which the buyer has taken possession of the samples, as part of the object purchased.[2] And in cases of inevitable accident,[3] the loss will fall upon the party entitled to receive it, and the party bound to deliver it is discharged: but if he had been guilty of negligence, he would be liable to an action for damages.[4]

---

[1] Co. Lit. 264, n. 2; Cage v. Acton, 1 Ld. Raym. 515; Milbourn v. Ewart, 5 T. R. 381; Goodright v. Wells, Dougl. 771; Lord Compton v. Oxenden, 2 Ves. J. 261.

[2] Noy's Maxims, p. 88; Hind v. Whitehouse, 7 East, 558, 571; 3 Smith, 528.

[3] See Thompson v. Mills, 7 T. R. 384; Medeiros v. Hill, 5 C. & P. 182; 8 Bing. 231; Williams v. Lloyd, Sir Wm. Jones, 179; by the name of Williams v. Hill, Palmer, 179.

[4] If a person engaged to give me a dozen of wine, and to supply me with the best wine in his cellar, though he had no wine in his cellar, the obligation would not be void for want of an object; nor, consequently, if all the wine was used would it become void by extinction.—Ev. Pot. n. p. 434.

It seems clear, that a debtor may charge himself not only with risks that may be foreseen, but also those which there could be no room to apprehend.—Pot. Ev. n. p. 439. See the law where the contractor had not the article.—Vin. Ab. Contract M. p. 21; and see Hitchcock v. Giddings, 4 Price, Exc. P. 135; Sugden, Vendor and Purchaser, 553.

Parallel Articles of the French Code.

Section 7.

Of Rescinding and Setting Aside Agreements.

In considering the rescission of contracts, the distinction between void and voidable must be kept in view.[1] Where an agreement is void, it may be so pleaded in bar to any action for breach.[2] When it is only voidable, if a party wish to impeach or rescind a contract, he must do so within a reasonable time;[3] or if a party wish to compel performance of a contract, which the other party has given notice of his intention not to perform, he must proceed within reasonable time.[4] When a payment has been made on a contract, which is rescinded, or put an end to, the money may be recovered back again; but if it continue open, damages arising out of it can only be recovered.[5] Where a contract is not carried into execution, by reason of some negligence or default of one party, the other party, not having done anything which can be considered as an execution of the contract in part, may abandon the contract, and recover back the money he has paid on it:[6] but this rule holds only where the contract can be rescinded in toto, so as to place both parties in the same situation they were in before.[7] 1304. 1305.

1 Co. Lit. 295 b. Where a party has the option of rescinding he must exercise it in reasonable time.—Doe v. Smith, 2 T. R. 43.

2 Sel. N. P.

3 Hodgson v. Davies, 2 Camp. 530; Ellis v. Mortimer, 1 N. R. 257; Prosser v. Hooper, 1 Moore, 106; Chalmers v. Bradley, 1 Jac. & Walk. 51.

4 Heaphy v. Hill, 2 Sim. & Stu. 29; Reynolds v. Nelson, Madd. & Geld. 18. When no time is limited, the law appointeth the most convenient.—Wing. Quam longum debet esse rationabile tempus non definitur in lege, sed pendet ex discretione justiciariorum. — Co. Lit. 56. Quam rationabilis debet esse finis, non definitur, sed omnibus circumstantiis inspectis, pendet ex justiciariorum discretione.—11 Rep. 44.

5 Towers v. Barrett, 1 T. R. 133.

6 Giles v. Edwards, 7 T. R. 181.

7 Hunt v. Silk, 5 East, 449; Cook v. Munstone, 1 Bos. & Pul. 351. Non debet adduci exceptio ejus rei cujus petitur dissolutio.—Jenk. Cent. 37.

Parallel Articles of the French Code.

The privilege of avoiding contracts, which the law allows to such as enter on them during their minority, is personal, and cannot be exercised for the minor by
1306. to 1310. any other person:[1] and infancy will not operate as a bar to a contract for necessaries supplied to a minor.[2] The question of what are necessaries,[3] is governed by the fortune and circumstances of the infant.[4] Contracts entered into by infants for the maintenance of their trade,
1311. are not binding on them.[5] If an infant, after he come of age, expressly and voluntarily confirm the promise, he cannot plead infancy.[6]

CHAPTER VI.

Of the Proof of Contracts and Discharges.

1315. The general rule with regard to the burden of proof (onus probandi) is, that the party who asserts[7] the affirmative[8] of the issue,[9] or point in dispute, must prove it: and the party who claims the benefit of a contract, must prove it.[10] Where a contract is not evidently on the face

---

1 Keane v. Boycot, 2 H. Bl. 515; Taylor v. Croker, 4 Esp. 187.

2 Co. Lit. 172 a.

3 Where the bond of an infant be void or voidable appears to be a vexata questio.—Morning v. Knopp, Cro. Eliz. 700; Baylis v. Dinely, 3 M. & S. 477.

4 Ford v. Fothergill, 1 Esp. 212.

5 Whittingham v. Hill, Cro. Jac. 494; Williams v. Harrison, Carth. 160.

6 Thrupp v. Fielder, 2 Esp. 628; Harmer v. Killing, 5 Esp. 102.

7 Actori incumbit onus probandi.—Hob. 103. According to, probandi necessitas incumbit illi qui agit.—Just. Inst. l. 2, tit. 20, 4.

8 No proof to be made of a negative; but when the law presumes the affirmative, then the negative is to be proved.—Law Max.

9 The common law system of pleading, which narrows the evidence necessary by bringing the parties to a certain issue, is peculiar to the English system, and merits the eulogiums passed on it. The precision of allegation which is required by it, is particularly well calculated to ascertain the incumbency of the proof which is to be made by the respective parties.

10 Starkie or Roscoe on Evidence: for the rules of evidence. In general, he who alleges himself to be the creditor of another, is obliged to prove the fact or agreement upon which his claim is founded, when it is contested. On the other hand, when the obligation is proved, the debtor who alleges that he has discharged it is obliged to prove the payment.—Ev. Pot.

Parallel Articles of the French Code.

of it void, the party who claims to be excused or exonerated[1] must prove a discharge, or such facts as justify his not peforming it.

It is by the evidence which supports them, as well as their different degrees of solemnity, that the kinds of contracts (viz. of record, special and simple) mentioned as recognised by the English law, are characterized. There are two kinds of proof, probatio duplex; viz. viva, as by witnesses, vivâ voce; and mortua, as by deeds, writings, and instruments.[2] The rules which relate to the proof of records, specialties, and parol agreements; to parol evidence, presumptions, and the acknowledgments of the parties respecting contracts, are contained in following sections. 1316.

Section 1.

Of Written Evidence.

Sub-sections 1 and 2.

Of Records and Deeds under Seal.

Records and contracts of record prove themselves, either 1317.
by mere inspection, by certificate, or writ of certiorari.[3] 1319.
Ancient deeds[4] and wills of thirty years' standing prove themselves,[5] while they remain in the possession of the persons entitled to their custody;[6] but if there be any material blemish in the deed, by erasure or interlineation, the deed ought to be proved, though above thirty years.[7] Modern

---

[1] The law will not require a man to make proof of that which he cannot be intended to know.—2 Bl. Com. 367; Tidd, 801.

[2] Co. Lit. 6 b.

[3] Lex non requirit verificari quod apparet curiæ.—9 Rep. 54. Manifesta probatione non indigent.—7 Rep. 40. Perspicuà vera non sunt probanda.—Co. Lit. 16.

[4] Ex diuturnitate temporis omnia præsumuntur esse solemniter acta.—Jenk. Cent. 185. Chartarum super fidem, mortuis testibus, ad patriam, de necessitudine, recurrendum est.—Co. Lit.

[5] 2 Bl. Com. 367; B. N. P. 255; M'Kensie v. Frazer, 9 Ves. 5; 4 T. R. 709, n.

[6] Bul. N. P. 255.

[7] Bul. ib.; Gilb. Ev. 89.

Parallel Articles of the French Code.

deeds and other writings must be verified by parol evidence.[1] It is not, in general, absolutely essential to the validity of a deed or instrument, except formerly
1318. devise of real property and now all wills, that it should be executed in the presence of witnesses:[2] but wherever a deed or other instrument is subscribed by an attesting witness, such witness must be called to prove the execution.[3] Where the attesting witness is dead, incompetent to be a witness, or cannot be found after diligent search, evidence of the witness's handwriting is admissible;[4] where there has been no attesting witness, or where he is unable to prove the execution,[5] proof of the handwriting of the party is admitted.

An instrument not under seal is, in some cases (as a receipt for money), only primâ facie evidence, and may be contradicted and explained.[6] In general, parol evidence is not admissible to vary or contradict a written instrument.[7]

1320. A statement in a deed may become evidence against all the parties to it by estoppel, even though merely a recital:[8] and a party will not be allowed to gainsay an averment in his own deed.[9]

1322. All secret defeasances must be contemplated with suspicion; and if resisted can only be made available in a court of equity, upon evidence that the transaction between the parties was a fair one, and not executed with a fraudulent design to prejudice others.

---

1 2 Bl. Com. 368.

2 Grellier v. Neale, Peake, 147; Com. Dig. Fait. B. 4; Phil. on Evid. 413, 4th edit.

3 Call v. Dunning, 4 East, 53.

4 Anon. 12 Mod. 607; Wood v. Drury, 1 Ld. Raym. 734; Jones v. Mason, 2 Stra. 833; Cunliffe v. Sefton, 2 East, 183.

5 Grellier v. Neale.

6 Skaife v. Jackson, 3 B. & C. 421; Graves v. Key, 3 B. & Ad. 318.

7 Meres v. Ansell, 3 Wils. 275; Dawson v. Walker, 1 Stark. 361.

8 Com. Dig. Evid. (B. 5); Rees v. Lloyd, Wightw. 23; Lampon v. Corke, 5 B. & A. 607.

9 Doe v. Sherlock, 1 Fox & Smith, 78.

Parallel Articles of the French Code.

If a party refuse or neglect to admit his contract or handwriting, when formally called upon to do so in the course of an action, he is to pay the expenses of proving it, if the judge think it reasonable he should do so:[1] but 1322.
neither he nor his representatives are under any other 1323.
necessity of formally admitting or denying it; and if 1324.
not admitted, the other party proceeds to prove the contract by witnesses.

Whatever be the number of respective parties, more than 1325.
one original deed or instrument is not indispensable; but it is generally advisable to have a counterpart for each party, unless the expense is a very great object; and when there is only one original instrument, it may be desirable to make special provision for the inspection of it by all parties, and for taking attested copies. In no 1326.
case is it essential to the validity or proof of a written note or promise, provided the party know the contents, that it, or even the sum or amount for which it is given, should be in the party's handwriting; it is sufficient that he sign it, or some person do so for him by his direction. As to the signature, it is provided by the statute of frauds,[2] that no action shall be brought whereby to charge any person, upon any special promise, to answer for the debt, default, or miscarriage of another person; or upon any contract or sale of lands, tenements, and hereditaments, or any interest in or concerning them; or upon any agreement not to be performed within the space of one year from the making thereof, unless the agreement upon which such action shall be brought, or some memorandum or note thereof, shall be in writing, and signed by the party to be charged therewith, or some other person thereunto by him lawfully authorized.[3] And no contract for the sale of any goods for the price of 10*l.* and upwards, shall be allowed to be good, except the

[1] Prac. R. Hil. Term, 3 & 4 Wm. IV.

[2] 29 Car. II. c. 3, entitled, An Act for Prevention of Frauds and Perjuries.

[3] Ib. s. 4.

Parallel Articles of the French Code.

buyer shall accept part of the goods so sold, and actually receive them, or give something in earnest to bind the bargain or in part payment; or that some note or memorandum in writing of the said bargain, be made and signed by the parties to be charged by such contract, or their agents lawfully authorized.[1]

1329 to 1332. What a man writes or says for himself cannot be evidence for himself or his representative.[2] A tradesman's own entries in his shop-book are no evidence against his customers, that the goods therein entered were delivered; but the entries of a deceased shopman or servant in his master's books, stating the delivery of goods, are evidence for the master of such delivery.[3] By 7 Jac. I. c. 12, the shop-book of a tradesman shall not be evidence in any action for wares delivered or work done above one year before the bringing of the action, except the tradesman or his executor shall have obtained a bill of defendant, or obligation of his debtor, for his said debt.[4] But, in a variety of cases, the declarations of deceased persons have been admitted when against their own interest.[5]

Sub-section 3.

Of Tallies.

1333. The use of tallies is so rare in England, that there are no modern cases to be found on the subject: but it should seem, that tallies, being mere arbitrary signs, would be no evidence in themselves, and would require a witness to explain the signification of them and of their various marks; and then, if the duplicate were produced

---

1 29 Car. II. c. 3, s. 17, entitled, An Act for Prevention of Frauds and Perjuries.

2 Glyn v. Bank of England, 2 Ves. 42; R. v. Debenham, 2 B. & A. 187.

3 3 Bl. Com. 368; Price v. Ld. Torrington, 1 Salk. 285; Cooper v. Marsden, 1 Esp. 1.

4 Sikes v. Marshall, 2 Esp. 705; 2 Salk. 690.

5 2 Russ. 67 (n.)

from custody of the debtor, they might be allowed as evidence against him; but when from the custody of the creditor, they could only be used in the same way as a creditor's books.

Parallel Articles of the French Code.

Sub-section 4.

Of Copies of Documents.

It is a general rule, that the best evidence must be given, that the nature of the case admits;[1] and, therefore, where a contract has been reduced to writing, and been signed by the parties, as the writing is the best evidence of it, it must be produced;[2] and secondary evidence of its contents is inadmissible, unless it is proved to be lost, or in the possession of another party who has been required by notice to produce it, and not complied. 1334.

When the original document is proved to be lost, or accidentally destroyed, evidence may be given of its contents in the best manner the party can;[3] and the unstamped part, executed at the same time as the stamped one, or the draft of the document, or a copy, are admissible as secondary evidence of the contents.[4] 1335.

Where a deed requiring enrolment is enrolled, proof of the enrolment, by a copy examined with the enrolment will dispense with evidence of the execution by any of the parties to the deed.[5] So where a deed not requiring enrolment is enrolled on the acknowledgment of one of the parties, it seems evidence against that party without calling the attesting witnesses.[6] 1336.

The memorial of a registered deed is not evidence of

---

[1] 3 Bl. Com. 368; B. N. P.

[2] Brewer v. Palmer, 3 Esp. 213; Doe v. Griffith, 6 Bing. 533.

[3] Tussen v. Clarke, Lofft. 496.

[4] 3 Bl. Com. 368; Waller v. Horsfall, 1 Camp. 501; Munn. v. Godbold, 3 C. & P. 97; 3 Bing. 292.

[5] Thurle v. Madison Styles, 462; Smarke v. Williams, 3 Lev. 387; 10 Ann. c. 18, s. 3.

[6] Ibid.

Parallel Articles of the French Code.

the contents of such deed, unless notice has been given to produce the original.[1]

If the probate of a will be lost, an exemplification is granted, and may be given in evidence.[2]

Sub-section 5.

Of Acknowledgments and Confirmation.

1337. The contents of a written instrument cannot be proved against a party by his admission or acknowledgment, unless the non-production be accounted for;[3] but an acknowledgment of the debt by the defendant, will enable the plaintiff to recover upon the count on an account stated.[4] No acknowledgment is sufficient evidence of a new or a continuing contract to take a case out of the statute of limitations, unless in writing, signed by the party charged therewith.[5]

1338. A deed or agreement only voidable may be established by a deed of confirmation, but if it is void it cannot;[6] for a confirmation is an approbation of or assent to an estate, interest, or right in existence.[7] And a contract once dissolved, cannot be set up by a subsequent agreement.[8]

1339. A confirmation cannot strengthen a void estate, and where a donation is void,[9] a deed of confirmation is totally ineffectual.[10]

---

1 Nolton v. Harris, 2 Esp. 549.

2 Ramsbottom's case, 1 Leach, 30 (n.)

3 Bloxam v. Elsie, R. & M. 187.

4 Highmore v. Primrose, 5 M. & S. 65.

5 9 G. IV. c. 14, s. 1.

6 2 Bl. Com. 325; Shep. Touch. 311; Co. Lit.

7 Co. Lit. 295 b, n. 1.

8 Rex v. Inhabitants of Gresham, 1 T. R. 101.

9 Confirmatio est nulla ubi donum præcedens est invalidum et ubi donatio nulla omnino nec valebit confirmatio.

10 Co. Lit. 295 b.

Parallel Articles of the French Code.

Section 2.

Of Parol Evidence.

We have already seen what agreements relating to lands or goods of 10*l.* value, not partly executed by earnest, delivery, or payment, are void under the statutes of frauds, unless in writing, and signed.[1] 1341.

When the statute of frauds does not require an agreement to be in writing, as in cases of part performance of a sale of goods, or where the goods are under the value of 10*l.*, the agreement may be proved by parol evidence.[2]

Although parol evidence is not admissible at law or in equity, to disannul or substantially vary a written agreement,[3] it is allowed to show circumstances of fraud, or of mistake, or surprise.[4] With regard to the mode in which the amount of 10*l.* is made up, interest is payable on simple contract debts only when they are in writing, or where there has been a demand.[5] 1342.

Where several articles were bought at a shop at the same time, but at different prices, each under 10*l.*, but amounting together to 70*l.*, it was held to be one contract, and within the statute.[6] 1345

It is not an entire or joint order, if as to one article the party is to have an option and time for consideration.[7] But otherwise, if the contract were complete, it would be within the statute of frauds, although the delivery may not be intended to be made until some future period.[8]

---

1 29 Car. II. c. 3. s. 17; and ante, p. 493, 4.

2 Bennett v. Henderson, 2 Stark. 550.

3 3 & 4 Wm. IV. c. 42.

4 Sug. Ven. & Par. c. 3. s. 4; and ante, p. 492, n. 7.

5 1 Ves. & B. 527; Joynes v. Statham, 3 Atk. 388; Garrard v. Grinley, 2 Swanst. 224.

6 Baldey v. Parker, 2 B. & C. 37.

7 Price v. Lea, 1 B. & C. 156.

8 9 Geo. IV. c. 14, s. 7.

Parallel Articles of the French Code.

In some cases, where goods have been taken wrongfully, the party may waive the tort, and sue on the implied contract.[1]

Section 3.

Of Presumptions.

1349. There are three kinds of presumption: 1st, legal presumption made by the law itself, and said to be præsumptio juris et de jure;[2] 2ndly, legal presumption to be made by a jury, of law and fact,[3] said to be præsumptio juris; 3rdly, natural presumptions, or presumptions of mere fact,[4] called præsumptio hominis vel judicis. Of the latter there appear to be three distinguishable species, or rather three degrees: 1st, such as are violent, and afford competent legal evidence; 2ndly, such as are proper subjects of deliberation for a jury; and thirdly, such as are inadmissible. Lord Coke says, many times juries, together with other matter, are much induced by presumptions, whereof there be three sorts: viz. violent, probable, and light or temerary. Violenta presumptio,[5] which necessarily attend the fact, is many times plena probatio. Presumptio probabilis, arising from circumstances which usually attend the fact, moveth little; but presumptio levis seu temeraria moveth not at all.[6]

---

[1] Hill v. Perrot, 3 Taunt. 274. recog.; Abbotts v. Barry, 3 B. & B. 369.

[2] The law will admit no proof against its own presumptions.

[3] Omnia præsumuntur legitime facta donec probetur in contrarium.—Co. Lit. 232. Stabit præsumptio donec probetur in contrarium.—Hob. 297.

[4] Injuria non præsumitur.—Co. Lit. 232. Malum non præsumitur.—4 Rep. 72. Nullum iniquum est præsumendum in jure.—4 Rep. 71. Nulla impossibilia odiosa, aut inhonesta sunt præsumenda; vera autem et honesta et possibilia.—Co. Lit. 78. In facto quod se habet ad bonum et malum, magis de bono quam de malo præsumendum est.—Co. Lit. 78.

[5] Præsumptio violenta valet in lege.—Jenk. Cent. 56.

[6] Co. Lit 6 b

Parallel Articles of the French Code.

Sub-section I.

Of Presumptions of Law.

Legal presumptions are those which are attached by law to certain acts or certain facts, such as— 1350.

1st. Fraud (in cases of voluntary conveyances, by persons indebted to the extent of general insolvency[1]), which makes the transaction void.[2]

2nd. Negligence in certain cases from accident.[3]

3rd. Right of property from possession.[4]

4th. Payment and discharge of debts not acknowledged after length of time.[6]

5th. A verdict or judgment will operate by estoppel, if so pleaded in a second action; but if only offered in evidence and not so pleaded, it is not conclusive.[7]

6th. In favour of innocence, and of the legality and regularity[8] of acts.[9]

7th. The admissions of a party to a suit, express or implied from his conduct, are strong evidences against him; but he is at liberty to prove that such admissions are mistaken or untrue, and he is not estopped or concluded by them, unless the person has been induced by them to alter his conduct.[10] Admissions in an answer in chancery are only secondary evidence.[11]

---

1 3 B. & Ad. 362; 5 Ves. 384; Sim. & Stu. 315.

2 13 Eliz. c. 5. (Fraudulent preferences).

3 Christie v. Griggs, 2 Camp. 79; Curtis v. Drinkwater, 3 B. & Ad. 169.

4 Co. Lit. 15 a; B. N. P. 103; Jayne v. Price, 4 Taunt. 326.

5 An acquittance for the last payments is a discharge of former arrears.—Noy's Max.

6 Gilb. Ev. 137, 8; Gibbon v. Featherstonehaugh, 1 Stark. 225; Colsel v. Budd, 1 Camb. 27.

7 Outram v. Morewood, 3 East, 365; Stafford v. Clark, 2 Bingh. 381; Hooper v. Hooper, M. Cl. & Y. 509.

8 Omnia præsumitur solemniter esse acta. Co. Lit. 6.

9 2 B. & A. 386; Rodwell v. Ridge, 1 C. & P. 220; R. v. Verelst 3 Camp. 432

10 Per Bailey J., Hearne v. Rogers, 9 B. & C. 586.

11 Call v. Dunning, 4 East, 53; Doe v. Watson, 2 Stark. 23.

Parallel Articles of the French Code.

A judgment or verdict[1] is conclusive evidence between the same parties in the same character upon the same cause of action.[2]

1351. A judgment or verdict is only evidence where it is directly upon the point in question; and it is not evidence of any matter which came collaterally in question, nor of any matter incidentally cognizable, or of any matter to be inferred by argument from the judgment.[3]

1352. Legal presumptions dispense with the necessity of proof by the party for whose benefit it exists.[4] But in general, presumptive evidence may be rebutted, and is only to be relied upon until the contrary is actually proved.[5]

Sub-section 2.

Of Presumptions not established by Law.

1353. It is the peculiar province of a jury to deal with presumptions of mere facts or natural presumptions; yet where the facts are inseparably connected according to the course of nature, the courts themselves will draw the inference without the aid of the jury.[6]

Section 4.

Of the Admissions of Party.

1354. Admissions which can be produced against a party are either judicial or extra-judicial, expressed or implied. A

[1] Interest reipublicæ res judicatas non rescindi.—2 Inst. 360. In præsumptione legis judicium redditur in invitum.—Co. Lit. 248 b. Judicia in Curia Regis non adnihilentur sed stent in robore suo quousque per errorem aut attinctum adnullentur.—2 Inst. 359. Judicia pro veritate accipiuntur.—2 Inst. 573. Res judicata pro veritate accipitur.—Co. Lit. 103.

[2] Hitchin v. Campbell, 2 Bl. 827; Robinson's case, 5 Rep. 321.

[3] Duchess of Kingston's case, 20 How. St. T. R. 533; Blackham's case. 1 Salk. 290.

[4] Banbury Peerage, 2 Selw. N. P. 709; R. v. Hawkins, 10 East, 216.

[5] 3 Bl. Com. 371 (Chr.)

[6] Rex v. Suffer, 8 East, 193.

Parallel Articles of the French Code.

party may expressly admit extra-judicially any act, as his handwriting to a contract:[1] but concessions made for the purpose of settling matters in dispute are not legal admissions.[2]

A judicial admission is an acknowledgment of a fact or facts by the pleadings (of record), or by an express consent of the party or his attorney, or by implication, as the payment of money into court.[3] Admissions of record cannot be disputed, and though untrue, the jury may not find a verdict contrary to them.[4] Admissions by consent are conclusive between the parties, as to the points admitted. 1356.

Section 5.

Of the Examination of the Parties themselves.

At common law, accusare nemo se debet, nisi coram Deo.[5] An oath is not lawful whereby any person may be compelled to confess or accuse himself: and a person may not swear for himself, except where he has some particular power by act of parliament.[6] 1357 to 1369.

In chancery the defendant is put upon his oath in answer to the plaintiff's bill of complaint; but he has no means of compelling the plaintiff to answer on his oath, except by a cross or other bill filed against him.

An answer in chancery is good evidence against the defendant as an admission upon oath, and it must all be taken together. 1365.

---

[1] Waldridge v. Kerrison, 1 Esp. 143; Westlake v. Collard, Bul. N. P. 236.

[2] Gregory v. Howard, 3 Esp. 113.

[3] See, however, what it admits.—Rucher v. Palgrave, 1 Camp. 557; 1 Taunt. 419.

[4] Blackburn v. Scholes, 2 Camp. 341; B. N. P. 298; Winbish v. Tailbois, Plow. 48; Watkins v. Towers, 2 T. R. 275.

[5] Goddard's case, 2 Co. 46. [6] Hard. 139. [7] 4 Co. 9.

Parallel Articles of the French Code.

The answer of a guardian is no evidence against an infant, nor the answer of a trustee against a cestui qui trust.[1]

An answer is evidence against privies.[2]

The answer of one defendant is not evidence against a co-defendant;[3] but of partners it may be.[4]

---

[1] B. N. P. 237; Gilb. Ev. 50.

[2] B. N. P. 237

[3] Dartmouth v. Roberts, 16 East, 334.

[4] Wych v. Mead, 3 P. Wms. 311.

[5] Grant v. Jackson, Peake, 203.

APPENDIX.

APPENDIX.

FRENCH CIVIL CODE.

PRELIMINARY TITLE.

OF THE PUBLICATION, EFFECT, AND APPLICATION OF THE LAWS IN GENERAL.

DECREED 5TH MARCH, 1803. PROMULGATED 15TH OF THE SAME MONTH.

ARTICLE I.

The laws are executory throughout the whole French territory, by virtue of the promulgation thereof made by the king.*

They shall be in force in every part of the kingdom, from the moment at which their promulgation can have been known.†

The promulgation made by the king shall be held to be known in the department of the royal residence, one day after the promulgation; and in each of the other departments, after the expiration of the same interval augmented one day for every ten myriameters (about twenty ancient leagues) between the town in which the promulgation shall have been made, and the chief place of each department.‡

* For the English law as to promulgation, see p. 192.

† For the English law on this point, see p. 193.

‡ As to the French mode of promulgation (by insertion in the official bulletin), see ordonnance 27th November, 1816. In many cases it must be necessary to bring a new law into immediate operation, in a part the most distant in the kingdom. By this ordonnance, and another 17th January, 1817, the execution of the laws may be hastened by the mode pointed out in the latter.

The English lawyer may sometimes have occasion to refer to the authentic edition of the Codes of France: M. Dupin, in his Bibliotheque, will give him some light. He says, on the official editions of the Codes it is necessary to remark, that the official edition under the imperial government ceased to be so after the restoration; and that the only edition of the Codes which can now be cited and quoted in pleadings, writings, consultations, and public documents, is that printed at the royal press, in execution of the ordonnance of 30th August, 1816, and inserted in the Bulletin, 7th series, No. 109, bis: "imprimée a l'imprimerie royale, en execution de l'ordonnance du 30 Août, 1816, et inserée au Bulletin, 7e serie, No. 109, bis."

It will be seen that the royal edition has been resorted to, in preference to the consular or imperial.

2.

The law ordains for the future only; it has no retrospective operation.

For a similar principle in the English law, see p. 193.

3.

The laws of police and public security bind all inhabiting the territory.*

Immoveable property, although in the possession of foreigners, is governed by the French law,†

The laws relating to the condition and capacity of persons govern Frenchmen, although residing in a foreign country.‡

* For a similar principle in English law, see p. 194.

† For a similar principle in English law, see p. 195.

‡ As to the English law on this point, see p. 195, 6.

4.

The judge who shall refuse to determine, under pretext of the silence, obscurity, or insufficiency of the law, shall be liable to be proceeded against as guilty of a refusal of justice.

See a contrary principle in the English law, p. 196.

5.

The judges are forbidden to pronounce, by way of general and legislative determination, on the causes submitted to them.

See a somewhat similar principle in the English system, p. 197.

6.

Private agreements must not contravene the laws which concern public order and good morals.

See a similar principle in the English law, p. 198, 9.

BOOK I.

OF PERSONS.

DECREED 8TH MARCH, 1803. PROMULGATED 18TH OF THE SAME MONTH.

TITLE I.

OF THE ENJOYMENT AND PRIVATION OF CIVIL RIGHTS.

CHAPTER I.

Of the Enjoyment of Civil Rights.

7.

The exercise of civil rights is independent of the quality of citizen, which is only acquired and preserved conformably to the constitutional law.

A similar general principle appears in the English law. See p. 205.

8.

Every Frenchman shall enjoy civil rights.

A similar rule of English law, see p. 206, and see p. 202, 3, 4.

9.

Every individual born in France of a foreigner,* may, during the year which shall succeed the period of his majority, claim the quality of Frenchman: provided, that if he be resident in France, he declares that his intention is to fix his domicile in that country, and that in case he shall reside in a foreign country, he give security to become domiciled in France, and do establish himself there within a year, to be computed from the date of that undertaking.†

* On this point, see p. 206.

† The English law has no similar regulation. No act or declaration is required by the English law; the actual administration of the oath of allegiance to the mass of people in general having become obsolete.

10.

Every child born of a Frenchman in a foreign country is French.* Every child born in a foreign country of a Frenchman who shall have lost the quality of Frenchman, may at any time recover this quality by complying with the formalities prescribed in the ninth article.†

* See a similar principle, p. 207.

† See note † to art. 9.

11.

A foreigner shall enjoy in France the same civil rights as are or shall be accorded to Frenchmen by the treaties of that nation to which such foreigner shall belong.

See parallel, but not similar, law of England, p. 207. It may be as well here to observe, that an important law was passed in France, 19th July, 1819, to permit foreigners to succeed, take, and dispose of property in France, like natives.

12.

A foreign woman who shall have married a Frenchman shall follow the condition of her husband.

See a contrary principle in the English law, p. 209, and p. 207.

13.

A foreigner who shall have been permitted, by the licence of the king, to establish his domicile in France, shall enjoy in that country all civil rights so long as he shall continue to reside there.

See the mode for aliens acquiring civil rights in England, p. 209.

14.

A foreigner, even though not resident in France,* may be cited before the French courts, to enforce the execution of engagements contracted by him in France with a Frenchman; he may be summoned before the tribunals of France, on account of engagements entered into by him with Frenchmen in a foreign country.†

* See as to persons not resident, p. 210.

† See as to engagements contracted in England, or abroad, p. 210, 211.

15.

A Frenchman may be summoned before a French court, for engagements contracted by him in a foreign country, though with a foreigner.

See a similar principle in the English law, p. 210, 211,

16.

In all causes other than those of commerce, in which a foreigner shall be plaintiff, he shall be required to give security for the payment of the costs and damages incident to the suit, unless he possess in France immoveable property of value sufficient to guarantee such payment.

See a similar principle in the English law, p. 211, 212.

CHAPTER II.

Of the Privation of Civil Rights.

Section 1.

Of the Privation of Civil Rights by the Loss of the Quality of Frenchman.

17.

The quality of Frenchman shall be lost, 1st, by naturalization acquired in a foreign country;* ¶2nd, by accepting, without the authority of the king, public employments bestowed by a foreign government;† 3dly, [by adoption into any foreign corporation which shall require distinctions of birth; 4thly,‡] in short, by any settlement made in a foreign country, without intention of returning.

Commercial establishments shall never be considered as having been made without intention of return.§

* A very great difference was created by a decree of 26th August, 1811, between those authorised by the French government and those not so authorized to be naturalized. There seems, however, to be some doubt as to how far that decree is still operative.

¶ See parallel but dissimilar English law, p. 214, 215.

† See parallel law in the English system, p. 213, 214.

‡ Omitted in the present French code.

§ As to the consequences, according to the English law, of residence for commercial or other purposes in a foreign country, see p. 214.

18.

A Frenchman, who shall have lost his quality of Frenchman, may at any time recover it by returning* to France with the licence of the king, and declaring that he intends to settle there, and he renounces every distinction inconsistent with the law of France.†

* See English law on this subject, p. 215.

† See note † to article 9.

19.

A Frenchwoman, who shall marry a foreigner, shall follow the condition of her husband.*

If she become a widow, she shall recover the quality of Frenchwoman, provided she reside in France, or that she return thither with the licence of the king, and declare her intention to fix there.†

* See contrary principle in the English law, p. 216.

† In consequence of the principles of the English law on the subject of the foregoing part of this article being different, no law on this point is required in the English system.

20.

The individuals who shall recover the quality of Frenchman or Frenchwoman in the cases provided for by articles 10, 18, and 19, shall not be permitted to avail themselves of it until they have fulfilled the conditions imposed upon them by those articles, and only for the exercise of rights open for their advantage after that period.

In consequence of the English law

being different to the French on the points laid down in these articles, no law similar to this is necessary in the English system. See note † to article 9.

21.

The Frenchman who, without the licence of the king, shall engage in the military service of a foreign power, or shall enrol himself in any foreign military association, shall lose his quality of Frenchman.

He can re-enter France only with the permission of the king, and recover the quality of Frenchman only by complying with the conditions required of a foreigner in order to become a citizen; and then without prejudice to the punishments denounced by the criminal law against Frenchmen who have borne or shall bear arms against their country.

See the penalties imposed by the English law in these cases, p. 216.

Section II.

Of the Deprivation of Civil Rights, in consequence of Judicial Sentences.

22.

Sentences to punishment, the effect of which is to deprive the party condemned of all participation in the civil rights hereafter mentioned, shall carry with them civil death.

See the English law on this subject, p. 216, 7.

Decrees, 6th April, 1809, and 26th August, 1811, make the total deprivation of civil and political rights one of the punishments of the French law in certain cases of entering the service of foreign states. See Code Penal, art. 42.

23.

Sentence to natural death shall carry with it civil death.

See similar law of England, p. 218.

24.

Other perpetual corporal punishments shall not imply civil death, except so far as the law shall have attached that consequence.

See, consequence of transportation and imprisonment according to the English law, p. 218, 219.

25.

By civil death, the party condemned loses his property in all the goods which he possessed; and the succession is open for the benefit of his heirs, on whom his property devolves, in the same manner as if he were naturally dead and intestate.*

He can no longer inherit any estate, nor transmit, by this title, the property which he has acquired in consequence.†

He can neither dispose of his property, in whole or in part, either by way of gift during his life, or by will, nor receive by similar title, except for the purpose of subsistence.‡

He cannot be nominated guardian, nor concur in any acts relative to guardianship.§

He cannot be a witness in any act, formal or authenticated, nor be admitted to give evidence in any court.||

He cannot engage in any suit, whether as defendant or plaintiff, except in the name and by the intervention of a special curator, who is appointed him by the court in which the action is brought.¶

He is incapable of contracting a marriage attended by any civil consequences.

If he have previously contracted marriage, it is dissolved, as respects all civil consequences.

His wife and his heirs shall respectively exercise those rights and demands to which his natural death would have given rise.**

* See, as to forfeiture of real and personal property by the English law, p. 219, 220.

† See, as to corruption of blood, p. 220.

‡ See a similar English law, p. 221.

§ See a similar English law, p. 220.

|| See a similar English law, p. 220.

¶ See the English law on this point, p. 220.

** See a contrary principle as to marriages already contracted, p. 220, 221.

26.

Peremptory sentences only import civil death, reckoning from the day of their execution, whether real or by representation.

As to the commencement of operation of a sentence, see p. 221.

27.

Condemnations for contumacy shall not imply civil death until after five years from the execution of the sentence by representation, and during which the condemned party may make his appearance.

As to the time of commencement of the penalties inflicted by the English outlawry for contumacy, see p. 222.

28.

Those condemned for contumacy shall, during the five years, or until they shall make appearance or until their arrest during that period, be deprived of the exercise of civil rights.

Their property shall be administered and their rights exercised in the same manner as those of absent persons.

As to the consequence of outlawry, see p. 222.

29.

When the party under sentence for contumacy shall appear voluntarily during the five years, to be reckoned from the day of the execution, or when he shall have been seized and made prisoner during that interval, the judgment shall be entirely reversed; the accused shall be restored to the possession of his property; he shall be tried afresh; and if, by the new judgment, he is condemned to the same punishment or a different punishment equally drawing after it civil death, it shall only take place from the date of the execution of the second judgment.

As to reversing outlawry and its consequent restoration, see p. 224.

30.

When a party condemned for contumacy, who shall not have appeared or who shall not have been made prisoner until the expiration of the five years, shall be acquitted by this new judgment, or shall only be sentenced to a punishment that does not carry with it civil death, he shall re-enter into the full enjoyment of his civil rights for the future, reckoning from the day on which he shall have reappeared in court; but the first judgment shall preserve, as regards the past, the consequences produced by civil death during the interval which elapsed between the period of the expiration of the five years and the day of appearance in court.

As to the effect of reversing the outlawry on acts done while it continued, see p. 224, 225.

31.

If the party under sentence for contumacy dies during the five years interval of grace without having appeared, or without having been seized or arrested, he shall be deemed dead as to the entirety of his rights. Judgment of contumacy shall be reversed entirely, without prejudice nevertheless to the action of a private party, which shall not be entered against the heirs of the party condemned, except according to the civil form.

As to the consequences of the death of an outlaw, see p. 225.

32.

In no case shall the becoming free from the punishment by lapse of time restore a party condemned to his civil rights except for the future.

See a similar English law on this point, see p. 225.

33.

Property acquired by a condemned person, after incurring civil death, and of which he shall be found possessed at the date of his natural death, shall belong to the state by right of escheat.* Nevertheless it shall be lawful for the king to make for the benefit of the widow, children, or relations of the party condemned, such

* See the English law to the same effect, see p. 225, 6.

disposition as humanity shall suggest to him.*

* See the power of the English Crown for this purpose, p. 226.

TITLE II.

OF REGISTERS ([a]) OF THE CIVIL STATE OR CONDITION.

Decreed 12th March, 1803. Promulgated 21st of the same Month.

CHAPTER I.

General Ordonnance.

34.

The registers of the civil state shall declare the year, the day, and hour, at which they shall be received; the Christian name, surname, age, profession, and domicile of all those who shall be therein mentioned.

See similar general principles in the English law, p. 227.

35.

The officers of the civil state may insert nothing in the registries which they shall make, either by way of note or of any explanation whatsoever, other than what is declared by the parties causing it to be made.

See the English law on this point, p. 227, 8.

36.

In the cases where the parties interested are not bound to appear in person, they may be represented by means of a special and authentic power of attorney.

In the English law it rests with the registrar to satisfy himself before he registers, see p. 227.

37.

Witnesses to registers of the civil state can be of the male sex only, of the age of 21 years, at the least, relations or others; they shall be chosen by the parties interested.

Any credible witness seems sufficient in the English law, see p. 228.

38.

The officers of the civil state shall read over their acts to the parties appearing or to their attornies, and also to the witnesses.

The performance of this formality shall be mentioned therein.

No similar obligation on the part of the English registrar.

39.

These entries shall be signed by the officer of the civil state, by the parties appearing, and by the witnesses; or mention shall be made of the cause which may prevent the parties and the witnesses from signing.

See a similar provision in the English law, p. 228.

40.

The registers of the civil state shall be inserted in every commune, in one or more registers kept in duplicate.

See the English provision on this point, p. 228.

41.

The registers shall have the beginning and end marked, and a sign put on each page, by the president of the court of first instance, or by the judge who shall supply his place.

See an enactment, similar in principle though not in form, in the English law, p. 228.

42.

The entries shall be inscribed on the registers in succession, without any blank. Rasures and references shall be approved and signed in the same manner as the body of the act. No abbreviations shall be used, nor any date inserted in figures.

See parallel English enactment, p. 228.

43.

The registers shall be closed by the officer of the civil state at the end of every year; and within the month, one of the duplicates shall be depo-

([a]) The records which enable a person to establish his state in society, are called in French, Des Actes de l' Etat Civil (Acts or Records of the Civil State), and are analagous to the instruments of the Roman law.

sited among the archives of the commune, the other among the rolls of the court of first instance.

See the provision of the English law on this point, p. 229.

44.

The warrants of attorney and other papers which ought to continue annexed to the records of the civil state, shall be deposited, after being marked by the person who shall have produced them and by the officer of the civil state, among the rolls of the tribunal, with the duplicate of the registers which shall be deposited among the said rolls.

No English enactment on this point. See note to art. 36.

45.

Every person may cause to be delivered to him by the depositaries of the registers of the civil state extracts from those registers. The extracts delivered, corresponding with the registers and authenticated by the president of the court of first instance, or by the judge who shall supply his place, shall be evidence, until set aside as false (jusqu' a l'inscription de faux).

See similar laws on these points in the English system, p. 229.

46.

Where no registers exist, or where they shall be lost, proof of them shall be received, as well by written documents as by witnesses; and in such cases marriages, births, and deaths, may be proved as well by registers and papers coming from the possession of fathers and mothers deceased, as by witnesses.

See the parallel English law on this point, p. 229.

47.

Every register of the civil state, either of Frenchmen or foreigners, made in a foreign country, shall be deemed valid, if reduced to writing according to the forms used in such country.

See a parallel but dissimilar law in the English system, p. 230.

48.

Every registry of the civil state of a Frenchman made in a foreign country shall be valid, if it has been acknowledged conformably to the French laws by the diplomatic agents, or by the consuls.

See a parallel but dissimilar English law, p. 230.

49.

In all cases where mention of an entry relating to the civil state ought to be made on the margin of another register already inserted, it shall be done, at the request of the parties interested, by the officer of the civil state, on the current registers, or on those which have been deposited among the archives of the commune, and by the keeper of the rolls of the tribunal of first instance, on the registers deposited among the rolls; to which end the officer of the civil state shall give notice within three days to the kings's attorney in the said court, who shall take care that such mention is made in a uniform manner on both registers.

No similar English enactment.

50.

Every offence against the preceding articles on the part of any of the officers therein named, shall be prosecuted before the tribunal of first instance, and punished with a fine not exceeding 100 francs.

See parallel English laws, p. 230, 1.

51.

Every officer entrusted with the registers shall be answerable civilly for any alterations made therein, saving his remedy, if he has any, against the authors of such alterations.

See the English law on this point, p. 231.

52.

Every alteration, every falsification of the registers of the civil state, every entry made upon a loose sheet and otheriwse than on the registers designed for this purpose, shall give a right of action for damages to the parties, over and above the punishments contained in the penal code.

See the English law on this point, p. 231.

53.

The king's attorney in the court of first instance shall be bound to verify the state of the registers at the time of their being deposited among the rolls of the court;* he shall draw up a concise statement of such verification, he shall denounce all contraventions or offences committed by the officers of the civil state, and shall demand sentence of fine against them.†

* No similar English enactment.

† As to suing for and recovering penalties under the registration acts, see p. 231.

54.

In all cases where a tribunal of first instance shall take cognizance of registries relating to the civil state, the parties interested may appeal against the judgment.

As to appeals against penalties, see p. 231.

CHAPTER II.

Of Registers of Birth.

55.

Declarations of birth shall be made, within three days after delivery, to the officer of the civil state of the place: the child shall be shown to him.

See the parallel English law, p. 231.

56.

The birth of the child shall be declared by the father, or, in his default, by the doctors in physic or surgery, the midwives, the officers of health, or other persons who shall have attended at the birth; and where the mother shall have been delivered out of her own house, by the party at whose house she was delivered.

The register of birth shall be immediately entered in the presence of two witnesses.

See the parallel English law, p. 231.

57.

The register of birth shall set forth the day, the hour, and the place of birth, the sex of the infant, and the names which shall be given it, the Christian and surnames, profession, and domicile of the father and mother, and those of the witnesses.

See parallel English law, p. 232.

58.

Every person who shall have found a new-born infant is called upon to carry it to the officer of the civil state, as well as the clothes and other effects found with the infant, and to declare all the circumstances of the time and place when and where it shall have been found; a detailed statement of which shall be drawn up, setting forth the apparent age of the child, its sex, the names which shall be given it, and the civil authority to which it shall be committed. This statement shall be inscribed upon the registers.

See a provision on this point in the English law, p. 233.

59.

If a child is born during a voyage at sea, the register of birth shall be drawn up within twenty-four hours, in presence of the father, if at hand, and of two witnesses selected from among the officers of the vessel, or for want of them from among the ship's crew. This register shall be reduced to writing, that is to say, on board the king's ships, by the officer for the administration of the marine; and on board vessels belonging to a privateer or merchant, by the captain, master, or commander of the ship. The register of birth shall be inserted at the end of the roll of the ship's crew.

See a similar English law, p. 233.

60.

At the first port at which the vessel shall touch, whether to refit, or for any other purpose, except for discharge, the officers for the administration of the marine, the captain, master, or commander, are bound to deposit two authentic copies of the registers of birth, which they shall have reduced to writing, that is to say, in a French port at the office of the prefect of maritime inscription, and in a foreign port in the hands of the consuls. One of these copies shall remain deposited in the office of maritime inscription, or in the chancery of the consulate; the other shall be sent to the minister of marine, who shall cause a copy of each of the said registers, certified by himself, to be transmitted to the officer of the state of the domicile of the father of the child, or of its mother, if the father is unknown: this copy shall immediately be inscribed on the registers.

See the English law on this point, p. 233.

61.

On the arrival of the ship at its port of discharge, the roll of the ship's crew shall be deposited in the office of the superintendent (preposé) of maritime inscription, who shall send a copy of the register of birth, with his signature, to the domicile of the child's father, or of its mother, if the father is unknown: this copy shall then be inscribed on the registers.

See the English law on this point, p. 333.

62.

The acknowledgment of a child shall be inscribed on the registers, at its date; and mention shall be made of this in the margin of the register of birth, if one exists.

No similar provision required by the English law.

CHAPTER III.

Of Registries of Marriage.

63.

Before the celebration of a marriage, the officer of the civil state shall make two publications; of eight days between them, one day being on a Sunday, before the gate of the town-hall. These publications, and the register which shall be drawn up relating to them, shall set forth the names, surnames, professions, and domiciles of the parties about to be married, the circumstances of their majority or minority, and the names, surnames, professions, and domiciles of their fathers and mothers. This register shall set forth, moreover, the days, places, and hours at which the publications shall have been made; it shall be inscribed on one single register, which shall be marked and signed as directed in article 41, and deposited at the end of every year among the rolls of the court of the arrondisment.

As to the necessity of publication of banns, and the mode according to the English law, see p. 234, 5, 6.

64.

An extract from the register of publication shall be affixed to the door of the town-hall, and remain so during the interval of eight days between the one and the other publication.* The marriage shall not be celebrated until the third day after, and not including that of the second publication.†

* See as to publication of banns and the mode according to the English law, p. 234, 5, 6.

† As to the time of celebrating after publication, see p. 234, 5, 6.

65.

Where a marriage has not been celebrated within a year, to be computed from the expiration of the interval between the publications, it cannot be celebrated until new publications shall have been made, according to the forms hereinbefore prescribed.

As to new notice and publication in England, see p. 236.

66.

Acts of opposition to a marriage shall be signed, both original and copy, by the parties opposing, or by their attornies, specially and authentically appointed; they shall be signified, with a copy of the appointment, to the party, or delivered at the domicile of the parties, and to the officer of the civil state, who shall put his mark of having received it (visa) on the original.

As to opposition to a marriage in England, see p. 236.

67.

The officer of the civil state shall, without delay, make mention concisely of the oppositions on the register of the publications; he shall likewise make mention, on the margin of the inscription of the said oppositions, of the judgments or acts of withdrawing the opposition which shall have been sent to him.

As to the entry of the opposition, see p. 236.

68.

Where opposition has been made, the officer of the civil state shall not be at liberty to celebrate a marriage, until he shall have had a withdrawal of it transmitted to him, upon pain of a fine of 300 francs, together with all damages.

As to the consequences of opposition, and the penalty of celebrating a marriage notwithstanding, see p. 236, 7.

69.

If there has been no opposition, a memorandum thereof shall be made in the act of marriage;* and where publications have been made in several communes, the parties shall transmit a certificate from the officer of the civil state of each commune, certifying that there is no opposition.†

* No similar provision required by the English law.

† See parallel English law, p. 237.

70.

The officer of the civil state shall cause to be transmitted to him the register of birth of each party about to be married. Where either party shall be unable to produce it to him, its place may be supplied by showing an act of notoriety delivered by the justice of the peace at the parties' place of birth, or at that of his domicile.

No similar provision required by the English law.

71.

The act of notoriety shall contain a declaration of seven witnesses of either sex, relations or not, the names, surnames, profession, and domicile of the future husband or wife, and those of the father and mother, if they are known; the place, and, as nearly as possible, the date of birth, and the causes which prevent the producing of the register of birth. The witnesses shall sign the act of notoriety with the justice of the peace; and if there are any witnesses who are unable or do not know how to sign their names, mention shall be made of that circumstance.

No similar proceeding required by the English law.

72.

The act of notoriety shall be presented to the court of first instance in the place where the marriage is to be celebrated. The court, after having heard the king's attorney, shall give or refuse its approval, accordingly as it shall find the declarations of the witnesses, and the causes which prevent the production of the act of birth sufficient or insufficient.

No similar proceeding acquired by the English law.

73.

The authentic act * of the consent † of fathers and mothers, or of grandfathers and grandmothers, or in defect of these, that of the family, shall contain the names, the surnames, the professions, and domiciles of the future husband, or wife, and of all those who shall have concurred in the act, together with their degree of relationship.

* No similar document required by the English law.

† See as to the consent of parents, p. 237.

74.

The marriage shall be celebrated in the commune in which one or other of the parties shall reside. This residence, as regards the marriage, shall be established by six months' continued habitation within the same commune.

As to the place of celebrating a marriage in England, see p. 238.

75.

On the day appointed by the parties after the intervals for the publications, the civil officer in the town hall, in the presence of four witnesses, relations or not, shall read to the parties the beforementioned documents, relating to their condition and to the formalities of the marriage, and from cap. 6. title "*Of marriage: on the respective rights and duties of married persons.*" He shall receive from each party, one after the other, a declaration that they are willing to take each other for husband and wife; he shall pronounce, in the name of the law, that they are united in marriage, and he shall forthwith draw up a registry to that effect.

As to the mode of solemnizing a marriage in England, see p. 238, 9.

76.

In the registry of a marriage shall be set forth,

1st. The names, surnames, professions, age, place of birth, and residences of the married persons.

2nd. If they are of full age, or minors.

3rd. The names, surnames, professions, and residences of the fathers and mothers.

4th. The consent of the fathers and mothers, grandfathers and grandmothers, and that of the family, in the cases in which they are requisite.

5th. The respective acts, if any have been made.

6th. The publications within the different places of residence.

7th. The oppositions, if any have been made; the relinquishment of them, or the mention that no opposition has been made.

8th. The declaration of the contracting parties of taking each other as husband and wife, and the declaration of their union by the public officer.

9th. The names, surnames, ages, professions, and residences of the witnesses, and their declaration if they are relations or allied to the parties, on which side, and in what degree.

As to the requisites of the registry of a marriage, see p. 239.

CHAPTER IV.

The Act of Decease.

77.

No interment shall be made without an authority on paper, free of duty, and with charge from the officer of the civil state, who may not deliver it until he shall have been conducted to the deceased person to assure himself of the death, and after twenty-four hours after decease, except in cases otherwise provided for by the regulations of the police.

As to burial without certificate of registration of death, see p. 239.

78.

The register of death shall be drawn up by the officer of the civil state, on the declaration of two witnesses. These witnesses shall, if possible, be the two nearest relations or neighbours; or where a party shall die out of his own residence, the person at whose house the party died, and a relation or other person.

On this point, see p. 240.

79.

The register of the death shall contain the names, surname, age, profession, and residence of the deceased person; the name and surname of the consort, if the deceased were married or widowed; the names, surnames, age, profession, and residence of the parties declaring the fact, and if they are relations, their degree of affinity.

The same register shall contain, moreover, as far as can be ascertained, the names, surnames, profession and residence of the father and mother of the deceased, and the place of his birth.

As to the requisites of an English register of death, see p. 241.

80.

In cases of death in military hospitals, civil or other public edifices, the governors, directors, managers, and masters of such edifices, are required to notify the same, within twenty-four hours, to the officer of the civil state, who shall repair to the place to satisfy himself of the death, and thereupon draw up the register conformably to the preceding article, upon the declarations which shall have been given him, and upon the observations he shall then make.

Registers shall, moreover, be kept in the aforesaid hospitals and edifices, for the purpose of inserting such depositions and observations.

The officer of the civil state shall transmit the register of death to the officer at the last residence of the deceased, who shall insert it in the registers.

As to the registry of deaths in English hospitals, see p. 241.

81.

When there shall be any signs or marks of violent death, or of other circumstances which give rise to suspicion, interment shall not take place until an officer of police, assisted by a doctor in physic or surgery, shall have drawn up a statement of the condition of the body, and of the circumstances relative thereto, as well as the information he shall have been able to collect respecting the name, surname, age, profession, place of birth, and residence of the deceased.

On this point see the English provisions, p. 241.

82.

The officer of police is required to transmit forthwith to the civil state,* at the place where the party died, all the informations set forth in his statement, after which the registry of the death shall be drawn up. The officer of the civil state shall transmit a copy thereof to the officer at the residence of the deceased, if known: this copy shall be inserted in the registers.

* See a similar provision of the English law, p. 241.

83.

The keepers of the criminal records are required, within twenty-four hours after the execution of judgments inflicting the punishment of death, to transmit to the officer of the civil state, at the place where the condemned party shall have been executed, all the informations enumerated in the 79th article, after which, the register of death shall be drawn up.

No similar enactment of the English law.

84.

In case of death in prisons or houses of seclusion or detention, intimation thereof shall immediately be given, by the gaolers and keepers, to the officer of the civil state, who shall repair thither as directed in article 80, and shall draw up the register of death.

As to deaths in prison in England, see p. 241.

85.

In all cases of death, by violence, or in prisons and houses of seclusion, or by execution, no mention shall be made in the registers of these circumstances, but the register of death shall be drawn up simply in the form prescribed by article 79.

See the English law on this point, p. 241, 2.

86.

In case of death during a sea-voyage, a registry shall be drawn up within twenty-four hours, in presence of two witnesses selected from the officers of the vessel, or in defect of them, from among the ship's crew. This act shall be drawn up in manner following, viz. on board the king's ships, by the officer for the administration of the marine, and on board vessels belonging to a merchant, or privateers, by the captain, master, or commander of the vessel. The register of death shall be inserted at the end of the roll of the ship's crew.

See the parallel English law on this point, p. 242.

87.

At the first port where a vessel shall touch, whether to refit, or for any other cause except to lay up, the officers for the administration of the marine, the captain, master, or commander, who shall have drawn up the registers of death, are required to deposit two copies thereof conformably to article 60. On the arrival of a vessel at her port of discharge, the roll of the ship's crew shall be deposited in the office of the superintendent of maritime inscription; he shall transmit one copy of the register of death, with his signature, to the officer of the civil state, at the residence of the deceased person: this copy shall be forthwith inserted in the registers.

See the parallel English law on this point, p. 242.

CHAPTER V.

Of Registers of the Civil State regarding the Military out of the Territory of the Kingdom.

88.

Registers of the civil state made out of the territory of the kingdom, concerning the military or other persons attached to the army, shall be drawn up in the forms prescribed by the preceding regulations: saving the exceptions contained in the following articles.

As to the records of the state of English soldiers, whether in or out of the realm, see p. 242.

89.

The quarter-master in every corps, consisting of one or more battalions or squadrons, and the captain commandant in other corps, shall discharge the functions of the officer of the civil state; the same functions shall be discharged for officers without troops, and for persons attached to the army, by the inspector of the muster rolls belonging to the army, or to a division of the army.

As to the duty of the adjutant in an English regiment, see p. 242.

90.

With every body of troops, a register shall be kept of registry of the civil state, relative to individuals of the corps, and another with the staff officer of the army, or division of the army,* for acts of a civil nature relative to officers without troops, and all others attached to the army; these registers shall be preserved in the same manner as other registers of the corps and staff, and deposited among the archives of the war, on the re-entrance of such corps or army into the territory of the kingdom.†

* See the English regulations as to regimental registry as to officers, p. 243.

† The regimental registry is kept at head quarters, p. 243.

91.

The registers shall be marked and signed, in every corps, by the commanding officer; and among the staff by the chief officer of the staff.

See the mode of certifying the English regimental register, p. 243.

92.

Declarations of birth in the army shall be made within ten days succeeding the delivery.

See parallel regulations in the English army, p. 243.

93.

The officer charged with the custody of the civil register must, within ten days following the inserting of a registry of birth in the said register, address an extract of it to the officer of the civil state, at the last residence of the father of the child, or of its mother, if the father is unknown.

No similar regulation in the English system.

93.

Publications of marriage among the military and those employed in following the army, shall be made at their last residence: they shall be put, moreover, twenty-five days before the celebration of the marriage, upon the order of the day of the corps, in the case of individuals who belong to such corps; and for officers without troops, and the employés attached to it, upon that of the army or division of the army.

No similar regulation in the English system. But as to marriage, see p. 244.

95.

Immediately after the insertion in the register of the registry of celebration of marriage, the officer charged with the custody of such register shall transmit a copy thereof to the officer of the civil state of the last residence of the married persons.

No similar regulation in the English system, p. 244.

96.

The registries of death shall be drawn up, in every corps, by the quarter-master; and in case of officers without troops, and their employés, by the inspector of the muster rolls of the army, on the attestation of three witnesses; and an extract from these registers shall be transmitted, within ten days, to the officer of the civil state of the deceased's last residence.

See the English regulations on this point, p. 244.

97.

In case of death in military hospitals, removeable or stationary, the registry thereof shall be drawn up by the director of the said hospitals, and sent to the quarter-master of the corps, or to the inspector of the muster rolls of the army or the division of the army of which the deceased formed part; these officers shall forward a copy thereof to the officer of the civil state of the last residence of the deceased.

No similar regulations on this point; but see p. 244.

98.

The officer of the civil state of the residence of the parties, to whom a copy of any registry of a civil nature shall have been transmitted from the army, is required forthwith to inscribe it on the registers.

No similar regulation in the English law.

CHAPTER VI.

Of the Amendments of Registers of the Civil State.

99.

When the amendment of a register of the civil state shall be demanded, it shall be decreed accordingly, saving an appeal, by a competent tribunal, and on the request of the king's attorney, parties interested shall be summoned, if there be ground.

As to the amendment of errors in a register, see p. 245.

100.

A judgment of amendment cannot at any time be opposed to parties interested who shall not have demanded it, or who shall not have been summoned thereto.

No similar principle is required in the English law, the register not being absolutely conclusive.

101.

Judgments of amendment shall be inscribed upon the registers by the officer of the civil state, as soon as they shall have been transmitted to him; and mention thereof shall be made on the margin of the amended register.

See, as to the immediate amendment of errors discovered in the English register, p. 245.

TITLE III.*

Of Domicile.

DECREED 14TH MARCH, 1803.—PROMULGATED 24TH OF SAME MONTH.

102.

The domicile of every Frenchman is, as far as regards the exercise of

* Formerly the provinces of France had each a different customary law and court; and being still divided into districts, each having its own tribunals, with, for most purposes, exclusive jurisdiction, questions of domicile have, and still do demand in that country, great attention.

his civil rights, in the place where he has his principal establishment.

See a similar principle in the English law, p. 249.

103.

The change of domicile shall be effected by the fact of a real habitation in another place, accompanied by an intention of fixing the principal establishment in such latter place.

See the English law on these points of fact and intention, p. 250.

104.

Proof of such intention shall be collected from an express declaration, made as well to the magistrates of the place which the party shall quit, as to those of the place to which he shall have transferred his domicile.

There is no similar declaration recognized in the English law.

105.

In default of express declaration, proof of intention shall depend on circumstances.

As to the proof of intention according to the English law, see p. 250, 1.

106.

A citizen called to a public office, temporary or revocable, shall preserve his former domicile, unless he has manifested a contrary intention.

See a nearly similar principle in the English law, p. 251.

107.

The acceptance of offices, bestowed for life, shall import an immediate transfer of the functionary's domicile to a place where he is to exercise his office.

See the English law in such case, p. 251.

108.

A married woman has no domicile but that of her husband. A minor not emancipated shall have his domicile with his father, mother, or guardian; one of full age, placed under restraint, shall have his with his legal committee.

See a similar principle in the English law, governing these cases, p. 251, 2.

109.

Persons of full age who constantly serve or labour at the house of others, shall have the same domicile as the person with whom they serve or labour, provided they lodge also under the same roof.

See a similar principle in the English law, p. 252.

110.

The place where succession shall open, is to be determined by the domicile.

See the parallel principle in the English law, p. 252, 3.

111.

When an act shall contain, on behalf of the parties, or one of them, an election of domicile for the execution of the same act in a different place from that of the real domicile, the notifications, demands, and proceedings, relative to such act, may be made at the domicile agreed on, and before the judge of that place.

The English courts, not being merely local, no principle exactly similar exists in the English law; but, as to the parties substituting another place for services of notices, &c., see p. 253.

TITLE IV.

Of Absent Persons.

DECREED 15TH OF MARCH, 1803.—PROMULGATED 25TH OF THE SAME MONTH.

CHAPTER I.

Of Presumption of Absence.

112.

If there be necessity to provide for the administration of the whole or part of the effects, left by a person presumed absent, or who has no accredited agent, it shall be determined on by a court of first instance, on the petition of the parties interested.

In the English, as in the Roman and the ancient French law, there are no proceedings for declaring a person absent, unaccountable absence being too rare to have received any great portion of legislative attention; but of course there are laws and proceedings to be adopted in the more common act of absconding for fraudulent purposes, and also rules for preserving the absent parties' rights, p, 255, 6, and 253 to 260.

113.

The court, on the request of the most diligent party, shall appoint a notary to represent the presumed absentees in the inventories, accounts, distribution, and payments, in which they shall be interested.

No similar principle in the English law.

114.

The public ministry is specially charged to watch over the interests of persons presumed absent; and shall be heard upon all demands which concern them.

No similar officer; but see the vigilance exercised by the courts, p. 258.

CHAPTER II.

Of the Declaration of Absence.

115.

Whenever a person shall have ceased to appear at the place of his domicile or residence, and when no tidings shall have been heard of him during four years, the parties interested may proceed before a court of first instance, in order that his absence may be declared.

No similar proceeding in England.

116.

In order to establish the absence, the court shall, after the production of papers and documents, order that an inquiry be made peremptorily with the king's attorney, in the circle of the domicile, and in that of actual residence, if they are distinct from each other.

No similar proceeding in England; but see, as to proclamations of outlawry, p. 267.

117.

The court, in adjudging upon the demand, shall moreover have regard to the motives of absence, and to the causes which may have prevented the receiving tidings respecting the individual presumed absent.

No similar provision in the English law.

118.

The king's attorney shall, as soon as they shall be given, transmit all judgments, as well preparatory as definitive, to the minister of justice, who shall make them public.

No similar provision in the English law.

119.

The judgment of declaration of absence shall not be given until the expiration of a year after that directing an inquiry.

See note to article 115.

CHAPTER III.

Of the Effects of Absence.

SECTION I.

Of the Effects of Absence, as respects the Property possessed by the Absentee at the Date of his Disappearance.

120.

In cases where an absent person shall not have left an authority for the administration of his property, his heirs presumptive at the date of his disappearance, or at the date of the last tidings respecting him, may, by virtue of the definitive judgment which shall have declared his absence, take upon themselves provisional possession of the property which belonged to the absentee at the date of his departure, or of the last tidings respecting him, on condition of giving security for the fidelity of their administration.

No similar provision in the English law; but see presumption of death, p. 258.

121.

If the absentee have left behind him a power of attorney, his heirs presumptive may not proceed for the declaration of absence, or entry on provisional possession, until after the lapse of ten years from the disappearance, or the last tidings respecting him.

No similar provision in the English law, and the party empowered might continue to act until the presumed death of the absent person, or the expiration of his authority, p. 259.

122.

The same rule shall prevail, if the power of attorney ceases; and, in such case, provision shall be made for the administration of the property of the absentee, as directed in the first chapter of the present title.

No similar provision in the English law, p. 259.

123.

When the heirs presumptive shall have obtained provisional possession, the will, if any exists, shall be opened on the requisition of the parties interested, or of the king's attorney of the court; and the legatees, donees, as well as all those who have any claims upon the property of the absentee, contingent upon his death, are empowered to exercise such claims provisionally, on condition of giving security.

The proceedings to execute a will after the presumed death of an absent person in England, would not differ from those in ordinary cases, except, perhaps, as to security for refunding. See p. 259, and n. 1.

124.

A married party in community of goods, if desirous of the continuance of the community, may prevent the provisional possession and the provisional exercise of all rights, subject to the contingency of the death of the absentee, and take, or retain by preference, the administration of the property of the absentee. If the married party demand provisional dissolution of the community, he shall exercise his claims, and all his legal and conventional rights, on condition of giving security for things susceptible of restitution. The wife, exercising an option for the continuance of community, preserves the right of renouncing it afterwards.

The English law has nothing resembling community, but as to the situation of parties married to persons presumed dead, see p. 260.

125.

Provisional possession shall only be regarded as a deposit, which shall confer on those who obtain it the administration of the property of the absentee, and which shall render them liable to account to him, in case of his re-appearance, or the receipt of tidings respecting him.

As there is no provisional possession recognized in the English law, of course there is no law respecting it; but as to the rights of the party on re-appearing, see p. 255, 260.

126.

The parties obtaining provisional possession, or a party married who shall have elected a continuance of community, must cause an inventory to be made of the moveable effects and papers of the absentee, in presence of the king's attorney of the court of first instance, or of a justice of the peace required by the said king's attorney.

The court shall order, if there be occasion, a sale of the whole or part of the moveable effects. In case of sale, the produce shall be employed the same as accrued profits.

Those who obtain provisional possession, may demand, for their own security, that a competent person, nominated by the court, proceed to view the immoveable property, in order to verify its condition. His report shall be allowed in presence of the king's attorney; the costs of it shall be paid from the property of the absentee.

No similar provision in the English law.

127.

They who, by means of provisional possession, or of legal administration, shall have enjoyed the property of the absentee, shall only be bound to render to him the fifth part of his revenues, in case he shall re-appear within fifteen complete years from the day of his disappearance; and the tenth part, in case he shall not re-appear until after fifteen years.

After thirty years' absence, the whole of his revenues shall belong to them.

A different principle governs in parallel cases in the English law. See p. 258. 9.

128.

None of those who shall only enjoy property by virtue of provisional possession, shall be at liberty to alienate or pledge the immoveable property of the absentee.

See the law of England, p. 258, 59, 60.

129.

Where the absence has continued during thirty years from the provisional possession, or from the date at which the married party in community shall have taken upon him the administration of the property of the absentee, or where a hundred years shall have elapsed since the birth of the absentee, the securities shall be discharged: all those who have right may demand a distribution of the property of the absentee, and have the definitive possession decreed by the court of first instance.

As to the time of the presumption of death by the English law, see p. 258, 9.

130.

A succession to the absentee shall be opened from the day of his decease proved, for the benefit of his next heirs at that date;* and they who shall have enjoyed the goods of the absentee are required to restore them, with reservation of the fruits acquired by them, by virtue of article 127.

* On this point see the English law, p. 259.

131.

If the absentee re-appears, or if his existence is proved during provisional possession, the effects of the judgment which shall have declared his absence shall cease: without prejudice, if there be ground, to the precautionary measures prescribed in the first chapter of the present title for the administration of his goods.

See the English law on this point, p. 260, and note to art. 125.

132.

If the absentee re-appears, or if his existence is proved, even after definitive possession, he shall recover his property in the state in which it shall then be, the price of that part of it which shall have been sold, or the profits accruing from the employment which shall have been made of the price of his property sold.

See the English law on this point, p. 260.

133.

The children and direct descendants of the absentee are empowered equally, within thirty years to be computed from final possession, to demand restitution of his property, as is mentioned in the preceding article.

See the same principle (perhaps restricted as to time by the statutes of limitation) in the English law, p. 260.

134.

After the judgment declaratory of absence, every person who shall have rights to exercise against the absentee, can only prosecute them against those who shall have been part in possession of his property, or who shall have the legal administration thereof.

No similar principle in the English law, p. 256.

Section II.

Of the Effects of Absence, with regard to eventual Rights which may belong to the Absentee.

135.

Whoever shall claim a right fallen to an individual whose existence shall not be known, must prove that the said individual was alive when the right was open: until such proof, his demand shall be declared not admissible.

See the parallel English law, p. 259, 60.

136.

If a succession opens to which an individual shall be called whose existence is not known, it shall devolve exclusively upon those with whom he would have had a right to participate, or upon those who shall be entitled to it in his default.

See the parallel English law, p. 259, 60.

137.

The dispositions of the two preceding articles shall take place without prejudice to the actions on petition of inheritance and other rights, which shall belong to the absentee or to his representatives or others having title, and shall only be extinguished by the lapse of time established for prescription.

See note to art. 131, 2, 3.

138.

As long as the absentee shall fail to appear, or that actions shall fail to be brought in his right, those who shall have got the succession shall gain the fruits bonâ fide received by them.

Section III.

Of the Effects of Absence, as they relate to Marriage.

139.

A married person absent, whose consort shall have contracted a new union, shall alone be admissible to impeach such marriage in person or by attorney furnished with proof of his existence.

See the parallel English law, p. 260

140.

If the married party absent has not left relations capable of succeeding to him, the consort may demand to be put into provisional possession of the property.

No similar principle in the English law.

CHAPTER IV.

Of the Superintendence of Minors whose Father has Disappeared.

141.

If a father has disappeared, leaving children minors, the issue of a marriage with his wife, who remains, the mother shall have the superintendence of them, and she shall exercise all the rights of her husband, as regards their education and the administration of their property.

See the remedy in this case by the English law, p. 260.

142.

Six months after the father's disappearance, if the mother were dead at the time of such disappearance, or if she shall die before the absence of the father is declared, the superintendence of the children shall be given, by the family council, to the nearest relation in the ascending line, and in their default to a provisional guardian.

No similar principle in the English law.

143.

The same shall be done in the case where one of the married parties who shall have disappeared, shall leave children under age the issue of a former marriage.

No similar provision in the English law.

TITLE V.

Of Marriage.

DECREED THE 17TH OF MARCH, 1803. PROMULGATED 27TH OF THE SAME MONTH.

CHAPTER I.

Of the Qualities and Conditions required in order to be able to Contract Marriage.

144.

A man before the age of eighteen, and a woman before fifteen complete, cannot contract marriage.

See the parallel English law, p. 262.

145.

Nevertheless it is lawful for the king, upon weighty reasons, to grant dispensations of age.

See the English law on this point, p. 262, 3.

146.

There is no marriage where there is no consent.

See similar English law, p. 263.

147.

A second marriage cannot be contracted before the dissolution of the first.

See similar English law, p. 263.

148.

A son who has not attained the full age of twenty-five years, a daughter who has not attained the full age of twenty-one years, cannot contract marriage without the consent of their father and mother; in case of disagreement, the consent of the father is sufficient.

See the parallel English law, p. 263.

149.

If one of the two be dead, or under an incapacity of manifesting his or her will, the consent of the other is sufficient.

See the parallel English law, p. 264.

150.

If the father and mother are dead, or if they are under an incapacity of manifesting their will, the grandfathers and grandmothers shall supply their place; if there be a disagreement between the grandfather and grandmother of the same line, the consent of the grandfather shall suffice.

If there be disagreement between the two lines, this division shall import consent.

See parallel English law, p. 264.

151.

The children of a family, having attained the majority fixed by article 148, are required, before contracting marriage, to demand, by a respectful and formal act, the advice of their father and mother, or that of their grandfathers and grandmothers when their father and mother are dead, or under an incapacity of manifesting their will.

No similar requirement in the English law. See p. 264.

ARTICLES 152, 3, 4, 5, 6, AND 7.

DECREED THE 12TH OF MARCH, 1824. PROMULGATED 22ND OF THE SAME MONTH.

152.

From the majority fixed by article 148 to the full age of thirty years for sons, and until the full age of twenty five years for daughters, the respectful act required by the preceding article and on which there shall have been no consent to the marriage, shall be renewed two several times, from month to month; and one month after the third, it shall be lawful to pass on to the celebration of the marriage.

No similar requirement in the English law. See p. 264.

153.

After the age of thirty years, it shall be lawful, in default of consent, upon one respectful act, to pass on, after the expiration of a month, to the celebration of the marriage.

No similar requirement in the English law. See p. 264.

154.

The respectful act shall be notified to such person or persons of the ascending line as are pointed out in article 151, by two notaries, or by one notary and two witnesses; and in the statement which shall be drawn up thereof, mention shall be made of the answer.

No similar English law. See p. 264.

155.

In case of the absence of the ancestor to whom the respectful act ought to have been made, the celebration of the marriage may be proceeded in, on producing a judgment given declaring absence, or in default of such judgment that which shall have ordered an inquiry, or if there has not yet been any act of notoriety delivered by the justice of the peace of the place where the ancestor had his last known domicile. This act shall contain the declaration of four witnesses officially summoned by the justice of the peace.

No similar English law required. See p. 264.

156.

The officers of the civil state who shall have proceeded to the celebration of marriages contracted by sons not having attained the full age of twenty-five years, or by daughters not having attained the full age of twenty-one years, without having the consent of the fathers and mothers, that of the grandfathers and grandmothers, and that of the family, in a case requiring them, declared in the act of marriage, shall, on the prosecution of the parties interested, and of the king's attorney in the tribunal of first instance of the place where the marriage shall have been celebrated, be condemned to the fine inflicted by article 192, and further, to an imprisonment of not less than six months.

See the English law on this point, p. 264.

157.

Where respectful acts shall have been omitted to be made in cases in which they are prescribed, the civil officer who shall have celebrated the marriage shall be condemned to the same fine, and to an imprisonment of not less than one month.

No similar English law required. see p. 264.

158.

The regulations contained in articles 148 and 149, and those of articles 151, 152, 153, 154, and 155, relative to the respectful act required to be made to the father and mother in the case contemplated by those articles, are applicable to natural children legally recognized.

See the English law, as to the marriage of an illegitimate minor. p. 265.

159.

The natural child who has not been acknowledged, and the child who, after having been so, has lost his father or mother, or whose father and mother are unable to manifest their will, shall be able, before the full age of twenty-one years, to marry only after obtaining the consent of a guardian ad hoc, who shall be nominated for him.

See the English law as to the marriage of an illegitimate minor, p. 265.

160.

If there is neither father nor mother, neither grandfathers nor grandmothers, or if they are all found to be under an incapacity of manifesting their will, male or female children under the age of twenty-one years cannot contract marriage without the consent of a family council.

See the English law on this point, p. 265.

161.

In a direct line, marriage is prohibited between all the ascending and descending branches, legitimate or natural, and the kindred in the same line.

See similar English law, p. 265.

162.

In the collateral line, marriage is

prohibited between brother and sister, legitimate or natural, and the kindred of the same degree.

See similar English law, p. 265.

163.

Marriage is further prohibited between the uncle and the niece, the aunt and the nephew.

See similar English law, p. 266.

164.

It shall be lawful, nevertheless. for the king, on weighty grounds, to remove the prohibitions contained in the preceding article.

See contrary English law, p. 266.

CHAPTER II.

Of the Formalities relative to the Celebration of Marriage.

165.

The marriage shall be celebrated publicly, before the civil officer of the domicile of one of the two parties.

See similar English law, p. 266.

166.

The two publications directed by article 63, under the title "*Of the registers of the civil state,*" shall be made to the municipality of the place where each of the contracting parties shall have his domicile.

See parallel English law, p. 266.

167.

Nevertheless, where the actual domicile is only established by six months' residence, the publication shall be further made to the municipality of the last domicile.

As to the residence required for marriage in the English law, see p. 267.

168.

If the contracting parties, or one of them, is or are, as regards the marriage, under the power of others, the publications shall besides be made to the municipality of the domicile of those under whose power they are.

As to the residence required for marriage in the English law, see p. 267.

169.

It shall be lawful for the king or his officers, on weighty reasons, to dispense with the second publication.

As to the marriage by licence, p. 267.

170.

A marriage contracted in a foreign country between natives of France and between natives of France and a foreigner, shall be valid, if celebrated according to the forms used in that country, provided that it has been preceded by the publications prescribed in article 63, under the title "*Of registers of the civil state,*" and that the Frenchman has not infringed the regulations contained in the preceding chapter.

See English law on his subject, p. 276.

171.

Within three months after the return of a Frenchman into the territory of the republic, the registry of the celebration of marriage contracted in a foreign country shall be transcribed into the public register of marriages, at the place of his domicile.

No similar English enactment.

CHAPTER III.

Of Oppositions to Marriage.

172.

The right of opposing the celebration of marriage belongs to persons connected by marriage with one of the two contracting parties.

As to who may oppose a marriage according to the English law, see p. 268.

173.

The father, and in default of the father, the mother, and in default of the father and mother, the grandfathers and grandmothers, may oppose the marriage of their children and descendants, although they are full twenty-five years of age.

As to who may oppose a marriage

according to the English law, see p. 268.

174.

In default of any ancestor, the brother or sister, the uncle or aunt, cousin or cousins-german, being of age, can make opposition only in the two following cases:

1st. Where the consent of the family council, required by article 160, has not been obtained.

2nd. Where the opposition is founded on a state of insanity in the future spouse: This opposition, which the court is empowered summarily to set aside, shall never be received, except on the condition of the opponent proceeding for interdiction, and causing a decree to be made thereon, within the interval which shall be fixed by the judgment.

As to who may oppose a marriage according to the English law, see p. 268.

175.

In the two cases contemplated by the preceding article, the guardian or curator shall not, during the continuance of the guardianship or curatorship, make opposition, except so far as he shall have been authorized by a family council, which he is at liberty to convoke.

As to who may oppose a marriage according to the English law, see p. 268.

176.

Every act of opposition shall set forth the quality which gives the opponent the right to make it; it shall contain the election of domicile in the place where the marriage ought to be celebrated; it ought equally, unless it be made at the request of an ancestor, to contain the motives of opposition: the whole on pain of nullity, and of suspension of the ministerial officer, who shall have signed the act containing the opposition.

As to the formalities to be observed by the English law in opposing a marriage, see p. 268.

177.

The tribunal of first instance shall pronounce within ten days on the petition in revocation.

There is no time limited by the English law. On this point, see p. 268, 9.

178.

If an appeal be made, a decision shall be made thereon within ten days from the citation.

There is no time limited for deciding an appeal by the English law.

179.

If the opposition be rejected, the opponents, other nevertheless than ancestors, may be sentenced to damages.

See on this point in the English law, p. 269.

CHAPTER IV.

Of Suits for Nullity of Marriage.

180.

A marriage which has been contracted without the free consent of the married persons, or of one of them, can only be impeached by the married persons,* or such one of them whose consent has not been free.†

When there has been a mistake as to the person, the marriage shall only be impeached by such one of the married persons as may have been led into the error.

* See the English law on these two points, p. 270, 1.

† See the parallel English law, p. 271.

181.

In the case mentioned in the preceding article, the suit of nullity is no longer admissible, wherever there has been cohabitation continued during six months after the married person has acquired full liberty, or after discovery made of the error.

See the parallel and nearly similar English law, p. 271.

182.

A marriage contracted without the consent of the father and mother, of the ancestors, or of the family council, in cases where such consent was necessary, can only be impeached by those whose consent was requisite, or by such of the two married persons as stood in need of that consent.

By the English law such a marriage is not voidable. See that point, and as to the penal consequences, p. 271, 2.

183.

A suit for nullity is no longer maintainable either by the married persons, or by the relations whose consent was required, in those cases where the marriage has been approved, either expressly or tacitly, by those whose consent was necessary; or when a year has elapsed without objection on their part, subsequently to their knowledge of the marriage. Such suit is no longer maintainable by a married party, after the lapse of a year without objection on his part, subsequent to his having attained the competent age for consenting for himself to the marriage.

See observation to the preceding article, and p. 271.

184.

Every marriage contracted in contravention of the regulations contained in articles 144, 147, 161, 2, and 3, may be impeached either by the married parties themselves, or by those having an interest therein, or by the public authorities.

On this point, see the English law, p. 273.

185.

Nevertheless a marriage contracted by parties who have not yet reached the required age, or of whom one has not attained that age, is no longer liable to be impeached, 1st, where six months have expired since the married person or persons have attained the competent age; 2nd, where the woman not having reached that age, has conceived before the expiration of six months.

See the English parallel and somewhat similar law on this first clause of this article. As to the second clause, see p. 272.

186.

The father, the mother, the ancestors, and the family who have consented to a marriage contracted under the circumstances mentioned in the preceding article, are inadmissible to sue for its nullity.

No parallel enactment in the English law.

187.

In all those cases where, conformably to article 114, a suit for nullity may be instituted by all those who have an interest therein, such suit cannot be maintained by collateral relations, or the children born of another marriage of the survivor of the parties, but only where they have an actual and existing interest therein.

Some such marriages being absolutely void, no such provision as this is necessary for them in the English law. As to the interest necessary or otherwise, see p. 270, and for incest, p. 273. Those for want of age, p. 271, 2.

188.

The married party, to the prejudice of whom a second marriage has been contracted, may demand the nullity thereof, even during the life of the party who was engaged with him or her.

Such a marriage being by the law of England absolutely void, see next article.

189.

If the new married parties oppose the nullity of the first marriage, the validity or nullity of such marriage must be decided previously.

See the English law on this point, p. 273.

190.

The king's attorney may and shall, in all cases to which article 184 can be applied, and subject to the modifications contained in article 185, demand the nullity of the marriage, during the lives of the two married persons, and cause them to be sentenced to separation.

There is no such provision in the English civil law, though the parties in some of those cases are liable to punishment by the criminal or ecclesiastical law.

191.

Every marriage not publicly contracted, and not celebrated before the competent public officer, may be impeached by the married parties themselves, by the father and mother, by the ancestors, and by all those who have an actual and existing interest therein, as well as by the public authorities.

See parallel English law, p. 273.

192.

If the marriage has not been preceded by the two publications required, or if the dispensations permitted by the law have not been obtained, or if the intervals prescribed between the publications and celebrations have not been observed, the king's attorney shall cause a fine to be awarded against the public officer, which shall not exceed 300 francs; and against the contracting parties, or those under whose control they have acted, a fine proportioned to their fortune.

See parallel English law, p. 273.

193.

The penalties awarded in the preceding article shall be incurred by the persons designated therein, for every contravention of the rules prescribed by article 165, even though such contraventions shall not be adjudged sufficient to cause nullity of the marriage to be pronounced.

See similar English law, p. 273.

194.

No person can claim the title of spouse, and the civil consequences of marriage, unless he shows a registry of celebration inscribed upon the register of the civil power, saving the cases provided for by article 46, under the tiile "*Of registers of the civil state.*"

See a different principle in the English law, p. 274.

195.

The marriage in possession (la possession d'etat) cannot dispense with the pretended spouses, who shall respectively claim to be such, producing the registry of celebration of the marriage before the officer of the civil state.

See a different principle in the English law, p. 274.

196.

Where there is an actual marriage, and the registry of celebration of the marriage before the officer of the civil state is produced, the married parties are respectively incapable of suing for a nullity of this instrument.

See the English parallel principle, p. 274.

197.

If, nevertheless, in the cases of articles 194 and 195, there are children, the issue of two individuals who have lived publicly together as husband and wife, and who are both deceased, the legitimacy of such children cannot be contested on the single ground of the non-production of the registry of celebration, whenever such legitimacy is proved by an actual marriage uncontradicted by the registry of birth.

See the English law on this point, p. 274.

198.

When the proof of a legal celebration of marriage is acquired by the result of a criminal procedure, the insertion of the judgment on the registers of the civil state assures to the marriage, computing from the day of its celebration, all its civil consequences, as well as regards the married parties as the children the issue of such marriage.

No similar principle required in the English law, see p. 274; but see the penalties and parties to an indictment against the public functionary, p. 280, 1.

199.

If the married parties are dead, or

one of them, without having discovered the fraud, the criminal suit may be instituted by all those who have interest in causing the marriage to be declared valid, and by the king's attorney.

No similar enactment required in the English law.

200.

If the public officer is dead at the time of the discovery of the fraud, the action shall be carried on in a civil form against his heirs by the king's attorney in the presence of the parties interested and on their accusation.

No similar enactment required in the English law.

201.

A marriage which has been declared null draws after it, nevertheless, civil consequences, as well with regard to the married parties as to their children, when it has been contracted in good faith.

See a contrary principle in the English law, p. 275.

202.

Where good faith exists only on the part of one of the married persons, the marriage only produces civil consequences in favour of such person, and the children of the marriage.

See a contrary principle in the English law, p. 275.

CHAPTER V.

Of the Obligations accruing from Marriage.

203.

Married persons contract together, by the single act of marriage, the obligation of nourishing, maintaining, and bringing up their children.

See the parallel English law, p. 275.

204.

A child has no action against his father and mother for an establishment in marriage or otherwise.

See the parallel English law, p. 275.

205.

Children owe a maintenance to their fathers and mothers, and other ancestors who are in want thereof.

See the parallel English law, p. 276.

206.

Sons-in-law and daughters-in-law owe equally, under the same circumstances, a maintenance to their fathers-in-law and mothers-in-law; but this obligation ceases, 1st, when the mother-in-law had entered into a second marriage; 2nd, when such of the married parties as produced the affinity and the children, the issue of the union of the other party, are dead.

See the parallel, but dissimilar English law, p. 276.

207.

The obligations resulting from these regulations are reciprocal.

See parallel principles of English law, p. 276.

208.

Maintenance is only allowed in proportion to the need of the party who claims it, and the fortune of the party who owes it.

See parallel English law, p. 276.

209.

When he who supplies or he who receives maintenance is placed in such a situation, that the one can no longer give, or the other has no longer a need thereof, in whole or in part, a discharge or reduction thereof may be demanded.

See parallel English law, p. 276.

210

If the person who is bound to supply maintenance can show that he is unable to pay an alimentary pension, the court shall, on being made acquainted with the cause, give orders that he shall receive into his house, and there nourish and maintain, the party to whom he owes maintenance.

See parallel but dissimilar English law, p. 276, 7.

211.

The court shall, in like manner, adjudge, whether a father or mother who shall offer to receive, nourish, and support within the house, a child to whom they owe maintenance, ought in this case to be discharged from paying an alimentary pension.

See the parallel English law as to the last article.

CHAPTER VI.

Of the respective Rights and Duties of Married Persons.

212.

Married persons mutually owe to each other fidelity, succour, assistance.

See parallel principle in the English law, p. 277.

213.

The husband owes protection to his wife, the wife obedience to her husband.

See similar English law, p. 278.

214.

The wife is obliged to live with her husband, and to follow him wherever he may judge fit to reside: the husband is obliged to receive her, and to furnish her with every thing necessary for the wants of life, according to his means and station.

See similar English law, p. 278.

215.

The wife cannot sue in her own name, without the authority of her husband, even though she should be a public trader, or not in community or separate in property.

See similar English law, p. 278, 9.

216.

The authority of the husband is not necessary when the wife is prosecuted in a criminal matter, or relating to police.

See similar English law, p. 279.

217.

A wife, although not in community or separate in property, cannot give, alienate, pledge, or acquire by free or chargeable title, without the concurrence of her husband in the act, or his consent in writing.

See similar English law, 279.

218.

If the husband refuse to authorize his wife to sue in her own name, the judge may give her authority.

No similar English law.

219.

If the husband refuse to authorize his wife to pass an act, the wife may cause her husband to be cited directly before the tribunal of first instance, of the circle of their common domicile, which may give or refuse its authority after the husband shall have been heard, or duly summoned before the chamber of council.

No similar English law.

220.

The wife, if she is a public trader, may, without the authority of her husband, bind herself for that which concerns her trade; and in the said case binds also her husband, if there be a community between them.*

She is not reputed a public trader, if she merely retail goods in her husband's trade, but only when she carries on a separate trade.†

† See parallel Engllsh law, p. 279, 80.
* See parallel English law, p. 279, 80.

221.

When the husband is subjected to a condemnation, carrying with it an afflictive or infamous punishment, even though it may have been pronounced merely for contumacy, the wife, though of age, cannot, during the continuance of such punishment, sue in her own name or contract, until after authority given by the judge, who may in such case give his authority, without hearing or summoning the husband.

See the English law in parallel cases, p. 280.

222.

If the husband is interdicted or absent, the judge, on cognizance of the cause, may authorize his wife either to plead in her own name or to contract.

See the English law in parallel cases, p. 280.

223.

Every general authority, though stipulated by the contract of marriage, is valid only as to the administration of the property of the wife.

See the English law on this subject, p. 280.

224.

If the husband is a minor, the authority of the judge is necessary for his wife, either to sue in her own name, or to contract.

See parallel English law, p. 281.

225.

The nullity, founded on defect of authority, can only be opposed by the wife, by the husband, or by their heirs.

See parallel English law, p. 281.

226.

The wife may make a will without the authority of her husband.

See dissimilar English law, p. 281.

CHAPTER VII.

Of the Dissolution of Marriage.

227.

Marriage is dissolved,

1st. By the death of one of the parties;

2nd. By divorce lawfully pronounced;

3rd. By condemnation become definitive of one of the married parties to a punishment implying civil death.

See the English law as to the dissolution of marriage, p. 281.

CHAPTER VIII.

Of Second Marriages.

A woman cannot contract a new marriage until ten months have elapsed from the dissolution of the preceding marriage.

See parallel, but dissimilar English law, p. 281.

TITLE VI.

Of Divorce.

DECREED THE 21ST MARCH, 1803.—PROMULGATED 31ST OF THE SAME MONTH.

[By a law passed 8th May, 1816, divorce was abolished, and suits for divorce for determinate causes were converted into suits for separation of person, which corresponds with our divorce, a mensa et thoro.]

CHAPTER I.

Of the Causes of Divorce.

229.

The husband may demand a divorce on the ground of his wife's adultery.

See the parallel English law, p. 283.

230.

The wife may demand divorce on the ground of adultery in her husband, when he shall have kept his concubine in their common residence.

See the parallel English law, p. 283.

231.

The married parties may reciprocally demand divorce for outrageous conduct, ill-usage, or grievous injuries, exercised by one of them towards the other.

See the parallel English law, p. 283.

232.

The condemnation of one of the married parties to an infamous punishment, shall be to the other a ground of divorce.

See the parallel English law, p. 283.

233.

The mutual and unwavering consent of the married parties, expressed in the manner prescribed by law, under the conditions, and after the proofs which it points out, shall prove sufficiently that their common life is insupportable to them; and that there exists, in reference to them, a peremptory cause of divorce.

See the parallel but dissimilar English law, p. 284.

CHAPTER II.

Of the Divorce for Cause determinate.

Section I.

Of the Forms of the Divorce for Causes determinate.

234.

Whatever may be the nature of the facts or offences which afford ground for a suit of divorce for cause determinate, such suit shall only be made in the court of the circle within which the married persons shall have their domicile.

As to the English court in which suits for divorce must be brought, see p. 284.

235.

If any of the facts alleged by the married party demandant, give ground for a criminal prosecution on the part of the public officers, the action for divorce shall remain suspended until after the judgment of the court of assizes; it may then be resumed, without permitting any objection or exception at law to be drawn from the criminal judgment prejudicial to the married party demandant.

See parallel English law, p. 285.

236.

Every petition for divorce shall detail the facts; it shall be sent back with the corroborating documents, if there be any, to the president of the court, or to the judge who shall perform its functions, by the married party demandant in person, unless prevented by illness; in which case, on his or her request, and the certificate of two doctors of physic or surgery, or of two officers of health, the magistrate shall repair to the residence of the demandant, there to receive his or her petition.

No similar English law, but see, as to the general course of proceeding, p. 285, 6.

237.

The judge, after having heard the petitioner, and having made such observations to him or her as he shall deem suitable, shall mark the petition and the documents, and draw up a statement of the adjournment of the whole in his hands. This statement shall be signed by the judge and by the petitioner, unless the latter is ignorant or unable to write, in which case mention shall be made thereof.

See the general course of proceeding in the English law, p. 285, 6.

238.

The judge shall make order, at the foot of his statement, that the parties shall appear in person before him, at the day and hour that he shall point out; and to this end, a copy of his order shall be addressed by him to the party against whom the divorce is demanded.

See as in the preceding.

232.

On the day appointed, the judge shall make to the two married parties, if both present themselves, or to the petitioner, if appearing alone, such representations as he shall deem likely to effect a reconciliation: if he is unable to accomplish this, he shall draw up a statement thereof, and shall direct the communication of the petition and of the documents to the public officer, and the report of the whole to the tribunal.

See as in the preceding.

240.

Within the three following days, the court, on the report of the president, or of the judge who shall have exercised his functions, and on the opinion of the public officer, shall award or suspend the permission of citation. The suspension shall not exceed the term of twenty days.

See as in the preceding.

241.

The petitioner may, by virtue of the permission of the court, cause the defendant to be summoned, in the ordinary form, to appear in person at a private hearing, within the interval prescribed at the head of his summons, of the petition of divorce, and of the documents produced in its support.

See as in the preceding.

242.

At the expiration of the interval, whether the defendant appear or not, the petitioner in person, assisted by a council, if he shall deem it expedient, shall set forth or cause to be set forth the grounds of his petition; he shall produce the documents which support it, and shall name the witnesses whom he proposes to have heard.

See as in the preceding.

243.

If the defendant appear in person or by an authorized agent, he may make his observations or cause them to be made, as well upon the grounds of the petition as upon the documents produced by the petitioner and on the witnesses named by him. The defendant shall name, on his part, the witnesses he proposes to have heard, and on them the petitioner in turn shall make his observations.

See as in the preceding.

244.

A statement shall be drawn up of the appearance, assertions, and observations of the parties, as well as of the confessions which either may make. The statement shall be read over to the aforesaid parties, who shall be required to sign it; and express mention shall be made of their signature, or of their declaration of inability or unwillingness to sign.

See as in the preceding.

245.

The court shall send the parties to a public hearing, of which it shall appoint the day and hour; it shall direct a communication of the proceeding to the public officer, and shall appoint a reporter. In case the defendant shall not have appeared, the petitioner shall be bound to signify to him the order of the court, within the interval which it shall appoint.

See as in the preceding.

246.

At the day and hour appointed, on the report of the judge nominated, the public officer being heard, the court shall decree first upon the points of not receiving it, if any have been propounded. In case they shall be found conclusive, the petition for divorce shall be rejected: in the opposite case, or if exceptions of law have not been offered, the petion for divorce shall be admitted.

See as in the preceding.

247.

Immediately after the admission of the petition for divorce, on the report of the judge appointed, the public officer being heard, the court shall adjudge fully. It shall give judgment on the petition, if it appear in a state to be decided on; if not, it shall admit the petitioner to proof of pertinent facts alleged by him, and the defendant to contrary proof.

See as in the preceding.

248.

At every stage of the cause, the parties shall be at liberty, after the reports of the judge, and before the public officer shall have begun to speak, to propose or cause to be proposed their respective arguments, first upon exceptions at law, and afterwards upon the whole; but in no case shall the counsel of the petitioner be heard, unless the petitioner be present in person.

See as in the preceding.

249,

Immediately after pronouncing the judgment which shall direct the inquiries, the registrar of the court shall read that part of the statement which contains the nomination already made of the witnesses whom the parties propose to have heard They shall be warned by the president that they are still at liberty to mention others, but that after this moment no more can be received.

See as in the preceding.

250.

The parties shall propose at once their respective exceptions against the witnesses of whom they desire to get rid. The court shall decide on these exceptions after having heard the public officer.

See as in the preceding.

251.

The relations of the parties, with the exception of their children and descendants, cannot be excepted to on the ground of their affinity, nor can the domestics of the parties by reason of such quality; but the court shall have such regard as reason requires to the depositions of relations and servants.

See as in the preceding.

252.

Every judgment which shall admit a proof by witnesses shall mention by name the witnesses who shall be heard, and shall fix the day and hour at which the parties are to present themselves.

See as in the preceding.

253.

The depositions of the witnesses shall be received by the court sitting with closed doors, in the presence of the public officer, the parties, and their counsel or friends to the number of three on each side.

See as in the preceding.

254.

The parties by themselves or by their counsel may make to the witness such observations and examinations as they shall judge suitable, without being allowed, nevertheless, to interrupt them in the course of their depositions.

See as in the preceding.

255.

Every deposition shall be reduced to writing, as well as the remarks and observations to which it shall have given rise. The statement of inquiry shall be read as well to the witnesses as to the parties: both shall be required to sign it; and mention shall be made of their signature, or of their declaration of inability or refusal to sign.

See as in the preceding.

256.

After the close of the two inquiries or of that of the petitioner, if the defendant has not produced witnesses, the court shall send the parties to a public hearing, for which it shall point out the day and hour; it shall order the communication of the proceeding to the public officer, and shall appoint a reporter. This order shall be signified to the defendant at the request of the petitioner, within the interval appointed therein.

See as in the preceding.

257.

On the day fixed for final judgment, the report shall be made by the judge commissioned: the parties shall be at liberty afterwards to make by themselves or by the instrumentality of their counsel, such observations as they shall judge useful to their cause; after which the public officer shall give his opinion.

See as in the preceding.

258.

Final judgments shall be pronounced publicly; when it shall establish the divorce, the petitioner shall be authorized to go before the officer of the civil state, and cause him to pronounce it.

See as in the preceding.

259.

When the petition for divorce shall have been founded on causes of excess, cruelty, or grievous injury, although they shall be well established, the judges shall be at liberty not to allow the divorce immediately. In such case, before judgment is given, they shall authorize the woman to quit the society of her husband, without being bound to receive him, if she judges it not expedient; and they shall sentence the husband to pay her an alimentary pension proportioned to his means, if the wife has not herself sufficient funds to supply her wants.

See as in the preceding.

260.

After a year of trial, if the parties are not reunited, the married person petitioning shall cause the other to be cited to appear before the court, within the intervals prescribed by law, there to hear final judgment pronounced, which shall then allow the divorce.

See as in the preceding.

261.

When the divorce shall be demanded by reason that one of the married persons is condemned to an infamous punishment, the only formalities to be observed shall consist of producing before the civil court a copy in correct form of the judgment of condemnation, with a certificate from the court of assizes, importing that the said judgment is no longer liable to be reviewed in any legal way.

See note to art. 235.

262.

In case of appeal from the judgment of admission, or from the final judgment given by the court of first instance in a cause of divorce, the cause shall be carried on and decided by the court of appeal, as an urgent affair.

As to appeals in English suits for divorce, see p. 287.

263.

The appeal shall not be receivable except where it shall have been lodged within three months, to be reckoned from the day of intimation given of the judgment rendered on the hearing or by default. The interval for making application to the court of cassation against a judgment in the last resort shall also be of three months, computing from the intimation. The application shall be suspensory.

As to the time of appealing by the English law, see p. 287.

264.

By virtue of every judgment given in the last resort, or passed into force as a matter decided, which shall authorise a divorce, the married person who shall have obtained it, shall be obliged to present himself, within an interval of two months, before the officer of the civil state, the other party being duly summoned, in order to cause him to pronounce the divorce.

No similar English law.

265.

These two months shall not begin to run, with regard to the judgments of first instance, until after the expiration of the interval for the appeal; with regard to judgments given for default in matters of appeal, not until after the expiration of the interval for opposition; and with regard to peremptory judgments in the last resort, not until after the expiration of the interval for application for cassation.

No similar English law.

266.

The married party petitioner who shall have suffered the interval of two months hereinbefore determined to pass by, without summoning the other party before the officer of the civil state, shall forfeit the benefit of the judgment which has been obtained, and shall not be permitted to resume his suit for divorce, except for new cause; in which case the ancient causes may be insisted on.

No similar English law.

Section 2.

Of the Provisional Measures to which a Suit for Divorce for Cause Determinate may give rise.

267.

The provisional management of the children shall rest with the husband, petitioner, or defendant in the suit for divorce, unless it be otherwise ordered by the court for the greater advantage of the children, on petition either of the mother, or the family, or the public officer.

See the English law on this subject, p. 287.

268.

The wife, petitioner, or defendant in divorce, shall be at liberty to quit the residence of her husband during the prosecution, and demand an alimentary pension proportioned to the means of the husband. The court shall point out the house in which the wife shall be bound to reside, and shall fix, if there be ground, the alimentary provision which the husband shall be obliged to pay her.

See the English law on this subject, p. 287.

269.

The wife shall be bound to prove her residence in the house appointed, as often as she shall be thereto required; in default of such proof, the husband may refuse the alimentary pension, and if the wife is the petitioner for divorce, may cause her to be declared incapable of continuing her prosecution.

No similar principle of English law.

270.

The wife having community of goods, plaintiff or defendant in divorce shall be at liberty, in every stage of the cause, commencing with the date of the order mentioned in article 238, to require, for the preservation of her rights, that seals should be affixed to the moveable goods in community. These seals shall not be taken off until an inventory and appraisement is made, and on the undertaking of the husband to produce the articles contained in the inventory, or to answer for their value, as their legal guardian.

The English law does not recognise this kind of partnership between the husband and wife, and therefore there is no similar English law. See the English law as to the wife's property, p. 287.

271.

Every obligation contracted by the husband at the expense of the community, every alienation made by him of immoveable property dependant upon it, subsequently to the date of the order mentioned in article 238, shall be declared void, if proof be given, moreover, that it has been made or contracted in fraud of the rights of the wife.

See as to the preceding article,

Section 3.

Of Exceptions at Law against the Suit for Divorce for Cause determinate.

272.

The suit for divorce shall be extinguished by the reconciliation of the parties, whether occurring subsequently to the facts which might have authorized such suit, or to the petition for divorce.

See the parallel English law, p. 288.

273.

In either case the petitioner shall be declared incapable of prosecuting the suit; a new one may, nevertheless, be instituted for cause accruing subsequently to the reconciliation, and the ancient causes may then be employed in support of such new petition.

See the parallel English law, p. 288.

274.

If the petitioner for divorce deny that a reconciliation has taken place, the defendant shall make proof thereof, either in writing or by witnesses, in the form prescribed in the first section of the present chapter.

See parallel English law, p. 288.

CHAPTER III.

Of Divorce by Mutual Consent.

275.

The mutual consent of married persons shall not be admitted, if the husband have not reached twenty-five years, or if the wife be under twenty-one.

See the English law on this point, p. 288, 9.

276.

The mutual consent shall not be received until two years from the marriage.

See note to article 275.

277.

It shall no longer be admissible after twenty years of marriage, nor where the wife shall have attained the age of forty-five years.

See note to article 275.

278.

In no case shall the mutual consent of married persons be sufficient, unless authorized by their fathers and mothers, or by their other living ancestors, according to the rules prescribed in article 150, under the title "*Of Marriage.*"

See note to article 275.

279.

Married persons determined to effect a divorce by mutual consent, shall be bound to make previously an inventory and estimate of all their property, moveable and immoveable, and to adjust their respective rights, on which, notwithstanding, it shall be free to them to enter into arrangements.

See note to article 275.

280.

They shall be bound in like manner to establish in writing their agreement on the three points following:

1st. To whom the children, the fruit of their union, shall be intrusted, as well during the period of the suit, as after divorce pronounced;

2d. To what house the wife is to retire and reside in, during the period of the suit;

3d. What sum the husband is to pay to his wife during the same period, if she has not an income sufficient to supply her wants.

See note to article 275.

281.

The married parties shall present themselves together and in person, before the president of the civil court of their circle, or before the judge who shall discharge his functions, and make a declaration to him of their desire, in presence of two notaries brought by themselves.

See note to article 275.

282.

The judge shall make to both the married parties together, and to each of them apart, in the presence of the two notaries, such representations and exhortations as he shall deem suitable: he shall read to them the fourth chapter of the present title, which regulates "*The Effects of Divorce,*" and shall disclose to them all the consequences of the step they are taking.

See note to article 275.

283.

If the married parties persist in their resolution, an act shall be given them, by the judge setting forth that they demand a divorce, and mutually consent to it: and they shall be required to produce and deposit on the instant, in the hands of the notaries, besides the acts mentioned in articles 279 and 280.

1st. The acts of their birth and that of their marriage;

2d. The acts of birth and of death, of all the children the fruit of their union;

3d. An authenticated declaration of their father and mother, or other living ancestors, to the effect, that for causes to them known, they authorize him or her, their son or daughter, grandson or granddaughter, married to such or such a person, to demand divorce and to consent thereto. The fathers, mothers, grandfathers, and grandmothers of the married parties shall be presumed living, until the production of the acts verify their decease.

See note to article 275.

284.

The notaries shall draw up at length a detailed statement of all that shall have been said or done in execution of the preceding articles; the minute thereof shall remain with the elder of the two notaries, as well as the documents produced, which shall be annexed to the statement, in which mention shall be made of intimation which shall be given to the wife to retire within twenty-four hours to the house agreed on between her and her husband, and to reside there until divorce pronounced.

See note to article 275.

285.

The declaration thus made shall be renewed within the first fortnight of the 4th, 7th, and 10th months following, observing the same formalities. The parties shall be bound each time to bring proof, by public act. that their fathers, mothers, or other living ancestors persist in their first determination; but they shall not be bound to repeat the production of any other act.

See note to article 275.

286.

Within a fortnight from the day on which a year shall have expired, computing from the first declaration, the married parties, attended each by two friends, persons of credit within the circle, of the age of fifty years at the least, shall present themselves together, and in person, before the president of the court, or the judge who shall discharge his functions; they shall hand to him copies, in correct form, of the four statements, containing their mutual consent, and of all the acts which shall have been annexed to it, and shall require of the magistrate, each separately, in the presence, nevertheless, of each other, and of the four persons of credit, sentence of divorce.

See note to article 275.

287.

After the judge and the attending parties shall have made their observations to the married persons, if they persevere, an act shall be delivered to them of their request, and of the presentation made by them of the documents in its support; the registrar of the court shall draw up a statement, which shall be signed as well by the parties (unless they shall declare they know not how or are incapable of writing, in which case mention shall thereof be made,) as by the four attending persons, the judge and the registrar.

See note to article 275.

288.

The judge shall then annex to this statement his decree, that within three days a report shall by him be made to the court in the council-chamber, upon the conclusions in writing by the public officer, to whom the documents shall be, for this purpose, communicated by the registrar.

See note to article 275.

289.

If the public officer finds in the documents proof that the married parties were of the age, the husband of twenty-five years, the wife of twenty-one years when they made their first declaration; that at this period they had been married during two years, and that their marriage had not subsisted more than twenty years; that the wife was under the age of forty-five years; that the mutual consent had been expressed four times in the course of the year, after the preliminaries hereinbefore prescribed, and with all the formalities required in the present chapter, more especially with the authority of the fathers and mothers of the married persons, or with that of their other living ancestors, in case of the previous decease of their fathers and mothers:—he shall give his conclusions in these terms, "the law permits;" in a contrary case, his conclusion shall be in these terms, "the law forbids."

See note to article 275.

290.

The court shall not upon the report enter into any other examinations than those pointed out in the preceding article. If the result shall be that, in the opinion of the court, the parties have satisfied the conditions, and complied with the formalities appointed by the law, it shall admit the divorce, and send the parties before the officer of the civil state, to have it pronounced: in the opposite case, the court shall declare that the divorce cannot be admitted, and shall set forth the grounds of their decision.

See note to article 275.

291.

The appeal against the judgment, declaring that there is no ground for directing a divorce, shall only be admissible where it is lodged by the two parties, but by separate acts, within ten days at the soonest, and at the latest within twenty days, from the date of the judgment of first instance.

See note to article 275.

292.

The acts of appeal shall be mutually signified as well to the other married party as to the public officer of the court of first instance.

See note to article 275.

293.

Within ten days, to be computed from the intimation given to him of the second act of appeal, the public officer in the court of first instance shall cause to be passed to the attorney-general of the Royal court a copy of the judgment, and the documents on which it has been founded. The attorney-general in the Royal court shall give his conclusions in writing, within ten days following the receipt of the documents; the president, or the judge officiating for him, shall make his report to the Royal court, in the chamber of council, and judgment shall be finally given within ten days following the remission of the conclusions of the attorney-general.

See note to article 275.

294.

In pursuance of the sentence establishing the divorce, and within twenty days from its date, the parties shall present themselves together and in person before the officer of the civil state, in order to cause him to pronounce the divorce. This interval exceeded, the judgment shall be as though it had never occurred.

See note to article 275.

CHAPTER IV.

Of the Effects of Divorce.

295.

Married parties who shall be divorced, for any cause whatsoever, shall never be permitted to be united again.

See parallel English law, p. 289.

296.

In a case of divorce pronounced for cause determinate, the wife divorced shall not be permitted to marry for ten months after divorce pronounced

See parallel but dissimilar English law, p. 290.

297.

In case of divorce by mutual consent, neither of the parties shall be allowed to contract a new marriage until the expiration of three years from the pronunciation of the divorce.

See note to art. 275, and the English law as to divorces not à vinculo matrimonii on this point, p. 290.

298.

In the case of divorce admitted by law for cause of adultery, the guilty party shall never be permitted to marry with his accomplice.* The wife adulteress shall be condemned in the same judgment; and, on the request of the public minister, to confinement in a house of correction, for a determinate period, which shall not be less than three months, nor exceed two years.†

* See contrary principle of the English law, p. 290.

† See the English law, p. 290.

299.

For whatever cause a divorce shall take place, except in the case of mutual consent, the married party against whom the divorce shall have been established shall lose all the advantage conferred by the other party, whether by their contract of marriage, or since the marriage contracted,

See the parallel English law, p. 290.

300.

The married party who shall have obtained the divorce shall preserve the advantages conferred by the other spouse, although they may have made mutual stipulations and such reciprocity have not taken place.

See the parallel English law, p. 290.

301.

If the married parties shall have conferred no advantage, or if those stipulated do not appear sufficient to secure the subsistence of the married party who has obtained the divorce, the court may award to such party, from the property of the other, an alimentary pension, which shall not exceed the third part of the revenues of such other. This pension shall be revocable in a case where it shall cease to be necessary.

See the English law of alimony, p. 290, and p. 286.

302.

The children shall be entrusted to the married party who has obtained the divorce, unless the court, on petition by the family, or by the public officer, gives order, for the greater benefit of the children, that all or some of them shall be committed to the care, either of the other married party, or of a third person.

See the parallel English law, p. 291.

303.

Whoever may be the person to whom the children shall be committed, their father and mother shall preserve respectively the right to watch over the maintenance and education of their children, and shall be bound to contribute thereto in proportion to their means.

See the parallel English law, p. 291.

304.

The dissolution of a marriage by divorce admitted by law shall not deprive children, the fruit of such marriage, of any of the benefits secured to them by the laws, or by the matrimonial covenants of their father and mother; but there shall be no admission of claims by the children, except in the same manner and in the same circumstances in which they would have been admitted if the divorce had not taken place.

See the parallel English law, p. 291.

305.

In the case of divorce by mutual consent, a property in half the possessions of each of the two married parties shall be acquired in full right, from the day of their first declaration, by the children born of their marriage: the father and mother shall nevertheless retain the enjoyment of such moiety until their children's majority, on condition of providing for their nourishment, maintenance, and education in a manner suitable to their fortune and condition; the whole without prejudice to the other advantages which may have been secured to the said children by the matrimonial covenants of their father and mother.

This kind of divorce being unknown in England, there is no similar provision of the English law.

CHAPTER V.

Of the Separation of Persons.

306.

In cases where there is ground for a petition in divorce for cause determinate, it shall be free to the married persons to make petition for separation of persons.

See the English law as to this point, p. 291, 2.

307.

It shall be entered, carried on, and determined in the same manner as every other civil action: it shall not take place in consequence merely of the mutual consent of married parties.

See English law, p. 292.

308.

The wife against whom separation of persons shall be pronounced for cause of adultery, shall be condemned by the same judgment, and, on the requisition of the public minister, to confinement in a house of correction during a fixed period, which shall not be less than three months nor exceed two years.

See parallel English law, p. 292.

309.

The husband shall continue empowered to arrest the effect of this sentence, by consenting to receive his wife again.

See parallel English law, p. 292.

310.

When the separation of persons, pronounced for any other cause than that of adultery in the wife, shall have continued three years, the married party who was originally defendant may demand divorce of the court, which shall allow it, unless the original plaintiff, present or duly summoned, consents immediately that such separation shall cease.

No English parallel.

311.

The separation of person shall carry with it in every case a separation of property.

See parallel English law, p. 292.

TITLE VII.

Of Paternity and Filiation.

DECREED 25TH MARCH, 1803. PROMULGATED THE 2ND OF APRIL.

CHAPTER I.

Of the Filiation of Legitimate Children, or those Born in Marriage.

312.

An infant conceived during marriage has the husband for its father.* Nevertheless, the latter may disavow such child, if he prove that, during the time which has elapsed from the three hundreth to the one hundred and eightieth day previous to the birth of such infant, he was either, by reason of absence, or by the effect of some accident, under a physical incapability of cohabiting with his wife.†

* See similar principle in the English law, p. 293.

† See similar principle in the English law, p. 293, 4.

313.

The husband shall not disavow an infant, on allegation of his natural impotence;* he shall not disavow it even for cause of adultery, unless the birth has been concealed from him, in which case he shall be permitted to bring forward all the facts proper to show that he is not the father.†

* See contrary principle in the English law, p. 294.

† See p. 294, and n. 1.

314.

A child born within one hundred and eighty days from the marriage, shall not be disavowed by the husband in the following cases:

1st. If he had knowledge of the pregnancy before the marriage.

2d. If he assisted at the act of birth, and if this act is signed by him, or contains his declaration that he does not know how to sign.

3d. If the child is declared not capable of living.

See parallel English law, p. 294, 5.

315.

The legitimacy of an infant born three hundred days after dissolution of marriage, may be contested.

See parallel English law, p. 295.

316.

In the different cases where the husband is authorized to disclam, he must do so within a month, if he be on the spot where the infant is born;

Within two months after his return, if he be absent at such time;

Within two months after discovery of the fraud, if the birth of the child have been concealed from him.

See English law on these points, p. 295.

317.

If the husband die before having made his disclaimer, but yet being within the interval allowed for making it, the heirs shall have two months to contest the legitimacy of the child, to be reckoned from the period at which such child would be put in possession of the property of the husband, or from the period at which the heirs shall be disturbed by the child in the possession.

See preceding note, and note to art. 319.

318.

Every extrajudicial act, containing a disavowal on the part of the husband or of his heirs, shall be as though not made, unless followed within the interval of one month, by an action at law, brought against a tutor ad hoc, appointed for the child, the mother being present.

See preceding note, and note to art. 319 and 321.

CHAPTER II.

Of the Proofs of the Filiation of Legitimate Children.

319.

The filiation of legitimate children is proved by the registry of birth inscribed upon the registers of the civil state.

See English law on this subject, p. 295, 6.

321.

The possession of this condition is established by a satisfactory combination of facts, which show the relationship of filiation and parentage between an individual and the family to which he claims to belong. The principal of these facts are: that the individual has always borne the name of the father to whom he claims to belong; that the father has treated him as his child, and in that character has provided for his education, his maintenance, and his establishment; that he has been uniformly received as such in society; that he has been acknowledged as such by the family.

See English law on this subject, p. 296.

322.

No one may claim a condition contrary to that conferred on him by his register of birth, and a possession conformable to such register;

And reciprocally, no one can contest the condition of him who has a possession conformable to his register of birth.

See parallel but contrary principle of English law, p. 296.

323.

In default of register and constant enjoyment, or if the child have been registered, either under false names, or as born of father and mother unknown, the proof of filiation may be made by witnesses.

This proof, however, cannot be admitted, except when there is a commencement of proof in writing, or when the presumptions and probable evidence resulting from facts unquestionable from the first, are sufficiently weighty to decide their admission.

See parallel English law, p. 296.

324.

The commencement of proof in writing is gathered from the documents of the family, from registers, and private papers of the father or the mother, from public acts, and likewise private ones emanating from one party engaged in the dispute, or who would have had interest therein if living.

See English law as to such proofs, p. 297.

325.

Contrary proof may be made by all means proper, to establish that the claimant is not the child of the mother he pretends to have; or even, the maternity being proved, that he is not the child of the husband of such mother.

See parallel English law, p. 297.

326.

The civil courts alone shall be competent to adjudicate on claims of condition.

See parallel English law, p. 297.

327.

A criminal action for an offence in concealing a condition, cannot be commenced until after final judgment on the question of condition.

See parallel English law, p. 297.

328.

The action in claim of condition is imprescriptible, with regard to the child.

See parallel English law, p. 297.

329.

An action cannot be brought by the heirs of a child who has not claimed, except he has died a minor, or within five years after his majority.

See parallel English law, p. 297.

330.

The heirs may pursue this action where it has been commenced by the child, unless he had formally discontinued it, or had let three years pass without any step taken, reckoning from the last act of procedure.

See parallel English law, p. 297.

CHAPTER V.

Of Natural Children.

Section 1.

Of the Legitimation of Natural Children.

331.

Children born out of wedlock, other than such as are the fruit of an incestuous or adulterous intercourse, may be legitimated by the subsequent marriage of their father and mother, when the latter shall have legally acknowledged them before their marriage, or shall have recognised them in the act itself of celebration.

See English law on this subject, p. 298.

332.

The legitimation may take place, in favour even of deceased children who have left descendants; and in such case, the benefit thereof accrues to such descendants.

See note to article 331.

333.

Children legitimated by subsequent marriage shall enjoy the same rights as if they were born of that marriage.

See note to article 331.

Section 2.

Of the Acknowledgment of Natural Children.

334.

The acknowledgment of a natural child shall be made by an authentic act, whenever it shall not have been done in its register of birth.

See note to article 331, and p. 298.

335.

This acknowledgment shall not take place for the benefit of children born of an incestuous or adulterous intercourse.

See note to article 334.

336.

The acknowledgment of the father, without the indication and avowal of the mother, has no effect, except as regards the father.

See note to article 334.

337.

An acknowledgment made during marriage, by one of the parties, to the advantage of a natural child, which such party shall have had before marriage by another person, shall not prejudice the other married party, nor the children born of such marriage. Nevertheless, its effect shall be produced after the dissolution of the marriage, where no children of it remain.

See note to article 334.

338.

A natural child acknowledged cannot claim the rights of a legitimate child. The rights of natural children shall be settled in the title "*Of Succesions.*"

See note to article 334.

339.

Every acknowledgment on the part of father or mother, as well as every claim on the part of the child, may be contested by all those who have any interest therein.

See note to article 334.

340.

Scrutiny as to paternity is forbidden. In the case of rape, when the period of such rape shall refer to that of conception, the ravisher may be declared, on the petition of the parties interested, the father of the child.

See note to article 334.

341.

Scrutiny as to maternity is admissible. The child who shall claim his mother, shall be bound to prove that he is identically the same child of whom she was delivered. He shall not be permitted to make this proof by witnesses, until he shall have already made a commencement of proof in writing.

See note to article 334.

342.

A child shall in no case be admitted to search whether for paternity or maternity, in cases where, according to article 335, acknowledgment would not have been admitted.

See note to article 334.

TITLE VIII.

Of Adoption and Friendly Guardianship.

DECREED 23RD MARCH, 1803. PROMULGATED 2ND OF APRIL.

CHAPTER I.

Of Adoption.

SECTION 1.

Of Adoption and its Effects.

343.

Adoption is permitted only to persons of either sex, above the age of fifty years, and who, at the period of adoption, shall have neither children nor legitimate descendants, and who shall be at the least fifteen years older than the individuals whom they propose to adopt.

See as to the English law on adoption, p. 299.

344.

No one can be adopted by more than one person, except by husband and wife.

Except in the case in article 366, no married person can adopt without the consent of the other conjunct.

See p. 299.

345.

The power of adoption shall only be exercised towards an individual, for whom, during minority, and for a period of at least six years, the party shall have furnished necessaries, and bestowed uninterrupted care, or towards one who shall have saved the life of the party adopting, either in a fight, or in rescuing him from fire or water.

It shall suffice, in this latter case, that the adopter have attained majority, be older than the adopted, without children, or lawful descendants; and if married, that his conjunct consent to the adoption.

See p. 299.

346.

Adoption shall not, in any case, take place before the majority of the adopted party. If the adopted, having father and mother, or one of them, has not completed his twenty-fifth year, he shall be bound to produce the consent of his father and mother, or the survivor, to his adoption; and if he is more than twenty-five years of age, to require their counsel.

See p. 299.

347.

The adoption shall confer the name of the adopter on the adopted, in addition to the proper name of the latter.

See p. 299.

348.

The adopted shall continue in his own family, and shall there retain all his rights: nevertheless, marriage is prohibited—

Between the adopter, the adopted, and his descendants;

Between adopted children of the same individual;

Between the adopted and the children who may be born to the adopter;

Between the adopted and the conjunct of the adopter, and reciprocally between the adopter and the conjunct of the adopted.

See p. 299.

349.

The natural obligation, which shall continue to exist between the adopted and his father and mother, to supply them with sustenance in cases determined by the law, shall be considered as common to the adopter and the adopted towards each other.

See p. 299.

350.

The adopted shall acquire no right of succession to the property of the relations of the adopter; but he shall enjoy the same rights with regard to succession to the adopter as are possessed by a child born in wedlock, even though there should be other children of the latter description, born subsequently to the adoption.

See p. 299.

351.

If the adopted child die without lawful descendants, things given by the adopter, or derived by inheritance from him, and which shall actually exist at the decease of the adopted, shall return to the adopter or to his descendants, on condition of contributing to debts, without prejudice to the rights of third persons.

The surplus of the property of the adopted shall belong to his own relations; and these shall always exclude, for the same objects specified in the present article, all the heirs of the adopter other than his descendants.

See p. 299.

352.

If during the life of the adopter, and after the decease of the adopted, children, or descendants left by the latter, shall themselves die without issue, the adopter shall succeed to donations made by him, as is directed in the preceding article; but this right shall be inherent in the person of the adopter, and not transmissible to his heirs, even in the descending line.

See p. 299.

Section 2.

Of the Forms of Adoption.

353.

The party who shall propose to adopt, with the one who shall be willing to be adopted, shall present themselves before the justice of the peace at the domicile of the adopter, there to pass an act of their respective consents.

See p. 299.

354.

A copy of this act shall be transmitted, within ten days following, by the more diligent party, to the king's solicitor in the court of first instance, within whose jurisdiction the domicile of the adopter shall be found, in order to be submitted to the approbation of that court.

See p. 299.

355.

The court, being assembled in the chamber of council, and having received suitable testimonials, shall examine, 1st, whether all the conditions of the law are complied with; 2nd, whether the party who proposes to adopt enjoys a good reputation.

See p. 299.

356.

After having heard the king's solicitor, and without any other form of proceeding, the court shall pronounce without giving its reasons, in these terms: "*there is place*" (il y a lieu), or, "*there is no place for adoption.*"

See p. 299.

357.

In the month succeeding the judgment of the court of first instance, this judgment shall, on the prosecution of the more diligent party, be submitted to the royal court, which shall deal with it in the same forms as the court of first instance, and shall pronounce without assigning reasons: "*the judgment is confirmed,*" or, "*the judgment is reversed; in consequence there is place,*" or, "*there is no place for adoption.*"

See p. 299.

358.

Every judgment of the royal courts which shall establish an adoption, shall be pronounced at the hearing, and posted in such places and in such a number of copies as the court shall judge expedient.

See p. 229.

359.

Within three months after this judgment, the adoption shall be enrolled, on the requisition of one or other of the parties, on the register of the civil state of the place where the adopter shall be domiciled.

This enrolment shall not take place but upon view of a copy, in form, of the judgment of the royal court; and the adoption shall remain without effect unless it be enrolled within this interval.

See p. 299.

360.

If the adopter happen to die after the act setting forth his inclination to form a contract of adoption has been received by the justice of the peace and carried before the courts, and before these have finally pronounced, the procedure shall be continued, and the adoption admitted if there be place. The heirs of the adopter may, if they believe the adoption inadmissible, remit to the king's solicitor all memorials and observations on this subject.

See p. 299.

CHAPTER II.

Of Officious or Friendly Guardianship.

361.

Every individual aged above fifty years, and without children or legitimate descendants, who shall be willing during the minority of an individual, to attach him to himself by a legal title, may become his friendly guardian, on obtaining the consent of the father and mother of the child, or of the survivor of them, or in their default, of a family council, or finally, if the child have no known relatives, on obtaining the consent of the directors of the hospital into which he shall have been received, or of the municipality of the place of his residence.

See p. 299.

362.

A married person cannot become a friendly guardian without the consent of the other conjunct.

See p. 299.

363.

The justice of the peace at the domicile of the child shall draw up a statement of the petitions and consent relative to the friendly guardianship.

See p. 299.

364.

This guardianship shall not have place except for the benefit of children under fifteen years of age.

It shall carry with it, without prejudice to any private stipulations, the obligation of supporting the ward, of bringing him up, and of putting him in a situation to gain his livelihood.

See p. 299.

365.

If the ward possess any property, and has been formerly under guardianship, the administration of his property as well as that of his person shall pass to the friendly guardian, who nevertheless shall not be permitted to throw the expenses of education on the funds of the ward.

See p. 299.

366.

If the friendly guardian, after the lapse of five years since his guardianship, and in the prospect of his decease before the majority of his pupil, confers on him adoption by testamentary act, such disposition shall be valid, provided the friendly guardian does not leave legitimate children.

See p. 299.

367.

In the case where a friendly guardian dies, either before the five years or after that time, without having adopted his ward, the latter shall be supplied with the means of subsistence, of which the quantum and the kind, unless provided for by some anterior formal agreement, shall be regulated either amicably between the respective representatives of the guardian and his ward, or judicially in case of dispute.

See p. 299.

368.

If, at the majority of the ward, his friendly guardian be willing to adopt him, and the former consent thereto, proceedings shall be taken for the adoption according to the forms prescribed in the preceding chapter, and the effects thereof shall be, in all points, the same.

See p. 299.

369.

If, within three months following the majority of the ward, the requests made by him to his friendly guardian on the subject of adoption, remain ineffectual, and the ward shall not find himself in a condition to gain his livelihood, the friendly guardian may be sentenced to indemnify his ward for the incapacity in which the latter finds himself of providing for his own subsistence.

This indemnification shall resolve itself into assistance adequate to procure him a trade; the whole without prejudice to stipulations which may have been made in prospect of this case.†

* See p. 299.

† See p. 299.

370.

The friendly guardian who shall have had the management of any of his ward's property, shall be bound in every case to render an account thereof.

See p. 299.

TITLE IX.

Of Paternal Power.

DECREED 25TH OF MARCH, 1803.—PROMULGATED 3RD OF APRIL.

371.

A child, at every age, owes honour and respect to his father and mother.

See parallel English law, p. 300.

372.

He remains subject to their control until his majority or emancipation.

See parallel English law, p. 300.

273.

The father alone exercises this control during marriage.

See parallel English law, p. 300.

374.

A child cannot quit his father's house without the permission of his father, unless for voluntary enlistment, after the full age of eighteen years.

See parallel English law, p. 300.

375.

A father who shall have heavy causes of dissatisfaction at the conduct of a child, shall have the following means of correction.

See the English law on this point, p. 300.

376.

If the child have not commenced his sixteenth year, the father may cause him to be confined for a period which shall not exceed one month; and to this effect the president of the court of the circle shall be bound, on his request, to deliver an order of arrest.

See as in note to 375.

377.

From the age of sixteen years commenced to the majority or emancipation, the father is only empowered to require the confinement of his child during six months at the most; he shall apply to the president of the aforesaid court, who, after having conferred thereon with the king's attorney, shall deliver an order of arrest or refuse the same, and may in the first case abridge the time of confinement required by the father.

See as in note to 375.

378.

There shall not be in either case, any writing or judicial formality, except the order itself for arrest, in which the reasons thereof shall not be set forth.

The father shall only be required to subscribe an undertaking to defray all expenses and to supply suitable support.

See as in note to 375.

379.

The father is always at liberty to abridge the duration of the confinement by him ordered or required. If the child after his liberation fall into new irregularities, his confinement may be ordered anew, according to the manner prescribed in the preceding articles.

See as in note to 375.

380.

If the father be remarried, he shall be bound to conform to article 377, in order to procure the confinement of his child by the first bed, though under the age of sixteen years.

See as in note to 375.

381.

The mother surviving and not married again is not empowered to cause the confinement of a child, except with the concurrence of the two nearest paternal relations, and by means of requisition, conformably to article 377.

See English law as to maternal authority, p. 301.

382.

When the child shall possess personal property, or when he shall exercise a state, his confinement shall not take place, even under the age of sixteen years, except by way of requisition in the form prescribed by art. 377.

The child confined may address a memorial to the attorney-general in the royal court, who shall cause an account to be rendered by the king's attorney in the court of first instance, and shall make his report to the president of the Royal court, who, after having given intimation thereof to the father, and after having collected the proofs, may revoke or modify the order delivered by the president of the court of first instance.

See as in note to art. 375.

383.

Articles 376, 377, 378, and 379, shall be common to fathers and mothers of natural children, legally recognised.

See as in note to art. 375; and p. 298, 301.

384.

The father during marriage, and, after the dissolution of marriage, the father or mother surviving, shall have the enjoyment of the property of their children, until the full age of eighteen years, or until such emancipation, as may take place before the age of eighteen years.

See parallel, but contrary English law, p. 301.

385.

The conditions of such enjoyment shall be—

1st. Those by which usufructuaries are bound.

2nd. Nourishment, maintenance, and education of children, according to their fortune.

3rd. The payment of arrears or interest on capital.

4th. Funeral expenses, and those of the last sickness.

See as in last note.

386.

This enjoyment shall not take place for the benefit of a father or mother against whom a divorce shall have been pronounced; and it shall cease with regard to the mother in the case of a second marriage.

See as in note to art. 385.

387.

It shall not extend to property which children may have acquired by separate labour and industry,* nor to such as shall be given or bequeathed to them under the express condition that their father and mother shall not enjoy it.†

* See English law on this point, p. 302.

† See English law as to this point, p. 301.

TITLE X.

Of Minority, Guardianship, and Emancipation.

DECREED 26TH OF MARCH, 1803.—PROMULGATED THE 5TH OF APRIL.

CHAPTER I.

Of Minority.

388.

A minor is an individual of either sex who has not yet attained the age of twenty-one years.

See parallel English rule of law, p. 302.

CHAPTER II.

Of Guardianship.

SECTION 1.

Of the Guardianship of Father and Mother.

389.

The father is, during marriage, administrator of the personal effects of his children being minors.*

He is accountable,† as regards the property and income of effects as he has not the enjoyment of: and as regards the property only, of such whereof the law gives him the usufruct.

* See parallel English law, p. 304.

† See parallel English law, p. 304.

390.

After the dissolution of marriage from the natural or civil death of one of the parties, the guardianship of children being minors, and not emancipated, belongs absolutely to the survivor of the father and mother.

See the English law as to the mother, p. 304.

391.

The father may, nevertheless, nominate to the mother surviving and being guardian, a special council, without whose advice she shall not have power to do any act relative to the guardianship. If the father specify the acts for which the council shall be nominated, the guardian shall be competent to do other acts without its assistance.

As to the father's power according to the law of England, when the mother survives, see p. 304, 5.

392.

This nomination of council can only be made in one of the modes following:

1st. By act of last will.

2nd. By a declaration made either before the justice of peace, assisted by his registrar, or before notaries.

See par. power of English law, p. 395; and note to art. 397.

393.

If at the time of the husband's decease, his wife is with child, a curator for the unborn child shall be named by a family council.

At the birth of the child the mother shall become its guardian, and the curator shall be its deputy guardian in full right.

As to the father's power, and the necessity by the English law of appointing a guardian in such case, see p. 305.

394.

The mother is not bound to accept the guardianship;* nevertheless, and in case she refuses it, she must discharge its duties, until she have caused a guardian to be appointed.

* See similar English law, p. 305, 6.

395.

If a mother being guardian desires to marry again, she is required before the act of marriage to convoke a family council, who shall decide whether the guardianship ought to be continued to her.

In defect of such convocation she shall lose the guardianship entirely; and her new husband shall be jointly and severally responsible for all the consequences of the guardianship which she shall have unduly continued.

See, as to the mother's second marriage, p. 306; the family council is unknown, see post sect. 4.

396.

When the family council, being duly convoked, shall continue the guardianship to the mother, it shall of necessity assign to her, as a conjoint guardian, her second husband, who shall with his wife become jointly and severally responsible for the administration subsequent to the marriage.

See as to the second husband, p. 306.

Section 2.

Of the Guardianship appointed by the Father or Mother.

397.

The individual right of choosing as guardian a relation or even a stranger, belongs only to the father or mother who shall last die.

See the English law on this point, p. 306.

398.

This right cannot be exercised except in the forms prescribed by article 392, and subject to the modifications and exceptions hereinafter mentioned.

See the English mode exercising this power, p. 306.

399.

The mother re-married, and not continued in the guardianship of the children of her first marriage, cannot choose them a guardian.

See as in note to art. 397.

400.

When the mother re-married, and continued in the guardianship, shall have made choice of a guardian for the children of her former marriage, such choice shall only be valid as far as it shall be confirmed by the family council.

Same as last article.

401.

The guardian elected by the father or the mother is not bound to accept the guardianship, if he be not in other respects within the class of persons, whom in default of such special election, the family council might have charged with it.

See similar English law, p. 306.

Section 3.

Of the Guardianship of Ancestors.

402.

Where a guardian has not been chosen for a minor by his father or mother who died last, the guardianship belongs of right to his paternal grandfather; and in default of such to his maternal grandfather, and so ascending, in such manner as that the paternal ancestor shall, in all cases, be preferred to the maternal ancestor in the same degree.

See the English law on these points, p. 306, 7.

403.

Where, in default of the paternal and the maternal grandfather of the minor, an equal claim shall appear to be established between two ancestors of a higher degree, who shall both belong to the paternal line of the minor, the guardianship shall pass of right to such of the two as shall be found to be paternal grandfather of the father of the minor.

See the English law on this point, p. 306, 7.

404.

If the same competition take place between two great-grandfathers of the maternal line, the nomination shall be made by the family council, who shall, nevertheless, only have power to choose one of such two ancestors.

See the English law on this point, p. 306, 7.

SECTION 4.

Of Guardianship appointed by the Family Council.

405.

When * a child a minor and not emancipated shall be without father or mother, or guardian elected by his father or mother, or without male ancestors, as also when the guardian of one of the descriptions above mentioned shall find himself either within the case of the exclusions hereinafter described, or validly excused, the nomination of a guardian shall be provided for by a family council.†

* As to the appointment, under the English law, of a guardian where no relative is entitled to have the wardship, see p. 307.

† The power of a family council is a thing unknown to the English law: the Court of Chancery supplies its place, see p. 307.

406.

This council shall be convoked either on the requisition and care of the relations of the minor, of his creditors, or of other parties interested, or even officially, and on the intervention of the justice of the peace at the domicile of the minor. Any person may declare before this justice of the peace, the fact which shall give occasion to the nomination of a guardian.

See note† to art. 405.

407.

The family council shall be composed, exclusive of the justice of the peace, of six relations or connexions, taken as well from the commune where the guardianship shall be opened, as within the distance of two myriameters, half on the father's side, and half on the mother's side, and according to the order of proximity in each line.

The relation shall be preferred to the connexion in the same degree; and amongst relations of the same degree, the elder to the younger.

See note† to art. 405.

408.

The brothers-german of the minor, and the husbands of sisters-german, are alone excepted from the limitation of the number laid down in the preceding article.

If they are six, or above, they shall all be members of the family council, which they shall compose alone, with the widows of ancestors, and ancestors validly excused, if there be any.

If they are in number too few, the other relations shall be summoned only for the purpose of completing the council.

See note† to art. 405.

409.

When the relations or connexions of either line shall find themselves insufficient in number on the spot, or within the distance pointed out by article 407, the justice of the peace shall summon either relations or connexions residing at greater distances, or citizens within the same commune, known as having had habitual friendly intercourse with the father or the mother of the minor.

See note† to art. 405.

410.

The justice of the peace is at liberty, even when there shall be on the spot a sufficient number of relations or connexions, to give permission to summon, at whatever distance they may be domiciliated, relations or connexions nearer in degree, or of the same degree as the relations and connexions present; in such manner, however, that it shall operate to withdraw some of the last, and without exceeding the number directed in the preceding articles

See note† to art. 405.

411.

The interval for appearance shall be regulated by the justice of the peace on a day fixed, but in such manner, that there shall always be an interval of three days at the least between the notification of the summons, and the day appointed for the assembling of the council, although all the parties summoned shall reside within the commune, or within the distance of two myriameters.

As often as any among the parties summoned shall be found to reside beyond that distance, the interval shall be augmented by one day for every three myriameters.

See note† to art. 405.

412.

The relations, connexions, or friends thus convened, shall be bound to appear in person, or cause themselves to be represented by especial proxy.

The proxy can only represent one person.

See note† to art. 405.

413.

Every relation, connexion, or friend convoked, and who without lawful excuse shall fail to appear, shall incur a fine not exceeding fifty francs, and which shall be awarded without appeal by the justice of the peace.

See note† to art. 405.

414.

If there be sufficient excuse, and it shall appear convenient either to wait for the absent member, or to supply his place; in such case, as in every other where the interest of the minor shall appear to require it, it shall be lawful for the justice of the peace to adjourn the assembly, or to postpone it.

See note† to art. 405.

415.

This assembly shall be held as of right at the house of the justice of the peace, unless he himself shall point out another place of meeting.

The presence of three-fourths at least of the members convoked shall be necessary in order to their deliberations.

See note † to art. 405.

416.

The justice of the peace shall preside over the family council, and shall have therein a deliberative voice, and the casting vote in case of division.

See note † to art. 405.

417.

When a minor, residing in France, shall possess property in the colonies, or *vice versâ*, special administration of his property shall be given to a supplementary guardian.*

In this case the guardian and supplementary guardian shall be independent, and not responsible to each other in regard to the discharge of their respective functions.†

* See parallel English law, p. 308.

† See parallel English law, p. 308.

418.

The guardian shall act and administer, in this capacity, from the day of his nomination, if it took place in his presence; if otherwise, from the day on which it was notified to him.

See parallel English law, p. 308.

419.

Guardianship is a personal charge, which does not pass to the heirs of the guardian.* They shall only be responsible for the conduct of their ancestor;† and if they are of age, they shall be bound to continue it until the nomination of a new guardian.

* See parallel English law, p. 308.

† See parallel English law, p. 308.

Section 5.

Of the Supplementary Guardian.

420.

In every guardianship there shall

be a supplementary guardian, nominated by the family council. His functions shall consist in acting for the interests of the minor, when they shall be in opposition to those of the guardian.

As to the mode of defending the interests of the infant, where they are in conflict with the guardians, see p. 309.

421.

When the functions of guardian shall devolve upon a person described under section 1, 2, or 3, of the present chapter, such guardian is bound, before entering upon his functions, to convoke a family council, composed as is pointed out in section 4, for the purpose of nominating a supplementary guardian.

If he intermeddle with the management before he has complied with this formality, the family council convened either on the requisition of the relations, creditors, or other parties interested, or officially by the justice of the peace, may, if there be fraud on the part of the guardian, withdraw him from the guardianship without prejudice to the indemnities due to the minor.

See note to art. 420.

422.

In other guardianships, the nomination of supplementary guardian shall have place immediately after that of guardian.

See note to art. 420.

423.

In no case shall the guardian vote for the nomination of supplementary guardian, who shall be selected, except in the case of brothers-german, in that of the two lines to which the guardian shall not belong.

See note to art. 420.

424.

The supplementary guardian shall not supply entirely the place of the guardian, when the guardianship shall become vacant, or when it shall be abandoned by absence; but he shall be bound in such case, under pain of damages which may accrue therefrom to the minor, to urge the nomination of a new guardian.

See note to art. 420.

425.

The functions of supplementary guardian shall cease at the same period as the guardianship.

See note to art. 420.

426.

The regulations contained in sections 6 and 7 of the present chapter, shall apply to supplementary guardians.

Nevertheless the guardian shall not be at liberty to urge the deprivation of the supplementary guardian, nor to vote in family councils, which shall be convened for that object.

See note to art. 420.

Section 6.

Of the Causes which excuse from Guardianship.

427.

Persons excused from guardianship are—

Those mentioned in titles 3, 5, 6, 7, 8, 9, 10, and 11 of the act of the 18th May, 1804;

The presidents and counsellors of the court of cassation, the solicitor-general and advocates-general of the same court;

The prefects;

All citizens, exercising a public function in a department different from that in which the guardianship is established.

This office not being compulsory (see p. 309), the regulations of the section have no parallel in the English law.

428.

Military men in active service, and all other citizens who are in the discharge of a commission of the king beyond the territory of the kingdom, are equally exempted from guardianship.

See note to art. 427.

429.

If the commission be unauthenticated and contested, the exemption shall not be pronounced until after production by the party excusing himself of the certificate of the minister for the department within which the commission alleged as excuse shall lie.

See note to art. 427.

430.

Citizens of the description contained in the preceding articles, who have accepted guardianship subsequently to the functions, services, and commissions, which exempt from it, shall not be permitted for such cause to procure their discharge from it.

See note to art. 427, and p. 310, as to those who have once acted in the office.

431.

Those, on the contrary, on whom the functions, services, and commissions shall have been imposed, subsequently to the acceptance and exercise of guardianship, may, if unwilling to continue it, cause a family council to be convoked within one month, and take measures therein for supplying their place.

If, at the expiration of these functions, services, and commissions, the new guardian claim his discharge, or the ancient one demand his guardianship again, it may be restored to the latter by a family council.

See note to art. 427 and 430.

432.

No citizen, not being a relation or connexion, can be compelled to accept guardianship, except in the case where there shall not be, within the distance of four myriameters, relations or connexions in condition to undertake the guardianship.

See note to art. 427.

433.

Every individual who has completed his sixty-fifth year may refuse to become a guardian. He who previously to this age shall have been nominated such, may at seventy years cause himself to be discharged from the guardianship.

See note to art. 427 and 430.

434.

Every individual attacked with a grievous sickness, being duly proved, is exempted from guardianship. He may moreover cause himself to be discharged therefrom, if this infirmity has come upon him since his nomination.

See note to art. 427 and 430.

435.

Two guardianships are, in the case of all persons, a sufficient excuse for not accepting a third.

The husband or father who shall be already charged with one guardianship, shall not be bound to accept a second, other than that of his children.

See note to art. 427.

436.

They who have five lawful children are exempted from every guardianship other than that of such children. Children who have died in active service in the armies of the republic shall be always reckoned as operating such exemption.

Other children being dead shall not be reckoned except so far as they shall themselves have left children in actual existence.

See note to art. 427.

437.

The event of children born during guardianship shall not authorize its resignation.

See note to art. 427 and 430.

438.

If the guardian nominated be present at the deliberation which imposes on him the guardianship, he ought at once, and on pain of being excluded from all ulterior objection, to state his excuses, on which the family council shall deliberate.

See note to art. 405 † and 427.

439.

If the guardian nominated has not assisted at the deliberation which imposed upon him the guardianship, he may cause a family council to be convoked in order to deliberate on his excuses.

His proceedings on this subject shall take place within an interval of three days, commencing with the intimation which shall have been given him of his nomination; this interval shall be augmented by one day for three myriameters of distance from the place of his domicile to that of the opening of the guardianship: this interval past, he shall not be heard.

See note to art. 438.

440.

If his excuses are rejected he may make application to the courts to have them admitted; but he shall be bound, during the litigation, to act as guardian provisionally.

See note to art. 427.

441.

If he succeed in causing himself to be exempted from the guardianship, they who shall have rejected his excuses shall be condemned in costs of suit.

If he fail, he shall himself be condemned therein.

See note to art. 429.

Section 7.

Of Incapacity, Exclusion, and Deprivation of Guardianship.

442.

Persons incapable of being guardians or members of family councils are, 1st, Minors, except the father or mother; 2nd, Interdicted persons; 3rd, Women, except the mother and female ancestors; 4th, All those who have, or whose father or mother has, a suit with the minor, in which the state of such minor, his fortune, or a considerable portion of his property, is brought in question.

See the parallel English law, p. 310.

443.

Condemnation to an afflictive or infamous punishment imports absolutely an exclusion from guardianship. It imports in like manner deprivation, in a case where the question is respecting a guardianship previously conferred.

See parallel English law, p. 310.

444.

Excluded also from guardianship, and deprivable if already in the exercise of it, are—

1st. Persons guilty of notorious misconduct.

2nd. Those whose management thereof betrays incapacity or want of fidelity.

See the parallel English law, p. 310.

445.

No individual who shall have been excluded or deprived of a guardianship, can be a member of a family council.

No parallel English law. See note to art. 427.

446.

As often as there shall be ground for the deprivation of a guardian, it shall be pronounced by a family council, convoked at the instance of the supplementary guardian, or officially by the justice of the peace.

Such guardian shall not be at liberty to neglect calling such convocation, when formally required thereto by one or more relations or connexions of the minor, of the degree of cousin-german or of still nearer degrees.

As to the removal of a guardian by judicial authority under the law of England, see p. 310, 11.

447.

Every resolution by a family council which shall pronounce the expulsion or deprivation of a guardian, shall recite its motives, and shall not be made until the guardian shall have been heard or summoned.

No parallel English law.

448.

If the guardian concur in the resolution, mention shall be thereof made, and the new guardian shall enter immediately upon his functions.

If he object, the supplementary guardian shall sue for a confirmation of the resolution before the court of first instance, which shall decree, saving the right of appeal.

The guardian excluded or deprived may himself, in such case, summon the supplementary guardian in order to procure himself to be confirmed in his guardianship.

No parallel English law.

449.

The relations or connexions who shall have required the convocation, may become parties in the cause, which shall be carried on and judged as an urgent affair.

No parallel English law.

Section 8.

Of the Guardian's Administration.

450.

The guardian shall have the care of the person of the minor, and shall represent him in all civil acts.*

He shall deal with his property like a good father of a family, and shall answer in damages for the consequences of his mismanagement.†

He must not buy the property of the minor, nor take it on lease, unless the family council have authorized the supplementary guardian to let it him to hire, nor accept an assignment of any claim or credit against his ward.

*See similar English law, p. 311, 12, 13.

†See similar English law, p. 311, 12, 13.

See parallel English law, p. 313.

451.

Within ten days following that of his nomination, duly notified to him, the guardian shall require the removal of seals, if any have been affixed, and shall proceed immediately to make an inventory of the goods of the minor, in presence of the supplementary guardian.

If anything be due to him from the minor, he must declare in his inventory, on pain of forfeiture, and this on the requisition which the public officer shall be bound to make thereon to him, and whereof mention shall be made in the statement.

See parallel English law, p. 313, 14.

452.

Within the month following the close of the inventory, the guardian shall cause to be sold at an auction, held by a public officer in presence of the supplementary guardian, and after notices or publications, of which mention shall be made in the statement of sale, all the moveable goods other than those which the family council shall have authorized him to preserve in kind.

See parallel English law, p. 314.

453.

The father and mother, as long as they have the personal and legal enjoyment of the property of the minor, are excused from selling the moveable goods, if they prefer preserving them in order to their restoration in kind.*

In this case they shall cause an estimate to be made, at their own expense, of their just value, by an experienced person named by the supplementary guardian, and who shall be sworn before the justice of the peace.†

They shall render the estimated value of such of the moveable goods as they are unable to produce in kind.‡

* As to occupying ward's property, see English law, p. 313.

† No exact parallel English enactments.

‡ See English law on this subject, p. 314.

454.

At the period of entering upon the exercise of every guardianship, other than that of the father and mother, the family council shall regulate by observation, and according to the importance of the property administered, the amount of the minor's annual expense, as well as that of the administration of his property.

The same act shall specify whether the guardian is authorized to procure the assistance in his management of one or more private administrators, paid by salaries and acting under his responsibility.

As to the annual expenses, see p. 313, 14.

455.

The council shall determine positively the sum at which the tutor's obligation shall commence, of employing the surplus of the revenues above the expenditure; this employment must be made within the interval of six months, which after the guardian shall become debtor for interest in default of employing it.

As to investing surplus at interest, according to the English law, see p. 312, 13, 14.

456.

If the guardian have not caused the sum at which the employment shall commence to be determined by a family council, he shall, after the interval expressed in the preceding article, become debtor for the interest of the whole sum unemployed, however small it may be.

See English law as to investing surplus, p. 314.

457.

The guardian, even though father or mother, may not borrow for the minor, nor alienate, nor mortgage his immoveable property, without being authorized thereto by a family council.*

This authority ought not be accorded except in case of an absolute necessity, or an evident advantage.†

In the first case, the family council shall not grant its authority until it shall have been proved, by a succinct account presented by the guardian, that the money, personal effects, and revenues of the minor, are insufficient.‡

The family council shall point out, in all cases, the immoveable property which ought to be sold by preference, and all the conditions which it shall deem useful.§

*See parallel English law, p. 314, 15.
† See parallel English law, p. 315.
‡ See note to art. 405; and see p. 313, 14.
§ See note to art. 405; and see p. 313, 14.

458.

The resolutions of the family council relative to this object shall not be executed until after the guardian shall have demanded and obtained confirmation thereof before the civil court of first instance, which shall decree thereon in the chamber of council, and after having heard the king's solicitor.

No parallel English law; but see as to application to the Court of Chancery, p. 313.

459.

The sale shall be made publicly, in presence of the supplementary guardian, at an auction held by a member of the court of first instance, or by a notary appointed for this purpose, and after the publication of three notices, in three consecutive weeks, in the usual place within the district.

No parallel English law.

460.

The formalities required by articles 457 and 458, in order to the alienation of the property of a minor, do not apply to the cases in which a judgment shall have directed an auction on the application of a co-proprietor indivisibly.

Provided only in such case, that the auction do not take place except in the form prescribed by the preceding article: strangers shall, of necessity, be admitted thereto.

See parallel English law, p. 314, 15.

461.

The guardian shall not be at liberty

to accept or to repudiate a succession fallen to the minor, without a previous authority from the family council. The acceptance shall only take place under benefit of inventory.

No parallel English law. See post b. 3, title 1, c. 5.

462.

In a case where a succession repudiated in the name of the minor shall not have been accepted by another, it may be resumed either by the guardian, authorized to this end by a new resolution of the family council, or by the minor himself when arrived at full age, but in the state in which it shall be found at the time of the resumption, and without power to impeach any sales and other acts which shall have legally taken place during the interval.

No parallel English law. See b. 3, tit. 1, c. 5.

463.

A donation made to a minor shall not be accepted by the guardian, except with the authority of a family council.

It shall have, with regard to the minor, the same effect as with regard to an adult.

No parallel English law. See post par. art. 932; and see as to receiving a legacy, p. 315.

464.

No guardian shall be at liberty to bring an action respecting real claims* of the minor, nor to acquiesce in a demand relative to such claims, without the authority of a family council.†

* See as to suits by infant, p. 313.

† No parallel English law.

465.

The same* authority shall be necessary to a guardian in order to claim a partition;† but it is competent to him without such authority to answer a claim for partition directed against the minor.

* See note to art. 405.

† See English law as to guardian making partition, p. 315.

466.

In order to obtain against the minor the whole effect which would follow between adults, the partition should be made judicially, and should be preceded by an estimate made by qualified persons named by the tribunal of the first instance at the place of the opening the succession.

Such qualified persons after having taken an oath well and faithfully to fulfil their office, before the president of the same court, or another judge delegated by him, shall proceed to the division of the inheritance and the formation of lots, which shall be taken by lot, and in the presence either of a member of the court, or of a notary commissioned by him, who shall deliver the lots.

Every other partition shall be considered merely as provisional.

See English law on this subject, p. 315.

467.

The guardian shall not be at liberty to compound* for the minor, until he shall be thereto authorised by the family council,† and under the advice of three jurisconsults, appointed by the king's solicitor in the court of first instance.

No composition shall be valid, except so far as it shall have been confirmed by the court of first instance, after having heard the commissioner of government.

* See parallel English law, p. 312, 15, 16.

† See note to art. 405.

468.

The guardian who shall have heavy causes of dissatisfaction respecting the conduct of the minor, may lay his complaints before a family council, and if thereto authorized by such council, may claim the confinement of the minor, conformably to what has been decreed on this subject under the title "*Of Paternal Power.*"

No exactly parallel English law. See, as to the guardian's power, p. 311, 12.

Section 9.

Of the Accounts of the Guardianship.

469.

Every guardian is accountable for his management at the close of it.

See parallel English law, p. 316.

470.

Every guardian, other than the father and mother, may be required, even during the guardianship, to submit to the supplementary guardian accounts of the state of his administration, at such periods as the family council shall deem it proper to fix upon, provided, nevertheless, that the guardian shall not be bound to furnish more than one of them each year.

These accounts of state of administration shall be drawn up and remitted free of charge on unstamped paper, and without any legal formality.

No exactly parallel English law; but see p. 316.

471.

The final account of the guardianship shall be rendered at the expense of the minor, when he shall have reached his full age, or obtained his emancipation. The guardian shall advance the expenses.

The guardian shall be allowed therein every charge satisfactorily verified, and the object of which shall be useful.

See parallel English law, p. 316.

472.

Every treaty which may be made between the guardian and the minor after coming of age shall be null, unless preceded by the rendering of a detailed account, and the production of vouchers; the whole approved by the receipt of the party taking the accounts, ten days at least before such treaty.

See Parallel English law, p. 317.

473.

If the account afford ground for disputes, they shall be prosecuted and determined like other disputes on a civil matter.

See parallel English law, p. 317.

474.

The sum to which the balance of the account due from the guardian shall amount, shall carry interest without demand, to be computed from the close of the account.

The interest on what shall be due to the guardian from the minor, shall only run from the day of the demand of payment subsequent to the close of the account.

See parallel English law, p. 317.

475.

Every action by a minor against his guardian, relative to the transactions of the guardianship, ceases by prescription after ten years, computing from the majority.

See parallel English law, p. 317.

CHAPTER III.

Of Emancipation.

476.

The minor is emancipated to all intents and purposes by marriage,

See English law as to emancipation, p. 318.

477.

The minor, even though not married, may be emancipated by his father, or, in default of father, by his mother, when he shall have attained the full age of fifteen years.

This emancipation shall be effected by the simple declaration of the father or mother, received by the justice of the peace, assisted by his registrar.

See note to art. 476.

478.

A minor left without father or mother may likewise be emancipated, if the family council judge him capable thereof, provided only he have completed his eighteenth year.

In such case, the emancipation shall result from the resolution which shall have authorized it, and from the declaration of the justice of the peace, as president of the family council, made in the same act, that the minor is emancipated.

See note to art. 476; and note to art. 405.

479.

When the guardian shall not have taken any measures for the emancipation of the minor, of which mention is made in the preceding article, and when one or more relations, or connexions of such minors of the degree of cousin-german, or of other nearer degrees, shall judge him capable of being emancipated, they may require the justice of the peace to convoke the family council in order to deliberate on this subject.

The justice of the peace is bound to yield his assent to this requisition.

See note to art. 476.

480.

The accounts of the guardianship shall be rendered to the minor emancipated, assisted by a curator, who shall be nominated for him by the family council.

See note to art. 476.

481.

A minor emancipated shall make leases, whose duration shall not exceed nine years; he shall receive his revenues and shall therefore give discharge, and shall do all acts consisting only of pure administration, without being liable to have such acts reversed in all cases in which an adult would not be so himself.

See note to art. 476.

482.

He shall not bring a real action, or be defendant therein, even to receive and give discharge for a personal capital, without the assistance of a curator, who in the last case shall superintend the employment of the capital received.

See note to art. 476.

483.

A minor emancipated is not permitted to borrow, under any pretext, without a resolution of the family council, confirmed by the court of the first instance, after having heard the king's solicitor.

See note to art. 476.

484.

He shall not be permitted to sell or alienate his immoveable property, or to do any other act than those of pure administration, without observing the forms prescribed to an unemancipated minor.

With regard to obligations contracted by him in the way of purchases or otherwise, they shall be reducible in case of excess; the courts shall on this subject take into consideration the fortune of the minor, the good or bad faith of the persons who shall have contracted with him, the utility or inutility of the expenses.

See note to art. 476.

485.

Every emancipated minor, whose engagements shall have been reduced by virtue of the preceding article, may be deprived of the benefit of emancipation, which shall be withdrawn from him in pursuing the same forms as those which shall have taken place in conferring it upon him.

See note to art. 476.

486.

The minor shall re-enter into guardianship from the day on which his emancipation shall have been revoked, and so continue until his majority shall be accomplished.

See note to art. 476.

487.

The minor emancipated who enters into trade, is reputed an adult for the acts relative to such trading.

See note to art. 476.

TITLE XI.

Of Majority, Interdiction, and the Judicial Adviser.

DECREED, 29TH MARCH, 1803. PROMULGATED 18TH OF APRIL.

CHAPTER I.

Of Majority.

488.

Majority is fixed at twenty-one years completed; at this age a person is capable of all acts regarding civil life, saving the restriction contained under the title "*Of Marriage.*"

See parallel English law, p. 318.

CHAPTER II.

Of Interdiction.

489.

An adult, who is in an habitual state of imbecility, idiotcy, or madness, must be interdicted, even though such state present some lucid intervals.

See parallel English law, p. 319.

490.

Any person is competent to claim the interdiction of a relative. It is the same of one spouse with regard to the other.

See parallel English law, p. 319.

491.

In the case of madness, if the interdiction is not claimed, either by the spouse or by the relatives, it must be claimed by the king's solicitor, who may also claim it in cases of idiotcy or insanity against an individual who is unmarried, and without known relatives.

No parallel English law.

492.

Every demand of interdiction shall be made before the court of first instance.

See parallel English law as to the court, p. 320.

493.

Acts of idiotcy, insanity, or madness shall be detailed in writing. They who prosecute the interdiction shall produce witnesses and documents.

As to the petition, &c., under the English law, see p. 320.

494.

The court shall order that the family council, formed according to the mode pointed out in section 4 of chap. 2, of the title "*Of Minority, Guardianship, and Emancipation,*" shall give its judgment on the state of the person whose interdiction is demanded.

See the English law for making this decision, p. 320, note to art. 405.

495.

They who shall have claimed the interdiction shall not form part of the family council: however, the husband or wife, and the children of the person whose interdiction shall be claimed, may be admitted thereto without having a deliberative voice therein.

See note to art. 405.

496.

After having received the judgment of the family council, the court shall interrogate the defendant in the chamber of council; if he cannot be present there, he shall be interrogated at his dwelling, by one of the judges commissioned for this purpose, assisted by his registrar. In all cases the king's solicitor shall be present at the interrogation.

As to affirming or reversing verdict to lunacy by English law, see p. 320.

497.

After the first interrogatory, the court shall, if there be ground, appoint a provisional administrator, to take care of the person and goods of the defendant.

No parallel English law.

498.

Judgment on a petition for interdiction shall only be given at a public hearing, the parties being heard or summoned.

As to verdict of English jury, see p. 320.

499.

In rejecting the petition for interdiction, the court shall be empowered nevertheless, if the circumstances require it, to order that the defendant shall not thenceforward plead, make agreement, borrow, receive a moveable capital, nor give discharge therefore, alienate, nor encumber his property by mortgages, without the assistance of a council, who shall be nominated for him by the same judgment.

As to power of Lord Chancellor in such case, see p. 320.

500.

In case of appeal from the judgment given in the first instance, the court Royal may, if it judge necessary, interrogate anew the party whose interdiction is demanded, or cause him to be interrogated by a commissioner.

As to new inquisition under the English law, see p. 320.

501.

Every judgment importing interdiction or nomination of an adviser shall, on the instance of the petitioners, be entered, signified to the party, and inscribed within ten days on the schedules, which shall be hung up in the hall of audience, and in the offices of the notaries of the circle.

No parallel English law.

502,

Interdiction or the nomination of a council shall have its effect from the day of the judgment. All acts passed subsequently by the interdicted person, or without the assistance of the adviser, shall be void in law.

See parallel English law, p. 320.

503.

Acts anterior to interdiction may be annulled, if the cause of interdiction existed notoriously at the period of making such acts.

See parallel English law, p. 320.

504.

After the death of an individual, acts done by him cannot be impeached for cause of insanity, except so far as his interdiction shall have been pronounced or claimed before his decease; unless the proof of insanity is derived from the very act impeached.

See parallel English law, p. 320.

505.

If there be no appeal from the judgment of interdiction given in the first instance, or if it is confirmed on appeal, application shall be made for the nomination of a guardian and of a supplementary guardian for the interdicted person, according to the rules prescribed under the title, "*Of Minority, Guardianship, and Emancipation.*" The provisional administrator shall suspend his duties, and render his accounts to the guardian, unless he be such himself.

As to the English committees, see p. 320, 1.

506.

The husband is of right the guardian of his wife under interdiction.

See parallel English law, p. 320, 1.

507.

The wife may be nominated guardian of her husband: in such case the family council shall regulate the form and conditions of the administration, saving the remedy which shall be allowed in the courts to the wife, who shall conceive herself injured by the resolution of the family.

See parallel English law, p. 321.

508.

No person, with the exception of the husband or wife, ancestors and descendants, shall be bound to hold the guardianship of a person interdicted beyond ten years. At the expiration of that period, the guardian may demand and shall obtain the substitution of another.

No parallel English law, this office not being compulsory.

509.

A person interdicted bears likeness

to a minor, as regards his person and his property; the laws on the guardianship of minors shall be applicable to the guardianship of persons under interdiction.

A similar principle governs this portion of the English law, see p. 319 to 321.

510.

The revenues of a person interdicted ought particularly to be employed in alleviating his misfortune and accelerating his cure. According to the symptoms of his malady, and the state of his fortune, the family council shall be empowered to pass a resolution that he shall be attended in his own house, or that he shall be placed in a house of health or even in an hospital.

See parallel English law, p. 321.

511.

When there shall be question concerning the marriage of the child of a person under interdiction, the dowry, or the advancement of the inheritance, and the other matrimonial stipulations, shall be regulated by the opinion of the family council, confirmed by the court on the conclusions of the king's solicitor.

See parallel English law, p. 321.

512.

The interdiction ceases with the causes which produced it; nevertheless the liberation shall not be pronounced without the observation of the formalities prescribed in order to obtain the interdiction, and the party under interdiction shall not re-assume the exercise of his rights until after judgment of liberation.

See parallel English law, p. 321.

CHAPTER III.

Of the Judicial Adviser.

513.

Prodigals may be forbidden to plead, to compound, to borrow, to receive any moveable capital, and to give a discharge therefore, to alienate, or to encumber their property by mortgages, without the assistance of an adviser nominated to them by the court.

See the English law on this subject, p. 321.

514.

Prohibition from proceeding without the assistance of an adviser, may be claimed by such as have a right to demand interdiction; their petition must be prosecuted and determined in the same manner.

This prohibition cannot be obtained without observing the same formalities.

See note to art. 513.

515.

No judgment, in matter of interdiction, or of nomination of adviser, shall be given either in the first instance or by way of appeal, except upon the conclusions by the public functionary.

See note to art. 513.

BOOK II.

OF PROPERTY, AND THE DIFFERENT MODIFICATIONS OF PROPERTY.

DECREED 25TH OF JANUARY, 1804.—PROMULGATED FEBRUARY 4TH.

TITLE I.

Of the Distinction of Property.

516.

All property is moveable or immoveable.

See parallel English law, p. 323.

CHAPTER I.

Of Immoveable Property.

517.

Property is immoveable, either by its nature* or by its destination, or by the objects to which it is applied.†

* See parallel English law, p. 324.

† The English law does not recognise this sort; but see, as to effect of intention of converting, p. 324.

518.

The soil of the earth and buildings are immoveable by their nature.

See similar principle recognised by the English law, p. 324, 5.

519.

Wind or watermills, fixed on pillars and forming part of a building, are also immoveable by their nature.

See similar English law, p. 325, 6.

520.

Crops hanging by the roots, and fruits not yet gathered from the trees, are in like manner immoveable.*

As soon as grain is cut and the fruits plucked, although not carried away, they become moveable.†

If one part only of the crop is cut, such part alone is moveable.‡

* See similar English law, p. 327.

† See similar English law, p. 327.

‡ See similar English law, p. 327.

521.

The cuttings of underwood of the ordinary kind or forest trees made up in regular fagots, only become moveable in proportion as the trees are felled.

See parallel English law, p. 328.

522.

The live stock which the proprietor of a farm gives up to the farmer, or metayer,* for the purposes of cultivation, whether valued or not, are regarded as immoveable as long as they continue attached to the farm in pursuance of the agreement.†

Such as may be given in cheptel to others than the farmer or metayer are moveable.

* The metayer system is unknown in England.

† See parallel, but dissimilar English law, p. 328.

523.

Pipes which serve to conduct water in a house, or other possession, are immoveable, and form part of the estate to which they are attached.

See parallel English law, p. 328.

524.

Articles which the proprietor of a farm has placed thereon, for the service and management of such a farm, are immoveable by destination.*

Thus immoveables by destination, having been placed by the proprietor for the use and management of his farm, are,—beasts required for agricultural purposes; implements of husbandry; seeds given to farmers or other cultivators;† pigeons belonging to dove-houses; rabbits in warrens; bee-hives; fish in ponds;‡ presses, coppers, stills, vats, and tubs; implements necessary for the working of forges, paper-mills, and other machinery.§

Straw and manure. || All moveable effects which a proprietor has attached to a farm to continue so for ever, are immoveable also by destination.

* See the principle of English law on this point, p. 328.

† See parallel, but dissimilar English law, p. 328.

‡ See parallel and similar English law, p. 329.

§ See parallel English law, p. 329.

|| See parallel English law, p. 329.

525.

A proprietor is considered to have attached moveable effects to his estate for ever, when they are fastened thereto by plaster, lime, or cement, or when they cannot be separated without being broken and damaged, or without breaking or injuring that part of the estate to which they are attached. The mirrors of an apartment are considered as fixed for perpetual continuance, when the framework on which they are fastened forms part of the body of the wainscot. It is the same with respect to pictures and other ornaments. As regards statues, they are immoveable when they are placed in a niche formed expressly to receive them, although they may be capable of removal without breaking or damage.

See parallel English law, p. 329, 330.

526.

Immoveable in respect of the object to which they are applied are—

The usufruct of immoveable things;

Servitudes or agricultural services;

Actions whose object is the recovery of immoveable property.

See parallel similar English law, p. 330.

CHAPTER II.

Of Moveables.

527.

Property is moveable in its nature, or by the determination of the law.

See parallel similar English law, p. 330.

528.

Bodies which may be transported from place to place, whether they move themselves like animals, or whether, like inanimate things, they are incapable of changing their place without the application of extrinsic force, are moveables in their nature.

See parallel English law, p. 330.

529.

Bonds and actions relating to sums demandable or personal effects, actions and interests in companies for objects of finance, commerce, or industry, although immoveables depending on such undertakings, belong to the companies, are moveables by determination of law. These actions or interests are reputed moveable with respect to each individual member, as long as the society exists.

Perpetual or life annuities, whether granted by the republic or by private persons, are also moveable by determination of law.

See parallel English law, 330, 1.

ARTICLE DECREED 21ST OF MARCH, 1804. PROMULGATED THE 31ST OF MARCH.

530.

Every annuity granted in perpetuity as the price of the sale of immoveable property, or as the condition of ceding an immoveable fund by free or chargeable title, is in its nature redeemable.

The creditor is allowed to regulate the provisions and conditions of redemption.

He is permitted to stipulate that such annuity shall not be redeemed until after a certain term, which shall in no case exceed thirty years; every stipulation to the contrary is void.

See parallel English law, p. 331.

531.

Boats, ferry-boats, vessels, mills, and floating-baths, and generally all machinery not fixed on piles, and not forming part of the building, are moveable: the seizure of some articles of this kind may, nevertheless, on account of their importance, be subject to particular forms, as shall be explained in the code of civil procedure.

See parallel English law, p. 331.

532.

The materials arising from the demolition of an edifice, and those collected for the construction of a new one, are moveable until they are employed by the artificer in building.

See parallel English law, p. 331, 2.

533.

The word "*moveables*," employed alone in the regulations of the law or an individual, without other addition or designation, does not comprehend ready money, jewels, credits, books, medals, instruments of science, art, and trade, body-linen, horses, equipages, arms, grain, wine, hay, and other commodities; in like manner, it does not comprehend objects of commerce.

Sea parallel definitions of the English law, p. 332.

534.

The words "*goods moveable*," only comprehend moveables destined for the use and ornament of apartments, as tapestries, beds, seats, mirrors, clocks, tables, china, and other objects of that nature.

Pictures and statues which form part of the furniture of an apartment, are also comprised therein, but not collections of pictures which may be in galleries or private rooms.

It is the same with respect to pieces of porcelain: such only as form part of the decoration of an apartment are comprised under the denomination of "*goods moveable*."

See parallel definitions of the English law, p. 332.

535.

The expression "*moveable goods*," that of "*personalty*," or of "*personal property*," comprehend generally all that is deemed "*moveable*," according to the rules heretofore established.

The sale or gift of a furnished house only comprehends the "*moveable goods*."

See parallel definitions of English law, p. 332.

536.

The sale or gift of a house, with all therein contained, does not comprehend cash, nor credits, and other rights of which the titles may be deposited within the house; all other personal effects are contained therein.

See similar principles of English law, p. 333.

CHAPTER III.

Of Property, with Reference to those who are in the Possession of it.

537.

Private persons have the free disposition of the property belonging to them, subject to the modifications established by the laws.*

Property not belonging to private persons is administered, and cannot be alienated, except in the forms and in pursuance of the regulations peculiar to it.†

* See parallel English law, p. 332.

† See parallel English law, p. 333.

538.

Highways, roads, and streets at the national charge, rivers and streams which will carry floats, shores, ebb and flow of the sea, ports, harbours, roads for ships, and generally all portions of the national territory, which are not susceptible of private proprietorship, are considered as dependencies on the public domain.

See parallel English law, p. 334.

539.

All property unclaimed and without owner, and that of persons who die without heirs, or of which the succession is abandoned, belongs to the nation.

See parallel English law, p. 334.

540.

Gates, moats, ramparts of places of war, and fortresses, form also part of the national domain.

See parallel English law, p. 334.

541.

It is the same with respect to soils, fortifications, and ramparts of places which are no longer places of war; they belong to the nation unless they have been validly alienated, or unless their proprietorship has been barred by prescription.

See parallel English law, p. 334.

542.

Communal property is that to the ownership or produce of which the inhabitants of one or more communes have an acquired right.

See parallel definition of the English law, p. 334, 5.

543.

A person may have over property either a right of ownership, or a simple right of enjoyment, or only claims for ground-services.

See parallel English legal distinctinction, p. 335.

TITLE II.

Of Property.

DECREED THE 27TH OF JANUARY, 1804. PROMULGATED THE 6TH OF FEBRUARY.

544.

Property is the right of enjoying and disposing of things in the most absolute manner, provided they are not used in a way prohibited by the laws or by any bye-law.

See parallel definition of the English law, p. 335, 340.

545.

No one can be compelled to give up his property, except for the public good, and for a just and previous indemnity.

See parallel principle of English law, p. 340,

546.

Property in a thing, whether real or personal, confers a right over all which it produces, and over all connected with it by accession, whether naturally or artificially. This right is termed the "*right of accession*."

See parallel rule and definition of English law, p. 340.

CHAPTER I.

Of the Right of Accession over the Produce of any Thing.

547.

The natural or artificial fruits of the earth,

Civil advantages,

The increase of animals, belong to the proprietor by right of accession.

See parallel English law, p. 341.

548.

The fruits produced by anything only belong to the proprietor on condition of reimbursing the expenses of labour, tillage, and seed, incurred by third persons.

See parallel, but dissimilar, English law, p. 341.

549.

A mere possessor does not acquire the fruits unless he is in possession by good faith; in the opposite case he is bound to render the produce with the thing itself to the proprietor who claims it.

See parallel English law, p. 342.

550.

He is in possession by good faith who possesses, as proprietor, by virtue of a conveyance of the defects of which he is not aware.

He ceases to be in possession by good faith from the moment when he discovers such defects.

See parallel English law, p. 342.

CHAPTER II.

Of the Right of Accession over what is connected and incorporated with any Thing.

551.

Everything which is connected and

incorporated with anything belongs to the proprietor, according to rules which shall be hereafter established.

See parallel article, p. 342.

Section I.

Of the Right of Accession relatively to Things immoveable.

552.

Property in the soil gives the property above and beneath.*

The proprietor may make above all kinds of plantations and buildings which he shall judge convenient, saving the exceptions established under the title "*Of Servitude and Services relating to Land.*"

He may make beneath all buildings and excavations which he shall judge convenient, and draw from such excavations all the products which they are capable of furnishing, saving the restrictions resulting from the laws and statutes relating to mines, and from the laws and regulation of police.†

* See parallel principle of English law, p. 343.

† See parallel English law, p. 343.

553.

All buildings, plantations, and works upon the soil or beneath the surface, are presumed to have been made by the proprietor at his own expense, and to belong to him, until the contrary be shown; without prejudice to the property which a third person may have acquired or may acquire by prescription, whether it be a vault beneath the building of another, or any other part of the building.

See parallel English law, p. 343.

554.

The proprietor of the soil having made buildings, plantations, and works with materials which did not belong to him, must pay the value thereof; he may also be condemned in damages, and interest if there be ground; but the owner of such materials is not allowed to remove them.

See parallel English law, p. 343.

555.

When plantations, buildings, and works have been made by a third person and with his own materials, the proprietor of the soil has a right either to retain them, or to oblige such third person to remove them.*

If the proprietor of the soil demand the demolition of the plantations and buildings, it must be done at his charge who made them and without any indemnity; he may moreover be condemned in damages and interest, if there be ground, for the injury which may have been sustained by the proprietor of the soil.†

If the proprietor prefer preserving such plantations and buildings, he owes a reimbursement for the value of the materials and the price of the work, without regard to the greater or less augmentation of value which the soil has received. Nevertheless if the plantations, buildings, and works have been made by a third person evicted but not condemned to a restitution of profits on account of his good faith, the proprietor shall not demand the demolition of the said works, plantations, and buildings: but he shall have his election, either to repay the value of the materials and the price of workmanship, or to reimburse a sum equal to the augmented value of the estate.‡

* See parallel English law, p. 343.

† See parallel English law, p. 343.

‡ See parallel English law, p. 343.

556.

The accumulations and increase of mud formed successively and imperceptibly on the soil bordering on a river or other stream, is denominated "*alluvion.*"*

Alluvion is for the benefit of the proprietor of the shore, whether in respect of a river, a navigable stream, or one admitting floats, or not; on condition, in the first case, of leaving a landing-place or towing-path conformably to regulations.†

* See parallel English definition, p. 344.

† See parallel rule of English law, p. 344.

557.

It is the same with regard to derelictions occasioned by a running stream retiring insensibly from one of its banks, and encroaching on the other; the proprietor of the bank discovered profits by the alluvion, without giving the proprietor on the opposite side a right to reclaim the land which he has lost.

This right does not take place with regard to derelictions of the sea.

See parallel English law, p. 344.

558.

Alluvion does not take place with respect to lakes and ponds, the proprietor of which preserves always the land which the water covers when it is at the pond's full height, even though the volume of water should be diminished.

In like manner the proprietor of a pond acquires no right over land bordering on his pond which may happen to be covered by an extraordinary flood.

See parallel English law, p. 344.

559.

If a river or a stream, navigable or not, carries away by a sudden violence a considerable and distinguishable part of a field on its banks, and bears it to a field lower, or on its opposite bank, the owner of the part carried away may reclaim his property; but he is required to make his demand within a year: after this interval it is inadmissible, unless the proprietor of the field to which the part carried away has been united, has not yet taken possession thereof.

See parallel English law, p. 344.

560.

Islands, islets, and accumulations of mud formed in the bed of rivers or streams navigable, or admitting floats, belong to the nation, if there be no title or prescription to the contrary.

See parallel English law, p. 344.

561.

Islands and accumulations of mud formed in rivers and streams not navigable, and not admitting floats, belong to the proprietors of the shore on that side where the island is formed; if the island be not formed on one side only, it belongs to the proprietors of the shore on the two sides, divided by an imaginary line drawn through the middle of the river.

See parallel English law, p. 345.

562.

If a river or other stream in forming itself a new arm, divide and surround a field belonging to the proprietor of the shore, and thereby form an island, such proprietor shall retain the ownership of his land, although the island be formed in a river or in a navigable stream or one admitting floats.

See parallel English law, p. 343.

563.

If a river or a navigable stream, capable of admitting floats or not, form a new course, abandoning its ancient bed, the proprietors of the land newly occupied take, by title of indemnity, the ancient bed abandoned, each in proportion to the land of which he has been deprived.

See parallel English law, p. 345.

564.

Pigeons, rabbits, and fish passing to another dove-house, warren, or pond, belong to the proprietors of the latter, provided they have not been attracted by fraud and artifice.

See parallel English law, p. 345.

Section 2.

Of the Right of Accession relatively to moveable Property.

565.

The right of accession having for its object two things moveable which belong to different masters, is entirely subordinate to the principles of natural equity.

The following rules shall serve as examples to guide the judge in determing, in cases not provided for, according to the peculiar circumstances.

See parallel English article, p. 345.

566.

When two objects appertaining to different masters, which have been united in such a manner as to form one whole, are nevertheless separable, so that one can subsist without the other, the whole belongs to the master of that which forms the principal part, on condition of paying to the other the value of the one which was united to it.

See the English law on this point, p. 345.

567.

That is to be deemed the principal part to which the other was only united for the use, ornament, or completion of the first.

The English law, proceeding on a totally different principle, p. 345, 6, requires no such rule. See note 6, p. 345.

568.

Nevertheless, when the object united is much more valuable than the principal one, and when it has been employed unknown to the proprietor, the latter may demand that the object united shall be separated in order to be restored to him, even though it may be attended with some deterioration of that to which it was joined.

Same observation as to the preceding article.

569.

If of two objects united in order to form one whole, the one cannot be regarded as accessory to the other, that shall be deemed the principal which is most considerable in value, or in size if the value of both is nearly equal.

Same observation as to art. 567.

570.

If an artizan or any person whatsoever has employed a material which did not belong to him, in order to form something of a new description, whether the material can or cannot be restored to its original shape, the proprietor thereof has a right to claim the thing* which has been formed from it, on paying the price of the workmanship.†

* See parallel English law, p. 346.

† No similar principle.

571.

If however the workmanship were so important, that it surpassed by much the value of the material employed, the labour shall then be deemed the principal part, and the artificer shall have a right to retain the thing wrought, on paying the price of the material to the proprietor.

See the English law on this point, p. 346.

572.

Where a person has made use of materials which partly belong to him and in part do not, in order to form an object of a new description, without having destroyed any of the materials, but in such a way that they cannot be separated without inconvenience, the object is common to both proprietors; by reason as respects the one of the materials belonging to him, and in regard to the other by reason at once of the material belonging to him, and the price of his workmanship.

See parallel English principle, p. 346.

573.

When an object has been formed by the mixture of many materials belonging to different proprietors, but of which no one can be regarded as the principal material; if such materials are capable of being separated, he without whose knowledge such materials were mingled, may demand the division thereof.

If the materials are incapable of separation without inconvenience, they acquire therein a common property proportioned to the quantity, quality, and value of the material belonging to each of them.

See the English law in case of voluntary intermixture, p. 345, 6.

574.

If the material belonging to one of the proprietors were far superior in quantity or value to the other, in such case the proprietor of the material superior in value may claim the thing produced by the mixture, on paying to the other the price of his material.

See p. 345, note 6, and p. 346.

575.

When an object remains in common between the proprietors of the materials of which it has been formed, it ought to be sold by auction for their mutual advantage.

See parallel but dissimilar English law, p. 346.

576.

In all cases where a proprietor, whose material has been made use of without his knowledge, in order to form an object of a different description, can claim a property in such object, he has the election of demanding restitution of his material, in kind, in the same quantity, weight, measure, and goodness, or its value.

See note to art. 566.

577.

Persons who shall have employed materials belonging to others and without their knowledge, may also be condemned in damages and costs if there be ground, without prejudice to prosecution in an extraordinary manner if there be occasion.

See parallel English law, p. 346.

TITLE III.

Of Usufruct, Use, and of Habitation.

DECREED THE 30TH OF JANUARY, 1804. PROMULGATED THE 9TH OF FEBRUARY.

CHAPTER I.

Of Usufruct.

578.

Usufruct is the right of enjoying things of which the property is in another, in the same manner as the proprietor himself, but on condition of preserving them substantially.

See parallel kind of English right, p. 347.

579.

Usufruct is established by the law, or by the consent of man.

See parallel English law, p. 348.

580.

Usufruct may be established either simply, or to a certain day, or conditionally.

See parallel English law, p. 348.

581.

It may be established over every species of property, moveable or immoveable.

See parallel English law, p. 348.

Section 1.

Of the Rights of the Usufructuary.

582.

The usufructuary has a right to the enjoyment of every species of benefit, whether natural, or artificial, or civil, which the object of usufruct is capable of producing.

See parallel English law, p. 349.

583.

Natural benefits are those which the earth produces spontaneously. The production and increase of animals are also natural fruits.*

The artificial fruits of the soil are those which are obtained by cultivation.†

*See parallel definition in the English law, p. 349.

† See parallel definition in the English law, p. 349.

584.

Civil fruits are rents of houses, interest on sums due, arrears of rent. The value of farms is also ranged under the class of civil fruits.

See parallel definition in the English law, p. 349.

585.

Natural and artificial fruits, hanging by branches and roots at the period when the usufruct commences, belong to the usufructuary.*

Those which are in a similar state at the period when the usufruct closes, belong to the proprietor, without recompense on either side for tillage and sowing, but without prejudice also to such portion of the fruits as may be acquired by the joint cultivator, if there were one at the commencement or cessation of the usufruct.†

* See parallel English law, p. 349.

† See parallel English law, p. 349.

586.

Civil fruits are reputed to accrue from day to day, and belong to the usufructuary, in proportion to the duration of his usufruct. This rule applies to the rent of farming leases, as well as to rents of houses and other civil fruits.

See parallel English law, p. 349.

587.

If the usufruct comprises objects which cannot be used without destroying them, as money, grain, and liquors, the usufructuary has a right to make use of them, but on condition of restoring them at the end of the usufruct in similar quantity, quality, and goodness, or their estimated value.

See parallel English law, p. 350.

588.

The usufruct of an annuity confers likewise on the usufructuary, during the continuance of his usufruct, a right to the perception of the arrears, without rendering him liable to any restitution.

See parallel English law, p. 350.

589.

If the usufruct comprehend things which, without being immediately consumed, are deteriorated by little and little in the using, as linen and moveable furniture, the usufructuary has a right to employ them for the purposes to which they were destined, and is only compelled to restore them at the end of his usufruct in the state in which they may then be, not being damaged by his fraud or fault.

See parallel English law, p. 350.

590.

If the usufruct comprehend underwood, the usufructuary is bound to observe the order and proportionate quantity of his cuttings, conformably to the established usage and custom of proprietors, without indemnity, however, to be made to the usufructuary or his heirs, for ordinary cutting, whether of underwood, poles, or timber, which may have been omitted during his enjoyment.*

Trees which can be removed from a nursery-ground without injuring it, do not therefore form part of the usufruct except on the condition that the usufructuary shall conform to the usage of such places in restoring them.†

* See parallel English law, p. 350.

† See parallel English law, p. 350.

591.

The usufructuary receives the benefit likewise, always conforming to the seasons and custom of the ancient proprietors, of those parts of a wood of tall trees as have been placed in regular cuts, whether such cuts are made periodically over a certain extent of ground, or whether they are made of a certain number of trees taken indiscriminately over the whole surface of the domain.

See parallel English law, p. 350, 51.

592.

In no other cases can the usufructuary touch full grown timber-trees: he can only employ trees blown down or broken by accident, for the reparations to which he is bound: he may, however, for that object cause some to be felled in case of necessity, but on condition of making such necessity appear to the proprietor.

See parallel English law, p. 351.

593.

He may take also in the woods

props for vines: he may take also from the trees, their annual or periodical produce: the whole, according to the usage of the country, or the custom of the proprietors.

See parallel English law, p. 351.

594.

Fruit-trees which die, those likewise which are torn down or broken by accident, belong to the usufructuary, on condition of replacing them by others.

† See parallel English law, p. 351.

595.

The usufructuary may enjoy in his own person, let on lease to another, or even sell or transfer, his right by gratuitous title. If he lets on lease, he must conform, with regard to the seasons at which leases ought to be renewed and as respects their duration, to the regulations established relative to a husband with regard to the property of a wife, under the title "*Of the Contract of Marriage, and of the respective Rights of married Persons.*"

See parallel English law, p. 351.

596.

The usufructuary is entitled to the enjoyment of the augmentation accruing by alluvion to the object of his usufruct.

* See parallel English law, p. 351.

597.

He enjoys the right of servitude, toll, and generally all the rights which the proprietor is capable of enjoying, and he enjoys them in the same manner as the proprietor himself.

See parallel English law, p. 351.

598.

He enjoys also in the same manner as the proprietor, such mines and quarries as are in a course of working at the commencement of the usufruct; nevertheless, if there be question concerning a work which cannot be made without a grant, the usufructuary shall not have the enjoyment thereof until he shall have obtained the permission of government.

He has no right over mines and quarries not yet opened, nor over peat-bog, nor over treasure which may be discovered, during the continuance of his usufruct.

See parallel English law, p. 352.

599.

The proprietor cannot, by his own deed, nor in any possible manner, injure the rights of the usufructuary.

The usufructuary on his part cannot at the conclusion of his usufruct claim any indemnity for improvements which he may pretend to have made, although the value of the thing may have been augmented thereby.

He or his heirs may, however, carry away mirrors, pictures, and other ornaments, which he may have caused to be put up, but on condition of restoring their places to the original state.

See parallel English law, p. 352.

Section 2.

Of the Obligations of the Usufructuary.

600.

The usufructuary takes things in the state in which they are; but he cannot enter into the enjoyment of them, until he has caused an inventory of the moveable, and a statement of the immoveable objects of the usufruct, to be drawn up in the presence of the proprietor, or after having duly summoned him.

See parallel English law, p. 352.

601.

He must give security to enjoy like a careful husbandman, unless he be dispensed therefrom by the act constituting the usufruct: nevertheless, the father and mother having the legal usufruct of the property of their children, the seller or donor with a reservation of usufruct, are not bound to give security.

See parallel but dissimilar English law, p. 352.

602.

If the usufructuary cannot find

security, the immoveables are let on lease or put in sequestration;*

Sums comprehended in the usufruct are placed out;

Commodities are sold, and the price received therefrom is in like manner placed out;†

The interest on such sums and the prices of such leases belong in this case to the usufructuary.‡

* See note to art. 601.

† See parallel English law, p. 353.

‡ See parallel English law, p. 353.

603.

In default of security on the part of the usufructuary, the proprietor may require that such moveables as perish in the using should be sold, in order that the price thereof may be placed out like that of the commodities; and then the usufructuary enjoys the interest during his usufruct; the usufructuary, however, may demand, and the judges are empowered to order, according to circumstances, that one portion of the moveables necessary for his use should be left for him, on his simple security on oath, and on condition of producing them at the expiration of the usufruct.

See note to art. 601.

604.

Delay in giving security does not deprive the usufructuary of the fruits to which he may have claim; they are his due from the moment at which the usufruct commences.

See note to art. 601.

605.

The usufructuary is only bound to necessary reparations.*

Substantial reparations are at the charge of the proprietor, unless they have been occasioned by the neglect of necessary repairs, since the commencement of the usufruct: in which case the usufructuary is also bound to them.

* See parallel English law, p. 353.

606.

Substantial repairs are those of the main walls and vaults, the re-establishment of beams, and entire roofs;

That of ditches and of buttresses, and enclosing walls in entirety:

All other reparations are necessary repairs.

No parallel English law.

607.

Neither the proprietor nor the usufructuary is bound to rebuild what falls down through age, or what is destroyed by mere accident.

See parallel English law, p. 353.

608.

The usufructuary is bound, while his enjoyment continues, to all annual charges on the estate, such as contributions and others, which by custom are considered charges on the fruits.

See parallel English law, p. 353.

609.

With respect to charges which may be imposed on property during the continuance of the usufruct, the usufructuary and the proprietor contribute thereto in manner following:

The proprietor is obliged to pay them, and the usufructuary must account to him for the interest;

If they are advanced by the usufructuary, he has a right to recover them at the end of the usufruct.

See parallel English law, p. 353.

610.

A legacy given by a testator, of an annuity or alimentary pension, may be acquitted by the general legatee of the usufruct in its entirety, and by the legatee having the general title of usufruct in the proportion of his enjoyment, without any second payment on their part.

See parallel, but dissimilar English law, p. 354.

611.

The usufructuary by particular title is not bound by debts for which the estate is mortgaged; if he be compelled to pay them he has his remedy against the proprietor, saving what is said in article 1020, under the title

"*Of Donations during Life and of Wills.*"

See parallel English law, p. 354.

612.

The usufructuary either general or by general title must contribute with the proprietor to the payment of debts in manner following:

An estimate is made of the value of the estate the subject of usufruct, a rate of contribution to debts is then fixed in proportion to such estimate.

If the usufructuary is willing to advance the sum which the estate must contribute, the capital is restored to him at the termination of the usufruct without any interest.

If the usufructuary is not willing to make such advance, the proprietor has the election either to pay such sum (and in this case the usufructuary must account to him for the interest during the continuance of his usufruct), or to cause a portion of the property subject to usufruct, to the required amount, to be sold.

See parallel English law, p. 354.

613.

The usufructuary is only liable for the charges of such proceedings at law as regard the enjoyment, and of other judgments to which such proceedings may give rise.

See parallel English law, p. 354.

614.

If during the continuance of the usufruct a third person is guilty of any usurpation on the estate, or any other attempt against the rights of the proprietor, the usufructuary is bound to give him information against such intruder; in default thereof he is himself responsible for all damage which may result therefrom to the proprietor, as he would be with respect to injuries committed by himself.

See parallel English law, p. 354.

615.

If the usufruct be established only over an animal which happens to perish without the fault of the usufructuary, the latter is not bound to restore another for it, nor to pay its value.

See parallel English law, p. 354.

616.

If a flock over which an usufruct has been established perishes entirely by accident or by disease, and without the fault of the usufructuary, the latter is not bound towards the proprietor except to account for the skins or their value.

If the flock does not entirely perish, the usufructuary is bound to replace them, until the increase amounts to the number of those animals which perished.

See parallel English law, p. 354, 5.

SECTION 3.

Of the Manner in which Usufruct is put an end to.

617.

Usufruct is extinguished—

By the natural and civil death of the usufructuary;

By the expiration of the time for which it has been granted;

By the consolidation or union in the same person of the two qualities of usufructuary and proprietor;

By the non-exercise of the right during thirty years;

By the total loss of the object over which usufruct was established.

See parallel English law, p. 355.

618.

Usufruct may likewise cease by the abuse of which the usufructuary is guilty in his enjoyment, either by committing spoliation upon the estate, or by suffering it to fall to decay for want of repair.

The creditors of the usufructuary may interfere in controversies, for the preservation of their rights; they may offer amends for spoliation committed, and guarantee for the future.

The judges may, according to the importance of the circumstances, either pronounce the absolute extinction of the usufruct, or give order for the re-entry of the proprietor into the enjoyment of the object encumbered therewith, on condition of paying annually, to the usufructuary or his agent, a fixed sum up to the period at which the usufruct would have ceased.

See parallel English law, p. 355.

619.

Usufruct which is not granted to particular persons, only lasts for thirty years.

See parallel English law, p. 355.

620.

Usufruct granted until a third person has reached a fixed age, continues until such period, although such third person die before the age fixed.

For the English law in such case, see parallel article 1183, p. 459.

621.

The sale of a thing which is the subject of usufruct makes no alteration in the right of the usufructuary; he continues to enjoy his usufruct unless he has formally renounced it.

See parallel English law, p. 355, 6.

622.

The creditors of an usufructuary may cause a renunciation made to their prejudice to be annulled.

See the English parallel principle of law, p. 356.

623.

If one part only of the thing subject to usufruct be destroyed, the usufruct is preserved over the remainder.

A similar principle recognised in the English law.

624.

If the usufruct be established over a building only, and such building be destroyed by a fire or other accident, or if it have fallen down through age, the usufructuary shall have no right to the enjoyment either of the soil or the materials.

If the usufruct be established over a domain of which a building forms a part, the usufructuary shall enjoy the soil and the materials.

See parallel English law, p. 356.

CHAPTER II.

Of Use and Habitation.

625.

The rights of use and of habitation are established and forfeited in the same manner as those of usufruct.

See the English law on this subject, and the totally different signification of the term "use," p. 356, 7, 8.

626.

A person is incapable, as in the case of usufruct, of enjoying them without previously giving security, and without making lists and inventories.

See note to preceding article.

627.

The person entitled to use, and he who has a right of habitation, ought to enjoy them like careful husbandmen.

See note to art. 625.

628.

The rights of use and of habitation are governed by the document which has established them, and receive, according to its regulations, more or less extension.

See note to art. 625.

629.

If that document is not explicit on the extent of these rights, they are regulated as follows.

See note to art. 625.

630.

He who has the use of the fruits of an estate, cannot exact from thence more than is necessary to him for his own wants and those of his family.

He may exact therefrom for the wants likewise of children who have come to him subsequently to the grant of use.

See note to art. 625.

631.

The person enjoying use cannot assign or let his right to another.

See note to art. 625.

632.

He who has the right of habitation in a house, may dwell there with his family, even though he should not have been married at the period when such right was conferred upon him.

See note to art. 625.

633.

The right of habitation is confined to what is necessary for the habitation of him to whom such right is conceded, and of his family.

See note to art. 625.

634.

The right of habitation can neither be assigned nor hired.

See note to art. 625, and p. 357.

635.

If the person enjoying the use absorb the whole fruits of an estate, or if he occupy the entirety of a house, he is subjected to the charges of culture, to necessary reparations, and to the payment of contributions, like an usufructuary.

See note to art. 625.

636.

The use of woods and forests is regulated by particular laws.

See note to art. 625.

TITLE IV.

Of Servitudes or Ground Services.

DECREED 31ST OF JANUARY, 1804.—PROMULGATED THE 10TH OF FEBRUARY.

637.

A servitude is a charge imposed upon an estate for the use and benefit of an estate belonging to another proprietor.

See parallel definition of the English law, p. 358, 9.

638.

Servitude does not establish any pre-eminence of one estate over another.

See the parallel principle of English law, p. 359.

639.

It is derived either from the natural situation of places, or from obligations imposed by law, or from agreements between proprietors.

See parallel English law, p. 359.

CHAPTER I.

Of Servitudes derived from the Situation of Places.

640.

Inferior lands are subjected, as regards those which lie higher, to receive the waters which flow naturally therefrom, to which the hand of man has not contributed.

The proprietor of the lower ground cannot raise a bank which shall prevent such flowing.

The proprietor of the higher lands cannot do anything to increase the servitude of the lower.

See parallel principle of English law, p. 359, 60.

641.

He who possesses a spring within his field may make use of it at his pleasure, saving the right which the proprietor of a lower field may have acquired by title or by prescription.

See parallel principle of English law, p. 360.

642.

Prescription in such case can only be acquired by an uninterrupted enjoyment during the space of thirty years; to be computed from the moment at which the proprietor of the lower field has made and completed the works apparently designed to facilitate the fall and course of the water within his property.

See parallel English law, p. 360.

643.

The proprietor of a spring cannot change the course thereof when it supplies the inhabitants of a commune, village, or hamlet, with water for their necessary use; but if the inhabitants have not acquired the use of it by prescription or otherwise, the proprietor may claim an indemnity, to be settled by competent persons.

See parallel English law, p. 360, 61.

644.

He whose property borders on a running water, other than that which is declared a dependency on the public domain by article 538, under the title "*Of the Distinctions of Property,*" may employ it in its passage for the irrigation of his property.

He whose estate is intersected by such water, is at liberty to make use of it within the space through which it runs, but on condition of restoring it, at the boundaries of his field, to its ordinary course.

See parallel principle of English law, p, 361.

645.

If a dispute arise between proprietors to whom such waters may be useful, the courts, in pronouncing their judgment, must reconcile the interest of agriculture with the respect due to property; and in all cases particular and local regulations on the course and use of waters must be observed.

See parallel principle of English law, p. 361.

646.

Every proprietor may compel his neighbour to determine the boundaries of their contiguous properties. Such determining of boundaries must be at their common expense.

See parallel principle of English law, p. 361.

647.

Every proprietor may enclose his estate, saving the exception contained in article 682.

See parallel principle of English law, p. 362.

648.

The proprietor who is desirous of enclosing his land, loses his right to the free pasturage and waste land, in proportion to the land which he withdraws.

See parallel principle of English law, p. 362 and 361; parallel article 646.

CHAPTER II.

Of Servitudes established by Law.

649.

Servitudes established by law have for their object the public benefit, or that of the commune, or of private persons.

See parallel English article, p. 362.

650.

Those established for the public benefit, or that of the commune, have for their object footways by the side of navigable rivers or streams admitting floats,* the construction or reparation of roads, and other public works, or those relating to the commune.†

Everything relating to this species of servitude, is determined by the laws, or by particular regulations.

* See parallel but dissimilar English law, p. 362, 63.

† See parallel English law, p. 362, 63.

651.

The law subjects proprietors to different obligations as respects each other, independently of all convention.

See parallel English law, p. 363.

652.

Part of these obligations is regulated by the laws touching rural police.

Others relate to party-walls and ditches, and the cases in which supporting walls are necessary, to views over the property of the neighbour, to the dropping of water from house-eaves, to rights of way.

This is merely an explanation, and can scarcely be called a law.

SECTION 2.

Of a Party-Wall and Ditch.

653.

In towns and fields every wall which serves as a boundary between buildings, even to its base, or between courts and gardens, or even between enclosures in the fields, is presumed party, if there be no title or mark to the contrary.

See parallel English law, p. 361, 63.

654.

It is a mark of non-partition when the summit of the wall is straight and perpendicular with its base on one side, and presents on the other an inclined plane. Again, when there is on one side only a coping, or ridges, and shouldering-pieces of stone, which might have been placed there in building the wall.

In such cases the wall is deemed to belong exclusively to the proprietor on whose side are the eaves or corbels, and ridges of stone.

See parallel principle of English law, p. 361, 63, 64.

655.

The reparation and rebuilding of the party-wall are at the expense of all those who have claim thereto, and in proportion to the claim of each.

See a local parallel enactment in the English law, p. 364.

656.

Nevertheless, each joint-proprietor of a party-wall may relieve himself from contributing to the reparations and rebuilding by abandoning his claim of partition, provided that the party-wall do not sustain a building belonging to him.

See parallel English law, p. 364, and note to art. 655.

657.

Every joint-proprietor is at liberty to build against a party-wall, and to place beams and joists in the whole thickness of the wall, except fifty-four millimetres (two inches), without prejudice to the right which his neighbour has to cause the beam to be reduced by the chisel to half the thickness of the wall, in case the latter shall desire to fix beams in the same place, or to build a chimney against it.

See a parallel English law, p. 364, and note to art. 655.

658.

Every joint-proprietor may cause a party-wall to be built higher, but he must alone defray the expense of such elevation, of the necessary reparations above the height of the common enclosure; and furthermore, of an indemnity against the expense in the rate of the additional building, and according to the value.

See a parallel English law, p. 364, and note to art. 655.

659.

If the party wall is not in condition to support the additional building, he who desires to elevate it must cause it to be entirely rebuilt at his own expense, and the excess in thickness must be taken from his own side.

See a parallel English law, p. 364, and note to art. 655.

660.

The neighbour who has not contributed to the elevation may acquire right of partition by paying half of the expense it has cost, and the value of one moiety of the soil furnished for the excess of thickness, if there be any.

See a parallel English law, p. 364.

661.

Every proprietor joining a wall has in like manner the power of rendering it common, in whole or part, by paying to the owner of the wall the half of its value, or the half of the value of that portion which he desires to make common, and the half of the value of the soil on which the wall is built.

See note to art. 655 and 659.

662.

One of two neighbours must not form in the body of a party-wall any hollow, nor apply or lean any work against it without the consent of the other, or, on his refusal, without having directed, under the advice of competent persons, the necessary means for erecting such new work without injury to the rights of the other.

See a parallel English law, p. 364, 5; and note to art. 655.

663.

Each inhabitant of a town or suburb can compel his neighbour to contribute to the construction and reparation of the enclosure forming the boundary of their houses, courts, and gardens situated within the said towns and suburbs: the height of the enclosure shall be fixed according to particular regulations or constant and acknowledged usages; and in defect of such usages or regulations, every boundary-wall between two neighbours, which shall for the future be constructed or rebuilt, must be at least thirty-two decimeters (ten feet) high, including the coping, within towns containing fifty thousand souls and upwards, and twenty-six decimeters (eight feet) in others.

See note to art. 655, and p. 361, 2.

664.

When the different stories of a house belong to different proprietors, if the titles to the property do not regulate the mode of reparations and reconstructions, they must be made in manner following:

The main walls and roof are at the charge of all the proprietors, each in proportion to the value of the story belonging to him.

The proprietor of each story makes the floor belonging thereto.

The proprietor of the first story erects the staircase which conducts to it; the proprietor of the second story carries the stairs from where the former ends to his apartments; and so of the rest.

This mode of possessing property is unknown in England.

665.

On the re-building a partition-wall or a house, the servitudes, active and passive, continue with respect to such new wall or house, without power nevertheless to increase them, and provided the reconstruction have taken place before a right by perscription has been acquired.

See parallel art. 675, p. 366.

666.

All ditches between two estates are presumed common if there be no title or proof to the contrary.

See parallel English law, p. 365, and reference in note to art. 655.

667.

It is a proof that a ditch is not common when the bank or earth thrown up is found only on one side of it.

See parallel principle of English law, p. 365, as in the preceding article.

668.

The ditch is deemed to belong exclusively to him on whose side the earth is found to be thrown up.

See parallel principle of English law, p. 365.

669.

A common ditch must be maintained at the common charge.

See reference in note to art. 655.

670.

Every hedge which separates two estates is reputed common, unless there be only one of the estates in an enclosed condition, or unless there be vouchers or sufficient possession to prove the contrary.

See parallel principle of English law, p. 365.

671.

It is not allowable to plant trees of lofty trunk, but at the distance prescribed by particular regulations actually existing, or by constant and acknowledged usages; and in default of regulations and usages, only at the distance of two metres from the line which separates the two estates in the case of trees of lofty trunk, and at the distance of half a metre in the case of other trees and quick hedges.

See parallel principle of English law, p. 365.

672.

A neighbour may require trees and hedges planted at a less distance to be pulled up.

He whose property is overshadowed by the branches of his neighbour's trees, may compel the latter to cut off such branches.

If it be the roots which encroach on his estate, he has a right to cut them therein himself.

Same reference as to preceding article.

673.

Trees which are found in a common hedge are common like the hedge; each of the two proprietors has the right to require that they should be felled.

See parallel principle of English law, p. 365.

Section 2.

Of the Distance and intermediary Works required for certain Buildings.

674.

He who causes a well or a cess-pool to be dug near a wall partition or not;

He who wishes a chimney to be built there, or a hearth, a forge, or oven, or a kiln;

To build a stable against it;

Or to form against such wall a magazine of salt, or a heap of corrosive substance;

Is obliged to leave the distance prescribed by particular regulations and usages on such subjects, or to form the works prescribed by the same regulations and usages, in order to avoid injury to his neighbour.

See parallel principles of English law, p. 365, 6.

Section 3.

Of Views over a Neighbour's Property.

675.

One of two neighbours cannot without the consent of the other form in the partition-wall any window or aperture, in any manner whatsoever, even a fan-light.

See parallel English law, p. 366.

676.

The proprietor of a wall which is not common, joining immediately the estate of another, may form in such wall lights or windows of wire-lattice, and fan-lights.*

These windows must be furnished with a lattice-work of iron, the meshes of which shall extend to an opening of one decimeter (about three inches eight lines at the most), and with a dormant window.†

* See parallel dissimilar English law, 366, 7.

† No parallel enactment of English law. See previous note.

677.

These windows or lights must not be less than twenty-six decimeters (eight feet) above the floor or base of the chamber which is desired to be lighted, if it be the ground-floor, and nineteen decimeters (six feet) above the floor for the upper stories.

No parallel enactment of English law, note * to art. 676.

678.

A party must not have direct views nor windows for sight, nor balconies or other similar projections over the estate, enclosed or unenclosed, of his neighbour, within the decimeters (six feet) between the wall on which they are formed and the aforesaid estate.

See note * to art. 676, and p. 366.

679.

A party shall not have side or oblique views over the same estate within the distance of six decimeters (two feet).

See note * to art. 676.

680.

The distance mentioned in the two preceding articles is computed from the exterior basement of the wall in which the aperture is made, or if there be balconies or other similar projections from their exterior line to the boundary line of the two properties.

See note * to art. 676.

Section 4.

Of the Droppings of House-Eaves.

681.

Every proprietor must so form his roofs, that the rain-water shall drop upon his own land or the public way; he must not suffer it to flow upon his neighbour's land.

See parallel principle of English law, p. 367.

Section 5.

Of the Right of Way.

682.

Every proprietor whose fields are surrounded, and who has no outlet to the *public road*, may claim a passage over the fields of his neighbours for the agricultural purposes of his estate, on condition of an indemnity proportioned to the injury which he may occasion.

See where a way of necessity arises in England, p. 367, 8.

683.

The road ought regularly to be taken on that side where the passage is the shortest from the *farm surrounded to the public highway*.

See note to preceding article.

684.

Nevertheless it ought to be fixed in that spot where it can occasion the least injury to him over whose farm it is granted.

See note to art. 682.

685.

The action for indemnity, in the case provided for in article 682, may be prescribed against; and the road must be continued though the action for indemnity be no longer admissible.

See note to art. 682.

CHAPTER III.

Of Servitudes established by the Act of Man.

Section 1.

Of the different Species of Servitudes which may be established over Property.

686.

It is allowed to proprietors to establish over their property, or in favour of their property, such servitudes as seem good to them,* provided nevertheless that the services established be not imposed either on a person, or in favour of a person,† but only on an estate and for the benefit of an estate, and provided moreover such services contain nothing contrary to public order.

The mode of using and extent of servitudes thus established, are governed by the document which constitutes them;‡ in default of such document, by the rules hereafter given.

* See similar principle of English law, p. 368.

† See parallel but dissimilar English principle, p. 368.

‡ See parallel principle of English law, p. 368.

687.

Servitudes are established either for the use of buildings, or for that of landed estates.

Those of the first species are called *urbane*, whether the buildings to which they are due are situated in a town or in a field;

Those of the second species are called *rural*.

This distinction is unimportant in the English law, p. 368.

688.

Servitudes are either continual or interrupted.

Continual servitudes are those whose use is or may be continual without having a necessity for the positive act of man: such are water-pipes, house-eaves, windows, and other things of that description.

Interrupted servitudes are those which require the positive act of man for their exercise: such are rights of way, of drawing water, of pasture, and other similar ones.

This distinction is not formally recognised in the law of England, but see p. 369.

689.

Servitudes are apparent or non-apparent.

Apparent servitudes are those which are manifested by external works; such as a gate, a window, or aqueduct. Non-apparent servitudes are those which have no external sign of their existence, as for example a prohibition to build upon a field, or against building beyond a determinate height.

This distinction is unimportant in the English law, and not formally recognised.

SECTION 2.

Of the Mode of establishing Servitudes.

690.

Continual and apparent servitudes are acquired by deed, or by possession for thirty years.

See parallel English law, p. 369.

691.

Continual non-apparent servitudes, and interrupted servitudes whether apparent or not, can only be established by deeds.

Even immemorial possession does not suffice to establish them; without power nevertheless to impeach at the present time servitudes of this nature already acquired by possession in districts where they may have been acquireable in this manner.

See parallel principle of English law, p. 369.

692.

The appointment of the father of a family is equivalent to a deed as regards continual and apparent servitudes.

The English law does not recognise this mode of creating easements other than by deed, p. 369.

693.

There is no appointment by the father of a family but when it is proved that the two farms actually divided have belonged to the same proprietor, and that it is by him that things have been put into the state whence results the servitude.

See note to preceding article.

694.

If the proprietor of two estates, between which there exists an apparent sign of servitude, disposes of one of these estates, without inserting in the contract any stipulation relative to the servitude, it continues to exist actively or passively in favour of the land alienated, or over the land alienated.

See parallel principle of English law, p. 370.

695.

The deed constituting servitude, as far as respects those which cannot be acquired by prescription, can only be supplied by a document acknowledging the servitude, and emanating from the proprietor of the estate subject to servitude.

See parallel article 690, p. 369.

696.

When a servitude is established, it is considered that everything is granted which is necessary in order to make use of it.

Thus the servitude of drawing water at another's fountain necessarily imports a right of way.

See parallel principle of English law, p. 370.

SECTION 3.

Of the Rights of the Proprietor of the Estate to which the Servitude is due.

697.

He to whom a servitude is due has a right to form all the works necessary to make use of and preserve it.

See parallel principle of English law, p. 370.

698.

These works are at his own expense, and not at that of the proprietor of the estate subjected to servitude, unless the deed establishing the servitude declare the contrary.

See note to preceding article.

699.

In the case even where the proprietor of an estate subjected to servitude is charged by the deed with the construction at his own expense of works necessary for the usage or preservation of the servitude, he may always get rid of such charge, by abandoning the estate subjected to servitude to the proprietor of that estate to which the servitude is due.

See note to preceding article.

700.

If the estate for the benefit of which the servitude has been established happens to be divided, the servitude remains due for each portion, provided always, nevertheless, that the burden of the estate subjected to servitude shall not be aggravated.

Thus, for example, if the case be respecting a right of way, all the joint proprietors shall be obliged to exercise it by the same path.

See parallel principle of English law, p. 370, 1.

701.

The proprietor of an estate from which a servitude is due can do nothing which tends to diminish the usage thereof or to render it less commodious.

Thus he cannot change the condition of places, nor transport the exercise of the servitude into a place different from that in which it has been originally assigned.

Nevertheless, if this original assignment has become more burdensome to the proprietor of the estate subjected to the servitude, or if he is prevented from making there advantageous repairs, he may offer to the proprietor of the other estate a place equally commodious for the exercise of his rights, and the latter shall not be at liberty to refuse.

See parallel principle of English law, p. 371.

702.

On the other hand, he who claims the servitude, can only use it according to his title, without power to effect either in the estate which owes the servitude, or in the estate to which it is due, any change which aggravates the condition of the former.

See parallel principle of English law, p. 371.

Section 4.

Of the Manner in which Servitudes are extinguished.

703.

Servitudes cease, when things are in such a state that it is impossible any longer to make use of them.

See parallel principle of English law, p. 371, parallel article 705.

704.

They revive if things are re-established in such a manner that they can be made use of; unless a sufficient space of time have already elapsed to raise a presumption that the servitude has been extinguished, as is described in article 707.

See parallel principle of English law, p. 371.

705.

Every servitude is extinguished when the estate to which it is due, and that which owes it, are united in the same hands.

See parallel principle of English law, p. 371.

706.

Servitude is extinguished by nonusage during thirty years.

See parallel principle of English law, p. 371.

707.

The thirty years begin to run according to the different species of servitudes, either from the day on which they have ceased to be enjoyed, when the case regards interrupted servitudes, or from the day on which an act has been made contrary to the servitudes, in the case of continual servitudes.

See parallel articles, 689, 690, p. 369.

708.

The mode of servitude is subject to prescription like the servitude itself, and in the same manner.

See parallel principle of English law, p. 370, parallel article 697.

709.

In the estate in favour of which the servitude is established belong to several coparceners, the enjoyment by one precludes prescription with regard to all.

See parallel principle of English law, p. 373.

710.

If among the joint-proprietors there be one against whom the prescription has not been able to run, as a minor, he shall have preserved the right for all the others.

See parallel principle of English law, p. 373.

BOOK III.

OF THE DIFFERENT MODES OF ACQUIRING PROPERTY.

DECREED THE 19TH OF APRIL, 1803.—PROMULGATED THE 29TH OF THE SAME MONTH.

General Dispositions.

711.

Ownership in goods is acquired and transmitted by succession, by donation between living parties, or by will, and by the effect of obligations.

See parallel principle of English law, p. 373.

712.

Ownership is acquired also by accession or incorporation, and by prescription.

See the parallel English law, p. 373.

713.

Property which has no owner belongs to the nation.

See the parallel English law, p. 374.

714.

There are things which belong to no one, and the use whereof is common to all.

The laws of police regulate the manner of enjoying such.

See the parallel principle of English law, p. 374.

715.

The right of hunting and fishing is alike regulated by particular laws.

See parallel English law, p. 374,

716.

Property in a treasure belongs to him who discovers it in his own field: if discovered in another person's field, it belongs, by halves, to him who discovered it and the proprietor of the field.

Treasure is everything concealed or hidden in the earth over which no one can prove property, and which is discovered purely by the effect of chance.

See the parallel English law, p. 374, and p. 334, and n 9.

717.

Rights over property thrown into the sea, over objects which the sea casts up, of what nature soever they may be, over plants and herbage which grow on the banks of the sea, are also regulated by particular laws.

It is the same with regard to things lost whereof the owner does not appear.

See parallel principle of English law, p. 374.

TITLE I.

Of Successions.

DECREED THE 19TH OF APRIL, 1803. PROMULGATED THE 29TH OF THE SAME MONTH.

CHAPTER I.

Of the Opening of Successions, and of the Seisin of Heirs.

718.

Successions are opened by natural death, and by civil death.

See parallel principle of English law, p. 375.

719.

A succession is opened by civil death from the moment at which that death is incurred, conformably to the regulations of chap. 2, section 2, of the title, "*Of the Enjoyment and Privation of Civil Rights.*"

See parallel principle of English law, p. 375.

720.

If several persons, respectively called to the succession of each other, perish by one and the same accident, so that it is not possible to ascertain which of them died first, the presumption of survivorship is determined by the circumstances of the event, and in defect of such, by force of age and sex.

See the English law on this subject, p. 375, 6.

721.

If those who perished together were under fifteen years, the eldest shall be presumed to have survived.

If they were all above sixty, the youngest shall be presumed to have survived.

If some were under fifteen years, and others more than sixty, the former shall be presumed to have survived.

See the English law on this subject, p. 375, 6.

722.

If those who perished together were of the age of fifteen years complete, but less than sixty, the male is always presumed to have survived, where there is equality of age, or if the difference which exists does not exceed one year.

If they were of the same sex, the presumption of survivorship which gives rise to succession according to the order of nature must be admitted; thus the younger is presumed to have survived the elder.

See the English law on this subject, p. 375, 6.

723.

The law regulates the order of succeeding between legitimate heirs; in defect of such, the property passes to natural children, afterwards to the husband or wife surviving; and if there be neither of those, to the state.

See parallel English law, p. 376.

724.

The lawful heirs are seised in full right of the property, rights, and actions of the deceased, under the obligation to discharge all the expenses of the succession: natural children, the spouse surviving, and the state, must cause themselves to be put in possession by act of law, in the forms which shall be determined.

See the parallel principle of English law, p. 376, 7.

CHAPTER II.

Of the Qualities requisite to succeed.

725.

In order to succeed, the party must necessarily be in existence at the moment at which the succession is opened.

Those incapable of succeeding are,

1st. He who is not yet conceived.

2nd. The child who is not born capable of living.

3rd. He who is civilly dead.

See the parallel English law on these points, p. 377, 8.

726.

A foreigner* is not permitted to succeed to property which his relation, foreigner or Frenchman, possesses in the territory of the republic, except in those cases and in the manner in which a Frenchman succeeds to his relation possessing property within the country of such foreigner, conformably to the regulations of article 11, under the title "*Of the Enjoyment and Privation of Civil Rights.*"†

* By a law of 14th July, 1810, foreigners are capable of succeeding to property in France.

† See parallel principle of English law, p. 378.

727.

1st, He who shall be condemned for having caused or attempted to cause the death of the defunct; 2nd, He who has brought against the defunct a capital charge adjudged calumnious; and 3rd, The heir being of age, who, being informed of the murder of the defunct, shall not have denounced it to the officers of justice, are unworthy to succeed, and as such excluded from successions.

See the English law on such points, p. 378.

728.

This failure of denunciation cannot be objected to the ancestors and descendants of the murderer, nor to his connexions in the same degree, nor to the husband or wife, nor to his brothers or sisters, nor to his uncles and aunts, nor to his nephews and nieces.

See note to article 727.

729.

The heir excluded from the succession for cause of unworthiness, is bound to restore all the fruits and revenues of which he has had the enjoyment since the opening of the succession.

See note to article 727.

730.

The children of such unworthy person, coming to the succession in their own right, and without the aid of representation, are not excluded by the fault of their father; but the latter cannot in any case claim, over the property of such succession, the usufruct which the law allows to fathers and mothers over the property of their children.

See note to article 727, and p. 378, note 4.

CHAPTER III.

Of the different Orders of Succession.

Section 1.

General Dispositions.

731.

Successions are offered to the children and descendants of the deceased, to his ancestors and collateral relations, in the order and according to the rules hereafter determined.

See parallel English article, p. 378.

732.

The law considers neither the nature nor the origin of the property in order to regulate the succession thereto.

See parallel, but dissimilar English principle, p. 378, 9.

733.

Every succession, which falls to ancestors or collaterals, is divided into two equal parts; one for the relations of the paternal line, the other for relations of the maternal line.

Uterine relations, or children of the same father, are not excluded by germanes; but they only take share in their own line, saving what shall be declared in article 752. Germanes take part in the two lines.

There is no devolution from one line to another, except when no ancestor or collateral can be found in one of the two lines.

See parallel principles of English law, p. 379.

734.

This first division being effected between the paternal and maternal lines, no further division is made between the different branches; but the moiety devolved upon each line belongs to the heir or heirs nearest in degree, saving the case of representation, as shall be spoken of hereafter.

See parallel principle of English law, p. 379, 380.

735.

The proximity of relationship is established by the number of generations; every generation is called a degree.

See parallel rule of English law, p 380.

736.

The series of degrees forms the line; the series of degrees between persons descending from each other is called the *line direct*; the *line collateral* is the series of degrees between persons who do not descend from each other, but who are descended from a common author.

The line direct is distinguished into the line direct descending and the line direct ascending.

The first is that which connects the head with those who descend from him; the second is that which connects a person with those from whom he descends.

See parallel rules of English law, p. 380.

737.

In the direct line are computed as many degrees as there are generations between the persons: thus the son is, with respect to his father, in the first degree; the grandson in the second; and in like manner the father and grandfather with respect to sons and grandsons.

See parallel rule of English law, p. 380.

738.

In the collateral line the degrees are computed by generations, from the one relative to, but not including their common author, and from the latter to the other relative.

Thus two brothers are in the second degree; the uncle and the nephew are in the third degree; cousins-german in the fourth; and so of the rest.

See parallel rule of English law, p. 380, 1.

Section 2.

Of Representation.

739.

Representation is a fiction of law, of which the effect is to cause representatives to enter into the place, the degree, and the rights of the party represented.

See parallel definition of English law, p. 381.

740.

Representation takes place to infinity in the direct descending line.

It is admitted in all cases, whether the children of the deceased come in competition with the descendants of a child previously dead; or whether all the children of the deceased having died before him, the descendants of such children are found to be in equal or unequal degrees toward them.

See parallel principle of English law, p. 381.

741.

Representation does not take place in favour of ancestors; the nearest in each of the two lines always excludes the more distant.

See parallel rule of English law, p. 382.

742.

In the collateral line, representation is admitted in favour of children and descendants of brothers and sisters of the deceased, whether they come to the succession concurrently with uncles or aunts, or whether all the brothers and sisters of the deceased being previously dead, the succession is found to be devolved upon their descendants in equal or unequal degrees.

See parallel rule of English law, p. 382.

743.

In all cases where representation is admitted, the petition is effected by stocks: if one original stock have produced several branches, the subdivision is made also by stocks in each branch, and the members of the same branch make distribution between themselves by heads.

See parallel principle of English law, p. 382.

744.

There is no representation of persons living, but only of those who are civilly or naturally dead.

There can be no representation of a person, the succession to whom is renounced.

See parallel principle of English law, p. 382.

Section III.

Of Successions Devolving upon Descendants.

745.

Children or their descendants succeed to their father and mother, grandfathers, grandmothers, or other ancestors, without distinction of sex or primogeniture, and although they be the issue of different marriages.

They succeed by equal portions and by heads when they are all in the first degree and called in their own right: they succeed by stocks, when they come all or in part by representation.

See parallel principle of English law, p. 382, 3.

Section IV.

Of Successions devolving upon Ancestors.

746

If the deceased has left neither posterity, nor brother, nor sister, nor descendants from them, the succession is divided into moieties between the ancestors of the paternal line and the ancestors of the maternal line.

The ancestor who is found in the nearest degree receives the moiety allotted to his line, to the exclusion of all others.

Ancestors in the same degree succeed by heads.

See parallel principle of English law, p. 383.

747.

Ancestors succeed, to the exclusion of all others, to things by them given to their children or descendants dead without issue, when the objects given are found again in kind in the succession.

If the objects have been alienated, the ancestors receive the price which may be therefore due. They succeed also to the action for recovery which the donee may have.

No parallel English principle.

748.

When the father and mother of a party dead without issue have survived him, if he has left brothers, sisters, or descendants from them, the succession is divided into two equal portions, of which a moiety only devolves upon the father and mother, who share it equally between them.

The other moiety belongs to the brothers, sisters, or descendants from them, as shall be explained in section 5 of the present chapter.

See parallel principle of English law, p. 383.

749.

In the case where a person dead without issue leaves brothers, sisters, or descendants from them, if the father or the mother be previously dead, the portion which in such case would have devolved conformably to the preceding article, is re-united to the moiety accruing to the brothers, sisters, or their representatives, as shall be explained in section 5 of the present chapter.

See parallel principle of English law, p. 384.

Section V.

Of Collateral Successions.

750.

In case of the previous decease of the father and mother of a person dead without issue, his brothers, sisters, or their descendants are called to the succession, to the exclusion of the ancestors and other collaterals.

They succeed, either in their own right, or by representation, as has been regulated in section 2 of the present chapter.

See parallel rule of English law, p. 384.

751.

If the father and mother of the party dead without issue have survived him, his brothers, sisters, or their representatives are only called to a moiety of the succession.

If the father or the mother only has survived, they are called to the enjoyment of three-fourths.

See parallel rule of English law, p. 384.

752.

The distribution of the moiety or of the three-fourths devolved upon the brothers or sisters, according to the terms of the preceding article, is effected between them by equal portions, if they are all by the same bed; if they are by different beds, a division is made of a moiety between the two lines paternal and maternal of the deceased; the germanes take part in both lines, and the uterine relations and those on the father's side each in their own line only; if there are brothers and sisters on one side only, they succeed to the whole, to the exclusion of all the other relations of the other line.

See parallel rule of English law, p. 384.

753.

In default of brothers or sisters, or descendants from them, and in default of ancestors in one or other of the lines, the succession devolves as regards one moiety on the surviving ancestors; and as regards the other moiety, on the nearest relations of the other line.

If there be a competition of collateral relations in the same degree, they share by heads.

See parallel rule of English law, p. 384,

754.

In the case of the preceding article, the father or mother surviving has the usufruct of a third of the goods to which he does not succeed in property.

See parallel rule of English law, p. 384.

755.

Relations beyond the twelfth degree do not succeed. In default of relations capable of succeeding in one line, the relations of the other line succeed as regards the whole.

See parallel rule of English law, p. 384.

CHAPTER IV.

Of irregular Successions.

SECTION 1.

Of the Rights of Natural Children over the Property of their Father or Mother, and of the Succession to Natural Children dead without Issue.

756.

Natural children are not heirs; the law does not grant to such any rights over the property of their father or mother deceased, except when they have been legally recognised. It does not grant to them any right over the property of relations of their father or mother.

See the English law as to the rights of bastards to take an inheritance or distributive share, p. 384, 5.

757

The right of the natural child over the property of the father or mother deceased, is regulated in the following manner:

If the father or mother has left lawful descendants, such right extends to one-third of the hereditary portion which the child would have had if he had been legitimate: it extends to a moiety when the father or mother does not leave descendants, but ancestors, or brothers or sisters; to three-fourths when the father or mother does not leave either descendants or ancestors, or brothers or sisters.

See note to article 756.

758.

The natural child has a right to the whole of the property, when his father or mother does not leave relations of a degree capable of succeeding.

See note to article 756.

759.

In case of the previous decease of the natural child, his children or descendants may claim the rights fixed by the preceding articles.

See note to article 756.

760.

The natural child or his descendants are bound to deduct from what they have the right to claim, all which they have received from the father or the mother whose succession is opened, and which shall be subject to account, according to the rules established in section 2 of chapter 6 of the present title.

See note to article 756.

761.

All claim is forbidden them, when they have received in the lifetime of their father or mother, the half of what is allowed them by the preceding articles, with an express declaration on the part of their father or mother, that their intention is to reduce the natural child to the portion which they have assigned him.

In the case in which this portion shall be inferior to the half of what ought to come to the natural child, he shall not be at liberty to claim more than the additional sum necessary to complete such moiety.

See note to art. 756.

762.

The regulations of articles 757 and 758 are not applicable to children who are the fruit of adulterous or incestuous intercourse.

The law awards to them a subsistence merely.

See note to art. 756.

763.

This subsistence is regulated by consideration of the ability of the father or mother, and the number and quality of legitimate heirs.

See note to art. 756.

764.

When the father or mother of an adulterous or incestuous child shall have caused him to learn a mechanical art, or when one of them shall have secured to him a subsistence while living, the child cannot set up any claim against their succession.

See note to art. 756.

765.

The succession to a natural child deceased without issue, devolves upon his father or mother who may have acknowledged him; or by moieties to both, if he has been acknowledged by both.

See note to art. 756.

766.

In case of the previous decease of the father and mother of the natural child, the property which he has received from them passes to the legitimate brothers or sisters, if found in kind in the succession: actions for recovery, if any exist, on the price of such property alienated, if still due, revert equally to the legitimate brothers and sisters.

All other property passes to the natural brothers or sisters, or their descendants.

See note to art. 756.

Section 2.

Of the Rights of the Husband or Wife surviving, and of the State.

767.

When the deceased leaves neither relations of a degree capable of succeeding, nor natural children, the property of his succession belongs to the husband or wife (conjunct), not being divorced, who survives.

See the rights of the surviving husband or wife under the English law, p. 385.

768.

In default of husband or wife (conjunct) surviving, the succession is acquired by the state.

See the English parallel law, p. 385.

769.

The husband or wife (conjunct) surviving, and the administration of the domains, who claim right to the succession, are bound to cause seals to be affixed, and to have an inventory made in the forms prescribed for the acceptance of successions under privilege of inventory.

See note to art. 782, 93, 4.

770.

They must demand the being put in possession in the court of first instance within the jurisdiction of which the succession is opened. The court cannot decree on such petition until after three publications and notices in the usual forms, and after having heard the king's attorney.

See note to preceding article.

771.

The spouse surviving is also bound to convert into money the personal property, or to give sufficient security to assure its restoration, in case heirs of the deceased should present themselves within the space of three years: after such delay, the security is discharged.

See note to art. 767.

772.

The spouse surviving, or the administration of the domains who shall not have complied with the formalities respectively prescribed to them, may be condemned to damages and interest towards the heirs, if any such appear.

See note to art. 769 and 771.

773.

The regulations of articles 769, 770, 771, and 772 are common to natural children summoned for want of relations.

See parallel English law, p. 384, 5,

CHAPTER V.

Of the Acceptance and Repudiation of Successions.

Section 1.

Of Acceptance.

774.

A succession may be accepted simply and absolutely, or under privilege of inventory.

The English law proceeds on an entirely different footing from the French and Civil law; but see as parallel, p. 386.

775.

No one is bound to accept a succession which has fallen to him.

See the parallel English law, p. 386, and note to preceding article.

776.

Married women are incapable of a valid acceptance of a succession without the authority of their husbands or of act of law, conformably to the regulations of chapter 6, under the title "*Of Marriage.*"

Successions falling to minors and interdicted persons, cannot be validly accepted but in conformity to the regulations of the title "*Of Minority, Guardianship, and Emancipation.*"

See note to art. 774, and parallel English law, p. 387.

777.

The effects of acceptance have relation back to the day of the opening of the succession.

See parallel English law, p. 387.

778.

Acceptance may be express or tacit; it is express, when the title or quality of heir is assumed in an authentic or private act; it is tacit when the heir makes an act which necessarily supposes his intention of accepting, and which he would have no right to do but in his quality of heir.

See note to art. 774, and p. 387.

779.

Acts purely conservatory, of attention and provisional administration, are not acts of acceptance (addition) of heirship, if the title or quality of heir have not been assumed.

See note to art. 774, and a parallel principle of English law, p. 387.

780.

Donation, sale, or conveyance of his successional rights made by one coheir, either to a stranger, or to all the other coheirs, or to some one of them, imports on his part acceptance of the succession.

It is the same 1st, With a renunciation, though gratuitous, made by one of the heirs, in favour of one or more of his coheirs.

2nd. With a renunciation made even to the advantage of all the coheirs without distinction, when he receives the price of his renunciation.

See note to art. 774, and parallel principle of English law, p. 387.

781.

When he to whom a succession has fallen is dead without having repudiated it, or without having accepted it expressly or tacitly, his heirs may accept or repudiate it in his right.

See note to art. 774, and a parallel principle of English law, p. 388.

782.

If the heirs cannot agree in accepting or rejecting the succession, it must be accepted under privilege of inventory.

This species of possession under benefit of inventory, is totally unknown to the English law.

783.

One of full age cannot impeach an express or tacit acceptance made by him of a succession, except in the case where such acceptance shall have been the consequence of a fraud practised against him: he can never disclaim it under pretext of hardship, excepting only in the case where the succession is found to be absorbed or diminished more than half, by the discovery of a will unknown at the moment of acceptance.

See note to art. 774, and a parallel principle of English law, p. 388.

Section 2.

Of the Renunciation of Successions.

784.

Renunciation of a succession is not to be presumed: moreover, it can only be made at the registry of the court of first instance within the circle where the succession is opened, or a particular register kept for this purpose.

See the parallel English law, p. 388, and note to art. 774.

785.

The heir who renounces, is considered as never having been heir.

See note to art. 774, and p. 388.

786.

The share of the party renouncing is added to his coheirs; if he be the only one, it devolves upon the next degree.

See note to art. 774 and 784.

787.

Parties can never come in as representatives of an heir who renounces: if the party renouncing is the sole heir in his own degree, or if all his coheirs renounce, the children come in, in their own right, and succeed by heads.

See note to art. 774 and 784.

788.

The creditors of a party renouncing to the prejudice of their rights, may cause themselves to be authorized by law to accept the succession in right of their debtor, in his place and stead.

In such case, the renunciation is annulled merely in favour of the creditors, and up to the amount only of their claims; it is not so as respects the advantage of the heir who has renounced.

No parallel principle of English law; and see note to art. 784.

789.

The power of accepting or repudiating a succession, is prescribed by the lapse of time required for the longest prescription respecting claims to real property.

No parallel principle of English law; and see note to art. 784.

790.

So long as prescription of the right to accept has not been acquired against heirs who have renounced, they have the ability still of accepting the succession, if it has not been already accepted by other heirs: without prejudice, nevertheless, to the rights which may be acquired by third persons over the property of the succession, whether by prescription, or by acts validly made with the curator to the vacant succession.

See note to preceding article.

791.

A party cannot, even by contract

of marriage, renounce the succession to a living person, nor alienate the eventual claims which he may have to such succession.

See parallel principle of English law, p. 388.

792.

The heirs who shall have conveyed away or concealed the goods of a succession are deprived of the power of renouncing it: they become heirs simply and absolutely, notwithstanding their renunciation, without power to claim any share in the objects conveyed away or concealed.

See a parallel principle of English law, p. 388, 9.

SECTION 3.

Of the Privilege of Inventory, of its Effects, and of the Obligations of the Beneficiary Heir.

793.

The declaration of an heir, that he does not mean to assume this quality except under the privilege of an inventory, ought to be made at the registry of the civil court of first instance of the circle in which the succession is opened: it must be inscribed on the register destined to receive acts of renunciation.

The benefit of inventory is unknown to the English law. See p. 389.

794.

This declaration has no effect unless it is preceded or followed by a faithful and exact inventory of the goods of the succession, in the forms regulated by the laws upon that proceeding, and within the intervals which shall be hereafter determined.

See note to preceding article.

795.

The heir has three months to form an inventory, computing from the day on which the succession is opened.

He has moreover, for the purpose of deliberating on his acceptance or renunciation, a delay of forty days, which began to run from the day on which the three months allowed for the inventory expire, or from the day of closing the inventory, if it has been finished before the three months.

See note to article 793.

796.

If, however, there are in the succession objects liable to perish, or expensive in their preservation, the heir may, in his quality of capable to succeed, and without being liable to inference of an acceptance on his part, cause himself to be authorized by act of law to proceed to a sale of such effects.

Such sale ought to be made by the public officer, after notices and publications regulated by laws relating to that procedure.

See note to article 793.

797.

During the continuance of the intervals for making the inventory and for the deliberation, the heir cannot be compelled to assume this quality, and sentence cannot be obtained against him; if he renounce when those intervals are expired, or before, the expenses legally incurred by him up to that period are to be charged upon the succession.

See note to article 793.

798.

After the expiration of the intervals above mentioned, the heir, in case of suit against him, may demand a new delay, which the court which has possession of the suit may grant or refuse according to circumstances.

See note to article 793.

799.

The expenses of the prosecution, in the case of the preceding article, are at the charge of the succession, if the heir can prove either that he had not any knowledge of the death, or that the delays were insufficient, whether by reason of the situation of the property, or by reason of disputes having arisen; if he can bring no proof thereon, the expenses remain at his personal charge.

See note to article 793.

800.

The heir preserves nevertheless, after the expiration of the delays granted by art. 795, and also of those allowed by the judge conformably to article 798, the faculty of still making an inventory and of constituting himself heir beneficiary, if he has not otherwise done an act of heirship, or if there does not exist against him a judgment passed by force of a matter decided, which condemns him in the quality of simple and absolute heir.

See note to article 793.

801.

The heir who is found guilty of concealing or who has omitted knowingly of bad faith, to comprehend in the inventory some effects of the succession, is deprived of the privilege of the inventory.

See note to article 793.

802.

The effect of the privilege of the inventory is to give to the heir the advantage—

1st. Of not being bound to payment of the debts of the succession except to the amount of the value of the goods collected by him, besides the power of discharging himself from the payment of the debts, by abandoning all the goods of the succession to the creditors and legatees.

2nd. Of not confounding his personal property with that of the succession, and of preserving towards it the right of claiming the payment of his own demand.

See note to article 793, and p. 389.

803.

The beneficiary heir is charged to administer the goods of the succession, and must render an account of his administration to the creditors and legatees.

He cannot be compelled by his own property until after he has been in arrear in rendering his account, and in default of having satisfied this obligation.

After the settling of the account, he can only be answerable in his own personal property to the amount of the sums remaining in his hands.

See note to article 793.

804.

He is only responsible for serious faults in the administration with which he is invested.

See note to article 793.

805.

He cannot sell the moveables of the succession but by the agency of a public officer, by auction, and after public notices and the accustomed publications.

If he present them in kind he is only responsible for the depreciation or deterioration caused by his own negligence.

See note to article 793.

806.

He can only sell the immoveable property in the forms prescribed by the laws on this procedure; he is bound to pay over the price thereof to the mortgage creditors who make themselves known.

See note to article 793.

807.

He is bound, if the creditors or other persons interested require it, to give good and sufficient security for the value of the moveables comprised in the inventory, and for the portion of the price of the immoveable property not paid over to mortgage creditors.

In failure of this security to be furnished by him, the moveable property is sold, and the price is deposited, as well as the unappropriated portion of the price of the immoveable property, to be employed in the acquittance of the charges on the succession.

See note to article 793.

808.

If there are opposing creditors, the beneficiary heir can only pay in the order and in the manner directed by the judge.

If there are not opposing creditors,

he pays the creditors and the legatees as soon as they present themselves.

See note to article 793.

809.

Creditors not opposing, who do no appear until after the settling of the account and the payment of the balance, have no redress to exercise except against the legatees.

In both cases such redress is prescribed by the lapse of three years, to be computed from the day of the settling of the accompt and from the payment of the residue.

See note to article 793.

810.

The expenses of the seals, if any have been affixed, of the inventory and of the account, are at the charge of the succession.

See note to article 793.

Section 4.

Of vacant Successions.

811.

When after the expiration of the delays for making the inventory and for deliberating, no person appears who claims a succession, there is no heir known, or the known heirs have renounced, such succession is taken to be vacant.

See the English law in such case, p. 390, and p. 385.

812.

The court of first instance within the circle in which it is opened, names a curator on the petition of the persons interested, or on the requisition of the king's attorney.

See note to preceding article.

813.

The curator in a vacant succession is bound, before everything, to certify the state thereof by an inventory: he exercises and prosecutes the rights belonging to it: answers demands formed against it: he administers on condition of causing the money arising from the succession, as well as that produced by the sale of the moveables or immoveables, to be paid into the hands of the receiver of royal revenues, for the preservation of their rights, and on condition of rendering account to whomsoever it shall belong.

See note to article 812.

814.

The regulations of section 3 of the present chapter, on the forms of the inventory, on the mode of administration, and on the account to be rendered on the part of the heir beneficiary, are furthermore common to the curators of vacant successions.

See note to article 811, and to article 793.

CHAPTER VI.

Of Division and Restitution.

Section 1.

Of the Action for Division and of its Form.

815.

No one can be compelled to remain without division, and distribution may be always sued for, notwithstanding prohibitions and conventions to the contrary.

The distribution may nevertheless be suspended by agreement during a limited time; such agreement cannot be made obligatory beyond five years; but it may be renewed.

See parallel English law, p. 390.

816.

The distribution may be demanded even though one of the coheirs shall have enjoyed separately a part of the goods of the succession, if there have not been an act of distribution, or sufficient possession to acquire a prescriptive right.

See parallel English law, p. 390, 1.

817.

The action for distribution, with respect to coheirs, minors, or interdicted persons, may be exercised by their guardians, specially authorized by a family council.

With respect to absent coheirs, the action belongs to the relations put in possession.

See parallel English law, p. 391; and as to family council, note to article 405.

818.

The husband may, without the concurrence of his wife, claim a distribution of objects, moveable or immoveable, fallen to her and which come into community: with respect to objects which do not come into community, the husband cannot claim the distribution thereof without the concurrence of his wife; he can only demand a provisional distribution in case he has a right to the enjoyment of her property.

The coheirs of the wife cannot claim final distribution without suing the husband and his wife.

See parallel English law, p. 391.

819.

If all the heirs are present and of age, the affixing of the seals on the effects of the succession is not necessary, and the distribution may be made in the form and by such act as the parties interested judge convenient.

If all the heirs are not present, if there are among them minors or interdicted persons, the seal must be affixed with the least possible delay, whether at the request of the heirs, or on the prosecution of the king's attorney in the court of first instance, or officially by the justice of the peace within the circle in which the succession is opened.

No parallel English law.

820.

Creditors may also require the affixing of seals, by virtue of an executory title or of a permission from the judge.

No parallel English law.

821.

When the seal has been affixed, all creditors may make opposition thereto, although they have neither executory title nor permission from the judge.

The formalities for the removal of the seals and the formation of the inventory are regulated by the laws on the procedure.

No parallel English law.

822.

The action for distribution and the disputes which arise in the course of the proceedings, are submitted to the court of the place where the succession is opened.

It is before this court that auctions are held, and that petitions ought to be brought relative to the warranty of lots between copartners, as well as those for rescinding of the distribution.

See parallel English law, p. 391.

823.

If one of the coheirs refuse to consent to the distribution, or if disputes arise, either respecting the mode of proceeding therein, or on the manner of completing it, the court pronounces as in a summary matter, or commissions, if there be ground, one of the judges for the proceedings in the distribution, on whose report it decides the dispute.

See parallel English law, p. 392.

824.

The estimate of the immoveable property is made by competent persons (experts) chosen by the parties interested, or on their refusal nominated officially.

The statement of these persons must present the basis of the estimate: it must show whether the thing estimated can be conveniently divided; in what manner; in short to fix, in case of division, each of the parts which may be formed of it and their value.

See parallel English law, p. 392.

825.

The valuation of the moveables, if there have not been an appraisement made in a regular inventory, ought to be made by people conversant with these affairs, at a fair price, and without increase.

See English law on this subject, p. 392.

826.

Each of the coheirs may demand his own share in kind of the moveables and immoveables of the succession; nevertheless, if there are seising or opposing creditors, or if the majority of the coheirs deem a sale necessary for the discharge of the debts and incumbrances on the succession, the moveables must be sold publicly in the ordinary form.

See a parallel English law, p. 392; parallel article, 825, 6.

827.

If the immoveables cannot be commodiously divided, a sale by auction must be proceeded in before the court.

Nevertheless the parties, if all of age, may consent that the auction should be made before a notary, on the choice of whom they can agree.

See the rule of English law in parallel cases, p. 392.

828.

After the moveables and immoveables have been valued and sold, the judge appointed sends the parties (if there be ground for doing so) before a notary respecting whom they can agree, or one officially nominated if the parties cannot agree upon the choice.

They proceed before this officer to the accounts which the copartners may owe, to the formation of the general mass, to the composition of the lots, and to the supplies to be made to each of the copartners.

No exact English parallel law, but see parallel section throughout.

829.

Every coheir makes restitution of the estate according to rules which shall be hereafter established, of gifts he may have received, and of sums for which he is debtor.

See a parallel English law, p. 392, and post article 843 et seq.

830.

If the restitution is not made in kind, the coheirs to whom it is due may deduct a correspondent portion from the mass of the succession.

The deductions are made as far as possible, in objects of the same nature, quality, and goodness as the objects not restored in kind.

See note to article 829, and a parallel principle, p. 392.

831.

After these deductions, recourse is had on what remains in the mass, to the formation of so many equal lots as there are coheirs or stocks in coparcenary.

See note to article 829, and a parallel principle, p. 392, 3.

832.

In the formation and arrangements of the lots, parties must avoid as much as possible, disjointing estates and dividing works; and it is expedient, if it can be, to dispose in each lot the same quantity of moveables and immoveables, of rights or credits of the same nature and value.

See parallel principle of English law, p. 392, parallel art. 827.

833.

The inequality of the lots in kind is balanced by a return either in rent or in money.

See parallel principle of English law, p. 393.

834.

The lots are formed by one of the coheirs, if they can agree between themselves on a choice, and if the party elected accepts the commission; in the opposite case, the lots are made by a competent person appointed by the judge-commissary.

They are afterwards drawn at hazard.

See parallel principle of English law, p. 393.

835.

Before proceeding to draw the lots, each coparcener is admitted to offer his objections against their formation.

See parallel principle of English law, p. 393.

836.

The rules established for the division of the masses to be distributed are equally observed in the subdivision to be made between the coparcenary stocks.

A similar rule applies in the English law.

837.

If in the operations sent before a notary disputes should arise, the notary shall draw up a statement of the difficulties and of the respective allegations of the parties, and shall send them before the commissary nominated for the distribution; and, further, the forms shall be pursued which are prescribed by the laws on that procedure.

No exactly parallel English law.

838.

If all the coheirs are not present, or if there are amongst them interdicted persons, or minors although emancipated, the distribution must be made by act of law, conformably to the rules prescribed by article 819, and those following up to and including the preceding one. If there are many minors who have opposing interests in the distribution, a special and particular guardian must be appointed for each.

See a parallel principle of English law, p. 393.

839.

If there be ground for an auction, in the case of the preceding article, it cannot be made except by act of law with the formalities prescribed for the alienation of the property of minors. Strangers are always admitted thereto.

No exactly parallel English law.

840.

Distributions made conformably to the rules above prescribed, whether by guardians with the authority of a family council, or by minors emancipated, assisted by their curators, or in the name of absentees or persons not present, are final: they are only provisional, if the rules prescribed have not been observed.

See the parallel principle of English law, p. 393.

841.

Every person, even a relation of the deceased, not being in the order of succession (qui n'est pas son successible), and to whom a coheir shall have ceded his claim upon the succession, may be excluded from the division, either by all the coheirs, or by one only, on reimbursing him the price of such cession.

See parallel but dissimilar English law, p. 393.

842.

After the distribution, delivery must be made to each of the coparceners, of the particular titles to the objects which may have devolved to him. The titles to a property divided remain with him who has the greatest share, on condition of aiding therewith such of the coparceners as shall be interested therein, when it shall be required of him. Titles common to a whole inheritance are delivered to him whom all the heirs have chosen to be the depositary thereof, on condition of aiding therewith the coparceners, on every requisition. If there be a difficulty in the choice, it is regulated by the judge.

See parallel English law, p. 394.

Section 2.

Of Restitutions.

843.

Every heir, even beneficiary, coming to a succession, must restore to his coheirs, all he has received from the deceased by donation during life directly or indirectly: he cannot retain such gift nor claim a legacy left him by the deceased, unless such gifts and legacies have been given him expressly in addition (par preciput), and not subject to partition, or with a dispensation of restitution.

See the parallel English law on this subject, p. 394, 5.

844.

In the case even where gifts and legacies shall have been made in addition and with dispensation of restitution, the heir coming to distribution cannot retain them except to the amount of the disposable proportion : the excess is subject to restitution.

See note to preceding article.

845.

The heir who renounces a succession, may, nevertheless, retain a donation made during life, or claim a legacy given him, to the amount of his disposable proportion.

See note to article 843.

846.

A donee who was not heir presumptive at the time of the donation, but who has come into the order of succession on the day of opening the succession, must equally make restitution, unless the donor have dispensed therewith.

See note to article 183.

847.

Donations and legacies given to the son of him who is found to be successor at the period of opening the succession, are always taken to have been made with dispensation of restitution.

The father coming to the succession of the donor is not bound to make restitution.

See note to article 843.

848.

In like manner, the son coming in his own right to the succession of the donor, is not bound to restore a donation made to his father, even though he shall have accepted the succession to the latter: but if the son only comes by representation, he must restore a donation made to his father, even in the case where he shall have repudiated the succession.

See note to article 843.

849.

Donations and legacies made to the husband or wife of a party succeeding, are deemed to have been made with dispensation of restitution.

If the donations and legacies are made conjointly to the two married parties of whom one only is capable of succeeding, the other restores a moiety thereof; if donations are made to the married party capable of succeeding, restitution must be made of the whole.

See note to article 843.

850.

Restitution is only made to the succession of the donor.

See note to article 843.

851.

Restitution is due from him who has been employed for the establishment of one of the coheirs, or for the payment of his debts.

See note to article 843.

852.

The expenses of nourishment, of maintenance, of education, of apprenticeship, the ordinary expenses of equipment, those of marriage and customary presents, must not be restored.

See note to article 843.

853.

It is the same with respect to profits which the heir may have derived from contracts made with the deceased, if such contracts did not present any indirect advantage when they were made.

See note to article 843.

854.

In like manner restitution is not due in respect of partnerships formed without fraud between the deceased and one of his heirs, when the conditions thereof have been regulated by an authentic act.

See note to article 843.

855.

Immoveable property which has perished by accident, and without the fault of the donee, is not subject to restitution.

See note to article 843.

856.

The fruits and interests of things

subject to restitution are only due computing from the day on which the succession is opened.

See note to article 843.

857.

The restitution is due only from one coheir to another: it is not due to legatees nor to the creditors of the succession.

See note to article 843.

858.

The restitution is made in kind or by taking less.

See note to article 843.

859.

It may be demanded in kind, in the case of immoveables, as often as the immoveable given has not been alienated by the donor, and there are not in the succession immoveables of the same nature, value, and goodness, of which may be formed lots nearly equal for the other coheirs.

See note to article 843.

860.

The restitution only takes place by taking less when the donee has alienated the immoveable before the opening of the succession; it is due to the value of the immoveable at the date of the opening.

See note to article 843.

861.

In all cases reimbursements ought to be made to the donee of the expenses at which the object has been improved, regard being had to the augmented value as found at the time of distribution.

See note to article 843.

862.

Reimbursement should be made also to the donee of expenses necessarily incurred in the preservation of the object, although they have not improved the bulk.

See note to article 843.

863.

The donee on his part must give account of the injuries and deteriorations which have diminished the value of the immoveable, by his own act or through his fault and negligence.

864.

In the case where the immoveable has been alienated by the donee, the improvements or injuries caused by the purchaser must be charged conformably to the three preceding articles.

See note to article 843.

865.

When the restitution is made in kind, the property is re-united to the stock of the succession, free and quit of all charges created by the donee; but the mortgage-creditors may intervene in the distribution for the purpose of preventing a restitution being made in fraud of their claims.

See note to article 843.

866.

When the donation of an immoveable made with dispensation of restitution to one capable of succeeding exceeds his disposable portion, restitution of the excess is made in kind, if the retrenchment of such excess can operate advantageously.

In the contrary case, if the excess is above one moiety of the value of the immoveable, the donee must restore it in entirety, saving a deduction from the stock to the amount of his disposable portion; if such portion exceed half the value of the immoveable, the donee may retain the immoveable in entirety, on condition of taking less, and of recompensing the coheirs in money or otherwise.

See note to article 843.

867.

The coheir who makes restitution in kind of an immoveable, may retain the possession thereof until he has been reimbursed the sums due to him for expenses or improvements.

See note to article 843.

868.

The restitution of moveables is only made by taking less.

It is regulated on the basis of the value of the moveables at the time of the donation according to the estimatory statement annexed to the act; and in defect of such statement, according to a valuation by competent persons, at a fair price and without increase.

See note to article 843.

869.

The restitution of money given is made by taking less in the money of the succession.

In case of deficiency, the donee may free himself from restitution of the money by abandoning to the due amount the moveables, or in default of moveables, the immoveables of the succession.

See note to article 843.

Section 3.

Of Payment of Debts.

870.

The coheirs contribute among them to the payment of the debts and charges on the succession, each in the proportion to what he takes therein.

See the same principle, though differently carried into effect, in the English law, p. 395.

871.

The legatee by general title (a titre universel) contributes with the heirs proportionably to his emolument; but the particular legatee is not bound by debts and charges, saving, however, a mortgage on the immoveable bequeathed.

See the parallel principle of English law, p. 395, 6.

872.

When some of the immoveables of a succession are encumbered with rents by a special mortgage, each of the coheirs may require that the rents should be redeemed, and the immoveables rendered free, before they proceed to the formation of lots. If the coheirs make distribution of the succession in the state in which they find it, the immoveable encumbered ought to be estimated at the same rate as the other immoveables; a deduction of the capital of the rent is made from the total valuation; the heir within whose lot such immoveable falls, alone remains charged with the encumbrance of the rent, and he must indemnify his coheirs against it.

See the parallel principles of English law, p. 396.

873.

The heirs are bound by the debts and charges on the succession, personally for their part and individual portions, and conditionally for the whole; saving the remedy either against their coheirs, or against the general legatees, in proportion to the part in which they are bound to contribute thereto.

See the principle of English law on this point, p. 396, 7.

874.

The particular legatee who has discharged the debt with which the immoveable bequeathed was encumbered, enters by substitution into the rights of the creditor against the heirs and successors by general title (a titre universel).

See parallel principles of English law, p. 397.

875.

The coheir or successor by general title, who has paid, in consequence of the mortgage, more than his share of the common debt, has no resource against the other coheirs or successors by general title, except for such part as each of them ought personally to sustain, even in the case where the coheir having paid the debt shall have caused himself to be substituted into the rights of the creditors; without prejudice nevertheless to the rights of a coheir, who, by the effect of the privilege of inventory, shall have preserved the power of claiming payment of his personal demand, like every other creditor.

See the parallel principle of English law, p. 397.

876.

In case of the insolvency of one of the coheirs or successors by general title, his share in the mortgage debt is assessed upon all the others, in their respective proportions.

See the parallel principle of English law, p. 397.

877.

Executory demands against the deceased are in like manner executory against the heir personally; but the creditors nevertheless shall not be at liberty to pursue the execution thereof until eight days after the notification of such demands in person, or at the domicile of the heir.

See the parallel principle of English law, p. 397.

878.

They may demand, in all cases, and against every creditor, the separation of the patrimony of the deceased from that of the heir.

No parallel rule of English law.

879.

This right however can be no longer exercised, when there is a transfer in the claim against the deceased, by the acceptance of the heir as debtor.

No parallel rule of English law.

880.

Prescription takes place, with reference to moveables, by the lapse of three years.

With regard to immoveables, an action may be maintained as long as they are in the hands of the heir.

See the parallel principles of English law, p. 397.

881.

The creditors of the heir are not permitted to demand a separation of the patrimonies against the creditors of the succession.

See the English law on this subject, p. 397.

882.

The creditors of one coparcener, in order to prevent the making of distribution in fraud of their rights, may oppose its being done out of their presence; they have a right of interposing therein at their own charge; but they cannot impugn a distribution completed, provided however it has not been proceeded in without them, and in prejudice of an opposition formed by them.

See the English law on this subject, p. 397.

SECTION 4.

Of the Effects of Distribution and of the Warranty of the Lots.

883.

Each coheir is deemed to have succeeded alone and immediately to all the effects comprised in his lot, or fallen to him by auction, and never to have had any property in the other effects of the succession.

See a parallel principle of English law, p. 398.

884.

The coheirs are respectively sureties for each other, against those molestations and evictions only which proceed from a cause anterior to the distribution.

The guarantee does not take effect if the species of eviction suffered be excepted by a particular and express clause in the act of distribution; it ceases if it is by his own fault that the coheir suffers eviction.

See parallel principle of English law, p. 398.

885.

Each of the coheirs is personally bound, in proportion to his hereditary share, to indemnify his coheir against the loss which his eviction has caused him.

If one of the coheirs is found to be insolvent, the portion in which he is bound must be equally assessed upon the party indemnified and all the solvent coheirs.

See note to preceding article.

886.

The guarantee of the solvency of one who owes a rent cannot be made use of beyond the five years succeeding the distribution.

There is no ground for the warranty on account of the insolvency of a debtor where it has occurred subsequently to the distribution completed.

No parallel rule of English law.

SECTION 5.

Of Annulment of Distributions.

887.

Distributions may be rescinded for cause of violence or fraud.

There may also be ground for annulment where one of the coheirs establishes, to his own prejudice, an inequality of more than one-fourth. The simple omission of an object in the succession does not give room for an action for annulment, but merely for a supplement to the act of distribution.

See parallel principle of English law on this subject, p. 397, 8

888.

The action for annulment is admitted against every act which has for its object the putting an end to non-division (l'indivision) between the coheirs, although it be ratified by sale, by exchange, by composition, or in any other manner.

But after the distribution, or the act which supplies its place, the action for recision is no longer admissible against a composition founded upon the real difficulties presented by the first act, even though there should not have been process commenced upon this subject.

No exactly parallel English law.

889.

The action is not admitted against a sale of a successional right made without fraud to one of the coheirs, at his own risk and peril, by his other coheirs, or by one of them.

A similar principle would prevail in the English law.

890.

In order to judge if damage have been done, a valuation is made of the objects according to their value at the period of the distribution.

No exactly parallel English law.

891.

The defendant on a petition for annulment may arrest the progress thereof and prevent a new distribution, by tendering and furnishing to the plaintiff the supplement of his hereditary portion, either in money or in kind.

No parallel English law.

892.

The coheir who has alienated his lot in whole or in part, is no longer admissible to sustain an action for annulment on the ground of fraud or violence, if the alienation which he has made is subsequent to the discovery of the fraud, or to the cessation of the violence.

No exactly parallel English law, but see parallel article 1115.

TITLE II.

Of Donations during Life, and of Wills.

DECREED THE 3RD OF MAY, 1803. PROMULGATED THE 3RD OF THE SAME MONTH.

CHAPTER I.

General Regulations.

893.

A man may only dispose of his property by gratuitous title, by donation during life, or by will, in the form hereafter established.

See a parallel article of English law, p. 399.

894.

A donation during life (entre-vifs) is an act by which the donor deprives himself actually and irrevocably of the thing given, in favour of the donee who accepts it.

See definitions of the English law, p. 399, 400.

895.

A will is an act by which the testator disposes for the time when he shall no longer exist, of the whole or of part of his property, and which he is at liberty to revoke.

See parallel definition of English law, p. 400.

896.

Substitutions are prohibited.*

Every disposition by which the donee, the heir appointed, or the legatee, shall be charged to preserve and render to a third person, shall be null, even with regard to the donee, the heir appointed, and the legatee.†

* A material alteration in favour of substitutions was effected by a law of the 17th May, 1826, allowing them for the benefit of the children of the donor, born or to be born, to the second degree inclusively.

† See parallel but dissimilar principle of English law, p. 400.

897.

Excepted from the preceding article are those dispositions permitted to fathers and mothers, to brothers and sisters, in the sixth chapter of the present title.

See the English law on this point, p. 400.

898.

The disposition by which a third person shall be called to receive the donation, the inheritance, or legacy, in the case where the donee, the heir appointed, or the legatee, will not receive it, shall not be regarded as a substitution, and shall be valid.

No parallel English law.

899.

It shall be the same with a disposition during life or by will, by which the usufruct shall be given to one and the naked property to another.

See parallel English law, p. 400.

900.

In every disposition during life or by will, impossible conditions, such as shall be contrary to the laws and to morals, shall be reputed not written.

See parallel English law, p. 400, 1.

CHAPTER II.

Of the Capacity of disposing or of receiving by Donation during Life or by Will.

901.

In order to make a donation during life or by will, it is necessary to be of sane mind.

See parallel principle of English law, p. 401.

902.

All persons may dispose or receive, either by donation during life, or by will, excepting such as are declared incapable of doing so by the law.

See parallel principle of English law, p 401.

903.

A minor under the age of sixteen years is capable of disposing in no way, saving that which is ordained in chapter 9 of the present title.

See parallel principle of English law, p. 401.

904.

A minor who has reached the age of sixteen years can make disposition by will only, and to the amount of not more than half the property of which the law permits an adult to dispose.

See parallel principle of English law, p. 401.

905.

A married woman cannot make donation during life without the assistance or the special consent of her husband, or without being thereto authorized by the law, conformably to what is prescribed by articles 217 and 219, under the title "*Of Marriage.*"

She shall not need either the consent of her husband, or the authorization of the law, in order to dispose by will.

See parallel principle of English law, p. 401.

906.

In order to be capable of receiving during life, it suffices to be conceived at the moment of the donation.

In order to be capable of receiving by will, it suffices to be conceived at the period of the testator's death.

Nevertheless the donation or the will shall not have their effect except so far as the infant shall be born likely to live.

See parallel principle of English law, p. 401, 2.

907.

A minor, although arrived at the age of sixteen years, shall not be permitted, even by will, to make disposition for the benefit of his guardian.

A minor shall not be permitted, on arriving at majority, to make disposition either by donation during life, or by will, for the benefit of him who was formerly his guardian, unless the final accompts of the guardianship have been previously rendered and settled.

Excepted in the two cases above mentioned are the ancestors of minors, who are or who have been their guardians.

See parallel principle of English law, p. 402.

908.

Natural children shall not be permitted, by donation during life, or by will, to receive anything beyond what is accorded to them under the title "*Of Successions.*"

See a parallel principle of English law, p. 402.

909.

Doctors in physic or in surgery, officers of health and apothecaries, who shall have attended a person during the malady of which he dies, shall not be allowed to profit by donations during life, or by will, which such person shall have made in their favour in the progress of the disorder.

Excepted 1st, are remunerative dispositions made by particular documents, regard being had to the ability of the disposer and to the services rendered.

2nd. General dispositions, in the case of relationship even to the fourth degree inclusive, provided however the deceased has not heirs in direct line; unless he to whose profit the disposition has been made shall be himself among the number of such heirs.

The same rules shall be observed with regard to the minister of religion.

See parallel principle of English law, p. 402.

910.

Dispositions during life, or by will, for the benefit of hospitals, of the poor of a commune, or of establishments of public utility, shall not take effect, except so far as they shall be authorized by an ordinance of the government.

See parallel principle of English law, p. 402.

911.

Every disposition for the benefit of an incapacitated person shall be null, whether disguised under the form of a chargeable contract, or made under the name of substituted persons.

The fathers and mothers, the children and descendants, and the husband or wife of the incapacitated person shall be deemed substituted.

See parallel principle of English law, p. 402, 3.

912.

Dispositions shall not be allowed for the benefit of a foreigner, except in a case where such foreigner might be allowed to make disposition for the benefit of a Frenchman.

See parallel principle of English law, p. 403.

CHAPTER III.

Of the Portion of Goods that may be Disposed of, and of Reduction.

SECTION 1.

Of the Disposable Portion of Goods.

913.

Free gifts, whether by acts during life, or by will, shall not exceed the half of the property of the disposer, if he leave at his decease but one legitimate child; the third part if he leave two children; the fourth part if he leave three or more of them.

See parallel but totally dissimilar English law, p. 403.

914.

Comprehended in the preceding article, under the name of children, are descendants in any degree whatsoever; nevertheless they are only reckoned for the child whom they represent in the succession of the disposer.

See note to preceding article.

915.

Free gifts, by acts during life, or by will, shall not exceed a moiety of the property, if in default of children the deceased leaves one or more ancestors in both the paternal and maternal line; and three-fourths if he leave ancestors only in one line.

The property thus preserved for the benefit of ancestors shall be received by them in the order in which the law calls them to succeed; they shall alone enjoy the right to this reservation, in all cases in which a distribution in competition with the collaterals shall not have given them their disposable proportion of the goods at which it is fixed.

See note to article 913.

916.

In default of ancestors and descendants, free gifts by acts during life, or by will, may exhaust the whole of the property.

See note to article 913, and p. 403.

917.

If the disposition by act during life or by will is of an usufruct or life-annuity, of which the value exceeds the disposable proportion, the heirs for whose benefit the law makes a reservation, shall have the option either of executing such disposition, or of abandoning the property of the disposable proportion.

See note to article 913.

918.

The value in full property of goods alienated, whether charged with a life-annuity, or in purchase of an annuity (a fonds perdu), or with reservation of usufruct, to one succeeding in the direct line, shall be counted against the disposable proportion; and the excess, if there be any, shall fall into the mass. Such reckoning and such return cannot be demanded by such of the other persons succeeding in direct line as shall have consented to those alienations, nor in any case by those succeeding in the collateral line.

See note to article 913.

919.

The disposable proportion may be given in whole or in part, either by act during life, or by will, to children or others, successors of the donor, without being subject to restitution by the donee or legatee coming to the succession, provided the disposition have been made expressly by title of addition (preciput) or beyond the share,

The declaration that the gift or legacy is by title of addition or beyond the share, may be made, either by the act which shall contain the disposition, or subsequently in the form of dispositions during life, or by will.

See note to article 913.

Section 2.

Of the Reduction of Donations and Legacies.

920.

Dispositions, either during life or by reason of death, which shall exceed the disposable proportion, shall be reducible to such proportion at the opening of the succession.

See note to article 913.

921.

The reductions of dispositions during life shall not be demanded except by those for whose profit the law makes the reservation, by their heirs or assigns; the donees, legatees, and creditors of the deceased shall not be allowed to demand such reduction, nor to profit by it.

See note to article 913.

922.

The reduction is settled by forming one mass of all the property existing at the decease of the donor or testator. Such property is fictitiously added thereto as he shall have disposed of by donations during life, according to their condition at the period of such donations, and their value at the time of the donor's death. A calculation is made upon the whole property, after having deducted the debts, what with regard to the quality of the heirs whom he leaves, is the portion he was empowered to dispose of.

See note to article 913.

923.

Donations during life shall never be reduced, until after having exhausted the value of all the property comprised in the testamentary dispositions; and when such reduction shall be necessary, it shall be made by commencing with the last donation, and so proceeding backwards from the later to the earlier ones.

See note to article 913.

924.

If the reducible donation during life has been made to one succeeding, he may retain, out of the property bestowed, the value of the portion which belongs to him as heir, in goods not disposable if they are of the same nature.

See note to article 913.

925.

When the value of the donations during life shall exceed or equal the disposable proportion, all the testamentary dispositions shall be lapsed.

See note to article 913.

926.

When the testamentary dispositions shall exceed either the disposable portion, or the part of such portion which shall remain after having deducted the value of the donations during life, the reduction shall be made proportionably, without any distinction between universal and particular legacies.

See note to article 913.

927.

Nevertheless in all cases where the testator shall have expressly declared his intention to be, that any legacy should be discharged in preference to others, such preference shall take place; and the legacy which shall be the object thereof shall not be reduced, except by so much as the value of the others shall not make up the legal reservation.

See note to article 913.

928.

The donee shall restore the fruits of that which shall exceed the disposable portion, computing from the day of the donor's decease, if the demand for reduction has been made within the year; if not, from the day of such demand.

See note to article 913.

929.

Immoveables recovered by the effect of the reduction shall be so unencumbered by the debts or mortgages of the donee.

See note to article 913.

930.

The action for reduction or reclaim may be maintained by the heirs, against third persons detaining immoveables forming part of donations and alienated by the donees, in the same manner and in the same order as against the donees themselves, execution on the donees' goods having been previously levied. This action must be maintained in the order of the dates of the alienations, beginning with the most recent.

See note to article 913.

CHAPTER IV.

Of Donations during Life.

SECTION I.

Of the Form of Donations during Life.

931.

All acts forming donation during life shall be passed before notaries, in the ordinary form of contracts;* and an original minute thereof shall remain (with the notary), on pain of nullity.†

* See parallel rule of English law, p. 403, 4.

† The notarial system being unknown to the English law for civil, though otherwise for some commercial purposes, there is no parallel to this clause.

932.

A donation during life shall not bind the donor, or produce any effect, except from the day on which it shall have been accepted in express terms.

The acceptance may be made, while the donor is living, by a subsequent and authentic act, of which an original (minute) shall remain; but then the donation shall only have effect with regard to the donor, from the day on which the act which shall verify such acceptance shall have been notified to him.

See parallel but dissimilar English law, p. 404.

933.

If the donee be of age, the acceptance must be made by him, or in his name, by a person constituted by his power of attorney, giving a power to accept the donation made, or a general power of accepting donations which shall have been or which may be made.

Such authority ought to be executed before notaries; and a copy thereof must be annexed to the original of the donation, or to the original of an acceptance made by a separate act.

See note to preceding article.

934.

A married woman cannot accept a donation without the consent of her husband, or, in case of her husband's refusal, without the authority of the law, conformably to what is prescribed by articles 217 and 219, under the title "*Of Marriage*."

See note to article 932.

935.

A donation made to a minor not emancipated, or to an interdicted person, must be accepted by his guardian, conformably to article 463, under the title "*Of Minority, Guardianship, and Emancipation.*"

A minor emancipated may accept with the assistance of his curator.

Nevertheless the father and mother of the minor emancipated or not emancipated, or the other ancestors, even during the life of the father or mother, may, though neither the tutors nor curators of the minor, accept from him.

See note to article 932.

936.

A person deaf and dumb, who knows how to write, may accept himself, or by power of attorney.

If he is unable to write, the acceptance must be made by a curator nominated for this purpose, according to the rules established under the title "*Of Minority, Guardianship, and Emancipation.*"

See note to article 932.

937.

Donations made for the benefit of hospitals, of the poor of a commune, or of establishments for public utility, shall be accepted by the managers of such communes or establishments, having been thereto duly authorized.

See note to article 932.

938.

A donation duly accepted shall be perfect by the simple consent of the parties; and the property in the objects bestowed shall be transferred to the donee without necessity of any other conveyance.

See note to article 932.

939.

When there shall be a donation of property capable of being mortgaged, the transcription of the documents containing the donation and acceptance, as well as the notification of the acceptance which shall have taken place by separate act, ought to be made at the offices for mortgages within the circle in which the property is situated.

See note to article 932.

940.

Such transcription shall be made at the instance of the husband, when the property shall have been given to his wife; and if the husband does not satisfy such formality, the wife may proceed to do so without authority.

When the donation shall be made to minors, to interdicted persons, or to public establishments, the transcription shall be made at the instance of the guardians, curators, or managers.

See note to article 932.

941.

The want of transcription may be objected by all persons having interest, except those however whose duty it is to cause the transcription to be made, or their assigns, and the donor.

See note to article 932.

942.

Minors, interdicted persons, married women, shall not be reinstated after default of acceptance or transcription of donations; saving the remedy against their guardians or husbands, if occasion be, and without restitution being allowed even in the case where the said guardians and husbands shall be found insolvent.

See note to article 932.

943.

A donation during life shall only comprehend the present property of the donor; if it comprehend future property, it shall in that respect be null.

See parallel rule of English law, p. 404.

944.

Every donation during life made under conditions, the execution of which depends on the single will of the donor, shall be void.

See parallel principle of English law, p. 405.

945.

It shall be in like manner null, if it have been made under the condition of discharging other debts or encumbrances than those which existed at the period of the donation, or which shall be expressed either in the act of donation, or in the statement which ought to be thereto annexed.

See a parallel English law, p. 405.

946.

In a case where the donor has reserved to himself the liberty of disposing of an article comprehended in the donation, or of a fixed sum in the property bestowed; if he dies without having disposed thereof, the said article or the said sum shall belong to the heirs of the donor, notwithstanding any clauses or stipulations to the contrary.

See parallel English law, p. 405.

947.

The four preceding articles do not apply to donations whereof mention is made in chapters 8 and 9 of the present title.

See the notes to the articles in those chapters.

948.

An act of donation of moveable property shall be valid only for effects of which an estimatory statement, signed by the donor and the donee, or those who accept for him, shall have been annexed to the minute of the donation.

No parallel English law.

949.

The donor is permitted to make a reserve for his own benefit, or to dispose, for the benefit of another, of the enjoyment or usufruct of the moveable or immoveable property bestowed.

See parallel English law, p. 405, 6.

950.

When the donation of moveable effects shall have been made with a reservation of usufruct, the donee shall be bound, at the expiration of the usufruct, to take the goods bestowed which shall be found in being, in the state in which they are; and he shall have an action against the donor or his heirs, by reason of articles not in existence to the amount of the value which shall have been given them in the estimatory statement.

See parallel principle of English law, p. 406.

951.

The donor may stipulate for the right of a return of the objects bestowed, either in case of the previous decease of the donee only, or in case of the previous decease of the donee and of his descendants.

This right shall not be contracted for except for the benefit of the donor only.

See parallel principle of English law, p. 406.

952.

The effect of the right of return shall be to rescind all alienations of property bestowed, and to cause such property to revert to the donor, free and quit of all charges and mortgages, saving nevertheless the mortgage of dowry and of matrimonial contracts, if the other property of the married party donor does not suffice, and in the case only where the donation shall have been made to the party by the same contract of marriage, from which result such rights and mortgages.

See parallel principle of English law, p. 406.

SECTION 2.

Of Exceptions to the Rule on the Irrevocability of Donations during Life.

953.

A donation during life shall not be revoked except for cause of the non-performance of the conditions under which it shall have been made,* for cause of ingratitude,† and by reason of the unexpected birth of children.

* See parallel principle of English law, p. 406, 7.

† No parallel principle of English law.

954.

In the case of revocation on account of non-performance of conditions, the property shall return into the hands of the donor, free of all charges and mortgages on account of the donee; and the donor shall have, against third persons detaining immoveable property bestowed, all the rights which he would have had against the donee himself.

See parallel principle of English law, p. 407.

955.

A donation during life shall not be revoked on account of ingratitude, except in the following cases. 1st, If the donee have attempted the life of the donor; 2nd, If he have become guilty of cruelty, crimes, or heinous injury towards him; 3rd, If he refuses him subsistence.

No parallel principle of English law.

956.

The revocation for non-performance of conditions, or for cause of ingratitude, shall never take place absolutely.

See parallel principle of English law, p. 407.

957.

Petitions for revocation on account of ingratitude ought to be made within a year, to be computed from the date of the crime imputed by the donor to the donee, or from the date at which the crime might have been known to the donor.

Such revocation cannot be petitioned for by the donor against the heirs of the donee, nor by the heirs of the donor against the donee, unless in the last case the action have been instituted by the donor, or unless he have died within a year after the crime.

No parallel principle of English law.

958.

Revocation on account of ingratitude shall prejudice neither alienations made by the donee, or mortgages and other real charges which he was able to impose on the object of the donation, provided that the whole be anterior to the inscription which shall have been made of the extract of the petition for revocation in the margin of the transcription prescribed by article 939.

In case of revocation, the donee shall be condemned to restore the value of the objects alienated, regard being had to the time of the petition and the fruits, computing from the day of such petition.

No parallel English law.

959.

Donations in favour of marriage shall not be revocable on account of ingratitude.

No parallel principle of English law.

960.

All donations during life made by persons who had no children or descendants actually living at the time of the donation, of what value soever such donations may be, and by what title soever they may have been made, and although they may have been mutual or remuneratory, even such as shall have been made in favour of marriage by others than the ancestors of the married parties, or by the married parties to each other, shall be absolutely revoked by the birth of a legitimate child to the donor, even of a posthumous one, or by the legitimation of a natural child by subsequent marriage, if it be born subsequently to the donation.

See parallel but dissimilar English law, p. 407.

961.

Such revocation shall take place although the child of the donor were conceived at the time of the donation.

See note to preceding article.

962.

A donation shall be in like manner revoked, even when the donee shall have entered into possession of the property bestowed, and when it shall have been suffered to remain by the donor after the birth of the child; without, nevertheless, the donee being bound to restore the profits received by him, of what nature soever they may be, except from the day on which the birth of the child, or his legitimation by subsequent marriage, shall have been notified to him by summons or other act in regular form; and this, although the petition for re-entry into the property bestowed shall only have been formed subsequently to such notification.

See note to article 960.

963.

The property comprised in the donation absolutely revoked, shall return to the patrimony of the donor, free of all charges and mortgages on the part of the donee, without liability to be affected, even subsidiarily, by the restitution of the dowry of the wife of such donee, by her previous claims or other matrimonial contracts; which shall take place even though the donation shall have been made in favour of the marriage of the donee and inserted in the contract, and though the donee shall be bound by way of security, by the donation, to the execution of the contract of marriage.

See note to article 960.

964.

Donations thus revoked shall not be revived or take effect anew, either by the death of the child of the donor or by any confirmatory act; and if the donor is desirous of conferring the same property on the same donee, either before or after the death of the child by whose birth the donation was revoked, he can only accomplish it by a new disposition.

See note to article 960.

965.

Every clause or agreement by which the donor shall have renounced his right to revoke a donation on account of the birth of a child, shall be regarded as null, and shall be incapable of producing any effect.

See note to article 960.

966.

The donee, his heirs or assigns, or others detaining things bestowed, cannot object prescription to make valid a donation revoked by the birth of a child, until after a possession of thirty years, which shall only begin to run from the day of the birth of the last child of the donor, though posthumous; and this, without prejudice to interruptions, such as of right.

See note to article 960.

CHAPTER V.

Of Testamentary Dispositions.

SECTION 1.

Of general Rules on the Form of Wills.

967.

Every person may dispose by will, either under the title of appointment of an heir, or under the title of legacy, or under any other denomination proper to manifest his will.

See parallel principle of English law, p, 408.

968.

A will cannot be made in the same document by two or more persons, either for the benefit of a third person, or under the title of a reciprocal and mutual disposition.

See parallel principle of English law, p. 408.

969.

A will may be an olographe, or made by public act, or in the mystic form.

The English law does not recognise these distinctions. See the English law as to the form of wills, p. 408, 9.

970.

An olographic will shall not be valid unless it be written throughout, dated and signed by the hand of the testator: it is not subjected to any other formality.

See note to preceding article.

971.

A will by public act is that which is received by two notaries in the presence of two witnesses, or by one notary in the presence of four witnesses.

See note to articles 969 and 931†.

972.

If the will is received by two notaries, it must be dictated to them by the testator, and it must be written by one of such notaries, as it is dictated.

If there be only one notary, it must equally be dictated by the testator, and written by such notary.

In both cases, it must be read over to the testator, in presence of the witnesses.

Express mention of the whole must be made.

See note to preceding article.

973.

This will must be signed by the testator; if he declare that he knows not how or is unable to sign, express mention shall be made of his declaration in the act, as well as of the cause which prevents him from signing.

See note to article 971.

974.

The will must also be signed by the witnesses; nevertheless in the country it shall suffice that one of the two witnesses signs, if the will is received by two notaries, and that two of the four witnesses sign if it is received by one notary.

See note to article 971.

975.

Neither of the legatees by what title soever they are so, nor their relations nor connexions even to the fourth degree inclusively, nor the clerks of the notaries by whom the acts shall be taken, shall be capable of being received as witnesses of the will by public act.

See parallel principle of English law, p. 409.

976.

When the testator shall be desirous of making a mystic or secret will, he shall be bound to sign his dispositions, whether he has written them himself, or whether he has caused them to be written by another. The paper which shall contain his dispositions, or the paper which shall serve as envelope, if there be one, shall be closed and sealed. The testator shall present it thus closed and sealed to the notary and to six witnesses at the least, or he shall cause it to be closed and sealed in their presence; and he shall declare that the contents of such paper are his will, written and signed by himself, or written by another and signed by him: the notary shall thereon draw up the act of superscription, which shall be written on the paper or on the sheet which shall serve for envelope; this act shall be signed as well by the testator as by the notary, together with the witnesses. All the above shall be done immediately and without diversion to other acts; and in case the testator, by an impediment happening subsequently to the signature of the will, is rendered unable to sign the act of superscription, mention shall be made of the declaration he shall have made on that subject, without it being necessary, in such case, to augment the number of witnesses.

See note to article 969.

977.

If the testator knows not how to sign, or if he were unable to sign when he caused his dispositions to be written, a witness shall be called to the act of superscription in addition to the number contained in the preceding article, who shall sign the act with the other witnesses; and mention shall be made therein of the cause for which such witness was called.

See note to article 969.

978.

Those who do not know how or who are unable to read, shall not be allowed to make dispositions in the form of a mystic will.

See note to article 969.

979.

In the case where a testator cannot speak but is able to write, he may make a mystic will, on condition that such will shall be written throughout, dated and signed with his own hand; that he shall present it to the notary and to the witnesses; and that at the head of the act of superscription, he shall write in their presence, that the paper which he presents is his will; after which the notary shall write the act of superscription, in which mention shall be made of the testator having written these words in presence of the notary and of the witnesses; and moreover everything observed which is prescribed in article 976.

See note to article 969.

980.

The witnesses called to be present at wills must be males, of age, subjects of the king, enjoying civil rights.

See parallel rule of English law p. 409.

SECTION 2.

Of particular Rules touching the Form of certain Wills.

981.

The wills of military men and of individuals employed in the armies, in whatever country, may be received by a commander of a batalion or squadron, or by any other officer of a superior rank, in presence of two witnesses, or by two military commissaries, or by one of such commissaries in presence of two witnesses.

See the English law as to nuncupative wills p. 410, 11; and further 1 Vict. c. 26, abolishing nuncupative wills.

982.

They may moreover be received, if the testator be sick or wounded, by the chief officer of health, assisted by the military commandant charged with the police of the hospital.

See note to preceding article.

983.

The dispositions of the above articles shall take place only in favour of those who shall be on a military expedition, or in quarters, or in garrison out of the French territory, or prisoners in an enemy's country; but those who are in quarters, or in garrison in the interior, shall not have the benefit thereof unless they shall be in a place besieged, or in a citadel or other place of which the gates shall be closed, and the communications cut off by reason of war.

See note to art. 981.

984.

The will made according to the form established above, shall be void six months after the testator shall have returned into a place in which he shall have the liberty of employing the ordinary forms.

See note to art. 981.

985

Wills made in a place with which all communication shall be intercepted, on account of the plague or other contagious distemper, may be made before the justice of the peace, or before one of the municipal officers of the commune in presence of two witnesses.

See note to art. 981.

986.

This disposition shall take place as well with respect to those who shall be attacked by such disorders, as to those who shall be in the places infected therewith, although they be not actually sick.

See note to art. 981.

987.

The wills mentioned in the two preceding articles, shall become void six months after the communications shall have been re-established in the place where the testator remains, or six months after he shall have passed into a place where they shall not be interrupted.

See note to art. 981.

988.

Wills made at sea, in the course of a voyage, may be received in manner following:

On board ships and other vessels of the king, by the officer commanding the vessel, or in his absence by him who supplies his place in the order of the service, one or other conjointly with the officer of administration, or with him who fulfils his functions.

And on board commercial vessels, by the supercargo of the ship, or him who performs his functions, one or other conjointly with the captain, the master or the commander, or in their absence by those who replace them.

In all cases such wills must be received in the presence of two witnesses.

See the English law on this point, embodied in the stat. 55 Geo. III., c. 60.

989.

On board the king's ships, the will of the captain or that of the officer of administration, and on board commercial vessels, that of the captain, of the master or commander, or that of the supercargo, may be received by those who stand next them in the order of service, on conforming themselves as to other points to the regulations of the preceding article.

See note to preceding article.

990.

In all cases, a double original shall be made of the wills mentioned in the two preceding articles.

See note to art. 988.

991.

If the vessel touch at a foreign

port in which resides a French consul, they who shall have received the will are bound to deposit one of the originals, closed or sealed, in the hands of such consul, who shall cause it to be transmitted to the minister of marine; and the latter shall cause it to be deposited among the rolls of the justice of the peace at the place where the testator was domiciled.

See note to article 988.

992.

On the return of the vessel to France, whether into the port of her fitting out, or into a different port from that of her fitting out, the two originals of the will, alike closed and sealed, or the one which shall remain, if the other have been deposited during the course of the voyage in conformity with the preceding article, shall be remitted to the office of the overseer of maritime inscription; such overseer shall transmit them without delay to the minister of marine, who shall order the deposit thereof according to the directions of the preceding article.

See note to article 988.

993.

Mention shall be made on the roll of the ship, in the margin, of the name of the testator, of the disposal which shall have been made of the originals of the will, whether into the hands of a consul, or to the office of an overseer of maritime inscription.

See note to article 988.

994.

The will shall not be regarded as made at sea, although it be in the course of a voyage, if at the time when it was made the ship had touched land, either foreign, or within the French dominion, where there was a French public officer; in which case it shall not be valid except so far as it shall have been drawn up according to those usual in the countries where it shall have been made.

See note to article 988.

995.

The above regulations shall be common to wills made by mere passengers, who shall not form part of the ship's crew.

See note to article 988.

996.

A will made at sea, in the form prescribed by article 988, shall only be valid where the testator shall die at sea, or within three months after he shall have landed, and in a place where he shall be able to renew it in the ordinary forms.

See note to article 988.

997.

A will made at sea must not contain any dispositions for the benefit of the officers of the vessel, unless they are relations of the testator.

See note to article 988.

998.

The wills comprehended in the preceding articles of the present section, shall be signed by the testators and by those who shall have taken them.

If the testator declare that he does not know how to or cannot sign, mention of his declaration shall be made, as well as of the cause which prevents his signing.

In cases where the presence of two witnesses is requisite, the will shall be signed at least by one of them, and mention shall be made of the cause for which the other shall not have signed.

See note to article 988.

999.

A Frenchman who shall be in a foreign country, may make his testamentary dispositions by act under his private signature, as is prescribed in article 970, or by authentic act, in the forms used in the place where such acts shall be made.

See parallel principle of English law, p. 410, parallel article 1000.

1000.

Wills made in a foreign country

can only be carried into effect on property situated in France, after having been registered in the office of the testator's domicile, if he have preserved one, otherwise at the office of his last known domicile in France; and in case the will shall contain dispositions of immoveables which shall be situated there, it must be moreover registered at the office of the place of such immoveables, without being chargeable with a double duty for it.

See parallel principle of English law, p, 410, 11.

1001.

The formalities to which different wills are subjected by the regulations of the present and of the preceding section, must be observed on pain of nullity.

See the notes to the preceding articles.

Section 3.

Of Institutions of Heir, and of Legacies in general.

1002.

Testamentary dispositions are either universal (universelles) or by universal title (a titre universel), or by particular title. Each of these dispositions, whether it have been made under the denomination of institution of heir, or whether made under the denomination of legacy, shall produce its effect according to the rules hereafter established for universal legacies (legs universels), for legacies by universal title, and for particular legacies.

The English law does not recognise any distinctions precisely similar to these, but see nearly parallel rules, p. 411.

Section 4.

Of the Universal Legacy.

1003.

A universal legacy is the testamentary disposition by which the testator gives to one or more persons the entirety (universalité) of the property which he leaves at his death.

See parallel definition of the English law, p. 411.

1004.

When at the decease of the testator there are heirs to whom a portion of his property is reserved by the law, such heirs are fully seised (saisie de plein droit) by his death of all the property of the succession; and the universal legatee is obliged to demand of them a delivery of the property comprehended in the will.

See the parallel English law, p. 412.

1005.

Nevertheless, in such cases, the general legatee shall have the enjoyment of the property comprehended in the will, computing from the day of the death, if the demand of delivery was made within a year from that event; if otherwise, such enjoyment shall only commence from the day of the demand legally made, or from the day on which such transfer shall have been voluntarily consented to.

No parallel English law; but see parallel articles, 1027 and 1015.

1006.

When at the decease of the testator there shall be no heirs, to whom a portion of his property shall be reserved by the law, the universal legatee shall be fully seised by the death of the testator, without being bound to demand a transfer.

See note to article 1004.

1007.

Every olographic will shall, before it is put in execution, be presented to the president of the court of first instance of the circle in which the succession is opened. Such will shall be opened, if it has been sealed. The president shall draw up a statement of the presentation, of the opening, and of the state of the will, which he shall order to be deposited in the hands of a notary appointed by himself.

If the will is in the mystic form, its presentation, its opening, its description, and its deposit, shall be made in the same manner; but the opening shall not be permitted except in the presence of those of the notaries and witnesses who signed the act of superscription, as shall be found on the spot, or those summoned.

See note to article 969, and parallel principle, p. 412.

1008.

In the case in article 1006, if the will is olographic or mystic, the universal legatee shall be obliged to procure himself to be put in possession by an ordinance of the president, placed at the bottom of a request, to which shall be joined the act of deposit.

See note to preceding article.

1009.

A universal legatee, who shall be concurrently with an heir to whom the law reserves a portion of the property, shall be liable for the debts and charges on the succession of the testator, personally for his own share and portion, and by way of mortgage for the whole; he shall also be bound to discharge all the legacies, saving the case of reduction, as it is explained in articles 926 and 927.

See parallel principle of English law, p. 412, and the notes to article 793.

Section 5.

Of Legacy by Universal Title.

1010.

A legacy by universal title is that by which the testator bequeaths part of the whole [quote part] of the property of which the law allows him to dispose, such as a half, a third, or all his immoveables, or all his moveables, or a certain share of all his immoveables, or of all his personalty.

Every other legacy forms only a disposition by particular title.

See note to article 1003, and p. 411.

1011.

Legatees by universal title shall be bound to demand delivery from the heirs to whom a portion of the property is reserved by the law; in their default from the general legatees, and in default to the latter, from the heirs called in the order established under the title "*Of Successions.*"

See note to article 1004.

1012.

The legatee by universal title shall be bound like the universal legatee, by the debts and charges of the succession of the testator, personally for his own share and portion, and by way of mortgage for the whole.

See note to article 1009.

1013.

When the testator shall only have disposed of part of the disposable portion, and shall have done so by universal title, the legatee shall be bound to discharge the particular legacies by contribution with the natural heirs.

See note to article 1002, and parallel article 793.

Section 6.

Of Particular Legacies.

1014.

Every free and simple legacy shall give to the legatee, from the day of the testator's decease, a right to the thing bequeathed, a right transmissible to his heirs or assigns.

Nevertheless, the particular legatee can only put himself in possession of the thing bequeathed, or claim the fruits or interests of it, to be computed from the day of his demand of delivery, made according to the order established by article 1011, or from the day on which such delivery shall have been voluntarily agreed to.

See parallel principle of English law, p. 412.

1015.

The interest or fruits of the thing bequeathed shall accrue for the benefit of the legatee, from the day of the death, and without his having sued at law.

1st. When the testator shall have expressly declared his desire, in this respect, in the will.

2nd. When an annuity or a yearly allowance shall have been bequeathed under title of maintenance.

See parallel principle of English law, p. 413.

1016.

The expenses of the demand of delivery shall be at the charge of the succession, provided nevertheless that it shall not cause any reduction of the legal reserve. The fees on registration shall be borne by the legatee: The whole if it have not been otherwise directed by the will. Every legacy may be registered separately, although such registration may profit no one but the legatee or his assigns.

No exactly parallel principle of English law; but see p. 413.

1017.

The heirs of the testator, or other persons bound to pay a legacy, shall be personally bound to discharge it, each in proportion to the share and portion in which he shall have been benefited by the succession. They shall be bound by way of mortgage for the whole to the extent of the value of the immoveables of the succession of which they shall be detainers.

No exactly parallel English law; but see p. 413.

1018.

The thing bequeathed shall be delivered with all necessary accessories, and in the state in which it shall be found on the day of the donor's death.

See parallel principle of English law; but see p. 413.

1019.

When he who has bequeathed the property of an immoveable, has afterwards augmented it by acquisitions, such acquisitions, though they be contiguous, shall not be deemed to form part of the legacy without a new disposition.

It shall be otherwise with embellishments, or new buildings formed on the estate bequeathed, or an enclosure with which the testator shall have enlarged the circumference.

See parallel English law, p. 414.

1020.

If before or after the will, the thing bequeathed has been mortgaged for a debt of the succession, or even for the debt of a third person, or if it is encumbered with an usufruct, he who ought to acquit such legacy is not bound to redeem it, unless he have been charged to do so by an express disposition of the testator.

See parallel English law, p. 414.

1021.

Where a testator shall have bequeathed an object belonging to another, the legacy shall be void, whether the testator were aware or not that it did not belong to him.

See parallel English law, p. 414.

1022.

When the legacy shall be of a thing undetermined, the heir shall not be bound to give it of the best quality, nor may he offer the worst.

See parallel principle of English law, p. 414.

1023.

A legacy made to a creditor shall not be deemed a compensation for his debt, nor the legacy made to a domestic a compensation for his wages.

See parallel English law, p. 414.

1024.

The legatee by particular title shall not be bound by the debts of the succession; * saving the reduction of the legacy as is said above, and saving the mortgage right of creditors. †

* No parallel English law.

† See parallel English law, p. 396, 7.

Section 7.

Of Testamentary Executors.

1025.

The testator may nominate one or more testamentary executors.

See parallel English law, p. 415.

1026

He may give them seisin of the whole or only of one part of his moveables; but it cannot continue beyond a year and a day, computing from his death.

If he has not given it them, they cannot demand it.

See parallel principle of English law, p. 415.

1027.

The heir may put an end to the seisin, by offering to place in the hands of the testamentary executors a sum sufficient for the payment of the personal legacies, or by guaranteeing such payment.

See parallel dissimilar principle of English law, p. 415.

1028.

He who cannot bind himself, cannot be a testamentary executor.

See parallel principle of English law, p. 415.

1029.

A married woman can accept testamentary executorship only with her husband's consent.

If she has separate property, either by the marriage contract or by judgment, she may accept it with her husband's consent, or upon his refusal, with legal authority, conformably to what is prescribed by articles 217 and 219, under the title "*Of Marriage.*"

See parallel principle of English law, p. 415.

1030.

A minor cannot be testamentary executor even with the authority of his guardian or curator.

See parallel principle of English law, p. 415.

1031.

Testamentary executors shall cause the seals to be affixed if there are minor, interdicted, or absentee heirs.

They shall cause to be made in the presence of the heir presumptive, or having duly summoned him, an inventory of the property of the succession.

They shall proceed to a sale of the moveables, on failure of sufficient money to pay the legacies.

They shall see that the will be executed; and they may, in case of dispute respecting its execution, interfere in order to sustain its validity.

They must, at the expiration of a year from the death of the testator, render an account of their management.

See parallel principles of English law, p. 416.

1032.

The powers of a testamentary executor shall not pass to his heirs.

See parallel principle of English law, p. 416.

1033.

If there are several testamentary executors who have accepted, one may act alone in default of the others; and they shall each be responsible for the whole of the account of the moveables, which was confided to them, unless the testator have divided their functions, and unless each of them is confined in that which has been allotted him.

See parallel principle of English law, p. 416.

1034.

The expenses incurred by a testamentary executor for the affixing of the seals, the inventory, the account, and the other expenses relative to their functions, shall be at the charge of the succession.

See parallel principle of English law, p. 416, 7.

Section 8.

Of the Revocation and of the Lapse of Wills.

1035.

Wills cannot be revoked, in whole or in part, except by a later will, or by an act before notaries, containing a declaration of the change of intention.

See the parallel English law, p. 417.

1036.

Later wills, not revoking in an express manner the preceding ones, shall only annul such dispositions contained in the latter, as shall be found incompatible with the new ones, or which shall be contrary.

See parallel similar principle of English law, p. 417.

1037.

A revocation made by a latter will shall produce its complete effect, although the new act remain unexecuted by reason of the incapacity of the heir instituted or of the legatee, or by reason of their refusal to accept.

No parallel English principle.

1038.

Every alienation, even that by sale with power of repurchase (rachat), or by exchange, which the testator shall make of the whole or of part of the thing bequeathed, shall import revocation of the legacy as respects all which has been alienated, although the posterior alienation be null, and the object be returned into the hands of the testator.

See parallel principle of English law, p. 417, 8.

1039.

Every testamentary disposition shall lapse if he in whose favour it has been made does not survive the testator.

See parallel similar principle of English law, p. 418.

1040.

Every testamentary disposition made under a condition dependant on an uncertain event, and such that, in the testator's intention, it must not be executed except so far as such event shall happen or not happen, shall be lapsed, if the heir instituted or the legatee dies before the accomplishment of the condition.

See parallel rule of English law, p. 418.

1041.

The condition which, in the testator's intention, only suspends the execution of the disposition, shall not prevent the instituted heir, or the legatee, from having a right vested and transmissible to his heirs.

See parallel principle of English law, p. 418.

1042.

The legacy shall lapse, if the thing bequeathed have totally perished during the life of the testator.

The same rule holds, if it have perished subsequently to his death, without the act and fault of the heir, although the latter has unduly delayed delivering it, when it would have perished in the hands of the legatee.

See parallel principle of English law, p. 418.

1043.

A testamentary disposition shall lapse, when the instituted heir or the legatee shall reject it, or shall be found incapable of receiving it.

See parallel principle of English law, p. 418.

1044.

There shall be accruer (accroissement) for the benefit of legatees, in the case where the legacy shall be made to several conjointly

The legacy shall be taken to be made conjointly when it shall be so by one single and the same disposition, and when the testator shall not have assigned the share to any of the co-legatees in the thing bequeathed.

See parallel principle of English law, p. 419.

1045.

It shall also be taken to be made

conjointly, when a thing which is not capable of being divided without deterioration, shall have been given by the same act to several persons, although separately.

No exactly parallel enactment in the English law; but the intention in such case would govern.

1046.

The same causes which, according to article 954 and the first two regulations of article 955, shall authorize the petition for revocation of the donation during life, shall be admitted for petition for revocation of testamentary dispositions.

See note to those articles, and parallel principle of English law, p. 419.

1047.

If such petition be founded on a serious injury done to the memory of the testator, it must be instituted within the year, to be computed from the date of the crime.

See note to preceding article.

CHAPTER VI.

Of Dispositions permitted in favour of the Grandchildren of the Donor or Testator, or of the Children of his Brothers and Sisters.

1048.

The property of which fathers and mothers have the power of disposing, may be given by them in whole or in part, to one or more of their children, by instruments during life or by will, with the charge of rendering such property to the children of the said donees, born or to be born, in the first degree only.

It must be remarked that the English law stands on a totally different footing, but as far as there can be any similarity, see parallel principle of English law, p. 419.

1049.

In case of death without children, the disposition shall be valid which a deceased shall have made by act during life or testamentary, for the benefit of one or more of his brothers or sisters, of the whole or part of his property not reserved by the law in the succession, with a charge of rendering such property to children born and to be born, in the first degree only, to the said donees' brothers and sisters.

See note to preceding article.

1050.

The dispositions allowed by the two preceding articles, shall only be valid as far as the condition of restitution shall be for the benefit of all the children born and to be born of the party subjected thereto, without exception or preference of age or sex.

See note to article 1048.

1051.

If in the cases mentioned above, the party charged with restitution for the benefit of his children dies, leaving children in the first degree and descendants of a child previously deceased, such last shall receive, by representation, the portion of the child previously deceased.

See the English law on this point, p. 420.

1052.

If the child, the brother or the sister to whom property shall have been given by act during life, without charge of restitution, accept a new gift made by act during life or testamentary, on condition that the property previously given shall be subject to such charge, they are no longer permitted to divide the two dispositions made for their benefit, or to renounce the second in order to hold the first, even though they should offer to render the property comprised in the second disposition.

See parallel principle of English law, p. 420.

1053.

The claims of parties appointed (in remainder) shall be opened at the period when, for any cause whatsoever, the enjoyment of the child, of the brother or sister charged with restitution, shall cease :* the previous renunciation of the enjoyment for the benefit of the parties appointed, shall not be permitted to prejudice the creditors of the party charged anterior to the abandonment. †

* See parallel principle of English law, p. 420.

† See parallel principle of English law, p. 774, 881, 2.

1054.

The wives of the parties charged cannot have, over the property to be rendered, subsidiary redress, in case of insufficiency of free property, except for the capital of dotal money, and in the sole case where the testator has expressly ordered it.

See parallel principle of English law, p. 420.

1055.

He who shall make the dispositions authorized by the preceding articles, shall be allowed to nominate, by the same act or by a later one, in authentic form, a guardian charged with the execution of such dispositions; such guardian cannot be excused except for one of the causes expressed in section 6 of chapter 2, of the title "*Of Minority, Guardianship, and Emancipation.*"

See parallel principle of English law, p. 420.

1056.

In default of this guardian, one shall be named at the instance of the party charged, or of his guardian if he be a minor, within the interval of a month, to be computed from the day of the decease of the donor or testator, or from the day subsequent to such death, on which the act containing the disposition shall have been known.

No parallel principle of English law.

1057.

The party charged, who shall not have satisfied the preceding article, shall be deprived of the benefit of the disposition; and in such case the right may be declared open for the benefit of the parties appointed in remainder, at the instance either of the parties appointed if they are of age, or of their guardian or curator if they are minors or interdicted persons, or of any relation of the party in remainder of age, minors or interdicted persons, or even officially at the instance of the king's attorney in the court of first instance in the place where the succession is opened.

No parallel principle of English law.

1058.

After the decease of one who shall have made disposition with charge of restitution, proceedings shall be taken in the ordinary forms, for forming the inventory of all the property and effects which shall compose his succession, excepting, however, the case where it relates to only one particular legacy. This inventory shall contain a valuation at a fair price of the moveables and moveable effects.

See the English law on this point, p. 420.

1059.

It shall be made at the request of the party charged with restitution, and within the delay fixed under the title "*Of Successions,*" in presence of the guardian named for its execution. The expenses shall be deducted from the property comprehended in the disposition.

See note to preceding article.

1060.

If the inventory has not been made by the request of the party charged within the interval above mentioned, proceedings shall be taken in the month following, at the instance of the guardian named for its execution, in presence of the party charged, or of his guardian.

No exact parallel Engish law; but see note to article 1058.

1061.

If the two preceding articles have

not been satisfied, the same inventory shall be proceeded in at the instance of the persons designated in article 1057, by calling thereto the party charged or his guardian, and the guardian named for the execution.

See note to preceding article.

1062.

The party charged shall be bound to take proceedings for a sale, by notices, and to the highest bidder, of all the moveables and effects comprised in the disposition, with the exception, however, of those of which mention is made in the two following articles.

No exact parallel in the English law; but see p. 421.

1063.

Household goods, and other moveable effects which shall have been comprised in the disposition, with the express condition of preserving them in kind, shall be restored in the state in which they shall be found at the period of restitution.

See ante, p. 350, the English principle governing in such case.

1064.

Cattle and implements serving for the cultivation of lands, shall be taken to be comprised in donations of such lands during life or testamentary; and the party charged shall only be bound to get them appraised and estimated, in order to render an equal value at the period of restitution.

See note to articles 522 and 524, on which this article is based.

1065.

An investment shall be made by the party charged, within the interval of six months, computing from the day of closing the inventory, of the ready money, of such as arises from the price of the moveables and effects which shall have been sold, and of that which shall have been received from debts owing.

Such interval may be prolonged, if there be ground for it.

No exactly parallel English law; but see p. 421.

1066.

The party charged shall be in like manner bound to invest money arising from debts owing which shall be recovered and from payments of rents, and this within three months at the latest, after he shall have received such money.

See note to preceding article.

1067.

This investment shall be made in conformity to what shall have been directed by the author of the disposition, if he have pointed out the nature of the effects in which the investment is to be made; if not, it can only be in immoveables, or with privilege over immoveables.

See note to article 1065.

1068.

The investment directed by the preceding articles shall be made in presence and at the instance of the guardian named for the execution.

See note to article 1065.

1069.

Dispositions by acts during life or testamentary, on condition of restitution, shall be, at the instance either of the party charged or of the guardian named for the execution, made public; that is to say, as regards immoveables, by the transcription of the acts into the registers of the office of mortgages of the place where they are situated; and as regards sums placed out with priority of claim over immoveables, by inscription on the property subject to such priority.

No exact parallel English law.

1070.

The want of transcription of the act containing the disposition, may be objected by creditors and third persons purchasers, even to minors or interdicted persons; saving the remedy against the party charged and against the guardian for the execution, and without minors and interdicted persons being capable of being reinstated against such failure of transcription, even though the tenant for life and the guardian be found insolvent.

No parallel English law.

1071.

The want of transcription cannot be supplied nor regarded as cured by the knowledge which creditors, or third persons creditors, might have had of the disposition by other means than that of transcription,

No parallel English law.

1072.

Neither donees, legatees, nor even the legitimate heirs of him who shall have made the disposition, nor in like manner their donees, legatees, or heirs, can in any case object to parties in remainder the want of transcription or inscription.

No parallel English law.

1073.

The guardian named for the execution shall be personally responsible, unless he has, in every point, conformed to the rules above established for verifying the property, for the sale of the moveables, for the investment of the money, for transcription and inscription, and in general if he have not used all necessary diligence, in order that the charge of restitution be well and faithfully performed.

See parallel principle of English law, p. 421.

1074.

If the party charged is a minor, he cannot, even in case of the insolvency of his guardian, be reinstated against failure in complying with the rules prescribed to him by the articles of the present chapter.

No exact parallel of English law required. See, by notes to each article on this chapter, whether there can be any such failure of complying.

CHAPTER VII.

Of Divisions made by the Father, Mother, or other Ancestors, among their Descendants.

1075.

The father and mother and other ancestors may make the division and distribution of their property among their children and descendants.

See the English law as to the power of person in such case, p. 421, and parallel article 1048.

1076.

These distributions may be made by acts during life or testamentary, with the formalities, conditions, and rules prescribed for donations during life and wills.

Divisions made by acts during life can only have present property for their object.

See the parallel English law, p. 421.

1077.

If all the property which the ancestor shall leave on the day of his death has not been comprised in the division, that portion of property which shall not have been comprehended therein shall be distributed conformably to law.

See as to intestacy book 3, tit. 1, which applies in the cases most similar in the English law.

1078.

If the division has not been made among all the children who shall exist at the time of the death and the descendants of those who have previously died, the division shall be entirely null. A new one may therefore be claimed in legal form, either by the children or descendants who shall not have received any portion thereof, or even by those among whom the distribution shall have been made.

See parallel English law, p. 421.

1079.

A division made by the ancestor may be impeached on account of inequality of more than a fourth; it may also be so in case it should result from the division and from the dispositions made in preciput, that one of the coparceners shall have an advantage greater than the law permits him.

No exactly parallel English law; but see the nearly reverse, p. 421.

1080.

The child who, for one of the causes expressed in the preceding article, shall impeach the division made by the ancestor, must advance the expenses of the estimate; and he shall bear them eventually, as well as the charges of the contest, if the objection is not founded.

See note to preceding article.

CHAPTER VIII.

Of Donations made by the Marriage Contract to the Parties, and to Children to be born of the Marriage.

1081.

Every donation during life of present property, though made by contract of marriage to the married parties, or to one of them, shall be subject to the general rules prescribed for donations * made under this title.

It shall not take place for the benefit of children to be born, except in the cases set forth in chapter 6 of the present title. †

* See the English view taken of a marriage contract, p. 421.

† See the parallel English law, p. 422.

1082.

The fathers and mothers, the other ancestors, the collateral relations of the married parties, and even strangers, may, by the contract of marriage, dispose of the whole or of part of the property which they shall leave at the day of their death, as well for the benefit of the married parties as for the benefit of children to be born of their marriage, in the case in which the donor shall survive the married party donee.

A similar donation, although made for the benefit only of the married parties or of one of them, shall be always, in the said case of survivorship by the donor, presumed to have been made for the benefit of the children and descendants to be born of the marriage.

See parallel principle of English law, p. 422.

1083.

The donation, in the form contained in the preceding article, shall be irrevocable, in this sense only, that the donor can no longer dispose of, by gratuitous title, the objects comprised in the donation, unless it be for moderate sums under the title of recompense or otherwise.

See parallel principle of English law, p. 422.

1084.

The donation by marriage contract may be made cumulatively of present and future property, in whole or in part, on condition that there shall be annexed to the act a statement of the debts and charges of the donor existing at the day of the donation; in which case it shall be competent to the donee, at the death of the donor, to take the present property, renouncing the residue of the property of the testator.

This is an arrangement unknown to the English law; but see a somewhat parallel principle, p. 422, and the notes to the whole chapter on successions in this Appendix.

1085.

If the statement of which mention is made in the preceding article has not been annexed to the act containing the donation of the present and future property, the donee shall be compelled to accept or reject such donation for the whole. In case of acceptance, he can only claim the property which shall be found in existence at the day of the donor's decease, and he shall be subject to the payment of all the debts and incumbrances of the succession.

See note to preceding article.

1086.

The donation by marriage contract in favour of married persons and of children to be born of their marriage, may furthermore be made, on condition of paying without distinction all the debts and incumbrances on the succession of the donor, or under other conditions, the execution of which might depend on his will, by whomsoever the donation shall have been made; the donee shall be bound to fulfil such conditions, unless he prefer renouncing the donation; and in case the donor, by the marriage contract, shall reserve to himself the liberty of disposing of an article comprised in the donation of his present property, or of a fixed sum to be taken out of the same property, the article or the sum, if he die without having disposed thereof, shall be taken to be comprised in the donation, and shall belong to the donee or to his heirs.

See note to articles 1084, and 953, 954, et seq.

1087.

Donations made by contract of marriage shall not be impeached, or declared null, under pretence of want of acceptance.

See ante parallel articles 932 to 942.

1088.

Every donation made in favour of marriage shall be lapsed, if the marriage do not follow.

See principle of English law in parallel cases, p. 422.

1089.

Donations made to one of the married parties, in the terms of articles 1082, 1084, and 1086, above-mentioned, shall become void, if the donor survive the married party donee and his posterity.

See principle of English law in parallel cases, p. 422.

1090.

All donations made to married persons by their marriage contract, shall, at the time of opening the succession of the donor, be reducible to the portion of which the law shall permit him to dispose.

See parallel English law, p. 422 and 403, parallel article 913.

CHAPTER IX.

Of Dispositions between Married Persons, either by Contract of Marriage, or during Marriage.

1091.

Wedded persons can, by the marriage contract, make reciprocally, or one of the two to the other, such donation as they shall deem proper, subject to the modifications hereafter expressed.

See parallel principle of English law, p. 423.

1092.

Every donation during life of present property, made between wedded persons by the marriage contract, shall not be deemed to have been made with condition of survivorship by the donee, unless such condition has been formally expressed; and it shall be subject to all the rules and forms above prescribed touching donations of this description.

See parallel principle of English law, p. 423,

1093.

The donation of future property, or of present and future property, made between wedded persons by marriage contract, whether single or mutual, shall be subject to the rules established by the preceding chapter, with regard to similar donations which shall be made to them by a third person; saving that it shall not be transmissible to the issue of such marriage, in case of the death of the wedded person donee before the other.

See notes to preceding chapter, and p. 423.

1094.

The husband can, either by marriage contract, or during the marriage, in case he shall leave neither children nor descendants, dispose in favour of his wife, absolutely, of every thing which he might dispose of in favour of a stranger, and in addition of the usufruct of the entirety of the portion of which the law prohibits the disposition to the prejudice of heirs.

And in case the husband donor shall leave children or descendants, he may give to his wife either a fourth absolutely, and another fourth in usufruct, or the moiety of all his property in usufruct only.

See note to preceding article, and p. 423.

1095.

A minor cannot by marriage contract give to his wife, either by single or mutual donation, except with the consent and assistance of those whose consent is requisite for the validity of his marriage; but with such consent he may give all that the law allows a husband of full age to give to his wife.

See parallel principle of English law, p. 423.

1096.

All donations, although entitled as during life, made between wedded persons during marriage, shall be always revocable.

The revocation may be made by the wife, without being thereto authorized by the husband, or by judicial authority.

Such donations shall not be revoked by the subsequent birth of children.

See parallel principle of English law, p. 423.

1097.

Wedded persons shall not be permitted during marriage to make to each other, either by act during life or by will, any mutual and reciprocal donation by one and the same act.

See parallel principle of English law, p. 423.

1098.

The husband or wife who, having had children by another bed, shall contract a second or subsequent marriage, can only give to such new spouse the portion of a legitimate child, taking least, and provided that in no case such donations exceed a fourth of the property.

See parallel but dissimilar principle of English law, p. 423.

1099.

Wedded persons cannot give each other indirectly beyond what is allowed them by the above regulations.

Every donation, either disguised, or made to intermediate persons, shall be null.

No parallel restriction. See note to articles 913, 1048, and 1091.

1100.

Donations by one of the wedded persons to the children or to one of the children of the other, the issue of a former marriage, and those made by the donor to relations to whom the other wedded party shall be heir presumptive on the day of the donation, although the latter may not have survived his relation donee, shall be deemed to have been made to intermediate persons.

No parallel principle of English law.

TITLE III.

Of Contracts, or Conventional Obligations in general.

DECREED 7TH OF FEBRUARY, 1804. PROMULGATED THE 17TH OF THE SAME MONTH.

CHAPTER I.

Preliminary Regulations.

1101.

A contract is an agreement, by which one or more persons are bound towards one or several others, to give, to do, or not to do something.

See a similar definition, p. 424.

1102.

A contract is *synallagmatical* or

bilateral when the contractors bind themselves reciprocally the one to the other.

See the parallel English law in substance, p. 427, in form, 428; and see note to article 1107.

1103.

It is *unilateral* when one or several persons are bound towards one or several others, without there being any engagement on the part of such latter.

See the parallel English law, though it should seem this kind of obligation can scarcely be called a contract; and see note to article 1107.

1104.

It is *commutative* when each of the parties binds himself to give or to do a thing which is regarded as the equivalent for that which is given him, or for that which is done for him.

When the equivalent consists in the chance of gain or loss for each of the parties, in consequence of an uncertain event, the contract is *aleatory*.

See note to article 1107.

1105.

The contract of *beneficence* is that in which one of the parties procures for the other an advantage purely gratuitous.

See note to article 1107.

1106.

The contract by *onerous title* is that which subjects each of the parties to give or do something.

See note to article 1107.

1107.

Contracts, whether they have a particular denomination, or whether they have not, are subject to general rules, which are the objects of the present title.

The rules applicable to certain contracts are established under the titles relating to each of them; and the rules applicable to commercial transactions are established by the laws relating to commerce.

The English law does not recognise as distinct kinds of contracts those called in this code commutative, aleatory, of beneficence or by onerous title. These distinctions, and those of nominate and innominate, perfectly or imperfectly reciprocal, syllagmatic contracts, contracts bonâ fide, and contracts stricti juris, were important in the civil law (which the French adopt) on account of the different kinds of action adapted to them (the actio directa to the principal obligation, and the actio contraria to the incidental), to which the English law has nothing analogous. See note by Mr. Evans, to Pothier on Contracts. See however the various distinctions made by the law of England, p. 424 to 429.

CHAPTER II.

Of Conditions essential to the Validity of Agreements.

1108.

Four conditions are essential to the validity of an agreement:

The consent of the party who binds himself;

His capacity to contract;

A certain object forming the matter of the contract;

A lawful cause of obligation.

See parallel article of English law, p. 429.

Section 1.

Of Consent.

1109.

There can be no valid consent if such consent have been only given through mistake (par erreur), or have been extorted through violence or surreptitiously obtained by fraud.

See parallel English law, p. 430.

1110.

Mistake is a cause for annulling the agreement only when it relates to (tombe sur) the very substance of the thing which is the subject thereof.*

It is not a cause for nullity when it relates only to the person with whom the contract was intended to be made, unless the consideration of such person were the principal cause of the agreement.†

* See parallel English law, p. 430.

† See parallel English law, p. 431.

1111.

Violence exercised towards him who has contracted the obligation, is a cause of nullity, although it have been exercised by a third person, other than him for whose benefit the agreement has been made.

See parallel English law, p. 431.

1112.

That is violence which is of a nature to make an impression on a reasonable person, and which may inspire him with fear of exposing his person or his fortune to a considerable and present injury.

Regard must be had, on this subject, to the age, to the sex, and condition of persons.

See parallel English law, p. 431, 2.

1113.

Violence is a cause of nullity of contract, not only when it has been exercised towards the contracting party, but also when it has been so over his or her husband or wife, over their descendants or ancestors.

See parallel English law, p. 432.

1114.

Mere reverential fear towards a father, or mother, or other ancestor, without any violence having been exercised, does not suffice to annul a contract.

See parallel principle of English law, p. 432.

1115.

A contract can no longer be impeached on account of violence, if, subsequently to the cessation of the violence, such contract have been approved, either expressly or tacitly, or by suffering the time fixed by the law for restitution to pass by.

See parallel English law, p. 432.

1116.

Fraud is a cause of nullity of the agreement when the manœuvres practised by one of the parties are such, that it is evident that without such stratagems the other party would not have contracted.*

It is not to be presumed, but must be proved.†

* See parallel English law, p. 433.

† See parallel English principle, p. 433.

1117.

The agreement contracted by mistake, violence, or fraud, is not void absolutely (de plein droit); it only affords ground for an action of nullity or rescision, in the cases and in the manner explained in section 7 of chapter 5 of the present title.

See parallel English law, p. 433.

1118.

Inequality of consideration (lesion) does not vitiate agreements except in certain cases, or with regard to certain persons, as will be explained in the same section.

See English law on this point, p. 434.

1119.

A man cannot, in general, bind himself or stipulate in his own name except for himself.

See parallel principle of English law, p. 434.

1120.

Nevertheless a man may vouch (se porte fort) for a third person, by promising the deed of the latter; saving the indemnity against him who has vouched, or who has promised to get it ratified, if the third party refuse to keep the engagement.

See parallel principle of English law, p. 435.

1121.

A man may in like manner stipulate for the benefit of a third person, when such is the condition of a stipulation that a man makes for himself, or of a donation which he makes to another. He who has made such stipulation can no longer revoke it, if the third party has declared his intention to profit by it.

See parallel principle of English law, p. 435.

1122.

A man is deemed to have stipulated for himself and for his heirs and assigns, unless the contrary be expressed, or result from the nature of the agreement,

See parallel principle of English law, p. 435.

SECTION 2.

Of the Capacity of the Contracting Parties.

1123.

Every person may contract if he has not been declared incapable by the law.

See parallel principle of English law, p. 435.

1124.

Minors are incapable of contracting;

Interdicted persons;

Married women, in the cases expressed by the law;

And all those generally to whom the law has forbidden certain contracts.

See parallel English law, p. 436.

1125.

The minor, the interdicted person, and the married woman cannot, under pretext of incapacity, impeach their own engagements, except in the cases provided for by the law. Persons capable of binding themselves cannot object the incapacity of the minor, of the interdicted person, or of the married woman, with whom they have contracted.

See parallel principle of English law, p. 436.

SECTION 3.

Of the Object and Matter of Contracts.

1126.

Every contract has for its object a thing which one party binds himself to give, or which one party binds himself to do or not to do.

See parallel principle of English law, p. 437.

1127.

The simple use or the simple possession of a thing may be, like the thing itself, the object of contract.

See parallel principle of English law, p. 437.

1128.

Only things which are objects of commerce can be the object of agreements.

See parallel principle of English law, p. 437.

1129.

It is necessary that the obligation have for its object a thing at least determinate as regards its species.

The individuality (quotite) of the thing may be uncertain, provided it is capable of being determined.

See parallel English law, p. 438.

1130.

Things future may be objects of an obligation.

A man cannot, however, renounce a succession not opened, nor make any stipulation regarding such a succession, even with his consent whose succession was dealt with.

See parallel but dissimilar English law, p. 438.

SECTION 4.

Of the Cause.

1131.

An obligation without a cause, or upon a false cause, or upon an unlawful cause, can have no effect.

See parallel English law, p. 439.

1132.

The agreement is not less valid although the cause be not expressed therein.

See parallel English law, p. 440.

1133.

The cause is unlawful when it is prohibited by the law, when it is concontrary to good morals or to public order.

See parallel English law, p. 440.

CHAPTER III.

Of the Effect of Obligations.

Section 1.

General Regulations.

1134.

Agreements legally formed hold the place of law to those who have made them.*

They cannot be revoked except with their mutual consent,† or for causes which the law authorizes.

They ought to be executed with good faith.‡

* See parallel axiom of English law, p. 441.

† See parallel principle of English law, p 441.

‡ A similar moral principle prevails in the English law.

1135.

Agreements bind not only as to what is expressed therein, but further as regards all the consequences which equity, usage, or law gives to an obligation from its nature.

See parallel principle of English law, p. 442.

Section 2.

Of the Obligation of Giving.

1136.

The obligation of giving imports that of delivering the thing* and of preserving it up to delivery, under pain of damages and interest towards the creditor.†

* See parallel English law, p. 442.

† See parallel but somewhat different principle of English law, p. 442, 3.

1137.

The obligation of looking to the preservation of the thing, whether the agreement have for its object the advantage of one of the parties, or whether its object be their common advantage, calls on him who is charged therewith to apply all the care of a good father of a family.

This obligation is more or less extended in relation to certain contracts, the effects of which, in this respect, are explained under the titles which relate to them.

See parallel principle of English law, p. 443, 4

1138.

The obligation to deliver the thing is perfect by the consent merely of the contracting parties.

It renders the creditor proprietor, and puts the thing upon his risk from the instant at which it ought to have been delivered, although the delivery have not been actually made unless the debtor should have delayed (soit en demeure) delivering it; in which case the thing remains at the risk of the latter.

See parallel principle of English law, p, 444.

1139.

The debtor is judged to be in delay (constitué en demeure), either by a summons or other equivalent act, or by the effect of the agreement, when it imports that, without need of a document and by the sole lapse of the term, the debtor shall be in delay.

See parallel principle of English law, p. 444, 5.

1140.

The effects of the obligation of giving or delivering an immoveable are regulated in the title "*Of Sales,*" and in the title *"Of Privileges and Mortgages."*

This is a mere explanation of arrangement.

1141.

If the thing which a party is bound to give or to deliver to two persons successively is purely moveable, he of the two who has been put in actual possession of it is preferred, and remains proprietor of it, although his title should be posterior in date, provided however that the possession be in good faith.

See parallel principle of English law, p. 445.

SECTION 3.

Of the Obligation to do or not to do.

1142.

Every obligation to do or not to do resolves itself into damages and interest, in case of non-performance on the part of the debtor.

See parallel principle of English law, p. 444, 5.

1143.

Nevertheless the creditor has a right to demand that whatever shall have been done in contravention of the engagement, shall be destroyed; and he may procure himself to be authorized to destroy it at the expense of the debtor, without prejudice to his damages and interests, if there be ground.

See parallel principle of English law, p. 446.

1144.

The creditor may also, in case of non-performance, be authorized to procure the obligation to be executed himself at the expense of the debtor.

See parallel principle of English law, p. 446.

1145.

If the obligation is not to do, he who contravenes it therein is indebted in damages and interest by the single act of contravention.

See parallel principle of English law, p. 446.

SECTION 4.

Of Damages and Interest resulting from the Non-performance of the Obligation.

1146.

Damages and interest (dommages et interets*) are only due when the debtor is in arrear in fulfilling his obligation; except nevertheless when the thing which the debtor has bound himself to give or to do cannot be given or done but within a certain time, which he has suffered to pass by.†

* These terms together most closely correspond with that of damages in the English law.

† See parallel principle of English law, p. 447.

1147.

The debtor is condemned, if there be ground, to the payment of damages and interest, either by reason of the non-performance of the obligation or by reason of delay in its execution, as often as he cannot prove that such non-performance arises from a foreign cause which cannot be imputed to him, although there be no bad faith on his part.

See parallel principle of English law, p. 447, 8.

1148.

There is no ground for damages and interest, when by consequence of a superior force or of a fortuitous occurrence, the debtor has been prevented from giving or doing that to which he has bound himself, or has done that from which he was interdicted.

See parallel principle of English law, p. 447, 8.

1149.

The damages and interest due to the creditor are, in general, to the amount of the loss which he has sustained or of the gain of which he has been deprived; saving the exceptions and modifications following.

See parallel principle of English law, p. 447, 8.

1150.

The debtor is only bound for the damages and interest which were foreseen, or which might have been foreseen at the time of the contract, when it is not in consequence of his fraud that the obligation has not been executed.

See parallel but dissimilar principle of English law, p. 447, 8.

1151.

Even in the case where the non-performance of the contract results from the fraud of the debtor, the damages and interest must only comprehend, as regards the loss sustained by the creditor and the gain of which he has been deprived, what is the immediate and direct consequence of the non-performance of the contract.

See parallel principle of English law, p. 447, 8.

1152.

When the agreement provides that he who shall fail in executing it shall pay a certain sum under the title of damages (dommages-intérêts), there can be allowed to the other party neither a greater nor a less sum.

See parallel principle of English law, p. 448.

1153.

In the obligations which are limited to the payment of a certain sum, the damages and interest resulting from delay in the performance consist only of a condemnation to the interest fixed by the law; saving the rules peculiar to commerce and security. Such damages and interest are due without the creditor being bound to prove any loss. They are only due from the day of the demand, except in cases wherein the law makes them run absolutely.

See parallel principle of English law, p. 448.

1154.

Interest accruing from capital sums may produce interest either by a judicial demand or by a special agreement, provided that, whether in the demand or in the agreement, relation is had to interest due for one entire year at least.

See parallel principle of English law, p. 448.

1155.

Nevertheless revenues falling due, such as rents of farms, lettings, arrears of perpetual or life annuities, produce interest from the day of demand or by the agreement. The same rule applies to restitution of fruits, and to interest paid by a third person to the creditor in discharge of the debtor.

See parallel principle of English law, p. 497, parallel article 1342.

Section 5.

Of the Interpretation of Agreements.

1156.

In agreements,* the mutual intention of the contracting parties must be sought after rather than to stop at the literal sense of terms.†

* The following rules are taken from Pothier on Contracts, pl. 1, c. 1, s. 1.

† See parallel principle of English law, p. 448, 9.

1157.

When a clause is susceptible of two meanings, it must rather be understood in that according to which it may have some effect, than in that whereby it cannot produce any.

See parallel principle of English law, p. 449.

1158.

Expressions susceptible of two meanings, must be taken in that which agrees best with the matter of the contract.

See parallel principle of English law, p. 449.

1159.

Whatever is ambiguous must be interpreted by what is the usage in the country where the contract is made.

See parallel principle of English law, p. 449, 50.

1160.

In a contract clauses which are usual must be supplied therein, although they are not expressed.

See parallel principle of English law, p. 450.

1161.

All the clauses of agreements interpret themselves, the ones by the others, by giving to each the sense derived from the entire act.

See parallel principle of English law, p. 450.

1162.

In case of doubt, the agreement is interpreted against him who has stipulated, and in favour of him who has contracted the obligation.

See parallel but contrary principle of English law, p. 450.

1163.

However general the terms may be in which an agreement is couched, it only comprehends things respecting which it appears that the parties proposed to contract.

See parallel principle of English law, p. 450.

1164.

When in a contract a case has been expressed for explaining the obligation, it is not to be deemed to have been designed to restrict the extension the engagement receives of right as regards cases not expressed.

See parallel principle of English law, p. 450, 1.

SECTION 6.

Of the Effect of Agreements as respects Third Persons.

1165.

Agreements have effect only between the contracting parties; they do not work injury to a third person, and they only benefit him in the case provided for by article 1121.

See parallel principle of English law, p. 451.

1166.

Nevertheless creditors may exercise all the rights and suits belonging to their debtor, with the exception of those which are exclusively attached to the person.

See parallel principle of English law, p. 451.

1167.

They may also, in their proper name, impeach acts made by their debtor in fraud of their rights.

They must nevertheless, as regards their rights, set forth under the title "*Of Successions*," and under the title "*Of the Marriage Contract, and of the respective Rights of Married Persons*," conform themselves to the rules which are therein prescribed.

See parallel principle of English law, p. 451.

CHAPTER IV.

Of the different Species of Obligations.

SECTION 1.

Of Conditional Obligations.

§ 1. *Of Conditions generally, and of their different Kinds.*

1168.

The obligation is conditional when it is made to depend on an event future and uncertain, either by suspending it until the event happens, or by resiling it accordingly as the event shall happen or not.

See parallel definition of English law, p. 452, 3, 4.

1169.

A *casual* condition is that which depends on chance, and which is in no respect in the power of the creditor or of the debtor.

See the English law, p. 454.

1170.

A *potestative* condition is that which makes the performance of the agreement depend on an event which it is in the power of one or other of the contracting parties to cause to happen or to prevent.

See the English law, p. 454.

1171.

A *mixed* condition is that which depends at once on the will of one of the contracting parties, and on the will of a third person.

See the English law, p. 454.

1172.

Every condition of a thing impossible, or contrary to good morals, or prohibited by the law, is void, and renders null the agreement which depends on it.

See parallel principle of English law, p. 455.

1173.

The condition of not doing an impossible thing does not render void the obligation contracted subject to such condition.

See parallel principle of English law, p. 455.

1174.

Every obligation is void when it has been contracted under a potestative condition on the part of him who binds himself.

See parallel but contrary English law, p. 455.

1175.

Every condition must be accomplished in the manner in which the parties have apparently wished and intended that it should be.

See parallel English law, p. 456.

1176.

When an obligation is contracted under the condition that an event shall happen within a fixed time, such condition is deemed to have failed when the time is expired without the event having taken place. If there be no time fixed, the condition may always be accomplished; and it is not taken to have failed until it has become certain that the event will not happen.

See parallel principle of English law, p. 456.

1177.

When an obligation is contracted under the condition that an event shall not happen within a fixed time, such condition is accomplished when the time is expired without the event having occurred; it is equally so, if before the time limited, it is certain that the event will not occur; and if there have been no determinate period, it is not accomplished until it is certain that the event will not happen.

See parallel principle of English law, p. 456.

1178.

The condition is taken to be accomplished, when it is the debtor, bound under such condition, who has prevented the accomplishment thereof.

See parallel principle of English law, p. 457.

1179.

A condition accomplished has an effect retroactive to the day on which the engagement was contracted. If the creditor be dead before the accomplishment of the condition, his rights pass to his heir.

See parallel English law, p. 457.

1180.

A creditor may, before the condition is accomplished, put in force all acts preservative of his rights.

No parallel English law.

§ 2. *Of the Suspensive Condition.*

1181.

The obligation contracted under a suspensive condition is that which depends either on an event future and uncertain, or on an event actually happened, but still unknown to the parties. In the first case, the obligation cannot be performed until after the event. In the second case, the obligation takes effect from the day on which it was contracted.

See parallel principle of English law, p. 457, 8.

1182.

When the obligation has been contracted under a suspensive condition, the thing which forms the matter of the agreement remains at the risk of the debtor, who is not bound to deliver it except in case of the event of the condition. If the thing have entirely perished without the fault of the debtor, the obligation is extinguished.

If the thing be deteriorated without the fault of the debtor, the creditor has the choice either to dissolve the obligation, or to demand the thing in the state in which it shall be found, without diminution of price. If the thing be deteriorated by the fault of the debtor, the creditor has a right either to dissolve the obligation, or to demand the thing in the state in which it shall be found, with damages and interest.

See parallel principle of English law, p. 458.

§ 3. *Of the Resolutory Condition.*

1183.

A resolutory condition is that which, when it is accomplished, operates the revocation of the obligation, and which again puts affairs in the same state as if the obligation had never existed. It does not suspend the performance of the obligation; it merely obliges the creditor to restore what he may have received, in the case the event provided for by the condition happens.

See parallel English law, p. 458, 9.

1184.

A resolutory condition is always understood in synallagmatic contracts, for the case in which one of the two parties shall not satisfy his engagement. In this case the contract is not dissolved absolutely. The party towards whom the engagement has not been performed, has his election either to compel the other to performance of the agreement where it is possible, or to demand the dissolution thereof with damages and interest. The dissolution may be demanded at law, and a delay may be granted to the defendant according to circumstances.

See parallel principle of English law, p. 459, 60.

Section 2.

Of Obligations for a Term.

1185.

A term differs from a condition, in that it does not suspend the engagement, of which it retards the execution only.

See the English law on this point, p, 460, 1.

1186.

That which is not due until after a term, cannot be demanded until the expiration of the term; but that which has been paid in advance, cannot be recovered.

See the English law on this point, p. 460, 1.

1187.

The term is always presumed to be stipulated in favour of the debtor, unless it result from the stipulation, or from circumstances, that it has been also agreed in favour of the creditor.

See the English law on this point, p. 460, 1.

1188.

A debtor can no longer claim the benefit of the term when he has become bankrupt, or when by his own act he has diminished the security which he had given by the contract to his creditor.

See the English law on this point, p. 460, 1.

Section 3.

Of alternative Obligations.

1189.

A debtor of an alternative obligation is discharged by the delivery of one of the two things which were comprehended in the obligation.

See parallel principle of English law, p. 461.

1190.

The choice belongs to the debtor, if it have not been expressly accorded to the creditor.

See parallel principle of English law, p. 461, 2.

1191.

A debtor may discharge himself by delivering one of two things promised; but he cannot compel the creditor to receive one part of one, and one part of the other.

See parallel principle of English law, p. 462.

1192.

An obligation is pure and simple, although contracted in an alternative manner, if the one of two things promised could not be the subject of obligation.

See parallel principle of English law, p. 462.

1193.

The obligation alternative becomes pure and simple, if one of the things promised perishes and is no longer capable of being delivered, even with the fault of the debtor. The price of such thing cannot be offered in its place. If both have perished, and the debtor is in fault with respect to one of them, he must pay the price of that which perished last.

See parallel principle of English law, p. 462.

1194.

When in the cases contemplated in the preceding article, the election has been given by agreement to the creditor, one of the things only has perished; then if it is without the fault of the debtor, the creditor must have that which remains; if the debtor is in fault, the creditor may demand the thing which remains, or the price of that which has perished: or both the things have perished; and then if the debtor is in fault with regard to both, or even with regard to one of them only, the creditor may demand the price of either at his election.

See the general parallel principle of English law, p. 462.

1195.

If both the things have perished without the fault of the debtor, and before he is in delay, the obligation is extinguished, conformably to article 1302.

See parallel principle of English law, p. 462.

1196.

The same principles apply to cases in which there are more than two things comprehended in the alternative obligation.

See parallel principle of English law, p. 462.

Section 4.

*Of Obligations in Solido.**

§ 1. *Of Solidarity between Creditors.*

1197.

The obligation is in solido among several creditors when the instrument gives expressly to each of them the right to demand payment of the whole of the debt, and when payment made to one of them discharges the debtor, although the benefit of the obligation be divisible and distributable between the different creditors.†

* Obligations in solido, between several creditors are, I conceive (says Mr. Evans), wholly unknown in the law of England. An obligation may be joint, and all obliged to join in an action.—Ev. Pot.

† As to what is most nearly analogous to this in the English law, see p. 462, 3.

1198.

It is within the election of the debtor to pay to one or other of the creditors in solido, so long as he is not anticipated by the prosecution of one of them Nevertheless postponement, which is only made by one of the creditors in solido, does not discharge the debtor, except on the part of such creditor.

See note to preceding article.

1199.

Every act which interrupts prescription with regard to one of the creditors in solido, benefits the other creditors.

See note to article 1197, and p. 462, 3,

§ 2. *Of Solidarity on the part of Debtors.*

1200.

There is solidarity on the part of debtors when they are bound to one and the same thing, in such manner that each one may be arrested for the entirety, and when payment made by one discharges the other towards the creditor.

See note to article 1197, and p. 464.

1201.

The obligation may be in solido, though one of the debtors be bound differently from the other to the payment of the same thing: for example, if one be bound only conditionally, while the engagement of the other is absolute, or if one has taken a term which is not granted to the other.

See note to article 1197, and p. 464.

1202.

Solidarity is not to be presumed; it is necessary that it should be expressly stipulated.

This rule is only suspended where the solidarity takes place absolutely, by virtue of a regulation of the law.

See note to article 1197, and p. 464.

1203.

The creditor of an obligation contracted in solido, may address himself to such one of the debtors as he may choose, without the latter being able to object the benefit of division.

See note to article 1197, and p. 464.

1204.

Suits instituted against one of the debtors do not prevent the creditor from pursuing the like against the others.

See note to article 1197, and p. 465.

1205.

If the thing due have perished by the fault or during the delay of one or of several of the joint and several debtors, the other joint debtors are not discharged from the obligation of paying the price of such thing; but the latter are not subject to damages. A creditor can only recover damages and interest, as well against the debtors by whose fault the thing has perished as against those who were in delay.

See note to article 1197, and p. 465.

1206.

Suits instituted against one of the debtors in solido interrupt prescription with respect to all.

See a parallel principle of English law, p. 465.

1207.

A demand for interest made against one of the debtors in solido causes interest to run with respect to all.

See a parallel principle of English law, p. 465.

1208.

A co-debtor in solido sued by the creditor, must oppose all the objections which flow from the nature of the obligation, and all those which are personal to himself, as well as those which are common to all the joint debtors. He cannot oppose objections which are purely personal to some of the other codebtors.

See note to article 1197, and p. 465.

1209.

When one of the debtors becomes sole heir of the creditor, or when the creditor becomes sole heir of one of the debtors, the confusion does only extinguish the credit in solido for the part and portion of such debtor or creditor.

See note to article 1197, and parallel article 1300, p. 487.

1210.

A creditor who consents to a division of the debt with regard to one of the codebtors, preserves his action in solido against the others, but subject to a deduction of the share of the debtor who was discharged from the solidarity.

See note to article 1197.

1211.

A creditor who receives by division the share of one of the debtors, without reserving in the quittance the solidarity or his rights in general, only renounces the solidarity with regard to such debtor.

A creditor is not deemed to relinquish the solidarity to the debtor by receiving from him a sum equal to the portion in which he is bound, if the acquittance do not import that it is for his share. It is the same with regard to a simple demand made against one of the co-debtors for his share, if the latter have not acquiesced in the demand, or if a judgment of condemnation have not intervened.

See note to article 1197.

1212.

The creditor who receives dividedly and without reserve the portion of one of the codebtors in the arrears or interest of the debt, does not lose his joint and several obligation, except as regards the arrears or interest fallen due, and not for those to fall due, nor as regards the capital, unless the divided payment have continued during ten consecutive years.

See note to article 1197.

1213.

The obligation contracted in solido towards the creditor divides itself absolutely among the debtors, who are not bound for it among themselves except each for his own share and portion.

See note to article 1197.

1214.

The co-debtor of a debt in solido, who has paid it in entirety, can only recover against the others the part and portion of each of them. If one of them is found to be insolvent, the loss which his insolvency occasions, is subdivided by contribution among all the other joint debtors being solvent and him who has made the payment.

See note to article 1197, and p. 465.

1215.

In the case in which a creditor has renounced the action in solido against one of the debtors, if one or more of the remaining co-debtors become insolvent, the portion of the insolvents shall be proportionably subdivided among all the debtors, even among those previously discharged from the solidarity by the creditor.

See a parallel principle of English law, p. 466.

1216.

If the matter for which the debt has been contracted in solido relates only to one of the co-obligors *in solido*, the latter shall be bound in the whole debt as respects the other joint debtors, who shall only be considered with reference to him as his sureties.

See note to article 1197. A parallel rule would govern in analogous cases.

SECTION 5.

Of Obligations divisible and indivisible.

1217.

The obligation is divisible or indivisible* accordingly as it has for its object, either a thing which in its delivery, or an act which in its execution, is or is not susceptible of division, either material or intellectual.†

* Most of this section applies only to the case of heirs according to the French law, and therefore has no parallel in the English system. The divisibility or indivisibility of obligations among the heirs is a subject on which there is nothing analogous in the English law, nor does our system apply to a stipulation or promise from a particular heir. The division of obligations into divisible and indivisible, in the Roman and French sense of the

terms, can have very little immediate application to the practice of the English law.—Ev. Pot., p. 171, n.

| For analogous principles, see p. 466.

1218.

The obligation is indivisible although the thing or the act which is the object thereof is divisible in its nature, if the relation under which it is considered in the obligation does not render it susceptible of partial execution.

See notes to preceding article.

1219.

Stipulated solidarity does not confer the character of indivisibility.

See note to articles 1197 and 1217.

§ 1. *Of the Effects of the divisible Obligation.*

1220.

The obligation which is susceptible of division, must be executed between the creditor and the debtor as if it were indivisible. The divisibility has no application but with regard to their heirs, who can demand the debt, or who are bound to pay it, only for the portions of which they are seized, or in which they are bound as representing the creditor or the debtor.

See note to article 1217, and p. 467, 8.

1221.

The principle laid down in the preceding article receives exceptions with regard to the heirs of the debtor. 1st. In the case where the debt is by way of mortgage. 2nd. When it is of a certain thing. 3rd. When it relates to an alternative debt regarding things in the election of the creditor, one whereof is indivisible. 4th. When one of the heirs is charged alone, by the document, with the execution of the obligation. 5th. When it results, either from the nature of the engagement, or from the thing which forms the object thereof, or from the end which is proposed by the contract, that the intention of the contracting parties was, that the debt should not be partially discharged. In the first three cases, the heir who possesses the thing due or the estate pledged for the debt, may be sued for the whole out of the thing due or out of the estate pledged, saving the remedy against his coheirs. In the fourth case the heir alone charged with the debt, and in the fifth case every heir, may also be sued for the whole; saving his remedy against his coheirs.

See note to article 1217, and p. 467, 8.

§ 2. *Of the Effects of an indivisible Obligation.*

1222.

Each one of those who have contracted conjointly an indivisible debt, is bound for the total thereof, although the obligation have not been contracted in solido.

See note to article 1217, and p. 468.

1223.

The same rule applies to the heirs of him who has contracted a similar obligation.

See note to preceding article.

1224.

Every heir of the creditor may demand in totality the execution of the indivisible obligation. He cannot alone remit the entirety of the debt; he cannot alone receive the value instead of the thing. If one of the heirs have alone remitted the debt or received the price of the thing, his coheir can only demand the indivisible thing by giving credit for the portion of the coheir who has made remittance or received the price.

See note to article 1222.

1225.

The heir of the debtor, charged with the entirety of the obligation, may demand a delay in order to sue his coheirs, unless the debt should be of a nature not capable of being acquitted except by the heir charged, who may then be condemned alone;

saving his remedy for indemnification against his coheirs.

See note to article 1222.

Section 6.

Of Obligations with Penal Clauses.

1226.

A penal clause is that by which a person, in order to assure the performance of an agreement, binds himself for something in case of non-performance.

See parallel article of English law, p. 468, 9.

1227.

The nullity of the principal obligation carries with it that of the penal clause. The nullity of the latter does not draw after it that of the principal obligation.

See parallel principle of English law, p. 469.

1228.

The creditor, in lieu of demanding the penalty stipulated against the debtor who is in delay, may sue for performance of the principal obligation.

See parallel principle of English law, p. 469.

1229.

The penal clause is the compensation for the damages and interest which the creditor is subjected to from the non-performance of the principal obligation. He cannot demand at the same time the principal and the penalty, unless the latter have been stipulated for delay only.

See parallel principles of English law, p. 469, 70, 1.

1230.

Whether the original obligation contain, or whether it do not contain a term within which it must be accomplished, the penalty is not incurred until he who is bound either to deliver, or to take, or to do, is in delay.

See parallel principle of English law, p. 471.

1231.

A penalty may be modified by the judge when the principal obligation has been executed in part.

See parallel principle of English law, p. 469, 70.

1232.

When the original obligation contracted with a penal clause relates to a thing indivisible, the penalty is incurred by the contravention of one only of the heirs of the debtor, and it may be demanded, either in entirety against him who has committed the breach, or against each of the coheirs for their part and portion, and by way of mortgage for the whole, saving their remedy against him who has actually incurred the penalty.

See note to article 1217.

1233.

When the original obligation contracted under a penalty is divisible, the penalty is only incurred by that one of the heirs who contravenes such obligation, and in the proportion only for which he was bound in the principal obligation, without any action against those who have performed it. This rule admits exception when the penal clause having been added with the intention that the payment should not be made partially, one coheir has prevented the performance of the obligation in totality. In such case the entire penalty may be demanded against him and against the other coheirs for their portion only, saving their remedy.

See note to article 1217.

CHAPTER V.

Of the Extinction of Obligations.

1234.

Obligations are extinguished,—by payment,—by novation,—by voluntary remission,—by compensation,—by confusion,—by the loss of the thing,—by nullity or rescission,—by the effect of the resolutory condition, which has been explained in the preceding chapter,—and by prescription, which shall form the subject of a particular title.

See parallel article of English law, p. 472.

Section 1.

Of Payment.

§ 1. *Of Payment in general.*

1235.

Every payment supposes a debt; that which has been paid without being due is subject to recovery. The recovery is not permitted with respect to natural obligations which have been voluntarily discharged.

See parallel principle of English law, p. 472, 3.

1236.

An obligation may be discharged by every person who is interested therein, such as a co-obligor or a surety. The obligation may even be discharged by a third person who is not interested therein, provided such third person act in the name and in discharge of the debtor, or that if he act in his own proper name, he is not substituted into the rights of the creditor.

See parallel principle of English law, p. 472, 3.

1237.

The obligation to do an act cannot be discharged by a third person against the consent of the creditor, when the latter has an interest in its being performed by the debtor himself.

See parallel principle of English law, p. 473.

1238.

In order to pay validly, it is necessary to be proprietor of the thing given in payment, and capable of alienating it. Nevertheless the payment of a sum in money or other thing which is consumed by using, cannot be recovered against the creditor who has consumed it bonâ fide, although payment thereof have been made by him who was not the proprietor thereof, or who was not capable of alienating it.

See parallel principle of English law, p. 473, 4.

1239.

The payment must be made to the creditor or to some one having authority from him, or authorized by the court or by the law to receive for him. Payment made to one who shall not have authority to receive for the creditor, is valid, if the latter ratify it or if he have profited thereby.

See parallel principle of English law, p. 474.

1240.

Payment made boná fide to him who is in possession of the credit, is valid, although the possessor be afterwards evicted.

See parallel principle of English law, p. 474, 5.

1241.

Payment made to the creditor is not valid if he were incapable of receiving it, unless the debtor can prove that the thing paid has turned to the benefit of the creditor.

See parallel principle of English law, p. 475.

1242.

Payment made by the debtor to his creditor, to the prejudice of a seizure or opposition, is not valid with regard to the creditors seizing or opposing; these latter may, according to their right, compel him to pay afresh, saving in such case only, his remedy against the creditor.

We have no exact parallel to seizure and opposition in the English law; but see a somewhat similar principle, p. 475.

1243.

The creditor cannot be compelled to accept a thing different from that which is due to him, although the value of the thing tendered should be equal or even greater.

See parallel principle of English law, p. 476.

1244.

The debtor cannot oblige the creditor to receive part payment of a debt, although divisible. The judge may, nevertheless, in consideration of the debtor's situation, and using this power with great caution, grant moderate delays for the payment, and suspend the execution of the suit, all things remaining in the same state.

See parallel principle of English law, p. 476.

1245.

A debtor in a certain and determinate object is discharged by the remittance of the thing in the state in which it may be at the time of delivery, provided that the deteriorations which have occurred therein do not proceed from his act or fault, nor from that of persons for whom he is responsible; provided also that previously to such deteriorations he were not in delay.

See parallel principle of English law, p. 476.

1246.

If the debt consists of a thing which is to be determined only as to its kind, the debtor shall not be bound, in order to his discharge, to give it of the best kind; but he must not offer the worst.

See parallel principle of English law, p. 476.

1247.

The payment must be performed in the place appointed by the agreement. If the place be not designated therein, payment, when a certain and determinate property is in question, must be made in the place where the thing which is the object of the obligation was at the date thereof. Except in these two cases, the payment must be made at the domicile of the debtor.

See parallel principle of English law, p. 476.

1248.

The expenses of the payment are at the charge of the debtor.

A similar principle in the English law.

§ 11. *Of Payment with Subrogation.*

1249.

Subrogation into the rights of the creditor, for the benefit of a third person who pays him, is either conventional or legal.

See parallel principles of English law, p. 476, 7.

1250.

Such subrogation is conventional; 1st. When the creditor receiving his payment from a third person substitutes (subroge) him into his rights, actions, privileges, or mortgages against the debtor, such substitution must be express, and made at the same time as the payment. 2nd. When the debtor borrows a sum with the effect of paying his debt, and of substituting the lender into the rights of the creditor. It is necessary to the validity of such substitution, that the act of borrowing and the acquittance should be made before a notary; that in the document of borrowing it should be declared that the sum has been borrowed in order to make payment, and that in the quittance it should be declared that the payment has been made with money furnished for that purpose by the new creditor. Such substitution is operative without the concurrence of the creditor's assent.

See parallel English law, p. 476, 7.

1251.

Subrogation takes place absolutely: 1st. For the benefit of him who being himself a creditor pays another creditor who has a preferable claim on account of his privileges or mortgages. 2nd. For the benefit of the purchaser of an immoveable, who employs the value of his purchase in payment of creditors to whom such inheritance was mortgaged. 3rd. For the benefit of him who being bound with others or for others for the payment of the debt, had an interest in discharging it. 4th. For the benefit of the beneficiary heir who has paid out of his own funds the debts of the succession.

See parallel principle of English law, p. 477, 8.

1252.

The subrogation established by the preceding articles takes place as well against sureties as against debtors; it must not work injury to the creditor where he has only been paid in part; in such case he may exercise his rights, as respects what remains due to him, in preference to him from whom he has only received a partial payment.

See note to preceding articles.

§ 3. *Of the Imputation of Payments.*

1253.

He who owes several debts has the right to declare, when he pays, which debt it is his purpose to discharge.

See parallel principle of English law, p. 478, 9.

1254.

He who owes one debt bearing interest or producing arrears cannot, without the consent of the creditor, apply the payment which he makes to the capital in preference to the arrears or interest: the payment made on the capital and interest, but which is not entire, is applied at first to the interest.

See parallel principle of English law, p. 478, 9.

1255.

When he who owes divers debts has accepted an acquittance by which the creditor has imputed what he has received to one of the debts specifically, the debtor can no longer demand the imputation to a different debt, unless there have been fraud or surprise on the part of the creditor.

See parallel principle of English law, p. 478, 9.

1256.

When the quittance does not contain any application, the payment must be applied to the debt which the debtor had at that time the most interest in acquitting among those which are equally due; otherwise, to the debt due, though less burdensome than those which are not so. If the debts are of equal nature, the imputation is made to the oldest: all things being equal, it is made proportionably.

See parallel principle of English law, p. 478, 9.

§ 4. *Of Offers of Payment, and of Consignation.*

1257.

When the creditor refuses to receive his payment, the debtor may make him real offers, and on the refusal of the creditor to accept them, may consign (*i. e.* deposit with a third person) the sum or the thing offered.

Real offers followed by a consignation discharge the debtor; they have with respect to him the effect of payment, when validly made, and the thing thus deposited remains at the risk of the creditor.

See parallel principle of English law, p. 479.

1258.

In order that real offers should be valid, it is necessary — 1st. That they should be made to the creditor, having the capacity to receive, or to a person who has authority to receive for him. 2nd. That they should be made by a person capable of paying. 3rd. That they should consist of the whole sum demandable, of arrears or interest due, of ascertained expenses, and of a sum for unliquidated expenses, without prejudice to perfect it. 4th. That the term be expired, if it have been stipulated in favour of the creditor. 5th. That the condition under which the debt has been contracted has occurred. 6th. That the offers were made at the place agreed on for the payment, and that, if there be no special agreement on the place of payment, they should be made personally to the creditor, or at his domicile, or at the domicile chosen for the performance of the agreement. 7th. That the offers be made by a ministerial officer having authority for these descriptions of acts.

See parallel principle of English law, p. 479, 80.

1259.

It is not necessary to the validity of the consignation that it should have been authorized by the judge; it suffices—1st. That it have been preceded by a summons signified to the creditor, and containing an indication of the day, the hour, and the place, where and when the thing offered will be deposited. 2nd. That the debtor divest himself of the thing offered, by placing it in the depôt marked out by the law for the reception of consignation, with the interest up to the day of the deposit. 3rd. That a statement have been drawn up by the ministerial officer, of the nature of the things offered, of the refusal which the creditor has made to receive them, or of his non-appearance, and finally of the deposit. 4th. That in case of non-appearance on the part of the creditor, the statement respecting the deposit have been signified to him with a summons to take away the thing deposited.

See parallel principle of English law, p. 479, 80.

1260.

The expenses of the real offers and of the consignation are, if valid, charged upon the creditor.

See parallel principle of English law, p. 479, 80.

1261.

So long as the consignation is not accepted by the creditor, the debtor may withdraw it; and if he do withdraw it, his coheirs and his sureties are not discharged.

See parallel principle of English law, p. 480.

1262.

When the debtor has himself obtained a judgment passed with force of a matter decided, which has declared his offers and his deposit good and valid, he is no longer at liberty, even with the consent of the creditor, to withdraw his deposit, to the prejudice of his codebtors, or of his sureties.

See parallel principle of English law, p. 480.

1263.

A creditor who has consented that the debtor should withdraw his consignation after it has been declared valid, by a judgment which has acquired the force of a matter decided, can no longer, with a view to the payment of his demand, exercise the privileges or mortgages which were attached thereto: there is no mortgage except from the day on which the act, by which he consented that the deposit should be withdrawn, shall be revested with the forms requisite to establish a mortgage.

No parallel English law.

1264.

If the thing due is a certain object which must be delivered in the place where it is found, the debtor must give the creditor notice to remove it, by act notified to him personally or at his domicile, or at the domicile elected for the execution of the agreement. Such notice having been given, if the creditor do not remove the thing, and the debtor wants the place in which it is situated, the latter may obtain from the court permission to put it in deposit in some other place.

See parallel English law, p. 480.

§ 5. *Of the Cession of Property.*

1265.

The cession of property is the abandonment made by a debtor to his creditors of all his property, when he finds himself not in condition to pay his debts.

See parallel principle of English law, p. 481.

1266.

The cession of property is voluntary or judicial.

See parallel principle of English law, p. 481.

1267.

The voluntary cession of property is that which the creditors accept voluntarily, and which has no effect but that which results from the contract entered into between them and the debtor.

See parallel principle of English law, p, 481.

1268.

Judicial cession is a benefit which the law accords to the unfortunate and *bonâ fide* debtor, to whom it is allowed, in order to secure the liberty of his person, to make judicially an abandonment of all his property to his creditors, notwithstanding any stipulation to the contrary.

See parallel principles of English law, p. 482.

1269.

Judicial cession confers no property on the creditors; it gives them the right only of making sale of the property for their own benefit, and of enjoying the revenues thereof until the sale.

See parallel principles of English law, p. 482.

1270.

Creditors cannot refuse a judicial cession unless it be within the cases excepted by the law. It produces a discharge from corporeal restraint. Beyond that, it only liberates the debtor to the amount of the value of the property abandoned; and in the cases where that shall prove insufficient, if other property shall come to his hands, he is compelled to abandon it until complete payment.

See parallel principle of English law, p. 481, 2.

SECTION 2.

Of Novation.

1271.

Novation is effected in three ways: 1st. When the debtor contracts towards his creditor a new debt that is substituted for the ancient one, which is extinguished.* 2nd. When a new debtor is substituted for the ancient one who is discharged by the creditor.† 3rd. When, by the effect of a new engagement, a new creditor is substituted for the ancient one, towards whom the debtor becomes discharged.‡

* See parallel principle of English law, p. 482.

† See parallel principle of English law, p. 483.

‡ See parallel principle of English law, p. 483.

1272.

Novation can only be effected between persons capable of contracting.

See parallel principle of English law, p. 483.

1273.

Novation is not to be presumed; it is necessary that the intention to effect it should clearly result from the act.

See parallel English law, p. 484.

1274.

Novation by the substitution of a new debtor, may be effected without the concurrence of the first.

See parallel but dissimilar principle of English law, p. 484.

1275.

The delegation by which a debtor gives to a creditor another debtor who binds himself towards the creditor, does not operate as a novation, if the creditor has not expressly declared that he intended to discharge his debtor who has made the delegation.

See parallel principle of English law, p. 484.

1276.

The creditor who has discharged the debtor by whom delegation has been made, has no remedy against such debtor, if the delegated person become insolvent, unless the acts contain an express reservation thereof, or that the delegated party was already openly a bankrupt, or had fallen into embarrassment at the moment of the delegation.

See note to preceding article.

1277.

The simple indication made by the debtor, of a person who is to pay in his place, does not operate as a novation. It is the same as to the simple indication made by the creditor, of a person who is to receive for him.

See note to article 1276.

1278.

The privileges and mortgages of an ancient debt do not pass to that which is substituted for it, unless the creditor have expressly reserved them.

See parallel principle of English law, p. 484.

1279.

When the novation is effected by the substitution of a new debtor, the original privileges and mortgages of the debt cannot pass to the property of the new debtor.

See parallel principle of English law, p. 484.

1280.

When the novation is effected between the creditor and one of the debtors in solido, the privileges and mortgages of the ancient debt can only be reserved upon the property of him who contracts the new debt.

See note to article 1197, and parallel principle of English law, p. 484.

1281.

By novation made between the creditor and one of the debtors in solido, the codebtors are discharged. Novation operating with respect to the principal debtor discharges his securities. Nevertheless, if the creditor have required in the first case the addition of the codebtors, or in the second that of the securities, the ancient debt subsists, if the codebtors or the securities refuse to accede to the new arrangement.

See a parallel principle of English law, p. 484.

SECTION 3.

Of the Remission of a Debt.

1282.

Voluntary remittance of the original document under private signature, by the creditor to the debtor, forms proof of discharge.

See parallel principle of English law, p. 485.

1283.

Voluntary surrender of the engrossment of a deed forms presumption of the remission of the debt or payment, without prejudice to contrary proof.

See parallel principle of English law, p. 485.

1284.

The surrender of the original document under private signature, or of an engrossed copy of the document to one of the debtors in solido, has the same effect for the benefit of his codebtors.

See parallel principle of English law, p. 485.

1285.

Conventional remittance or discharge for the benefit of one of the debtors in solido, liberates all the rest, unless the creditor have expressly reserved his rights against them: in which latter case, he can no longer recover the debt without deduction made of his share to whom he has made remittance.

See note to preceding article.

1286.

Delivery up of a thing given by way of security, does not suffice to raise presumption of the remission of the debt.

See parallel principle of English law, p. 485, 6.

1287.

Conventional remission or discharge accorded to the principal debtor discharges the sureties; that accorded to the surety does not liberate the principal debtor; that accorded to one of the sureties does not discharge the others.

See parallel principle of English law, p. 486.

1288.

What a creditor has received from a surety in discharge of his suretyship, must be imputed to the debt, and applied to the discharge of the principal debtor and of the other sureties.

See parallel principle of English law, p. 486.

SECTION 4.

Of Compensation.

1289.

When two persons find themselves debtors to each other, a compensation is effected between them extinguishing both debts in the manner and in the cases hereafter expressed.

See parallel principle of English law, p. 486.

1290.

Compensation is effected absolutely by force of law only, even without the knowledge of the debtors; the two debts are reciprocally extinguished the instant at which they are found to exist at the same time to the amount of their respective proportions.

See parallel principle of English law, p. 486.

1291.

Compensation only takes place between two debts which have equally for their object a sum of money, or a certain quantity of articles capable of being replaced by others, of the same species, and which are equally liquidated and demandable.

Loads of grain or commodities not contested, and of which the value is regulated by the prices current, may be set off against sums liquidated and demandable.

With regard to the kind of debts allowed to be set off, see parallel principle of English law, p. 486, 7

1292.

The term of grace is not an obstacle to compensation.

See parallel principle of English law, p. 487.

1293.

Compensation takes place whatever may be the causes of one or other of the debts, except in the case—1st. Of a demand for restitution of a thing of which the proprietor has been unjustly deprived. 2nd. Of the demand of restitution of a deposit and of a loan for use. 3rd. Of a debt for maintenance declared not seisable.

See parallel principles of English law, p. 486, 7.

1294.

The surety may oppose the compensation of that which the creditor owes to the principal debtor; but the principal debtor cannot oppose the compensation of that which the creditor owes to the surety. The debtor in solido may in like manner oppose the compensation of that which the creditor owes to his codebtor.

See parallel principle of English law, p. 487.

1295.

The debtor who has accepted absolutely and simply the cession which a creditor has made of his rights to a third person, can no longer oppose to the assignee the compensation, which he might before acceptance have opposed to the ceder.

With respect to cession which has not been accepted by the debtor, but which has been notified to him, it only prevents the compensation of debts posterior to such notification.

See the parallel principle of English law, p. 486, 7.

1296.

When the two debts are not payable in the same place, compensation thereof can only be opposed by accounting for the expenses of the remission.

See the parallel principle of English law, p. 486, 7.

1297.

When there are several debts subject to compensation due from the same person, the rules must be followed for their compensation, which are established touching imputation by article 1256.

See the parallel principle of English law, p. 486, 7.

1298.

Compensation does not take place to the prejudice of rights acquired by a third person. Thus he who, being a debtor, is become creditor subsequently to the opposition (saisie-arrêt) made by a third person into his hands, cannot oppose compensation to the prejudice of such seiser.

See the parallel principle of English law, p. 486, 7.

1299.

He who has paid a debt which was of right extinguished by compensation, can no longer, by pursuing the demand the compensation of which he has neglected to oppose, avail himself, to the prejudice of third persons, of the privileges and mortgages which were attached thereto, unless he had a sufficient excuse for not being aware of the claim which was to compensate his debt.

See the parallel principle of English law, p. 486, 7.

Section 5.

Of Confusion.

1300.

When the characters of debtor and creditor are united in the same person, a confusion arises by law which extinguishes the two claims.

See a parallel principle of English law, p. 486, 7.

1301.

The confusion which is effected in the person of the principal debtor, benefits his sureties. The same effected in the person of the surety does not draw after it the extinction of the principal obligation; that which is effected in the person of the creditor, does not benefit his codebtors in solido, except for the portion in which he was debtor.

See ante parallel rule of English law, p. 487.

Section 6.

Of the Loss of the Thing due.

1302.

When the certain and determinate property which was the object of the obligation happens to perish, is put out of commerce, or is lost in such manner that its existence is absolutely unknown, the obligation is extinguished if the thing have perished, or have been lost without the fault of the debtor, and before he have been in delay. Even when the debtor is in delay, and if he have not been charged with fortuitous occurrences, the obligation is extinguished in the case where the thing would equally have perished at the house of the creditor if it had been delivered to him. The debtor is bound to prove the fortuitous occurrence which he alleges. In whatsoever manner a thing stolen have perished, or have been lost, its loss does not exonerate him who has sustained it from restitution of the price.

See parallel principle of English law, p. 488.

1303.

When the thing has perished, been put out of traffic, or lost, without fault on the part of the debtor, he is bound, if there are any claims or actions for indemnity in reference to to such thing, to yield them to his creditor.

See the English law in such cases, p. 488.

Section 7.

Of the Action for Nullity, or for Rescission of Agreements.

1304.

In all cases in which the action for nullity or for rescission of an agreement is not limited to a less time by a particular law, such action enures for ten years. Such time does not run, in the case of violence, except from the day on which it ceases; in the case of mistake or fraud, from the day on which they have been discovered; and as respects acts passed by married women unauthorized, from the day of the dissolution of the marriage. The time does not run with respect to acts made by interdicted persons, except from the day on which the interdiction is removed; and with respect to those made by minors, only from the day of majority.

See parallel principles of English law, p. 489.

1305.

Simple inequality (lesion) gives ground for rescission in favour of the minor not emancipated, against all kinds of agreements; and in favour of the minor emancipated against all agreements which exceed the bounds of his capacity, as was determined under the title "*Of Minority, Guardianship, and Emancipation.*"

See ante those titles, and p. 489.

1306.

The minor is not relievable for cause of inequality, when it was merely the result of a casual and unforeseen event.

See parallel principle of English law, p. 490.

1307.

The simple declaration of majority, made by the minor, forms no obstacle to his relief.

See parallel principle of English law, p. 490.

1308.

The minor being in trade, banker, or artisan, is not relievable against engagements to which he is liable in respect of his trade or craft.

See parallel principle of English law, p. 490.

1309.

The minor is not relievable against agreements contained in his contract of marriage, when they have been made with the consent and assistance of those whose consent is requisite for the validity of his marriage.

See parallel principle of English law, p. 490.

1310.

He is not relievable against obligations resulting from his own wrong or quasi wrong.

See parallel principle of English law, p. 490.

1311.

He is no longer permitted to disclaim an engagement which he subscribed in minority, when he has ratified it in majority, whether such engagement were null in its form, or whether it were only liable to be relieved against.

See parallel principle of English law, p. 490.

1312.

When minors, interdicted persons, or married women are admitted in such capacities to obtain relief against their engagements, the reimbursement of what, in consequence of such engagements, shall have been paid during minority, interdiction, or marriage, cannot be exacted from them, unless it be proved that what has been paid has turned to their advantage.

See parallel principle of English law, p. 489, 90.

1313.

Persons of full age are not relieved for cause of inequality of price, except in the cases and under the conditions especially mentioned in the present code.

See parallel article, p. 431, 2.

1314.

When the formalities required with respect to minors or interdicted persons, either for alienation of immoveables, or in a distribution of succession, have been complied with, they are in reference to such acts considered as having done them during majority or before interdiction.

See parallel article, p. 311, 2, 3, 8.

CHAPTER VI.

Of the Proof of Obligations and of that of Payment.

1315.

The party who claims performance of an obligation must prove it.* On the other hand, he who claims to be exonerated must establish payment, or verify the act which led to the extinction of his obligation.†

* See parallel principle of English law, p. 490.

† See parallel principle of English law, p. 489, 90.

1316.

The rules which relate to literal proof, testimonial proof, presumptions, acknowledgment, and oath of parties, are explained in the following sections.

See parallel article of English law, p. 491.

Section 1.

Of Literal Proof.

§ 1. *Of an Authentic Document.**

1317.

An authentic act is that which has been taken by public officers, whose duty it is to draw up instruments in the place where the act was reduced to writing, and with the requisite solemnities.†

* In England, the presence of notaries or other public officers not being necessary to the validity of documents, except a few mercantile ones, there does not exist anything exactly corresponding with the authentic document of the French law. Matters of record bear the most resemblance.

† No exact parallel in the English law; but see, as to records and ancient deeds, p. 491.

1318.

The act which is not authentic through the incompetence or incapacity of the officer, or through a defect of form, is equivalent to a private writing, if it were signed by the parties.

No exact parallel; but as to what are modern deeds, see p. 492, and preceding note.

1319.

The authentic act supplies full credit to the agreement which it contains between the contracting parties and their heirs or assigns. Nevertheless, in case of complaint of capital fault, the execution of the act charged to be faulty shall be suspended by the institution of the charge; and in case of inscription of fault incidentally made, the courts may, according to circumstances, suspend provisionally the execution of the act.

As to what documents prove themselves, see p. 491.

1320.

The act, whether authentic or under private signature, affords proof between the parties even of that which is expressed therein only in declaratory terms, provided the declaration have a direct reference to the disposition. Declarations foreign to the disposition can only serve as commencement of proof.

See as to recital in deeds, p. 492.

1321.

Defeasances can only produce their effect between the contracting parties; they have no operation against third persons.

See parallel principle of English law, p. 492.

§ 2. *Of an Act under Private Signature.*

1322.

The act under private signature,* acknowledged by the party against whom it is produced, or held by law to have been acknowledged, obtains between those who have subscribed it, their heirs and assigns, the same credit as an authentic act.†

* This corresponds with the English deed, p. 491, 2.

† As to the evidence of deeds, see p. 493.

1323.

The party against whom an act under private signature is produced, is obliged formally to avow or disavow his writing or signature. His heirs or assigns may content themselves with declaring that they do not know the writing or the signature of their principal.

See parallel principle of English law, p. 493.

1324.

In the case in which the party disavows his writing or his signature, and in the case in which his heirs or assigns declare they do not know it, the verification thereof is ordered by the court.

See parallel principle of English law, p. 493.

1325.

Acts under private signature which contain synallagmatical agreements are only valid so far as there has been made as many originals as there are parties who have a distinct interest. One original is sufficient for all the parties having the same interest. Every original must contain the mention of the number of originals which have been made thereof. Nevertheless, failure in mentioning that the originals have been made double, triple, &c., cannot be objected by him who has executed on his part the agreement contained in the act.

See parallel principle of English law, p. 493.

1326.

A note or promise under private signature, by which one single party binds himself towards another in the payment of a sum of money, or of a thing (appreciable) capable of being valued, must be written throughout by the hand of the subscriber; or at least, it is necessary that besides his signature, he should write "*bon*," or "*approuvé*," bearing all in letters the sum or the quantity of the thing, excepting in the case where the act proceeds from merchants, artisans, labourers, vine dressers, day labourers, and servants.

See parallel principle of English law, p. 493.

1327.

When the sum expressed in the body of the instrument is different from that which is expressed in the "*bon*," the obligation is presumed only to extend to the smaller sum, even when the act, as well as the "*bon*," is written throughout by the hand of the party bound, unless it can be proved on whose part the mistake lies.

See note to preceding article.

1328.

Acts under private signature only take date against third persons from the day on which they have been registered, from the day of the death of the subscriber, or one of the subscribers, or from the day on which the substance of them is verified in acts drawn up by public officers, such as statements of sealing or of inventory.

No parallel principles of English law.

1329.

The journals or day-books of tradesmen (marchands) do not supply against those who are not in trade, proof of goods furnished as contained therein, saving what shall be said with respect to the oath.

See English law on this point, p. 494.

1330.

The books of tradesmen afford proof against them; but the party who desires to derive advantage therefrom, cannot divide them as to what they contain contrary to his claim.

See parallel principle of English law, p. 494.

1331.

Domestic registers and papers do not form any evidence for the party who has written them. They furnish proof against him, 1st, in all cases where they formally declare payment received; 2nd, where they contain express mention that the memorandum has been made to supply the want of a document in favour of him for whose benefit they declare an obligation.

See parallel principle of English law, p. 494.

1332.

Writing inserted by the creditor at the end, in the margin, or on the back of a document which has always remained in his possession, is evidence, though not signed and dated by him, when it tends to establish the liberation of the debtor. The same applies to writing inserted by the creditor on the back, or in the margin, or at the end of the duplicate of a document or quittance, provided such duplicate be in the hands of the debtor.

See parallel principle of English law, p. 494.

§ 3. *Of Tallies.*

1333.

Tallies correllative to their patterns afford proof between parties who are in the habit of thus verifying commissions which they make and receive in retail.

See parallel article of English law, p. 494, 5.

§ 4. *Of Copies of Documents.*

1334.

Copies, where the original document is in existence, only afford proof of what is contained in such document, the production of which may always be required.

See parallel principle of English law, p. 495.

1335

When the original document no longer exists, copies furnish proof, agreeably to the following distinctions:

1st. Copies of the minutes (grosses), or first copies of the document (expedition), supply the same proof as the original. It is the same with regard to copies which have been taken by authority of the magistrate, the parties having been present or duly summoned; or with regard to such as have been taken in presence of the parties, and with their mutual consent.

2nd. Copies which, without the authority of the magistrate, or without the consent of the parties, and subsequently to the deliverance of the copies of the minutes or first copies of the document, shall have been taken from the minute of the act by the notary who received it, or by one of his successors, or by public officers, who in such capacity are the depositaries of the minutes, may, in case of the loss of the original, be made evidence when they are ancient. They are considered as ancient when they are more than thirty years old. If they are less than thirty years old, they can only be made use of as commencement of proof in writing.

3rd. When copies taken from the minutes of an act shall not have been so by the notary who received it, or by public officers who are in such capacity depositaries of the minutes, they can only be made use of, notwithstanding any degree of antiquity, as the commencement of proof in writing.

4th. Copies of copies may, according to circumstances, be considered as simple notes.

No parallel English law; but see p. 495, and note to article 1317.

1336.

The transcription of an act upon the public registers shall only be made use of as commencement of proof in writing; and it is necessary even for that—

1st. That it be manifest that all the minutes of the notary, of the year in which the act appears to have been made, are lost, or that it be proved that the loss of the minute of this act have arisen from a particular accident.

2nd. That there exist a regular docket of the notary, proving that the act was made at the same date. When, by reason of the concurrence of these two circumstances, proof by witnesses shall be admitted, it shall be necessary that those who were witnesses of the act, if they are still in existence, should be heard.

See parallel principle of English law, p. 495.

§ 5. *Of Recognitive and Confirmative Acts.*

1337.

Recognitive acts do not dispense with the production of the original document, unless its tenor be therein specially set forth. That which they contain in addition to the original document, or that which is found therein different from it, has no effect. Nevertheless, where there are several corresponding acknowledgments confirmed by possession, and of which one is thirty years old, the creditor may be excused from producing the original document.

See parallel English law, p. 496.

1338.

An act of confirmation or ratification of an obligation against which the law admits an action for nullity or rescission is only valid when it contains within it the substance of such obligation, mention of the motive for the action for rescission, and an intention to remedy the defect on which such action was founded. Failing such act of confirmation or ratification, it is sufficient that the obligation be executed voluntarily after the period at which the obligation may be validly confirmed or ratified. Confirmation, ratification, or voluntary execution, in the forms and at the period determined by the law, imports renunciation of the arguments and exceptions which may be opposed to such act, without prejudice nevertheless to the right of third persons.

See parallel English law, p. 496.

1339.

The donor cannot remedy by any confirmative act the defects of a donation during life; null in form, it is necessary that it should be re-executed in legal form.

See parallel English law, p. 496.

1340.

Confirmation, ratification, or voluntary execution of a donation by the heirs or assigns of the donor, after his decease, imports their renunciation of opposition either to defects of form or any other objection.

See parallel English law, p. 496.

SECTION 2.

Of Testimonial Proof.

1341.

There must be an act made before notaries or under private signature, respecting all things exceeding the sum or value of one hundred and fifty francs, even in the case of voluntary deposits; and no proof can be received by witnesses against or beyond what is contained in such acts, nor touching what shall be alleged to have been said before, at the time of or subsequently to such acts, although there may be question as to a sum or value less than one hundred and fifty francs; the whole without prejudice to what is prescribed in the laws relative to commerce.

See parallel principle of English law, p. 497.

1342.

The above rule applies to the case in which the action contains, besides the demand of capital, a demand for interest, which, added to the capital, exceeds the sum of one hundred and fifty francs.

See parallel principle of English law, p. 497.

1343.

The party who has a demand exceeding one hundred and fifty francs, can no longer be admitted to testimonial proof even on giving up his original demand.

The English law says such contracts are void. See parallel article 1326, p. 493.

1344.

Proof testimonial, on the demand of a sum even less than one hundred and fifty francs, cannot be admitted when such sum is declared to be the residue, or to form part of a larger credit which is not proved by writing.

See note to preceding article.

1345.

If in the same suit a party make several demands, of which there is no evidence in writing, and where, if united together, they exceed the sum of one hundred and fifty francs, proof by witnesses cannot be admitted thereon, although the party allege that such credits arise from different causes, and that they accrued at different times, unless it be that such claims proceed from succession, donation, or otherwise from different persons.

See parallel English law, p. 497.

1346.

All demands, of whatsoever description they may be, which shall not be entirely proved by writing, shall be sued for by the same action, after which, other demands, of which there shall be no proof in writing, shall not be admitted.

See note to preceding article.

1347.

The rules above mentioned admit of exception when there is a commencement of proof in writing. This is applied to every act in writing which emanates from the party against whom the demand is made, or from him whom such party represents, and who renders probable the fact alleged.

See parallel article 1326, p. 493.

1348.

They admit, moreover, of exception in all cases where it is impossible for the creditor to obtain a literal proof of the obligation which has been contracted with him. This second exception applies — 1st. To obligations which spring from quasi-contracts and from crimes or quasi-crimes. 2nd. To necessary deposits made in case of fire, fall of buildings, tumult, or shipwreck, and to those made by travellers lodging at an inn, the whole according to the condition of the persons and the circumstances of the act. 3rd. To obligations contracted on the occurrence of unforeseen accidents, in which it would have been impossible to have had acts in writing. 4th. In the case where the creditor has lost the document which served him for literal proof, in consequence of a fortuitous circumstance, unforeseen, and resulting from superior force.

See the parallel article, 1326, p. 493; and a parallel principle, p. 498.

Section 3.

Of Presumptions.

1349.

Presumptions are the conclusions which the law or the magistrate draws from a fact known as to a fact unknown.

See parallel definition of English law, p. 498.

§ 1. *Of Presumptions established by Law.*

1350.

A legal presumption is that which is attached by a special law to certain acts or to certain facts; such are— 1st. Acts which the law declares null, as presumed to have been made in fraud of its regulations, from their quality only. 2nd. Cases in which the law declares property or liberation to result from certain determinate circumstances. 3rd. The authority which the law attributes to a matter decided. 4th. The force which the law attaches to the confession of the party or to his oath.

See parallel principles of English law, p. 499.

1351.

The authority of a matter decided has no place except with regard to that which formed the object of the judgment. It is necessary that the thing demanded should be the same;

that the demand should be founded on the same cause; that the demand should be between the same parties, and made by and against them in the same capacity.

See a parallel rule of English law, p. 500.

1352.

Legal presumption dispenses with all proof on his part for whose benefit it exists. No proof is admitted against presumption of law, when, on the basis of such presumption, it annuls certain acts or restrains an action, unless it have reserved contrary proof, and saving what shall be said touching the oath and judicial confession.

See parallel English law, p. 500.

§ 2. *Of Presumptions which are not established by Law.*

1353.

Those presumptions which are not established by law are left to the sagacity and prudence of the magistrate, who must only admit presumptions grave, precise, and concordant, and in those cases only in which the law admits testimonial proofs, unless the act should be impeached for cause of fraud or deceit.

See parallel English law, p. 500.

SECTION 4.

Of the Acknowledgment of the Party.

1354.

The acknowledgment which is objected to a party is either judicial or extrajudicial.

See parallel article of English law, p. 500.

1355.

The allegation of an extrajudicial acknowledgment purely is useless in all cases where it relates to a demand of which testimonial proof would not be admissible.

See parallel English law, p. 500, 1.

1356.

Judicial acknowledgment is a declaration made in court by the party or his attorney specially appointed. It furnishes complete proof against the party who made it. It cannot be divided against him. It cannot be revoked, unless it can be proved that it proceeded from a mistake of fact. It cannot be revoked under pretext of a mistake in law.

See parallel principle of English law, p. 501.

SECTION 5.

Of Oath.

1357.

The judicial oath is of two species: 1st. That which one party takes (defere) of the other in order to make the judgment of the cause depend thereon: it is called "*decisory*." 2nd. That which is taken by the direction of the judge to either of the parties.

In England, at Common law, this kind of examination is not admitted; but in Chancery the defendant answers on oath. See p. 501.

§ 1. *Of the Oath Decisory.*

1358.

The oath decisory may be tendered in any description of dispute whatsoever.

The serment decisoire is a proceeding which has but a partial analogy to our answers in Chancery. Ev. Pot. p. 11 (n.); and see note to preceding article.

1359.

It can only be taken touching a fact personal to the party to whom it is put.

See note to article 1357, and p. 501.

1360.

It may be taken in every stage of a cause, and although there exist no commencement of proof of the demand or of the objection on which it is claimed.

See note to articles 1357, 8, and p. 501.

1361.

The party to whom the oath is tendered, who refuses it or who does not consent to tender it in return to his adversary, or the adversary to whom it has been tendered in return and who refuses it, must yield in his claim or in his objection.

See note to articles 1357, 8, and p. 501.

1362.

The oath cannot be tendered in return when the fact which is the object thereof does not lie between the two parties, but is purely personal to him to whom the oath was originally tendered.

See note to articles 1357, 8, and p. 501.

1363.

When the oath tendered or offered in return has been taken, the adversary is not admissible to prove the falsity thereof.

See note to articles 1357, 8, and p. 501.

1364.

The party who has tendered the oath or offered it in return, is not allowed to retract after the adversary has declared that he is ready to make such oath.

See note to articles 1357, 8, and p. 501.

1365.

The oath when taken only affords proof in favour of the party taking it, or against him and in favour of his heirs and assigns, or against them. Nevertheless, the oath tendered by one of the creditors in solido to the debtor, only discharges the latter as regards the share of such creditor; the oath tendered to the principal debtor discharges equally his sureties; the same tendered to one of the debtors in solido benefits his co-debtors; and the same tendered to a surety benefits the principal debtor. In the two latter cases, the oath of debtor in solido or of the surety does not benefit the other codebtors or the principal debtor, except when it has been tendered touching the debt, and not in respect of the fact of the solidarity or security.

See note to articles 1357, 8, and parallel principle, p. 501, 2.

§ 2. *Of the Oath administered officially.*

1366.

The judge may take the oath of one of the parties, either to make the decision of the cause depend thereon, or simply in order to determine the amount of the sentence.

See note to article 1357.

1367.

The judge cannot administer the oath officially, either upon the demand, or on the objection which is opposed thereto, except under the two following conditions: it is necessary, 1st, That the demand or the objection should not be fully proved; 2nd, that it be not totally destitute of proofs. Except in these two cases, the judge must either admit or reject the demand absolutely and unconditionally.

See note to article 1357.

1368.

The oath administered officially by the judge to one of the parties cannot be offered in return by such party to the other.

See note to article 1357.

1369.

The oath touching the value of the thing demanded cannot be administered by the judge to the demandant, except where it is impossible by other means to verify such value. The judge must, even in this case, determine the sum up to the amount of which the demandant shall be believed upon his oath.

See note to article 1357.

PALMER and CLAYTON Printers, 9, Crane Court, Fleet Street.

A DIGEST

OF

PRINCIPLES OF ENGLISH LAW;

ARRANGED IN THE ORDER

OF

THE CODE NAPOLEON.

Catalogue

OF

LAW WORKS

PUBLISHED BY

MESSRS. BUTTERWORTH,

Law Publishers to the Queen's Most Excellent Majesty.

" Now for the Laws of England (if I shall speak my opinion of them " without partiality either to my profession or country), for the matter and " nature of them, I hold them wise, just and moderate laws: they give to God, " they give to Cæsar, they give to the subject what appertaineth. It is true " they are as mixt as our language, compounded of British, Saxon, Danish, " Norman customs. And surely as our language is thereby so much the richer, " so our laws are likewise by that mixture the more complete."—LORD BACON.

LONDON:
7, FLEET STREET, E.C.
1860.

Contents of Catalogue.

Christie's Crabb's Conveyancing.—Fifth Edit. by Shelford.

Two vols. royal 8vo., 3*l.* cloth.

CRABB'S COMPLETE SERIES of PRECEDENTS in CONVEYANCING and of COMMON and COMMERCIAL FORMS in Alphabetical Order, adapted to the Present State of the Law and the Practice of Conveyancing; with copious Prefaces, Observations and Notes on the several Deeds. By J. T. CHRISTIE, Esq., Barrister-at-Law. The Fifth Edition, with numerous Corrections and Additions, by LEONARD SHELFORD, Esq., of the Middle Temple, Barrister-at-Law.

*** The *Law of Property Amendment and Relief of Trustees Act*, 1859, has been added to the present edition.

From the Law Times.

"Great changes have been made in the law since Crabb's Precedents obtained their well deserved popularity. Hence the necessity for a new edition, and the preparation of it could not have been confided to more able hands than those of Mr. Shelford, the veteran authority on real property law. With the industry that distinguishes him he has done ample justice to his task. He has rewritten the greater portion of the introductions or prefaces, and remodelled such of the precedents as required reform to meet the exigencies of new statutes, new decisions or new practice. In carefulness we have in him a second Crabb, in erudition Crabb's superior, and the result is a work of which the original author would have been proud, could it have appeared under his own auspices. It is not a book to be quoted, nor indeed could its merits be exhibited by quotation. It is essentially a book of practice, which can only be described in rude outline and dismissed with applause, and a recommendation of it to the notice of those for whose service it has been so laboriously compiled."

From the Solicitors' Journal and Reporter.

"Mr. Shelford has shown remarkable industry and faithfulness in noting up recent decisions relating more immediately to the *practice* of conveyancing. The collection of precedents contained in these two volumes are all that could be desired. They are particularly well adapted for Solicitors, being of a really practical character. They are moreover free from the useless repetitions of common forms that so much increase the bulk and expense of some collections that we could name. We know not of any collection of conveyancing precedents that would make it so possible for a tyro to put together a presentable draft at an exigency, or which are more handy in every respect, even for the experienced draftsman. Mr. Shelford has proved himself in this task to be not unworthy of his former reputation. To those familiar with his other works it will be a sufficient recommendation of this work that Mr. Shelford's name appears on the title page; if there be any who are not well acquainted with them, we venture to recommend to such the work before us, as the most generally useful and convenient collection of precedents in conveyancing, and of commercial forms for ordinary use, which are to be had in the English language."

From the Law Magazine and Review.

"Those who have been in the habit of using Crabb's work will allow that his 'Prefaces' contain practical observations of considerable utility to the professional man. The flow of time carrying with it many changes, and some reforms in the law relative to conveyancing, have imposed the obligation upon Mr Shelford of carefully revising all, and in many instances has rendered it expedient for him to re write not a small portion of some of these Prefaces. Mr. Shelford has also had to exercise, and we doubt not with correct judgment has exercised, his discretion as to where he should reject Forms which he deemed it advisable to omit, and where he should revise them or introduce new ones, to meet the modern exigencies and characteristics of conveyancing. To this important part of his duty—the remodelling and perfecting of the Forms—even with the examination which we have already been able to afford this work, we are able to affirm, that the learned editor has been eminently successful and effected valuable improvements."

From the Law Chronicle.

"It possesses one distinctive feature in devoting more attention than usual in such works to forms of a commercial nature. We are satisfied from an examination of the present with the immediately preceding edition that Mr Shelford has very considerably improved the character of the work, both in the prefaces and in the forms. The two volumes contain several hundred pages of additional matter, and both the latest cases and decisions appear to be noticed in the prefaces. Indeed it is evident that Mr. Shelford has modernized the whole work, and thus given it an additional value. On the whole the two volumes of Crabb's Precedents, as edited by Mr. Leonard Shelford, will be found extremely useful in a solicitor's office, presenting a large amount of real property learning, with very numerous precedents. Indeed we know of no book so justly entitled to the appellation of 'handy' as the fifth edition of Mr. Crabb's Precedents."

Hunter's Property Amendment & Trustees Relief Act, 1859.

12mo. 5s. 6d. boards.

THE ACT to AMEND the LAW of PROPERTY and to RELIEVE TRUSTEES, 22 & 23 VICT. c. 35; with Introductions and Practical Notes. By SYLVESTER JOSEPH HUNTER, of Trinity College, Cambridge, B.A., and of Lincoln's Inn, Esq., Barrister-at-Law, Author of "An Elementary View of a Suit in Equity."

"His statement of the objects designed by the several sections is singularly clear and concise." —*[illegible] Times.*

"We have seldom perused a treatise of similar compass and pretension that has so thoroughly met our views of what it ought to be." —*Legal [illegible].*

"Having [illegible] the work with some attention, we can conscientiously express an approval of the labours of Mr. Hunter, and we recommend all our readers to purchase the volume." —*Law Chronicle.*

May's Parliamentary Practice.—Fourth Edition.

One thick volume, 8vo., 31s. 6d. cloth.

A PRACTICAL TREATISE on the LAW, PRIVILEGES, PROCEEDINGS and USAGE of PARLIAMENT. By THOS. ERSKINE MAY, Esq., of the Middle Temple, Barrister-at-Law; Clerk Assistant of the House of Commons. Fourth Edition, revised and enlarged.

CONTENTS.—Book I. Constitution, Powers and Privileges of Parliament.—II. Practice and Proceedings in Parliament.—III. The Manner of Passing Private Bills; showing the Practice in both Houses, with the latest Standing Orders, and the most recent Precedents.

From the Times.

"Mr. May's work upon this very important subject is one of those books which have not now to gain, but only to sustain, a reputation. This book has been a guide, and a very good guide. Many alterations in the forms of the House have taken place since the last edition was published, and the work seems to have been carefully brought down to the present day."

From the Law Times.

"As it is now perfected this work is the one great and recognized authority on Parliamentary Law and Practice, and therefore an indispensable addition to the library of all who enjoy that pleasant and profitable business."

From the Daily News.

"Mr. May's work is too well known to need any statement of its contents, being a standard of reference not only in England but in the United States, and in every part of the world where our Parliamentary institutions have been imitated.

From the Observer.

"The value of this excellent work is greatly increased by the thorough revision it has undergone at the hands of the author, as well as by additions made to it so as to bring it up to the last point of time. It possesses moreover, a copious index, which facilitates beyond measure the researches of those whose avocations or whose pleasure cause them to study the subject of which it so lucidly treats. Too much, therefore, cannot be said in praise of the production for its accuracy and for excellence nor can it be too strongly or too earnestly recommended to the attention of all persons in anywise connected with or interested in the business of legislation."

From the Solicitors' Journal.

"The great value of the work, and what best explains the success which has carried it already to the fourth edition, is the abounding information in the practice and proceedings in Parliament which it contains. The subject matter is so clearly and so logically arranged, that even without the aid of the index one can always lay his finger in a moment on the information which he requires."

"Any Member of Parliament will find as a rule all he wants in Mr. May's Treatise, and members of our Profession, who consult the book for practical purposes, will be most interested by the pages which are devoted to an account of the manner of passing Private Bills. No Solicitor who has or desires Parliamentary practice should omit to read at least so much of this treatise."

From the Economist.

"Mr. Erskine May's treatise on the usages and privileges of the English Parliament is a work of standard value. It requires no eulogy from the periodical press to raise its value in the eyes of English readers both at home and in the colonies. We heartily welcome the fourth edition of this very important work, because every fresh edition which brings up the precedents it quotes and all changes in law or practice, to a more recent date, greatly adds to its immediate value. In this edition we are brought up to the end of the Session of 1858."

From the Press.

"Mr. May's new publication is the fourth edition of a work on the most interesting and important subject, the forms and procedure by which the business of the Legislature of either House of Parliament is carried on, and Mr. May, in preparing it, has added so much fresh matter, that this edition is invested with all the characteristics and value of a new work. The work, in fact, in its present form is something more than a treatise, and nearly amounts to a history of constitutional organization."

From the Morning Post.

"The Treatise on the whole contains every information which can be valuable to Members of Parliament, to practitioners of the law, and to students of the most important branch of the constitutional history of this country. It possesses one merit which cannot be too highly appreciated, the correctness and clearness with which the point of each precedent is stated.

MR. SERJEANT STEPHEN'S

New Commentaries on the Laws of England.—Fourth Edition.

Four Volumes, 8vo., Four Guineas cloth.

(*DEDICATED, by permission, to HER MAJESTY THE QUEEN.*)

NEW COMMENTARIES ON THE LAWS OF ENGLAND, in which are interwoven, under a new and original Arrangement of the general Subject, all such parts of the Work of Blackstone as are applicable to the present times; together with full but compendious Expositions of the Modern Improvements of the Law up to the latest period; the original and adopted Materials being throughout the Work typographically distinguished from each other. By HENRY JOHN STEPHEN, Serjeant at Law. Fourth Edition. Prepared for the press by the learned Author in conjunction with JAMES STEPHEN, LL.D., of the Middle Temple, Barrister at Law, and Professor of English Law and Jurisprudence at King's College, London.

From the Law Times.

"That Mr. Serjeant Stephen has succeeded in maintaining the reputation of Blackstone as the hand-book of the Law Student, and establishing his edition as that which takes the place of the original, to the exclusion of a host of competitors for the same honour, is due in great part to his having caught the spirit of his master and even something of his style, and thus prevented that abruptness of transition from one writer to the other which occurs many times in almost every page, and sometimes even in the same sentence. There is none of the stiffness that might be expected from this striated composition, and that is a merit which belongs only to Mr. Stephen, and which has secured for him the almost undisputed possession of the field. Even since the last edition many changes have been made, which are carefully noted, so that the new one presents an outline of the law of England precisely at this moment. It must be the first text book read by the Law Student, but we would recommend the Practitioner to refresh his memory by sometimes dipping into its pages if he has not leisure to read it through. He will be astonished to find how much information he will gather from it."

From the Leguleian.

"In our opinion the key to the Examination is that admirable work Stephen's Commentaries, and no Student ought to take his seat at the hall of the Incorporated Law Society, to undergo the ordeal with any hope of obtaining honours, or even a certificate to pass, until he was conscious he had mastered its contents. Some may consider this a bold dictum; but no one who is at all acquainted with the character of the education of a Law Student, the nature of the examination itself, extending over all the branches of the law, the number and massive description of the various works published, after making those searches, will repudiate our statement, that a work which brings the whole mass of law in one clear and distinct focus of excellence is the most valuable that could be placed in the hands of a Student. We are the more anxious to impress candidates with the solid benefits and advantages that can be derived from the study of Stephen's Commentaries, since we know that many articled clerks are deceived into the perusal of other works compiled in a more or less imperfect manner, and bearing the name of *Commentaries on Blackstone*. Let them read Blackstone and all his Commentators from the first to the last, if they have time and appetite for such a task, but, on the completion of this undertaking, do not let them suppose that they have thereby become possessors of the contents of *Stephen's Commentaries*."

From the Solicitors' Journal.

"A fourth edition has appeared of Serjeant Stephen's Commentaries, prepared for the press by his son, Mr. James Stephen, the Professor of English Law and Jurisprudence at King's College, London. The character of the book is so well known and its reputation so thoroughly established, that we have no further inquiry to make than whether each new edition brings down the law to the date of publication. Mr. Stephen is a very worthy editor of his father's work, and has evidently bestowed the greatest care and industry on fulfilling his task as perfectly as possible. The last edition appeared in 1853, and on turning to different parts of the new edition we find the acts of parliament and the chief cases of a later date noted up very accurately. Where Mr. Kerr, in his Blackstone, refers to two cases, Mr. Stephen refers to twenty. This is the great merit of Stephen's Commentaries. It not only arranges the subject clearly and connectedly, but it shows the Student how he may prosecute the inquiry for himself, and carry his knowledge beyond what can possibly be conveyed within the limits of a general treatise."

From the Law Chronicle.

"We cannot but repeat, that the New Commentaries of Mr. Serjeant Stephen deserve the reputation which they have gained; that the fourth edition appears to have been very carefully prepared, bringing the law down to the end of the last session of parliament; that it is a work which will be found useful not only to the law student, but to the practitioner; that the notes alone contain very much practical matter, the value of which is enhanced by the references to the recent statutes and reported decisions; and above all, that the work, which may be relied on for accuracy, contains an excellent summary of the law in its present state: a sure foundation on which the student may safely build."

Stephen's Questions on the Commentaries.

1 vol. 8vo., 10s. 6d. cloth.

QUESTIONS for LAW STUDENTS on the FOURTH EDITION of Mr. Serjeant STEPHEN'S NEW COMMENTARIES. By JAMES STEPHEN, LL.D., Barrister at Law, &c. &c.

Wharton's Articled Clerk's Manual.—Eighth Edition.

1 thick vol. 12mo., 20s. cloth.

A MANUAL for ARTICLED CLERKS; containing Courses of Study as well in Common Law, Conveyancing, Equity, Bankruptcy and Criminal Law, as in Constitutional, Roman-Civil, Ecclesiastical, Colonial, and International Laws, and Medical Jurisprudence; a Digest of all the Examination Questions; with the General Rules, Forms of Articles of Clerkship, Notices, Affidavits, &c., and a List of the proper Stamps and Fees: being a comprehensive guide to their successful Examination, Admission and Practice as Attornies and Solicitors of the Superior Courts. Eighth Edition. By J. J. S. WHARTON, Esq., M.A., Oxon, Barrister at Law, Author of "The Law Lexicon."

"We cheerfully acknowledge and record much that deserves approbation. Throughout the Work there are traces of a well regulated and orthodox mind, well adapted to produce confidence in an instructor of youth. To conclude, we would tell our younger readers that by using this Manual judiciously, and not relying upon it to the exclusion of other reading, they may gain much. Everyone must judge for himself whether such assistance is suitable for him in reference to his own individuality, and if he decides in the affirmative, we know not where he could turn with more advantage than to the 'Articled Clerk's Manual.'"—*Solicitors' Journal and Reporter.*

"We think any articled clerk, commencing his studies, will find Mr. Wharton's book of assistance, as it will aid him in ascertaining to what matters he should direct his attention, and at the same time furnish him with information serving for the groundwork of further study. There is certainly no other work of the kind, and that is some merit in these days of imitation."—*Law Chronicle.*

"Mr. Wharton's book still continues to grow in public favour and in bulk. The 8th edition is now before us much enlarged in size, but its additional contents have been well selected and well digested, and they have consequently produced a healthy rotundity of which no one can complain. The new edition has not appeared before it was required. The merits of the book are undoubted, and each edition increases the esteem in which it is held."—*Leguleian.*

Drewry's Equity Pleader.

12mo., 6s. cloth.

A CONCISE TREATISE on the PRINCIPLES of EQUITY PLEADING; with Precedents. By C. STEWART DREWRY, of the Inner Temple, Esq., Barrister at Law.

CONTENTS. What Persons are entitled to sue in Equity, and in what manner to sue; of the Modes of instituting a Suit in Equity; of the Defence of Suits; of Pleas; of Answers; of Amended Bills; of Revivor and Supplemental Bills; of Interlocutory Applications; of the Proceedings on going into Evidence; of Appeals; Conclusion; Appendix of Precedents.

"Mr. Drewry will be remembered by many as the author of the very popular and excellent Treatise on the Practice in Equity. He has now contributed to the library of the lawyer another work of equal value, written for younger members of the profession, and for students, in which he describes the principles and general rules of equity pleading. It will be found of great utility as introductory to the more elaborate treatises, or to refresh the memory after the study of the larger books."—*Law Times.*

"If, however, a knowledge of Equity Pleading be desired by any of our readers, we can refer them to the above work for a very simple and concise outline. On the whole it appears to us that, keeping in view Mr. Drewry's design, namely, to produce a work on Equity Pleading for the information of students, he has successfully accomplished his professed object."—*Law Chronicle.*

"Such a book, since the recent reforms effected in that branch of the law, will be found useful to a large class of readers. As an introduction to pleadings as they now subsist in the Equity Courts the book is well timed."—*Law Magazine and Law Review.*

"As it is penned in an easy and readable style, and is as free from technical terms as possible, it is qualified to form a first book or introduction to its subject matter."—*Leguleian.*

Fry's Specific Performance of Contracts.

8vo., 16s. cloth.

A TREATISE on the SPECIFIC PERFORMANCE of CONTRACTS, including those of Public Companies, with a Preliminary Chapter on the Provisions of the Chancery Amendment Act, 1858. By EDWARD FRY, B.A., of Lincoln's Inn, Esq., Barrister at Law.

"It will be seen what a masterly grasp the author has taken of his subject, and his treatment of the various parts of it equally exhibits the hand of a man who has studied the law as a science. He is skilful in the extraction of principles, precise in the exposition of them, apt in their application to the particular case, but in that he is thoroughly practical. The practitioner who uses it as a text book will find in it an adviser who will tell him not only what the law is, but how it may be enforced."—*Law Times.*

"Mr. Fry's work presents in a reasonable compass a large quantity of modern learning on the subject of contracts, with reference to the common remedy by specific performance, and will thus be acceptable to the profession generally."—*Law Chronicle.*

"There is a closeness and clearness in its style, and a latent fulness in the exposition, which not only argue a knowledge of the law, but of those varying circumstances in human society to which the law has to be applied."—*Spectator.*

"Mr Fry's elaborate essay appears to exhaust the subject, on which he has cited and brought to bear, with great diligence, some 1,500 cases, which include those of the latest reports." *Law Magazine and Review.*

"Although a professional work, it is sufficiently popular in style to be serviceable to all persons engaged in commerce or joint stock undertakings." *The Times, July 20th,* 1858.

"This is a thoroughly satisfactory law book. No practising barrister should be without it, and its clearness, precision and methodical arrangement render it as good a text book for the legal student. The law of specific performance is a growing law just now, and the characteristic which gives its special value to Mr. Fry's work is, that the recent cases are as well digested in his mind as the older ones. Mr. Fry's is one of the best specimens of the modern law book."—*The Economist.*

"Mr Fry's treatise is succinct and comprehensive, evidencing patient study, and containing sound practical deductions supported by principle and authority."—*Leguleian.*

Bainbridge on Mines and Minerals.—Second Edition.

8vo., 24s. cloth.

A TREATISE on the LAW of MINES and MINERALS. By WILLIAM BAINBRIDGE, Esq., F.G.S., of the Inner Temple, Barrister at Law. Second Edition, carefully revised, and much enlarged by additional matter relating to manorial rights—rights of way and water and other mining easements—the sale of mines and shares—the construction of leases—cost book and general partnerships—injuries from undermining and inundations—barriers and working out of bounds. With an Appendix of Forms and Customs and a Glossary of English Mining Terms.

"Among recent publications has been a Second Edition of Mr. Bainbridge's elaborate Treatise on the Law of Mines and Minerals."—*Times.*

"Strange to say, until the publication of Mr. Bainbridge's Treatise, there was no law book dedicated to a subject so vast, so difficult, and involving so many interests. No wonder, then, that an endeavour to supply the defect should have received a cordial welcome, or that, when it was found to be so well done, there should be a demand for a second edition of it."—*Law Times.*

"Beyond the general revision and incorporation of recent decisions, which every New Edition implies, the Work has been much improved by the addition of much new matter. The Glossary of Mining Terms is more complete than any we have seen."—*Jurist.*

"We are glad to see that a New Edition of this Work, which has become an authority in relation to the Law of Mines and Minerals. We think that this volume will be servicable to many without the pale of the legal profession, it will assuredly be so to lawyers." *Law Magazine.*

Coote's New Admiralty Practice.

8vo. 12*s.* cloth.

THE NEW PRACTICE of the HIGH COURT of ADMIRALTY of ENGLAND; with the New Rules of 1859, and a Collection of Original Forms, and Bills of Costs. By HENRY CHARLES COOTE, Proctor of the Court, Author of "The Practice of the Court of Probate," "The Practice of the Ecclesiastical Courts," &c.

"Mr Coote is already very generally known to the Profession by his valuable books on the New Practice of the Court of Probate and the Practice of the Ecclesiastical Courts, which we have had occasion to notice. The work before us is characterized by lucid arrangement of the subject matter, as well as by a constant appreciation of what suits the convenience of practitioners. The merest tyro in this department of the law need hardly be afraid to undertake the ordinary business of the Court with such a book to guide him.'—*Solicitors' Journal and Reporter.*

"Mr. Coote has promptly entered the new field thus opened to him, and laid the first modern book on the subject before the new comers. He has the great advantage of experience, he has been long a practitioner in the Court as a Proctor, he is consequently familiar with those minutiæ of practice which mark the distinction between the student and the practical man"—*Law Times.*

"Mr Coote has, in a volume of convenient size, furnished the practitioner in the Admiralty Court with an invaluable manual. It is not merely that Mr Coote's volume is the only existing book of practice that it is to be recommended, but that it is a very excellent and complete production, leaving little chance of there being any successful rival" *Law Chronicle.*

"Mr. Coote has done his work well by doing it carefully and unaffectedly. He has kept himself most sensibly to the letter of his promise, and, by compressing into a reasonable space such information as the profession stood in need of, has succeeded in furnishing a work which has only to be perused to be appreciated and approved of."—*Shipping and Mercantile Gazette.*

Tudor's Leading Cases on Real Property, Conveyancing, &c.

One thick vol., royal 8vo., 36*s.* cloth.

A SELECTION of LEADING CASES on the LAW relating to REAL PROPERTY, CONVEYANCING, and the CONSTRUCTION of WILLS and DEEDS; with Notes. By OWEN DAVIES TUDOR, Esq., of the Middle Temple, Barrister at Law, Author of "A Selection of Leading Cases in Equity."

"The selection of cases in the volume before us has been judiciously made, and the notes are the result of much learning and industry. Mr. Tudor is also entitled to praise for having kept the notes within moderate dimensions, and for not having overburthened them with cases. Among the subjects are Tenancies at Sufferance, at Will, and from Year to Year; Freeholds of Inheritance and not of Inheritance; the Rights of Common; Easements; Advowsons; Rents; Uses and Trusts; Powers; Perpetuities; Mortmain; the Rule in Shelley's Case; Estates by Implication of Law; Escheats; Vested and Contingent Interests; Estates in Parcenary; Joint Tenancy; Tenancy in Common; and Tenancy by Entireties; Lapsed Legacies; Extrinsic Evidence in Construing Wills; Extinguishment and Merger; and Conditions and Restraints upon the Alienation of Property."—*Jurist.*

"It is a work which will repay perusal, and we would recommend those of our readers who are anxious for instruction on some of the most abstruse points of the Law of Real Property, to purchase and carefully read the volume of Mr. Tudor, and then we are satisfied that they will recognise the utility of the labours of the Annotator, and find themselves much improved thereby."—*Law Chronicle.*

"The manner in which Mr. Tudor has executed his task is beyond all praise."—*Morning Advertiser.*

"The work will doubtless be a valuable addition to the library of the working lawyer as well as that of the student."—*Legal Observer.*

"Mr. Tudor has done a substantial service to the Profession. The plan adopted is the same as in the Equity Cases. Mr. Tudor has exhibited his usual knowledge and clearness in the conveying of it to his readers, and his volume should be studied by the student, and will be useful for reference to the practitioner."—*Law Times.*

Francillon's Law Lectures.—First Series.

8vo., 8s. cloth.

LECTURES, ELEMENTARY and FAMILIAR, on ENGLISH LAW. FIRST SERIES. By JAMES FRANCILLON, Esq., County Court Judge, to be continued by subsequent volumes.

"We may say with confidence they are extremely well adapted to the use for which they are intended. We can therefore cordially recommend these Lectures to law students; but we are very much mistaken if Mr. Francillon will not find a class of readers greatly more numerous than even the numerous body of law students."—*Solicitors' Journal and Reporter.*

"Mr. Francillon has produced a very readable volume, which in this respect forms a striking contrast with ordinary law books. If the other portions are as ably done, Mr. Francillon will confer a benefit on the rising generation of lawyers, and of those laymen who may desire to acquire some knowledge of the principles of the law."—*Law Chronicle.*

"Mr. Francillon writes in a popular easy style and his little volume will be found both interesting and instructive to the general reader as well as the student."—*Bell's Messenger.*

"If all instructors were as agreeable and improving as Mr. Francillon is in these Lectures, law students would have no cause to complain of the dryness or the difficulty of their studies. Law students want a little more of this order of tuition and a few more such instructors as Mr. Francillon."—*Leguleian.*

"We can safely recommend them. They are prepared with considerable care and ability, and the language is so clear and simple that, but for the evidence which is offered by the substance of the work, we should have doubted whether the writer could be a lawyer. The substance is, moreover, rendered interesting so far as this is possible."—*Athenæum.*

Davis's County Courts Practice and Evidence.—Second Edition.

Post 8vo., 24s. cloth.

A MANUAL of the PRACTICE and EVIDENCE in ACTIONS and other Proceedings in the County Courts; with the Statutes and Rules. By JAMES EDWARD DAVIS, Esq., of the Middle Temple, Barrister-at-Law. SECOND EDITION. With a SUPPLEMENT, containing the Practice under the Statute 19 & 20 Vict. c. 108, and the New Rules and Orders, &c., together with a new and complete Index to the entire Work.

* *This is the only work on the County Courts which treats fully of the Law and Evidence in actions and other proceedings in these Courts.*

"We are glad to see that the excellent little work written some time since by Mr. Davis has reached a second edition. We may indeed congratulate Mr. Davis on the judgment he has throughout displayed in selecting and arranging the materials of which his present volume is composed."—*Law Magazine.*

"Mr. Davis's book will be found a very useful Manual, not only in the County Courts, but also in the superior tribunals."—*Jurist.*

"Mr. Davis has availed himself of the call for a second edition to enlarge and improve his useful little book. We prophesied the success of this book on its first appearance. There remains now only the pleasing duty of recording it and congratulating Mr. Davis upon his well-earned honour."—*Law Times.*

"The work of Mr. Davis may justly be said to be useful to the student and practitioner, independently of its application to the County Courts. Indeed, we know of no work of its size which can be *so* useful to the student or practitioner desirous of knowing what the common law is at the present time."—*Law Chronicle.*

"In its present form this single volume may be safely relied upon as an accurate and complete guide to every branch of County Court Practice and Evidence."—*Morning Post.*

"The work is now a correct compendium of the current Law and Practice on the subjects most frequently occurring in the County Courts, and will be found a most useful companion to the practitioner."—*Morning Chronicle.*

Davis's County Courts New Practice.

Post 8vo., 12s. cloth.

THE NEW PRACTICE of the COUNTY COURTS, in ACTIONS and other Proceedings, with the Statute 19 & 20 Vict. c. 108, and the Rules, &c., thereon: forming a Work complete in itself, or a SUPPLEMENT to the Second Edition of "The Manual of the Practice and Evidence in the County Courts." By JAMES EDWARD DAVIS, Esq., of the Middle Temple, Barrister at Law.

"This New Practice will not be found inferior to the Manual its predecessor. This publication will prove valuable to the profession generally on many points which fall within their practice, as in the case of a certiorari, or a prohibition, or a replevin. These subjects appear to be well handled."—*Leguleian.*

Stephen's Lush's Common Law Practice. Second Edition.

One thick volume, 8vo., 42s. cloth

LUSH'S PRACTICE of the SUPERIOR COURTS of COMMON LAW at WESTMINSTER, in Actions and Proceedings connected therewith over which they have a common Jurisdiction: with FORMS; also Introductory Treatises respecting Parties to Actions; Attornies and Town Agents; Suing in Person, by Attorney, or in Forma Pauperis, &c.: and an Appendix, containing the General Rules, the Authorized Table of Costs, Fees, &c. Second Edition. By JAMES STEPHEN, LL.D., of the Middle Temple, Barrister-at-Law, and Professor of English Law and Jurisprudence at King's College, London.

"An examination of the work enables us to pronounce a very favourable opinion on the manner in which Mr. Stephen has executed his laborious task. Mr. Stephen's editorship has not been of the ordinary kind."—*Law Magazine.*

"The law as well as the practice is set forth with extraordinary elaboration, indeed, we have never seen a law book which is such a monument of industry as this. We have no hesitation in pronouncing this to be by far the best 'Practice' that has yet appeared, and that Mr. Stephen has fully maintained the reputation achieved by Mr. Lush."—*Law Times.*

"The work has fallen into excellent hands. It is not too much to say that the work fully accomplishes its objects, and must necessarily become not only a standard authority, but a recognized manual in the matters which it so ably and lucidly treats."—*Morning Chronicle.*

"Mr. Lush has been fortunate in his editor. Painstaking, methodical and conscientiously cautious, Mr. Stephen has executed a most laborious task in a manner eminently useful and satisfactory. We dismiss his work with a hearty commendation to the attention of those whom it more particularly concerns."—*Daily News.*

"A work which is a complete text-book of the actual Practice, and is invaluable to the Practitioner and the Student. Indeed, we know not where the latter could find so *readable* a book on subjects ordinarily so little inviting as points of Practice; at the same time that the work furnishes all that the busiest Practitioner could desire."—*Law Chronicle.*

"The duty of remodelling Mr. Lush's Common Law Practice has been assigned by the publishers to Mr. James Stephen, and the result of his labours leaves them no ground to regret their selection. Nothing has been omitted which was necessary to complete the work of renovation."—*Morning Advertiser.*

"A careful examination of its contents has satisfied us that it combines in a remarkable degree the qualities of accuracy and conciseness. The new Practice is now clearly and succinctly explained and illustrated within the convenient compass of a single volume, and we cannot doubt that lawyers will rapidly evince their estimation of so great a boon."—*Morning Post.*

"We have compared it with the first edition, and we have no hesitation in saying that the work itself will be a permanent monument of the industry of the learned editor."—*Legal Observer.*

"We predict that it will be the standard authority on the Common Law Practice. Its Author has not adopted the plan pursued in other modern Practice books; but he has bestowed an earnest diligence and appropriate care on his subject, the result is a masterly treatise, exhibiting due accuracy."—*Leguleian.*

Oke's Magisterial Synopsis.—Seventh Edition.

IN THE PRESS. One thick volume, 8vo., cloth.

THE MAGISTERIAL SYNOPSIS: a Practical Guide for Magistrates, their Clerks, Attornies and Constables, in all Matters out of Quarter Sessions; containing Summary Convictions and Indictable Offences, with their Penalties, Punishment, Procedure, &c., Tabularly arranged. By GEORGE C. OKE, Assistant Clerk to the Lord Mayor of London, Author of "*The Magisterial Formulist*," "*The Law of Turnpike Roads*," &c. &c. Seventh Edition, enlarged and improved.

"I am aware that the Lord Mayor has at present an able assistant in the person of a gentleman of the name of Oke, author of the 'Magisterial Synopsis,' a very enterprising, able and learned man."—*The Lord Chancellor, in the House of Lords, February 23, 1860.*

Oke's Magisterial Formulist.—Second Edition.

8vo., 21*s.* cloth.

The MAGISTERIAL FORMULIST: being a complete collection of Forms and Precedents for practical use in all Cases out of Quarter Sessions, and in Parochial Matters, by Magistrates, their Clerks and Attornies: with an Introduction, Explanatory Directions, Variations and Notes. By GEORGE C. OKE, Author of "The Magisterial Synopsis," &c. &c. Second Edition, enlarged and improved.

"It is enough to announce the publication of a New Edition of this work, so well known to Magistrates' Clerks. It is a valuable Collection of the Forms and Precedents required in all cases out of Quarter Sessions and in Parochial Matters, with an Introduction explaining how they are to be used. Very considerable additions have been made to this New Edition, which consists of no less than 600 closely printed pages."—*Law Times.*

"This Collection of Forms and Precedents for Practical Use in all Cases out of Quarter Sessions and in Parochial Matters is deservedly esteemed. It is complete and well arranged, and we rejoice to see that a New Edition of it, which has for some time been demanded, has at length appeared."—*Law Magazine.*

Oke's Solicitor's Book-keeping.

8vo., 5*s.* cloth,

AN IMPROVED SYSTEM of SOLICITORS' BOOK-KEEPING, practically exemplified by a Year's supposed Business, with Directions for Posting, Balancing, Checking, &c. Adapted to small, moderate and large Offices; to Partnership and sole Concerns. By GEORGE C. OKE, Author of "*The Magisterial Synopsis*" and "*The Magisterial Formulist.*"

Scriven on Copyholds.—Fourth Edition, by Stalman.

Two vols., royal 8vo., 2*l.* 10*s.* boards.

A TREATISE on COPYHOLD, CUSTOMARY FREEHOLD and ANCIENT DEMESNE TENURE; with the Jurisdiction of Courts Baron and Courts Leet; also an Appendix containing Rules for holding Customary Courts, Courts Baron and Courts Leet, Forms of Court Rolls, Deputations, and Copyhold Assurances, and Extracts from the relative Acts of Parliament. By JOHN SCRIVEN, Serjeant at Law. THE FOURTH EDITION, embracing all the authorities to the present period, by HENRY STALMAN, Esq. of the Inner Temple, Barrister at Law.

Rouse's Practical Conveyancer.—Second Edition.

Two vols., 8vo., 26s. cloth.

THE PRACTICAL CONVEYANCER: a Companion to ROUSE'S PRACTICAL MAN, giving, in a mode combining facility of reference with general utility, upwards of Four Hundred Precedents of Conveyances, Mortgages and Leases; a Collections of Miscellaneous Forms; and (added in the present edition) Forms of Settlement and Separation Deeds. By ROLLA ROUSE, Esq., of the Middle Temple, Barrister-at-Law, author of "The Practical Man," &c. &c. &c. Second Edition, greatly enlarged.

"The work has been materially enlarged, expanded indeed into two volumes, and the references throughout have been carefully verified and tested. We entertain no sort of doubt that 'The Practical Conveyancer' will, in its present improved form, be acceptable to and appreciated by the profession." *Law Magazine and Review.*

"It may truly be said to offer more facilities to the draftsman than any other work comprising Conveyancing Precedents. Mr. Rouse's work is one which an intelligent clerk may readily adopt to any required draft. *Law Chronicle.*

"The changes are decided improvements. The arrangement is extremely convenient. If the first edition found favour with the profession, much more is this second edition entitled to their regard.'—*Law Times.*

"It is not often in these days when so much has been already written and so much more is being constantly poured from the press, that one comes across a book that can in any sense be called original. Nothing in legal literature bears the faintest resemblance to the 'Practical Conveyancer.' There is this special advantage in Mr Rouse's thoroughly systematic arrangement, that it is possible to get at home with his precedents much more quickly than with any other work of the kind. Altogether the book strikes us as a very effective labour saving machine, and one that will be found of special value to practitioners, the extent of whose business compels them to delegate a good deal of their conveyancing to clerks, who need some little preliminary instruction to enable them to set about a complicated draft in the right way. The book in short deserves its title, and may, we think, be relied on as a really Practical Conveyancer." *Solicitors' Journal and Reporter.*

"This is a new and materially improved edition in two vols. of a work whose practical utility we had occasion to notice two years ago. We think it well adapted not only for an aid to the practitioner, but also as a guide to the student of practical conveyancing." *Leguleian.*

"We ventured to predicate that the success of the work would be very great. And so it has proved. The work is really one of great utility, the forms are so arranged, that by means of skeleton drafts reference is made to the intended portions of a conveyance, so that a conveyancer has only to decide upon the construction of his deed, and he can then, by referring to the numbers, have the deed at once copied out by a clerk, and save an infinity of trouble. To the general, and especially the country practitioner, this work will prove very useful." *Bell's Messenger.*

Fisher's Law of Mortgage and Priority.

8vo., 25s. boards.

The LAW of MORTGAGE as applied to the REDEMPTION, FORECLOSURE and SALE in EQUITY of ENCUMBERED PROPERTY, with the Law of the PRIORITY of INCUMBRANCERS. By WILLIAM RICHARD FISHER, of Lincoln's Inn, Esq., Barrister at Law.

"Those who are concerned in mortgage transactions, whatever text book they use,—on the subjects of Redemption, Foreclosure and Sale will nowhere find so much, so careful, and such recent information as that which Mr. Fisher has collected. His work is skilfully planned and very clearly expressed. To write law well is a special faculty possessed by few, and Mr. Fisher is one of the few." —*Law Times.*

Glen's Poor Law Orders.—Fourth Edition.

12mo., 12s. cloth.

The CONSOLIDATED and other ORDERS of the POOR LAW COMMISSIONERS and the POOR LAW BOARD, together with the General Orders relating to Poor Law Accounts; the Statutes relating to the Orders, Audit of Accounts, Appeals and the Payment of Parish Debts. With Explanatory Notes elucidating the Orders and the Decisions thereon; Tables of Statutes, Cases and Index. By WILLIAM CUNNINGHAM GLEN, Esq., of the Middle Temple, Barrister at Law, and of the Poor Law Board. Fourth Edition.

"Mr. Glen, the editor of this volume, is officially connected with the Board, he has made the subject the study of his life, he is familiar with every part of it, and therefore he is able to give his readers information which no other man possesses, or could produce. Hence a volume whose utility has received the practical proof of four editions, each an improvement on its predecessor." *Law Times.*

Glen's Public Health and Local Government.

12mo. 12s. cloth.

THE LAW RELATING TO THE PUBLIC HEALTH AND LOCAL GOVERNMENT, in relation to SANITARY and other MATTERS, together with the PUBLIC HEALTH ACT, 1848, and the LOCAL GOVERNMENT ACT, 1858, and the Incorporated Acts, with Tables of Statutes, Cases and Index. By WILLIAM CUNNINGHAM GLEN, Esq., of the Middle Temple, Barrister-at-Law, and of the Poor Law Board.

"We anticipate for the above mentioned volumes a very considerable sale, because the information which they profess to give is needed by every town in the kingdom." *Law Magazine and Review.*

"The work is well done, and likely to prove generally useful." *Daily News.*

"A work which will in a convenient and accessible form furnish a lucid and informing guide and commentary to the statutes in question." *Builder.*

"There can be no doubt from the methodical and perspicuous manner in which Mr. Glen has performed his task that his book will be a standard one on the important matters comprised therein."—*Law Chronicle.*

"Its aim is declared to be to furnish those engaged in the administration of the law, and in the advancement of sanitary reforms, with a practically useful exposition of the statutes relating to the public health. This aim, it is but justice to say, it has completely accomplished, and there can be no question, therefore, that the work will be favourably received by the public." *Observer.*

"Both treatises are clearly, succinctly and ably written, and will prove safe and unerring guides in the administration of these branches of our municipal government." *Morning Herald.*

"They are well arranged and carefully executed, and the author shows throughout an extensive knowledge of the subjects of which he treats with considerable ability in imparting such knowledge." *Athenæum.*

"As expositions of the several Acts mentioned in the above titles we regard these as very useful works." *Standard.*

Glen's Nuisances Removal and Diseases Prevention.

12mo. 5s. cloth.

THE LAW RELATING TO THE REMOVAL OF NUISANCES INJURIOUS TO HEALTH, and to the PREVENTION OF EPIDEMIC AND CONTAGIOUS DISEASES, with the STATUTES, including the PUBLIC HEALTH ACT, 1858, and Tables of Statutes, Cases and Index. By WILLIAM CUNNINGHAM GLEN, Esq., of the Middle Temple, Barrister-at-Law, and of the Poor Law Board.

"Mr. Glen's little treatise on the Law relating to the Removal of Nuisances and the Prevention of Diseases will be of great service in guiding local authorities safely through the intricacies of the many statutes which more or less affect the subject." *Solicitors' Journal.*

"It will be found a full exposition of the law as it exists on this important subject." *Law Magazine and Review.*

"It is calculated to be eminently serviceable to local authorities for whose use it is principally compiled." *Daily News.*

"To all professional men concerned in the administration of the Laws relating to the Removal of Nuisances and the Preservation of the Public Health this little work of Mr. Glen will be found very useful, and as we know of no other work on the same matters, we might with truth say that it is indispensable to them." *Law Chronicle.*

"It contains a full exposition of the law as it exists upon this most important subject, arranged in such a manner as to enable those who consult it readily to comprehend the course of action which the law directs for the removal of nuisances, and is in every respect the complement of the preceding publication in point of utility as well as in point of practice." *Observer.*

"The Nuisances Removal Law is treated in the same manner as his Public Health and Local Government Law—simply, clearly and minutely—so that whatever information is sought is surely and readily found. In both works he has embodied all the decisions of his time, which have been very numerous." *Law Times.*

Shelford's Succession, Probate and Legacy Duties.

12mo., 12s. cloth.

THE LAW relating to the PROBATE, LEGACY and SUCCESSION DUTIES, including all the Statutes and the Decisions on those Subjects: with Forms and Practical Directions. By LEONARD SHELFORD, Esq., of the Middle Temple, Barrister-at-Law.

"The present work has had bestowed upon it that painstaking care which is the distinguishing feature of Mr. Shelford's labours." *Jurist.*

"The present volume will fully sustain the high reputation of its Author."—*Law Magazine.*

"A work which gives a *complete* view of the law relating to the subject, by noticing the kindred subjects of probate and legacy duties, without a knowledge of which the Succession Duty cannot be understood." *Law Chronicle.*

"Mr. Shelford has rendered good service to the profession by his clear and methodical exposition of the whole law relating to the probate, legacy and succession duties." *Morning Post.*

"Mr. Shelford's object has been to present a ... arrangement of this branch of the Stamp Laws. The work contains some valuable practical directions regarding the payment of the Succession Duties, &c." *Legal Observer.*

Hunter's Elementary View of a Suit in Equity.

12mo., 7s. boards.

AN ELEMENTARY VIEW OF THE PROCEEDINGS IN A SUIT IN EQUITY; with an Appendix of Forms. By SYLVESTER JOSEPH HUNTER, B.A., of Lincoln's Inn, Esq., Barrister-at-Law, and Holder of the Studentship of the Inns of Court.

"One merit may fairly be predicated of it. It is a clear, concise compendium of information, which the student will ... else here ... in a separate form. It has a good deal of the simplicity of statement which gave so much popularity to Smith's Elementary View." *Solicitors' Journal and Reporter.*

"So far as we can judge from glancing at these pages, we think their author has conscientiously performed his task." *Law Magazine and Review.*

"We shall content ourselves by stating, that we are surprised to find so much really practical matter comprised in so comparatively small a space, and we know of no other work from which a student can glean so much instruction on the different heads of equity practice." *Law Chronicle.*

"This volume ... to be very acceptable to those for whose use it was written."—*Law Times.*

"Its clearness is remarkably conspicuous. Altogether it is one of the most satisfactory handbooks we have perused."—*Leg... ...ian.*

Pearce's Guide to the Inns of Court and English Bar.

(*Corrected in accordance with the latest Regulations of the Four Inns of Court.*)

8vo., 8s. cloth.

A GUIDE to the INNS of COURT and CHANCERY; with Notices of their Ancient Discipline, Rules, Orders, and Customs, Readings, Moots, Masques, Revels and Entertainments; including an Account of the Eminent Men of the Honourable Societies, Lincoln's Inn, the Inner Temple, the Middle Temple, and Gray's Inn, &c.; together with the Regulations of the Four Inns of Court as to the Admission of Students, Keeping Terms, Exercises, Call to the Bar, &c. &c. &c. By ROBERT R. PEARCE, Esq., of Gray's Inn, Barrister at Law.

Grant's Laws of Bankers and Banking.

Post 8vo., 18s. cloth.

The LAW of BANKING; BANKER and CUSTOMER; BANKER and CORRESPONDENT; PRIVATE BANKS; BANKING CO-PARTNERSHIPS and JOINT-STOCK BANKS, COLONIAL BANKS, SAVINGS BANKS: comprising the Rights and Liabilities, and the Remedies of and against Directors, Managers, Clerks, Shareholders, &c.: the rules as to Cheques, Orders, Bills payable at Bankers, Accountable Receipts, Bank Notes, Deposits of Securities, Guarantees, &c. By JAMES GRANT, M.A., of the Middle Temple, Esq., Barrister at Law, Author of "The Law of Corporations in General."

"This is a well-designed and well-executed work."—*Legal Observer.*

"The learning and industry which were so conspicuous in Mr. Grant's former work are equally apparent in this. The book supplies a real want, which has long been felt both by the Profession and by the public at large."—*Jurist.*

"No man in the Profession was more competent to treat the subject of Banking than Mr. Grant. This volume appears opportunely. To all engaged in the litigations, as well as to all legal advisers of Bankers, Mr. Grant's work will be an invaluable assistant. It is a clear and careful Treatise on a subject not already exhausted, and it must become *the* Text-Book upon it."—*Law Times.*

"The object of the Author has been to give an entirely practical exposition of the law as it stands according to statutory enactment, and as it has been developed, ascertained and explained by judicial decisions."—*Times.*

"This is a very able work, the appearance of which is especially to be welcomed at the present time. The law relating to the Bank of England has not been included in it, for that would, in fact, have doubled its already ample size, but so much of the law and practice of the National Bank as is necessary to be known in connection with the affairs of private and Joint Stock Bankers will be found clearly laid down: of the law governing private and Joint Stock Banks, Mr. Grant gives a complete and lucid exposition. Fully illustrated with cases, and well indexed, his book will be not only helpful to the lawyer for whose use it is immediately designed, but will be consulted with advantage by many who belong to the large community of bankers' customers, while it will be of most obvious service to directors and shareholders of Joint-Stock Banks."—*Examiner.*

"For such a task, industry and accuracy are the qualities which are principally required: and the Author appears to possess them in a high degree. His work is moreover well arranged and clearly expressed."—*Athenæum.*

Williams's Common Law Pleading and Practice.

8vo., 12s. cloth.

An INTRODUCTION to PRACTICE and PLEADING in the SUPERIOR COURTS of LAW, embracing an outline of the whole proceedings in an Action at Law, on Motion, and at Judges' Chambers; together with the Rules of Pleading and Practice, and Forms of all the principal Proceedings. By WATKIN WILLIAMS, Esq., of the Inner Temple, Barrister at Law.

"The Common Law Procedure Acts and the New Rules have almost entirely re-organized the system of Pleading in our Courts of Law. Until the appearance of the present work, however, no new treatise on the subject has been attempted. Mr. Williams is a young and unknown author, and has undertaken a work requiring great care in its treatment; but we have no hesitation in saying that he has brought to bear on his task powers of arrangement and clearness of expression of no ordinary character, and has produced a work creditable to himself and useful to the Profession. For the Student especially the book has features of peculiar value, it is at the same time scientific and practical, and throughout the work there is a judicious union of general principles with a practical treatment of the subject, illustrated by forms and examples of the main proceedings."—*Jurist.*

Brandt's Divorce and Matrimonial Causes Practice; a Treatise on the Law, Practice and Procedure of Divorce and Matrimonial Causes under the Act 20 & 21 Vict. c. 85; containing the Act, also the Rules, Orders and Forms issued thereunder; together with Precedents. By WILLIAM BRANDT, of the Inner Temple, Esq., Barrister-at-Law. 12mo., 7*s.* 6*d.* boards.

Sharkey's Hand-Book of the Practice of Election Committees; with an Appendix of Statutes, Forms and Precedents. By P. BURROWES SHARKEY, Solicitor and Parliamentary Agent. 12mo. 5*s.* boards.

"We can recommend the Hand-Book of Mr Sharkey as a convenient and, we doubt not, trustworthy compendium of the Practice of Election Committees."—*Solicitors' Journal.*

Norman's Treatise on the Law and Practice relating to Letters Patent for Inventions as altered and amended by Statutes 15 & 16 Vict. c. 83, and 12 & 13 Vict. c. 109, with the New Rules of Practice in the Offices of Commissioners of Patents, and in the Petty Bag Office in Chancery, and all the Cases down to the time of publication. By JOHN PAXTON NORMAN, M.A., of the Inner Temple, Barrister at Law. Post 8vo., 7*s.* 6*d.*, cloth.

Gray's Treatise on the Law of Costs in Actions and other Proceedings in the Courts of Common Law at Westminster. By JOHN GRAY, Esq., of the Middle Temple, Barrister at Law. 8vo., 21*s.* cloth.

*** This Work embraces the whole modern Law and Practice of Costs, including the important provisions of the Common Law Procedure Act and Rules, 1852, and the recent Statutes affecting the Jurisdiction of the County Courts. Among the numerous subjects treated of may be mentioned Costs of Issues, of Demurrers, Amendments, Costs of one of several Defendants, Costs between Attorney and Client, Costs in particular Actions, as Ejectment, Replevin, Patents, Feigned Issues, Actions by and against Executors, Bankrupts, Assignees, Justices of the Peace, &c., so also Costs when the Jury are discharged or a Juror withdrawn, Costs of the Day, Security for Costs and Staying Proceedings, Proof of Documents, Witnesses, upon Arrest, Costs of Special Juries, View, &c., New Trials, Arrest of Judgment, in Error, Effect of Death of Parties, Costs on Award and Arbitration, Mandamus, Prohibition, Indictments, Orders, &c. removed by Certiorari, Taxation of Costs, Actions by Attornies, &c. to recover Costs, &c. &c

Bennett's Dissertation on the Nature of the various Proceedings in the Masters' Offices of the Court of Chancery; with a Supplement, including the Provisions of Recent Acts and Table of Fees. By W. H. BENNETT, Esq., of Lincoln's Inn, Barrister at Law. 8vo. 14*s.* boards.

The South Australian System of Conveyancing by Registration of Title, with Instructions for the Guidance of Parties Dealing, illustrated by Copies of the Books and Forms in Use in the Land Titles Office. By ROBERT R. TORRENS. To which is added the South Australian Real Property Act, as amended in the Sessions of 1858; with a copious Index. By HENRY GAWLER, Esq., Barrister, Solicitor to the Land Titles Commissioners. 8vo. 4*s.* half cloth.

Sessions Cases at the Central Criminal Court. Taken in Shorthand by Messrs. J. D. BARNETT and A. BUCKLER, by appointment to the Court.

Annual Subscription, if paid in advance, £1 : 11*s.* 6*d.* sewed; but for the convenience of the profession and the public, single numbers may also be purchased.

Coote's Practice of the Ecclesiastical Courts, with Forms and Tables of Costs. By HENRY CHARLES COOTE, Proctor in Doctors' Commons, &c. 1 thick vol. 8vo. 1*l.* 8*s.* boards.

Greening's Forms of Declarations, Pleadings and other Proceedings in the Superior Courts of Common Law, with the Common Law Procedure Act, and other Statutes; Table of Officers' Fees; and the New Rules of Practice and Pleading, with Notes. By HENRY GREENING, Esq., Special Pleader. Second Edition. 12mo. 10*s.* 6*d.* boards.

Archer's Index to the Unrepealed Statutes connected with the Administration of the Law in England and Wales, commencing with the Reign of William the Fourth, and continued up to the close of the Session 1850. By THOMAS G. ARCHER, Esq. 8vo. 5*s.* boards.

Pulling's Practical Compendium of the Law and Usage of Mercantile Accounts: describing the various Rules of Law affecting them, the ordinary Mode in which they are entered in Account Books, and the various Forms of Proceeding, and Rules of Pleading, and Evidence for their Investigation, at Common Law, in Equity, Bankruptcy and Insolvency, or by Arbitration. With a SUPPLEMENT, containing the Law of Joint Stock Companies' Accounts, and the Legal Regulations for their Adjustment under the Winding-up Acts of 1848 and 1849. By ALEXANDER PULLING, Esq. of the Inner Temple, Barrister at Law. 12mo. 9*s.* boards.

The Laws of Barbados. (By Authority.) Royal 8vo. 21s. cloth.

Warren's Manual of the Parliamentary Election Law of the United Kingdom, with reference to the Conduct of Elections, and the Registration Court; including the very latest Statutes and Decisions; with a copious Index. By SAMUEL WARREN, D.C.L., M.P., Q.C., and Recorder of Hull. One thick vol. royal 12mo. 25*s.* cloth.

Warren's Manual of the Law and Practice of Election Com-mittees, being the concluding portion of a "*Manual of Parliamentary Election Law,*" and including the latest Decisions. By SAMUEL WARREN, D.C.L., M.P., Q.C., and Recorder of Hull. Royal 12mo., 15*s.* cloth.

Leigh's Abridgment of the Law of Nisi Prius. By P. Brady LEIGH, of the Inner Temple, Barrister at Law. 2 vols. 8vo. £2 : 8*s.* boards.

A Practical Treatise on the Law of Tolls; and therein of Tolls Thorough and Traverse; Fair and Market Tolls; Canal, Ferry, Port and Harbour Tolls; Turnpike Tolls; Rateability of Tolls; Exemption from Tolls; Remedies and Evidence in Actions for Tolls. By FREDERICK GUNNING, Esq. of Lincoln's Inn, Barrister at Law. 9*s.* boards.

A Complete Collection of the Treaties and Conventions, and Reciprocal Regulations, at present subsisting between Great Britain and Foreign Powers. By LEWIS HERTSLET, Esq. Librarian and Keeper of the Papers, Foreign Office. Vols. 1 to 10, 8vo. £11 : 5*s.* boards.

Dr. Deane's Law of Blockade, as contained in the Judgments of Dr. Lushington and the Cases on Blockade decided during 1854. By J. P. DEANE, D.C.L., Advocate in Doctors' Commons. 8vo. 10*s.* cloth.

Wills's Essay on the Principles of Circumstantial Evidence: illustrated by numerous Cases. Third Edition. By WILLIAM WILLS, Esq. 8vo. 9*s.* boards.

The New Practice of the Court of Chancery as regulated by the Acts and Orders for the Improvement of the Jurisdiction of Equity, 15 & 16 Vict. c. 86; for Abolishing the Office of Master, 15 & 16 Vict. c. 80; and for Relief of the Suitors, 15 & 16 Vict. c. 87; with INTRODUCTION, NOTES, the ACTS, together with all the New Orders in Chancery of 1852, including the latest, and a copious INDEX. By JAMES O'DOWD, Esq., Barrister at Law. Second Edition, corrected, greatly improved, and including the *recent Cases*. 12mo. 7*s*. 6*d*. boards.

The New System of Common Law Procedure according to the Common Law Procedure Act, 1852. By J. R. QUAIN, of the Middle Temple, Barrister at Law, and H. HOLROYD, of the Middle Temple, Special Pleader. 12mo. 7*s*. 6*d*. cloth.

Sewell's Municipal Corporation Acts, 5 & 6 Will. 4, c. 76, and 6 & 7 Will. 4, cc. 103, 104, 105, with Legal and Explanatory Notes, and a copious Index. By RICHARD CLARKE SEWELL, Esq., of the Middle Temple, Barrister at Law. 12mo. 9*s*. boards.

The Law relating to Transactions on the Stock Exchange. By HENRY KEYSER, Esq., of the Middle Temple, Barrister at Law. 12mo., 8*s*. cloth.

A Legigraphical Chart of Landed Property in England from the time of the Saxons to the present Æra, displaying at one view the Tenures, Mode of Descent, Power and Alienation of Lands in England at all times during the same period. By CHARLES FEARNE, Esq. of the Inner Temple, Barrister at Law. On a large sheet, 6*s*. coloured.

Dwyer's Compendium of the Principal Laws and Regulations relating to the Militia of Great Britain and Ireland; and of the Duties of Lords-Lieutenants, Lieutenants and Deputy-Lieutenants of Counties, and of Chief Magistrates and Deputy-Lieutenants of Cities and Towns, and of Justices of the Peace, in connection therewith. 12mo. 5*s*. 6*d*. cloth.

The Common Law of Kent; or the Customs of Gavelkind. With an Appendix concerning Borough English. By T. ROBINSON, Esq. THIRD EDITION, with Notes and References to modern Authorities, by JOHN WILSON, Esq. Barrister at Law. 8vo. 18*s*. boards.

The Marriage and Registration Acts, 6 & 7 Will. 4, caps. 85, 86; with Instructions, Forms, and Practical Directions for the Use of Officiating Ministers, Superintendent Registrars, Registrars. The Acts of 1837, viz. 7 Will. 4, c. 1, and 1 Vict c. 22, with Notes and Observations; and a full Index. By JOHN SOUTHERDEN BURN, Esq., *Secretary to the Commission*. 12mo. 6*s*. 6*d*. boards.

A Treatise on the Law of Gaming, Horse-Racing, and Wagers; with a Full Collection of the Statutes in force in reference to those subjects; together with Practical Forms of Pleadings and Indictments, adapted for the General or Professional Reader. By FREDERIC EDWARDS, Esq., Barrister at Law. 12mo. 5*s*. cloth.

Hamel's Laws of the Customs, consolidated by direction of the Lords Commissioners of her Majesty's Treasury, under the Acts of 1853 and 1854; with a Commentary, containing Practical Forms, Notes of Decisions in Leading Customs Cases, Appendix of Acts, and a copious Index. By FELIX JOHN HAMEL, Esq., Solicitor for her Majesty's Customs. 1 vol. royal 8vo. 16*s*. cloth.

A Digest of Principles of English Law; arranged in the order of the Code Napoleon, with an Historical Introduction. By GEORGE BLAXLAND, Esq. Royal 8vo. £1 : 4*s.* boards.

The Law Student's Guide; containing an Historical Treatise on each of the Inns of Court, with their Rules and Customs respecting Admission, Keeping Terms, Call to the Bar, Chambers, &c., Remarks on the Jurisdiction of the Benchers, Observations on the Study of the Law, and other useful Information. By P. B. LEIGH, Esq. of Gray's Inn, Barrister at Law. 12mo. 6*s.* boards.

Schomberg's Acts for the Commutation of Tithes in England and Wales, 6 & 7 Will. 4, c. 71, and 1 Vict. c. 69, with Notes, Observations, and an Epitome of the Law of Tithes, and an Appendix, containing Tables for calculating the Rent-Charge, Forms of Notices, Agreements, Apportionments, &c. By J. T. SCHOMBERG, Esq., of the Inner Temple, Barrister at Law. 12mo. 7*s.* boards.

Anstey's Pleader's Guide; a Didactic Poem, in Two Parts. The Eighth Edition. 12mo. 7*s.* boards.

A Treatise on the Law of Commerce and Manufactures, and the Contracts relating thereto; with an Appendix of Treaties, Statutes, and Precedents. By JOSEPH CHITTY, Esq. Barrister at Law. 4 vols. royal 8vo. £6 : 6*s.* boards.

An Essay on Charitable Trusts, under the Charitable Trusts Act, 1853. By HENRY JOHN PYE, Esq. Post 8vo. 6*d.* sewed.

A Practical Treatise on Life Assurance; in which the Statutes, &c., affecting unincorporated Joint Stock Companies are briefly considered and explained. SECOND EDITION. By FREDERICK BLAYNEY, Esq., Author of "A Treatise on Life Annuities." 12mo. 7*s.* boards.

A Report of the Bread Street Ward Scrutiny; with Introductory Observations, a Copy of the Poll, and a Digest of the Evidence, Arguments, and Decisions in each Case. By W. T. HALY, Esq., Barrister at Law. 12mo. 4*s.* boards.

The Judgment of the Right Hon. Stephen Lushington, D.C.L., &c. delivered in the Consistory Court of the Bishop of London in the Cases of Westerton against Liddell (Clerk) and Horne and others, and Beal against Liddell (Clerk) and Parke and Evans, on 5th Dec. 1855. Edited by A. F. BAYFORD, D.C.L. Royal 8vo. 2*s.* 6*d.* sewed.

The Judgment of the Right Hon. Sir John Dodson, Knight, Dean of the Arches, &c.; also the JUDGMENT of the JUDICIAL COMMITTEE of the PRIVY COUNCIL, in the cases of Liddell (clerk), and Horne and others against Westerton, and Liddell (clerk) and Park and Evans against Beal. Edited by A. F. BAYFORD, LL.D.: and with an elaborate analytical Index to the whole of the Judgments in these Cases. Royal 8vo., 3*s.* 6*d.* sewed.

The Law Magazine and Law Review—*continued.*

CONTENTS OF NO. 13, NEW SERIES.

1. Privileges of Parliament. 2. The Tenure of Real Property in the Island of Guernsey—3. Costs in the Probate Court. 4. Shakespeare in the Queen's Bench. 5. Mr. Locke King's Intestacy Bill—6. The Library of the Middle Temple. 7. Principles and Law of Banking. 8. Judicial Anticipation. 9. The Failure and Fate of the Statute Law Commission—10. Taylor on Poisons. 11. The Divorce Court. 12. Bankruptcy Law Reform. 13. Lord Murray. 14. Recent Attacks on Titles to Real Property. Conservative Landed Estates Bills.

No. 14.

1. Sir John Taylor Coleridge and Mr. Pickle. 2. The Law of Railways.—3. Curiosities of Law. An English Borough in the Fourteenth Century: Custumnal of Romney.—4. The Jury System in England. 5. Selwyn's Nisi Prius. 6. The Legal effect of War with reference to Contraband.—7. The Political Economical View of Rent by the late Richard Jones.—8. The Study of the Law in the Universities and Inns of Court. Dr. Leapingwell's Manual of Roman Civil Law.—Papers of the Law Amendment Society. I. The Annual Report of the Council for the Session 1858-9. II. On the present position of Executors and Trustees.—Bar Examination Questions: Trinity Term, 1859. Report of the Committee of the Inns of Court.

No. 15.

1. Baron Bramwell, the Press and the Bar.—2. A late Trial for Murder in Germany.—3. Church Discipline.—3. The Law of Slavery.—5. Extract of Lord Brougham's Letter to the Earl of Radnor.—6. Constitutional Relations between Great Britain and her Colonies.—7. The Reformation of Adults. 8. Modern Legislation: The Parliamentary Remembrancer.—9. Railway Accidents and their Prevention. 10. The Libraries of the Inns of Courts.—11. Last Session.—12. Smethurst's Trial. 13. Judicial Statistics.—14. Conveyancing in South Australia by Registration of Title. 15. The late W. J. Broderip.

No. 16.

1. The Temple and the Templars. No. I. The Temple Church. 2. Rowland's History of the English Constitution. 3. Blasphemy. 4. Justice and Justices. 5. Criminal Law of France. 6. Curiosities of Law: No. II. An English Borough in the Fourteenth Century: Custumnal of Romsey.—7. Brawling: St. George's in the East London. 8. The Jurisdiction and Practice of the Admiralty Court. 9. Lord St. Leonard's Property and Trustees Relief Act. Corporation Magistrates. Criminal Procedure, French and English.—Recent Leading Cases on the Right to the Support of Land and Buildings: Solomon *v.* The Vintners Company and Bonomi *v.* Backhouse. Notices of New Works, Events of the Quarter, List of New Publications, &c.

No. 17.

1. The Lunacy Law and its Defects.—2. The Inns of Court. No. II. Finance in the Temple—Lincoln's Inn Benchers. 3. The Consolidated Orders of the Court of Chancery. 4. The Liberty of the French Bar. 5. Hilliard's Law of Torts. 6. The Juridical Society. 7. Conveyancing in South Australia. Mystery in English Legislation. 8. Corrupt Practices at Elections. The Gloucester Bribery Commission. 9. Proposed Consolidation of the Joint Stock Companies Acts. 10. Law and Lawyers in the British Colonies.—11. The Bankruptcy and Insolvency Bill, 1860.—12. The Law and Equity Bill. Common Law Commission.—13. John Austin.—Judges' Chambers.—Arbitrations. Points recently decided under Lord St. Leonards' Act.—Notes of New Books. Events of the Quarter. Archæology in the Temple, &c.

Reports.

House of Lords Reports.

REPORTS of CASES decided in the HOUSE of LORDS on APPEALS and WRITS of ERROR—CLAIMS of PEERAGE and DIVORCES. By CHARLES CLARK, Esq., of the Middle Temple, Barrister at Law. (Reporter, by appointment, to the House of Lords.)

Vols. I., II., III., IV., V. and VI., and Vol. VII. Parts I. and II., containing all the Cases decided from 1847 to 1860, inclusive. (*These Reports will be regularly continued.*)

Probate, Divorce Court and Matrimonial Causes Reports.—*By Authority.*

REPORTS of CASES decided in HER MAJESTY'S NEW COURT of PROBATE, and in the COURT for DIVORCE and MATRIMONIAL CAUSES, commencing Hilary Term, 1858. By Dr. SWABEY, D.C.L., Advocate and Barrister at Law, of Gray's Inn, and Dr. TRISTRAM, D.C.L., Advocate in Doctors' Commons, and of the Inner Temple. Vol. I., Parts I. II. III. and IV., price £1 : 11*s.* sewed.

(*These Reports will be regularly continued.*)

Dr. Robinson's New Admiralty Reports.

REPORTS of CASES argued and determined in the HIGH COURT of ADMIRALTY, commencing with the Judgments of the Right Honourable Stephen Lushington, D.C.L. By WILLIAM ROBINSON, D.C.L. Advocate.

Vols. I. and II., and Vol. III. Parts I. and II., containing Cases decided from Michaelmas Term 1838 to Trinity Vacation 1850. £4 : 7*s.* sewed.

(*These Reports are in immediate continuation of* DR. HAGGARD'S.)

Dr. Swabey's Admiralty Reports.

REPORTS of CASES determined in the HIGH COURT of ADMIRALTY, commencing Mich. Term, 1855. By M. C. MERTTINS SWABEY, D.C.L., of Doctors' Commons and of Gray's Inn, Barrister at Law. Vol. I., Parts I. and II., price 18*s.* sewed. (*These Reports, in immediate continuation of those by* DR. W. ROBINSON *and by* DR. SPINKS, *will be regularly continued.*)

Printed in Dunstable, United Kingdom

91222343R00399